Toyota Corona & Corona Mark II Owners Workshop Manual

by J H Haynes
Associate Member of the Guild of Motoring Writers

and P. G. Strasman
MISTC

Models covered

UK: Corona Mark II 'Shaver nosed' 1858cc
    1969 to 1972
    Corona Mark II 1969 cc. 1972 on

USA: Corona 113 cu in & 120 cu in 1969 on
    Corona Mark II 'Shaver nosed' 113 cu in & 120 cu in
    1969 to 1972

Covers all models of above. Does not cover
6 cylinder Mark II models

ISBN 0 85696 230 9

© J H Haynes and Company Limited 1975

All rights reserved. No part of this book may be reproduced or transmitted in any form or by any means, electronic or mechanical, including photocopying, recording or by any information storage or retrieval system, without permission in writing from the copyright holder.

Printed in England

**J H HAYNES AND COMPANY LIMITED
SPARKFORD YEOVIL SOMERSET ENGLAND**

distributed in the USA by
**HAYNES PUBLICATIONS INC.
9421 WINNETKA AVENUE
CHATSWORTH LOS ANGELES
CALIFORNIA 91311 USA**

Acknowledgements

Toyota Motor Sales Company Limited kindly gave us permission to reproduce certain of their illustrations and also provided technical information castrol Limited supplied lubrication details.

Wiltshire Toyota Limited supplied the Corona Mark II model used in our workshop. Their representatives Mr Waterhouse and Mr Hart were very helpful.

Car Mechanics magazine provided many of the photographs which make up the bodywork repair sequence of Chapter twelve.

Special thanks are due to all of those people at Sparkford who helped with the production of this manual. Particularly, Martin Penny and Les Brazier, who carried out the mechanical work and took the photographs, respectively; Rod Grainger who edited the text and Stanley Randolph who planned the layout of each page.

About this manual

Its aim

The aim of this book is to help you get the best value from your car. It can do so in two ways. First it can help you decide what work must be done, even should you choose to get it done by a garage, the routine maintenance and the diagnosis and course of action when random faults occur. But it is hoped that you will also use the second and fuller purpose by tackling the work yourself. This can give you the satisfaction of doing the job yourself. On the simpler jobs it may even be quicker than booking the car into a garage and going there twice, to leave and collect it. Perhaps most important, much money can be saved by avoiding the costs a garage must charge to cover their labour and overheads.

Haynes Owner's Workshop Manuals are the *only* manuals, available to the public, which are actually written from practical experience. We buy a second-hand and well used example of the vehicle to be covered by the manual. Then, in our own workshops, the major components of that vehicle are stripped and rebuilt by the author and a mechanic: at the same time all sequences are photographed. By doing this work ourselves, we encounter the same problems as you will and having overcome these problems, we can provide you with practical solutions.

The book has drawings and descriptions to show the function of the various components so that their layout can be understood. Then the tasks are described and photographed in a step by step sequence so that even a novice can cope with complicated work. Such a person is the very one to buy a car needing repair yet be unable to afford garage costs.

The jobs are described assuming only normal spanners are available, and not special tools. But a reasonable outfit of tools will be a worthwhile investment. many special workshop tools produced by the makers merely speed the work, and in these cases guidance is given as to how to do the job without them, the oft quoted example being the use of a large hose clip to com**press the piston rings for insertion in the cylinder**. But on a very few occasions the special tool is essential to prevent damage to components, then their use is described. Though it might be possible to borrow the tool, such work may have to be entrusted to the official agent.

To avoid labour costs a garage will often give a cheaper repair by fitting a reconditioned assembly. The home mechanic can be helped by this book to diagnose the fault and make a repair using only a minor spare part. The classic case is repairing a non-charging dynamo by fitting new brushes.

The manufacturer's official workshop manuals are written for their trained staff, and so assume special knowledge; detail is left out. This book is written for the owner, and so goes into detail.

Using the manual

The manual is divided into twelve Chapters - each covering a logical sub-division of the vehicle. The individual Chapters are divided into Sections, and the Sections into numbered paragraphs.

Procedures, once described in the text, are not normally repeated. If it is necessary to refer to another Chapter the reference will be given in Chapter number and section number (eg; Chapter 1/16).

If it is considered necessary to refer to a particular paragraph in another Chapter the reference is given in the following form 'Chapter 1/5:5'. Cross-references given without use of the word 'Chapter' apply to Sections and/or paragraphs in the same Chapter (eg; 'see Section 8' means also in this Chapter').

There are two types of illustration: (1) Figures which are numbered according to Chapter and sequence of occurrence in that Chapter. (2) Photographs which have a reference number on their caption. All photographs apply to the Chapter in which they occur so that the reference figure pinpoints the pertinent Section and paragraph number.

When the left or right side of the car is mentioned it is as if looking forward from the rear of the car.

Great effort has been made to ensure that this book is complete and up-to-date. However, the vehicle manufacturers continually modify their cars, even in retrospect without giving notice.

Whilst every care is taken to ensure that the information in this manual is correct no liability can be accepted by the authors or publishers for loss, damage or injury caused by any errors in, or omissions from, the information given.

Contents

Chapter	Section	Page	Section	Page
Introductory Sections	Buying spare parts	5	Lubrication chart	14
	Routine maintenance	10	Recommended lubricants	14
1 Engine	Removal	19	Reassembly	37
	Dismantling	22	Installation	44
	Renovation	30	Fault diagnosis	45
2 Cooling system	Draining, flushing, filling	47	Thermostat	48
	Antifreeze	48	Water pump	49
	Radiator	48	Fault diagnosis	50
3 Carburation; fuel, exhaust and emission control systems	Air cleaner	52	Carburettors	56
	Fuel pump	53	Accelerator pedal	80
	Fuel tank	55	Exhaust system	81
	Emission control system	56	Fault diagnosis	83
4 Ignition system	Contact breaker points	85	Coil polarity	93
	Distributor	86	Spark plugs	93
	Timing	86	Fault diagnosis	93
5 Clutch	Adjustment	96	Pedal	99
	Master cylinder	96	Renovation	99
	Operating cylinder	98	Release bearing	101
	Bleeding hydraulic system	98	Fault diagnosis	102
6 Manual gearbox and automatic transmission	**Manual gearbox**		**Automatic transmission**	
	3 speed type TC1	109	Maintenance	143
	3 speed type N30/31	115	Two speed unit	143
	4 speed type SS1	123	A30 type	147
	4 speed type W40	131	A40 type	149
	5 speed type	137	Fault diagnosis	152
7 Propeller shaft and universal joints	Maintenance	155	Universal joints; dismantling and reassembly	155
	Propeller shaft: removal and refitting	155	Fault diagnosis	155
8 Rear axle	Halfshafts	156	Removal and refitting	160
	Pinion oil seal	159	Fault diagnosis	160
9 Braking system	Drum brakes	162	Master cylinder	173
	Disc brakes	162	Bleeding hydraulic system	176
	Disc caliper	171	Vacuum servo unit	180
	Drum wheel cylinders	172	Fault diagnosis	185
10 Electrical system	Battery	188	Switches	203
	Alternator	188	Windscreen wiper motor	205
	Starter motor	192	Horns	207
	Instruments	199	Fault diagnosis	214
11 Suspension and steering	Shock absorbers	218	Steering column	224
	Front hubs	219	Steering box	231
	Front suspension	220	Wheels and tyres	233
	Rear suspension	223	Fault diagnosis	233
12 Body and fittings	Maintenance	235	Doors	240
	Repairs	235	Heater	246
	Windscreen glass	239	Air conditioning system	248
Metric conversion tables				252
Index				253

Use of English

As this book has been written in England, it uses the appropriate English component names, phrases, and spelling. Some of these differ from those used in America. Normally, these cause no difficulty, but to make sure, a glossary is printed below. In ordering spare parts remember the parts list will probably use these words:

Glossary

English	American	English	American
Accelerator	Gas pedal	Roof rack	Car-top carrier
Alternator	Generator (AC)	Saloon	Sedan
Anti-roll bar	Stabiliser or sway bar	Seized	Frozen
Barrel	Choke/venturi	Side indicator lights	Side marker lights
Battery	Energizer	Side light	Parking light
Bonnet (engine cover)	Hood	Silencer	Muffler
Boot lid	Trunk lid	Spanner	Wrench
Boot (luggage compartment)	Trunk	Sill panel (beneath doors)	Rocker panel
Bottom gear	1st gear	Split cotter (for valve spring cap)	Lock (for valve spring retainer)
Bulkhead	Firewall	Split pin	Cotter pin
Camfollower or tappet	Valve lifter or tappet	Steering arm	Spindle arm
Carburettor	Carburetor	Sump	Oil pan
Catch	Latch	Tab washer	Tang; lock
Circlip	Snap ring	Tailgate	Liftgate
Clearance	Lash	Tappet	Valve lifter
Crownwheel	Ring gear (of differential)	Thrust bearing	Throw-out bearing
Disc (brake)	Rotor/disk	Top gear	High
Driveshaft	Propellor shaft	Trackrod (of steering)	Tie-rod (or connecting rod)
Drop arm	Pitman arm	Trailing shoe (of brake)	Secondary shoe
Drop head coupe	Convertible	Transmission	Whole drive line
Dynamo	Generator (DC)	Tyre	Tire
Earth (electrical)	Ground	Van	Panel wagon/van
Engineer's blue	Prussion blue	Vice	Vise
Estate car	Station wagon	Wheel nut	Lug nut
Exhaust manifold	Header	Windscreen	Windshield
Fast back (Coupe)	Hard top	Wing/mudguard	Fender
Fault finding/diagnosis	Trouble shooting		
Float chamber	Float bowl		
Free-play	Lash		
Freewheel	Coast		
Gudgeon pin	Piston pin or wrist pin		
Gearchange	Shift		
Gearbox	Transmission		
Halfshaft	Axle-shaft		
Handbrake	Parking brake		
Hood	Soft top		
Hot spot	Heat riser		
Indicator	Turn signal		
Interior light	Dome lamp		
Layshaft (of gearbox)	Counter shaft		
Leading shoe (of brake)	Primary shoe		
Locks	Latches		
Motorway	Freeway, turnpike etc.		
Number plate	Licence plate		
Paraffin	Kerosene		
Petrol	Gasoline		
Petrol tank	Gas tank		
'Pinking'	'Pinging'		
Quarter light	Quarter window		
Retread	Recap		
Reverse	Back-up		
Rocker cover	Valve cover		

Miscellaneous points

An "Oil seal" is fitted to components lubricated by grease!

A "Damper" is a "Shock absorber" it damps out bouncing, and absorbs shocks of bump impact. Both names are correct, and both are used haphazardly.

Note that British drum brakes are different from the Bendix type that is common in America, so different descriptive names result. The shoe end furthest from the hydraulic wheel cylinder is on a pivot; interconnection between the shoes as on Bendix brakes is most uncommon. Therefore the phrase "Primary" or "Secondary" shoe does not apply. A shoe is said to be Leading or Trailing. A "Leading" shoe is one on which a point on the drum, as it rotates forward, reaches the shoe at the end worked by the hydraulic cylinder before the anchor end. The opposite is a trailing shoe, and this one has no self servo from the wrapping effect of the rotating drum.

Introduction to the Toyota Corona

This manual covers the range of Corona and Corona Mark II models which are fitted with 4 cylinder OHC type engines. The models featured are as follows:

North America:
Corona Mark II (shaver nose) 1969 to 1972
Corona (post shaver-nose) 1969 to date.
Vehicles are available in saloon, hardtop and estate wagon versions with optional engine capacities of 1858 cc (series 8R) or 1968 cc (series 18R).

UK and other territories:
Corona Mark II (shaver-nose) 1969 to 1972 fitted with the series 8R (1858 cc) engine only.
Corona Mark II (new body) 1972 to date fitted with the series 18R (1968 cc) engine only.

Transmission may be by means of 3, 4 or 5 speed manual gearbox or by 'Toyotaglide' automatic transmission. All vehicles covered by this manual have their serial numbers prefixed 'RT'.

Buying spare parts and vehicle identification numbers

Buying spare parts

Spare parts are available from many sources, for example Toyota garages, other garages and accessory shops, and motor factors. Our advice regarding spare part sources is as follows:

Officially appointed Toyota garages - This is the best source of parts which are peculiar to your car and are otherwise not generally available (eg; complete cylinder heads internal gearbox components, badges, interior trim etc). It is also the only place at which you should buy parts if your car is still under warranty: non-Toyota components may invalidate the warranty. To be sure of obtaining the correct parts it will always be necessary to give the storeman your car's engine and chassis number, and if possible, to take the 'old' part along for positive identification. Remember that many parts are available on a factory exchange scheme - any parts returned should always be clean! It obviously makes good sense to go straight to the specialists on your car for this type of part for they are best equipped to supply you.

Other garages and accessory shops - These are often very good places to buy materials and components needed for the maintenance of your car (eg spark plugs, bulbs, fanbelts, oils and greases, touch-up paint, filler paste, etc). They also sell general accessories, usually have convenient opening hours, charge lower prices and can often be found not far from home.

Motor factors - Good factors will stock all of the more important components which wear out relatively quickly (eg cylinders/pipes/hoses/seals/shoes and pads etc). Motor factors will often provide new or reconditioned components on a part exchange basis - this can save a considerable amount of money.

Vehicle identification numbers

Vehicle serial numbers are stamped on the rear bulkhead of the engine compartment and repeated (on North American vehicles) on the top surface of the facia panel just inside the windscreen. *The engine number* is stamped in the top face of the cylinder block, adjacent to the fuel pump.

BSP 1 Serial number location on rear bulkhead

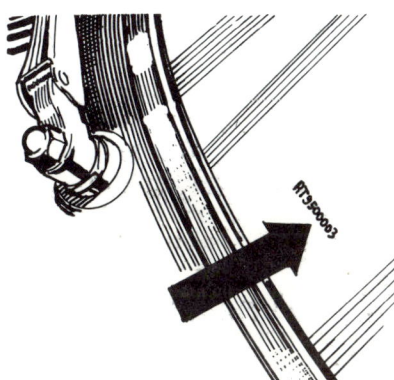

BSP 2 Serial number of facia panel top surface of North American vehicles

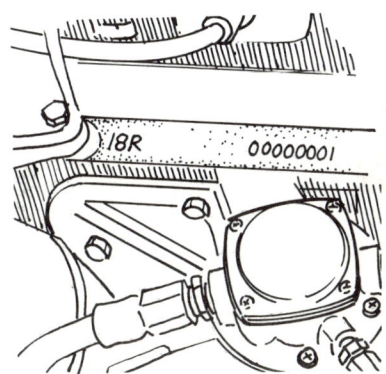

BSP 3 Location of engine number

BSP 4 Vehicle identification plate (other than North America)

Toyota Corona 2000 Mark II saloon - UK specification

Toyota Corona 2000 Mark II Estate - UK specification

Toyota Corona 2 - door - Hardtop - North American specification

1973 Toyota Corona Station Wagon - North American specification

1974 Toyota Corona Station Wagon - North American specification

Routine maintenance

Maintenance is essential for ensuring safety and desirable for the purpose of getting the best in terms of performance and economy from the car. Over the years the need for periodic lubrication - oiling, greasing and so on - has been drastically reduced if not totally eliminated. This has unfortunately tended to lead some owners to think that because no such action is required the items either no longer exist or will last for ever. This is a serious delusion. It follows therefore that the largest initial element of maintenance is visual examination. This may lead to repairs or renewals.

In the summary given here the essential for safety' items are shown in **bold type**. These **must** be attended to at the regular frequencies shown in order to avoid the possibility of accidents and loss of life. Other neglect results in unreliability, increased running costs, more rapid wear and more rapid depreciation of the vehicle in general.

Every 250 miles (400 km) travelled or weekly - whichever comes first

Steering
Check the tyre pressures.
Examine tyres for wear or damage.
Is steering smooth and accurate?

Brakes
Check reservoir fluid level.
Is there any fall off in braking efficiency?
Try an emergency stop. Is adjustment necessary?

Lights, wipers and horns
Do all bulbs work at the front and rear?
Are the headlamp beams aligned properly?
Do the wipers and horns work?
Check windscreen washer fluid level.

Engine
Check the sump oil level and top-up if required.
Check the radiator coolant level and top up if required.
Check the battery electrolyte level and top up to the level of the plates with distilled water as needed.

Every 6000 miles (9600 km) or six monthly - whichever comes first

Engine
Change oil.
Check distributor points gap.
Check and clean spark plugs.

Check fan belt tension and adjust if necessary.
Check cylinder head bolt torque setting.
Check valve clearances and adjust if necessary.
Renew oil filter.
Lubricate distributor.
Clean air cleaner element and set intake to seasonal position.
Clean fuel pump.

Gearbox (manual and automatic)
Check oil level and top-up if necessary.

Clutch
Check pedal free movement and for oil leakage at cylinders.
Check fluid reservoir level and top up if necessary.

Body
Lubricate all locks and hinges.
Check that water drain holes at bottom of doors are clear.

Steering
Examine all steering linkage rods, joints and bushes for signs of wear or damage.
Check front wheel hub bearings and adjust if necessary.
Check tightness of steering gear mounting bolts.
Move roadwheels to even out tread wear and rebalance if necessary.
Check and top-up if necessary, oil level in steering box.

Brakes
Examine disc pads and drum shoes to determine the amount of friction material left. Renew if necessary.
Examine all hydraulic pipes, cylinders and unions for signs of chafing, corrosion, dents or any other form of deterioration or leaks.
Check pedal free movement and for oil leakage at cylinders.

Suspension
Examine all nuts, bolts and shackles securing the suspension units, front and rear. Tighten if necessary.
Examine the rubber bushes for signs of wear and play.

Every 12000 miles (19000 km) or annually - whichever comes first

Engine
Check crankcase fume emission valve.
Check fuel storage evaporative emission control system and renew non-return valve.
Check exhaust emission control system.
Fit new spark plugs.

RM 1 Topping-up brake master cylinder

RM 2 Engine oil dipstick

RM 3 Topping-up engine oil

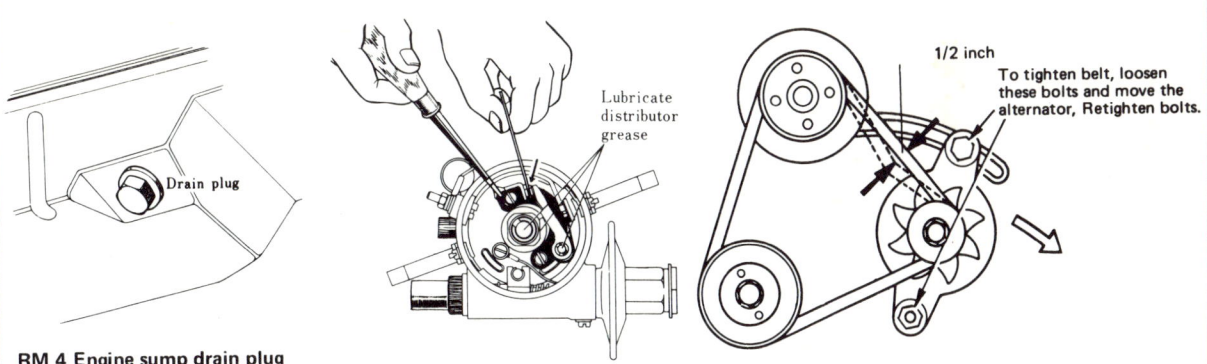

RM 4 Engine sump drain plug

Point gap : 0.018 inch

RM 5 Checking distributor points gap

RM 6 Alternator driving belt tension adjustment

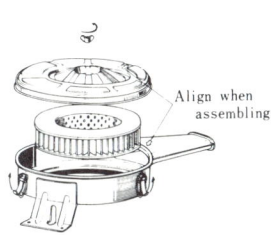

RM 7 Components of the air cleaner

RM 8 Air cleaner seasonal position arrows

RM 9 Winter/Summer air intake positions and control lever

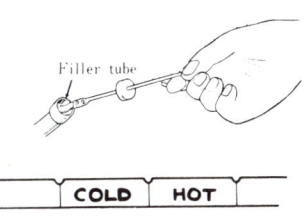

RM 10 Checking fluid level of automatic transmission

RM 11 Topping-up clutch master cylinder

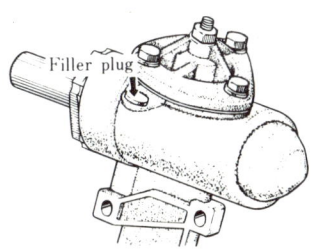

RM 12 Steering box filler plug

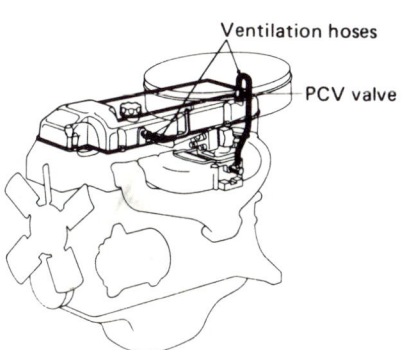

RM 13 Location of crankcase PCV valve (18R - C engine)

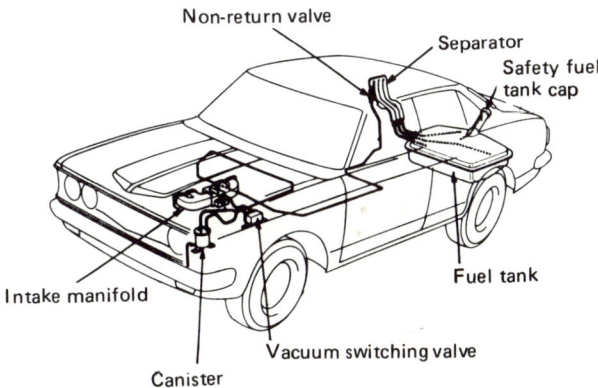

RM 14 Fuel evaporative emission control system layout

Fit new distributor points.
Clean carburettor float chamber and jets.
Check HT ignition leads for deterioration.

Steering
Check wheel alignment.

Suspension
Check efficiency of dampers

Transmission
Check security of propeller shaft bolts.
Check oil level in rear axle and top up if necessary.

Every 24000 miles (38000 km) or two yearly - whichever comes first

Engine
Flush cooling system and refill with anti-freeze mixture.
Renew air cleaner element.
Renew PCV valve.
Renew fuel line filter.

Suspension
Dismantle front hubs, clean out old lubricant and repack with fresh grease. Assemble and adjust.

Brakes
Lubricate handbrake linkage.

Transmission
Drain manual gearbox and refill with fresh oil.
Drain rear axle and refill with fresh oil.
Check propeller shaft universal joints for wear and recondition if necessary.

Steering
Grease ball joints.

Headlights
Check beams and adjust if required.

Every 48000 miles (77000 km) or four yearly - whichever comes first

Brakes
Drain hydraulic system, renew all cylinder seals and refill with fresh fluid. Bleed system.

Clutch
Drain hydraulic system, renew master and slave cylinder seals, refill with fresh fluid. Bleed system.

The following should be carried out at regular intervals

Cleaning
Examination of components requires that they be cleaned. The same applies to the body of the car, inside and out, in order that deterioration due to rust or unknown damage may be detected. Certain parts of the body frame, if rusted badly, can result in the vehicle being declared unsafe and it will not pass the annual test for roadworthiness.

Exhaust system
An exhaust system must be leakproof, and the noise level below a certain maximum. Excessive leaks may cause carbon monoxide fumes to enter the passenger compartment. Excessive noise constitutes a public nuisance. Both these faults may cause the vehicle to be kept off the road. Repair or replace defective sections when symptoms are apparent.

Quick reference maintenance capacities

Engine oil (including filter):
8R-C 7.4 Imp. pints 4.3 litres 4.3 U.S qts.
18R-C 9.1 Imp. pints 5.1 litres 5.3 U.S qts.

Gearbox
3 speed 3.1 Imp. pints 1.7 litres 1.8 U.S qts.
4 speed 4.1 Imp. pints 2.3 litres 2.4 U.S qts.
5 speed 4.7 Imp. pints 2.7 litres 2.7 U.S qts.

Automatic transmission:
Toyoglide 2 speed 5.9 Imp. qts 6.8 litres 7.2 U.S qts.
A30 5.6 Imp. qts 6.4 litres 6.8 U.S qts.
A40 5.1 Imp. qts 5.8 litres 6.1 U.S qts

Rear axle 2.4 Imp. pints 1.4 litres 1.5 U.S qts

Steering box 0.34 Imp. pints 0.19 litres 0.20 U.S qts.

Cooling system:
8R-C engine 13.4 Imp. pints 7.6 litres 7.8 U.S qts.
18R-C engine 14.3 Imp. pints 8.1 litres 8.3 U.S qts.

Fuel tank 11.4 Imp. gals. 52.0 litres 12.4 U.S gals.

Jacking and towing points
The jacking points on the saloon and hardtop models are located beneath the side body sills. On the estate wagon, the rear should be jacked under the centre of the road springs. These jacking points should be used for changing roadwheels only. Where work is being carried out under the vehicle then axle

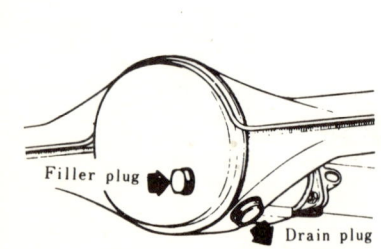

RM 15 Rear axle filler and drain plugs

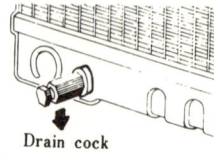
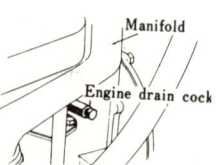

RM 16 Cylinder block and radiator drain cocks

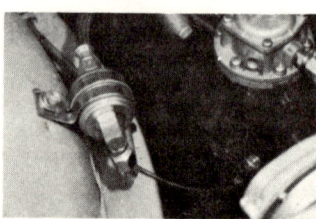

RM 17 Location of fuel line filter

Routine maintenance

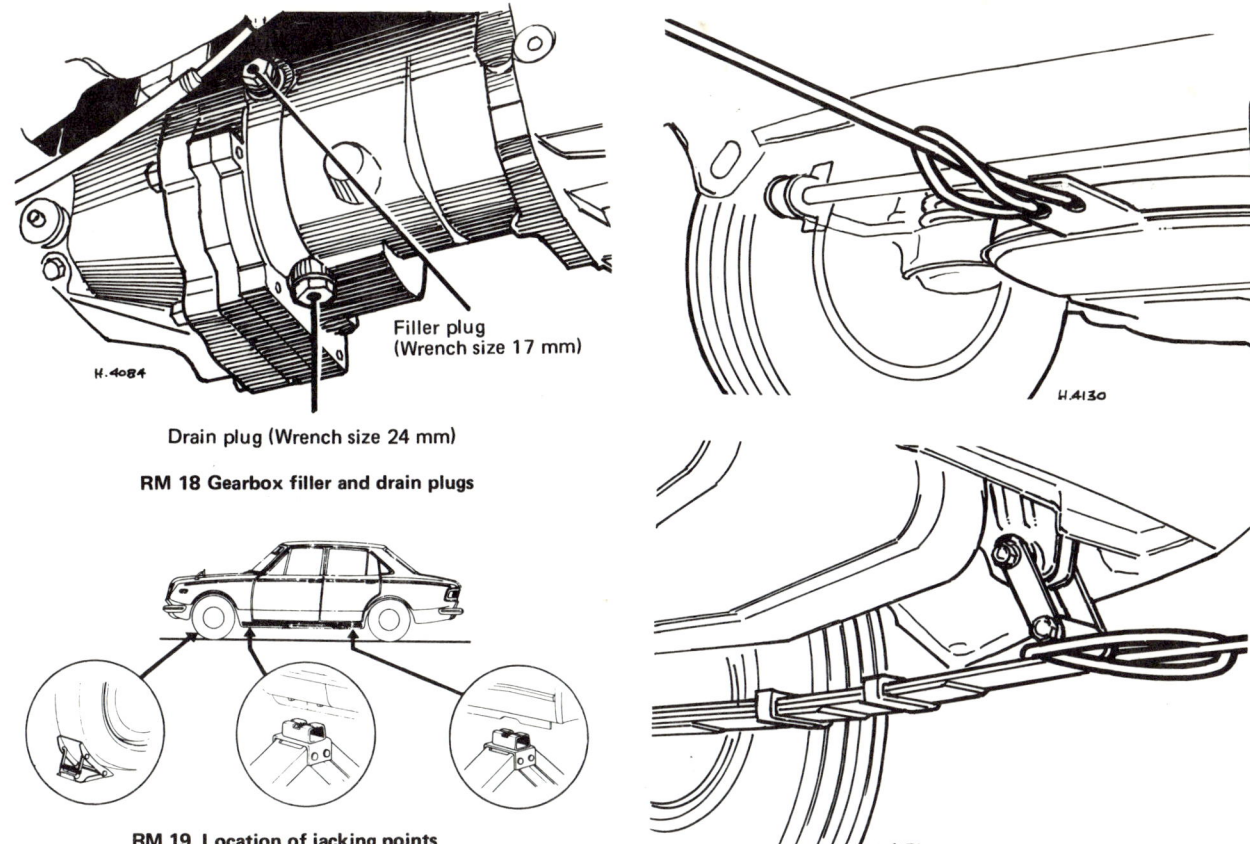

RM 18 Gearbox filler and drain plugs

RM 19 Location of jacking points

RM 20 Front and rear towing points

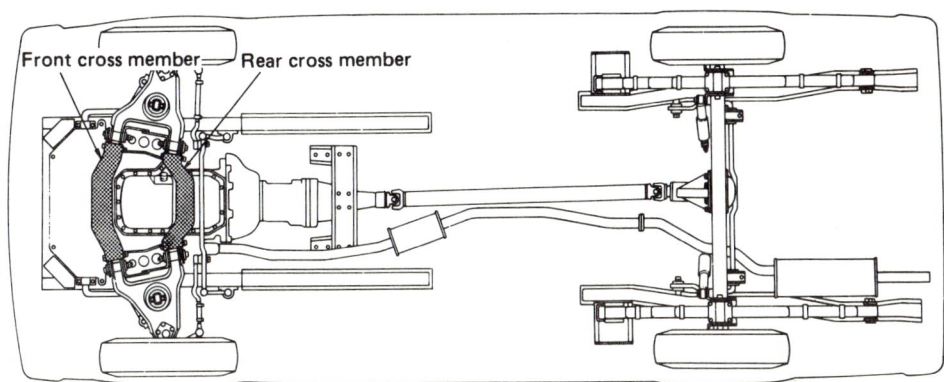

RM 21 Location of front cross members

stands or blocks should be positioned under the bodyframe members. To raise the complete front end for servicing or repair work, place the jack under the front crossmember; **on no account position it under the rear one**. The rear end may be jacked-up under the axle casing.

A towing eye is positioned at the front of all vehicles but attachment of a towline at the rear should be made at the rear spring shackle. When a vehicle fitted with automatic transmission is being towed, the propeller shaft must be disconnected from the rear axle pinion driving flange and the shaft tied up out of the way, otherwise the transmission unit will be damaged due to lack of lubrication as no rear oil pump is fitted to the unit.

Routine maintenance

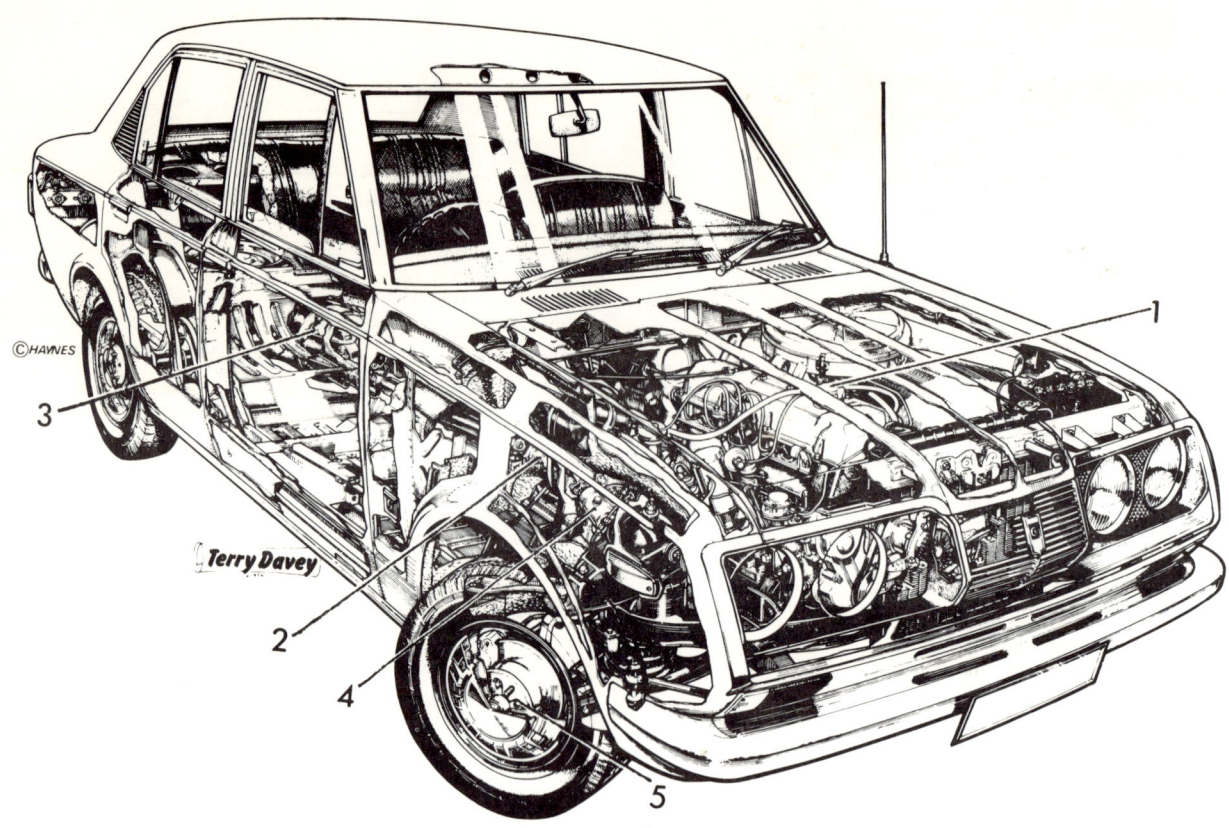

Recommended lubricants

Component	Castrol Grade
1 Engine	Castrol GTX
2 Gearbox	
Manual	Castrol Hypoy Light (80 EP)
Automatic	Castrol TQF
3 Rear axle	Castrol Hypoy B (90 EP)
4 Steering box	Castrol Hypoy Light (80 EP)
5 Wheel bearings/chassis	Castrol LM Grease

Note: The above are general recommendations. Lubrication requirements vary from territory-to-territory. Consult the operators handbook supplied with the vehicle.

Chapter 1 Engine

Contents

Camshaft and camshaft bearings - examination and renovation	24
Camshaft - removal	11
Connecting rods and bearings - examination and renovation	21
Crankshaft and main bearings - inspection and renovation	20
Crankshaft and main bearings - reassembly	34
Crankshaft and main bearings - removal	16
Crankcase ventilation system	18
Cylinder block - examination and renovation	32
Cylinder bores - examination and renovation	22
Cylinder head and valves - servicing	26
Cylinder head and valve mechanism - installation	39
Cylinder head - removal	12
Dismantling the engine - general	8
Driveplate (automatic transmission) - servicing	30
Engine ancillary components - removal	9
Engine ancillary components - refitting	40
Engine/automatic transmission - reconnecting	42
Engine/manual gearbox - reconnecting	41
Engine reassembly - general	33
Engine - separation from manual gearbox	6
Engine - separation from automatic transmission	7
Engine/transmission - installation	43
Engine/transmission - removal	5
Examination and renovation - general	19
Fault diagnosis - engine	45
Flywheel (or driveplate - automatic transmission) - refitting	37
Flywheel - servicing	29
General description	1
Initial start-up after major overhaul	44
Lubrication system, oil pump and filter	17
Method of engine removal	4
Major operations only possible with the engine removed	3
Major operations possible with engine in position	2
Oil pump and timing gear - reassembly	36
Oil pump drive shaft - servicing	28
Oil seals - renewal	31
Piston/connecting rod assemblies - removal	14
Pistons, rings and connecting rods - reassembly and refitting	35
Piston rings and gudgeon pins - removal	15
Piston and piston rings - examination and renovation	23
Rocker shaft and gear - removal	10
Rocker shaft - servicing	27
Sump and timing gear - removal	13
Sump - refitting	38
Timing components - examination and renovation	25

Specifications

Engine general

Engine type		4 cylinder in-line, single overhead camshaft (SOHC)
	8R series	**18R series**
Bore and stroke	3.39 x 3.15 in (86.0 x 80.0 mm)	3.48 x 3.15 in (88.5 x 80.0 mm)
Total piston displacement	113.4 cu in (1858 cc)	120.0 cu in (1968 cc)
Compression ratio	9.0 : 1 (8RB - 10 : 1)	8.5 : 1
Maximum BHP @ 5500 rev/min	108 (8RB - 120)	97
Maximum torque @ 3800 rev/min	117 lb/ft (16.2 kg/m) (8RB - 120 lb/ft - 16.6 kg/m)	106 lb/ft (14.6 kg/m)
Firing order	1 - 3 - 4 - 2	1 - 3 - 4 - 2

Cylinder head

Material	Cast-iron
Maximum permissible warpage	0.002 in (0.05 mm)

Cylinder block

Material	Cast-iron
Maximum permissible warpage	0.002 in (0.05 mm)
Bore:	
8R series	3.386 to 3.388 in (86.00 to 86.05 mm)
18R series	3.484 to 3.486 in (88.50 to 88.55 mm)
Maximum permissible cylinder bore wear	0.008 in (0.2 mm)
Maximum permissible bore difference between cylinders	0.002 in (0.05 mm)
Maximum permissible taper or out of round	0.0008 in (0.02 mm)

Chapter 1/Engine

	8R series	18R series
Pistons and rings		
Standard diameter	3.3846 to 3.3866 in (85.97 to 86.02 mm)	3.481 to 3.484 in 88.44 to 88.49 mm)
Oversize - 0.25	3.3941 to 3.3961 in (86.21 to 86.26 mm)	3.492 to 3.494 in (88.69 to 88.74 mm)
Oversize - 0.50	3.4039 to 3.4059 in (86.46 to 86.51 mm)	3.502 to 3.504 in (88.94 to 88.99 mm)
Oversize - 0.75	3.4138 to 3.4158 in (86.71 to 86.76 mm)	3.511 to 3.513 in (88.19 to 89.24 mm)
Oversize - 1.00	3.4236 to 3.4256 in (86.96 to 87.01 mm)	3.521 to 3.523 in 89.44 to 89.49 mm)
Gudgeon pin diameter	0.8663 to 0.8669 in (22.004 to 22.019 mm)	
Gudgeon pin bore in piston	0.8661 to 0.8667 in (22.00 to 22.015 mm)	
Piston ring end-gap	0.004 to 0.012 in (0.1 to 0.3 mm)	
Piston ring to groove clearance:		
Compression rings	0.0012 to 0.0028 in (0.03 to 0.07 mm)	
Oil control ring:		
8R series	0.0008 to 0.0028 in (0.02 to 0.07 mm)	
18R series	Zero (spring type)	
Connecting rods		
Length (between centres)	5.441 to 5.445 in (138.20 to 138.30 mm)	
Big-end bore	2.2047 to 2.2057 in (56.0 to 56.024 mm)	
Standard endfloat:		
8R series	0.0043 to 0.0097 in (0.110 to 0.246 mm)	
18R series	0.006 to 0.010 in (0.16 to 0.26 mm)	
Maximum endfloat	0.012 in (0.3 mm)	
Small end bush internal diameter (after reaming)	0.8666 to 0.8672 in (22.012 to 22.027 mm)	
Gudgeon pin to small end bush running clearance	0.0002 to 0.0004 in (0.005 to 0.011 mm)	
Maximum permissible gudgeon pin to small end bush clearance:		
8R series	0.0006 in (0.015 mm)	
18R series	0.0008 in (0.02 mm)	
Big-end bearing running clearance:		
8R series	0.0008 to 0.0020 in (0.02 to 0.05 mm)	
18R series	0.0010 to 0.0021 in (0.025 to 0.055 mm)	
Maximum permissible big-end bearing running clearance	0.003 in (0.08 mm)	
Crankshaft		
Number of main bearings	5	
End float:		
8R series	0.002 to 0.010 in (0.05 to 0.25 mm)	
18R series	0.0008 to 0.008 in (0.02 to 0.20 mm)	
Maximum permissible endfloat	0.12 in (0.3 mm)	
Maximum out-of-round or taper for journals and crankpins	0.0004 in (0.01 mm)	
Crankshaft journal and crankpin running clearance	0.0008 to 0.0020 in (0.02 to 0.05 mm)	
Maximum journal or crankpin running clearance	0.003 in (0.08 mm)	
Crankpin journal finished diameter:		
Standard bearing	2.3613 to 2.3622 in (59.976 to 60.000 mm)	
Undersize - 0.25	2.3504 to 2.3508 in (59.701 to 59.711 mm)	
Undersize - 0.50	2.3406 to 2.3410 in (59.451 to 59.461 mm)	
Undersize - 0.75	2.3307 to 2.3311 in (59.201 to 59.211 mm)	
Undersize - 1.00	2.3209 to 2.3213 in (58.951 to 58.961 mm)	
Flywheel		
Maximum permissible run-out	0.008 in (0.2 mm)	
Maximum regrind	0.04 in (1.0 mm)	
Camshaft		
Standard endfloat	0.0017 to 0.0066 in (0.042 to 0.168 mm)	
Maximum permissible endfloat	0.010 in (0.25 mm)	
Bearing running clearance	0.001 to 0.002 in (0.03 to 0.05 mm)	
Maximum bearing running clearance	0.004 in (0.1 mm)	
Cam lift (8R series):		
Inlet	0.4 in (10.0 mm)	
Exhaust	0.4 in (10.0 mm)	
Cam lift (18R series):		
Inlet	0.317 in (8.04 mm)	
Exhaust	0.319 in (8.10 mm)	
Camshaft journal finished diameter:		
Standard bearing	1.3768 to 1.3778 in (34.972 to 34.996 mm)	
Undersize 0.125	1.3718 to 1.3722 in (34.843 to 34.853 mm)	
Undersize 0.25	1.3670 to 1.3674 in (34.723 to 34.733 mm)	
Maximum journal out of round or taper	0.0004 in (0.01 mm)	

Chapter 1/Engine

Oil pump driveshaft
- Standard endfloat ... 0.002 to 0.005 in (0.06 to 0.13 mm)
- Maximum permissible endfloat ... 0.012 in (0.3 mm)
- Driveshaft bearing running clearance ... 0.0010 to 0.0026 in (0.025 to 0.066 mm)
- Maximum premissible driveshaft running clearance ... 0.003 in (0.08 mm)

Valves   8R series   18R series

- Head diameter:
  - Inlet ... 1.687 to 1.699 in (42.85 to 43.15 mm)   1.608 to 1.620 in (40.85 to 41.15 mm)
  - Exhaust ... 1.333 to 1.345 in (33.85 to 34.15 mm)   1.411 to 1.423 in (35.85 to 36.15 mm)
- Overall length ... 4.476 in (113.7 mm)   4.457 in (113.2 mm)
- Valve stem diameter:
  - Inlet ... 0.3140 to 0.3144 in (7.975 to 7.985 mm)
  - Exhaust ... 0.3132 to 0.3140 in (7.955 to 7.975 mm)
- Standard stem to guide clearance:
  - Inlet ... 0.0010 to 0.0022 in (0.025 to 0.055 mm)
  - Exhaust ... 0.0014 to 0.0030 in (0.035 to 0.075 mm)
- Maximum stem to guide clearance:
  - Inlet ... 0.003 in (0.08 mm)
  - Exhaust ... 0.004 in (0.10 mm)
- Valve head contact angle ... 45°
- Valve clearance (cold):
  - Inlet ... 0.007 in (0.18 mm)
  - Exhaust ... 0.013 in (0.33 mm)
- Valve clearance (hot):
  - Inlet ... 0.008 in (0.20 mm)
  - Exhaust ... 0.014 in (0.36 mm)
- Valve guide overall length:
  - Inlet ... 1.949 to 2.185 in (49.5 to 55.5 mm)
  - Exhaust ... 2.303 to 2.343 in (58.5 to 59.5 mm)
- Valve guide inner diameter (after reaming) ... 0.315 to 0.316 in (8.01 to 8.03 mm)
- Valve guide outer diameter:
  - Standard ... 0.5521 to 0.5528 in (14.023 to 14.041 mm)
  - Oversize (0.05) ... 0.5541 to 0.5548 in (14.073 to 14.091 mm)
- Valve guide projection ... 0.63 in (16.0 mm)
- Valve spring free length:
  - Inner ... 1.74 in (44.1 mm)
  - Outer ... 1.83 in (46.5 mm)

     8R series   18R series

- Valve rocker shaft outside diameter ... 0.7272 to 0.7277 in (18.470 to 18.483 mm)   0.7269 to 0.7277 in (18.464 to 18.483 mm)
- Rocker arm bush running clearance ... 0.0012 to 0.0015 in (0.030 to 0.038 mm)   0.0007 to 0.0020 in (0.017 to 0.051 mm)
- Maximum permissible running clearance ... 0.002 in (0.05 mm)   0.003 in (0.08 mm)

Timing chain tensioners
- Lower tensioner spring free length ... 2.70 in (67.4 mm)
- Upper tensioner spring free length ... 3.08 in (77.0 mm)

Torque wrench settings

	lb/ft	kg/m
Crankshaft main bearing cap bolts	75	10.4
Big-end bearing cap bolts	45	6.2
Camshaft bearing cap bolts	15	2.1
Crankshaft rear oil seal retainer bolts	15	2.1
Oil pump driveshaft thrust plate bolts	15	2.1
Camshaft sprocket to driveshaft bolt	70	9.7
Crankshaft pulley bolt	50	6.9
Sump bolts	5	0.7
Cylinder head bolts	70	9.7
Camshaft sprocket bolts	12	1.7
Rocker shaft pillar bolts	15	2.1
Rocker shaft oil pipe unions	15	2.1
Drive plate to torque converter bolts	32	4.4
Clutch bellhousing to cylinder block bolts:		
8R series	33	4.5
18R series	50	6.9
Timing cover bolts	15	2.1
Manifold bolts	35	4.8
Rocker cover bolts	7	0.9
Flywheel to crankshaft bolts	48	6.6

Driveplate (automatic transmission) to crankshaft bolts ...	45	5.9
Clutch pressure plate cover to flywheel:		
8R series	9	1.3
18R - C	16	2.2
Oil pump to crankcase bolts	15	2.1
Torque converter housing to engine bolts:		
8R	33	4.5
18R - C	50	6.9

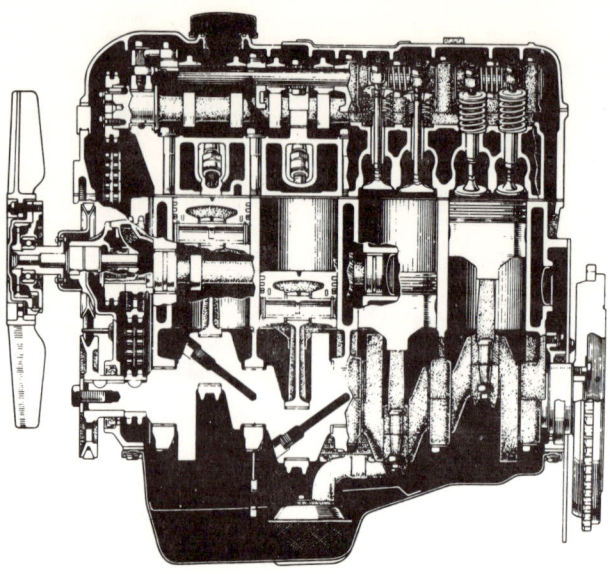

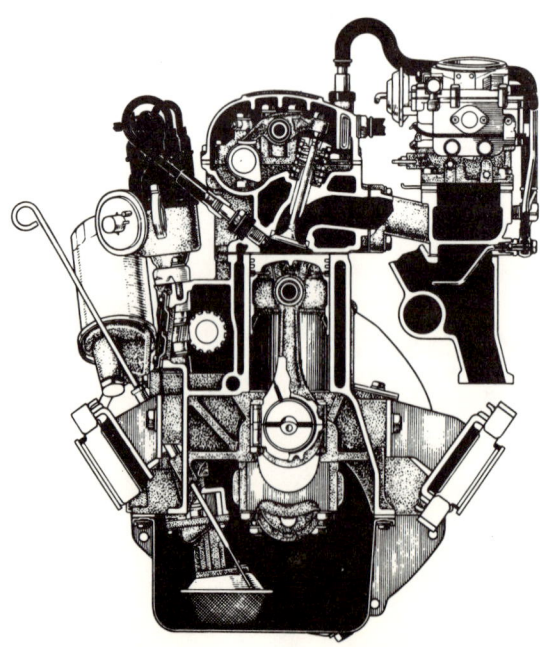

Fig 1.1 Sectional views of the 8R/18R series engine

Chapter 1/Engine

1 General description

The engine installed in all models is of four cylinder in-line overhead camshaft (ohc) type. The difference between the '8R' and '18R' series is that of capacity, the larger engine having an increased bore.

A five bearing crankshaft is employed and the overhead camshaft is driven by a double roller chain. A full-flow oil filter of disposable cartridge type is used and the lubrication system is by means of a trochoid type pump driven by a shaft connected to the crankshaft sprocket through the medium of a chain.

The '8R-C' and '18R-C' engines are equipped with full emission control systems. These systems are covered in Chapter 3, of this manual. The '8R-B' engine has twin SU type carburettors, otherwise it is similar to other models in the series.

2 Major operations possible with engine in position

1 The following operations can be carried out with the engine installed in the bodyframe:
A *Removal and replacement of camshaft cover. On vehicles equipped with air conditioning, the flexible pipe clamp must be removed from the camshaft cover and the pipe pulled away sufficiently far to provide clearance to withdraw the cover. On no account disconnect any of the air conditioning circuit pipes or unions.*
B *Removal and refitting of the camshaft and cylinder head.*
C *Removal and refitting of the timing chain and gears.*
D *Removal and refitting of the engine front mountings and the transmission rear mounting.*

2 If a hoist is attached to the engine lifting hooks and its weight is taken by the hoist, the engine mountings can be removed and the engine raised an inch or two. Disconnect the steering relay rod, drop arm and idler arm rods (Chapter 11) to permit the following operations to be carried out:
A *Removal and refitting of the sump (detach strengthener brackets first).*
B *Removal and refitting of the oil pump.*
C *Removal and refitting of the piston/connecting rod assemblies (through the top of the cylinder block).*

3 Major operations only possible with the engine removed

1 The following operations are only possible with the engine removed:
A *Removal and installation of the flywheel or driveplate.*
B *Removal and installation of the crankshaft and main bearings.*

4 Method of engine removal

The engine complete with gearbox or automatic transmission unit can be hoisted, at an angle, out of the engine compartment. Removal of the engine alone leaving the gearbox in position is not possible as the engine cannot be pulled far enough forward to clear the primary shaft of the gearbox or in the case of automatic transmission, the torque converter.

5 Engine/transmission - removal

1 Disconnect the lead from the battery negative terminal. (photo)
2 Drain the cooling system (see Chapter 3). (photo)
3 Drain the engine oil and the gearbox oil.
4 Drain the fluid if automatic transmission is fitted.
5 *On vehicles equipped with air conditioning:* the system must be discharged of refrigerant gas so that the compressor connecting pipes can be disconnected. This and the later recharging of the system are jobs for the service engineer.
6 Mark the position of the bonnet hinge plates, remove the securing bolts and with the help of an assistant, lift the bonnet from the vehicle. (photo)
7 Remove the radiator grille, the upper and lower shields and the fan shrouds. (photo)
8 Disconnect the upper and lower radiator hoses, unbolt the radiator and remove it from the engine compartment. On vehicles equipped with air conditioning, the condenser is located in front of the radiator and this too will have to be disconnected (system first discharged) and removed. On some models the headlight units may have to be removed to gain access to the condenser mountings. Where an oil cooler is fitted in conjunction with automatic transmission then the cooler hoses will also have to be removed from the radiator before it can be withdrawn. (photos)
9 Remove the air cleaner from the carburettor. (photo)
10 Disconnect the fuel inlet pipe from the fuel pump. (photo)
11 Disconnect the heater hoses. (photo)
12 Disconnect the controls from the carburettor. (photo)
13 Disconnect the brake servo unit vacuum hose from the inlet manifold.
14 Unbolt the clutch operating cylinder from the clutch bellhousing, also the hose support bracket and tie the cylinder up out of the way; there is no need to disconnect the hydraulic line. (photo)
15 Disconnect the leads from the following components: Starter solenoid, alternator, oil pressure switch, water temperature transmitter, emission control unit and coil (HT and LT leads). (photo)
16 Disconnect the vacuum hoses from the emission control unit. It is important that these are carefully identified to ensure exact refitting in their original positions.

5.1 Disconnecting lead from battery negative terminal

5.2 Sump drain plug

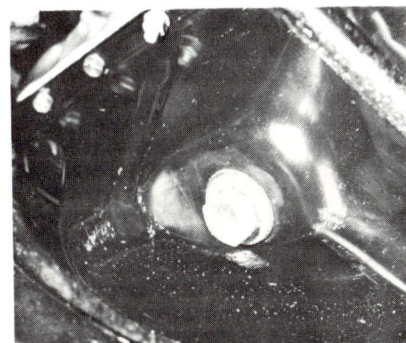

5.6 Bonnet hinge

5.7 Removing radiator grille

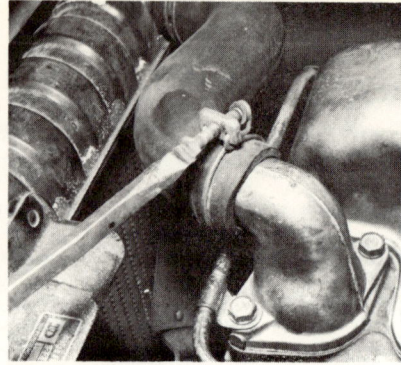
5.8a Disconnecting radiator top hose

5.8b Removing radiator

5.9 Removing air cleaner

5.10 Disconnecting fuel inlet hose from pump

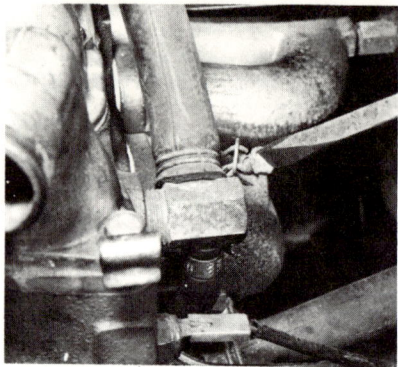
5.11 Disconnecting a heater hose

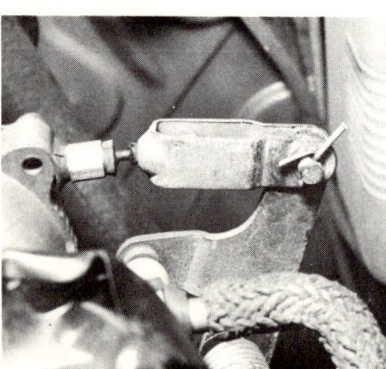
5.12 Throttle connection

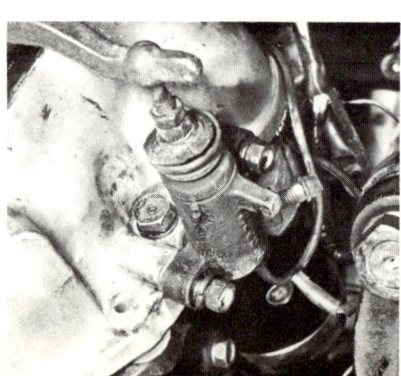
5.14a Removing clutch slave cylinder

5.14b Clutch hydraulic hose support bracket

5.15 Water temperature transmitter

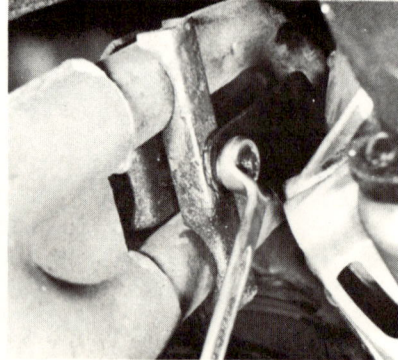
5.18 Removing exhaust pipe clamp

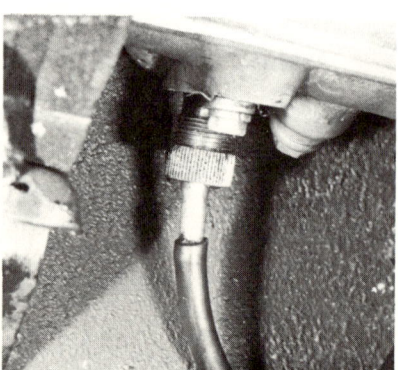
5.20 Speedo. cable connection to gearbox

Chapter 1/Engine

17 Working beneath the vehicle, disconnect the exhaust downpipe from the exhaust manifold.
18 Disconnect the exhaust pipe support bracket from the transmission housing. (photo)
19 Unbolt the handbrake cable equaliser and lower the equaliser complete with cables.
20 Disconnect the speedometer cable from the transmission housing. (photo)
21 *On vehicles with a three-speed manually operated gearbox:*
disconnect the high and low speed connecting rods and the cross-shaft from the lower end of the steering column type gearchange mechanism.
22 *On vehicles with a four or five-speed manually operated gearbox:* unscrew and remove the centre console within the vehicle and then remove the eight screws which secure the gearchange lever bellows retaining plate. Make sure that the lever is in neutral and then unscrew the lever lock bolt and the two lever bracket bolts (type SS1 gearbox). On type W40 and W50 gearboxes, remove the gear lever retainer plate and pull out the lever. (photos)
23 *On vehicles equipped with automatic transmission:* disconnect the speed selector rod from the selector lever on the transmission housing and remove the fluid filler tube and dipstick.
24 Mark the edges of the rear propeller shaft and rear axle pinion flanges so that they can be refitted in exactly the same relative positions to maintain balance. Unbolt the flanges and push the propeller shaft slightly forward to separate them and then withdraw the shaft to the rear.
25 Where the propeller shaft is of the three section, centre bearing type, then the connecting flanges at the front of the centre universal joint should be separated in addition to the rear pinion flange and the rear section of the shaft removed. Unbolt the centre flexible bearing from the bodyframe and withdraw the two front sections of the propeller shaft from the splined rear shaft of the transmission unit.
26 Using a suitable hoist and slings positioned securely round the engine, raise the hoist so that it just takes the weight of the engine. Unbolt the engine mountings from the crossmember. (photo)
27 Place a jack under the transmission housing and then unbolt and remove the rear mounting support crossmember and the mounting. (photos)
28 Remove the jack from below the transmission which will allow it to drop a few inches. Hoist the combined engine/transmission up and out of the engine compartment at a steeply inclined angle. (photo)

6 Engine - separation from manual gearbox

1 Remove the starter motor. (photo)
2 Unscrew and remove the bolts which connect the clutch bellhousing to the cylinder block.
3 Pull the gearbox from the engine in a straight line, supporting the gearbox so that its weight does not hang upon the gearbox input shaft, even momentarily, whilst it is still engaged with the clutch mechanism. (photo)

7 Engine - separation from automatic transmission

1 Unscrew and remove the oil cooler pipes.
2 Remove the starter motor.
3 Remove the 'kick-down' rod (two speed and A.30 type transmission) or disconnect the 'kick-down' cable (A.40 transmission).
4 Remove the two brackets which connect the sides of the

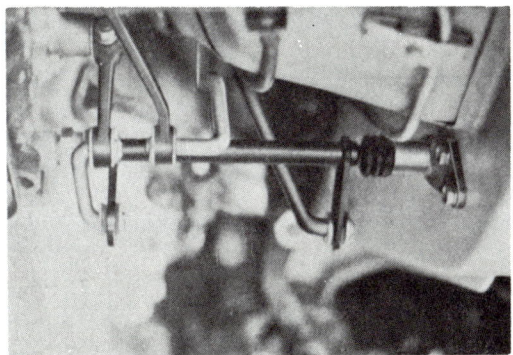

Fig 1.2 Steering column type gearchange (manual gearbox) cross-shaft and connecting rods (Sec 5)

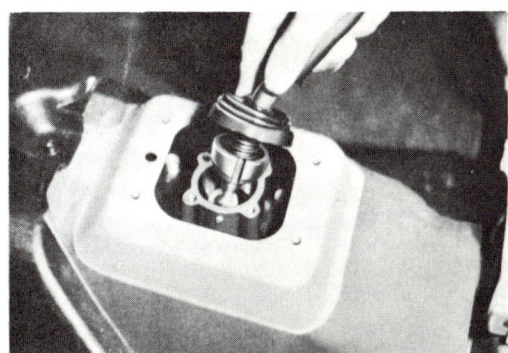

Fig 1.3 Removing gearchange lever from 4/5 speed type manual gearbox (Sec 5)

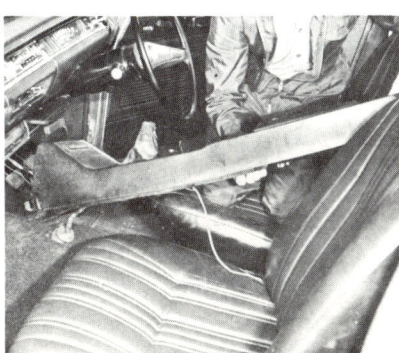

5.22a Removing centre console

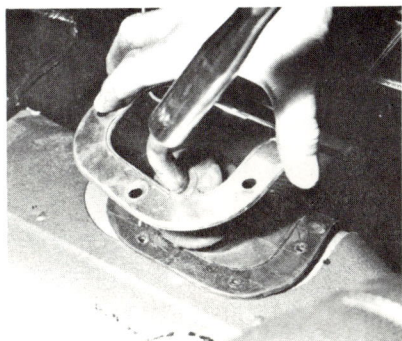

5.22b Removing gearchange lever boot retainer (type SS1 gearbox)

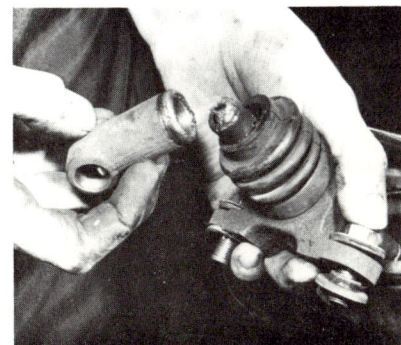

5.22c Disconnecting gearchange lever from swing arm (type SS1 gearbox)

5.26 An engine front mounting

5.27a Transmission rear mounting

5.27b Removing radiator support upper crossmember

5.28 Removing engine/transmission

6.1 Removing starter motor

6.3 Separating engine and gearbox

transmission casing to the cylinder block.
5 Remove the torque converter lower cover plate, then remove the torque converter to drive plate securing bolts. The drive plate will have to be rotated to reach each of the bolts in turn. Mark the relative position of the drive plate to the converter torque using a spirit pen or dab of quick drying paint so that they can be fitted in their original relative positions.
6 Unscrew and remove the bolts which secure the automatic transmission torque converter housing to the engine. Pull the automatic transmission unit from its connection with the engine, keeping it in a straight line and supporting its weight during the operation. There will probably be some loss of fluid from the torque converter during the separation procedure so be prepared to catch it in a suitable container.

8 Dismantling the engine - general

1 It is best to mount the engine on a dismantling stand but if one is not available, then stand the engine on a strong bench so as to be at a comfortable working height. Failing this, the engine will have to be stripped down on the floor.
2 During the dismantling process the greatest care should be taken to keep the exposed parts free from dirt. As an aid to achieving this, it is a sound scheme to thoroughly clean down the outside of the engine, removing all traces of oil and congealed dirt.
3 Use paraffin or a good water soluble grease solvent. The latter compound will make the job much easier, as, after the solvent has been applied and allowed to stand for a time, a vigorous jet of water will wash off the solvent and all the grease and filth. If the dirt is thick and deeply embedded, work the solvent into it with a wire brush.
4 Finally wipe down the exterior of the engine with a rag and only then, when it is quite clean should the dismantling process

begin. As the engine is stripped, clean each part in a bath of paraffin or petrol.
5 Never immerse parts with oilways in paraffin, ie; the crankshaft, but to clean, wipe down carefully with a petrol dampened rag. Oilways can be cleaned out with wire. If an air line is present all parts can be blown dry and the oilways blown through as an added precaution.
6 Re-use of old engine gaskets is false economy and can give rise to oil and water leaks, if nothing worse. To avoid the possibility or trouble after the engine has been reassembled **always** use new gaskets throughout.
7 Do not throw the old gaskets away as it sometimes happens that an immediate replacement cannot be found and the old gasket is then very useful as a template. Hang up the old gaskets as they are removed on a suitable hook or nail.
8 To strip the engine it is best to work from the top down. The sump provides a firm base on which the engine can be supported in an upright position. When this stage where the sump must be removed is reached, the engine can be turned on its side and all other work carried out with it in this position.
9 Wherever possible, replace nuts, bolts and washers fingertight from wherever they were removed. This helps avoid later loss and muddle. If they cannot be replaced then lay them out in such a fashion that it is clear where they came from.

9 Engine ancillary components - removal

1 With the engine removed from the vehicle and separated from the gearbox, the ancillary components should now be removed before dismantling proper begins.
2 Unbolt the clutch pressure plate assembly from the flywheel and remove the clutch mechanism complete with driven plate, (manual gearbox).
3 Bend back the tabs of the locking plates which are located

Chapter 1/Engine

under the bolts which secure the flywheel (or driveplate - automatic transmission) to the crankshaft rear flange. Remove the bolts and lift off the flywheel or driveplate as the case may be.

4 Where the vehicle is equipped with air conditioning, remove the air compressor and idler pulley, also the power steering hydraulic pump (if fitted).

5 From the right-hand side of the engine, remove the dipstick (1) the fuel pipes (2) and loosen the distributor clamp (3). Withdraw the distributor (4) complete with cap and HT leads. Remove the spark plugs followed by the fuel pump (5) and the oil filter/mounting assembly (6). If desired, the side cover (7), oil pressure switch (8) and engine mounting brackets (9) may also be removed. (Fig 1.4)

6 From the left-hand side of the engine, remove the heater pipes (1) which run to the automatic choke, the crankcase ventilation hose and then unbolt and remove the carburettor (2) complete with heat insulator (3) from the inlet manifold. Remove the manifold assembly (4), disconnect the inlet manifold water heater pipes (8R-B twin SU only), water pump bypass hose (6) drivebelt adjustment strap (7), alternator (8) and fan belt (9). The alternator mounting bracket and left-hand engine mounting bracket may be removed if desired. (Fig 1.5)

7 From the front of the engine, remove the water pump and fan assembly.

8 From the top of the engine, remove the thermostat housing (2) and the thermostat also the rocker box cover (1). (Fig 1.6)

9 The engine has now been stripped of ancillary components and is ready for dismantling, as described in the following Sections. On 8R-C engines before March 1971, an air pump (crankshaft driven by vee-belt) is fitted as part of the emission control system: this should be removed from its mountings.

10 Rocker shaft and gear - removal

1 Unscrew and remove the union bolts and withdraw the oil feed pipe.
2 Unscrew the rocker shaft pillar bolts in the sequence shown to ensure that the pressure of the valve springs is relieved gently to prevent distortion of the shaft. (Fig 1.7)
3 Remove the rocker shaft assembly from the cylinder head.

11 Camshaft - removal

1 Unbolt the gearwheel from the end of the camshaft. A semi-circular plastic plug is provided for access to the bolts.
2 Use a hooked piece of wire to support the chain while the gearwheel is removed and to prevent the chain becoming disconnected from the drive sprocket. This is particularly important when the camshaft is being removed with the engine in position in the car and further dismantling is not anticipated.

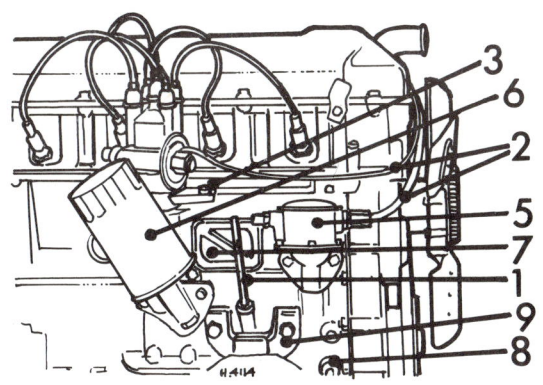

Fig 1.4 Location of ancillary components on right-hand side of engine (Sec 9)

1 Dipstick
2 Fuel pipes
3 Distributor clamp
4 Distributor
5 Fuel pump
6 Oil filter
7 Side cover
8 Oil pressure switch
9 Engine mounting bracket

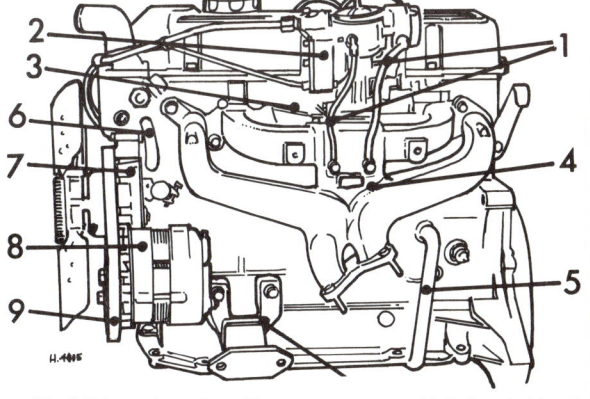

Fig 1.5 Location of ancillary components of left-hand side of engine (Sec 9)

1 Choke heater pipes
2 Carburettor
3 Heat insulating flange washer
4 Manifold assembly
5 Fume outlet (non EEC)
6 Water pump bypass
7 Drivebelt adjustment strap
8 Alternator
9 Fan belt

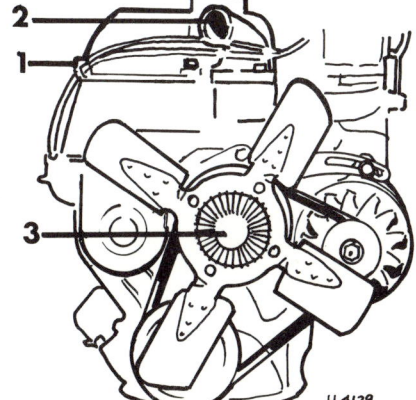

Fig 1.6 Engine front mounted components (Sec 9)
1 Rocker cover
2 Thermostat housing cover
3 Fan assembly

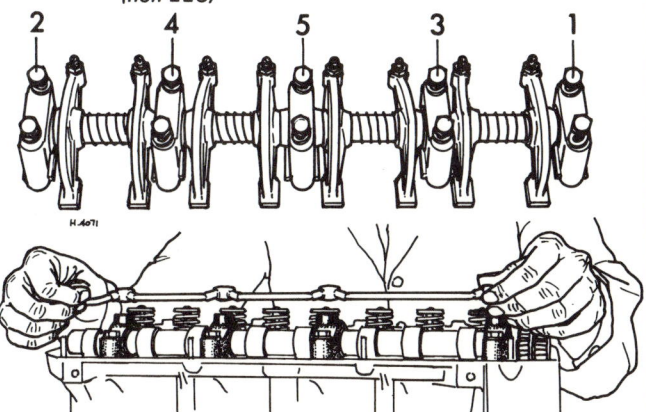

Fig 1.7 Loosening sequence for rocker shaft support pillar bolts and removing the oil pipe assembly (Sec 10)

Chapter 1/Engine

3 Remove the four camshaft bearing caps, keeping them in strict sequence for correct refitting (they are usually numbered 1 to 4).
4 Remove the camshaft.

12 Cylinder head - removal

1 Unscrew the cylinder head bolts half a turn at a time in the sequence shown in Fig 1.10.
2 Unscrew and remove the two bolts which secure the top end of the timing chain cover to the cylinder head.
3 Lift the cylinder head straight up to clear the locating dowels. If the cylinder head is stuck, do not attempt to prise it off by inserting a screwdriver or chisel in the gasket joint as this will only damage the machined faces of the head and block. Tap the sides of the head using a hammer and hardwood block or alternatively screw in the spark plugs and turn the engine by means of the crankshaft pulley bolt so that compression (all valves closed) will assist in breaking the seal.

13 Sump and timing gear - removal

1 Unscrew and remove the sump securing bolts and lift the sump from the crankcase.
2 Unscrew the crankshaft pulley bolt with the sump removed, jam the crankshaft with a piece of wood to prevent the engine

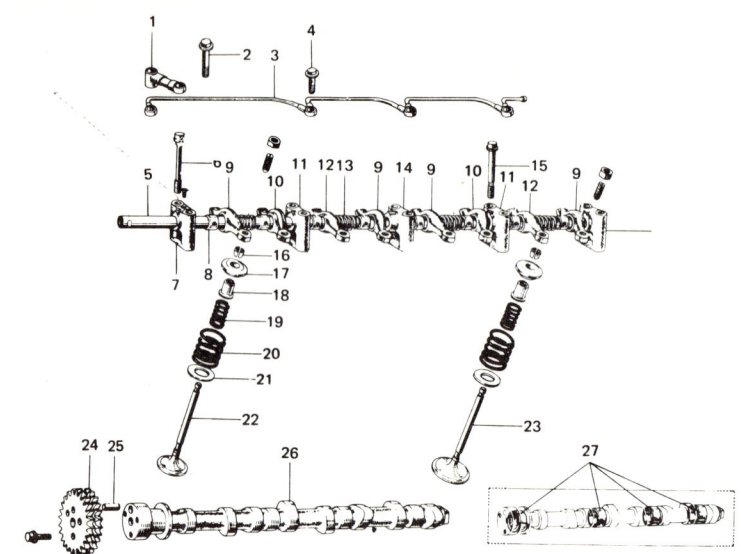

Fig 1.8 Exploded view of the rocker and valve gear and the camshaft (Secs 10 and 11)

1 Oil pipe union
2 Thermostat housing cover
3 Oil pipe assembly
4 Union bolt
5 Rocker shaft
6 Bolt
7 Rocker shaft support pillar
8 Bearing
9 Rocker arm
10 Rocker arm
11 Rocker shaft support pillar
12 Rocker arm
13 Spring
14 Rocker shaft
   support pillar
15 Bolt
16 Split collets
17 Valve spring retainer
18 Valve stem oil seal
19 Valve (inner) spring
20 Valve (outer) spring
21 plate
22 Exhaust valve
23 Inlet valve
24 Camshaft sprocket
25 Dowel pin
26 Camshaft
27 Camshaft shell bearings

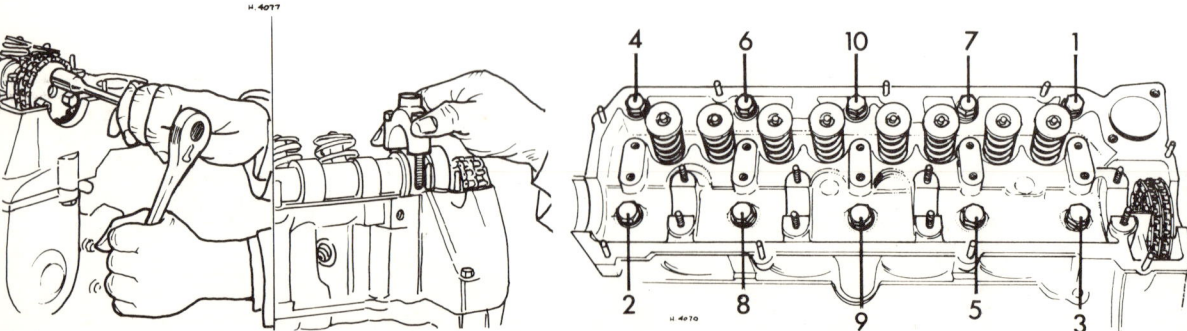

Fig 1.9 Removing the camshaft sprocket and bearing caps (Sec 11)

Fig 1.10 Bolt loosening sequence for the cylinder head bolts (Sec 12)

Chapter 1/Engine

turning as the bolt is loosened. If the pulley is being removed with the engine in position in the vehicle then *with manual gearbox vehicles,* engage a gear and apply the handbrake fully to prevent the crankshaft rotating. *With automatic transmission,* remove the starter and jam the ring gear with a large screwdriver or cold chisel.

3 Remove the crankshaft pulley. It will usually pull straight out but if necessary, remove it by placing two tyre levers behind it or use a puller (there are two holes tapped in the pulley for this purpose).

4 Unbolt and remove the timing cover. Note that the upper bolt is entered from the rear.
5 Remove the camshaft drive chain. The oil pump driveshaft sprocket and the chain tensioners should be withdrawn.
6 Remove the crankshaft sprocket (1) and oil pump driveshaft driven sprocket (2) complete with chain (3) as one assembly. Remove the chain damper. (Fig 1.15)
7 Remove the oil pump driveshaft thrust plate (1) and withdraw the driveshaft (2) and engine front plate. Unbolt and remove the oil pump assembly (4) from within the crankcase.

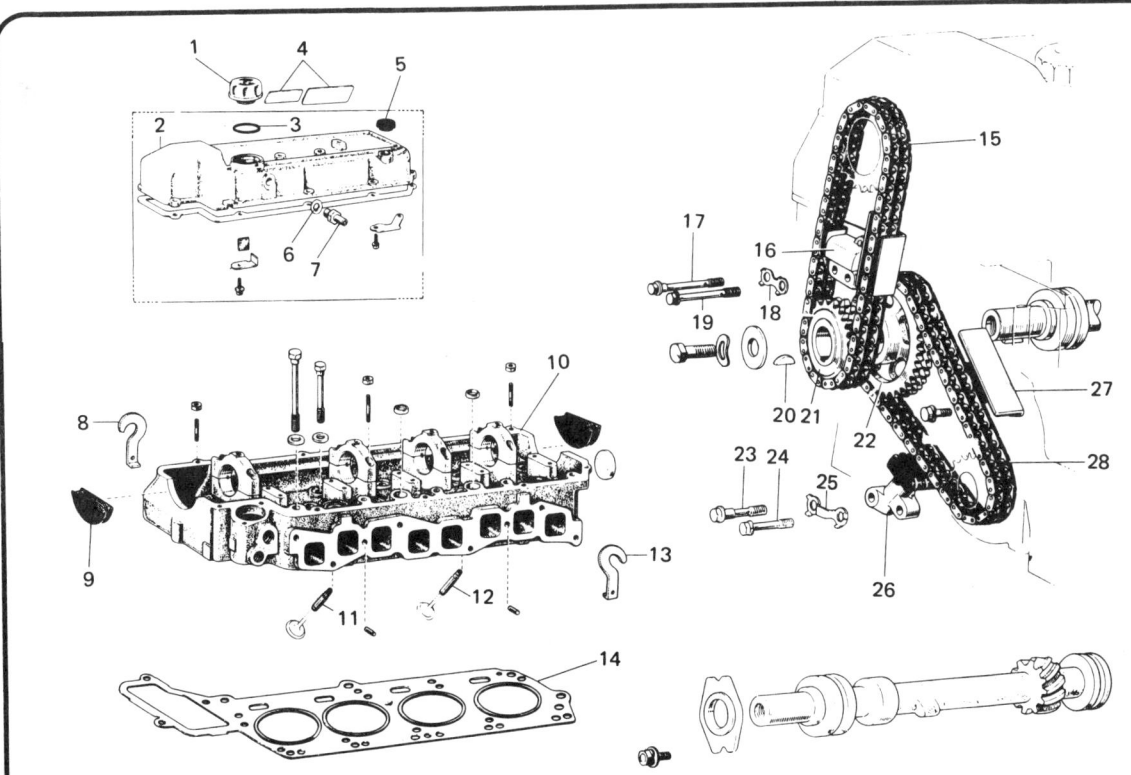

Fig 1.11 Exploded view of the cylinder head and timing gear (Secs 12 and 13)

1 Oil filler cap
2 Rocker cover
3 Seal
4 Plates
5 Grommet
6 Seal
7 Union
8 Lifting hook
9 Plug
10 Cylinder head
11 Valve guide
12 Valve guide
13 Lifting hook
14 Cylinder head gasket
15 Upper timing chain
16 Upper chain tensioner
17 Hollow bolts
18 Lockplate
19 Securing bolt
20 Woodruff key
21 Camshaft drive sprocket
22 Oil pump driveshaft
sprocket
23 Hollow bolt
24 Securing bolt
25 Lockplate
26 Lower chain tensioner
27 Chain slipper
28 Lower timing chain

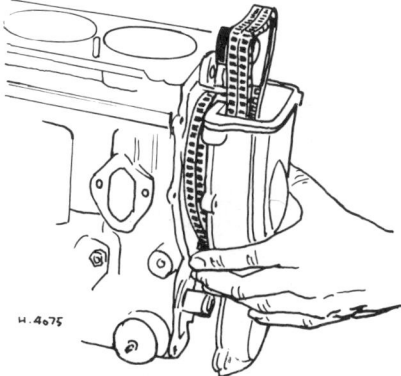

Fig 1.12 Removing the timing cover

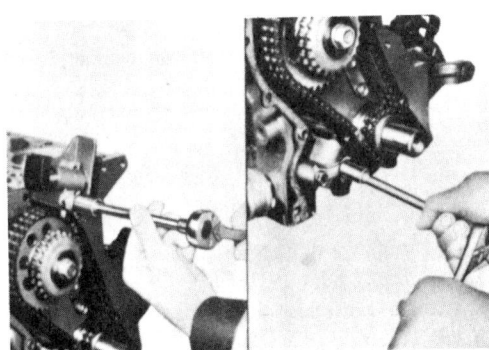

Fig 1.13 Unbolting the timing chain tensioner (Sec 13)

(Fig 1.17)

14 Piston/connecting rod assemblies - removal

1 Turn the crankshaft so that the pistons are all part way down their bores. Using a bearing scraper, carefully remove as much as possible of the 'wear' ridge at the top of each cylinder bore. This operation is essential to prevent the piston rings breaking as the pistons are extracted through the top of the block.

2 With quick-drying paint, mark each piston, connecting rod and big-end bearing cap. Number the components of each assembly 1 to 4 (from the front of the engine) and also the relative position of the components to each other and to the crankcase, so that if the original assembly is to be refitted it will be installed in its exact, previously located position.

3 Unbolt the big-end caps from the connecting rods and then push each piston/connecting rod assembly out through the top of the block. Take great care that the threads of the big-end studs do not score the cylinder bores during this operation.

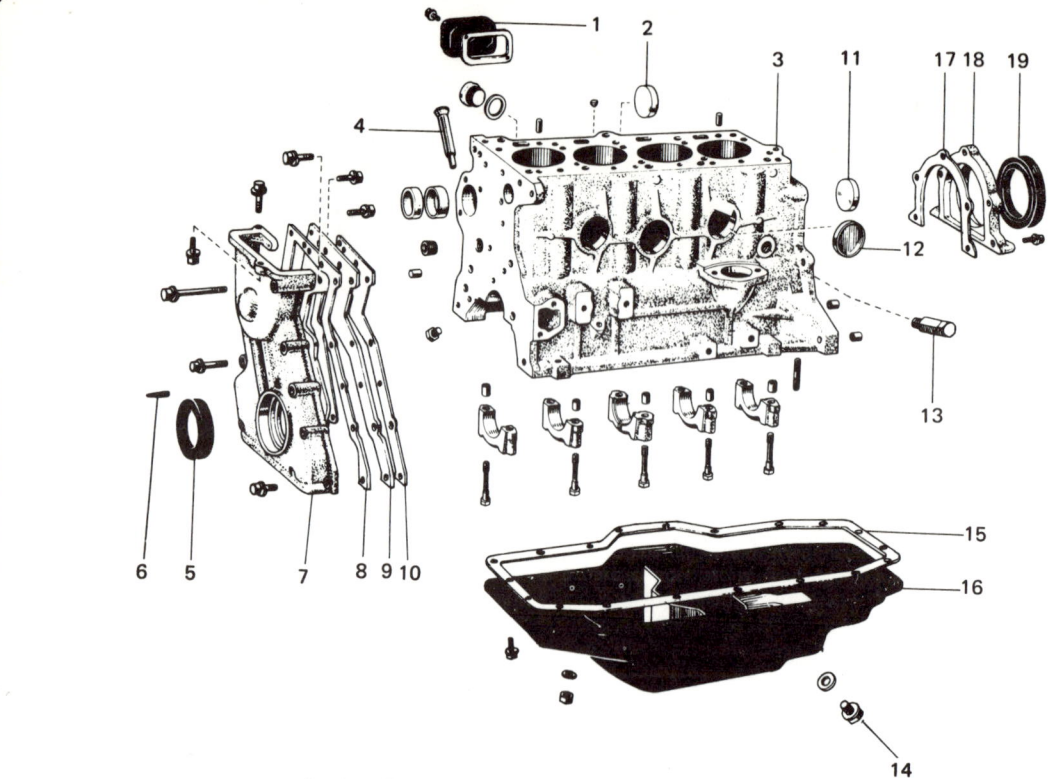

Fig 1.14 Exploded view of engine cylinder block (crankcase components)

1 Side cover
2 Core plug
3 Cylinder block
4 Dipstick guide
5 Timing cover oil seal
6 Timing index pointer
7 Timing chain cover
8 Gasket
9 Engine front plate
10 Gasket
11 Core plug
12 Core plug
13 Cylinder block drain plug
14 Sump drain plug
15 Sump gasket
16 Sump
17 Rear oil seal retainer gasket
18 Engine rear oil seal retainer
19 Crankshaft rear oil seal

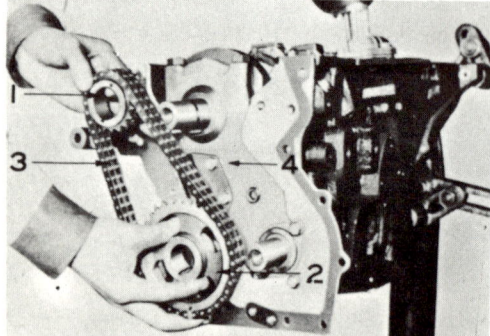

Fig 1.15 Removing the lower timing chain and sprockets (Engine inverted) as one assembly (Sec 13)

1 Crankshaft sprocket
2 Oil pump sprocket
3 Lower timing chain

Fig 1.16 Withdrawing the oil pump driveshaft from the front of the engine (Sec 17)

Chapter 1/Engine

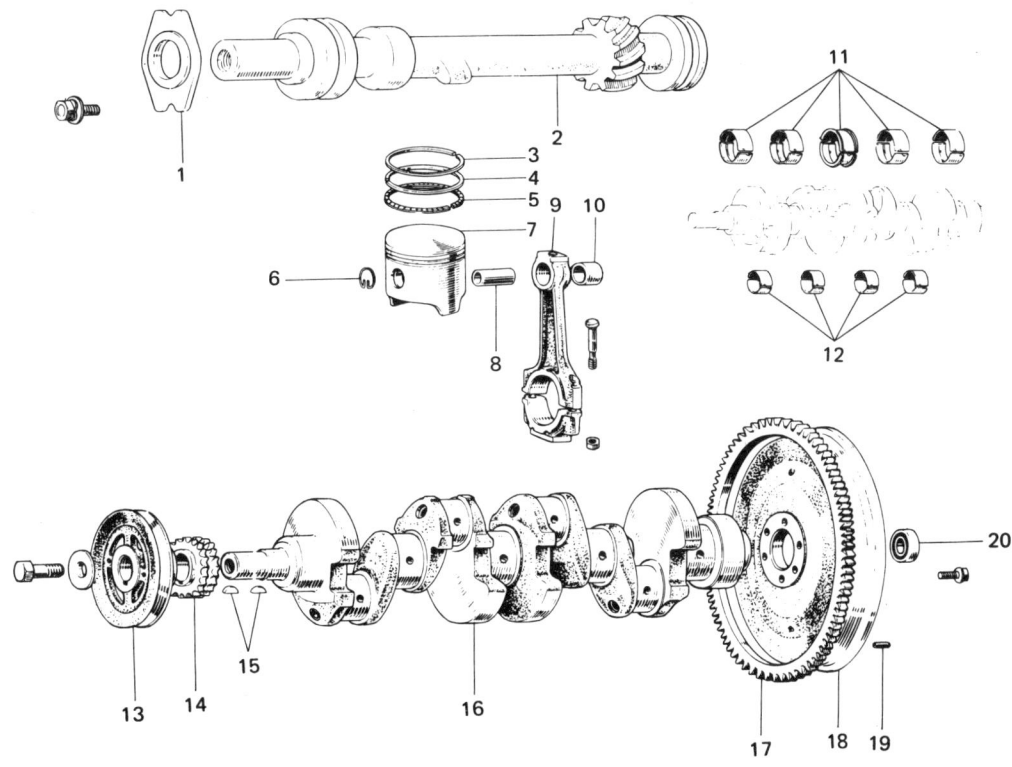

Fig 1.17 Exploded view of the crankshaft and oil pump driveshaft (Secs 16 and 17)

1 Oil pump driveshaft thrust plate
2 Oil pump driveshaft
3 Top compression ring
4 Second compression ring
5 Oil control ring
6 Circlip
7 Piston
8 Gudgeon pin
9 Connecting rod
10 Small end bush
11 Main shell bearings
12 Connecting rod bearings shells
13 Crankshaft pulley
14 Crankshaft sprocket
15 Woodruff keys
16 Crankshaft
17 Starter ring gear
18 Flywheel
19 Dowel pin
20 Input shaft spigot bearing

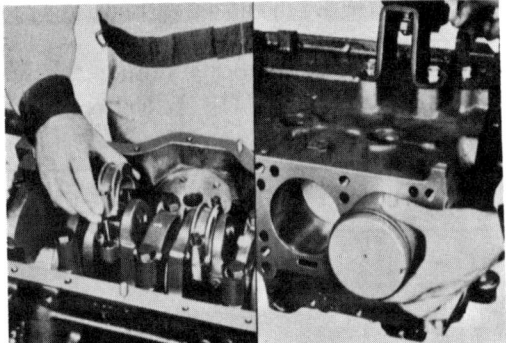

Fig 1.18 Unbolting big-end caps and removing piston/connecting rod assemblies (Sec 14)

15 Piston ring and gudgeon pin - removal

1 With the piston assemblies removed, the piston rings may be removed by opening each of them in turn, just enough to enable them to ride over the lands of the piston body.
2 In order to prevent the lower rings dropping into an empty groove higher up the piston as they are removed, it is helpful to use two or three narrow strips of tin or old feeler blades inserted behind the ring at equidistant points and then to employ a twisting motion to slide the ring from the piston.
3 To remove a gudgeon pin, first extract the circlips (one at each end) and then immerse the piston in hot water at a temperature of approximately 140° F (60°C). After a few minutes, the gudgeon pin will be able to be pushed out of the piston and connecting rod with finger pressure only.
4 Mark each gudgeon pin as it is removed with the piston sequence number (use masking tape) so that it can be refitted in its original location.

16 Crankshaft and main bearings - removal

1 Unbolt and remove the crankshaft rear oil seal retainer.
2 Mark each of the main bearing caps with quick-drying paint (numbered 1 to 5 from the front of the engine), making sure that the caps are also marked as to which way round they are to be refitted. Some caps are marked with a triangle, the apex of which points to the front of the engine and they are already numbered but check before removing them.
3 Unscrew the main bearing cap bolts and remove the caps complete with shell bearings. The centre main bearing shells incorporate thrust washers.
4 Lift the cranskhaft from the crankcase.

17 Lubrication system, oil pump and filter

1 Pressure for the engine lubrication system is generated by a trochoid type oil pump located within the crankcase. The pump is driven by an extension of the distributor driveshaft which in turn is meshed with a short driveshaft driven by chain from the

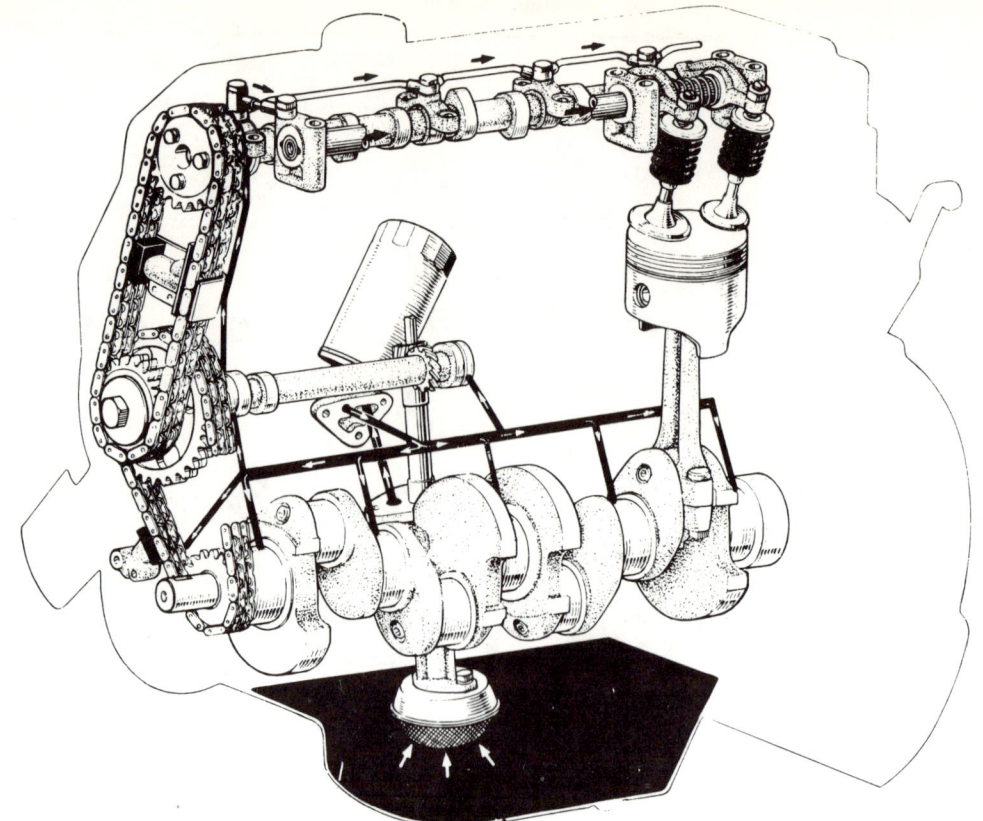

Fig 1.19 The engine lubrication system (Sec 17)

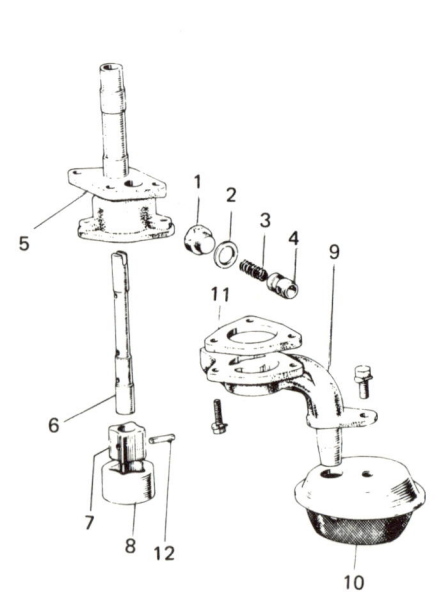

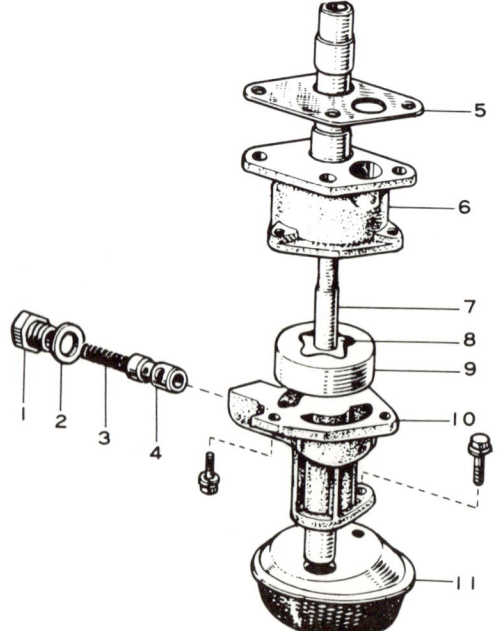

Fig 1.20 Exploded view of the oil pump (early type) (Sec 17)

1 Pressure relief valve plug
2 Gasket
3 Spring
4 Valve
5 Oil pump body
6 Shaft
7 Inner rotor
8 Outer rotor
9 Oil intake
10 Oil filter screen
11 Centre body section
12 Pin

Fig 1.21 Exploded view of the oil pump (later type) (Sec 17)

1 Pressure relief valve plug
2 Gasket
3 Spring
4 Valve
5 Gasket
6 Oil pump body
7 Shaft
8 Inner rotor
9 Outer (driven) rotor
10 Oil pump cover
11 Filter

Chapter 1/Engine

crankshaft sprocket. The pressurised oil is first passed through an externally mounted cartridge type disposable oil filter then to all the bearings and friction surfaces of the engine. Oil pressure also actuates the timing chain tensioners. Excess oil pressure is controlled by an integral relief valve within the oil pump.

2 The oil pump normally has a very long life but in the event of low oil pressure (not due to worn bearings or lack of oil) being observed, remove the pump for servicing. If the engine is in position in the vehicle, the sump will first have to be removed as described in Section 2.

3 To service the pump, first remove it from the crankcase (three screws) by pulling it straight down.

4 Unscrew and remove the pressure relief valve.

5 Unbolt the oil strainer.

6 Separate the cover from the pump body (three screws).

7 Withdraw the oil pump shaft and driven rotor from the body.

8 Examine all components for wear and using feeler blades, carry out the following clearance tests.

9 Measure the clearance between the tips of the drive and driven rotors. This should be between 0.004 and 0.006 in (0.10 and 0.15 mm). If the clearance exceeds 0.008 in (0.2 mm) renew both rotors as a matched set.

10 Using a straight-edge, check the clearance between the end faces of the rotors and the body flange. This should be between 0.001 and 0.003 in (0.03 and 0.07 mm). If the clearance exceeds 0.006 in (0.15 mm) the rotors should be renewed and possibly the pump body as well to achieve the correct tolerance.

11 Finally measure the clearance between the outer rotor and the inside of the pump body. The clearance should be between 0.004 and 0.006 in (0.10 and 0.16 mm). If the clearance exceeds 0.008 in (0.2 mm), renew the pump body.

12 Check the free length of the pressure relief valve. If it exceeds 1.85 in (47.0 mm) renew it.

13 Reassembly and installation are reversals of removal and dismantling but ensure that the rotor punch marks will face downwards when the pump is installed. Always use a new gasket when fitting the pump to the crankcase.

14 The cartridge type oil filter incorporates a non-return valve to prevent oil draining from the filter when the engine is switched off. A bypass valve is built into the filter base which opens in the

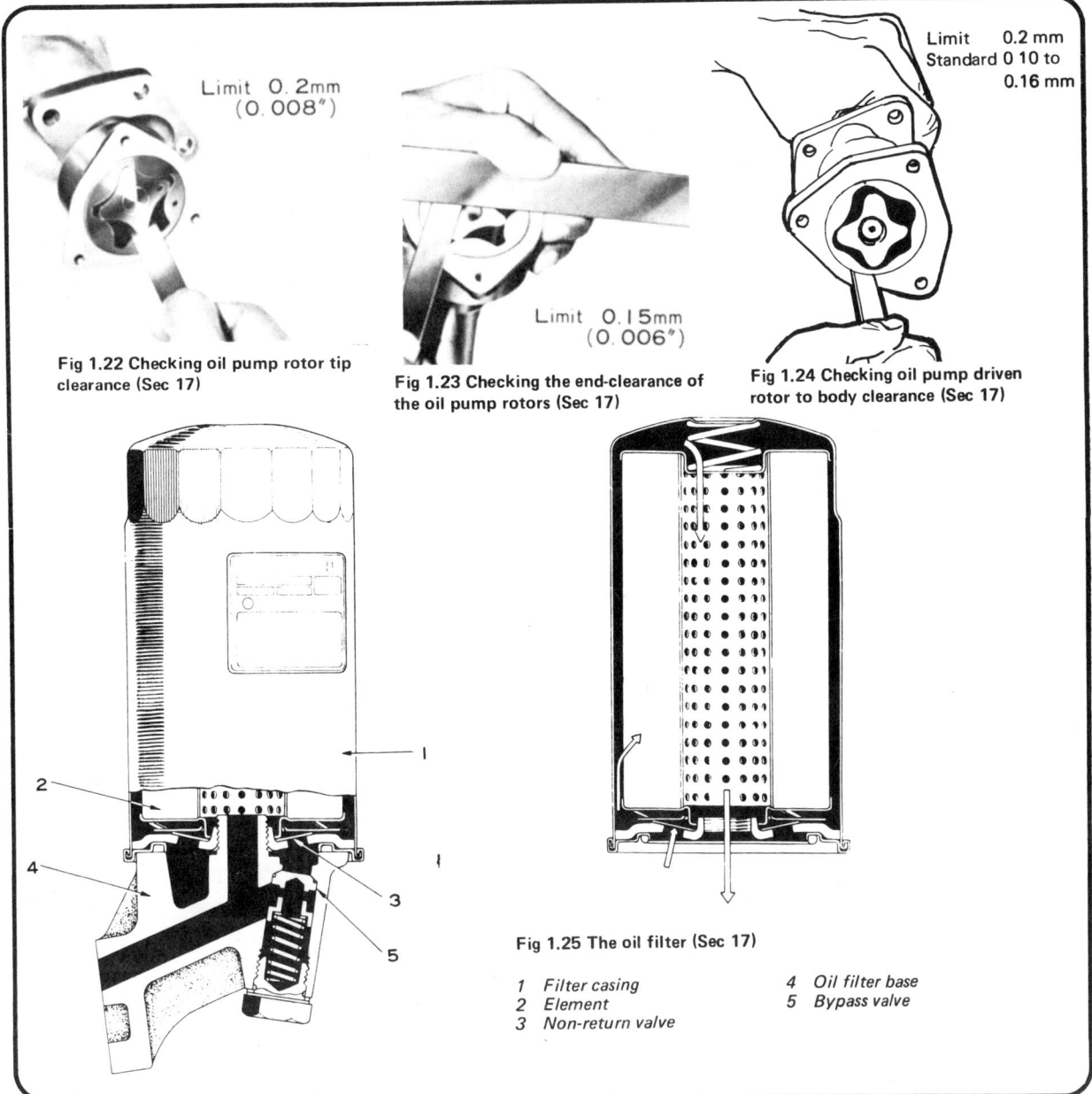

Fig 1.22 Checking oil pump rotor tip clearance (Sec 17)

Fig 1.23 Checking the end-clearance of the oil pump rotors (Sec 17)

Fig 1.24 Checking oil pump driven rotor to body clearance (Sec 17)

Fig 1.25 The oil filter (Sec 17)

1 Filter casing
2 Element
3 Non-return valve
4 Oil filter base
5 Bypass valve

event of the filter clogging to ensure normal (though unfiltered) oil circulation. (photo)

15 The filter cartridge can be removed using a chain wrench or special filter strap. Fit the filter using hand pressure only. Always use the new gasket supplied and smear its sealing face with grease before tightening. (photo)

18 Crankcase ventilation system

1 As part of the emission control system (described in Chapter 3), a positive crankcase ventilation system is fitted.
2 Every 12,000 miles (20,000 km) check the operation of the PCV valve. To do this, let the engine run at idling speed and first pinch and then release the hose just above the valve at the same time, listen for the sound of the valve seating. If it does not close or is sluggish in operation, remove it and wash it thoroughly in fuel. Other indications of a faulty PCV valve are evidence of oil at the air cleaner and rough idling.
3 Every 24,000 miles (38,000 km) renew the PCV valve and at all times make sure that the connecting hoses and clips are secure and in good condition, also the 'O' ring seal of the oil filler cap. (photo)

19 Examination and renovation - general

With the engine stripped down and all parts thoroughly cleaned, it is now time to examine everything for wear. The following items should be checked and where necessary renewed or renovated as described in the following Sections.

20 Crankshaft and main bearings - inspection and renovation

1 Examine the crankpin and journal surfaces for signs of scoring or scratches. Check the ovality of the crankpins at several different positions using a micrometer. If more than 0.001 in (0.0254 mm) out of round, the crankshaft will have to be reground. Check the journals in the same manner.
2 If it is necessary to regrind the crankshaft and to fit new bearings, your Toyota dealer will decide how much to grind off and he will supply new oversize shell bearings to suit. Details of regrinding tolerances and bearings are given in Specifications.
3 The main bearing running clearances may be established by using 'Plastigage' or a similar product inserted between the crankshaft journals and the main bearing shells.
4 With the crankshaft, Plastigage, bearing shells and caps in position, tighten the main bearing cap bolts to a torque of 75 lb/ft (10.4 kg/m). Remove the bearing caps and compare the Plastigage at its widest point with the index supplied. If the clearance is between 0.0008 and 0.0020 in (0.02 and 0.05 mm) then it is correct. If the clearance exceeds 0.003 in (0.08 mm) then the crankshaft must be reground and new oversize bearings fitted.

5 Remove the Plastigage and refit the main bearing caps and shell bearings. Tighten the main bearing cap bolts to 75 lb/ft (10.4 kg/m). Now check the crankshaft for endfloat either using

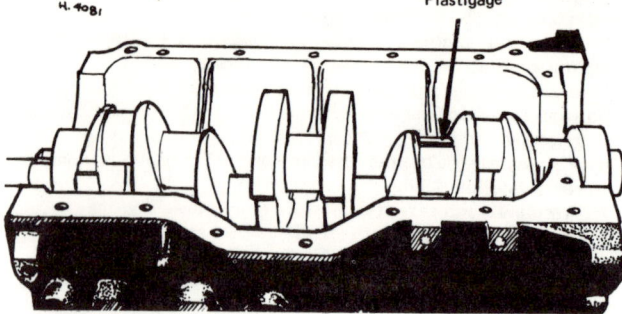

Fig 1.26 Checking crankshaft main bearing clearance with Plastigage (Sec 20)

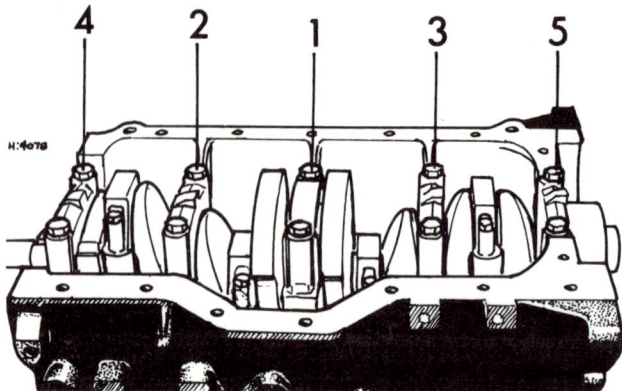

Fig 1.27 Tightening sequence for crankshaft main bearing cap bolts (Sec 20)

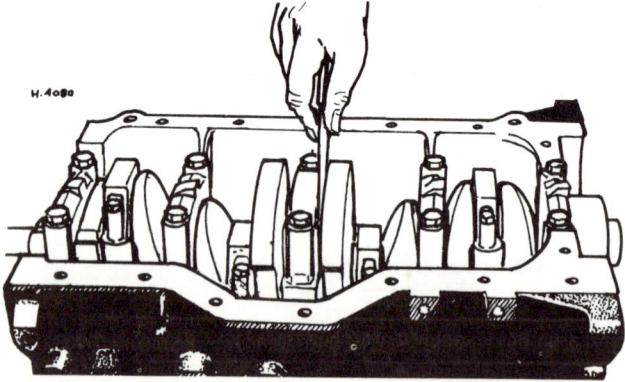

Fig 1.28 Checking crankshaft endfloat (Sec 20)

17.14 Removing the oil filter base

17.15 Installing oil filter

18.3 Oil filler cap 'O' ring seal

feeler blades or a dial gauge. Push and pull the crankshaft in both longitudinal directions and measure the total endfloat which should be between 0.002 and 0.010 in (0.05 and 0.25 mm) for the 8R series engine and between 0.0008 and 0.008 in (0.02 and 0.20 mm) for the 18R series engine.

6 Where the endfloat is incorrect, renew the centre main bearing shells which incorporate the thrust washers. (photo)

7 When carrying out the operations just described, make sure that the arrows on the main bearing caps point towards the front of the engine and that the caps and shells are located in their original sequence. Tighten the securing bolts in the sequence shown in Fig 1.27.

8 The clutch input shaft spigot bearing is located in the centre of the rear mounting flange of the crankshaft. Renew if worn, greasing its reverse side before fitting.

21 Connecting rods and bearings - examination and renovation

1 Big-end bearing failure is indicated by a knocking from within the crankcase and a slight drop in oil pressure.

2 Examine the big-end bearing surfaces for pitting and scoring. Renew the shells in accordance with the sizes specified in Specifications. Where the crankshaft has been reground, the correct undersize big-end shell bearings will be supplied by the repairer. (photo)

3 Check each connecting rod for bending or twist and then test the big-end running clearances in a similar manner to that described for the main bearings in the preceding Section.

4 The correct running clearance should be between 0.0008 and 0.0020 in (0.02 and 0.05 mm) with the big-end bolts tightened to a torque of 45 lb/ft (6.2 kg/m). Where the clearance exceeds 0.003 in (0.08 mm) the crankshaft will probably need regrinding and new shell bearings fitted.

5 With each connecting rod installed on its respective crankpin, check each rod for side-float. On the 8R series engine this should be between 0.0043 and 0.0097 in (0.110 and 0.236 mm) and for the 18R series between 0.006 and 0.010 in (0.16 and 0.26 mm). Where the side-float exceeds 0.012 in (0.3 mm) renew the connecting rod.

6 Check each small-end bush for wear or scoring. Each gudgeon pin should be a push fit in its bush using thumb pressure only. If the bush is worn it will have to be pressed out and a new one fitted, ensuring that the oil holes of the bush and the connecting rod coincide. As the bush will have to be reamed after fitting, this is probably a job best left to your Toyota dealer.

22 Cylinder bores - examination and renovation

1 The cylinder bores must be examined for taper, ovality, scoring and scratches. Start by carefully examining the top of the cylinder bores. If they are at all worn a very slight ridge will be found on the thrust side. This marks the top of the piston ring travel. The owner will have a good indication of the bore wear prior to dismantling the engine, or removing the cylinder head. Excessive oil consumption accompanied by blue smoke from the exhaust is a sure sign of worn cylinder bores and piston rings.

2 Measure the bore diameter just under the ridge with a micrometer and compare it with the diameter at the bottom of the bore, which is not subject to wear. If the difference between the two measurements is more than 0.0008 in (0.02 mm) then it will be necessary to fit special pistons and rings or to have the cylinders rebored and fit oversize pistons. If no micrometer is available remove the rings from a piston and place the piston in each bore in turn about ¾ in (19.05 mm) below the top of the bore. If an 0.0012 in (0.03 mm) feeler gauge slid between the piston and cylinder wall requires more than a pull of between 2.2 and 5.5 lbs (1.0 and 2.5 kg) to withdraw it, using a spring balance, then remedial action must be taken. Oversize pistons are available as listed in Specifications.

3 These are accurately machined to just below the indicated measurements so as to provide correct running clearances in bores bored out to the exact oversize dimensions.

4 If the bores are slightly worn but not so badly worn as to justify reboring them, then special oil control rings and pistons can be fitted which will restore compression and stop the engine burning oil. Several different types are available and the manufacturer's instructions concerning their fitting must be followed closely.

5 If new pistons or rings are being fitted and the bores have not been reground, it is essential to slightly roughen the hard glaze on the sides of the bores with fine glass paper so the new piston rings will have a chance to bed in properly.

6 If the cylinder bores have been bored out beyond the limit so that the maximum oversize pistons available cannot be fitted then sleeves can be supplied which after installation and boring will accept standard sized pistons. This again is a job for your Toyota dealer or motor engineering works.

23 Pistons and piston rings - examination and renovation

1 If the original pistons are to be refitted, carefully remove the piston rings as described in Section 15.

2 Clean the grooves and rings free from carbon, taking care not to scratch the aluminium surfaces of the pistons.

3 If new rings are to be fitted, then order the top compression ring to be stepped to prevent it impinging on the 'wear ring' which will almost certainly have been formed at the top of the cylinder bore.

4 Before fitting the rings to the pistons, push each ring in turn down to the bottom of its respective cylinder bore (use an inverted piston to do this so that the ring is kept square in its bore)

20.6 Centre main bearing shell incorporating thrust washer

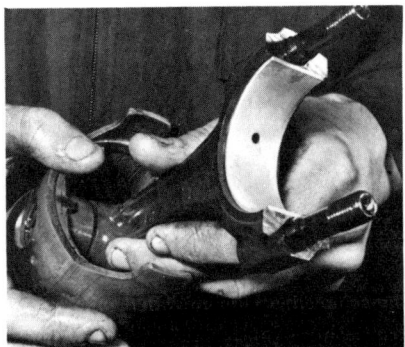

21.2 Big-end bearing shell and oil hole

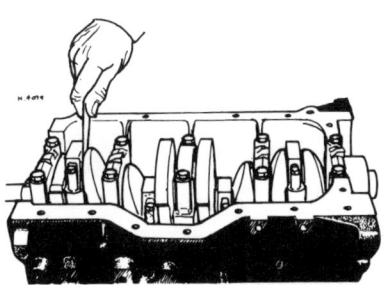

Fig 1.29 Checking a connecting rod for side-float (Sec 21)

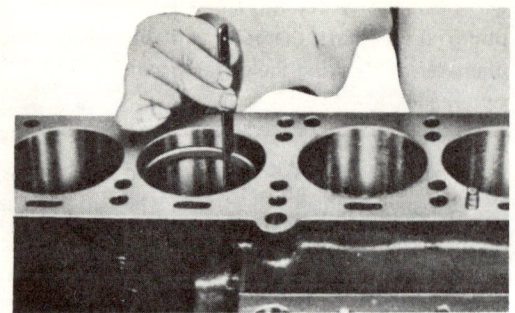

Fig 1.30 Measuring piston ring end-gap (ring located at top of bore for clarity) (Sec 23)

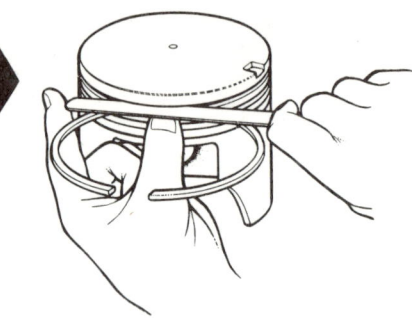

Fig 1.31 Measuring piston ring to groove clearance (Sec 23)

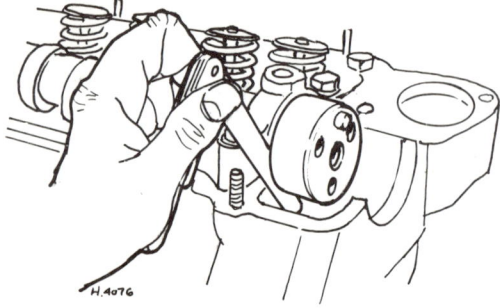

Fig 1.32 Checking camshaft endfloat (Sec 24)

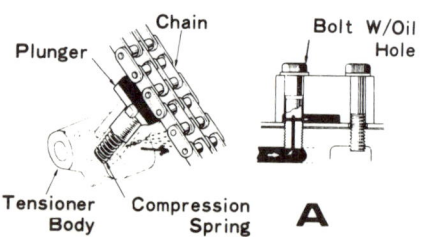 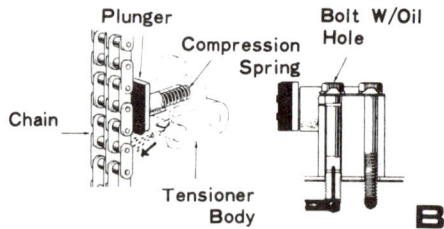

Fig 1.33 Chain tensioners components and cut-away diagrams showing oil flow (A) upper (B) lower (Sec 25)

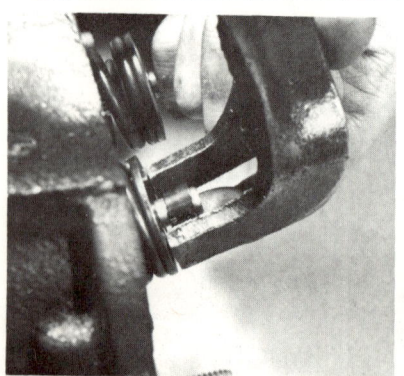

26.2 Compressing a valve spring

26.5a Valve stem oil seal

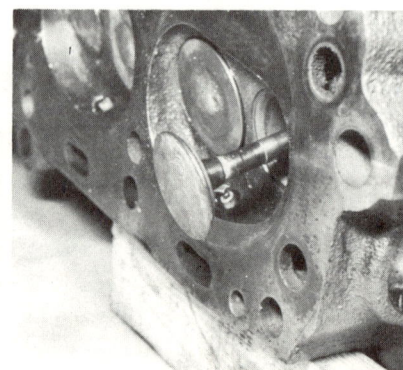

26.5b Removing a valve

and then measure the ring end gap. The gap for all rings should be between 0.004 and 0.012 in (0.1 and 0.3 mm). If the gap is incorrect, carefully grind the end of the ring.

5 Each ring should now be tested in its respective groove for side clearance. Using a feeler gauge, the clearance for compression rings should be between 0.0012 and 0.0028 in (0.03 and 0.07 mm) and for oil control rings between 0.0008 and 0.0028 in (0.02 and 0.07 mm). Where the side clearance is excessive, renew the piston as it will be the groove (width) that is worn.

6 Where necessary a piston ring which is slightly tight in its groove may be rubbed down holding it perfectly squarely on an oilstone or a sheet of fine emery cloth laid on a piece of plate glass. Excessive tightness can only be rectified by having the grooves machined out.

7 The gudgeon pin should be a push fit into the piston when heated in water to a temperature of 140° F (60° C). If it appears slack, then both the piston and gudgeon pin should be renewed.

24 Camshaft and camshaft bearings - examination and renovation

1 Check the camshaft journals for scoring or grooves and then measure each journal at several different points to detect any taper or out of round. If the difference between the measurements exceeds 0.0004 in (0.01 mm) the camshaft must be reground and oversize shell bearings fitted. This is a job for your Toyota dealer.

2 To check the camshaft bearing running clearances, use 'Plastigage' or a similar product in exactly the same way to that described for the crankshaft main and big-end bearings in previous Sections. Insert the Plastigage, fit the bearing caps complete with shell bearings and tighten the cap bolts to a torque of 15 lb/ft (2.1 kg/m). When the caps are removed and the Plastigage strip compared with the index, it should indicate a running clearance of between 0.001 and 0.002 in (0.03 and 0.05 mm). If the running clearance exceeds 0.004 in (0.1 mm), the camshaft must be reground and new oversize bearings fitted.

3 With the camshaft installed on the cylinder head complete with shell bearings and caps and the cap bolts tightened as previously specified, check the camshaft endfloat. This should be between 0.0017 and 0.0066 in (0.042 and 0.168 mm). Where the clearance exceeds 0.010 in (0.25 mm) renew all the camshaft shell bearings.

4 Finally examine the camshaft lobes for scoring or wear. Using a micrometer, check the overall lengths of the inlet valve lobes which should be a minimum of 1.721 in (43.70 mm). Now check the overall lengths of exhaust valve lobes which should be a minimum of 1.724 in (43.80 mm). Where the dimensions are less than those specified, renew the camshaft complete.

25 Timing components - examination and renovation

1 Examine all the sprocket teeth for wear or 'hooked' appearance and renew if necessary.

2 Wash the two timing chains thoroughly in paraffin and examine for wear or stretch. If the chain is supported at both ends so that the rollers are vertical then a worn chain will take on a deeply bowed appearance while an unworn one will dip slightly at its centre point.

3 Check the two chain tensioners for wear and renew the slippers if they are cut or grooved.

26 Cylinder head and valves - servicing

1 Each valve should be removed from the cylinder head using the following method:

2 Compress each spring using a valve spring compressor, until the split collets can be removed. Release the compressor slowly, remove it and then remove the retainer, double springs, oil seal from the valve stem and the washer. Finally withdraw the valve from its guide. (photo)

3 If, when the valve spring compressor is screwed down, the valve spring retaining cap refuses to free to expose the split collet, do not continue to screw down on the compressor as there is a likelihood of bending the valve stem.

4 Gently tap the top of the tool directly over the cap with a light hammer. This will free the cap. To avoid the compressor jumping off the valve spring retaining cap when it is tapped, hold the compressor firmly in position with one hand.

5 Slide the rubber oil control seal off the end of each valve stem and then drop out each valve through the combustion chamber. (photos)

6 It is essential that the valves are kept in their correct sequences unless they are so badly worn that they are to be renewed. If they are going to be kept and used again, place them in a sheet of card having holes numbered 1 to 8 corresponding with the relative positions the valves were in when fitted. Also keep the valve springs, washers etc in the correct order.

7 Examine the heads of the valves for pitting and burning, especially the heads of the exhaust valves. The valve seatings should be examined at the same time. If the pitting on valve and seat is very slight the marks can be removed by grinding the seats and valves together with coarse, and then fine, valve grinding paste.

8 Where bad pitting has occurred to the valve seats it will be necessary to recut them and fit new valves. Cut the valve seat in three stages as indicated, using first a 15° cutter than one of 65° and finally a 45° cutter to give a seat contact width of between 0.050 and 0.060 in (1.2 and 1.6 mm). In practice it is very seldom that the seats are so badly worn that they require renewal. Normally, it is the valve that is too badly worn to use again and the owner can easily purchase a new set of valves and match them to the seats by grinding. (Fig 1.34)

9 Valve grinding is carried out as followd: Smear a trace of coarse carborundum paste on the seat face and apply a suction grinder tool to the valve head. With a semi-rotary motion, grind the valve head to its seat, lifting the valve occasionally to redistribute the grinding paste. When a dull matt, even surface finish is produced on both the valve seat and the valve, wipe off the paste and repeat the process with fine carborundum paste, lifting and turning the valve to distribute the paste as before. A light spring placed under the valve head will greatly ease this operation. When a smooth unbroken ring of light grey matt finish is produced, on both valve and valve seat faces, the grinding operation is completed.

10 Scrape away all carbon from the valve head and the valve stem. Carefully clean away every trace of grinding compound, taking great care to leave none in the ports or in the valve guides. Clean the valves and valve seats with a paraffin soaked rag then with a dry rag, and finally, if an air line is available, blow the valves, valve guides and valve ports clean.

11 Wear in the valve guides can best be checked by inserting a new valve and testing for rocking movement in all directions. The clearance between the guide and valve stem must not exceed 0.003 in (0.08 mm) for inlet valves and 0.004 in (0.10 mm) for

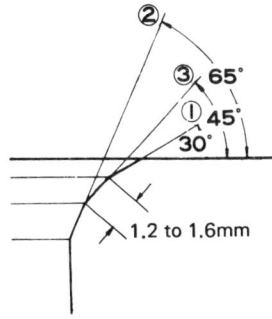

Fig 1.34 Valve seat cutting angles (Sec 26)

exhaust valves.

12 To renew a valve guide, drive it out from the valve spring side into the combustion chamber of the cylinder head. Drive in the new guide by reversing the process but the guide must protrude by 0.63 in (16.0 mm) on the valve spring side of the head.

13 Finally, ream the new guide to provide a clearance between valve stem and guide of between 0.0010 and 0.0022 in (0.025 and 0.055 mm) for inlet valves and between 0.0014 and 0.0030 in (0.035 and 0.075 mm) for exhaust valves.

14 The valve springs should be compared with their specified free lengths (inner 1.74 in - 44.1 mm, outer 1.83 in - 46.5 mm). Renew the springs as a set if they differ from their specified new length or have been in operation for more than 24,000 miles (38,000 km). Always renew the valve stem oil seals.

15 With the cylinder head removed, use a blunt scraper to remove all trace of carbon and deposits from the combustion spaces and ports. Scrape the cylinder head free from scale or old pieces of gasket or jointing compound. Clean the cylinder head by washing it in kerosene and take particular care to pull a piece of rag through the ports and cylinder head bolt holes. Any grit remaining in these recesses may well drop onto the gasket or cylinder block mating surface as the cylinder head is lowered into position and could lead to a gasket leak after reassembly is complete.

16 With the cylinder head clean test for distortion if a history of coolant leakage has been apparent. Carry out this test using a straight edge and feeler gauges or a piece of plate glass. If the surface shows any warping in excess of 0.002 in (0.05 mm) then the cylinder head will have to be resurfaced which is a job for a specialist engineering company.

17 Clean the pistons and top of the cylinder bores. If the pistons are still in the block then it is essential that great care is taken to ensure that no carbon gets into the cylinder bores as this could scratch the cylinder walls or cause damage to the piston and rings. To ensure this does not happen, first turn the crankshaft so that two of the pistons are at the top of their bores. Stuff rag into the other two bores or seal them off with paper and masking tape. The waterways should also be covered with small pieces of masking tape to prevent particles of carbon entering the cooling system and damaging the water pump.

18 There are two schools of thought as to how much carbon should be removed from the piston crown. One school recommends that a ring of carbon should be left round the edge of the piston and on the cylinder bore wall as an aid to low oil consumption. Although this is probably true for early engines with worn bores, on later engines the thought of the second school can be applied: which is that for effective decarbonisation all traces of carbon should be removed.

19 If all traces of carbon are to be removed, press a little grease into the gap between the cylinder walls and the two pistons which are to be worked on. With a blunt scraper carefully scrape away the carbon from the piston crown, taking great care not to scratch the aluminium. Also scrape away the carbon from the surrounding lip of the cylinder wall. When all carbon has been removed, scrape away the grease which will now be contaminated with carbon particles, taking care not to press any into the bores. To assist prevention of carbon build-up the piston crown can be polished with a metal polish. Remove the rags or masking tape from the other two cylinders and turn the crankshaft so that the two pistons which were at the bottom are now at the top. Place rag or masking tape in the cylinders which have been decarbonised and proceed as just described.

20 If a ring of carbon is going to be left round the piston then this can be helped by inserting an old piston ring into the top of the bore to rest on the piston and ensure that the carbon is not accidentally removed. Check that there are no particles of carbon in the cylinder bores. Decarbonising is now complete.

21 Reassembly is a reversal of dismantling but note that the closer coils of the valve springs must be nearer the cylinder head. (photo)

22 Check that the split collets are correctly seated and tap the retainers with a soft faced hammer to settle them. (photo)

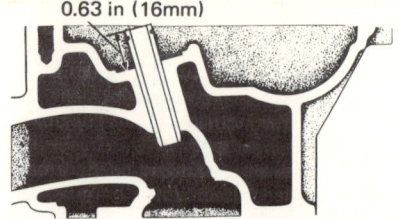

Fig 1.35 Correct projection of valve guide after installation (Sec 26)

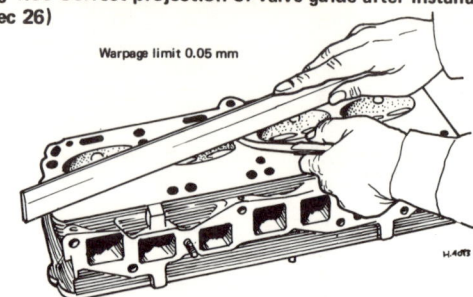

Fig 1.36 Checking the cylinder head for distortion (Sec 26)

26.21 Installing valve springs

26.22 Valve spring retainer and collets correctly installed

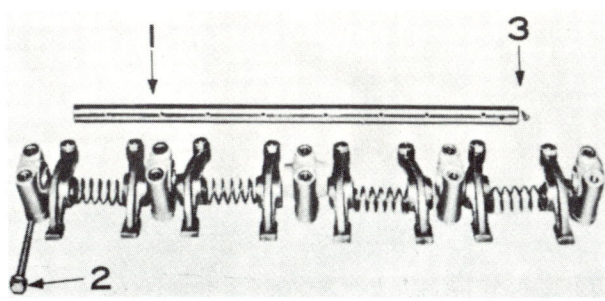

Fig 1.37 Exploded view of the rocker gear (Sec 27)

1 Rocker shaft
2 Pillar support bolt
3 Retaining screw

Fig 1.38 Rocker shaft support pillars front facing markings (Sec 27)

A Pillars 1,2,4,5 have recess on top of boss
B Pillar no. 3 has projection on top of boss

27 Rocker shaft - servicing

1 The rocker shaft does not normally require dismantling unless the heels of the rocker arms are scored or badly worn or one of the coil springs is broken.
2 If dismantling is essential, first remove the retaining screw (3) which secures the rocker shaft front support pillar to the shaft. (Fig 1.37). The rear pillar is retained to the shaft by means of the two securing bolts which engage in cut-outs in the shaft.
3 As each rocker arm, spring and pillar is withdrawn, keep it in strict sequence for refitting.
4 Reassembly is a reversal of dismantling but note that the rocker shaft pillars are marked at the top of their bearing bosses to indicate their front faces.

28 Oil pump driveshaft - servicing

1 The oil pump driveshaft bearings should be inspected for scoring or scratches.
2 The correct running clearance between the shaft and bearings is between 0.0010 and 0.0026 in (0.025 and 0.066 mm). Where the clearance exceeds 0.003 in (0.08 mm) the bearings must be renewed.
3 To do this, remove the plug at the back of the rear shaft bearing and using a suitably stepped mandrel, drive out the old and drive in the new bearings.
4 Check the endfloat of the driveshaft; this must not exceed 0.012 in (0.03 mm). If it does, renew the thrust plate to provide the standard endfloat of between 0.002 and 0.005 in (0.06 and 0.13 mm).

29 Flywheel - servicing

1 Examine the clutch driven plate contact surface of the flywheel for scoring or grooves. If they are deep, then the flywheel can be ground providing the flywheel thickness is not reduced by more than 0.04 in (1.0 mm).
2 Check the starter ring gear for cracks or chipped teeth. Where these are evident, it will be necessary to remove the ring and fit a new one or preferably exchange the flywheel for a reconditioned unit.
3 Either split the ring with a cold chisel after making a cut with a hacksaw blade between two teeth, or use a soft headed hammer (not steel) to knock the ring off, striking it evenly and alternately at equally spaced points. Take great care not to damage the flywheel during this process.
4 Heat the new ring in either an electric oven to about 200°C (392°F) or immerse in a pan of boiling oil.
5 Hold the ring at this temperature for five minutes and then

Fig 1.39 Measuring the bore of an oil pump driveshaft bearing (Sec 28)

quickly fit it to the flywheel so the chamfered portion of the teeth faces the gearbox side of the flywheel.
6 The ring should be tapped gently down onto its register and left to cool naturally when the contraction of the metal on cooling will ensure that it is a secure and permanent fit. Great care must be taken not to overheat the ring (indicated by the ring turning light metallic blue) as if this happens the temper of the ring will be lost.

30 Driveplate (automatic transmission) - servicing

1 Examine the starter ring gear for worn or broken teeth; where these are evident, renew the driveplate complete.
2 Check the torque converter securing bolt holes for elongation and if apparent, renew the driveplate.

31 Oil seals - renewal

1 During a major overhaul, discard the old oil seals and fit new ones as a matter of course.
2 With the engine timing cover removed, use a tubular drift to drive out the crankshaft pulley oil seal.
3 Refitting the new seal is a reversal of removal but make sure that the lips are facing inwards and coat the outer metal edge of the seal with gasket compound before driving it home. (photo)
4 The crankshaft rear oil seal is renewed in a similar manner to that just described. (Fig 1.41)
5 Smear the lips of new oil seals with multi-purpose grease before fitting the front cover or crankshaft rear oil seal retainer in position.

32 Cylinder block - examination and renovation

1 Examine the crankcase and cylinder block for cracks especially around bolt holes and between the cylinders.
2 Probe waterways and oil galleries to ensure that they are not blocked.

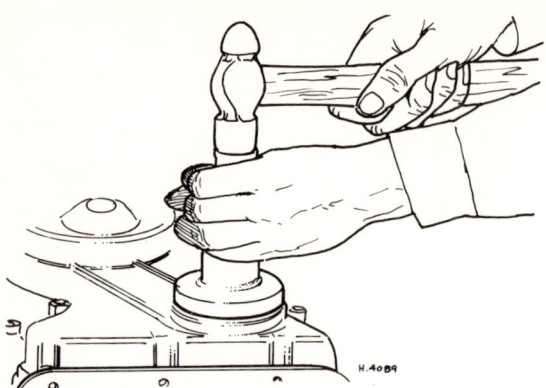

Fig 1.40 Fitting a timing cover oil seal (Sec 31)

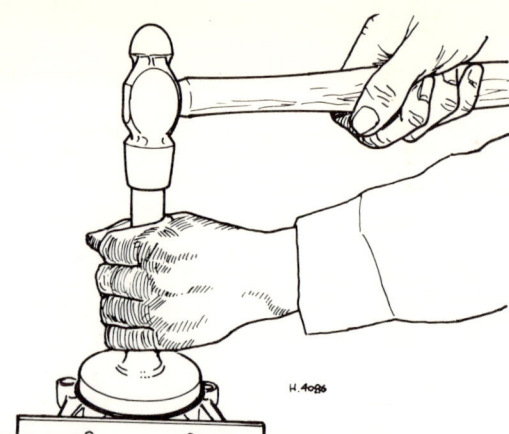

Fig 1.41 Fitting a new oil seal to the crankshaft rear oil seal retainer (Sec 31)

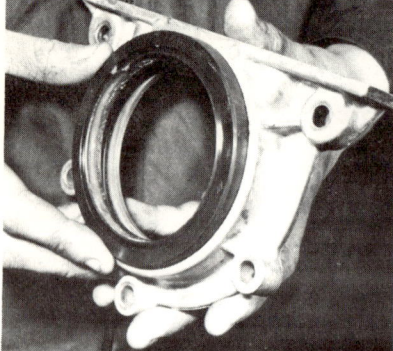

31.3 Installing crankshaft rear oil seal

34.1 Installing and lubricating main bearing shells

34.2 Installing crankshaft

34.3 Main bearing cap directional mark and number

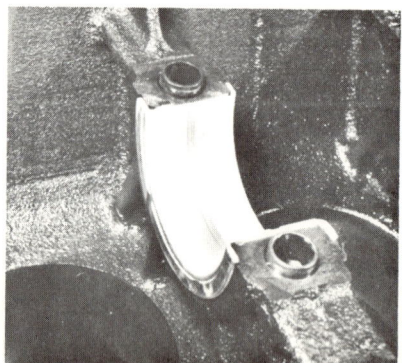

34.4a Centre main bearing shell

34.4b Installing centre main bearing cap

34.5 Tightening a main bearing bolt

34.6a Crankshaft rear oil seal retainer gasket

34.6b Installing crankshaft rear oil seal retainer

3 Check the security and condition of the core plugs. To renew a core plug, first drill a hole in its centre and lever it out. If it is particularly stubborn, tap a thread in the hole and screw in a bolt, using a piece of tubing and a large washer to act as a point of leverage and extract the plug as the bolt is tightened.

4 Where the cooling system has frozen due to the use of a weak antifreeze mixture, it is quite likely that one or more of the core plugs will have been partially dislodged from its seat by the expansion of the ice. In such an event, drive the plug fully home or better still, renew it. The engine side cover can be removed to gain access to the threaded type core plug located behind the oil pump driveshaft.

33 Engine reassembly - general

1 To ensure maximum life with minimum trouble from a re-built engine, not only must everything be correctly assembled but everything must be spotlessly clean, all the oilways must be clear, locking washers and spring washers must always be fitted where indicated and all bearing and other working surfaces must be thoroughly lubricated during assembly.

2 Before assembly begins renew any bolts or studs the threads of which are in any way damaged and whenever possible use new spring washers.

3 Apart from your normal tools, a supply of clean rag, an oil can filled with engine oil, a new supply of assorted spring washers, a set of new gaskets and a torque spanner, should be collected together.

34 Crankshaft and main bearings - reassembly

1 Locate the main bearing shells in their crankcase recesses and lubricate them with engine oil. (photo)
2 Carefully lower the crankshaft into position. (photo)
3 Fit the main bearing caps complete with shell bearings noting that the caps (previously numbered 1 to 5) should have their arrows pointing towards the front of the engine. (photo)
4 Note that the centre bearing incorporates the thrust washers. (photos)
5 Tighten the main bearing cap bolts in the sequence indicated and to the specified torque as given in Section 20. (photo)
6 Bolt on the crankshaft rear oil seal retainer complete with new seal (Section 31) and gasket. (photos) Tighten the securing bolts to a torque of 15 lb/ft (2.1 kg/m).

35 Pistons, rings and connecting rods - reassembly and refitting

1 Assemble the piston to the connecting rod so that the marks on the connecting rod and the piston crown are in alignment. These marks face the front of the engine when installed.
2 Connect the two components by pushing in the gudgeon pin by thumb pressure only (immerse the piston in hot water if necessary). Fit new circlips, one at each end of the gudgeon pin.
3 Fit the rings to the pistons, using the same method as for removal. It is vital that the rings are fitted in the correct order with their tapers running the correct way. This will be achieved if the ring markings face upwards. Stagger the piston ring gaps as indicated. (Fig 1.44)
4 Lubricate the piston rings liberally and the piston bore, fit a piston ring compressor. Using the handle of a hammer, tap the piston/connecting rod assembly into the cylinder bore so that the directional mark on the piston crown is towards the front of the engine. (photos)
5 Rotate the crankshaft so that the crankpin is at the lowest point, engage the connecting rod big-end with the crankpin and then fit the big-end bearing cap so that the marks made prior to dismantling on the rod and cap are adjacent and on the same side. (photo)
6 Tighten the big-end cap bolts to a torque of 45 lb/ft (6.2 kg/m). (photos)
7 Repeat the procedure with the other three piston/connecting rod assemblies and then check that the crankshaft turns smoothly.

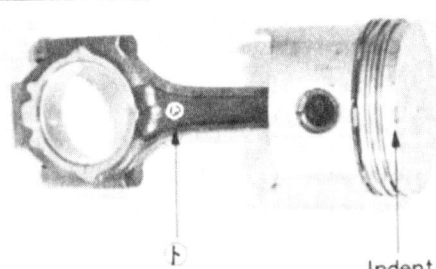

Fig 1.42 Piston and connecting rod correctly connected (Sec 35)

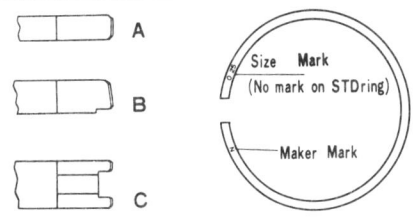

A = Compression Ring No. 1
B = Compression Ring No. 2
C = Oil Ring

Fig 1.43 Piston ring fitting diagram (marks face upwards) (Sec 35)

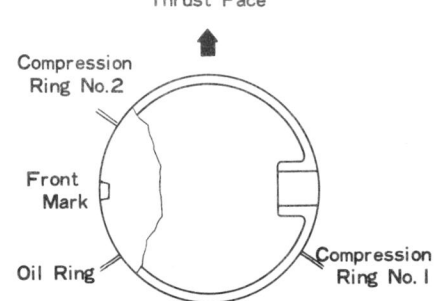

Fig 1.44 Piston ring end gap staggering diagram (Sec 35)

Fig 1.45 Inserting a piston/connecting rod assembly in the cylinder block (Sec 35)

35.4a Piston ring compressor in position

35.4b Piston crown showing forward directional mark

35.5 Installing a big-end cap

35.6 Tightening a big-end bearing nut

36.1a Oil pump flange gasket correctly located

36.1b Installing the oil pump

36.2 Installing engine front plate and gasket

36.3a Installing the oil pump driveshaft

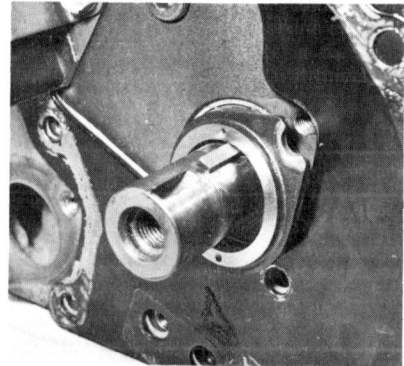
36.3b Oil pump driveshaft thrust-plate

36.4 Timing chain lower tensioner

36.5 Timing chain and sprockets correctly installed

36.7 Timing chain upper tensioner

36 Oil pump and timing gear - reassembly

1 Fit the oil pump to the crankcase using a new joint gasket. (photos)
2 Fit the front plate complete with new gasket. (photo)
3 Insert the oil pump driveshaft and the thrust plate, tightening it to a torque of 15 lb/ft (2.1 kg/m). (photos)
4 Fit the lower chain tensioner, so that the projection on the slipper is visible when installed. (photo)
5 Locate the crankshaft sprocket and the oil pump driveshaft sprocket within the loops of their chain and fit the complete assembly to crankshaft and oil pump driveshaft simultaneously. During this operation, take care not to drive the sprocket onto the oil pump driveshaft with too much force or the plug at the back of the rear bearing may be displaced. It is nut and a distance piece. Ignore any timing marks visible on the chain sprockets. (photo)
6 Fit the timing cover gasket, sticking it in position with jointing compound.
7 Fit the upper chain tensioner so that the projection on the slipper is at the rear. Note that one securing bolt of each chain tensioner is drilled with an oil hole; ensure that they are correctly located. (photo)
8 Bend up the lockplate tabs to secure the tensioner bolts.
9 Fit the camshaft drive sprocket to the oil pump driveshaft and tighten the retaining bolt to a torque of 70 lb/ft (9.7 kg/m). (photo)
engine is in the car or the correct way up, use a hooked piece of wire to keep the chain engaged with the sprocket teeth pending fitting the timing cover and cylinder head.
11 Fit the timing cover, using gasket cement on its mating faces (photo).
12 Tighten the timing cover bolts to a torque of 15 lb/ft (2.1 kg/m).
13 Fit the crankshaft pulley. A piece of tubing may be used to drive it into position.
14 Tighten the pulley securing bolt, with its washer, to a torque of 50 lb/ft (6.9 kg/m). (photo)

37 Flywheel (or driveplate - automatic transmission) - refitting

1 Bolt on the engine rear plate. (photo)

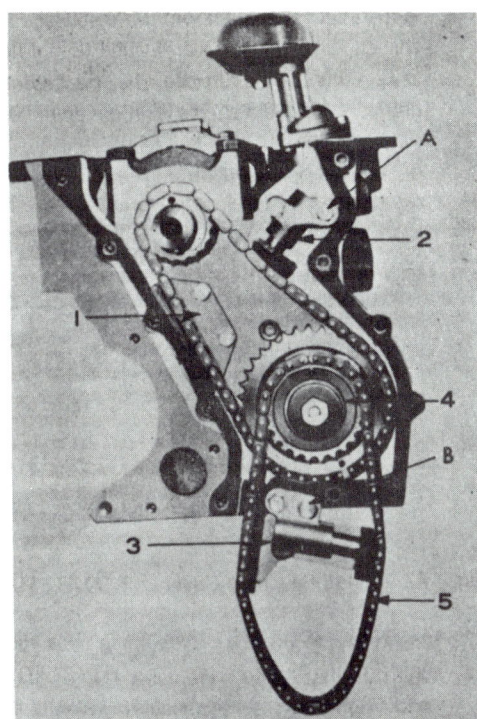

Fig 1.46 Layout of timing gear (engine inverted) (Sec 36)

1 Slipper
2 Lower chain tensioner
3 Upper timing tensioner
4 Camshaft drive sprocket
5 Upper timing chain
A and B securing bolts drilled with an oil hole

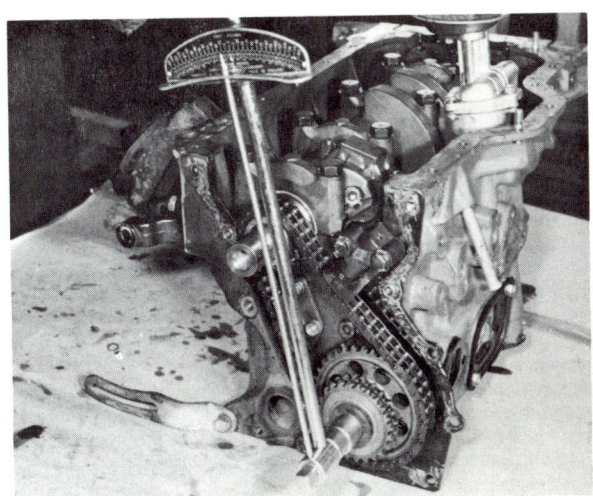

36.9 Tightening camshaft drive sprocket bolt

36.11 Fitting the timing cover

36.14 Tightening the crankshaft pulley bolt

37.1 Installing the engine rear plate

2 Refitting either the flywheel or driveplate is a reversal of removal but tighten the securing bolts to the specified torque and bend up the tabs of the locking plates. (photo)

38 Sump - refitting

1 Ensure that the mating faces of the sump and crankcase are quite clean and free from old pieces of gasket.
2 Smear the crankcase flange with jointing compound and stick a new gasket into position. (photo)
3 Smear the sump flange with jointing compound and bolt it into position. Do not overtighten the sump securing bolts (5 lb/ft - 0.7 kg/m). (photo)

39 Cylinder head and valve mechanism - installation

1 Check that the surfaces of the cylinder head and block are scrupulously clean.
2 Smear the top of the block with a thin film of gasket cement, making sure that none runs down into the oil or water passages or the bolt holes.
3 Lay a new gasket carefully into position on the block. (photo)
4 Smear the face of the cylinder head with a film of gasket cement and then lower the head straight down onto the block so that the positioning dowels engage first time. Do not slide the head about to position it as this will damage the gasket.
5 Make sure that the threads of the cylinder head bolts are clean and screw them in finger tight.
6 Tighten the bolts progressively (½ turn at a time) and in the sequence indicated to a torque of 70 lb/lb (9.7 kg/m). The timing chain will have been pulled through the aperture in the cylinder head with the hooked wire. (photo) (Fig 1.47)
7 Fit the lower bearing shells of the camshaft into their recesses on the top of the cylinder head.
8 Lubricate the bearings with engine oil and lower the camshaft into position.
9 Fit the bearing caps, complete with shell bearings. The caps should be numbered 1 to 4 (counting from the front of the engine) and the flat portion of their upper bosses must face the front. (photo)
10 Tighten the camshaft bearing cap bolts to a torque of 15 lb/ft (2.1 kg/m).
11 Rotate the crankshaft by means of the pulley bolt until No. 1 piston is at TDC on its compression stroke. To ascertain this position, place a finger over No. 1 spark plug hole and feel the compression being generated. When the second (TDC) notch in the crankshaft pulley is opposite the pointer on the timing cover, the setting is correct. (photo)
12 Turn the camshaft so that the dowel pin and punch mark are uppermost. Pull the timing chain upwards with the hooked piece of wire previously used to retain it on its drive sprocket.
13 Engage the camshaft sprocket within the upper loop of the chain so that the sprocket will fit on the dowel of the camshaft mounting flange without moving, **even fractionally,** the camshaft or the crankshaft. A certain amount of repositioning of the camshaft sprocket within the chain will probably be required before exact alignment with the dowel can be achieved. (photo)
14 Tighten the camshaft sprocket bolts to a torque of 12 ft/lb (1.7 kg/m). (photo)
15 Install the rocker shaft assembly, tighten the pillar bolts to a torque of 15 lb/ft (2.1 kg/m), progressively and in the sequence shown. (photo) (Fig 1.52)
16 Locate the oil feed pipe assembly and tighten the union bolts to a torque of 15 lb/ft (2.1 kg/m) (Fig 1.53)
17 Adjust the valve clearances in the following manner. The clearances will have to be readjusted when the engine has been fully reassembled and run to normal operating temperature.
18 Set No. 1 piston at TDC on its compression stroke and adjust valves 1, 2, 3 and 5. The inlet valves should be adjusted to give a

37.2 Tightening the flywheel bolts

38.2 Sump gasket correctly installed

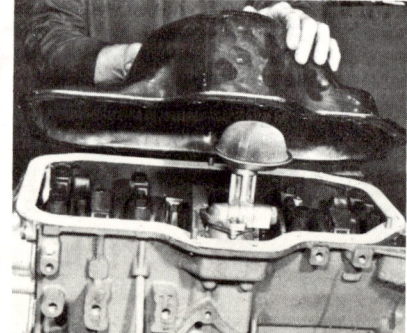
38.3 Installing the sump

39.3 Cylinder head gasket correctly installed

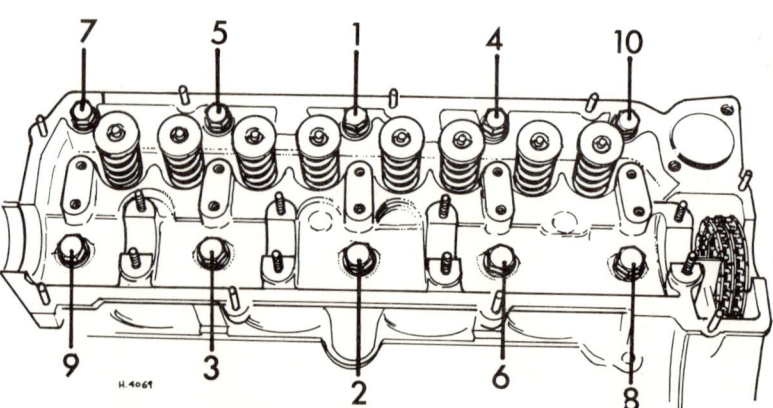
Fig 1.47 Cylinder head bolt tightening sequence (Sec 39)

39.6 Tightening a cylinder head bolt

39.9 Camshaft bearing cap correctly installed

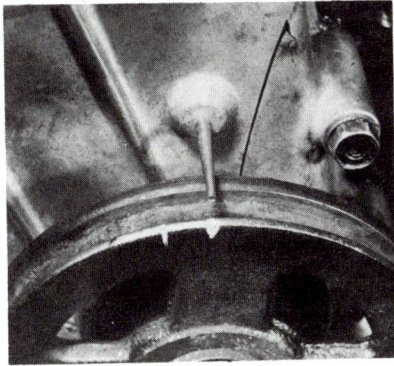

39.11 Timing marks (pointer opposite static ignition advance setting other mark is TDC)

39.13 Camshaft driven sprocket correctly set for installation to camshaft

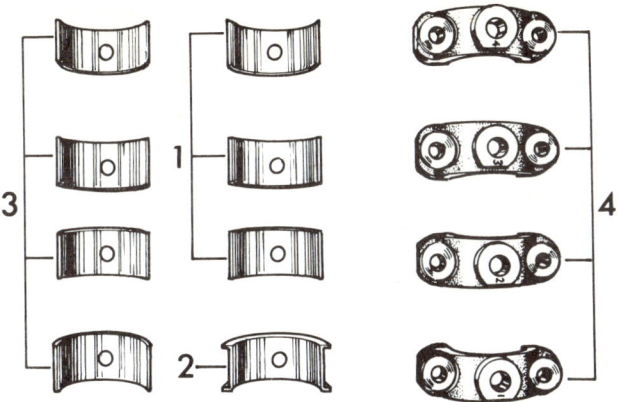

Fig 1.48 Camshaft bearings and caps (Sec 39)
1 & 2 Cylinder head half bearings
3 Upper bearings
4 Camshaft bearing caps, numbered 1 to 4

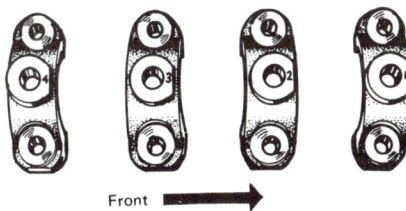

Fig 1.49 Correct installation of camshaft bearing caps (Sec 39)

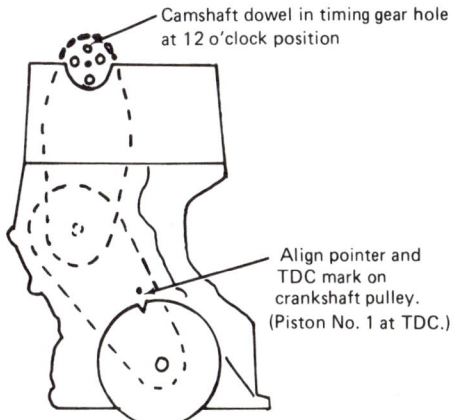

Fig 1.50 Timing gear setting diagram (Sec 39)

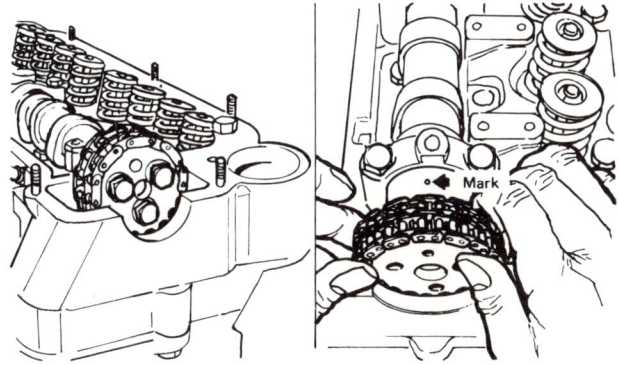

Fig 1.51 Fitting camshaft sprocket and chain to the camshaft (Sec 39)

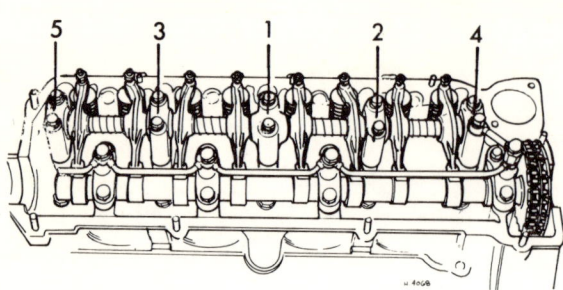

Fig 1.52 Rocker shaft support pillar securing bolt tightening diagram (Sec 39)

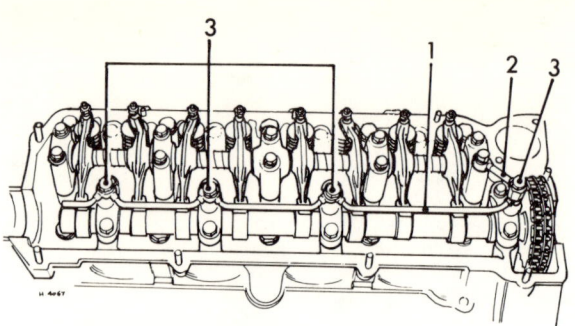

Fig 1.53 Oil delivery pipe installation (Sec 39)

1 Oil pipe assembly
2 Delivery pipe
3 Union bolt

39.14 Camshaft sprocket installed

39.15 Installing the rocker shaft

39.18 Adjusting a valve clearance

40.1 Tightening a thermostat housing bolt

40.2 Installing rocker cover

40.3a Location of water pump gasket

40.3b Water pump/fan unit installed

40.4 Left-hand engine mounting

40.5 Installing alternator

Chapter 1/Engine

clearance of 0.007 in (0.18 mm) and the exhaust valves to 0.013 in (0.33 mm). Turn the adjusting screw until the feeler blade is a stiff sliding fit between the end of the screw and the end of the valve stem. Tighten the locknut without moving the adjusting screw. (photo)

19 Rotate the crankshaft one complete turn so that the notch in the pulley is opposite to the TDC mark and adjust the valves 4, 6, 7 and 8. Numbering from the front of the engine, inlet valves are 2 - 3 - 6 - 7 and exhaust valves 1 - 4 - 5 - 8.

40 Engine ancillary components - refitting

1 Fit the thermostat and thermostat housing. (photo)
2 Fit the rocker cover, using a new gasket. (photo)
3 Stick a new gasket to the front face of the engine and then fit the water pump and fan assembly. (photos)
4 Fit the engine mounting brackets. It is a good idea at this stage to check the condition of the flexible mountings and renew them if they have deteriorated. (photo)
5 Fit the alternator mounting bracket, the alternator and adjustment strap. (photo)
6 Fit the alternator driving belt and adjust to give a maximum deflection of ½ in (12.7 mm) at the centre of its longest length. (photo)
7 Fit the water pump bypass hose. (photo)
8 Fit the manifold assembly using a new gasket. (photo) Note the lifting hook under the rear manifold bolt. (photos)
9 Refit the carburettor complete with heat insulator. (photo)
10 Fit the crankcase ventilation hose, the automatic choke heater pipes and on 8R-B engines (twin SU) reconnect the inlet manifold water heater hoses.
11 Fit the oil pressure switch and side cover (if removed). (photos)
12 Fit the fuel pump, using the two gaskets and insulator. (photos)

40.6 Correctly tensioned driving belt

40.7 Water pump bypass hose

40.8a Location of manifold gasket

40.8b Position of rear engine lifting hook

40.8c Position of front engine lifting hook

40.9 Installing manifold complete with carburettor

40.11a Location of oil pressure switch

40.11b Engine side cover (removable for access to core plug)

40.12a Fuel pump mounting flange gaskets and insulator

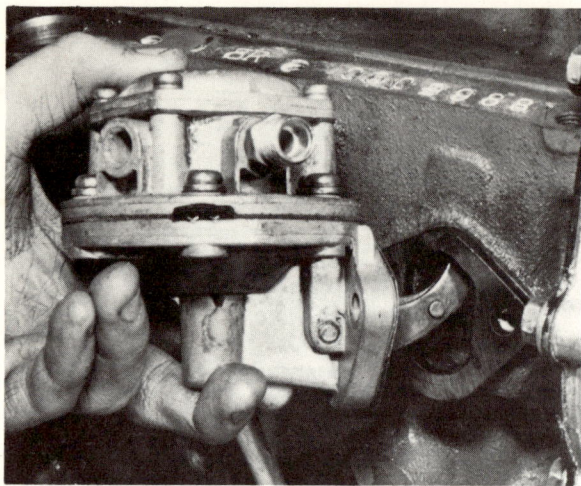

40.12b Installing the fuel pump

13 Install the distributor. To do this, refer to Chapter 4.
14 Fit the spark plugs and connect the HT leads between the distributor cap and the spark plug terminals (see Chapter 4 for sequence of fitting).
15 Insert the dipstick and connect the fuel pipe between the pump and carburettor.
16 Fit the air compressor, idler pulley and bracket (air conditioning system). If an air pump is used in conjunction with the emission control system (8R-C engines before March 1971 only) refit it and tension the driving belt (see Chapter 3).
17 For the correct tensioning of the various drivebelts; refer to the relevant Chapters, which are: alternator, Chapter 2, air pump (emission control) - Chapter 3, air conditioning compressor pump - Chapter 12.
18 Install the clutch mechanism to the flywheel ensuring that the driven plate is centralised as described in Chapter 5.
19 The power unit is now ready for coupling to the gearbox or automatic transmission unit prior to installation of the combined assembly.

41 Engine/manual gearbox - reconnecting

1 This is a reversal of the separation procedure, described in Section 6.
2 Tighten the clutch bellhousing to cylinder block bolts to a torque of 33 lb/ft (4.5 kg/m) on series 8R engines and to 50 lb/ft (6.9 kg/m) on series 18R engines.
3 Refit the starter motor.

42 Engine/automatic transmission - reconnecting

1 This is a reversal of the separation procedure, described in Section 7.
2 Check that the two projections on the torque converter key with the slots in the transmission fluid pump impeller, particularly if the torque converter has been partially withdrawn during dismantling operations.
3 Make sure that the driveplate is bolted to the torque converter with the marks made prior to dismantling in alignment. Tighten the bolts to a torque of 32 lb/ft (4.4 kg/m).
4 The torque converter housing to cylinder block bolts should be tightened according to engine series type as described for the clutch bellhousing in the preceding Section.
5 Check the security of the drain plug.
6 Refit the starter motor.

43 Engine/transmission - installation

1 Locate slings or chains round the engine and support the weight of the combined unit on suitable lifting tackle. Where a fixed hoist is being used, raise the power unit and roll the car under it.
2 Lower the unit into the engine compartment ensuring that nothing fouls during the operation.
3 With the front engine mountings roughly aligned, jack-up the transmission so that the rear crossmember and mounting can be installed. Remove the jack.
4 With the hoist still supporting the weight of the engine, the engine/transmission can be moved fractionally so that the front mountings can be aligned and bolted up.
5 Refit the propeller shaft making sure that the rear driving flanges have their marks (made before dismantling) in alignment.
6 Reconnect the gearchange or selector mechanism according to transmission type.
7 Reconnect the speedometer cable to the transmission housing.
8 Reconnect the handbrake equaliser and adjust if necessary, as described in Chapter 9.
9 Reconnect the exhaust downpipe to the manifold and secure the support bracket to the transmission housing.
10 Reconnect the vacuum hoses to the emission control unit.
11 Reconnect the emission control electrical leads.
12 Reconnect the choke and throttle controls.
13 Reconnect all electrical leads.
14 Bolt the clutch slave cylinder to the bellhousing (manual gearbox).
15 Reconnect the brake servo pipe to the inlet manifold.
16 Reconnect the heater hoses.
17 Reconnect the fuel inlet pipe to the fuel pump.
18 Refit the air cleaner.
19 Refit the radiator and connect the top and bottom hoses.
20 On vehicles equipped with air conditioning, install the condenser in front of the radiator and reconnect the pipes and hoses both to the condenser and the compressor pump.
21 Refit the radiator grille, upper and lower shields and the fan shrouds.
22 Refit the bonnet.
23 Refill the cooling system.
24 Refill the engine with oil.
25 Refill the gearbox or automatic transmission unit.
26 Connect the lead to the battery negative terminal.

44 Initial start-up after major overhaul

1 Start the engine and check for oil or water leaks. None should be apparent if new gaskets have been used throughout and the specified torque wrench settings adhered to.
2 Where an air conditioning system is installed, have the system professionally recharged with refrigerant gas.
3 Run the vehicle until normal operating temperature is reached and check the following:
(a) *Carburettor and emission control settings (Chapter 3).*
(b) *Ignition timing (with a stroboscope) Chapter 4.*
(c) *Check the torque of the cylinder head bolts (unscrew each bolt a quarter-turn and retighten to specified figure and in correct sequence). Check them again after 500 miles (800 km).*
(d) *Check the valve clearances (Section 39) but this time the clearances with the engine hot should be reset to inlet 0.008 in (0.20 mm) exhaust 0.014 in (0.36 mm).*
(e) *Recheck all oil levels and top-up the engine oil to make up for the amount absorbed by the new filter element.*

Chapter 1/Engine

45 Fault diagnosis - engine

Symptom	Cause
Engine will not turn over when starter switch is operated	Flat battery Bad battery connections Bad connections at solenoid switch and/or starter motor Starter motor jammed Defective solenoid Starter motor defective
Engine turns over normally but fails to start	No spark at plugs No fuel reaching engine Too much fuel reaching the engine (flooding)
Engine starts but runs unevenly and misfires	Ignition and/or fuel system faults Incorrect valve clearances Burnt out valves Worn out piston rings
Lack of power	Ignition and/or fuel system faults Incorrect valve clearances Burnt out valves Worn out piston rings
Excessive oil consumption	Oil leaks from crankshaft rear oil seal, timing cover gasket and oil seal, rocker cover gasket, oil filter gasket, sump gasket, sump plug washer Worn piston rings or cylinder bores resulting in oil being burnt by engine Worn valve guides and/or defective valve stem seals
Excessive mechanical noise from engine	Wrong valve to rocker clearances Worn crankshaft bearings Worn cylinders (piston slap) Slack or worn timing chain and sprockets
Poor idling	Leak in inlet manifold gasket Perforated or leaking PCV connecting pipe Perforated or leaking brake servo pipe

NOTE: When investigating starting and uneven running faults, do not be tempted into snap diagnosis. Start from the beginning of the check procedure and follow it through. It will take less time in the long run. Poor performance from an engine in terms of power and economy is not normally diagnosed quickly. In any event, the ignition and fuel systems must be checked first before assuming any further investigation needs to be made.

In addition to the foregoing, reference should also be made to the fault finding chart for emission control equipment which is to be found at the end of Chapter 3. Such a fault can have an immediate effect upon engine performance.

Chapter 2 Cooling system

Contents

Antifreeze and corrosion inhibiting mixtures 5	General description 1
Cooling system - draining 2	Radiator - removal, inspection and refitting 6
Cooling system - filling 4	Thermostat - removal, testing and refitting 7
Cooling system - flushing 3	Water pump and fluid coupling - renovation 9
Drivebelt - adjustment 10	Water pump - removal and refitting 8
Fault diagnosis - cooling system 12	Water temperature gauge and transmitter 11

Specifications

Water pump
Type ... ... Centrifugal with six blade impeller
Impeller to body clearance ... ... 0.012 to 0.028 in (0.3 to 0.7 mm)

Radiator
Type ... ... Pressurised, corrugated fin and tube
Radiator cap pressure rating ... ... 10.7 to 14.9 lb/in^2 (0.75 to 1.05 kg/cm^2)

Thermostat
Type ... ... Wax pellet
Opens ... ... 177 to 182°F (80.5 to 83.5°C)
Fully open ... ... 203°F (95°C)

Fluid fan coupling
Fluid type ... ... Silicone oil 10000 cst
Fluid capacity:
   8R series ... ... 0.39 to 0.42 oz (11 to 12 cc)
   18R series ... ... 0.85 to 0.92 oz (24 to 26 cc)

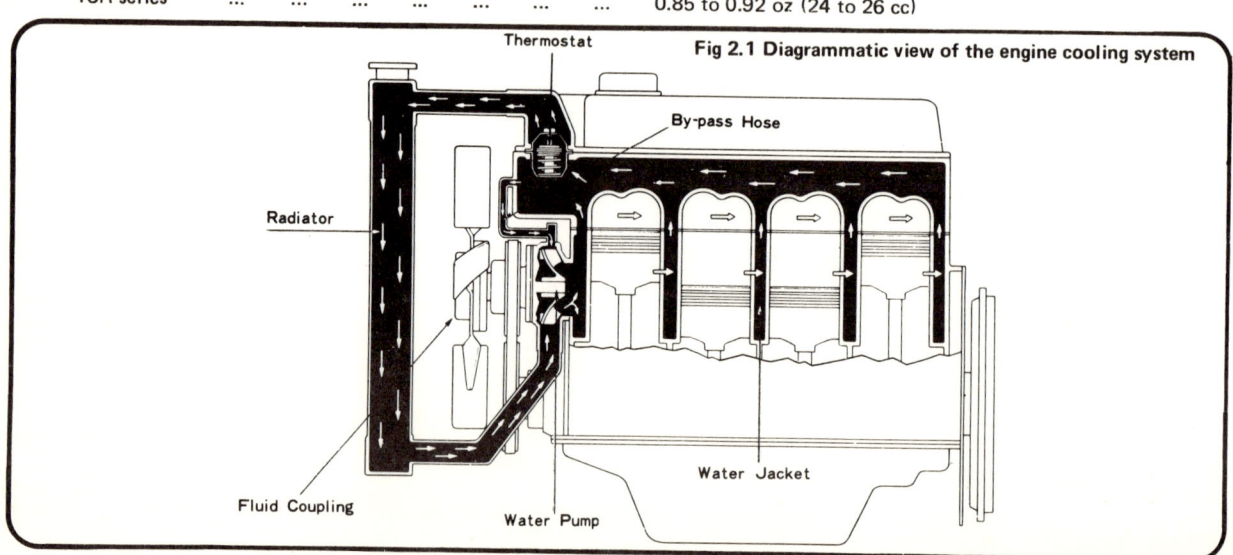

Fig 2.1 Diagrammatic view of the engine cooling system

Chapter 2/Cooling system

1 General description

The cooling system comprises the radiator, top and bottom water hoses, water pump, cylinder head and block water jackets, radiator cap with pressure relief valve and flow and return heater hoses. Some models are fitted with an expansion tank. The thermostat is located in a recess at the front of the cylinder head. The principle of the system is that cold water in the bottom of the radiator circulates upwards through the lower radiator hose to the water pump, where the pump impeller pushes the water round the cylinder block and head through the various cast-in passages to cool the cylinder bores, combustion surfaces and valve seats. When sufficient heat has been absorbed by the cooling water, and the engine has reached an efficient working temperature, the water moves from the cylinder head past the now open thermostat into the top radiator hose and into the radiator header tank.

The water then travels down the radiator tubes when it is rapidly cooled by the in-rush of air when the vehicle is in forward motion. A four bladed fan, mounted on the water pump pulley, assists this cooling action. The water, now cooled, reached the bottom of the radiator and the cycle is repeated.

When the engine is cold the thermostat remains closed until the coolant reaches a pre-determined temperature (see Specifications). This assists rapid warming-up.

The fan is of variable speed type having its central hub of fluid coupling design. (photo) At high engine speeds, the charge of silicone oil within the casing is thrown outwards by centrifugal force causing the disengagement of the fan so that it freewheels and does not absorb any engine power. As the engine speed drops to a pre-determined level, the fluid coupling is re-engaged and the fan resumes its rotation.

The heater is supplied with hot water from the engine cooling system and a water temperature transmitter unit and gauge are fitted.

1.1 Variable speed type fan assembly

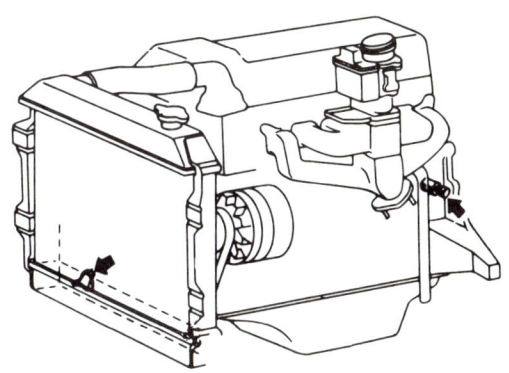

Fig 2.2 Radiator and cylinder block draining points (Sec 2)

2 Cooling system - draining

1 With the car on level ground drain the system as follows:
2 If the engine is cold remove the filler cap from the radiator by turning the cap anti-clockwise. If the engine is hot having just been run, then turn the filler cap very slightly until the pressure in the system has had time to disperse. Use a rag over the cap to protect your hand from escaping steam. If, with the engine very hot, the cap is released suddenly, the drop in pressure can result in the water boiling. With the pressure released the cap can be removed.
3 If anti-freeze is in the radiator drain it into a clean bucket or bowl for re-use.
4 Place the heater control in the 'HOT' position and unscrew the radiator drain plug and the one on the left-hand side of the cylinder block.

3 Cooling system - flushing

1 The radiator and waterways in the engine after some time may become restricted or even blocked with scale or sediment which reduce the efficiency of the cooling system. When this condition occurs or the coolant appears rusty or dark in colour the system should be flushed. In severe cases reverse flushing may be required as described later.
2 Place the heater controls to the 'HOT' position and unscrew fully the radiator and cylinder block drain taps.
3 Remove the radiator filler cap and place a hose in the filler neck. Allow water to run through the system until it emerges from both drain taps quite clear in colour. **Do not flush a hot engine with cold water.**
4 In severe cases of contamination of the coolant or in the system, reverse flush by first removing the radiator cap and disconnecting the lower radiator hose at the radiator outlet pipe.
5 Remove the top hose at the radiator connection end and remove the radiator as described in Section 6.
6 Insert the radiator and place a hose in the bottom outlet pipe. Continue flushing until clear water comes from the radiator top tank.
7 On some 2 door saloon models an aluminium radiator is used, in which case care must be taken when using any proprietary cleaner or descaler.

4 Cooling system - filling

Vehicles without a coolant reservoir/expansion tank
1 Place the heater control to HOT and check that the radiator and cylinder block taps are closed.
2 Pour coolant slowly into the radiator filler neck until it is 1 in (25.4 mm) below the filler neck. Refit the cap.

Vehicles with a coolant reservoir/expansion tank
3 Place the heater control in the HOT position and check that the radiator and cylinder block taps are closed. Pour coolant slowly into the radiator filler neck until it is full to the brim.
4 Run the engine at idling speed and watch the level of coolant at the filler neck drop, continuing to top up until the level no longer falls. Switch off the engine and refit the radiator pressure cap.
5 Remove the cap from the radiator reservoir tank and fill to the 'FULL' level with similar coolant.
6 Refit the reservoir cap.

5 Antifreeze and corrosion inhibiting mixtures

1 It is recommended that the system is filled with an antifreeze mixture where climatic conditions warrant its use. The cooling system should be drained, flushed and refilled every Autumn. The use of antifreeze solutions for periods of longer than a year is likely to cause damage and encourage the formation of rust and scale due to the corrosion inhibitors gradually loosing their efficiency. If the use of antifreeze mixture is not necessary because of favourable climatic conditions, never use ordinary water but always fill the system with a corrosion inhibiting mixture of recommended brand. Models having an aluminium radiator should use a coolant which contains special inhibitors for the protection of this part of the cooling system.

2 Before adding antifreeze to the system, check all hose connections and check the tightness of the cylinder head bolts as such solutions are searching. The cooling system should be drained and refilled with clean water as previously explained, before adding antifreeze.

3 The quantity of antifreeze which should be used for various levels of protection is given in the table below, expressed as a percentage of the system capacity.

Antifreeze volume	Protection to	Safe pump circulation
25%	−26°C (−15°F)	−12°C (10°F)
30%	−33°C (−28°F)	−16°C (3°F)
35%	−39°C (−38°F)	−20°C (−4°F)

4 Where the cooling system contains an antifreeze or corrosion inhibiting solution any topping-up should be done with a solution made up in similar proportions to the original in order to avoid dilution.

6 Radiator - removal, inspection and refitting

1 Drain the engine coolant.
2 Remove the lower shield to gain access to the bottom hose clamps. Remove the fan shroud.
3 Disconnect the top and bottom radiator hoses.
4 Unbolt the radiator and lift it from the engine compartment.
5 *On vehicles equipped with automatic transmission,* before the radiator can be removed, the oil cooler hoses will first have to be disconnected from the bottom of the unit.
6 *On vehicles equipped with an air conditioning system,* the condenser is mounted in front of the radiator and this must not be disconnected or damaged during the radiator removal operations.
7 Radiator repair is best left to a specialist but minor leaks may be temporarily rectified with a proprietary sealant.
8 With the radiator removed, brush accumulations of flies and leaves from the fins and examine and renew, if necessary, any hoses or clips which have deteriorated.
9 The radiator can be flushed as described in Section 3.
10 Check the pressure rating of the radiator cap and have its operation tested by a service station.

7 Thermostat - removal, testing, refitting

1 A faulty thermostat can cause overheating or slow engine warm-up. It will also affect the performance of the heater.
2 Drain off enough coolant through the radiator drain tap so that the coolant level is below the thermostat housing joint face. A good indication that the correct level has been reached is when the cooling tubes are exposed when viewed through the radiator filler cap.
3 Unscrew and remove the two retaining bolts and withdraw the thermostat cover sufficiently to permit the thermostat to be removed from its seat in the cylinder head.
4 To test whether the unit is serviceable, suspend the thermostat by a piece of string in a pan of water being heated. Using a thermometer, with reference to the opening and closing temperature in Specifications, its operation may be checked. The thermostat should be renewed if it is stuck open or closed or it fails to operate at the specified temperature. The operation of a thermostat is not instantaneous and sufficient time must be

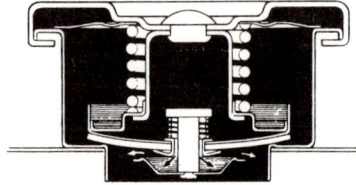

Vacuum valve operation

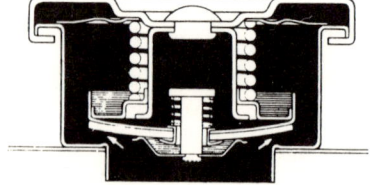

Pressure regulating valve operation

Fig 2.3 Sectional view of the radiator pressure cap (Sec 6)

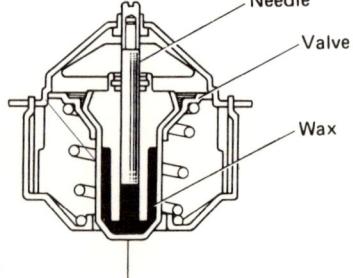 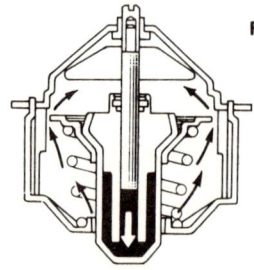

CLOSED   OPENED

Fig 2.4 Operational diagrams of the thermostat (Sec 7)

Chapter 2/Cooling system

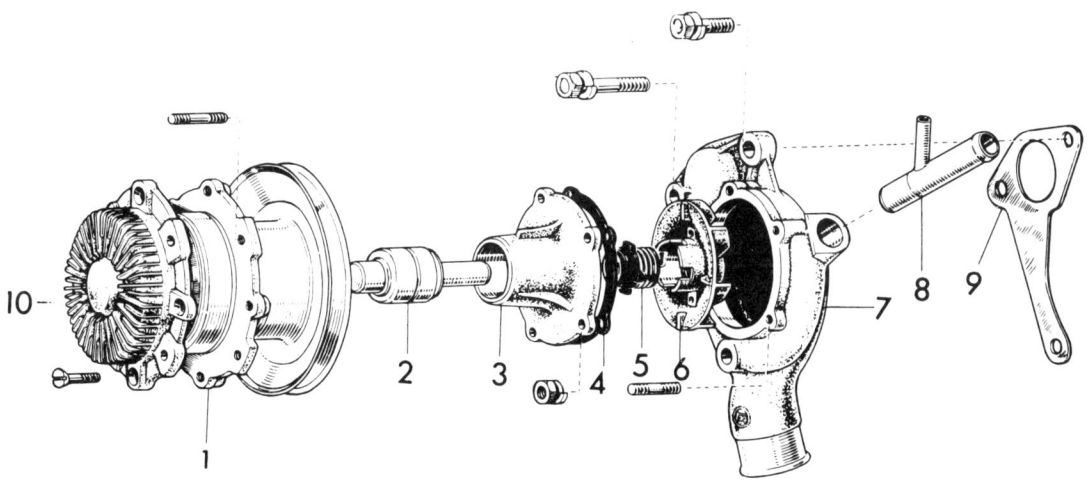

Fig 2.5 Exploded view of the water pump (Sec 8)

1 Fan fluid coupling
2 Shaft/bearing assembly
3 Cover
4 Cover gasket
5 Seal assembly
6 Impeller
7 Body
8 Union
9 Gasket
10 Fluid coupling case

allowed for movement during testing. Never replace a faulty unit - leave it out if no replacement is available immediately.
5 Replacement of the thermostat is a reversal of the removal procedure. Ensure the mating faces of the housing are clean. Use a new gasket with jointing compound. The word 'TOP' which appears on the thermostat face must be visible from above.

8 Water pump - removal and refitting

1 Drain the cooling system.
2 Remove the radiator.
3 Slacken the alternator mountings and remove the adjustment strap. Push the alternator in towards the engine and remove the driving belt.
4 On vehicles equipped with power steering or air conditioning systems, remove the driving belt in a similar manner to that described for the alternator/water pump drive belt.
5 Disconnect the water pump bypass hose and the heater hose.
6 Unscrew and remove the three water pump securing bolts and lift the pump and fan assembly from the front face of the cylinder block.
7 Refitting is a reversal of removal but always use a new gasket and check that pieces of old gasket are not adhering to the mating faces of either the pump or the cylinder block.
8 Adjust the drivebelt tension as described in Section 10. If power steering or air conditioning systems are installed, refer to Chapters 11 or 12 for details of tensioning the drivebelt.

9 Water pump and fluid coupling - renovation

1 It is recommended that when the water pump fluid coupling is in need of repair it should be exchanged for a factory reconditioned unit as spare parts availability is doubtful.

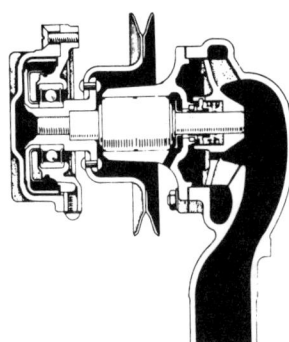

Fig 2.6 Sectional view of water pump and fluid coupling (Sec 9)

10 Drivebelt - adjustment

1 The drivebelt which runs between the crankshaft pulley, the water pump/fan pulley and the alternator pulley should be tensioned to provide a deflection of ½ in (12.7 mm) when pressed at the midway point between the alternator and the water pump.
2 To adjust the tension, slacken the alternator adjustment strap and mounting bolts and move the alternator towards or away from the engine. Retighten all bolts.

11 Water temperature gauge and transmitter

A description and testing procedure for these components is included with details of other instrumentation in Chapter 10.

12 Fault diagnosis

Symptom	Cause
Overheating	Insufficient water in cooling system
	Fan belt slipping (accompanied by a shrieking noise on rapid engine acceleration)
	Radiator core blocked or radiator grille restricted
	Bottom water hose collapsed, impeding flow
	Thermostat not opening properly
	Ignition advance and retard incorrectly set (accompanied by loss of power, and perhaps, misfiring)
	Carburettor incorrectly adjusted (mixture too weak)
	Exhaust system partially blocked
	Oil level in sump too low
	Blown cylinder head gasket (water/steam being forced down the radiator overflow pipe under pressure)
	Engine not yet run-in
	Brakes binding
Cool running	Thermostat jammed open
	Incorrect thermostat fitted allowing premature opening of valve
	Thermostat missing
Loss of cooling water	Loose clips on water hoses
	Top, bottom, or by-pass water hoses perished and leaking
	Radiator core leaking
	Thermostat gasket leaking
	Radiator pressure cap spring worn or seal ineffective
	Blown cylinder head gasket (pressure in system forcing water/steam down overflow pipe
	Cylinder wall or head cracked

Chapter 3 Carburation; fuel, exhaust and emission control systems

Contents

Accelerator pedal and linkage	35
Air cleaner (automatic temperture controlled) - servicing	4
Air cleaner (cleanable type) - servicing	2
Air cleaner (paper element type) - servicing	3
Air injection system (1971 - 8R–C engine) - description and maintenance	33
Air pump - servicing	34
Carburettors - general description	14
Dual barrel carburettor - accelerator pump adjustment	17
Dual barrel carburettor (18R engine series type) - adjustments and setting after dismantling and reassembly	23
Dual barrel carburettor (8R engine series type) - adjustments and setting after dismantling and reassembly	20
Dual barrel carburettor - automatic choke adjustment	15
Dual barrel carburettor (8R engine series type) - dismantling and reassembly	19
Dual barrel carburettor (18R engine series type) - dismantling and reassembly	22
Dual barrel carburettor (8R engine series type) - final adjustments after installation	21
Dual barrel carburettor (18R engine series) - final adjustments after installation	24
Dual barrel carburettor - removal and installation	18
Dual barrel carburettor - slow running adjustment	16
Emission control components - maintenance and testing	31
Emission control system (8R-C and 18R-C engines) - description and application	30
Emission control system circuits - testing	32
Exhaust systems and manifold	36
Fault diagnosis - carburation, fuel and emission control systems	37
Fuel contents gauge and transmitter unit	12
Fuel evaporative emission control (charcoal canister) system - dismantling and servicing	13
Fuel filter - servicing	5
Fuel pump - description	6
Fuel pump - dismantling, servicing and reassembly	9
Fuel pump - removal and refitting	8
Fuel pump - testing	7
Fuel tank - removal and refitting	10
Fuel tank - servicing and repair	11
General description	1
SU twin carburettors (8R-B engine) up to 1970 - adjustments	25
SU twin carburettors (8R-B engine) 1970 on - adjustments	26
SU twin carburettors (8R-B engine) up to 1970 - dismantling and reassembly	28
SU twin carburettors (8R-B engine) 1970 on - dismantling and reassembly	29
SU twin carburettors (8R-B engine) - removal and installation	27

Specifications

Fuel pump
Type	Mechanical
Discharge pressure	2.8 to 4.3 lb/in^2 (0.20 to 0.30 kg/cm^2)
Suction	In excess of 15.7 in Hg (400 mm Hg)

Dual barrel carburettors

Engine type	8R and 8R-C	18R and 18R-C
Throat diameter	2.64 in (67.0 mm)	as 8R type
Primary throttle bore diameter	1.34 in (34.0 mm)	as 8R type
Secondary throttle bore diameter	1.42 in (36.0 mm)	as 8R type
Primary venturi inner diameter:		
Main	0.98 in (25.0 mm)	0.91 in (23.0 mm)
Small	0.35 in (9.0 mm)	as 8R type
Secondary venturi inner diameter:		
Main	1.02 in (26.0 mm)	1.14 in (29.0 mm)
Large	0.61 in (15.5 mm)	as 8R type
Small	0.61 in (15.5 mm)	as 8R type
Main jet diameter:		
Primary	0.046 in (1.18 mm)	0.046 in (1.16 mm)
Secondary	0.053 in (1.35 mm)	0.065 in (1.65 mm)
Slow jet diameter:		
Primary	0.022 in (0.55 mm)	0.021 in (0.53 mm)
Secondary (8R)	0.022 in (0.55 mm)	0.033 in (0.85 mm)
Secondary (8R-C)	0.024 in (0.60 mm)	
Power jet diameter:		
(18R–C)	0.032 in (0.80 mm)	0.020 in (0.50 mm)
Pump jet diameter	0.032 in (0.80 mm)	0.020 in (0.50 mm)
Economiser jet diameter	0.042 in (1.06 mm)	0.042 in (1.06 mm)

Chapter 3/Carburation; fuel, exhaust and emission control systems

Main air bleed diameter:
- Primary ... 0.020 in (0.50 mm) ... 0.020 in (0.50 mm)
- Secondary ... 0.020 in (0.50 mm) ... 0.020 in (0.50 mm)

Slow air bleed diameter:
- (1) ... 0.028 in (0.70 mm) ... 0.033 in (0.85 mm)
- (2) ... 0.051 in (1.30 mm) ... 0.051 in (1.30 mm)
- Secondary ... ... 0.020 in (0.50 mm)

SU type carburettor
- Engine type ... 8R-B
- Throat diameter ... 1.59 in (40.5 mm)
- Throttle bore diameter ... 1.73 in (44.0 mm)
- Main jet diameter ... 0.10 in (2.5 mm)

Idling speeds:	8R	8R-B	8R-C	18R	18R-C
Manual gearbox	600 rev/min	750/850 rev/min	650 rev/min	600 rev/min	650 rev/min
Automatic transmission	650 rev/min in 'D'	—	650 rev/min in 'D'	600 rev/min in 'D'	800 rev/min in 'N'

Torque wrench settings

	lb/ft	kg/m
Manifold to cylinder head bolts	35	4.8
Carburettor to manifold	25	3.5
Fuel pump to crankcase	31	4.29

1 General description

The fuel system comprises a rear mounted fuel tank, a mechanically operated fuel pump which is actuated by an eccentric on the oil pump driveshaft and a carburettor. All models have a dual barrel single carburettor except those vehicles fitted with an 8R-B engine which has a twin SU type carburettor installation.

The dual barrel type carburettors have an automatic choke heated by air drawn from a tube located in the exhaust manifold. The inlet manifold on SU carburettors is heated by water from the engine cooling system.

A disposable element type air cleaner is used on 8R-C and 18R-C engines and a comprehensive fume emission control system is fitted, the components of which are fully described later in this Chapter. On other types of engine, the air cleaner element can be cleaned by washing in soap and water or fuel and thoroughly drying.

On 18R-C engine models operating in North America an automatic temperature controlled air cleaner is fitted.

2 Air cleaner (cleanable type) - servicing

1 Every 6,000 miles (9,000 km) remove the central wing nut from the top of the air cleaner cover and release the rim clamps.
2 Raise the cover and extract the felt type element.
3 Wash the element in soap and water or clean fuel and dry thoroughly. After three cleanings (18,000 miles, 30,000 km) the element must be renewed.
4 Wipe out the inside of the air cleaner casing and refit the components in the reverse order of dismantling.
5 Check that the condition of the rubber sealing gaskets has not deteriorated.
6 The twin air cleaners used with SU carburettors are serviced in a similar manner to the single type.

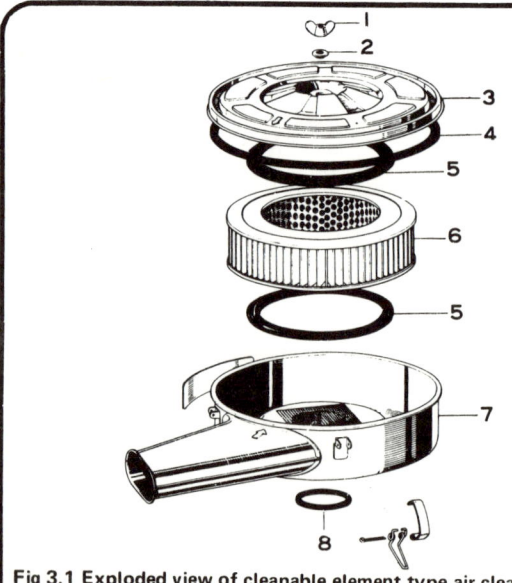

Fig 3.1 Exploded view of cleanable element type air cleaner (Sec 2)

1 Wing nut
2 Seal
3 Cover
4 Sealing ring
5 Element seals
6 Element
7 Casing
8 Gasket

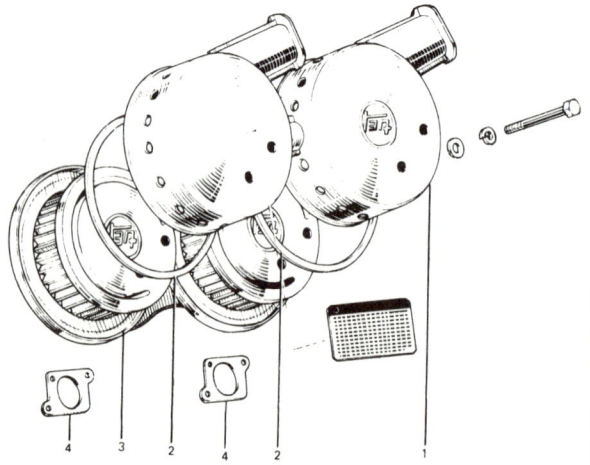

Fig 3.2 Exploded view of cleanable element type air cleaners (SU twin carburettor installation) (Sec 2)

1 Casing
2 Gasket
3 Element
4 Gasket

Chapter 3/Carburation; fuel, exhaust and emission control systems

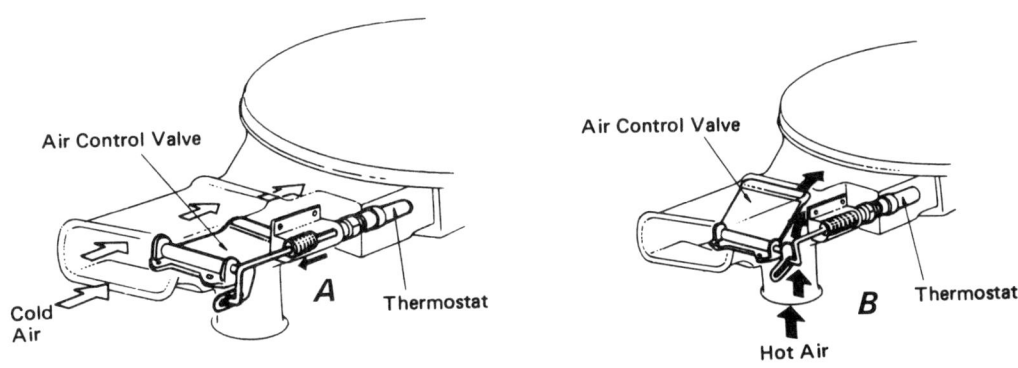

Fig 3.3 Automatic temperature controlled air cleaner shown in A cold mode B warm mode (Sec 4)

3 Air cleaner (paper element type) - servicing

1 Access to the paper element is obtained in exactly the same way as described in the preceding Section.
2 Every 6,000 miles (9,600 km), remove the element and tap off any adhering dust or blow compressed air from the inside of the element outwards.
3 Refit the element so that a clean fresh surface is presented to the air intake spout.
4 Check the gaskets and reassemble the components.

4 Air cleaner (automatic temperature controlled) - servicing

1 Servicing of this type of air cleaner is similar to that described for the paper element type in the preceding Section.
2 A thermostat is built into the air cleaner body and this controls, through the medium of a valve, the temperature of the air drawn through the air intake.
3 The valve is essentially a deflector which controls whether the air is drawn from the proximity of the exhaust manifold in order to prevent icing of the carburettor in cold weather and to maintain an even air intake temperature in the interest of reducing noxious gases emitted from the exhaust due to incomplete combustion.
4 Faulty operation of the device will be due either to the thermostat or the valve. In either case, renew the component complete.

5 Fuel filter - servicing

1 Two types of fuel filter may be encountered, on early models, a glass bowl type and on later models, a sealed, disposable cartridge type.
2 The bowl should be removed from the non-cartridge type filter whenever sediment is observed in the bottom of the bowl. Wipe out the bowl and refit it, do not overtighten the knurled securing nut.
3 Every 24,000 miles (38,000 km) both types of filter element should be renewed. This mileage should be regarded as a maximum. Under dirty or dusty operating conditions, renewal should be carried out at more frequent intervals.

6 Fuel pump - description

1 The fuel pump is of flexible diaphragm type and is actuated by a rocker arm which is in contact with an eccentric on the oil pump driveshaft.
2 The pump is located on the right-hand side at the forward end of the cylinder block and draws fuel from the rear mounted tank and supplies it under pressure to the carburettor.

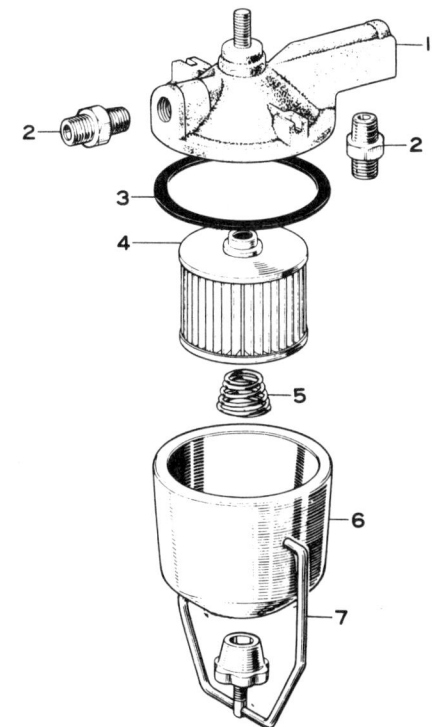

Fig 3.4 Early type fuel filter (Sec 5)

1 Body
2 Union
3 Gasket
4 Element
5 Spring
6 Bowl
7 Securing stirrup

Fig 3.5 Later type cartridge type fuel filter (Sec 5)

Fig 3.6 Exploded view of the fuel pump (Sec 9)

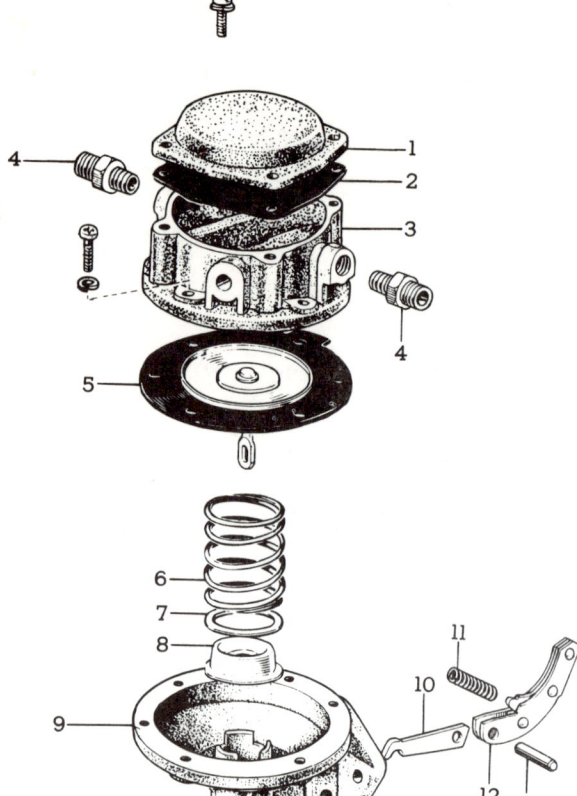

1. Cover
2. Gasket
3. Upper body
4. Union
5. Diaphragm/rod assembly
6. Spring
7. Oil seal retainer
8. Oil seal
9. Lower body
10. Rocker arm link
11. Spring
12. Rocker arm
13. Pivot pin
14. Gaskets
15. Insulator

7 Fuel pump - testing

Presuming that the fuel lines and unions are in good condition and that there are no leaks anywhere, check the performance of the fuel pump in the following manner: Disconnect the fuel pipe at the carburettor inlet union, and the high tension lead to the coil, and with a suitable container or a large rag in position to catch the ejected fuel, turn the engine over on the starter motor. A good spurt of petrol should emerge from the end of the pipe every second revolution.

8 Fuel pump - removal and refitting

1 Disconnect the inlet and outlet pipes from the pump by unscrewing the two unions.
2 Unscrew and remove the two bolts which secure the pump to the cylinder block. Withdraw the pump, together with insulator and gaskets.
3 Refitting is a reversal of removal but use a new gasket on each face of the insulating block.

9 Fuel pump - dismantling, servicing, reassembly

1 Remove the securing screws and lift off the cover (1) (Fig 3.7)
2 Remove the gasket (2).
3 Scratch an alignment mark on the flange edges of the upper and lower halves of the pump body and then remove the flange securing screws and separate the two halves.
4 From the lower body, unhook the diaphragm operating rod

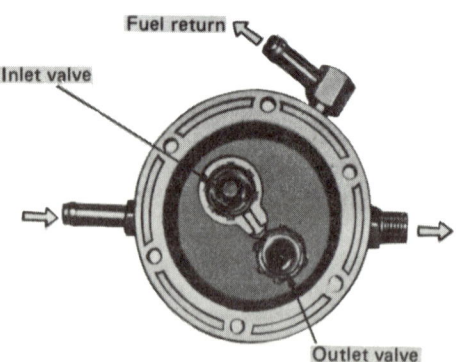

Fig 3.7 Fuel pump valves (Sec 9)

from the rocker arm by depressing the rod and twisting it sideways. Withdraw the diaphragm/rod assembly.
5 Remove the oil seal, retainer and spring.
6 If essential, due to a worn rocker arm, the pin (13) may be removed and the arm and spring removed.
7 Examine all components for wear. If this is severe, it will probably be more economical to renew the pump complete, on an exchange basis.
8 Check the operation of the valves in the upper body, by alternately sucking and blowing with the mouth at the inlet and outlet ports. When blowing (through the inlet port), the valve should open and close positively when sucked. When blowing (through the outlet port), the valve should close and

Chapter 3/Carburation; fuel, exhaust and emission control systems

open when sucked. The valves are staked in position and in the event of a fault it is recommended that a new upper body complete with valves is obtained.

9 If the pump components are in good order, obtain a repair kit which will contain all the necessary renewable items. The diaphragm/rod assembly cannot be dismantled and is renewed complete.

10 Reassembly is a reversal of dismantling. Align the flange mating marks and tighten the flange securing screws evenly and in opposite sequence. Final tightening should be carried out with the rocker arm fully depressed.

10 Fuel tank - removal and refitting

1 Drain the fuel from the tank into a suitable (capped) container.
2 Disconnect the fuel outlet pipe from the tank.
3 Remove the fuel tank shield.
4 Disconnect the lead from the terminal of the fuel contents transmitter unit.
5 *On models with a vented filler cap* remove the cap, the filler pipe grommet and the tank securing bolts and withdraw the tank.
6 *On models with a non-vented filler cap*, disconnect the vent pipes from the tank and also the flexible section of the filler tube before removing the tank securing bolts and the tank itself.
7 *On models with a fuel evaporative emission control system*, the breather hose from the tank contains a pressure equalising valve which must not be damaged or refitted the wrong way round.
8 On some late models fitted with 18R-C engines, a charcoal canister type evaporative emission control system is used (see Section 11). Fuel tanks on such models cannot be removed until the two hoses which run to the separator have been disconnected.
9 Refitting is a reversal of removal but scrape all the old sealing mastic from the mounting flanges and locate a new strip of sealer before bolting the tank into position.

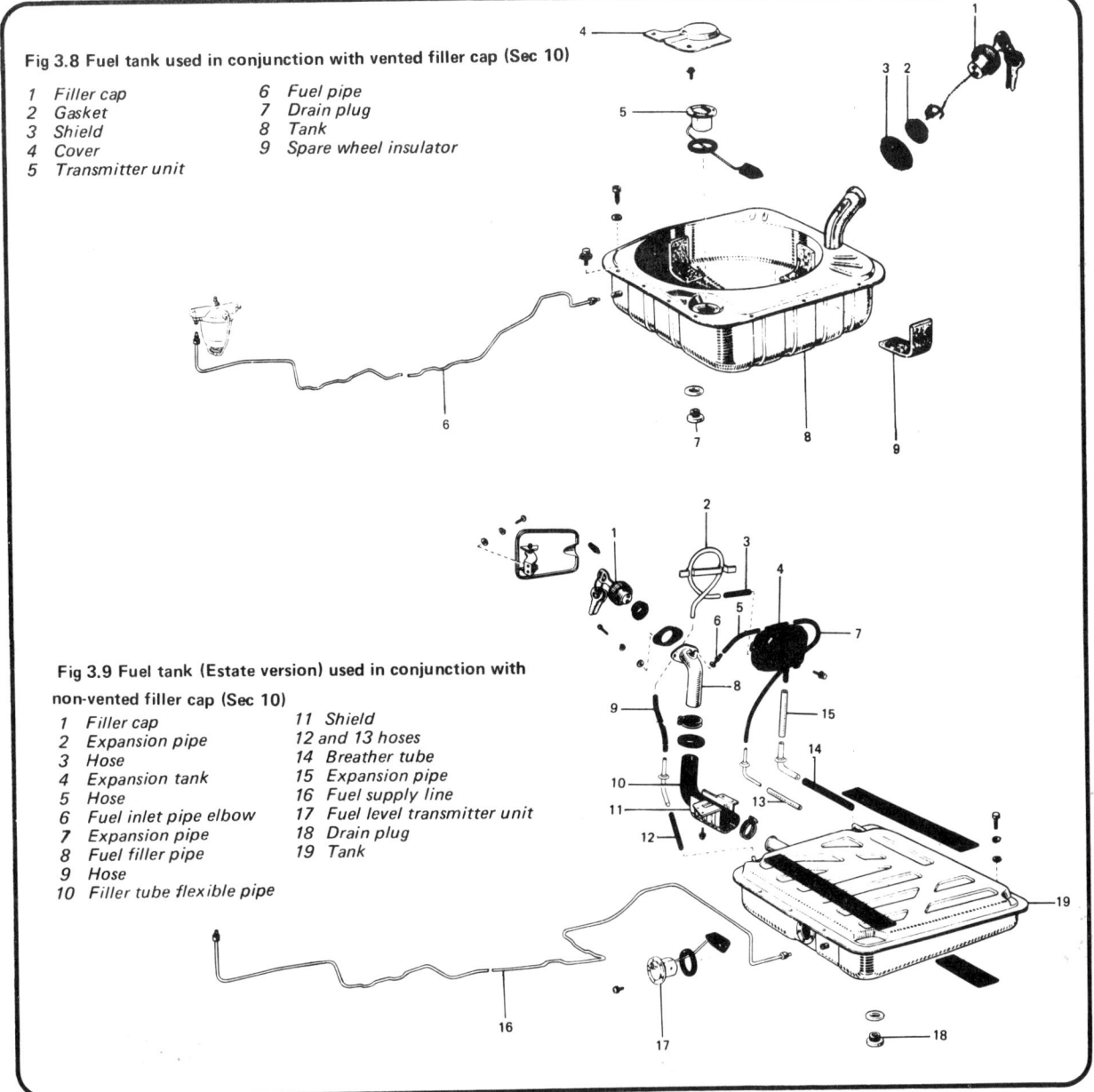

Fig 3.8 Fuel tank used in conjunction with vented filler cap (Sec 10)

1 Filler cap
2 Gasket
3 Shield
4 Cover
5 Transmitter unit
6 Fuel pipe
7 Drain plug
8 Tank
9 Spare wheel insulator

Fig 3.9 Fuel tank (Estate version) used in conjunction with non-vented filler cap (Sec 10)

1 Filler cap
2 Expansion pipe
3 Hose
4 Expansion tank
5 Hose
6 Fuel inlet pipe elbow
7 Expansion pipe
8 Fuel filler pipe
9 Hose
10 Filler tube flexible pipe
11 Shield
12 and 13 hoses
14 Breather tube
15 Expansion pipe
16 Fuel supply line
17 Fuel level transmitter unit
18 Drain plug
19 Tank

11 Fuel tank - servicing and repair

1 Over a period of time, sediment and water may accumulate in the bottom of the fuel tank. It is a good idea periodically when there is very little fuel left in the tank to remove the drain plug and drain the fuel and discard it.
2 If the tank is severely contaminated, withdraw the tank as previously described and remove the fuel level transmitter unit.
3 Use two or three changes of fuel and shake the tank vigorously until it is clean.
4 Should a leak develop, do not be tempted to solder over the hole. Fuel tank repair is a specialist job and unless lengthy safety precautions are observed, it can be a very dangerous procedure. It will probably be as economical to purchase a new tank as to have the original repaired.

12 Fuel contents gauge and transmitter unit

1 The testing of these units is described together with the other instrumentation in Chapter 10.

13 Fuel evaporative emission control (charcoal canister) system - description and servicing

1 This system installed on some late 18R-C engined models is designed to reduce the emission of fuel vapour to atmosphere by directing the vapour from the fuel tank through a separator to an absorbent charcoal canister. At vehicle speeds above 11 mph (17.7 kph) the vacuum switching valve operates and the vapour stored in the canister is drawn into the inlet manifold where it then burned as a controlled fuel/air mixture within the engine combustion chambers.
2 The fuel tank filler cap incorporates a valve which opens to admit air should a partial vacuum be created within the tank due to vapour removal.
3 The non-return valve maintains pressure in the fuel tank to prevent fuel entering the vapour extraction line when the tank is being filled.
4 Regularly inspect the condition and security of the system connecting hoses and the filler cap seal and renew as necessary.
5 Renew the non-return valve every 6,000 miles (9600 km).
6 Renew the charcoal canister every 5 years or at 50,000 miles (80,000 km) intervals, whichever occurs sooner.
7 Refer to Section 26, of this Chapter, for fault symptoms and their rectification.

14 Carburettors - general description

Models fitted with 8R and 18R engines are equipped with a dual barrel down draught carburettor except for those vehicles which have an 8R-B engine which has a twin SU type installation.

Reference should be made to Specifications Section for full details of jets and other components which differ between units when emission control systems are incorporated.

The operations in respect of the duel barrel carburettor apply to all models but any essential differences are noted.

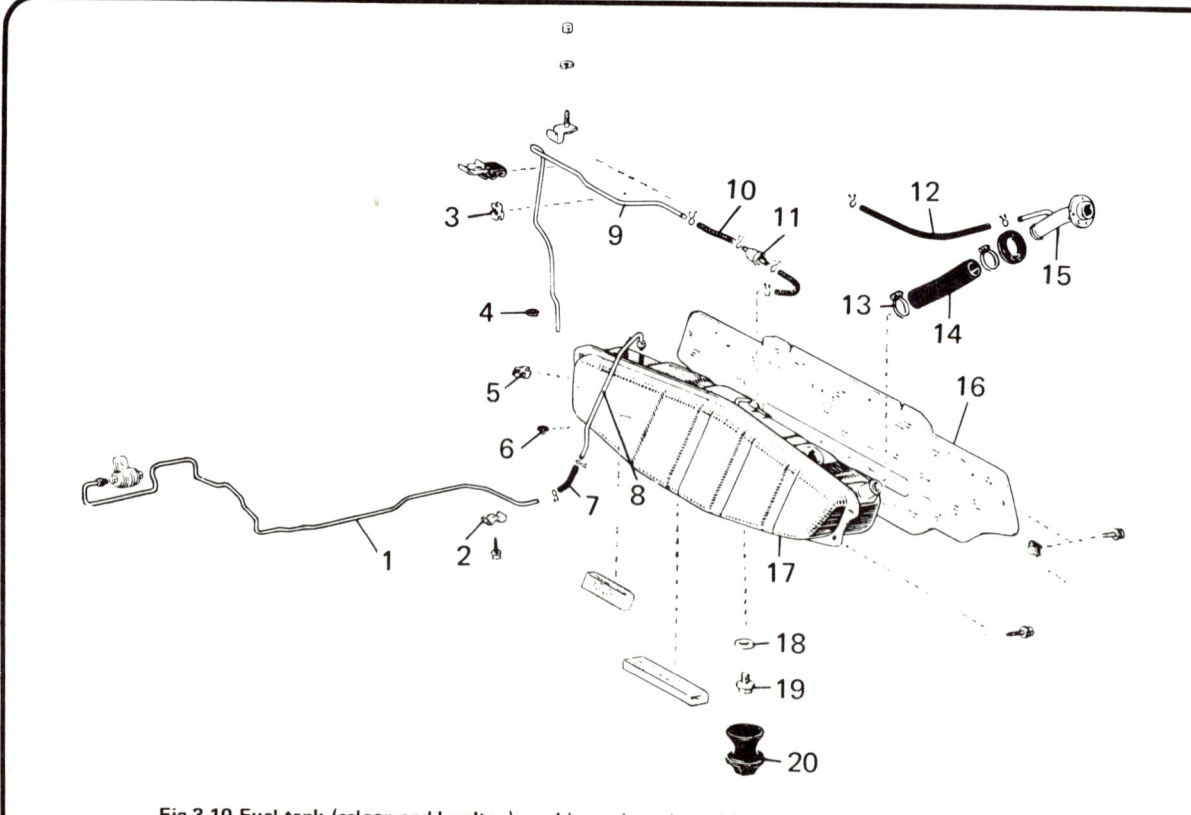

Fig 3.10 Fuel tank (saloon and hardtop) used in conjunction with evaporative emission control system (Sec 10)

1 Fuel supply line	7 Flexible connector	12 Hose	17 Tank
2 and 3 clamps	8 Fuel line	13 Clamp	18 Gasket
4 Grommet	9 Breather pipe	14 Flexible filler hose	19 Drain plug
5 Clamp	10 Flexible hose	15 Filler pipe	20 Drain plug shield
6 Grommet	11 Non-return valve	16 Shield	

15 Dual barrel carburettor - automatic choke adjustment

1 When the mark on the coil housing is in alignment with the centre index mark on the thermostat casing then the choke butterfly should be fully closed provided the ambient temperature is approximately 77°F (25°C).
2 Variations in air temperatures in which the vehicle is operating may be compensated for by turning the coil housing clockwise to richen the starting mixture in lower ambient temperatures and anti-clockwise to weaken it in high temperatures. Each graduation on the thermostat casing will vary the choke temperature setting by 9°F (5°C).

16 Dual barrel carburettor - slow running adjustment

1 The use of a vacuum gauge and a tachometer will be required for this operation.
2 Run the engine until normal temperature is reached.
3 Check that the valve clearances are correctly adjusted, the ignition timing is correct and all emission control settings are as specified.
4 Connect the tachometer in accordance with the maker's instructions and connect the vacuum gauge to the tapped hole in the inlet manifold.
5 Preset the mixture control screw by first screwing it into its seat and then unscrewing it between 2 and 2½ turns. **Do not force the screw into its seat.**
6 Start the engine and adjust the throttle control screw until the engine runs at 650 rev/min (indicated on the tachometer). On vehicles equipped with automatic transmission the speed selector should be in 'D' except those fitted with 18R-C engines which should be in 'N' (see Specifications).
7 Turn the mixture control screw until the maximum vacuum reading is obtained. Readjust the throttle control screw if necessary to make the engine resume its specified idling speed.

17 Dual barrel carburettor - accelerator pump adjustment

1 The correct accelerator pump stroke is when the centre of the pivot pin of the operating lever has a travel of 0.177 in (4.5 mm).
2 Where adjustment is required, carefully bend the connecting link (A - Fig 3.13).

18 Dual barrel carburettor - removal and installation

1 Remove the air cleaner.
2 Disconnect the fuel pipe from the carburettor.
3 Disconnect the distributor vacuum pipe from the carburettor, also the automatic choke heater pipes and the throttle control linkage.
4 Unscrew the carburettor flange securing bolts and lift the unit from the inlet manifold.
5 Installation is a reversal of removal but always use new gaskets and check the slow running adjustment after refitting, as described in Section 16.
6 On some 18R models a solenoid fuel cut off valve is fitted to the carburettor. Where fitted, disconnect the lead to the valve.

19 Dual barrel carburettor (8R engine series type) - dismantling and reassembly

1 *On early model carburettors,* remove the reloader connecting link cover and the connecting link.
2 Remove the reloader lever from the primary lever throttle shaft.
3 *On all carburettors,* remove the accelerator pump lever screw, the lever and the connecting links for the accelerator pump and

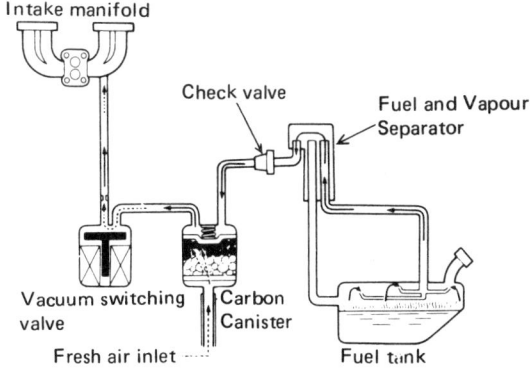

Fig 3.11 Diagrammatic layout of carbon canister type fuel evaporative emission control (Sec 13)

Fig 3.12 Automatic choke adjustment (dual barrel carburettor) 1 graduation on scale equals 9° F (Sec 15)

Fig 3.13 Accelerator pump stroke adjustment (dual barrel carburettor) (Sec 17)

Fig 3.14 Reloader link cover (1) connecting link (2) on early dual barrel carburettor (8R engine) (Sec 19)

Chapter 3/Carburation; fuel, exhaust and emission control systems

fast idle.
4 Remove the automatic choke connecting link and the flexible boot.
5 Remove the two screws which secure the throttle positioner diaphragm capsule and allow the unit to drop (applicable to emission control models only).
6 Disconnect the throttle positioner diaphragm capsule connecting link and withdraw the unit.
7 Remove the screws which secure the upper body to the main carburettor body and remove the upper body upwards to avoid damaging the accelerator pump plunger or float.
8 Remove the stop seal, the accelerator pump plunger and spring. (Fig 3.25)
9 Turn the main body upside down and catch the stop, the accelerator pump discharge weight and the ball.
10 If essential, the throttle positioner lever can be removed from the main body, also the stop lever spring, and the high speed valve stop lever.
11 Unscrew the main body from the throttle body/flange. There are three securing screws, two accessible from above and one

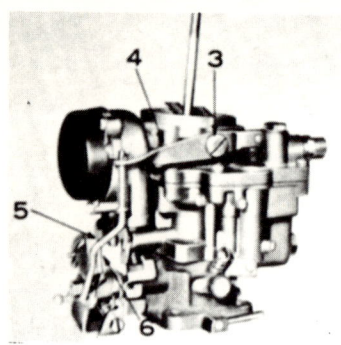

Fig 3.15 Location of accelerator pump lever screw (3) lever (4) pump connecting link (5) and fast idle link (6) - dual barrel carburettor (Sec 19)

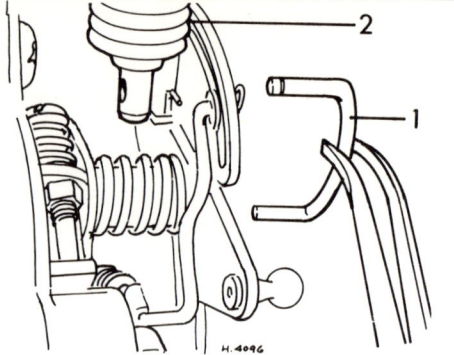

Fig 3.16 Removing automatic choke connecting link (1) and flexible boot (2) from dual barrel type carburettor (Sec 19)

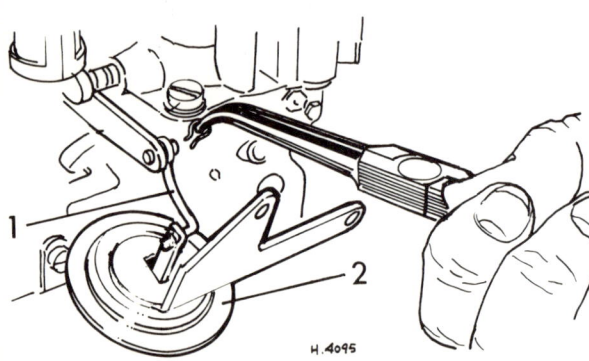

Fig 3.17 Removing throttle positioner diaphragm valve link (1) and valve (2) from dual barrel carburettor (Sec 19)

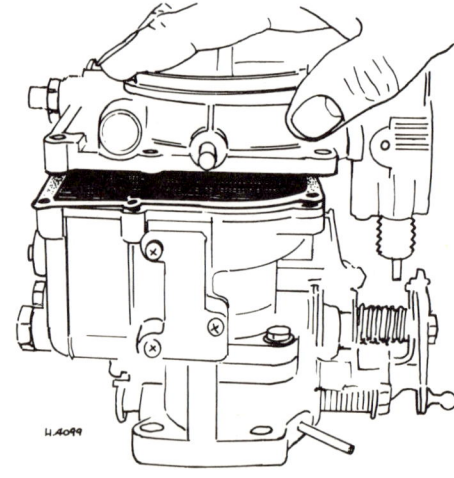

Fig 3.18 Removing upper body from dual barrel carburettor (Sec 19)

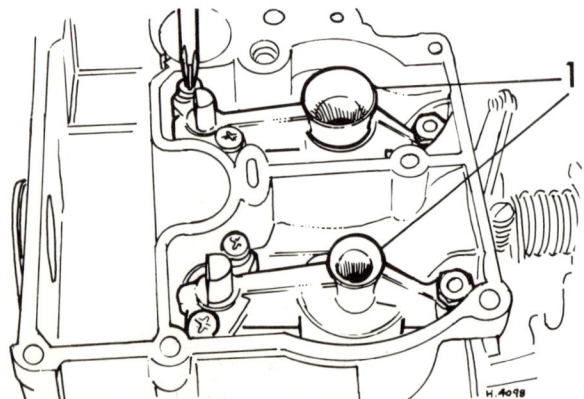

Fig 3.19 Removing the venturis (1) from dual barrel carburettor (Sec 19)

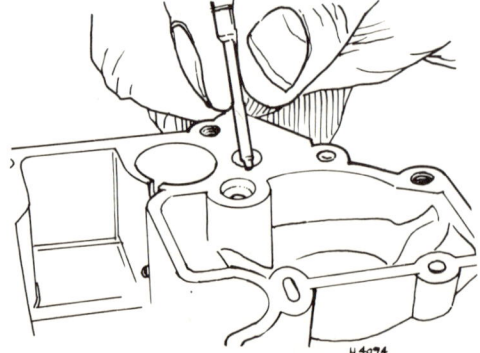

Fig 3.20 Removing the slow running jet from dual barrel carburettor (Sec 19)

from below.

12 Remove the primary and secondary venturis (large and small respectively) by unscrewing their securing screws. On some early model carburettors the venturis are interchangeable.

13 Remove the slow-running jet.

14 Extract the check ball retainer with a pair of long nosed pliers and then eject the ball by turning the carburettor upside down.

15 Remove the power valve assembly from the bottom of the float chamber. Unscrew the power jet from the power valve.

16 Remove the fuel level gauge assembly from the carburettor body by unscrewing the two securing screws.

17 Remove the plugs which cover the primary and secondary main jets and then unscrew the main jets.

18 Remove the thermostatic valve (three screws) from the main body. Do not dismantle the valve.

19 Unscrew and remove the mixture control and throttle speed screws and their springs.

20 Remove the throttle shaft link, the primary throttle shaft arm, connecting arm and the fast idle adjusting lever.

21 Only if essential, detach the secondary throttle return spring and remove the throttle lever from the shaft.

22 The primary secondary and high speed butterfly valves are better not disturbed unless the valve plates or shafts are worn. The valve plate securing screws are peened over and they will have to be filed before they can be unscrewed.

23 Remove the float pivot pin from the upper body and remove the float, at the same time extracting the fuel inlet needle valve component parts. Remove the fuel inlet union and filter gauze.

24 Remove the power piston stop and extract the power piston and spring.

25 Remove the automatic choke housing cover followed by the gasket and plate.

26 From within the automatic choke housing, remove the fast idle cam follower, the sliding rod and the piston connector.

27 The choke valve, shaft and lever should only be removed if essential as the valve plate securing screws are peened over and will have to be filed flat before they can be unscrewed.

28 The vacuum piston and connector can be extracted from the automatic choke housing if required but the unloader tab will have to be bent slightly to facilitate their withdrawal. (Fig 3.26)

29 If the automatic choke housing is removed from the carburettor upper body, retain the small 'O' ring type seal from the connecting vacuum passage.

30 With the carburettor now completely dismantled, wash all components in clean fuel and inspect for wear, damage or cracks.

31 Blow through jets and passages using a tyre pump. Never probe with wire or their calibration will be ruined. It is worth checking the jet calibrations against those listed in Specifications in case a previous owner has substituted any for incorrect sizes.

32 Obtain a repair kit which will contain all the essential gaskets, then discard the old items.

33 Commence reassembly by fitting the automatic choke

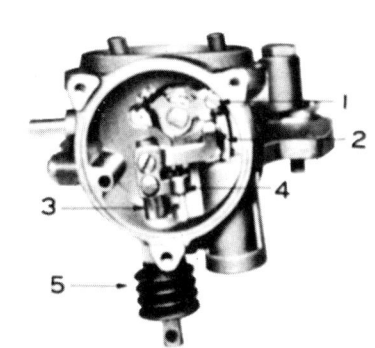

Fig 3.21 Removing the power valve and main jets (plugs removed) from the float chamber of a dual barrel carburettor (Sec 19)

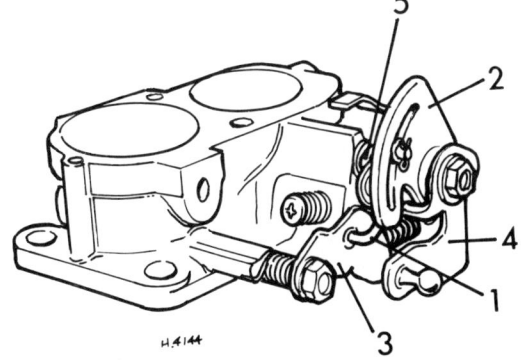

Fig 3.22 Removing the throttle shaft link (1) connecting arm (2) secondary throttle shaft lever (3) primary throttle shaft lever (4) and fast idle adjusting lever (5) from a dual barrel carburettor (Sec 19)

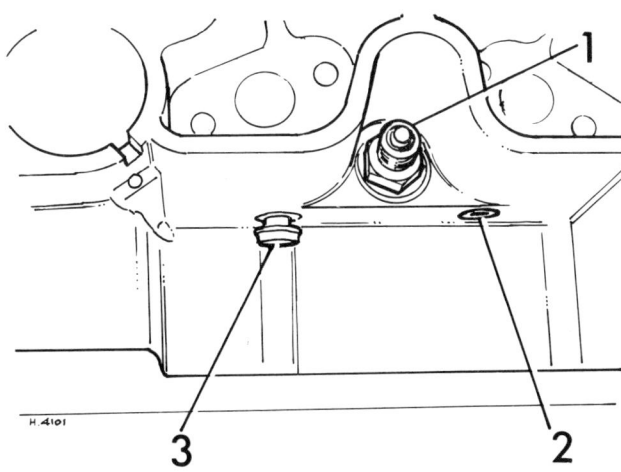

Fig 3.23 Removing the power piston (1) stop (2) and spring (3) from a dual barrel carburettor (Sec 19)

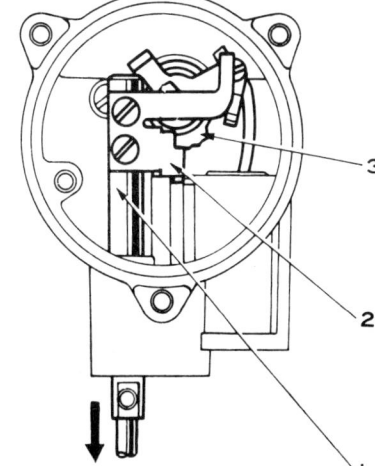

Fig 3.24 Internal components of the automatic choke of a dual barrel carburettor (Sec 19)

1 Sliding rod
2 Fast idle cam follower
3 Fast idle cam

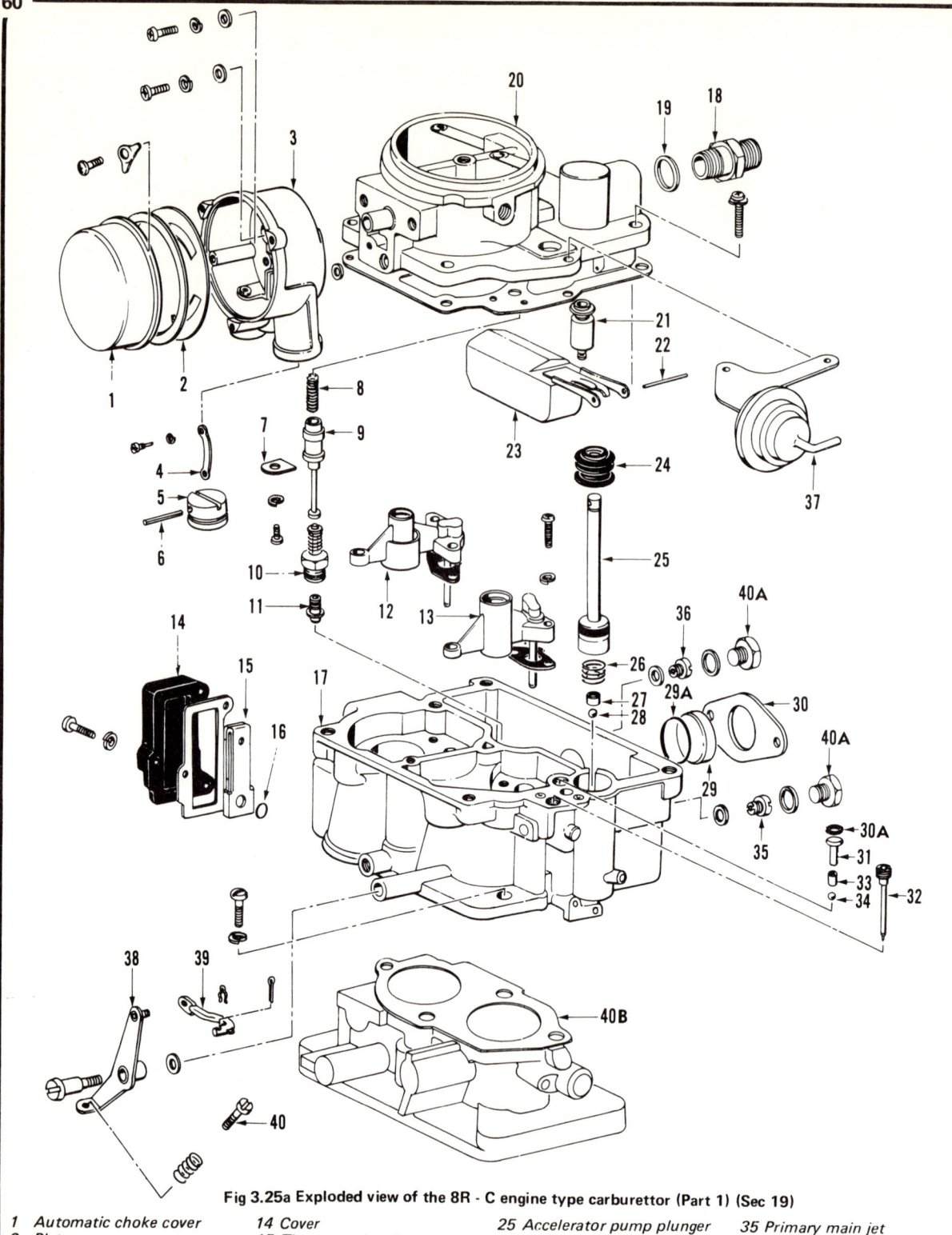

Fig 3.25a Exploded view of the 8R - C engine type carburettor (Part 1) (Sec 19)

1 Automatic choke cover
2 Plate
3 Automatic choke housing
4 Connecting link
5 Vacuum piston
6 Pivot pin
7 Power piston stop
8 Spring
9 Power piston
10 Power valve
11 Power jet
12 Secondary small venturi
13 Primary small venturi
14 Cover
15 Thermostatic valve
16 'O' ring
17 Main body
18 Fuel union and filter screen
19 Washer
20 Upper body
21 Fuel inlet needle valve
22 Float pivot pin
23 Float
24 Flexible boot
25 Accelerator pump plunger
26 Plunger spring
27 Check ball retainer
28 Check ball
29 Fuel level gauge glass
30 Glass retainer
30a Stop washer
31 Stop
32 Slow jet
33 Pump discharge weight
34 Check ball
35 Primary main jet
36 Secondary main jet
37 Throttle positioner diaphragm valve
38 Throttle positioner lever
39 Throttle positioner diaphragm valve connecting link
40 Throttle positioner adjusting screw
40a Plug
40b Gasket

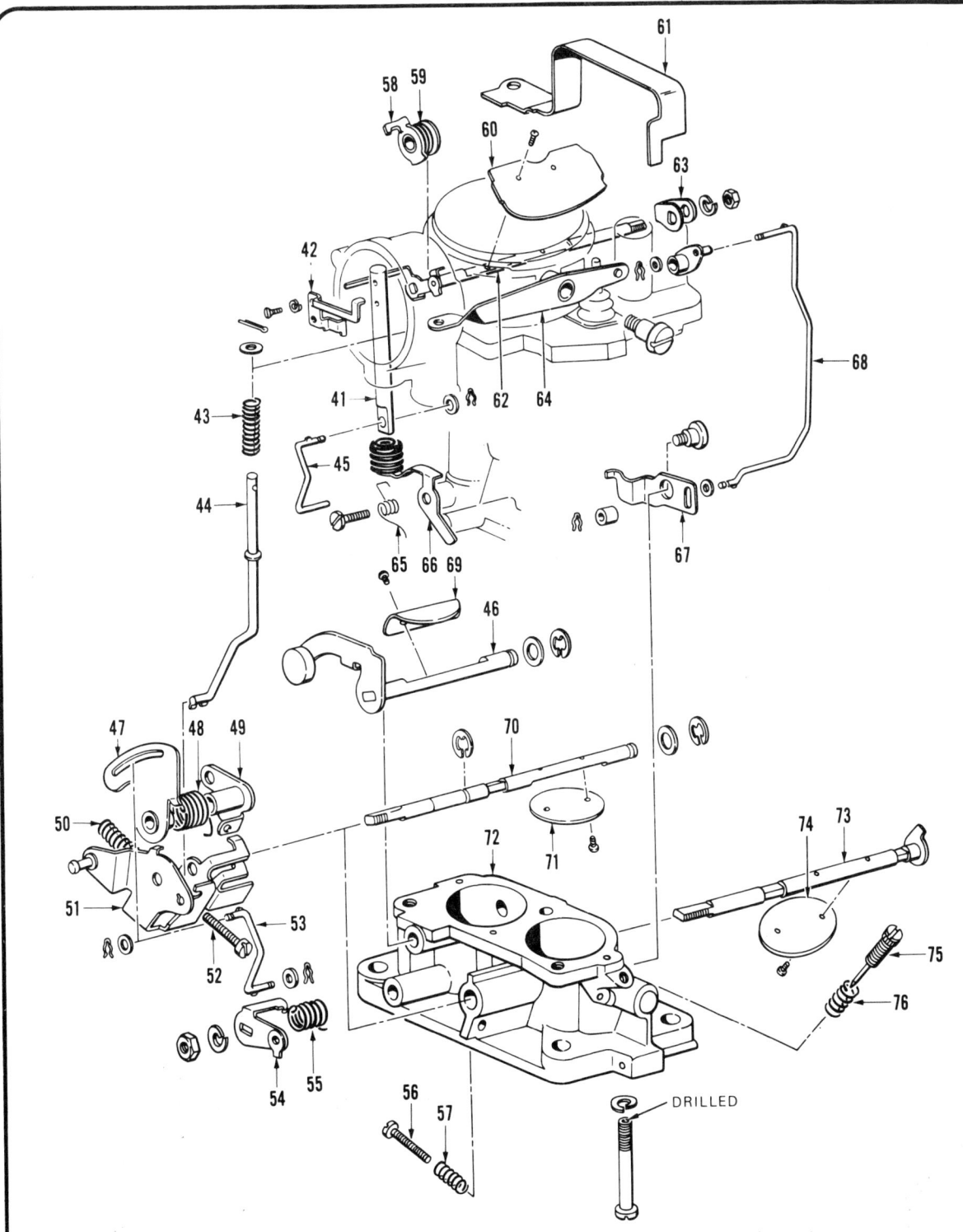

Fig 3.25b Exploded view of the 8R-C engine type carburettor (Part 2) (Sec 19)

41 Fast idle sliding rod
42 Fast idle cam follow
43 Accelerator pump rod spring
44 Accelerator pump connecting link
45 Fast idle connecting link
46 High speed valve shaft
47 Arm
48 Return spring
49 Fast idle adjusting lever
50 Spring
51 Primary throttle shaft arm
52 Fast idle screw
53 Throttle shaft link
54 Secondary throttle lever
55 Return spring
56 Throttle speed adjusting screw
57 Spring
58 Fast idle cam
59 Spring
60 Choke valve plate
61 Reloader cover
62 Choke shaft
63 Choke lever
64 Accelerator pump lever
65 Stop lever spring
66 High speed valve stop lever
67 reloader cover
68 Reloader connecting link
69 High speed valve
70 Primary throttle valve shaft
71 Primary throttle valve
72 Throttle body/flange
73 Secondary throttle valve shaft
74 Secondary throttle valve
75 Mixture adjusting screw
76 Spring

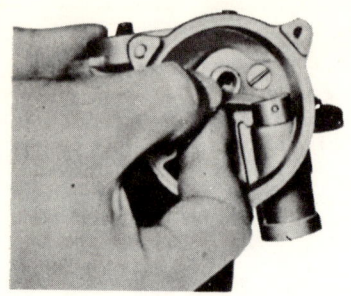

Fig 3.26 Removing the vacuum piston from automatic choke housing of dual barrel carburettor (Sec 19)

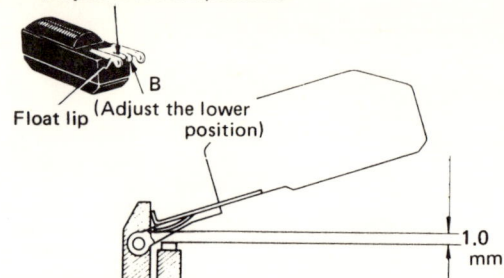

Fig 3.29 Float stroke adjustment on dual barrel carburettor (Sec 19)

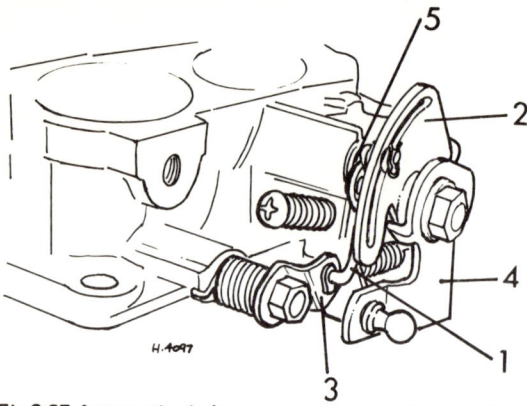

Fig 3.27 Automatic choke components correctly assembled (Sec 19)

1 Stepped screw
2 Piston connector
3 Sliding rod
4 Fast-idle cam follower
5 Flexible boot

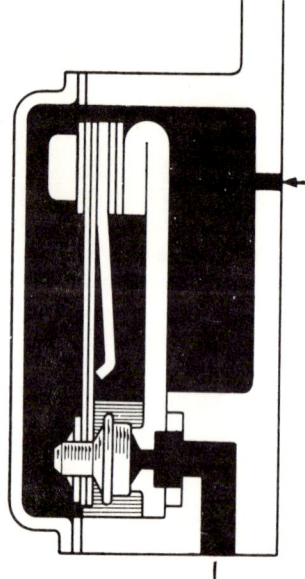

Fig 3.30 Sectional view of thermostatic valve on dual barrel carburettor (Sec 19)

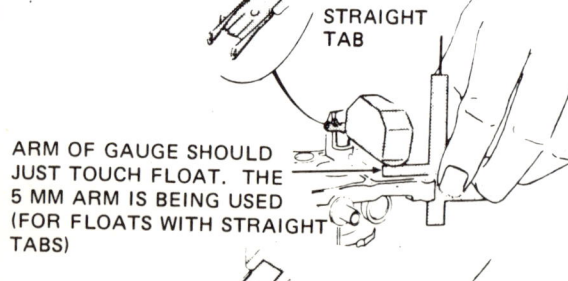

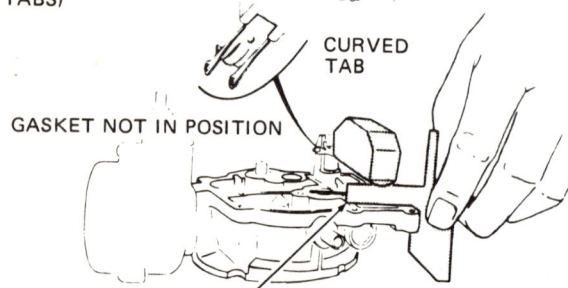

FLOAT LEVEL

NOTE: CURVED AND STRAIGHT TAB NEEDLE AND SEAT ASSEMBLIES ARE NOT INTERCHANGEABLE

Fig 3.28 Float level adjustment on dual barrel carburettor (Sec 19)

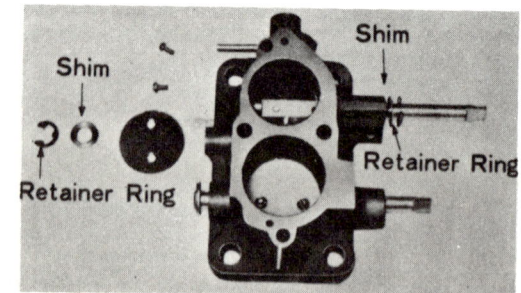

Fig 3.31 Components of throttle butterfly valve plates on dual barrel carburettor (Sec 19)

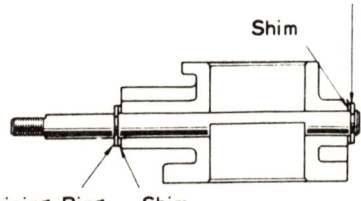

Fig 3.32 Sectional view of throttle shaft on dual barrel carburettor (Sec 19)

Chapter 3/Carburation; fuel, exhaust and emission control systems

housing to the carburettor upper body. Ensure that the vacuum connecting passage 'O' ring seal is in position and that the lower housing retaining screw is the longer one.

34 If the choke valve plate and shaft were dismantled, re-assemble the components using new screws and peening their ends.

35 Within the automatic choke housing, install the piston connector to the choke shaft using the screw with the shouldered head. Do not forget to include the screw lockwasher or the screw may project enough to cause the choke valve plate to bind. Now insert the sliding rod, the fast-idle cam follower and the flexible boot.

36 To the automatic choke housing fit the plate, gasket and housing cover, making sure that as the cover is offered up, the end of the bi-metal spring engages on the choke shaft lever. Secure the cover with three screws and their spring washers so that the mark on the cover aligns with the centre mark on the housing index.

37 Refit the fuel inlet union and filter to the upper body.

38 Turn the upper body upside down and install the power piston spring, power piston and its stop.

39 Fit the fuel inlet valve components, tightening the needle valve seat securely.

40 Fit the float and its pivot pin. Now check the float adjustment by letting the float hang by its own weight (upper body inverted). If the float arm is of straight tab design, a gauge, 0.1969 in (5.0 mm) in width should just slide between the lowest point of the float and the face of the upper body, no gasket being in position. Where the float arm is of curved tab design a gauge 0.3661 in (9.3 mm) in width should be used. A piece of flat steel strip can easily be made up into suitable gauges. Where the specified clearances are incorrect, bend the tab as required.

41 Now raise the float gently to the end of its stroke and measure the distance between the tip of the fuel inlet needle valve plunger and the operating tab of the float arm. Where this exceeds 0.04 in (1.0 mm) bend the two right-angled tabs at the end of the float arm as necessary.

42 Fit the fuel level gauge assembly to the main body noting that the glass must be installed so that the dot is to the inside with the bubble to the outside.

43 Fit a new 'O' ring seal and then the thermostatic valve assembly. This valve is designed to admit additional air directly to the inlet manifold to overcome any rich mixture problems which might occur when under bonnet temperatures are so high that they cause fuel to expand and overflow into the carburettor venturi.

44 Install the high speed valve stop and spring.

45 Refit primary and secondary main jets and the jet plugs and washers.

46 Refit the power valve complete with power jet (a washer is not installed under the power valve).

47 Install the primary and secondary venturis and gaskets. The secondary and smaller venturi fits in the right-hand aperture and the primary (large) venturi on the left-hand side when viewed from the float chamber end of the carburettor body. On later carburettors, there can be no mistake in assembly as the venturis are not interchangeable.

48 Insert the accelerator pump check ball, ball retainer, plunger spring and plunger.

49 If the primary and secondary throttle butterfly valve plates have been dismantled, refit them to their shafts (thinner valve plate to primary shaft). Do not peen the new valve plate securing screws or fit the throttle shaft circlips until the centralising shims have been fitted to provide perfect movement of the valve plates within their bores. The thicker shim should be on the throttle arm side.

50 Refit the mixture control screw and spring, screwing it in until it is lightly seated and then unscrewing it 2½ turns for a basic setting pending adjustment when the engine is started up.

51 Refit the throttle linkage and springs.

52 Assemble the high speed valve plate and shaft in a similar manner to that described for the primary and secondary valve plates.

53 Check the clearance between the edge of the high speed valve plate and the carburettor bore. A gauge which is between 0.014 and 0.030 in (0.35 and 0.75 mm) in thickness or diameter should be used for this. If adjustment is required, bend the tab on the arm of the high speed valve shaft.

54 On early carburettors, refit the reloader lever.

55 Refit the main body to the throttle body flange using a new gasket and making sure that it is fitted the correct way round and does not mask any drillings.

56 *On engines with emission control systems,* fit the throttle positioner lever and stop lever spring, also the throttle positioner diaphragm capsule connecting link.

57 Refit the check ball, weight, stop and seal into the pump discharge cavity in the main body.

58 Refit the upper body using a new gasket and secure the throttle positioner diaphragm capsule (emission control) beneath two of the upper body securing screws.

59 Connect the throttle positioner link.

60 Install the flexible boot on the fast idle sliding rod and fit the link between the sliding rod and the fast idle adjusting lever.

61 Fit the 'U' shaped lever to the choke shaft and connect the reloader link between the lever on the choke shaft and the re-loader lever. Ensure that the linkage rod washers are correctly positioned.

62 On early models, install the reloader cover.

63 Reconnect the accelerator pump link to the primary throttle

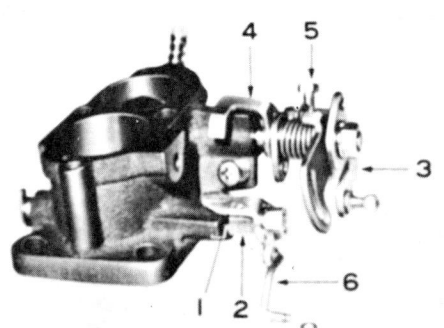

Fig 3.33 Throttle linkage on dual barrel carburettor (Sec 19)

1 Secondary throttle lever
2 Return spring
3 Primary throttle shaft arm
4 Fast idle lever
5 Fast idle screw
6 Throttle shaft link

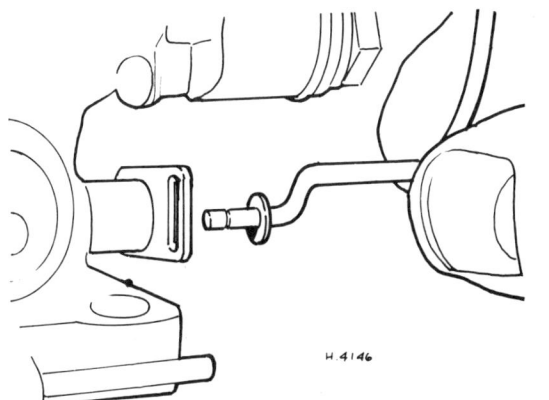

Fig 3.34 Installing reloader connecting link on dual barrel carburettor (8R engine) (Sec 19)

shaft arm making sure to include the spring.

64 Fit the flexible boot over the pump plunger shaft and tuck its end into the upper body.

65 Connect the accelerator pump lever to the plunger and then secure the pump lever to the upper body by means of its shouldered pivot screws.

20 Dual barrel carburettor (8R engine series type) - adjustments and setting after dismantling and reassembly

1 Check that the primary throttle butterfly valve plate opens fully (at 90° to carburettor bore). If necessary, bend the stop to

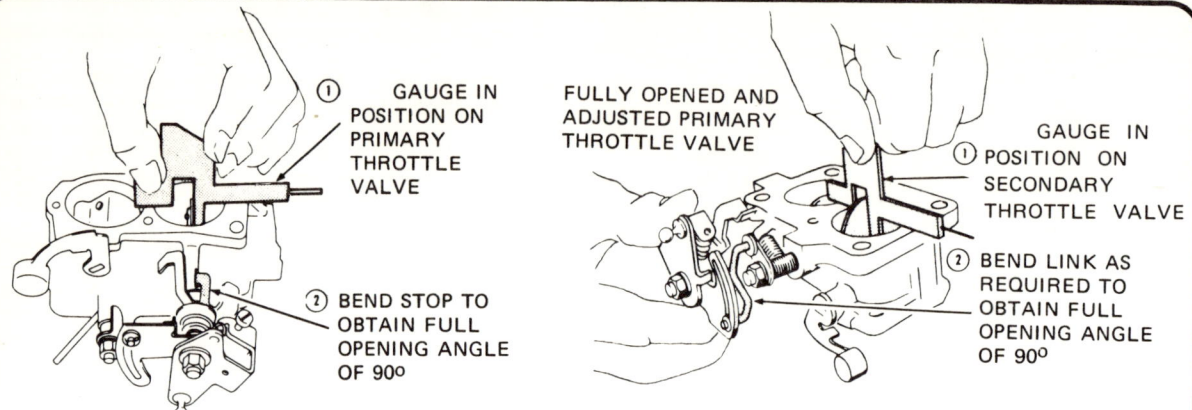

Fig 3.35 Checking opening of primary throttle valve plate on dual barrel carburettor (Sec 20)

Fig 3.36 Checking opening of secondary throttle valve plate on dual barrel carburettor (Sec 20)

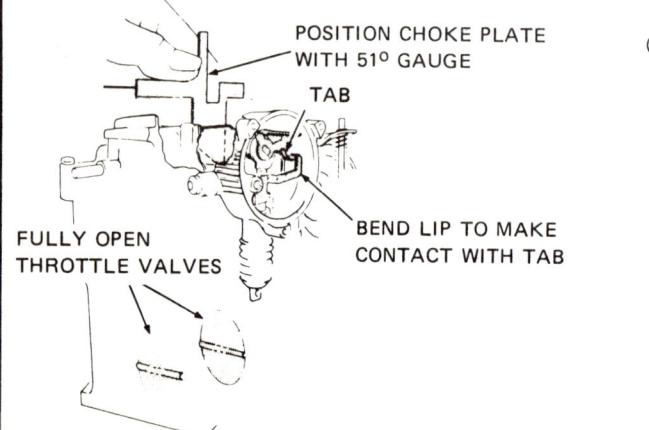

Fig 3.37 Checking unloader adjustment on dual barrel carburettor (Sec 20)

Fig 3.38 Checking secondary throttle stop adjustment on dual barrel carburettor (Sec 20)

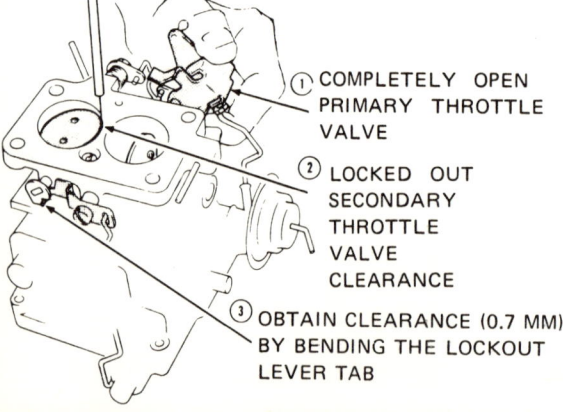

Fig 3.39 Adjusting primary to secondary throttle lockout clearance on dual barrel carburettor (Sec 20)

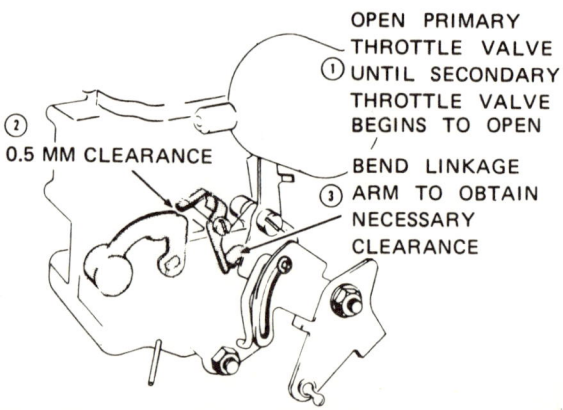

Fig 3.40 Adjusting clearance between high speed valve lockout lever and secondary valve stop lever on dual barrel carburettor (Sec 20)

adjust.

2 Check that the secondary throttle butterfly valve plate also opens fully and if necessary bend the link to achieve this.

3 Check and adjust the unloader if necessary by opening the primary and secondary throttle valve plates fully and checking that the choke valve plate is open through 51°. If adjustment is necessary, remove the automatic choke housing cover and bend the tab on the fast idle cam follower.

4 With both primary and secondary valve plates fully open, check that the stop is against the carburettor body. If not, bend the stop tab as necessary.

5 Open the primary throttle valve plate fully and check that the secondary valve plate to bore clearance is 0.028 in (0.7 mm) otherwise bend the lock-out lever tab.

6 Open the primary throttle valve plate until the secondary throttle valve plate just begins to open. At this point there should be a clearance of 0.020 in (0.5 mm) between the lock-out lever of the high speed valve plate shaft and the valve stop lever.

7 Open the choke valve plate through 20° when the clearance between the reloaded lever and the secondary throttle shaft should be between 0.06 and 0.12 in (1.5 and 3.0 mm). If necessary bend the reloader link.

8 Fully close the choke valve plate when the primary throttle valve plate should be open by between 0.0012 and 0.0410 in (0.03 and 1.03 mm). Screw the fast idle screw in or out to obtain the specified clearance measured between the edge of the valve plate and the bore surface.

9 Check that the throttle positioner adjusting screw is in alignment with the mark on the primary shaft arm tab. Bend the tab if necessary to obtain the correct alignment.

21 Dual barrel carburettor (8R engine series type) - final adjustments after installation

1 Start the engine and run it to normal operating temperature.

2 With the air cleaner removed, open the throttle quickly and check the fuel can be seen being sprayed from the accelerator pump jet into the primary (larger) venturi.

3 Have an assistant open the throttle fully by depressing the accelerator pedal to the limit of its travel and then check that the throttle valve plates are fully open.

4 Check that the choke valve plate is fully open.

5 On vehicles equipped with emission control systems, let the engine idle and remove the vacuum hose from the throttle positioner diaphragm capsule. If the distributor is fitted with a vacuum capsule, disconnect the vacuum pipe from the carburettor end.

6 Run the engine at a speed of 1400 rev/min and adjust the throttle positioner screw so that it just makes contact with the tab on the primary throttle shaft arm.

7 Reconnect the hose to the throttle positioner diaphragm capsule. The engine should now idle smoothly and the throttle positioner adjusting screw should be held just above the tab by the vacuum action of the diaphragm capsule unit.

8 Finally, adjust the slow running and mixture screws, as described in Section 16.

22 Dual barrel carburettor (18R engine series type) - dismantling and reassembly

1 The carburettor fitted to 18R series engines differs from that fitted to 8R series engines by not having a high speed valve or reloader mechanism. A diaphragm unit actuates the secondary throttle valve and the primary and secondary throttle linkage is of different design on the 18R type carburettor.

2 Although dismantling and reassembly are similar to the operations described for the 8R type carburettor in Section 19,

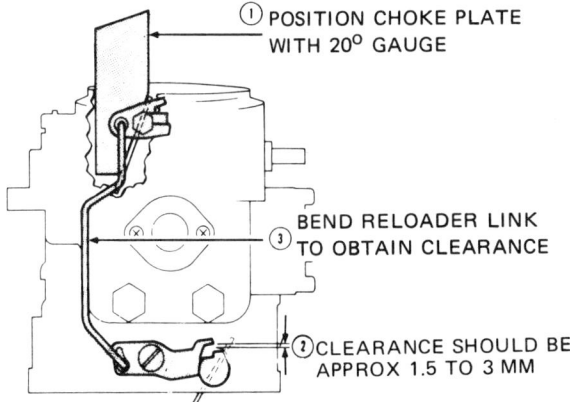

Fig 3.41 Checking reloader adjustment on dual barrel carburettor (Sec 20)

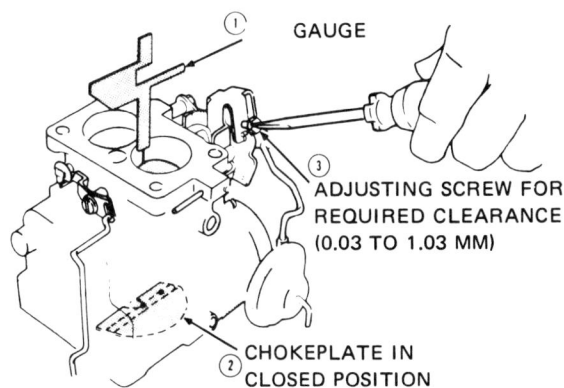

Fig 3.42 Making initial setting of fast idle screw for primary throttle plate opening on dual barrel carburettor (Sec 20)

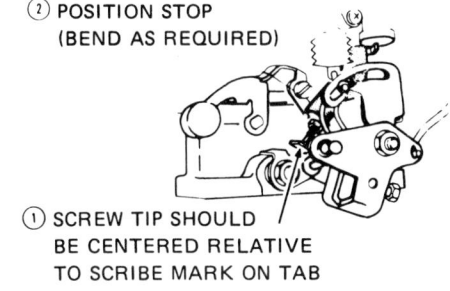

Fig 3.43 Adjusting throttle positioner linkage on dual barrel carburettor (Sec 20)

the following additional work will be required.

3 Remove the connecting link (5) from the sliding rod (1). (Fig 3.44)

4 Disconnect the diaphragm plunger shaft from the diaphragm lever (8) and detach the return spring (10).

5 Remove the diaphragm operating mechanism from the main body (89). Remove the gasket (81).

6 Dismantle the throttle operating mechanism by removing the four screws and lock washers which secure the diaphragm housing cap (74) to the housing (78). Separate the gasket (75) diaphragm spring (76) and diaphragm (77).

7 Although the reassembly operations are almost identical with those for the 8R type carburettor (Section 19), the following paragraphs describe the special procedure necessary when refitting the secondary throttle diaphragm and external throttle

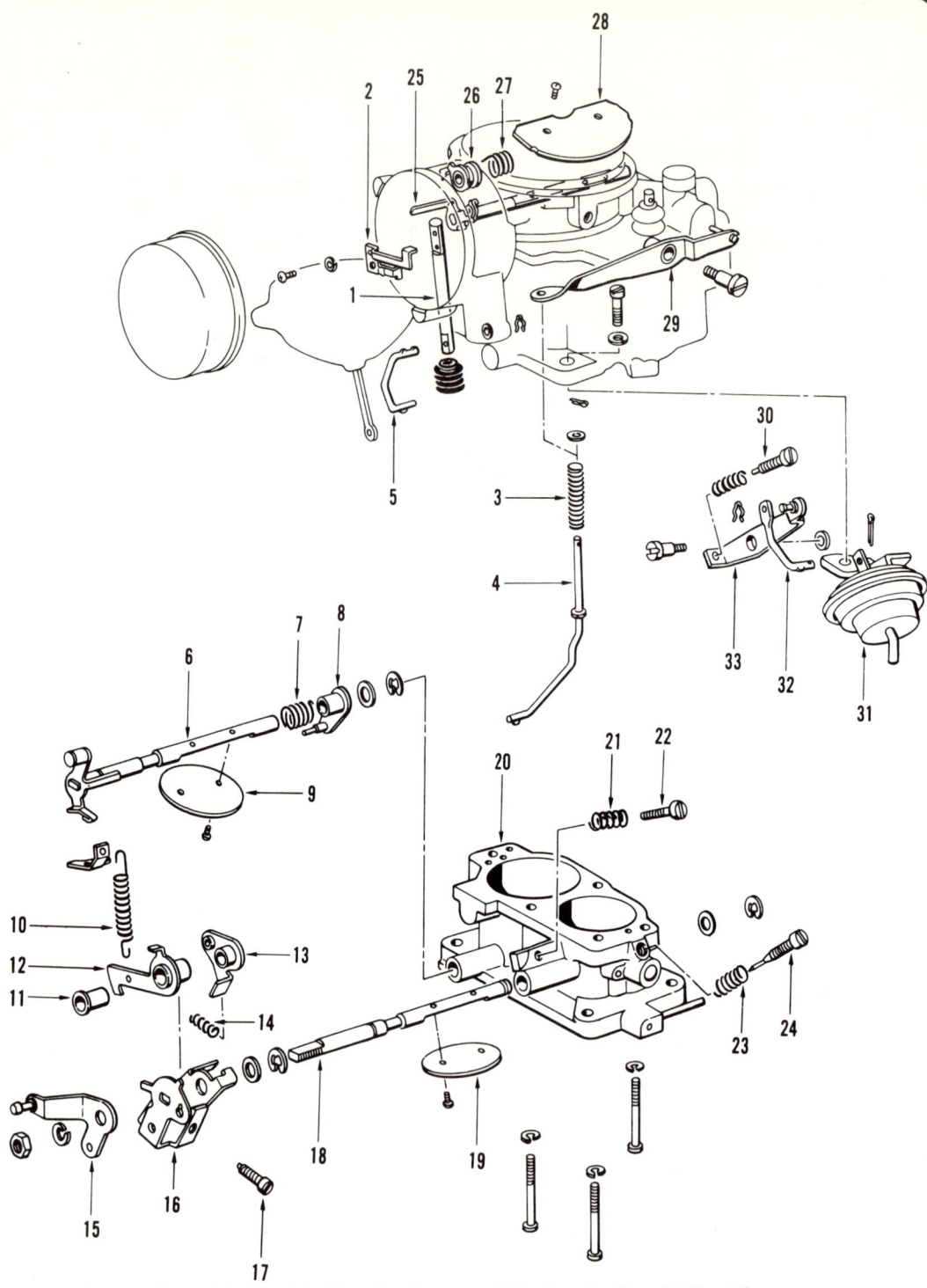

Fig 3.44a Exploded view of dual barrel carburettor - 18R - C engine (Part 1) (Sec 22)

1 Sliding rod
2 Fast idle cam follower
3 Accelerator pump rod spring
4 Accelerator pump link
5 Connecting link
6 Secondary throttle shaft
7 Diaphragm spring
8 Diaphragm lever
9 Secondary throttle valve plate
10 Spring
11 Collar
12 Secondary kick lever
13 Fast idle adjusting lever
14 Fast idle adjusting screw spring
15 Primary throttle lever
16 Primary throttle shaft arm
17 Fast idle adjusting screw
18 Primary throttle shaft
19 Primary throttle valve plate
20 Throttle body/flange
21 Throttle speed screw spring
22 Throttle speed screw
23 Mixture adjusting screw spring
24 Mixture adjusting screw
25 Choke shaft
26 Fast idle cam
27 Fast idle cam spring
28 Choke valve plate
29 Accelerator pump lever
30 Throttle positioner adjusting screw
31 Throttle positioner diaphragm valve
32 Throttle positioner link connector
33 Throttle positioner lever

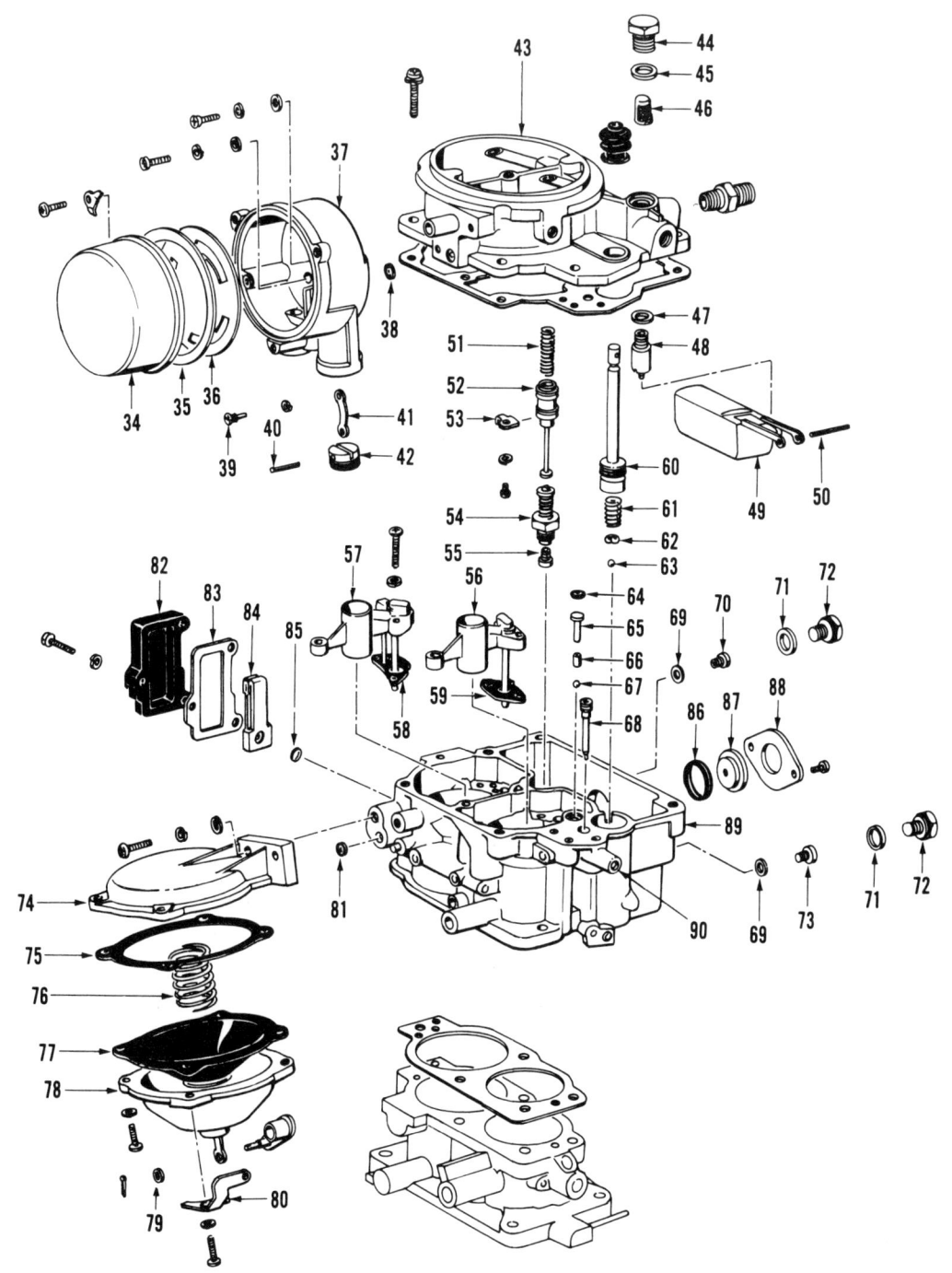

Fig 3.44b Exploded view of dual barrel carburettor - 18R - C engine (Part 2) (Sec 22)

34 Automatic choke cover
35 Gasket
36 Plate
37 Automatic choke housing
38 Gasket
39 Screw
40 Piston pin
41 Piston connector
42 Vacuum piston
43 Upper body
44 Plug
45 Gasket
46 Filter gauze
47 Gasket
48 Needle valve
49 Float
50 Float pivot pin
51 Power piston spring
52 Power piston
53 Power piston stop
54 Power valve
55 Power jet
56 Primary small venturi
57 Secondary small ventrui
58 Gasket
59 Gasket
60 Accelerator pump plunger
61 Spring
62 Check ball retainer
63 Ball
64 Gasket
65 Stop
66 Weight
67 Ball
68 Slow jet
69 Main jet gasket
70 Secondary main jet
71 Gasket
72 Plug
73 Primary main jet
74 Diaphragm unit cover
75 Gasket
76 Spring
77 Diaphragm
78 Diaphragm housing
79 Washer
80 Return spring bracket
81 Seal
82 Cover
83 Gasket
84 Thermostatic valve
85 'O' ring
86 Gaslet
87 Fuel level gauge glass
88 Glass retainer
89 Main body
90 Primary air bleed

linkage.

8 Locate the diaphragm in the diaphragm housing, centre the spring in the diaphragm and position the gasket on the housing.
9 Fit the diaphragm housing cap, using three screws and lockwashers and then locate the back spring stop under the fourth screw and lockwasher.
10 Use a new seal (81) in the recess in the upper body.
11 Connect the diaphragm operating rod to the lever (8) of the secondary throttle shaft.
12 On some models of this carburettor, a solenoid operated fuel cut-off valve is fitted to prevent engine run-on when the ignition is switched off.

23 Dual barrel carburettor (18R engine series type) - adjustments and setting after dismantling and reassembly

1 Adjust the secondary throttle valve initial kick-up mechanism

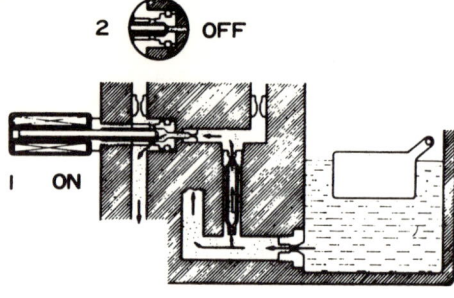

Fig 3.45 Solenoid operated fuel cut-off valve fitted to some dual barrel type carburettors (Sec 22)

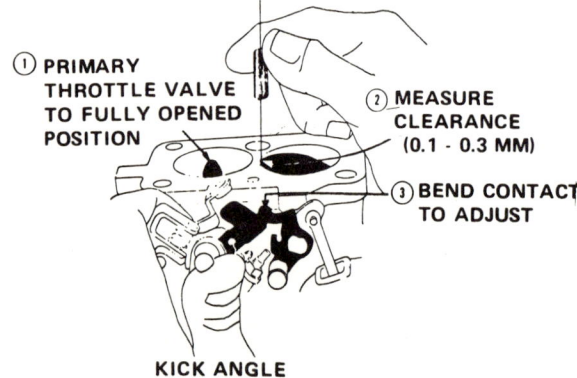

Fig 3.46 Checking adjustment of secondary throttle shaft kick-arm on 18R engine type dual barrel carburettor (Sec 23)

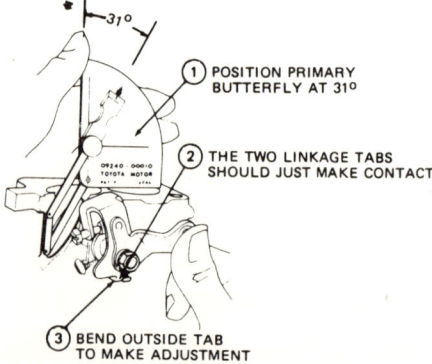

Fig 3.47 Checking the secondary contact angle on 18R engine type dual barrel carburettor (Sec 23)

in the following manner:
2 Hold the primary throttle butterfly valve plate in the fully open position and measure the clearance between the edge of the secondary throttle valve plate and the bore surface. This should be between 0.004 and 0.012 in (0.1 and 0.3 mm) otherwise bend the double folded tab of the secondary throttle shaft kick-arm.
3 Adjust the secondary contact angle. To do this, open the primary valve plate through 31° and observe whether the two linkage contact tabs are just touching. If not bend the outer tab as necessary.
4 Check the unloader adjustment, the accelerator pump stroke and the automatic choke setting in the same manner as described for the 8R series carburettor in Section 20, except that when carrying out the unloader adjustment, the choke valve plate should be open through 43°.

24 Dual barrel carburettor (18R engine series type) - final adjustments after installation

These are identical with those described for the 8R series carburettor in Section 21.

25 SU twin carburettors (8R-B engine) up to 1970 - adjustments

1 Remove the air cleaners.
2 Disconnect the choke control cable and throttle control cable.
3 Connect a tachometer and vacuum gauge to the engine.
4 Lift each of the carburettor pistons with the finger to check that they fall smoothly without any tendency to stick.

Fig 3.48 Testing piston movement on SU carburettor (Sec 25)

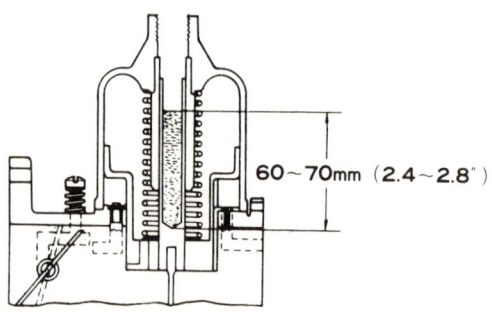

Fig 3.49 Damper oil lever in SU type carburettor (Sec 25)

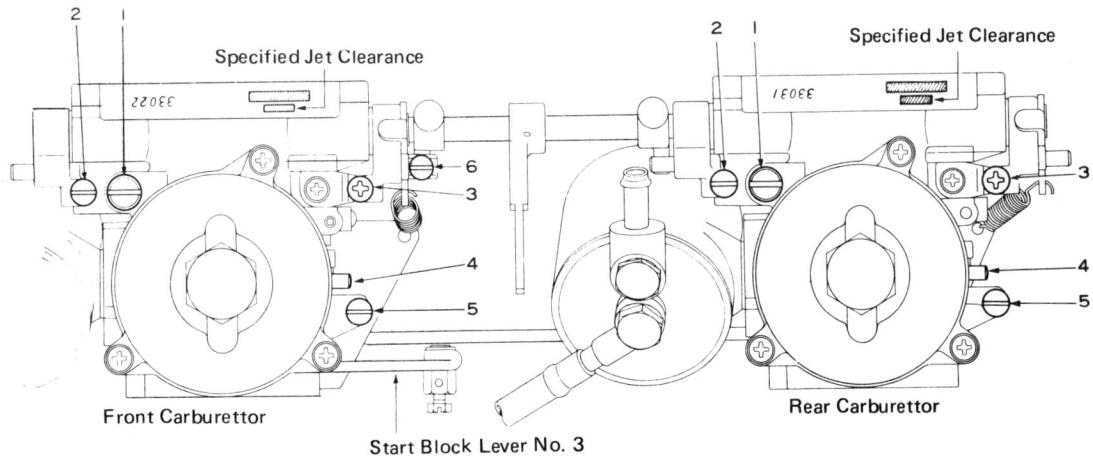

Fig 3.50 Location of SU type carburettor control screws (Sec 25)

1 Idle adjusting screws (not fitted to 8R - B engine from no. 328900)
2 Throttle speed adjusting screws
3 Fast idle adjusting screws
4 Lifting pins
5 Jet adjusting screws
6 Throttle shaft connector screw

5 Unscrew the damper and check and top-up if necessary the damper oil. Use only SAE 20 engine oil for this purpose.
6 On engines built up to No. '8R-328899' screw in each of the idle adjusting screws to close the idle ports of the front and rear carburettors. On engines from No. '8R-328900', idle adjusting screws are not fitted.
7 Check the setting of the jet adjusting screws. The specified clearance between the lever and starter block is stamped on the flange of the carburettor body and using feeler blades, the jet adjusting screws should be turned until the clearance conforms to Specification.
8 Unscrew the two throttle adjusting screws until they no longer contact the stops then screw them in until they just make contact with the stops. Now screw them in between 1 and 1½ turns to set both throttle valve plates equally.
9 Start the engine and run it until normal operating temperature is reached.
10 Unscrew both fast idle adjusting screws until they no longer contact the fast idle levers.
11 Using a flowmeter or other balancing device adjust the volume of air being drawn in at the carburettor intake by turning each of the throttle adjusting screws. When both readings are identical, lift the starter block lever and the engine will stall due to too rich a mixture. Hold the starter block lever in the raised position and screw in each of the fast idle adjusting screws until the ends of the throttle adjusting screws just lose contact with their stops.
12 Release the starter block lever and restart the engine.
13 Unscrew each of the throttle adjusting screws by the same amount so that the engine idling speed is between 750 and 850 rev/min.
14 Check the balance of the two carburettors again using the flowmeter (do not completely close the mouth of the carburettor when using this device) and if necessary turn the throttle adjusting screw of the unit with the lower air intake volume until it is equal to the other carburettor.
15 Raise the lifting pin of the front carburettor with the finger. If the idling speed drops momentarily and then resumes its normal level, the mixture (fuel/air ratio) is correct. If the engine stalls, the mixture is too weak and if the idling speed increases and then drops to normal, the mixture is too rich. To perform this test only lift the pin and release it immediately, do not hold it in the raised position. Do not repeat the test without first

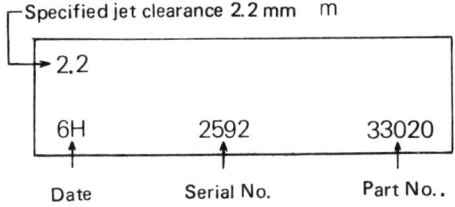

Fig 3.51 Interpetation of SU carburettor flange markings (Sec 25)

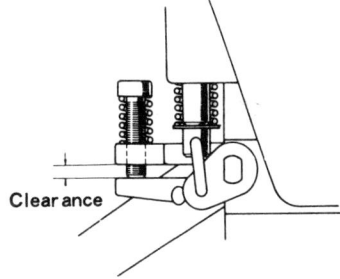

Fig 3.52 Jet clearance of SU type carburettor (Sec 25)

Fig 3.53 Balancing twin SU installation (Sec 25)

revving up the engine to clear the intake.

16 Remove the tachometer and vacuum gauge, reconnect the choke and accelerator controls and refit the air cleaners.

26 SU twin carburettors (8R-B engine) 1970 on - adjustments

1 As a result of modifications to this type of carburettor, the **adjustment procedure has been altered**.
2 Carry out the operations described in paragraphs 1 to 5 of the preceding Section.
3 Screw in the throttle adjusting screw until it just makes contact with the throttle shaft stop. Now screw it in one complete turn.
4 Start the engine and turn the throttle adjusting screws of both carburettors by the same amount until the engine speed is between 800 and 850 rev/min.
5 Using a flowmeter or other balancing device, adjust the air intake volume of both carburettors by fractionally adjusting both throttle adjusting screws.
6 Unscrew the idle adjusting screw on the front carburettor until the point is reached where the engine speed is at its highest. Now screw the idle adjusting screw in to the point where the engine speed would drop if the screw was turned any further.
7 Repeat the operation described in the preceding paragraph on the rear carburettor.
8 Should the engine not idle smoothly or perform properly over its entire speed range, check the setting of the main jet. If necessary, turn the main jet adjusting screw to give a measurement (carburettor bridge to main jet) of 1.22 in (31.0 mm).
9 Reconnect the accelerator linkage and adjust the screw on the accelerator link shaft so that both front and rear carburettor throttle valve plates will start to open at exactly the same time.
10 To adjust the fast idle, first check that the mark on the fast idle adjusting lever is in alignment with the centre line of the fast idle screw when the throttle valve plate is fully closed and the choke valve plate is fully open. Adjust if necessary by bending the connector.
11 Adjust the fast idle screw to give a clearance between the end of its threaded portion and the fast idle adjusting lever cam of **between 0 and 0.006 in (0 and 0.15 mm)** with the throttle valve plate fully closed and the choke valve plate fully open.
12 Pull the choke control fully out and check that the choke valve plate is open at 14.5° from the fully closed position. If necessary bend the connector to achieve this.

27 SU twin carburettor (8R-B engine) - removal and installation

1 Remove the air cleaners.
2 Disconnect the accelerator and choke control cables.
3 Disconnect the fuel inlet hoses.
4 Disconnect the vacuum hose (distributor advance capsule).
5 Disconnect the starter block lever connecting rod.
6 Remove the carburettor flange securing nuts and withdraw the twin carburettors as an assembly complete with the throttle connecting shaft.
7 Installation is a reversal of removal but carry out the checks and adjustments as described in Sections 25 or 26, according to type.

Fig 3.54 Checking mixture by raising lifting pin on SU type carburettor (Sec 25)

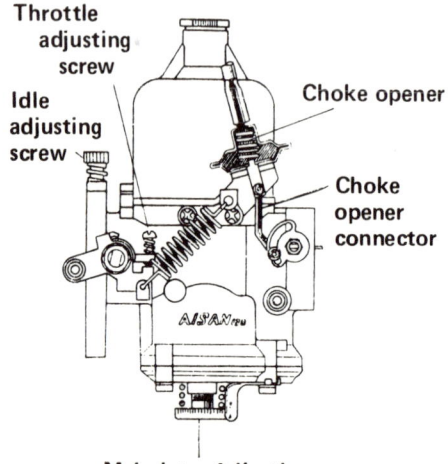

Fig 3.55 Location of control screws on 1970 onwards SU type carburettor (Sec 26)

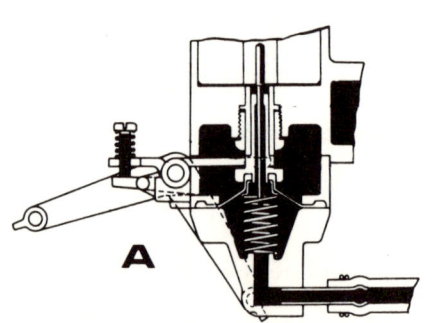
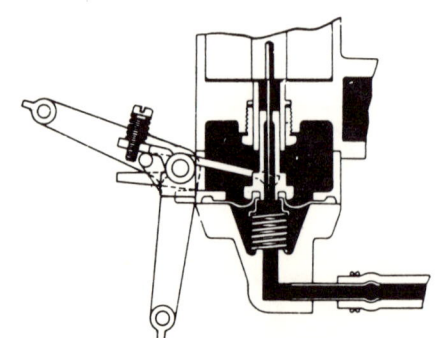

Fig 3.56 Choke valve plate position on SU type carburettor (Sec 26) A: Choke control released

28 SU twin carburettors (8R-B engine, up to 1970) - dismantling and reassembly

1 Unscrew the float chamber cover bolt and remove the cover.
2 To check the float level, turn the carburettor upside-down so and seat from the float chamber cover. (Figs 3.59 to 3.61)
3 Unscrew the main passage plug and extract the filter from the float chamber cover.
4 Extract the float from the float chamber.
5 Remove the pump connecting link, the hose which connects the float chamber to the diaphragm cover, the throttle return spring, and bracket. Unscrew the diaphragm cover screws and remove the diaphragm cover, the main jet return spring, the main jet and the starter block.
6 From the top of the depression chamber, remove the damper rod. The damper rod should not be dismantled unless essential (Fig 3.62)
7 Unscrew the suction chamber securing screws and lift off the chamber, extract the spring and piston.
8 Unscrew the main jet securing nut and remove the stop, gasket and main jet guide. (Fig 3.63)
9 If essential, remove the retaining circlip and remove the lifting pin and spring.
10 Remove the fast idle lever, spring and sliding rod, also withdraw the idle adjusting screw, spring and 'O' ring seal, then remove the fast idle screw and throttle screws together with their springs. (Fig 3.64)
11 Thoroughly clean all components in fuel and blow all holes and passages clear with air from a tyre pump. Inspect all parts for wear, particularly the body for cracks and renew as appropriate. Renew the diaphragm if it is split or has hardened.
12 Inspect the surface of the piston for scoring. Where evident, renew the component. If the piston is discoloured clean it only with fuel or metal polish, never attempt to clean it with emery cloth. Check the protrusion of the buffer pin. This is spring loaded and should project by between 0.012 and 0.016 in (0.3 and 0.4 mm) beyond the end face of the piston. (Fig 3.65)
13 Finally check that the jet needle is not bent and is correctly installed so that its shoulder is flush with the end face of the piston. If necessary, release the securing grub screw and adjust the position of the needle.
14 Obtain a new set of carburettor gaskets and seals.
15 Reassembly is a reversal of dismantling but note the following points:
16 Insert the main jet guide into the carburettor body followed by the gasket, stop and nut. Tighten the nut finger tight.

Fig 3.57 Location of starter block lever connecting rod (1) fuel inlet hoses (2) and throttle connecting shaft (3) on SU twin carburettor installation (Sec 27)

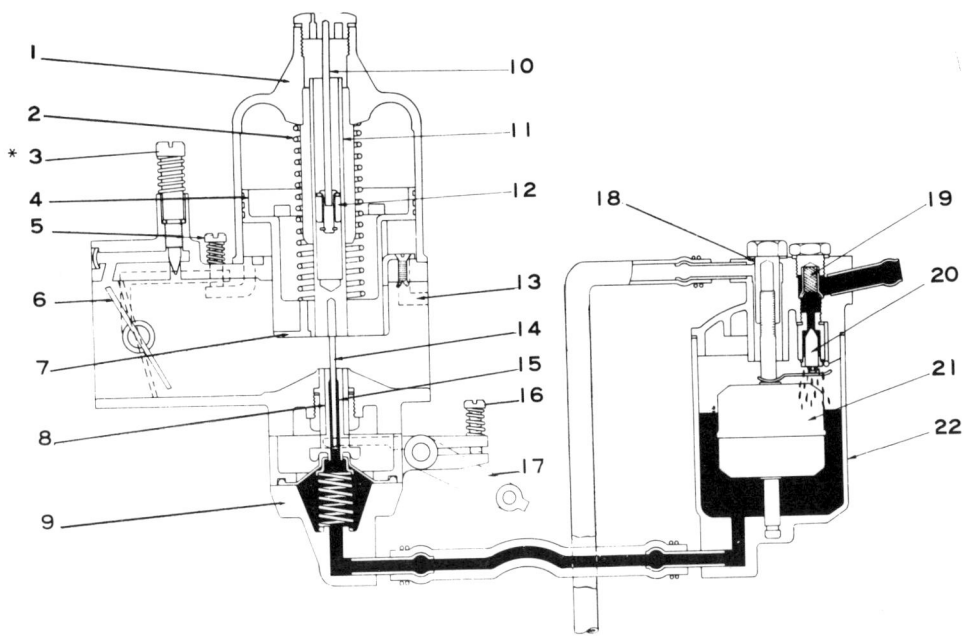

Fig 3.58 Sectional view of SU type carburettor (Sec 28)

1 Depression chamber
2 Spring
3 Idle adjusting screw (only on 8R - B engine up to no. 328899)
4 Piston
5 Throttle adjusting screw
6 Throttle valve
7 Suction passage
8 Main jet guide
9 Diaphragm cover
10 Damper
11 Guide
12 Piston guide
13 Air passage
14 Needle
15 Main jet
16 Jet adjusting screw
17 Starter block lever
18 Air vent
19 Inlet filter gauze
20 Fuel inlet needle valve
21 Float
22 Float bowl

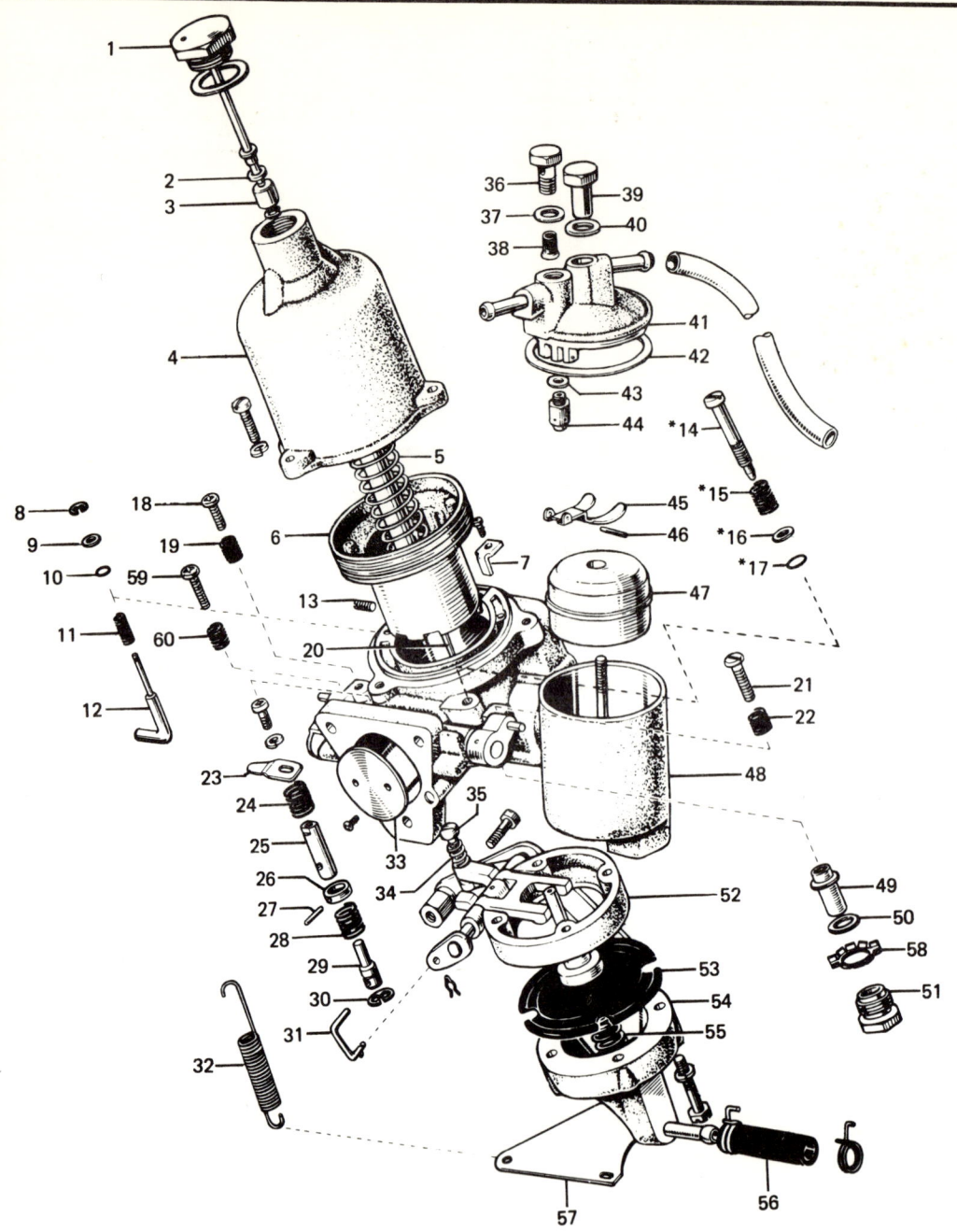

Fig 3.59 Exploded view of the SU type carburettor (Sec 28)

1. Damper
2. Damper valve
3. Damper piston
4. Depression chamber
5. Spring
6. Piston
7. Piston guide
8. Circlip
9. Washer
10. 'O' ring
11. Spring
12. Lifting pin
13. Needle grub screw
14. Idle adjusting screw
15. Spring
16. Washer
17. 'O' ring
18. Fast idle adjusting screw
19. Spring
20. Needle
21. Throttle adjusting screw
22. Spring
23. Fast idle lever
24. Spring
25. Sliding rod
26. Spring holder
27. Pin
28. Relief spring
29. Sliding relief rod
30. Circlip
31. Connecting link
32. Throttle return spring
33. Throttle valve plate
34. Spring
35. Jet adjusting screw
36. Plug
37. Gasket
38. Filter gauze
39. Float chamber bolt
40. Gasket
41. Float chamber cover
42. Gasket
43. Gasket
44. Needle valve assembly
45. Float lever
46. Pivot pin
47. Float
48. Body
49. Main jet guide
50. Gasket
51. Main jet securing nut
52. Starter block
53. Main jet/diaphragm assembly
54. Diaphragm cover
55. Return spring
56. Connecting hose
57. Throttle return spring bracket
58. Stop plate
59. Throttle speed screw
60. Spring

Items 14, 15, 16 and 17 are not fitted to engines no. 328900 onwards

Chapter 3/Carburation; fuel, exhaust and emission control systems 73

17 Insert the jet needle/piston assembly so that the needle passes into the main jet guide. Locate the piston spring and depression chamber cover, tightening the cover screws with the fingers only. Hold the carburettor in the vertical position and lift the piston and check that it falls smoothly without any tendency to stick. Tighten the main jet guide nut to a torque of 14 lb/ft (2.0 kg/m). Recheck the fall of the piston. If there is now a tendency for the needle to stick in the guide, release the guide nut and tap it on its side gently to centralise the guide. Retighten the nut and bend over the stop plate to lock it.

18 Tighten the depression chamber cover screws. Test the fall of the piston after raising it fully. Any tendency to stick can be overcome by releasing the depression chamber cover screws and moving the cover fractionally first in one direction and then in another until having retightened the screws, the tendency to stick has been eliminated.

19 When assembling the float chamber components, check the float level. To do this, invert the float chamber cover and measure the distance between the highest point of the curved section of the float lever and face of the cover rim. This dimension should be 0.63 in (16.0 mm) otherwise bend the lever at point A. (Fig 3.66)

20 Now raise the float lever gently with the finger to its highest point and measure the distance between the tip of the needle valve plunger and the float lever. This should be between 0.04 and 0.065 in (1.0 and 1.2 mm). If necessary bend the lever end

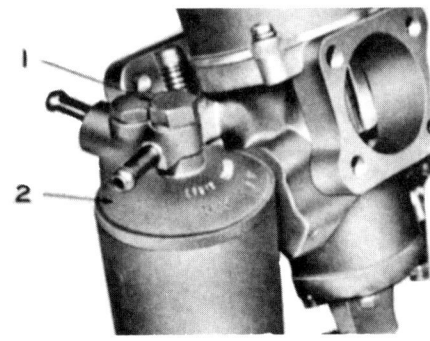

Fig 3.60 Float chamber cover securing bolt (1) and cover (2) on SU type carburettor

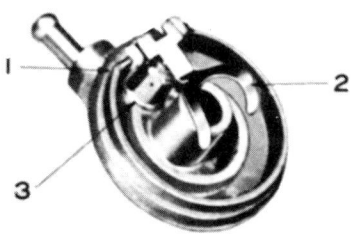

Fig 3.61 Float lever pivot pin (1) float lever (2) and fuel inlet needle valve assembly (3) in float chamber cover of SU type carburettor

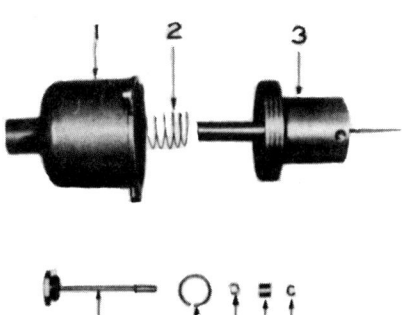

Fig 3.62 Depression chamber components (SU type carburettor)

1 Depression chamber
2 Spring
3 Piston
4 Damper rod
5 Seal
6 Valve
7 Piston
8 Circlip

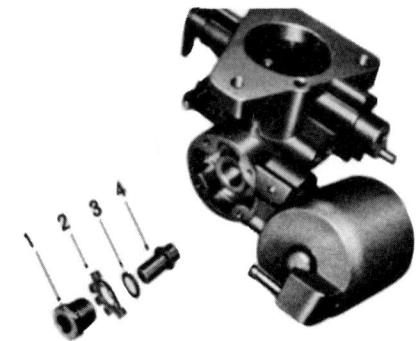

Fig 3.63 Main jet components on SU type carburettor

Fig 3.64 Lifting pin (1) fast idle lever securing screw (2) idle adjusting screw (3) fast idle adjusting screw (4) throttle speed screw (5) on SU type carburettor

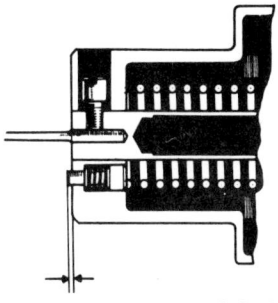

0.3~0.4mm (0.012~0.016")

Fig 3.65 Correct setting of piston buffer pin on SU type carburettor piston (Sec 28)

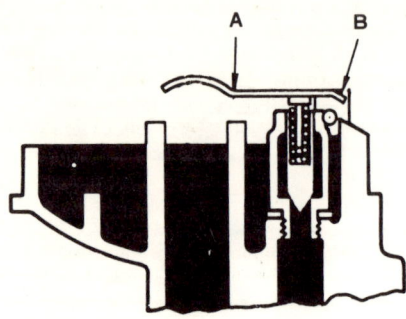

Fig 3.66 Float level adjustment diagram (SU type carburettor) (Sec 28)

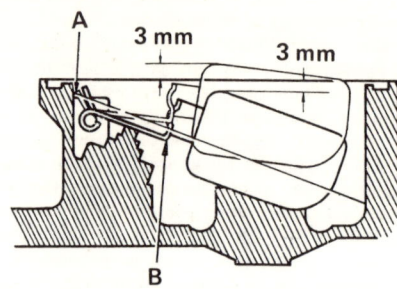

Fig 3.67 Float level adjustment diagram (SU type carburettor after 1970) (Sec 29)

Fig 3.68 Throttle adjusting screw initial setting on SU type carburettor (after 1970) (Sec 29)

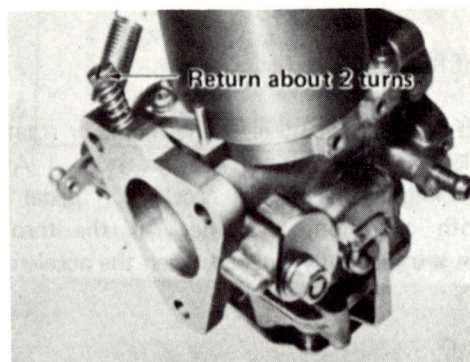

Fig 3.69 Idle adjusting screw initial setting on SU type carburettor (after 1970) (Sec 29)

tab at B.
21 Top-up the damper with oil and after installation, carry out the adjustment procedure described in Section 25.

29 SU twin carburettors (8R-B engine) 1970 on - dismantling and reassembly

1 The procedure is similar to that described for the earlier models in the preceding Section except that the float chamber components are of different design and the main jet is adjustable.
2 To check the float level, turn the carburettor upside-down so that the float hangs down under its own weight. The distance between the nearest point of the float and the face of the carburettor body should be 1.18 in (3.0 mm). If necessary, bend the float arm at B. Now hold the carburettor in the normal position so that the float hangs down by its own weight away from the fuel inlet needle valve. Check the distance between the lowest point of the float and the face of the carburettor which again should be 1.18 in (3.0 mm) otherwise bend the float arm at A. (Fig 3.67)
3 Initial setting of the main jet adjusting screw should be so that the distance between the upper face of the jet and the bridge (point of contact of lower face of piston) is 1.22 in (31.0 mm).
4 Set the throttle adjusting screw by screwing it in until it just contacts the throttle shaft stop and then screwing it in one further complete turn.
5 Set the idle adjusting screw two turns open from the lightly closed position.
6 Fill the damper with SAE 20 oil to the level marked on the damper rod.
7 When the carburettors have been refitted to the engine, carry out the adjustments described in Section 26.

30 Emission control system (8R-C and 18R-C engines) - description and application

Two systems are used (i) the improved combustion system (ICS) which is designed to reduce the emission of hydrocarbons and carbon monoxide from the exhaust system. The system depends upon a specially designed and calibrated carburettor, modified combustion chamber, special distributor, throttle positioner, speed sensor, speed marker relay and a vacuum switching valve.
(ii) The transmission controlled spark system (TCS) is a supplementary system which will also reduce emissions of oxides of nitrogen. Basically, the system controls the distributor advance and retard characteristics very precisely according to engine heat and vehicle speed. In addition to the components used in the ICS system, the TCS system includes a thermosensor, a computor and on some manual gearbox vehicles, a shift point sensor.
Applications of the two systems are as follows:
8R-C engine (North America) - ICS and TCS systems
8R-C engine (other territories) - ICS system
18R-C engine (standard equipment) - ICS and TCS systems
In addition to these systems, all vehicles are fitted with a positive crankcase ventilation system (PCV) (see Chapter 1) and a fuel evaporative emission control system (see Section 13, of this Chapter).
Certain early 8R-C engines were equipped with an air injection system (see Section 33).
The emission control system comprises three primary circuits:
(i) the throttle positioner circuit which controls exhaust emission during deceleration.
1 This circuit is designed to open the throttle valve plate very slightly when the accelerator pedal is released in order to

Chapter 3/Carburation, fuel, exhaust and emission control systems

increase the fuel/air supply to ensure complete combustion and minimize the discharge of exhaust contaminants.

2 When the vehicle is operating at medium and high speeds, the speed sensor causes the vacuum switching valve to be energized by the speed marker relay. The valve operates and allows air to be introduced into the throttle positioner diaphragm. The throttle positioner is then retained in this position by the tension of the return spring. If the accelerator pedal is now released, the throttle valve plate is held slightly open by the positioned mechanism instead of returning to the idling position.

3 When the vehicle speed enters the low speed range 14 to 11 mph (22 to 17 kmh) the speed sensor causes the vacuum switching valve to be de-energized and with the vacuum in the inlet manifold acting on the throttle positioner diaphragm, the positioner is released from the throttle valve plate which then returns to the normal idling position.

(ii) the thermosensor circuit which monitors the temperature of the engine coolant and if it is not within specified limits the information is relayed to the computer and the TCS system will not be actuated.

(iii) the TCS circuit controls the ignition timing to ensure optimum combustion at low speeds. This is achieved by the use of a vacuum switching valve (controlling the distributor through the diaphragm unit) and a speed sensor and marker. The distributor does not advance at speeds below 36 mph (58 kmp) unless the vehicle has just decelerated from a higher speed to not below 11 mph (17.7 kmh). At speeds below 11 mph (17.7 kmh) the TCS system is operational and the distributor is operating at the static timing position. At speeds over 36 mph (58 kmh) the TCS system is off and normal distributor advance characteristics are in operation. On some 1971 models with 8R-C engines and manual gearboxes, a shift point sensor was fitted. This is essentially a switch which switches off the TCS system when top gear is engaged.

31 Emission control components - maintenance and testing

1 No routine maintenance is specified beyond occasionally checking the security of the vacuum hoses and electrical leads.

2 It should be realised however, that correct setting and adjustment of the fuel system and ignition system components, also the valve clearances, are essential prerequisites to an emission controlled engine.

3 *The thermosensor* is screwed into the side of the cylinder head. To test its operation, have the engine idling at normal operating temperature and then disconnect the lead. Accelerate the engine and observe if the vernier adjuster on the distributor moves inwards (ignition advanced). This test simulates the conditions when engine coolant temperature is below 140°F (60°C) and the TCS system is off. Now reconnect the lead to the thermosensor and repeat the operation, the venier adjuster on

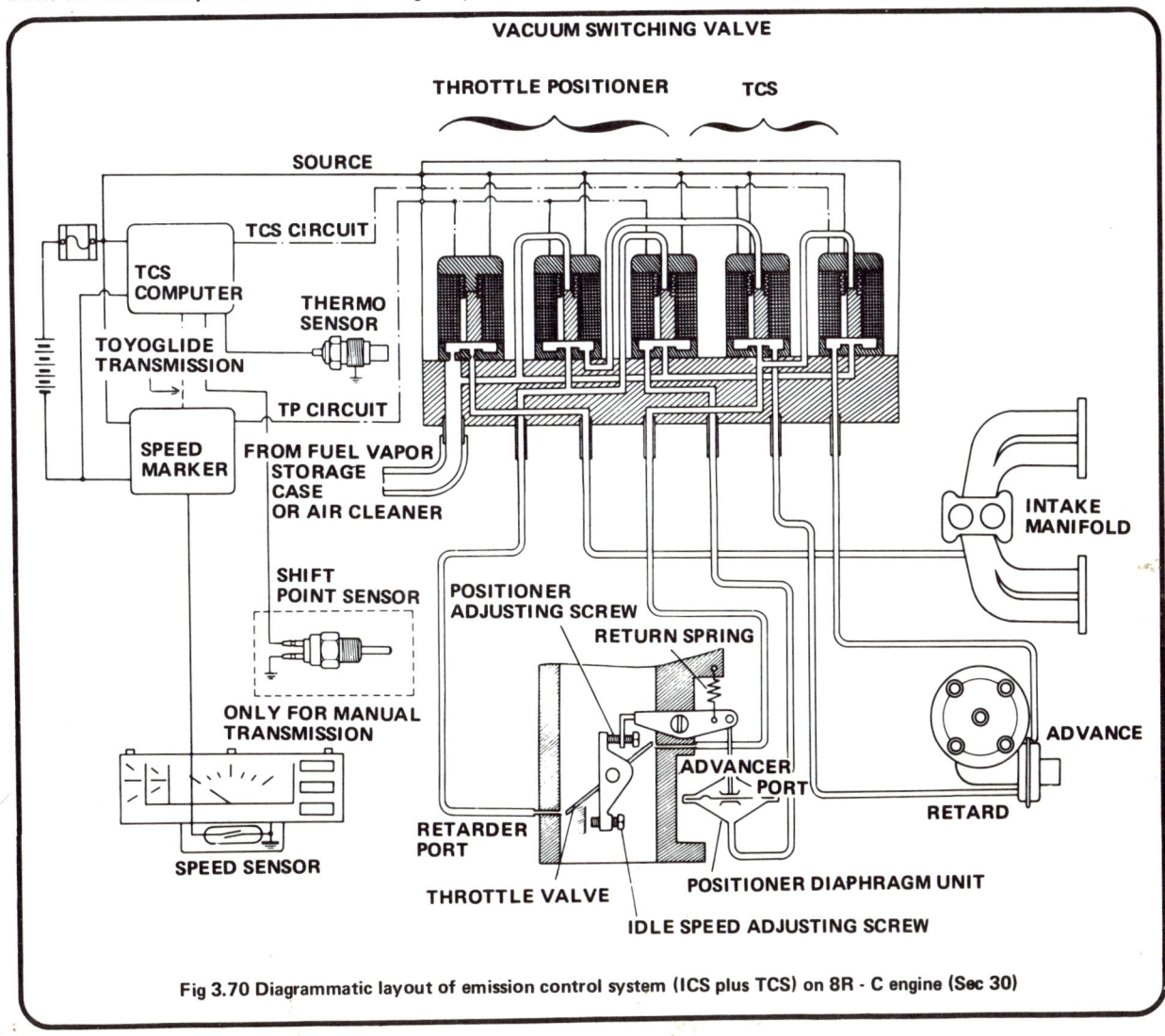

Fig 3.70 Diagrammatic layout of emission control system (ICS plus TCS) on 8R - C engine (Sec 30)

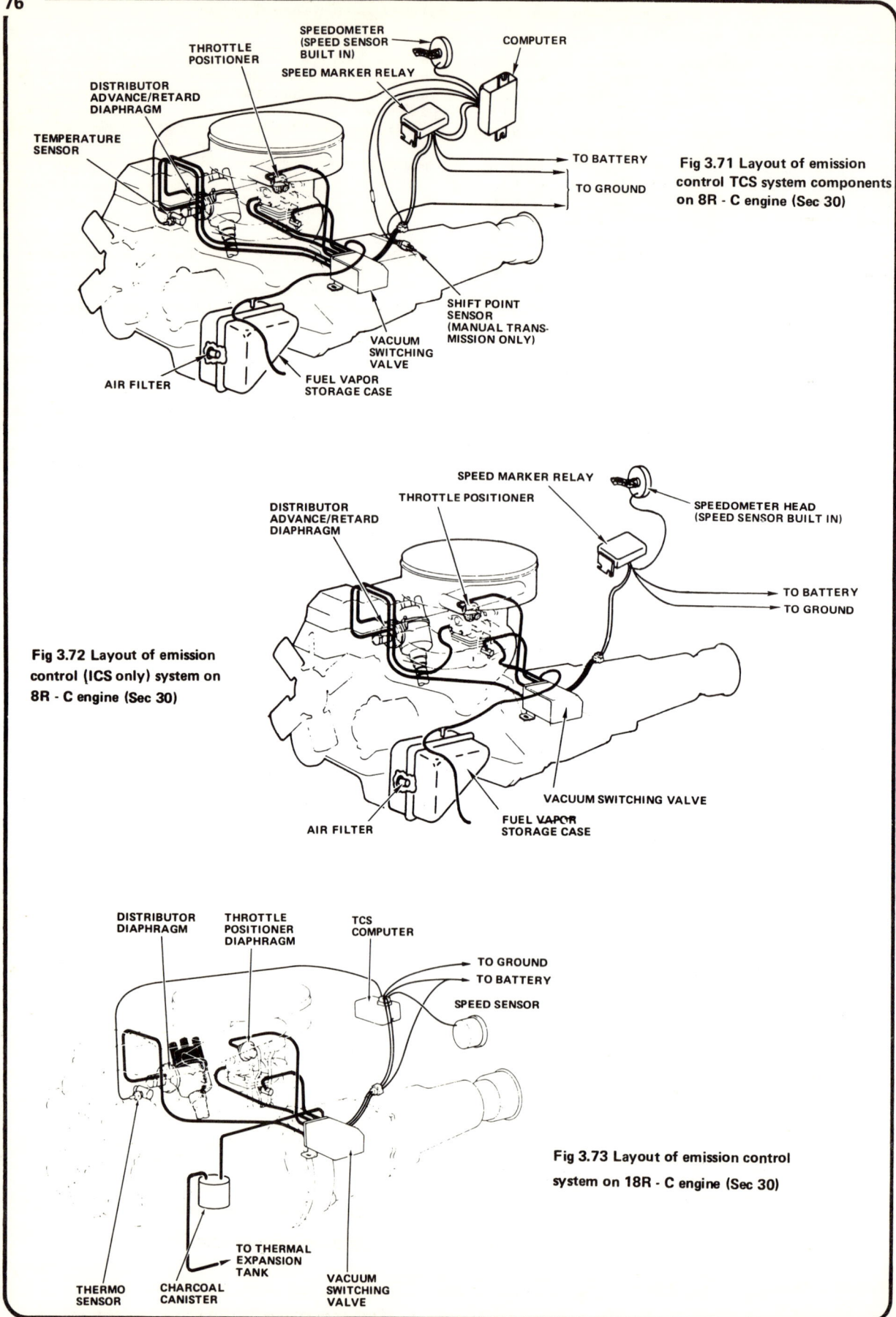

the distributor should move outwards (ignition retarded), TCS system on at temperatures between 140°F (60°C) and 203°F (95°C).

4 To test the operation of *the throttle positioner*, raise the rear wheels of the vehicle off the ground, chock the front wheels and have the engine idling at normal operating temperature. Engage 2nd gear ('2' selector position with automatic transmission). Now accelerate past 25 mph (40 km/h) but do not exceed 35 mph (56 km/h). Observe the throttle positioner which should engage. Release the throttle and the throttle positioner unit should delay the throttle valve closure down to a speed of 11 mph (18 km/h). Shift the gear lever or speed selector lever to neutral and the throttle positioner should disengage.

5 *TCS system*. A general check of the operation of the system may be carried out by again raising the rear wheels and letting the engine idle at normal operating temperature. Now engage 2nd gear (on 1971 8R-C with shift point sensor engage 4th gear to ensure TCS system off). Accelerate past 35 mph (56 km/h). and note distributor vernier adjuster moves inwards. Now decelerate and at speeds above 35 mph (56 km/h) the vernier adjuster should move outwards.

32 Emission control system circuits - testing

1 The following tests can only be carried out if you are in possession of a tachometer, vacuum gauge, ohmmeter and test lamp.

2 In the event of a fault developing in the system, first check that the engine oil, coolant and transmission oil levers are correct, also that the fanbelt tension is as specified and the ignition system is correctly timed and components properly maintained and set. The carburettor should be in perfect tune.

3 *Thermosensor*. With the engine running at normal operating temperature, disconnect and connect the lead from the thermosensor terminal several times. With the hand resting on the vacuum switching valve, actuation of the valve will be felt.

4 If the valve does not actuate, disconnect the lead from the thermosensor and insert the test lamp probe in the terminal of the vacuum switching valve connector plug. Withdraw and insert the test lamp probe several times and feel whether the vacuum switching valve actuates and the test lamp lights up. If neither happens, renew the switching valve.

5 Switch off the engine and disconnect the thermosensor wire. Use an ohmmeter to check the resistance of the thermosensor, this should be 2000 ohms (coolant temperature 178°F/81°C). If outside the specified resistance, drain the cooling system and renew the thermosensor. If the vacuum switching valve still does not actuate then the computer (mounted below the instrument panel on the driver's side) must be faulty and should be renewed.

6 *Throttle positioner*. With the engine running at normal operating temperature, insert the probe of the test lamp into the vacuum switching valve connector plug as shown. The test lamp should illuminate and the throttle positioner itself will drop because the vacuum source has been sealed off. Pinch the vacuum purge line and the throttle positioner should lift. Where these two tests prove positive then it can be assumed that the vacuum switching valve (TCS and throttle positioner sections), the thermosensor, the throttle positioner, the distributor and the computer (temperature circuit) are all functioning correctly. (Fig 3.79)

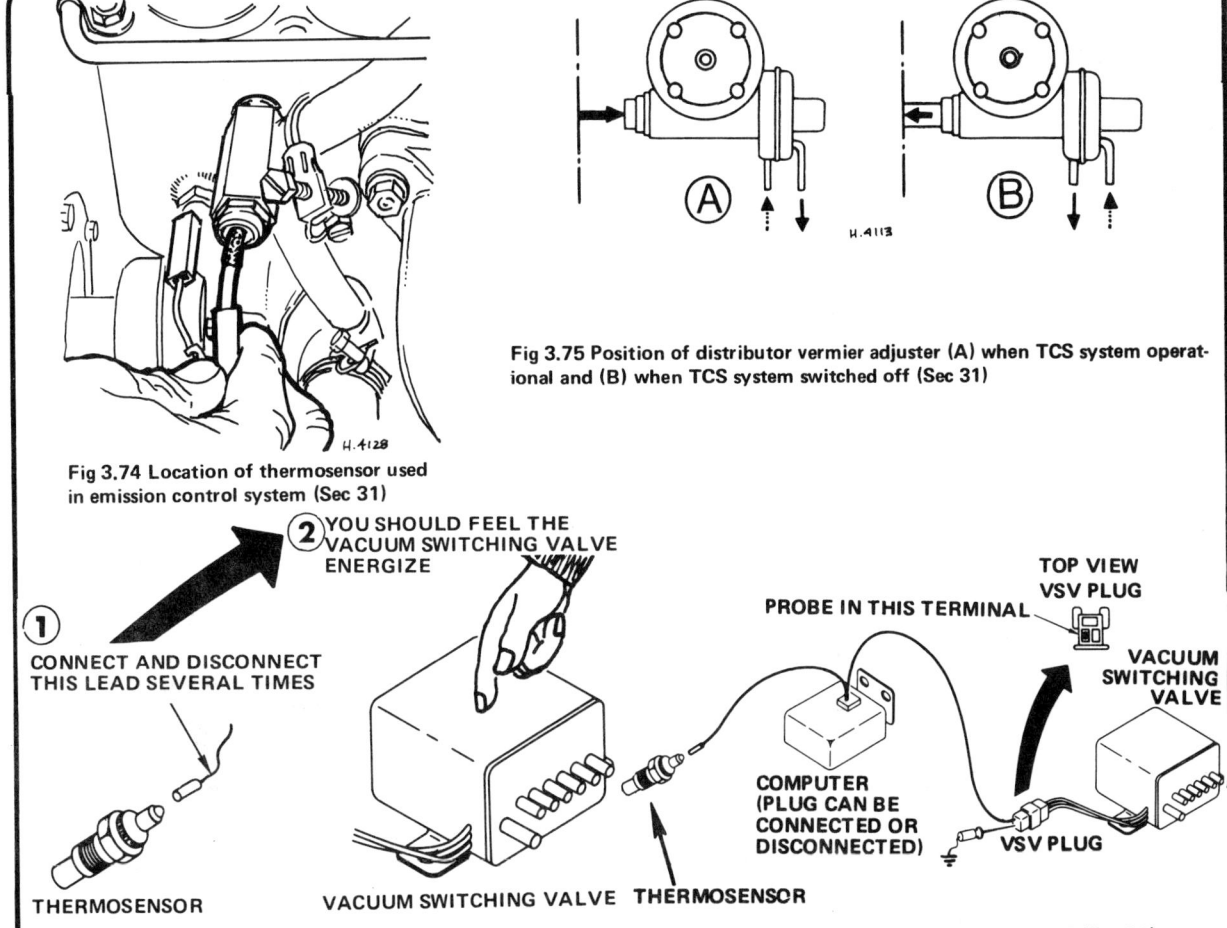

Fig 3.74 Location of thermosensor used in emission control system (Sec 31)

Fig 3.75 Position of distributor vermier adjuster (A) when TCS system operational and (B) when TCS system switched off (Sec 31)

Fig 3.76 Thermosensor test circuit no. 1 (Sec 32)

Fig 3.77 Thermosensor test circuit no. 2 (Sec 32)

7 *Speed marker and speed sensor.* With the engine running at normal operating temperature and the rear roadwheels raised, insert the test lamp probe into the vacuum switching valve connector plug as shown. The lamp should illuminate and the throttle positioner should drop. With second gear engaged accelerate slowly to over 25 mph (40 km/h) but under 35 mph (56 km/h) and observe that the test lamp goes out at 25 mph (40 km/h). Decelerate and check that the lamp comes on at 11 mph (18 km/h). If the lamp does not work as indicated then there is a fault in the speed marker or sensor or both. To check these components, switch off the engine and rotate one of the rear roadwheels in the forward direction of rotation, one complete revolution. Count the pulsations using the test lamp or ohmmeter. There should be either 4 or 6 evenly spaced pulsations according to the type of speedometer installed. If the pulsations are correct renew the speed marker relay but if they are incorrect, renew the speedometer head. (Figs 3.80 and 3.81).

8 *Computer.* With the engine running at normal operating temperature, the rear wheels raised and 2nd gear ('2' for automatic transmission) engaged, insert the test lamp probe into the vacuum switching valve connector plug as shown. The test lamp should remain extinguished indicating that the computer is on. Slowly accelerate to over 35 mph (50 km/h) when the test lamp should illuminate indicating that the computer is off. Now decelerate to below 14 mph (22.5 km/h) the test lamp should go out indicating that the computer is on. Where these tests do not prove positive, recheck the functioning of the speed marker and sensor (paragraph 7). Where no fault can be detected in these components, renew the computer. (Fig 3.82)

Emission control system components are sealed units and cannot be repaired but only renewed complete.

33 Air injection system (1971 8R-C engine) - description and maintenance

1 This system is designed to reduce the emission of toxic exhaust gases by mixing pressurised air, injected near each exhaust valve with the gases as they leave the engine combustion chambers.

2 The required air pressure is generated by an air pump which is driven by a belt from the crankshaft pulley.

3 Normal maintenance consists of checking the tension of the belt and keeping the connecting hoses tight and in good order. Adjust the tension of the driving belt to give a deflection of between 5/8 and 7/8 in (15.9 and 22.2 mm) at the centre of the belt between the air pump and crankshaft pulleys. Adjustment is carried out by slackening the air pump mountings and adjustment strap and moving the air pump as required.

4 Occasionally test the operation of the air bypass valve. To do this, run the engine at idling speed and listen for a hiss of escaping air from the valve. If evident, renew the valve. Run the engine at about half throttle and then suddenly release the accelerator control rod. A single ejection of air should be heard from

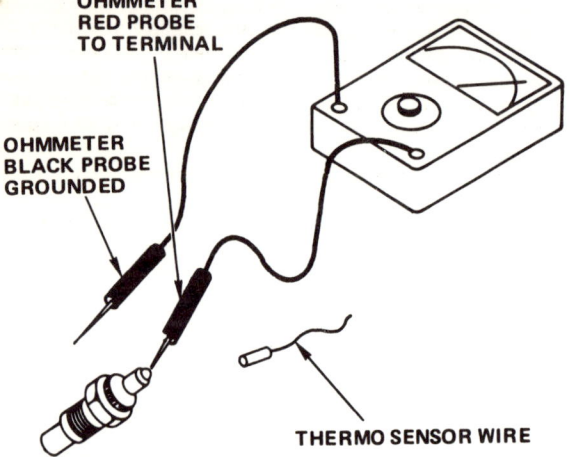
Fig 3.78 Thermonsenor test circuit no. 3 (Sec 32)

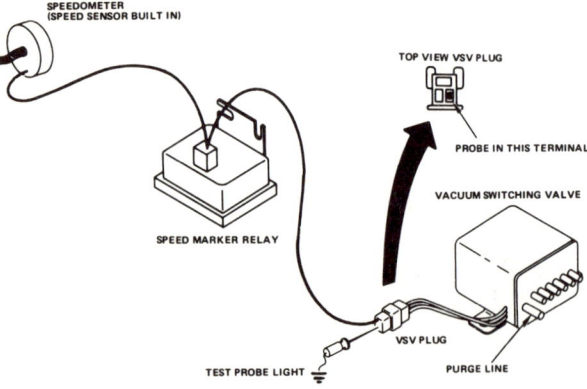
Fig 3.79 Throttle positioner test circuit (Sec 32)

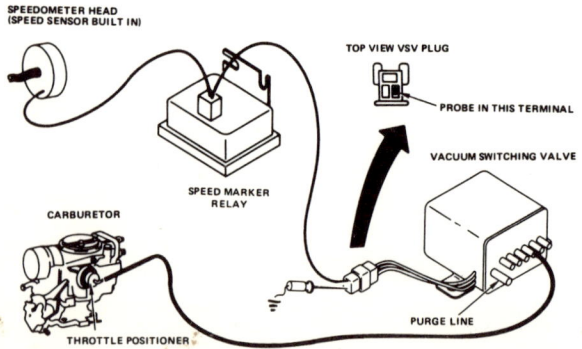
Fig 3.80 Speed marker and speed sensor test circuit no. 1 (Sec 32)

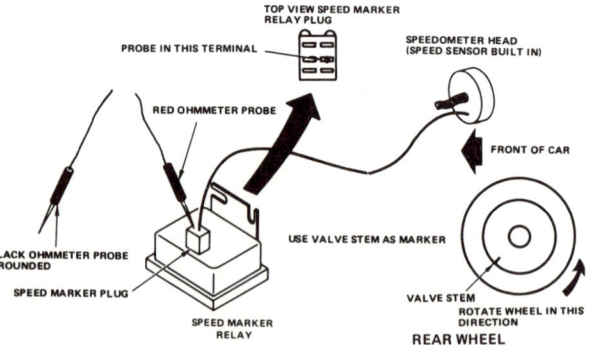
Fig 3.81 Speed marker and speed sensor test circuit no. 2 (Sec 32)

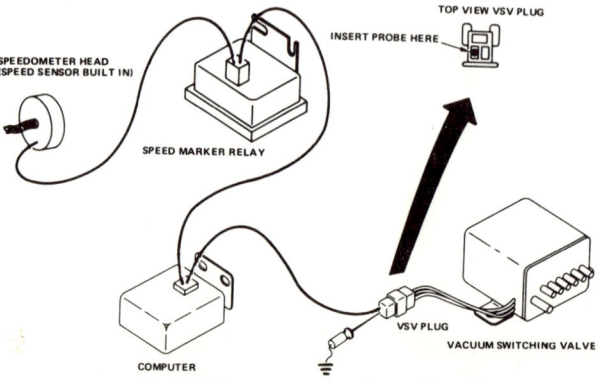
Fig 3.82 Computer test circuit (Sec 32)

Chapter 3/Carburation; fuel, exhaust and emission control systems

the valve. If no air is released or air keeps on escaping, then the
5 The non-return valve can be tested simply by blowing air in both directions and ensuring that air flow is restricted in one direction but not in the other.

34 Air pump - servicing

1 The pump used for the fume emission control air injection system is of rotary, sliding blade type. It draws air from the 'clean' side of the air cleaner and will normally give a long trouble-free life. In the event of a fault developing, an exchange unit is recommended but where suitable tools are available it can be repaired.
2 Prise the relief valve from the top of the pump using two sharpened levers located beneath the valve housing rim.
3 Turn the pulley so that its keyway is at right angles to a line drawn through the centres of the two cover locating dowels.
4 Place the pump, pulley downwards and drift out the two dowels towards the pulley.
5 Remove the pump cover retaining bolts and detach it from the pump housing by tapping it gently with a plastic faced hammer. Do not remove the pivot pin from the cover.
6 Hold the pulley still. This is best achieved by engaging a section of an old driving belt in the pulley and gripping the two ends of the belt as close to the pulley as possible in a vice. On no account grip any part of the air pump in the vice.
7 Using an Allen key, remove the socket screws from the rear rotor ring and detach the ring/bearing assembly and carbon seal.
8 Extract the blade assembly, carbon shoes and springs.
9 If essential the bearing can be pressed out from the rotor ring and a new one pressed in with its part number visible from the narrower diameter end of the ring.
10 The pulley must be removed with an extractor after unscrewing the securing nut (left-hand thread). No further dismantling should be carried out.

11 Clean the internal surfaces of the pump and examine for wear. The pump blades should be at least 2.35 in (59.69 mm) in width and the carbon shoes in excess of the minimum dimensions shown, otherwise renew them. (Fig 3.83)
12 Check that the rear seal has not worn below a thickness of 0.016 in (0.4064 mm) otherwise renew it.
13 Check that the shoe spring deflection at the highest point of its curvature when the spring is standing free on a flat surface is not less than 0.12 in (2.5908 mm) otherwise renew it.
14 Reassembly is a reversal of dismantling but observe the following points. Lubricate all roller bearings with recommended grease. Position each blade assembly so that they align with the centre of the division in the rotor housing which divides the air intake chamber from the exhaust chamber. Fit the carbon shoes so that the deeper one (white mark on its end) is installed in the deeper recess but having its coloured end mark towards the pump cover. The shoe springs are located in the deeper recess with their convex surface in contact with the carbon shoe. Tighten the rotor ring socket screws in diametrically opposite **sequence** to a torque of no more than 4 lb/ft (0.553 kg/m). (Fig 3.85)

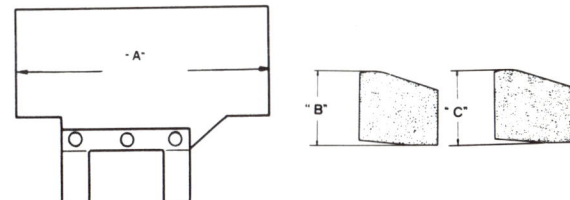

Fig 3.83 Air pump blade and carbon shoe dimensional (wear) diagram (see text for minimum dimensions) (Sec 34)

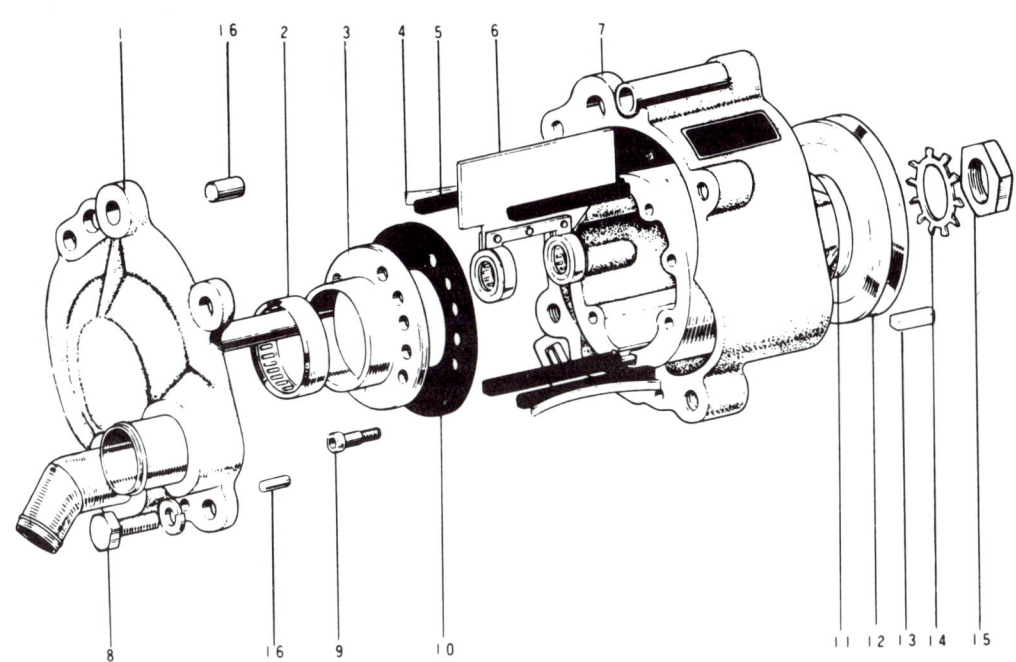

Fig 3.84 Exploded view of the emission control system air pump (Sec 34)

1 Cover	5 Carbon shoe	9 Socket screw	13 Key
2 Bearing	6 Blade	10 Carbon seal	14 Lockwasher
3 Rotor ring	7 Housing	11 Plate	15 Nut
4 Shoe spring	8 Securing bolt	12 Pulley	16 Dowel

Chapter 3/Carburation; fuel, exhaust and emission control systems

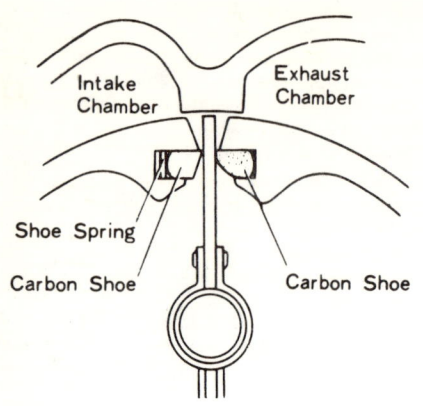

Fig 3.85 Installation diagram for air pump blades and shoes (Sec 34)

15 Finally, fit the pump cover, insert four securing bolts finger tight and drift in the dowels from the cover end. Tighten the cover bolts to a torque of 10 lb/ft (1.382 kg/m). The new blades may squeak for the first 100 miles (160 Km) until they have bedded in.

35 Accelerator pedal and linkage

1 The accelerator cable and linkage should not normally require adjustment unless the cable has stretched or new components have been fitted.
2 Adjustment should be carried out by moving the position of the cable in the rocker box cover clamp and if essential, altering the length of the link connecting rod by pulling the socket joints from their ball connectors and screwing the sockets in or out.
3 Ensure that with the pedal released, the throttle valve plate lever is against the throttle speed screw and when the pedal is

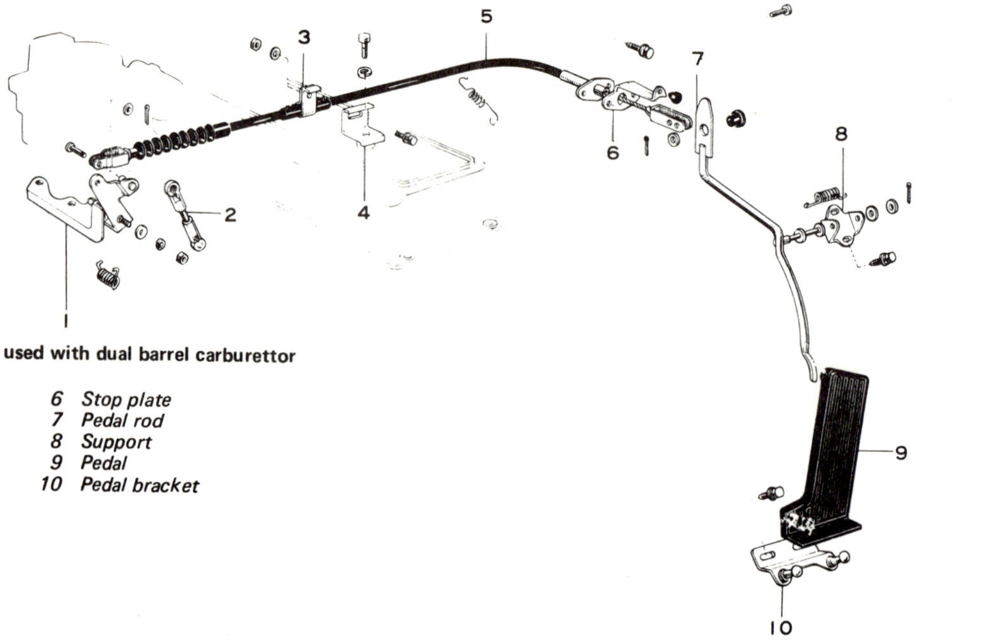

Fig 3.86 Accelerator linkage used with dual barrel carburettor

1 Bracket
2 Ball jointed rod
3 Cable clamp
4 Bracket
5 Outer cable
6 Stop plate
7 Pedal rod
8 Support
9 Pedal
10 Pedal bracket

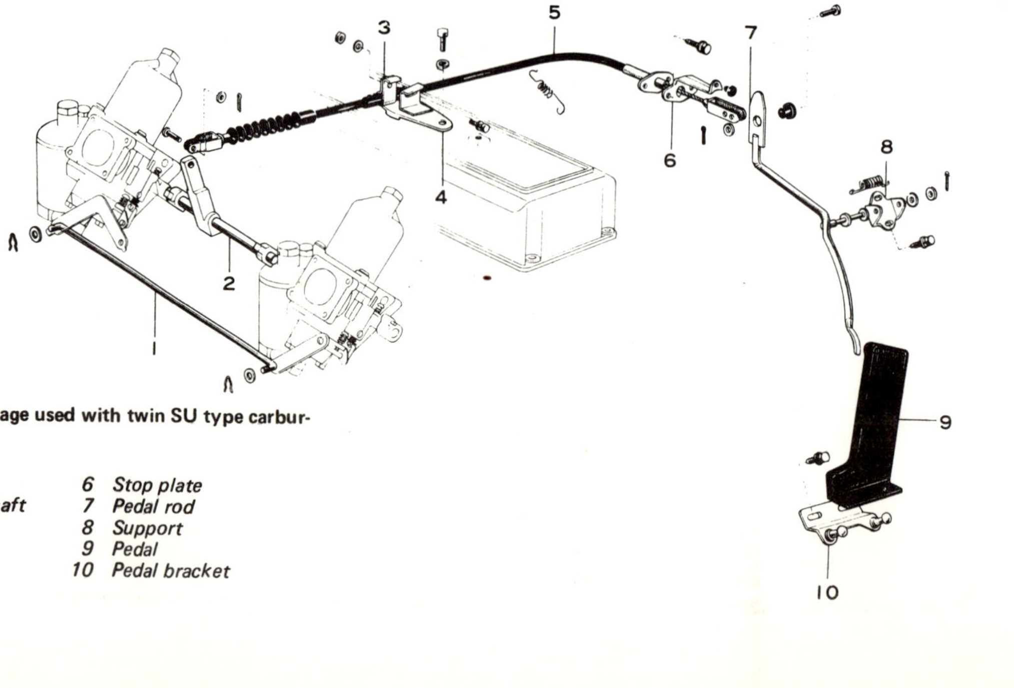

Fig 3.87 Accelerator linkage used with twin SU type carburettor

1 Connector rod
2 Throttle connector shaft
3 Cable clamp
4 Bracket
5 Outer cable
6 Stop plate
7 Pedal rod
8 Support
9 Pedal
10 Pedal bracket

fully depressed, the throttle valve plates are fully open. This is best checked by removing the air cleaner.

4 There are minor differences in the layout and components of the accelerator linkage as fitted to the different vehicle models but the adjustment procedure is similar.

36 Exhaust system and manifolds

1 The layout of the exhaust system is similar on all models although the individual components may vary in detail design.

2 The system is supported on flexible mountings and incorporates two main silencers and an expansion box.

3 Examination of the exhaust pipe and silencers at regular intervals is worthwhile as small defects may be repairable when, if left they will almost certainly require renewal of one of the sections of the system. Also, any leaks, apart from the noise factor, may cause poisonous exhaust gases to get inside the car which can be unpleasant, to say the least, even in mild concentrations. Prolonged inhalation could cause sickness and giddiness.

4 As the sleeve connections and clamps are usually very difficult to separate it is quicker and easier in the long run to remove the complete system from the car when renewing a section. It can be expensive if another section is damaged when trying to separate a bad section from it.

5 To remove the system, jack-up the car at front and rear and then disconnect the front downpipe from the exhaust manifold.

6 Disconnect all the flexible mountings and withdraw the complete system from below and to the rear of the vehicle.

7 Cut away the bad sections, taking care not to damage the good sections which are to be retained.

8 File off any burrs at the ends of the new sections of pipe and smear them with grease. Slip the clamps over the pipes and connect the sockets but do not tighten the clamps at this stage.

9 Push the complete system under the vehicle and jack it up so that the front pipe can be bolted to the manifold and the rear

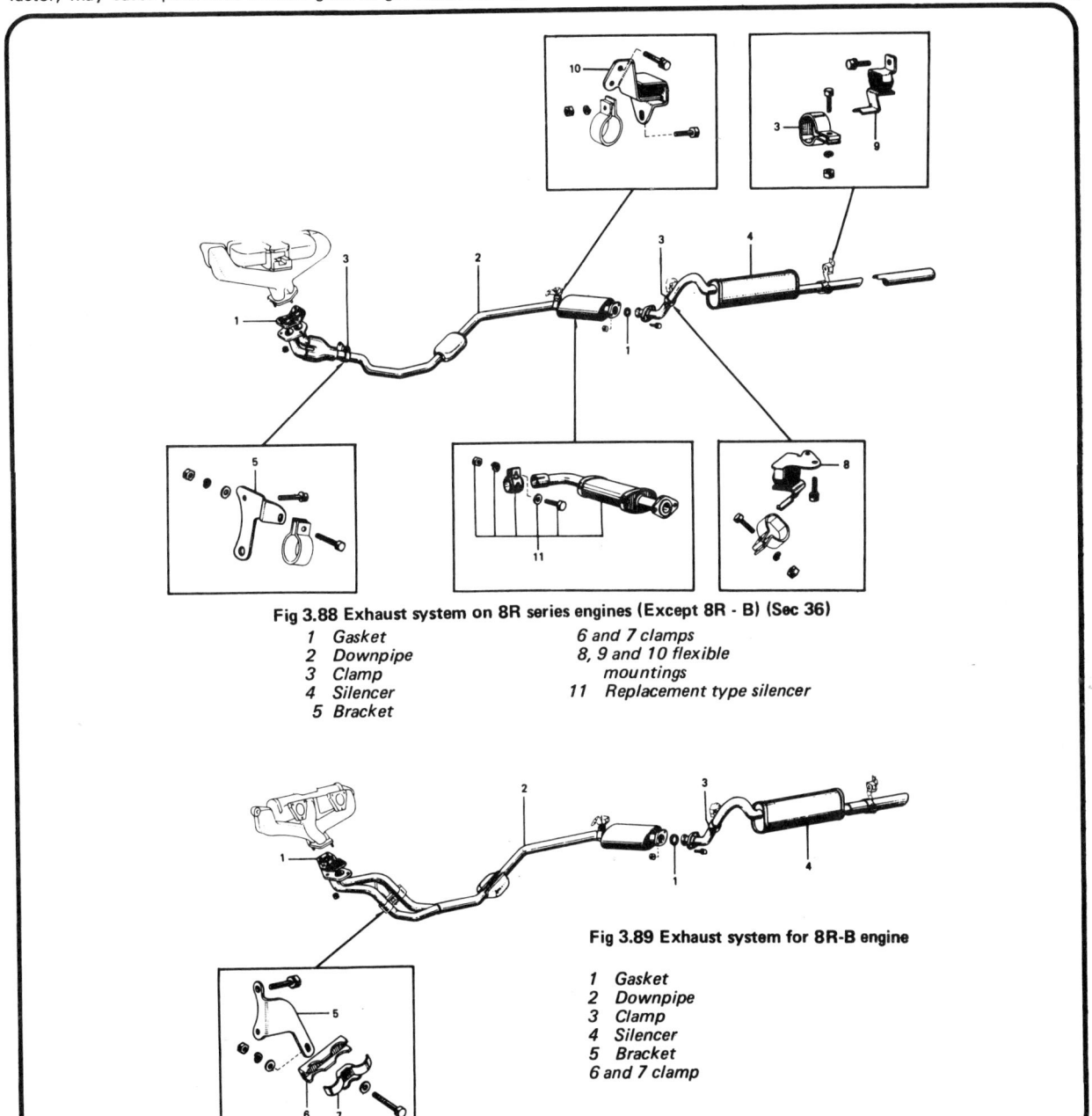

Fig 3.88 Exhaust system on 8R series engines (Except 8R - B) (Sec 36)

1 Gasket
2 Downpipe
3 Clamp
4 Silencer
5 Bracket
6 and 7 clamps
8, 9 and 10 flexible mountings
11 Replacement type silencer

Fig 3.89 Exhaust system for 8R-B engine

1 Gasket
2 Downpipe
3 Clamp
4 Silencer
5 Bracket
6 and 7 clamp

Chapter 3/Carburation; fuel, exhaust and emission control systems

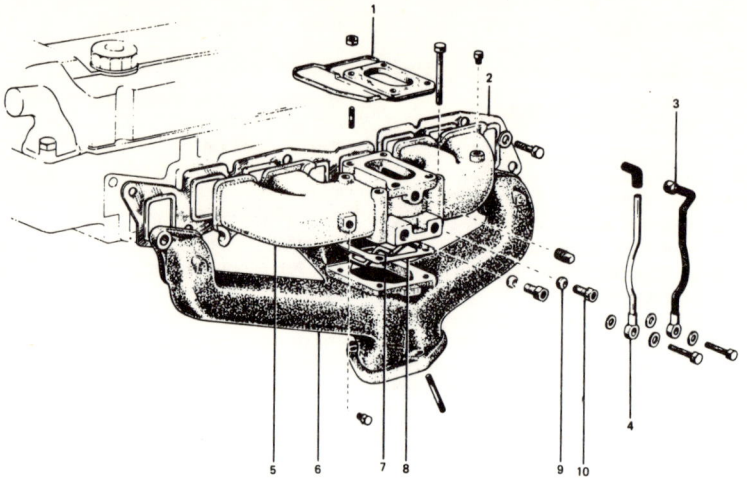

Fig 3.90 Manifold assembly used with dual barrel carburettor (Sec 36)

1 Heat insulator
2 Gasket
3 Choke heater pipe
4 Choke heater
5 Inlet manifold
6 Exhaust manifold
7 Choke heater
8 Gasket
9 Olive
10 Union

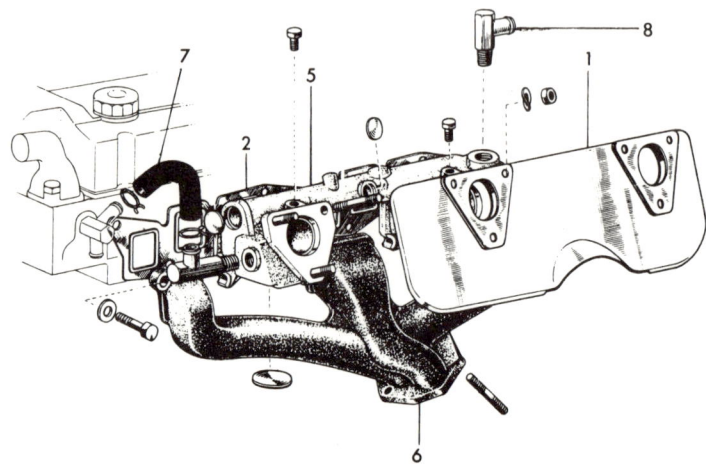

Fig 3.91 Manifold assembly used with twin SU type carburettors (Sec 36)

1 Heat insulator
2 Gasket
5 Inlet manifold
6 Exhaust
7 Water inlet
8 Water outlet

tail pipe mounting connected.
10 Now turn the silencer sections to obtain their correct attitudes so that they will not touch or knock against any adjacent parts when the system is deflected to one side or the other.
11 Tighten all clamps and flexible mountings.
12 The inlet and exhaust manifolds vary slightly between models, the main difference being that the inlet manifold on the 8R-B type engine (twin SU carburettors) is water heated from the cooling system. When disconnecting the water pipes, tie them up as high as possible to prevent loss of coolant.
13 The dual barrel carburettor fitted to other engines has an automatic choke heated by hot air from a heater pipe located within the exhaust manifold.
14 When removing or refitting the manifolds, always use new gaskets and do not tighten the inlet to exhaust manifold bolts until the bolts holding the assembly to the cylinder head have been fully tightened.

Chapter 3/Carburation; fuel, exhaust and emission control systems

37 Fault diagnosis - carburation, fuel and emission control systems

Fuel system and carburation

Symptom	Cause
Excessive fuel consumption	Air filter choked
	Leakage from pump, carburettor or fuel lines or fuel tank
	Float chamber flooding
	Distributor capacitor faulty
	Distributor weights or vacuum capsule faulty
	Mixture too rich
	Contact breaker gap too wide
	Incorrect valve clearances
	Incorrect spark plug gaps
	Tyres under inflated
	Dragging brakes
Fuel starvation or mixture weakness	Clogged fuel line filter
	Float chamber needle valve clogged
	Faulty fuel pump valves
	Fuel pump diaphragm split
	Fuel pipe unions loose
	Fuel pump cover leaking
	Inlet manifold gasket or carburettor flange gasket leaking
	Incorrect adjustment of carburettor

Emission control system

System or circuit	Symptom	Cause
Crankcase ventilation	Oil fume seepage from engine	Stuck or clogged PCV valve. Split or collapsed hoses.
Fuel evaporative emission control	Fuel odour	Choked canister. Stuck filler cap valve.
	Vapour will not be drawn into manifold	Collapsed or split hoses. Vacuum switching valve defective. Speed sensor defective
	Rough running engine	Defective check valve.
Transmission controlled spark (TCS)	TCS off when engine cold and raced	Defective distributor vacuum capsule, defective thermo sensor or vacuum switching valve.
	TCS on when engine hot and raced	Defective thermo sensor or vacuum switching valve.
	TCS off at incorrect speed ranges with engine hot	Defective vacuum switching valve or speed sensor.
Air injection system (early 8R-C engine)	Fume emission from exhaust pipe	Slack or broken air pump drive belt. Split or broken hoses. Clogged air filter. Defective air pump.
Throttle delay	System fails to operate at 25 mph (40 km/h) during acceleration	Adjust linkage, check vacuum hose to diaphragm unit.
	System fails to turn off during deceleration at 11 mph (18 km/h)	Defective diaphragm. Defective vacuum switching valve. Defective speed sensor.

Note: The efficiency of the fume emission control system is also dependent upon the correct setting and adjustment of all other engine components. These include the ignition, cooling and lubrication systems, the valve clearances and the condition generally of the engine. Refer to the appropriate Sections and Chapters of this manual for servicing procedures.

Chapter 4 Ignition system

Contents

Coil polarity and testing ... 12	assembly ... 11
Condenser (capacitor) - removal, testing and refitting ... 4	Distributor - removal and installation ... 5
Contact breaker - adjustment ... 2	Dwell angle - checking ... 7
Contact breaker points - removal and refitting ... 3	General description ... 1
Distributor (early type) - dismantling ... 8	Ignition system - fault diagnosis ... 14
Distributor (early type) - reassembly ... 10	Ignition system - fault symptoms ... 15
Distributor - inspection and servicing ... 9	Ignition timing - checking and adjustment ... 6
Distributor (late type) - dismantling, inspection and re-	Spark plugs and HT leads ... 13

Specifications

System type ... Battery, coil, distributor

Firing order ... 1–3–4–2

Distributor

Contact breaker points gap	0.016 to 0.020 in. (0.4 to 0.5 mm)
Dwell angle	50 to 54°
Condenser capacity	0.20 to 0.24 micro-farad
Static timing:	
8R engine	10° BTDC at 600 rev/min
8R-B engine	15° BTDC @ 800 rev/min
8R-C engine:	
Up to March 1971	0° (TDC) at 650 rev/min
After March 1971 and models with TCS system	10° BTDC at 650 rev/min
18R engine	7° BTDC at 600 rev/min (manual gearbox) or with automatic transmission in 'D'
18R-C engine	7° BTDC at 650 rev/min (manual gearbox) at 800 rev/min (auto transmission in 'N')

Centrifugal advance

	Engine speed (twice distributor speed) rev/min	Advance angle (degrees)
8R engine	800 to 1200	Begins
	2200	9 to 11
	5600	15 to 17
8R-B engine	800 to 1000	Begins
	1600	4.5 to 6.5
	5500	11 to 13
8R-C engine	800 to 1200	Begins
	2200	12.5 to 14.5
	4600	19 to 21
18R engine	800 to 1200	Begins
	3200	9 to 11
	5600	14 to 16
18R-C engine:		
Manual gearbox	1000 to 1400	Begins
	2640 to 2760	9 to 11
	5200	12 to 14
Automatic transmission	1200 to 1600	Begins
	3400	9.5 to 11.5
	5200	12 to 14

Chapter 4/Ignition system

Vacuum advance

8R engine	140 to 190	Begins
	240	1.5 to 3.5
	360	4.7 to 6.7
	620	9.5 to 11.5
8R-B engine	200 to 280	Begins
	440	3 to 5
	600	5.5 to 7.5
8R-C engine	130 to 200	Begins
	240	1 to 3
	360	3 to 5
	500	5 to 7
	640	6 to 8
18R engine	116 to 204	Begins
	270 to 290	2.6 to 4.6
	460 to 500	7.3 to 8.7
	710 to 730	11 to 13
18R-C engine		
Manual gearbox	1200	Begins
	2700	4.7
	5200	7.5
Automatic transmission	1400	Begins
	3400	6
	5200	9

Spark plugs

Type	NGK BP6ES 14 mm
Gap	0.028 to 0.032 in. (0.7 to 0.8 mm)

Torque wrench setting

	lb/ft	Kg/m
Spark plugs	15	2.1

1 General description

The ignition system comprises the following components:
The battery which provides a current of 2.3 amps to the coil when the engine is running.
The ignition/starter switch.
The coil which acts as a transformer to step up the 12 volt battery voltage to many thousands of volts, sufficient to jump the spark plug gaps.
The distributor which comprises: contact breaker, condenser, rotor arm, distributor cap with brush and centrifugal and vacuum advance and retard mechanism and is driven by the oil pump driveshaft at half crankshaft speed.
The spark plugs which ignite the compressed mixture in the combustion chambers.
Low and high tension leads connecting the various components.

When the ignition is switched on a current flows from the battery live terminal to the ignition switch through the coil primary winding to the moving contact breaker inside the distributor cap and to earth when the contact breaker points are in the closed position. During this period of points closure, the current flows through the primary windings of the coil and magnetises the laminated iron core which in turn creates a magnetic field through the coil primary and secondary windings.

Each time the points open due to the rotation of the distributor cam, the current flow through the primary winding of the coil is interrupted. This causes the induction of a very high voltage (25000 volts) in the coil secondary winding. This HT (high tension) current is distributed to the spark plugs in correct firing order sequence by the rotor arm and by means of the cap brush and HT leads.

A condenser is fitted to the distributor and connected between the moving contact breaker and earth to prevent excessive arcing and pitting of the contact breaker points.

The actual point of ignition of the fuel/air mixture which occurs a few degrees before TDC is determined by correct static setting of the ignition timing as described in Section 6. The ignition is advanced to meet varying operating conditions by the centrifugal counterweights fitted in the base of the distributor

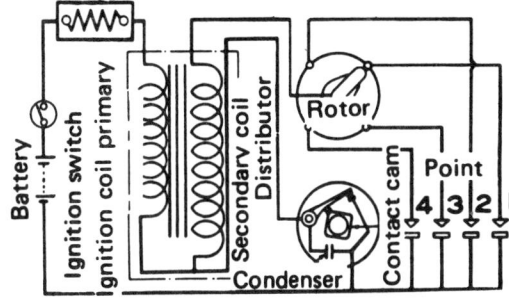

Fig. 4.1 Ignition circuit (Sec 1)

body and by vacuum from the inlet manifold operating though a capsule linked to the movable distributor baseplate.

Slight variations of the static ignition setting may be made by means of the vernier adjuster to compensate for different fuel qualities. To improve the intensity of the spark at the spark plug electrodes during high speed running, an external resistor is included in the ignition primary circuit.

2 Contact breaker - adjustment

1 Pull off the HT leads from the spark plugs and mark them 1 to 4 for easy refitting.
2 Spring back the distributor cover securing clips and lift the cover to one side. Withdraw the rotor and the dustproof cover.
3 Using a spanner on the crankshaft pulley securing bolt, rotate the engine in its normal direction of rotation until the heel of the movable contact breaker arm is on one of the 4 high points of the cam. Removal of the spark plugs will make turning the engine easier.
4 Examine the contact faces of the (now open) points and if they are pitted or burned then they must be removed and dressed as described in the next Section.

5 If the points are in good order, check the gap by inserting a feeler gauge of between 0.016 and 0.020 in (0.4 and 0.5 mm) in thickness. Insert the feeler blade in a vertical position and if the gap is correct, it will just fall by its own weight. If the gap is incorrect, adjust the fixed contact arm by loosening the retaining screw and moving it, as necessary, by means of a screwdriver blade inserted in the cut-out in the contact arm.
6 When the gap is correct, tighten the contact arm screw, remove the feeler blade, replace the dust proof cover, rotor arm and distributor cap. **Check that the ring spanner has been removed from the crankshaft pulley bolt.** Reconnect the HT leads.

3 Contact breaker points - removal and refitting

1 Carry out operations 1 and 2 of the preceding Section.
2 Detach the spring retaining clip from the top of the contact breaker arm pivot post.
3 Unscrew the nuts on the LT terminal on the outside of the distributor body just enough to enable the contact arm lead and spade terminal to be withdrawn, then lift the movable arm from the baseplate.
4 Remove the securing screw and lift the fixed contact breaker arm from the baseplate.
5 Examine the points. After a period of operation, one contact face should have a pip and the other a crater caused by arcing. This is a normal condition which should be removed by dressing the faces squarely on an oilstone.
6 Excessive pitting of the contact points may be caused by operation with an incorrect gap, the voltage regulator setting too high, faulty or wrong type of condenser, loose distributor baseplate or battery terminals.
7 Where contact breaker points are so badly worn or the pitting so deep that excessive rubbing would be required to eliminate it, then they should be renewed.
8 Wipe the faces of the points with methylated spirit before installing, smear the high points of the cam with petroleum jelly.
9 Refit the rotor, cap and HT leads.

4 Condenser (capacitor) - removal, testing, refitting

1 The condenser ensures that with the contact breaker points open, the sparking between them is not excessive, as this would cause severe pitting. The condenser is fitted in parallel and its failure will automatically cause failure of the ignition system as the points will be prevented from interrupting the low tension circuit.
2 Testing for an unserviceable condenser may be effected by switching on the ignition and separating the contact points by hand. If this action is accompanied by a blue flash then condenser failure is indicated. Difficult starting, missing of the engine after several miles running or badly pitted points are other indications of a faulty condenser.
3 The surest test is by substitution of a new unit.
4 To remove the condenser, unscrew its retaining screw and detach its lead from the LT terminal on the distributor body. Refitting is a reversal of removal.

5 Distributor - removal and installation

1 Remove No. 1 spark plug and place a finger over the hole to feel the compression being generated as the engine is rotated by means of the crankshaft pulley bolt.
2 As soon as compression is felt this will indicate that No. 1 piston is rising on its compression stroke. Continue turning the engine until the timing mark (not TDC mark) on the crankshaft pulley is in line with the pointer on the timing cover.
3 Remove the distributor cap and mark the rim of the distributor body at a point opposite to the centre line of the contact end of the rotor arm. This is equivalent to alignment with No. 1 contact in the distributor cap.
4 Disconnect the LT wire from the terminal on the distributor body.
5 Disconnect the vacuum tube from the distributor advance diaphragm unit.
6 Unbolt the distributor clamp plate and withdraw the distributor from the recess in the crankcase.
7 The distributor cap may be withdraw if the HT leads are first disconnected from the spark plugs and coil centre socket.
8 If the engine is turned while the distributor is removed, reset the crankshaft pulley timing mark opposite the timing cover pointer (No. 1 piston on compression stroke) as described in paragraph one, before installing the distributor. (photo)
9 Turn the rotor arm so that its centre line is in alignment with the mark made on the distributor body rim before removal. If a new distributor is being fitted then mark the rim of the body after the rotor arm has been aligned with No. 1 contact in the distributor cap.
10 Set the vernier adjuster so that its centre line is opposite the setting mark on the diaphragm unit.
11 Hold the distributor over its recess in the crankcase so that a line drawn through the vacuum diaphragm unit makes an angle of 30° with the centre line of the engine.
12 Using a screwdriver, turn the slot in the oil pump driveshaft (visible at the bottom of the distributor recess) so that it is in alignment with the tongue on the bottom of the distributor driveshaft.
13 Holding the distributor in the predetermined position, turn the rotor arm anticlockwise 30°.
14 Insert the distributor into the crankcase and as the gears mesh the rotor will rotate in a clockwise direction and become aligned with the mark made on the rim of the distributor body. The distributor should be pushed right down to fully engage the driveshaft tongue with the slot. The rotor will be opposite No. 1 spark plug contact in the distributor cap.
15 Rotate the distributor body until the contact breaker points are just about to open and then tighten the distributor clamp plate bolt. (photo)
16 Refit the distributor cap, connect the LT and HT leads and the vacuum pipe.
17 Check the timing with a stroboscope as described in the next Section.

6 Ignition timing - checking and adjustment

1 Check the ignition timing using a stroboscope. First paint the timing cover pointer and the timing notch on the pulley (not the TDC notch) with white paint. The position of this slot will vary in accordance with engine type and static advance setting (see Specifications Section).
2 Disconnect the vacuum pipe from the distributor diaphragm unit.
3 Start the engine and set the slow running speed to 650 rev/min preferably by using a tachometer.
4 Project the light from the stroboscope onto the timing cover pointer and pulley mark. Each flash of the stroboscope indicates that No. 1 cylinder has fired and if the timing is correct, the pulley mark will appear to be stationary and in alignment with the pointer.
5 Where the mark is not in alignment with the pointer, release the distributor clamp bolt and turn the distributor body until they do coincide. Tighten the clamp bolt.
    A useful check on the correct operation of the vacuum advance mechanism may be made by replacing the vacuum pipe to the distributor and still using the stroboscopic light as for checking the timing (just described), slowly increase the speed of the engine. The timing mark on the pulley should now move out of alignment with the timing cover pointer and the amount of misalignment should increase in proportion to the increase in engine speed. This proves correct operation of the vacuum advance mechanism. No movement between the pulley mark and

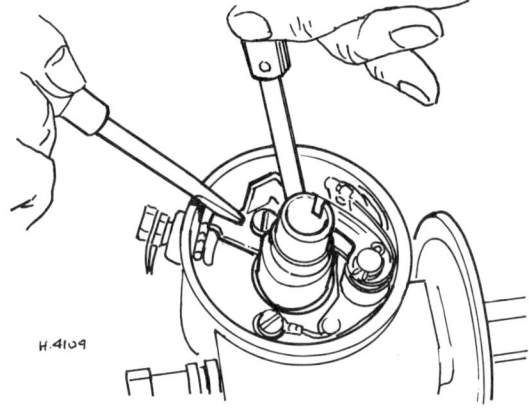

Fig. 4.2 Adjusting the contact breaker points gap (Sec 2)

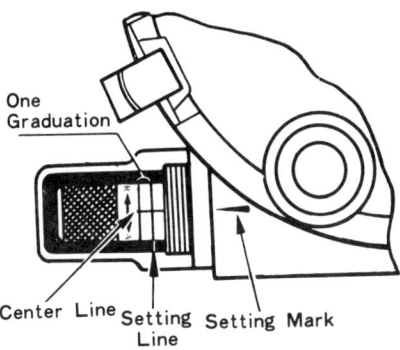

Fig 4.5 The distributor vernier adjuster (Sec 5)

Fig. 4.3 Removing the contact breaker points (Sec 3)

1 Spring clip
2 Moveable arm
3 Fixed contact

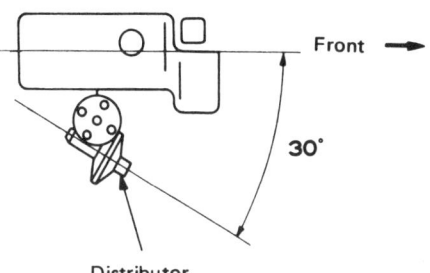

Fig 4.6 Distributor installation diagram (Sec 5)

Fig. 4.4 The timing marks (Sec 5)

Fig. 4.7 Rotor arm in alignment with No 1 spark plug contact in distributor cap after correct installation of distributor (Sec 5)

5.8 Ignition timing marks

5.15 Tightening distributor clamp bolt

pointer indicates either a break in the vacuum pipe or an unserviceable diaphragm unit.

6 Slight alterations to the ignition timing should be carried out by means of the vernier adjuster. This may be required when fuels of different octane ratings are used.

7 To adjust, drive the vehicle at a steady road speed (in top gear - manual gearbox or 'D' - automatic transmission) at about 25 mph (40 km/h). Suddenly depress the accelerator pedal to the floor and listen for the sound of 'pinking' (pre-deterioration). If evident, remove the plastic cap from the vernier adjuster and turn it in the 'R' direction only enough to prevent pinking on retest. Where the ignition timing is thought to be retarded or a fuel of higher octane rating is being used, turn the vernier adjuster in the 'A' direction until any further movement would cause the engine to 'pink'. Turning the vernier control through one graduation is equivalent to altering the ignition timing by 10 degrees.

8 With the engine switched off, it is a good idea to check the operation of the centrifugal advance mechanism. To do this, remove the distributor cap and turn the rotor arm fully clockwise. Release the rotor arm and ensure that it returns all the way to its original position. If it fails to do so, the counterweights are sticking or the return springs are broken or stretched.

7 Dwell angle - checking

1 On modern engines, setting the distributor contact breaker gap must be regarded as the initial setting. For optimum engine performance, the dwell angle must be checked. The dwell angle is the number of degrees through which the distributor cam turns between the closing and opening of the contact breaker points. It can only be checked with a dwell meter.

2 The correct dwell angle is between 50 and 54 degrees. If the angle is too large, increase the points gap, if too small, decrease the points gap.

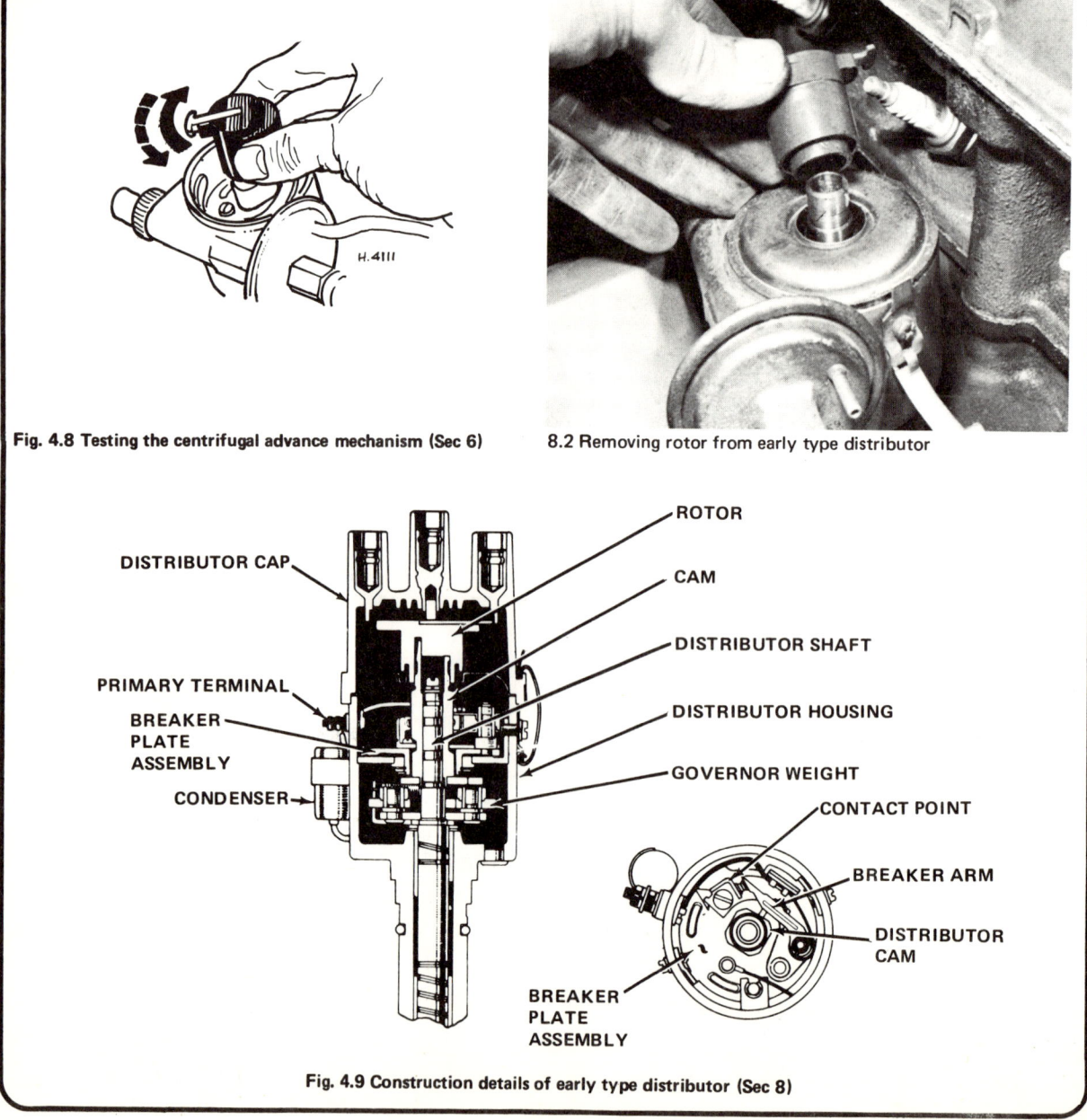

Fig. 4.8 Testing the centrifugal advance mechanism (Sec 6)

8.2 Removing rotor from early type distributor

Fig. 4.9 Construction details of early type distributor (Sec 8)

Chapter 4/Ignition system

8 Distributor (early type) - dismantling

1 Remove the distributor from the engine, as described in Section 5.
2 Remove the distributor cap, rotor arm and dust proof cover. (photo)
3 Remove the contact breaker assembly and the cap from the vernier adjuster.
4 Remove the vacuum diaphragm unit by withdrawing the retaining screws (1 and 2) and the circlip (3). (Fig 4.10)
5 Remove the distributor cap spring clips, the externally mounted condenser and the LT terminal from the distributor body.
6 Remove the contact breaker mounting plate (movable) and the baseplate (fixed) as an assembly. This is secured to the distributor body by screws.
7 Unscrew and remove the central cam screw and pull off the cam from the top of the distributor shaft.
8 Remove the mechanical advance counterweights and springs. Note carefully the positions of the two springs as they are not

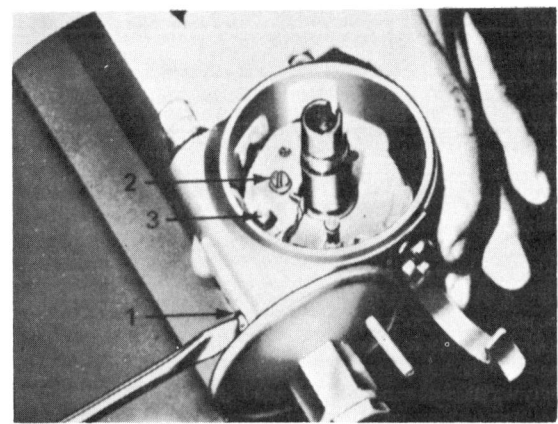

Fig. 4.10 Diaphragm unit retaining screw (1) earth lead (2) and circlip (3) on early type distributor (Sec 8)

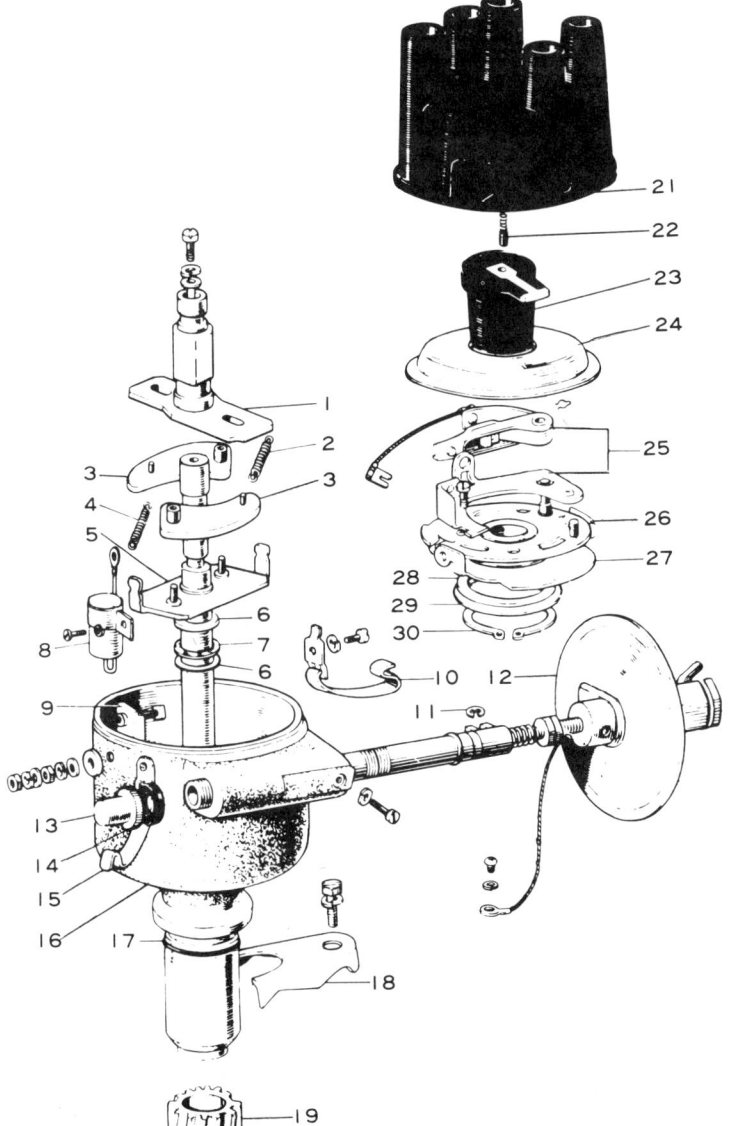

Fig. 4.11 Exploded view of early type distributor (Sec 8)

1 Cam
2 Counterweight spring
3 Counterweight
4 Counterweight spring
5 Shaft
6 Steel thrust washer
7 Plastic washer
8 Condenser
9 Terminal insulator
10 Cap spring clip
11 Circlip
12 Vacuum diaphagm unit
13 Plastic cover
14 Rubber washer
15 Cap spring clip
16 Body
17 'O' ring seal
18 Clamp plate
19 Spiral gear
20 Pin
21 Cap
22 Carbon brush
23 Rotor
24 Dust proof cover
25 Contact breaker arms
26 Movable plate
27 Baseplate
28 Thrust washer
29 Wave washer
30 Circlip

interchangeable.
9 Carefully drill out the rivetted end of the pin which secures the spiral gear/spacer to the bottom end of the distributor shaft.
10 Drive out the pin and withdraw the shaft upwards through the body, retaining any washers and shims.

9 Distributor - inspection and servicing

1 Check for wear between the shaft and the body. If evident it will be more economical to exchange the complete distributor unit for a reconditioned one rather than attempt to repair the old unit.
2 Check the fit of the counterweights on their pivot posts. The maximum clearance is 0.007 in (0.2 mm).
3 Examine the distributor cap for cracks and for burned or eroded contacts. Check the carbon brush in the centre of the cap interior; if it has worn below 0.28 in (7 mm) in length, renew it.
4 Separate the contact breaker swivel plate from the baseplate. Do this by removing the circlip and carefully detaching the small components. Do not lose the rolling balls. Renew any items which are worn or distorted. When the movable and fixed plates are assembled, prise them apart with the fingers; if the clearance is greater than 0.008 in (0.2 mm) adjust by means of different adjusting washers. A force of between 7.1 and 17.6 oz (200 and 500g) should be needed to turn the movable plate.
5 Check the teeth on the spiral gear and renew the gear if it is worn or chipped.

10 Distributor (early type) - reassembly

1 Lubricate the shaft with clean engine oil, locate the washers on the shaft (plastic between two steel ones) and then insert it into the distributor body.
2 Fit the spiral gear and insert the retaining pin but do not peen its end at this stage as the shaft endfloat must be checked. The correct endfloat is between 0.006 and 0.020 in (0.15 and 0.5 mm) tested with feeler gauges inserted between the spiral gear and the distributor body. Where the endfloat is outside that specified, add or remove the steel thrust washers as necessary.
3 When the correct endfloat is achieved, peen over the end of the spiral gear securing pin.
4 Apply engine oil to the counterweight pivot posts and then fit the counterweights and springs. Note particularly the position of the spring with the shorter number of coils and the longer hook.
5 Smear the distributor shaft with grease, fit the cam and secure with the central screw.
6 Refit the distributor cap spring clips.
7 Install the breaker plate assembly into the distributor body making sure that the diaphragm actuating link pivot is positioned correctly to receive the link.
8 Fit the vacuum diaphragm engaging its link with the baseplate pivot post and securing it with the circlip.
9 Fit the contact breaker assembly to the baseplate but do not tighten the securing screws at this stage.
10 Connect the diaphragm unit earth lead. The contact breaker lead and condenser lead should then be connected to the terminal on the distributor body.
11 Install the distributor to the engine (Section 5) and then adjust the contact breaker points as described in Section 2.
12 Check the ignition timing as described in Sections 6 and 7.
13 A smear of petroleum jelly should be applied to the high points of the cam when all adjustments are complete.

11 Distributor (late type) - dismantling, inspection and reassembly

1 Although there are detail differences in the components of the later type distributor, dismantling is very similar to the procedure described in Section 8 except that the cap securing clips

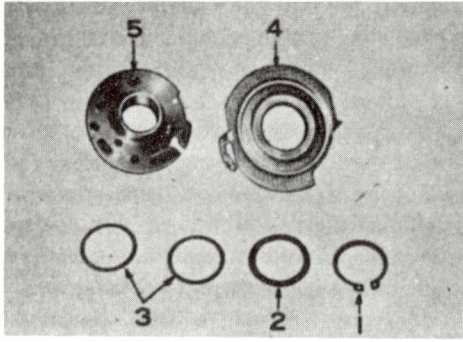

Fig. 4.12 Exploded view of baseplate assembly on early type distributor (Sec 9)

1 Circlip
2 Wave washer
3 Shims
4 Fixed baseplate
5 Movable plate

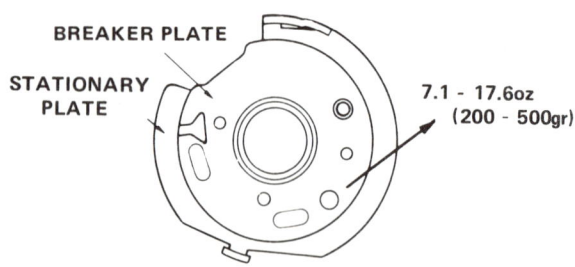

Fig. 4.13 Movable plate turning force diagram (early type distributor) (Sec 9)

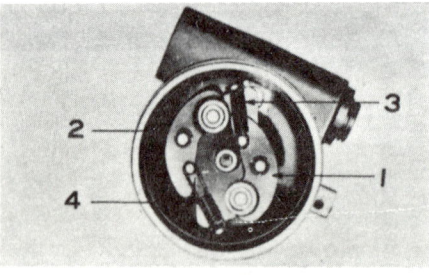

Fig. 4.14 Location of counterweights and springs on early type distributor (Sec 10)

1 and 2 Counterweight   3 and 4 Springs

are secured by internally located screws, the contact breaker assembly must not be dismantled and circlips are used to secure the counterweights.
2 Inspection of components for wear is similar to that described for the earlier type distributor except that if the force required to turn the movable baseplate exceeds 2.2 lbs (1.0 kg) when lubricated with engine oil, then the assembly must be renewed complete.
3 Reassembly is similar to the earlier type distributor, but if endfloat of the distributor shaft is outside that specified (0.006 to 0.020 in - 0.15 to 0.50 mm) a new single thrust washer must be selected from those available in thicknesses of 0.098 in (2.5 mm), 0.106 in (2.7 mm), 0.114 in (2.9 mm).
4 The baseplate assembly is secured to the distributor body with clips. Note carefully the location of the distributor cap positioner and that the earth lead is secured under the cap clip screw nearest the LT terminal on the distributor body.

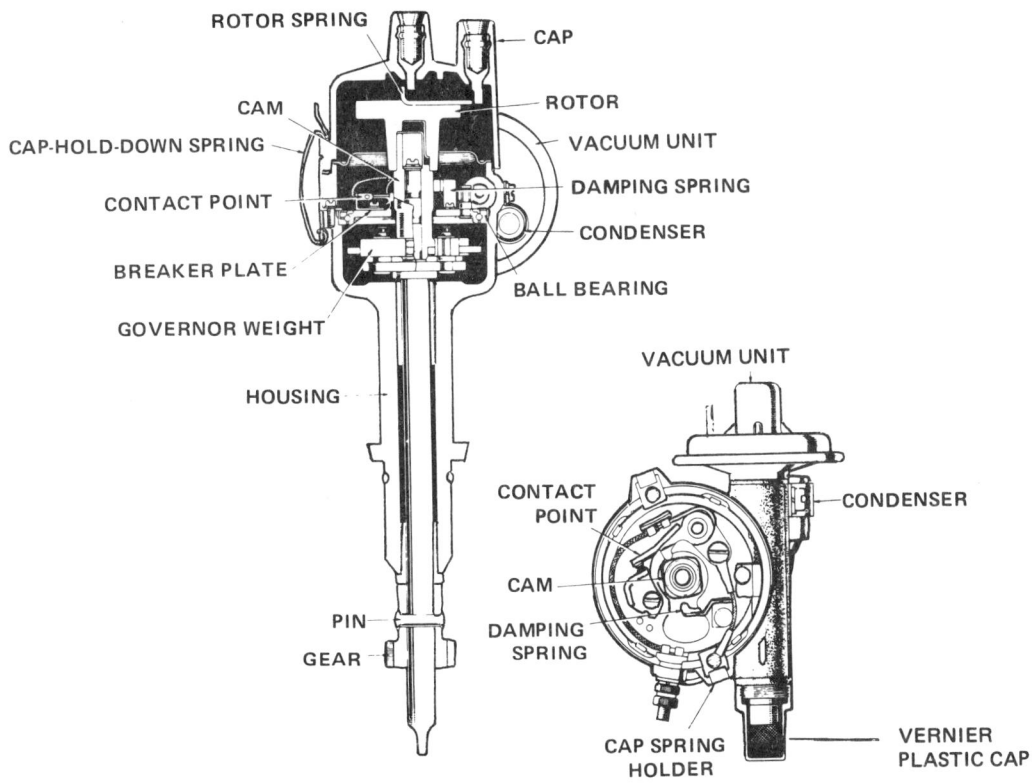

Fig. 4.15 Constructional details of later type distributor (Sec 11)

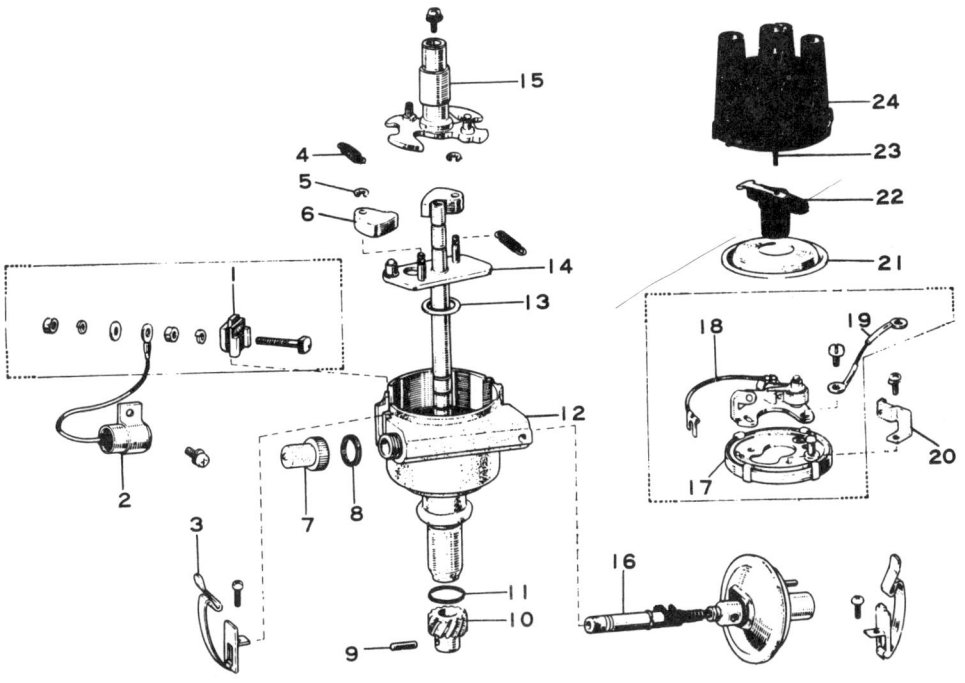

Fig. 4.16 Exploded view of later type distributor (Sec 11)

1 LT terminal assembly
2 Condenser
3 Cap clip
4 Counterweight spring
5 Circlip
6 Counterweight
7 Vernier control cap
8 Rubber washer
9 Pin
10 Spiral gear
11 'O' ring seal
12 Distributor body
13 Steel thrust washer
14 Shaft assembly
15 Cam
16 Diaphragm unit
17 Baseplate assembly
18 Contact breaker assembly
19 Earth lead
20 Distributor cap positioner
21 Dust proof cover
22 Rotor arm
23 Carbon brush
24 Cap

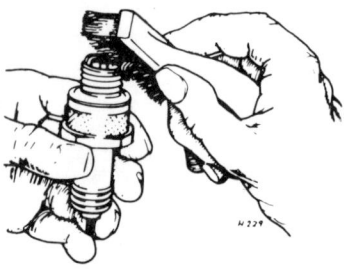
Cleaning deposits from electrodes and surrounding area using a fine wire brush.

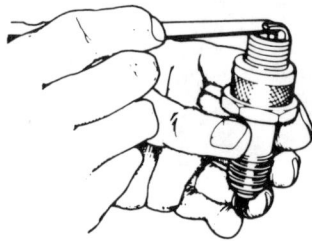
Checking plug gap with feeler gauges

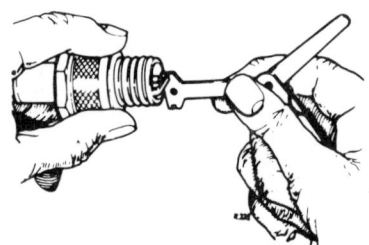
Altering the plug gap. Note use of correct tool.

Fig. 4.17 Spark plug maintenance (Sec 13)

White deposits and damaged porcelain insulation indicating overheating

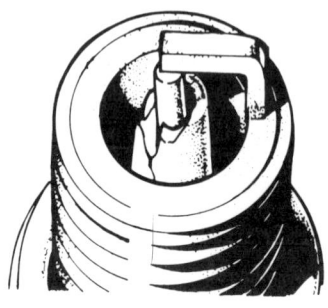
Broken porcelain insulation due to bent central electrode

Electrodes burnt away due to wrong heat value or chronic pre-ignition (pinking)

Excessive black deposits caused by over-rich mixture or wrong heat value

Mild white deposits and electrode burnt indicating too weak a fuel mixture

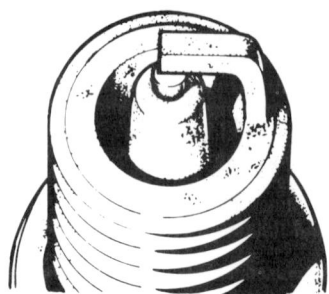
Plug in sound condition with light greyish brown deposits

Fig. 4.18 Spark plug electrode conditons (Sec 13)

12 Coil polarity and testing

1 High tension current should be negative at the spark plug terminals. If the HT current is positive at the spark plug terminals then the LT leads to the coil primary terminals have been incorrectly connected. A wrong connection can cause as much as 60% loss of spark efficiency and can cause rough idling and misfiring at speed.
2 With a negative earth electrical system, the LT lead from the distributor connects with the negative (primary) terminal on the coil.
3 The simplest way to test a coil is by substitution. If an ohmmeter is available use it to carry out the following checks but first apply a 12 volt current to the coil to bring it to normal operating temperature.
4 Check the primary resistance between the coil (+) and (−) terminals which should be between 3.3 and 4.3 ohms.
5 Check the secondary resistance (secondary to primary terminals) this should be between 7500 and 10000 ohms.
6 Insulation breakdown can only be satisfactorily tested using a megohmmeter between the coil casing and the primary terminals. The resistance should be in excess of 50 megohms.

13 Spark plugs and HT leads

1 The correct functioning of the spark plugs is vital for the correct running and efficiency of the engine. The plugs fitted as standard are listed in the Specification page.
2 At intervals of 6000 miles (9600 km) the plugs should be removed, examined, cleaned and, if worn excessively, renewed. The condition of the spark plug will also tell much about the overall condition of the engine.
3 If the insulator nose of the spark plug is clean and white, with no deposits, this is indicative of a weak mixture, or too hot a plug.
4 If the top and insulator nose is covered with hard black looking deposits, then this is indicative that the mixture is too rich. Should the plug be black and oily, then it is likely that the engine is fairly worn, as well as the mixture being too rich.
5 If the insulator nose is covered with light tan to greyish brown deposits, then the mixture is correct and it is likely that the engine is in good condition.
6 If there are any traces of long brown tapering stains on the outside of the white portion of the plug, then the plug will have to be renewed, as this shows that there is a faulty joint between the plug body and the insulator, and compression is being allowed to leak away.
7 Plugs should be cleaned by a sand blasting machine, which will free them from carbon more thoroughly than cleaning by hand. The machine will also test the condition of the plugs under compression. Any plug that fails to spark at the recommended pressure should be renewed.
8 The spark plug gap is of considerable importance, as, if it is too large or too small the size of the spark and its efficiency will be seriously impaired. The spark plug gap should be set to between 0.028 and 0.032 in (0.7 and 0.8 mm) for the best results.
9 To set it, measure the gap with a feeler gauge, and then bend open, or close the outer plug electrode until the correct gap is achieved. The centre electrode should never be bent as this may crack the insulation and cause plug failure.
10 The HT leads to the coil and spark plugs are of internal resistance, carbon core type. They are used in the interest of eliminating interference caused by the ignition system. They are much more easily damaged than copper cored cable and they should be pulled from the spark plug terminals by gripping the metal end fitting at the end of the cable. Occasionally wipe the external surfaces of the leads free from oil and dirt using a fuel moistened cloth.
11 Always check the connection of the HT leads to the spark plugs is in the correct firing order sequence 1-3-4-2.

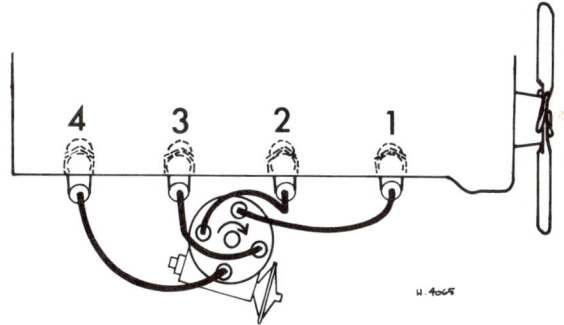

Fig. 4.19 Spark plug lead connecting diagram (Sec 13)

14 Ignition system - fault diagnosis

Failures of the ignition system will either be due to faults in the HT or LT circuits. Initial checks should be made by observing the security of spark plug terminals, switch terminals, coil and battery connection. More detailed investigation and the explanation and remedial action in respect of symptoms of ignition malfunction are described in the next Section.

15 Ignition system - fault symptoms

Engine fails to start
1 If the engine fails to start and the car was running normally when it was last used, first check there is fuel in the tank. If the engine turns over normally on the starter motor and the battery is evidently well charged, then the fault may be in either the high or low tension circuits. First check the HT circuit. Note: If the battery is known to be fully charged; the ignition light comes on, and the starter motor fails to turn the engine check the tightness of the leads on the battery terminals and also the secureness of the earth lead to its connection to the body. It is quite common for the leads to have worked loose, even if they look and feel secure. If one of the battery terminal posts gets very hot when trying to work the starter motor this is a sure indication of a faulty connection to that terminal.
2 One of the commonest reasons for bad starting is wet or damp spark plug leads and distributor. Remove the distributor cap. If condensation is visible internally, dry the cap with a rag and also wipe over the leads. Replace the cap.
3 If the engine still fails to start, check that current is reaching the plugs, by disconnecting each plug lead in turn at the spark plug end, and hold the end of the cable about 3/16th inch (4.7 mm) away from the cylinder block. Spin the engine on the starter motor.
4 Sparking between the end of the cable and block should be fairly strong with a regular blue spark. (Hold the lead with rubber to avoid electric shocks). If current is reaching the plugs, then remove them and clean and regap them. The engine should now start.
5 If there is no spark at the plug leads take off the HT lead from the centre of the distributor cap and hold it to the block as before. Spin the engine on the starter once more. A rapid succession of blue sparks between the end of the lead and the block indicate that the coil is in order and that the distributor cap is cracked, the rotor arm faulty, or the carbon brush in the top of the distributor cap is not making good contact with the spring on the rotor arm. Possibly the points are in bad condition. Clean and reset them as described in this Chapter.

6 If there are no sparks from the end of the lead from the coil, check the connections at the coil end of the lead. If it is in order start checking the low tension circuit.

7 Use a 12v voltmeter or a 12v bulb and two lengths of wire. With the ignition switch on and the points open test between the low tension wire to the coil (it is marked +) and earth. No reading indicates a break in the supply from the ignition switch. Check the connections at the switch to see if any are loose. Refit them and the engine should run. A reading shows a faulty coil or condenser, or broken lead between the coil and the distributor.

8 Take the condenser wire off the points assembly and with the points open, test between the moving point and earth. If there now is a reading, then the fault is in the condenser. Fit a new one and the fault is cleared.

9 With no reading from the moving point to earth, take a reading between earth and the (—) terminal of the coil. A reading here shows a broken wire which will need to be renewed between the coil and distributor. No reading confirms that the coil has failed and must be renewed, after which the engine will run once more. Remember to refit the condenser wire to the points assembly. For these tests it is sufficient to separate the points with a piece of dry paper while testing with the points open.

Engine misfires

10 If the engine misfires regularly run it at a fast idling speed. Pull off each of the plug caps in turn and listen to the note of the engine. Hold the plug cap in a dry cloth or with a rubber glove as additional protection against a shock from the HT supply.

11 No difference in engine running will be noticed when the lead from the defective circuit is removed. Removing the lead from one of the good cylinders will accentuate the misfire.

12 Remove the plug lead from the end of the defective plug and hold it about 3/16 inch (4.7 mm) away from the block. Restart the engine. If the sparking is fairly strong and regular the fault must lie in the spark plug.

13 The plug may be loose, the insulation may be cracked, or the points may have burnt away giving too wide a gap for the spark to jump. Worse still, one of the points may have broken off. Either renew the plug, or clean it, reset the gap, and then test it.

14 If there is no spark at the end of the plug lead, or if it is weak and intermittent, check the ignition lead from the distributor to the plug. If the insulation is cracked or perished, renew the lead. Check the connection at the distributor cap.

15 If there is still no spark, examine the distributor cap carefully for tracking. This can be recognised by a very thin black line running between two or more contacts, or between a contact and some other part of the distributor. These lines are paths which now conduct electricity across the cap thus letting it run to earth. The only answer is a new distributor cap.

16 Apart from the ignition timing being incorrect, other causes of misfiring have already been dealt with under the section dealing with the failure of the engine to start. To recap - these are that:

a) *The coil may be faulty giving an intermittent misfire.*
b) *There may be a damaged wire or loose connection in the low tension circuit.*
c) *The condenser may be short circuiting.*
d) *There may be a mechanical fault in the distributor (broken driving spindle or contact breaker spring).*

17 If the ignition timing is too far retarded, it should be noted that the engine will tend to overheat, and there will be a quite noticeable drop in power. If the engine is overheating and the power is down, and the ignition timing is correct, then the carburettor should be checked, as it is likely that this is where the fault lies.

18 Finally check the setting and adjustment of the fume emission control equipment, particularly the transmission controlled spark system (TCS) described in Chapter 3.

Chapter 5 Clutch

Contents

Clutch - adjustment ... 2	General description ... 1
Clutch - inspection and renovation ... 10	Hydraulic system - bleeding ... 7
Clutch - installation ... 12	Master cylinder - dismantling and reassembly ... 4
Clutch pedal - removal and refitting ... 8	Master cylinder - removal and refitting ... 3
Clutch release bearing - renewal ... 11	Operating cylinder - dismantling and reassembly ... 6
Clutch - removal ... 9	Operating cylinder - removal and refitting ... 5
Fault diagnosis - clutch ... 13	

Specifications

Type ... Single dry plate, diaphragm spring (coil springs on RT 72 S), hydraulically operated

Driven plate
Dimensions:
- Outside diameter ... 7.9 in. (200 mm)
- Inside diameter ... 5.51 in. (140 mm)
- Thickness ... 0.138 in. (3.5 mm)
- Total friction lining area (each side) ... 24.8 in^2 (160 cm^2)
- Number of torsional rubbers ... 4

Master cylinder
- Bore diameter ... 0.6248 in. (15.870 mm)

Operating cylinder
Bore diameter:
- RT 72 S ... 0.8465 in. (21.50 mm)
- RT 83 ... 0.7500 in. (19.05 mm)
- other models ... 0.5906 in. (15.0 mm)

Torque wrench settings

	lb ft	Kg/m
Pressure plate to flywheel bolts	11	1.5
Clutch bellhousing to engine bolts:		
8R series	33	4.5
18R series	50	6.9
Master cylinder reservoir bolt	20	2.8
Master cylinder cap	200	28.0
Release fork pivot ball stud	20	2.8
Clutch/brake pedal cross shaft nut	45	6.2

1 General description

All models except the RT 72 S which has a coil spring type pressure plate, are equipped with a single dry plate diaphragm spring type clutch. Operation is by means of a pendant foot pedal and hydraulic circuit.

Diaphragm spring type clutch

1 The unit comprises a pressure plate assembly which contains the pressure plate, diaphragm spring and fulcrum rings. The assembly is bolted by means of its cover to the rear face of the flywheel.
2 The driven plate (friction disc) is free to slide along the gearbox input shaft and it is held in place between the flywheel and pressure plate faces by the pressure exerted by the diaphragm spring. The friction lining material is rivetted to the driven plate which incorporates a rubber cushioned hub designed to absorb transmission rotational shocks and to assist in ensuring smooth take offs.
3 The circular diaphragm spring assembly is mounted on shouldered pins and held in place in the cover by two fulcrum rings. The spring itself is held in place by three spring steel clips.
4 Depressing the clutch pedal pushes the release bearing mounted on its hub retainer, forward to bear against the fingers of the diaphragm spring. This action causes the diaphragm spring outer edge to deflect and so move the pressure plate rearwards to disengage the pressure plate from the driven plate.
5 When the clutch pedal is released, the diaphragm spring forces the pressure plate into contact with the friction linings of the driven plate and at the same time pushes the driven plate fractionally forward on its splines to ensure full engagement with the flywheel. The driven plate is now firmly sandwiched between the pressure plate and the flywheel and so the drive is taken up.

Chapter 5/Clutch

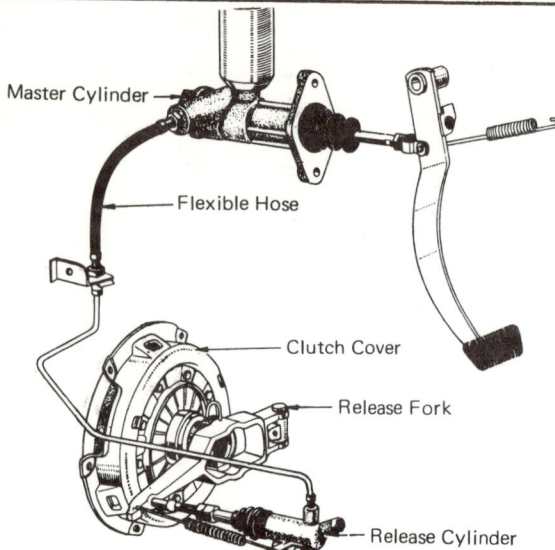

Fig. 5.1 Clutch component layout (diaphragm spring type) (Sec. 1)

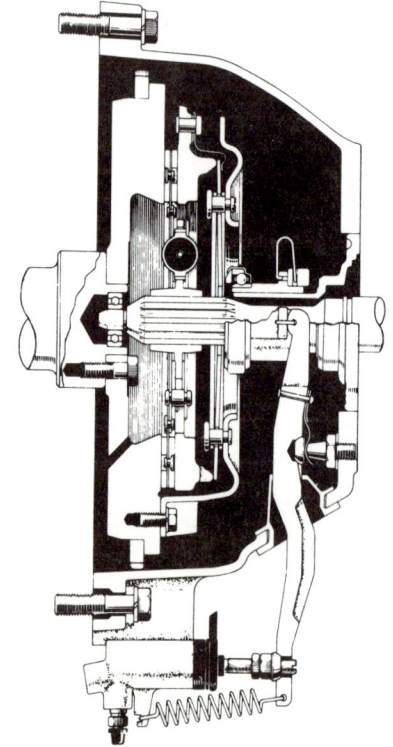

Fig. 5.2 Cross sectional view of diaphragm spring type clutch (Sec. 1)

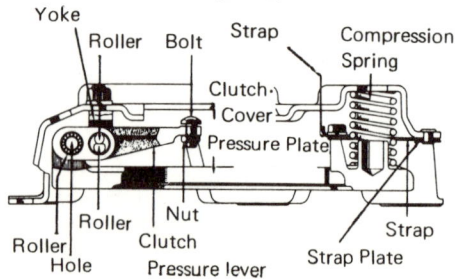

Fig. 5.3 Cross sectional view of coil spring type clutch (Sec. 1)

Coil spring type clutch

6 The operation of this type of clutch mechanism is similar to the diaphragm spring type but it requires rather high pedal pressures to compress the coil springs used in its construction.

2 Clutch - adjustment

1 For correct clutch operation, adjustment must be carried out to the pedal and to the hydraulic operating cylinder. Free-play at the clutch pedal is essential to ensure that the clutch engages and disengages fully, otherwise difficult gear changing or clutch slip can occur.

2 Adjust the pedal return stop bolt until the distance between the centre of the upper surface of the pedal pad and the floor (surface of anti-drumming sheet - carpet removed) is as shown in the following table according to model.

3 Working underneath the vehicle, check that the free movement between the end of the clutch operating cylinder pushrod and the release fork arm is between 0.08 and 0.14 in (2.0 and 3.5 mm). Establish this movement by detaching the release fork arm return spring and gently moving the arm back and forth. If necessary, adjust the clearance by loosening the locknut on the pushrod and rotating the pushrod.

4 Now measure the clutch pedal free-movement which should be in accordance with the figure shown in the table according to model. If it is not, loosen the locknut on the master cylinder pushrod and rotate the pushrod until the free-movement is correct.

5 Tighten all locknuts without altering the adjustment and reconnect the return springs.

Setting data

	All models with 8R series engines	All models with 18R series engines
Pedal height from floor (except RT 72S)	6in (152.5mm)	6.6in (168.0mm)
Pedal height from floor (RT 72S)		
Pedal free movement	0.9 to 2.2in (22.0 to 55.0mm)	0.04 to 0.28in (1.0 to 7.0mm)

3 Master cylinder - removal and refitting

1 Disconnect the master cylinder pushrod from the clutch pedal.

2 Disconnect the flexible hydraulic hose at its junction with the rigid fluid line. Plug or cap both the open hoses to prevent dirt entering the system.

3 Unbolt the master cylinder from the engine rear bulkhead taking care not to spill any hydraulic fluid onto the vehicle paintwork.

4 Refitting is a reversal of removal but after installation is complete, check the pedal free-movement as described in the preceding Section and bleed the hydraulic system (Section 7).

4 Master cylinder - dismantling and reassembly

1 The design of the master cylinder varies between models and date of manufacture but the operations described in this Section apply to all types.

2 Remove the reservoir cap and float and tip out the fluid.

3 Operate the pushrod two or three times to eject any fluid from the cylinder.

4 Unscrew the reservoir securing bolt (accessible within the reservoir) and remove the reservoir.

5 Unscrew and remove the flexible hose from the master cylinder.

6 Peel back the rubber boot from the end of the cylinder and remove the circlip.

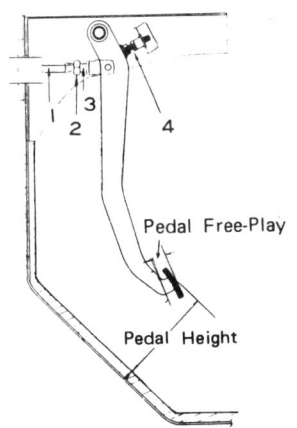

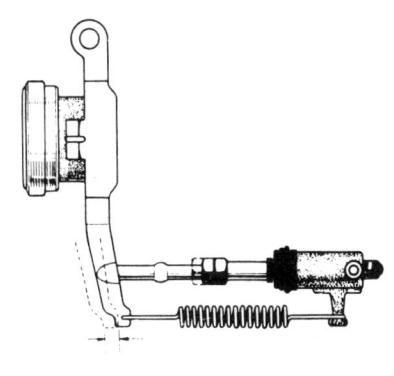

Fig. 5.5 Release fork arm free-movement diagram (Sec. 2)

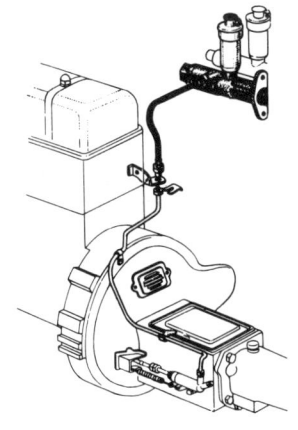

Fig. 5.4 Clutch pedal adjustment diagram (Sec. 2)

1 Master cylinder pushrod
2 Locknut 3 Clevis
4 Pedal stop

Fig. 5.6 Master cylinder installation and connections (Sec. 3)

Fig. 5.7 Exploded view of the clutch master cylinder (Sec. 4)

1 Reservoir cap
2 Float
3 Reservoir securing bolt
4 Washer
5 Reservoir
6 End cap
7 Gasket
8 Cup seal
9 Spacer
10 Fluid

11 Body
12 Spring
13 Piston
14 Seal
15 Washer
16 Circlip
17 Flexible boot
18 Pushrod
19 Clevis

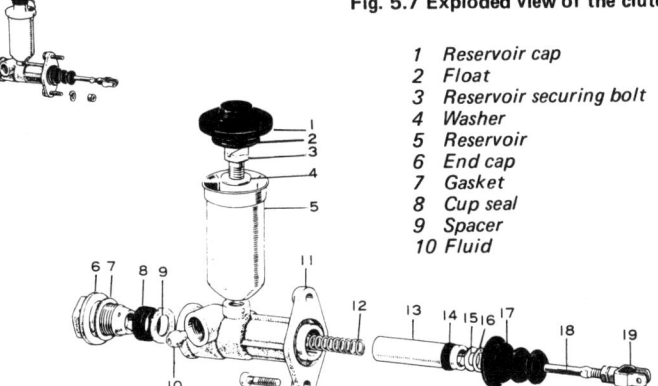

Fig. 5.8 Exploded view of alternative type master cylinder (Sec. 4)

1 Reservoir cap
2 Float
3 Reservoir securing bolt
4 Washer
5 Reservoir

6 Body
7 Inlet valve
8 Spring
9 Inlet valve casing
10 Connecting rod

11 Spring
12 Spring retainer
13 Piston
14 Cup seal
15 Plate

16 Circlip
17 Flexible boot
18 Pushrod
19 Clevis

7 On master cylinders with a threaded end cap at the forward end, secure the master cylinder body in a vice and unscrew it.
8 Extract the piston/seal assembly from the cylinder.
9 Wash all components in clean fluid and discard all rubber seals. If there are any 'bright' wear areas on the piston or cylinder bore surfaces, renew the complete unit.
10 If the components are in good condition, obtain a repair kit which will contain all the necessary seals and other items requiring renewal.
11 Reassembly is a reversal of dismantling but locate the rubber seals using the fingers only, to avoid damaging them, and noting that their lips face the cap end of the master cylinder. Dip each component in clean hydraulic fluid before fitting it into the cylinder. Tighten the end cap and reservoir securing bolt to the torque specified in Specifications.

5 Operating cylinder - removal and refitting

1 Disconnect the hydraulic pipe at its union on the operating cylinder body.
2 Disconnect the return spring.
3 Unscrew and remove the securing bolts and withdraw the cylinder.
4 Refitting is a reversal of removal but check the pushrod to release arm free-movement after the hydraulic system has been bled (Sections 2 and 7).

6 Operating cylinder - dismantling and reassembly

1 The design of the operating cylinder may vary slightly according to model and date of manufacture but the operations described in this Section apply to all types.
2 Depress the pushrod two or three times to eject any hydraulic fluid and then pull out the pushrod assembly complete with rubber boot.
3 Eject the piston assembly by applying air pressure at the fluid inlet or by tapping the end of the cylinder on a block of wood.
4 Wash components in clean hydraulic fluid and discard all rubber seals. If there are any 'bright' wear areas on the piston or cylinder bore surfaces, renew the complete unit.
5 If the components are in good condition, obtain a repair kit which will contain all the necessary seals and other items requiring renewal.
6 Reassembly is a reversal of dismantling but manipulate the seals into position using the fingers only to avoid damaging them. Dip each component in clean hydraulic fluid before inserting it into the cylinder.

7 Hydraulic system - bleeding

1 Gather together a clean glass jar, a length of rubber tubing which fits tightly over the bleed nipple on the operating cylinder, a tin of hydraulic brake fluid and someone to help.
2 Check that the master cylinder is full. If it is not, fill it and cover the bottom two inches of the jar with hydraulic fluid.
3 Remove the rubber dust cap from the bleed nipple on the operating cylinder, and with a suitable spanner open the bleed nipple approximately three quarters of a turn.
4 Place one end of the tube securely over the nipple and insert the other end into the jar so that its open end will remain submerged in the fluid.
5 Have your assistant depress the clutch pedal to the limit of its travel and then remove his foot so that the pedal can return to its normal position without being obstructed.
6 Repeat this operation until no more air can be seen being expelled from the end of the tube submerged in the jar. Keep the reservoir well topped-up with fluid to prevent air being drawn into the system again.
7 With the pedal fully depressed, tighten the bleed nipple.
8 Refit the dust cap. Always use new hydraulic fluid for topping-up the reservoir, which has been stored in an air tight tin and has not been shaken during the preceding 24 hours. Always discard fluid which has been bled from the system or retain it for bleed jar purposes only.

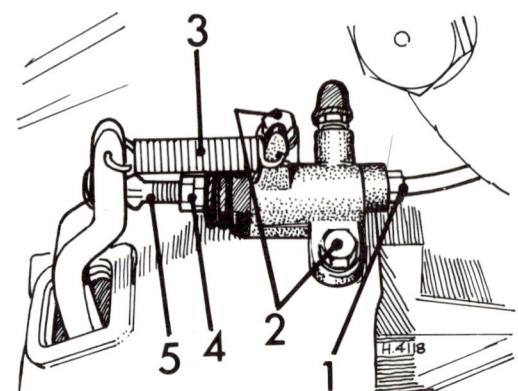

Fig. 5.9 Clutch operating cylinder removal points (Sec. 5)

1 Fluid pipe union
2 Securing bolts
3 Return spring
4 Locknut
5 Pushrod

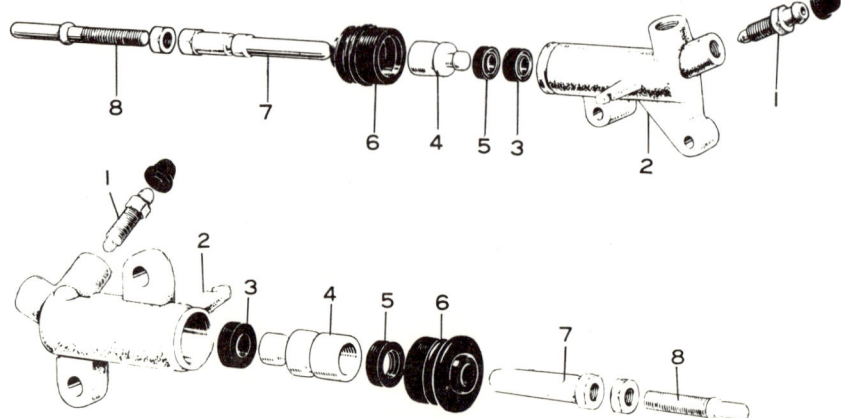

Fig. 5.10 Alternative types of clutch operating cylinders (Sec. 6)

1 Bleed nipple
2 Body
3 Cup seal
4 Piston
5 Cup seal
6 Flexible boot
7 and 8 pushrod assembly

Chapter 5/Clutch

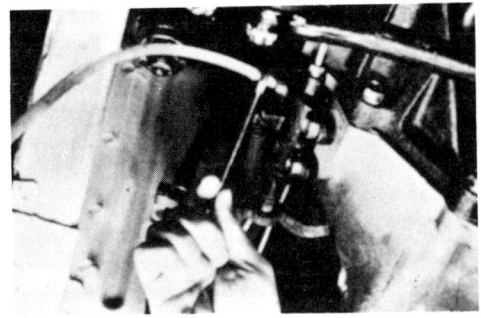

Fig. 5.11 Bleeding the clutch hydraulic system (Sec. 7)

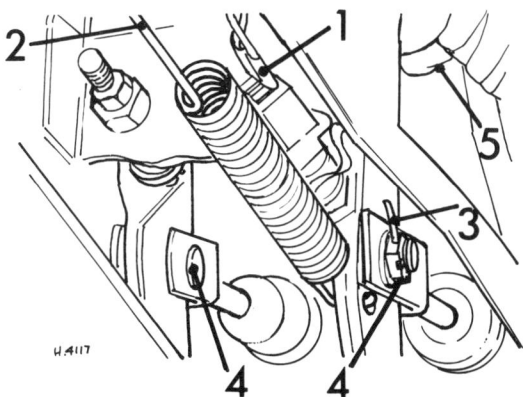

Fig. 5.12 Clutch pedal removal points (Sec. 8)

1 Stop lamp switch
2 Pedal return spring
3 Split pin
4 Clevis
5 Cross-shaft nut

8 Clutch pedal - removal and refitting

1 The clutch and brake pedals operate on a common cross-shaft and so they will be dismantled together.
2 Disconnect the leads from the stop lamp switch.
3 Detach the pedal return springs.
4 Withdraw the split pins and cotter pins which connect the brake and clutch master cylinder pushrods to the pedals.
5 Unscrew and remove the nut from the end of the cross-shaft and withdraw the cross-shaft from the clutch pedal side.
6 Examine all bushes and components for wear and renew as necessary.
7 Refitting is a reversal of removal but apply grease to the cross-shaft and pedal bushes and tighten the nut on the cross--shaft to a torque of 45 lb/ft (6.2 kg/m).
8 Check the pedal heights (Section 2 of this Chapter and Section 23 of Chapter 9).

9 Clutch - removal

1 Access to the clutch assembly and to the clutch release mechanism (Section 11) may be gained in one of two ways; (i) by removing the gearbox leaving the engine in position in the vehicle as described in Chapter 6 or (ii) by removing the engine/gearbox as one unit (at the time of major overhaul) and then separating the gearbox from the engine (Chapter 1).
2 Scribe a mating line from the clutch cover to the flywheel to ensure identical positioning on replacement and then remove the cover to the rear face of the flywheel. Unscrew the bolts diagonally half a turn at a time to prevent distortion to the cover flange.
3 With all the bolts and spring washers removed lift the clutch assembly off the locating dowels. The driven plate or clutch disc may fall out at this stage as it is not attached to either the clutch cover assembly or the flywheel.

10 Clutch - inspection and renovation

1 Examine the clutch disc friction linings for wear and loose rivets and the disc for rim distortion, cracks, perished torsion rubbers and worn splines. The surface of the friction linings may be highly glazed, but as long as the clutch material pattern can be clearly seen this is satisfactory. Compare the amount of lining

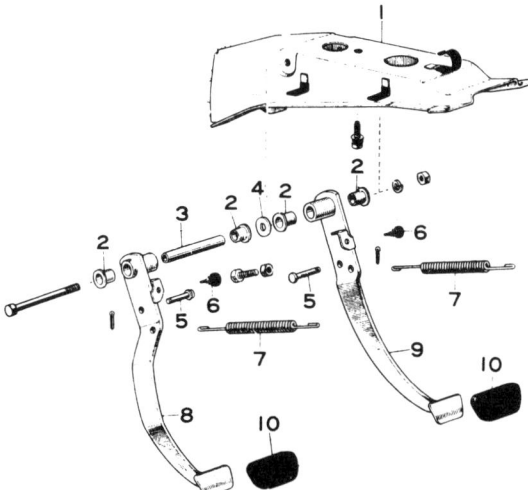

Fig. 5.13 Exploded view of the clutch/brake pedal assembly (Sec. 8)

1 Bracket
2 Bush
3 Spacer
4 Washer
5 Clevis
6 Rubber buffer
7 Pedal return springs
8 Clutch pedal
9 Brake pedal
10 Pedal pad

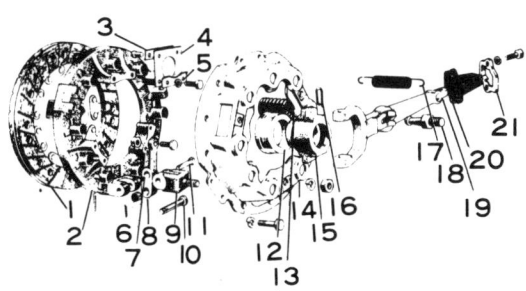

Fig. 5.14 Exploded view of coil spring type clutch

1 Driven plate
2 Pressure plate
3, 4 and 5 Strap components
6 and 7 Rollers
8 Lever
9 Lever yoke
10 Bolt
11 Pin
12 Release bearing
13 Spring
14 Cover
15 Bearing hub
16 Release bearing clip
17 Return spring
18 Ball pivot stud
19 Release fork arm
20 Dust excluding
21 Boot retaining plate

Chapter 5/Clutch

wear with a new clutch disc at the stores in your local garage, and if the linings are more than three quarters worn replace the disc.

2 It is always best to renew the clutch driven plate as an assembly to preclude further trouble but if it is wished to merely renew the linings, the rivets should be drilled out and not knocked out with a punch. The manufacturers do not advise that only the linings are renewed and personal experience dictates that it is far more satisfactory to renew the driven plate complete than to try and economise by only fitting new friction linings.

3 Check the machined faces of the flywheel and the pressure

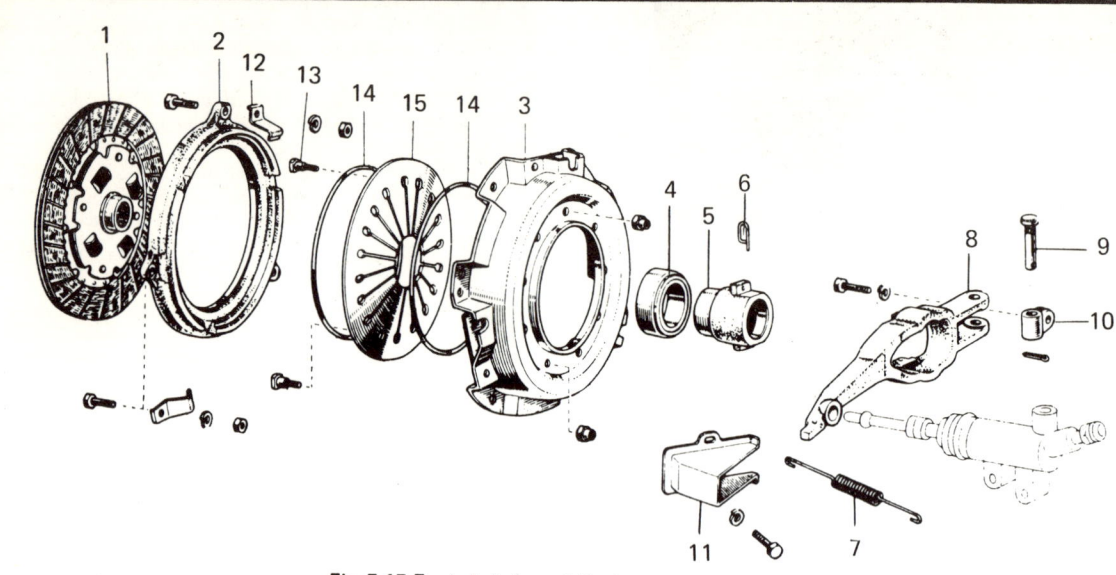

Fig. 5.15 Exploded view of diaphragm spring type clutch (Sec. 10)

1 Driven plate	5 Release bearing hub	9 Pin	13 Bolt
2 Pressure plate	6 Release bearing clip	10 Release fork support	14 Ring
3 Cover	7 Return spring	11 Dust excluder	15 Diaphragm spring
4 Release bearing	8 Release fork	12 Spring	

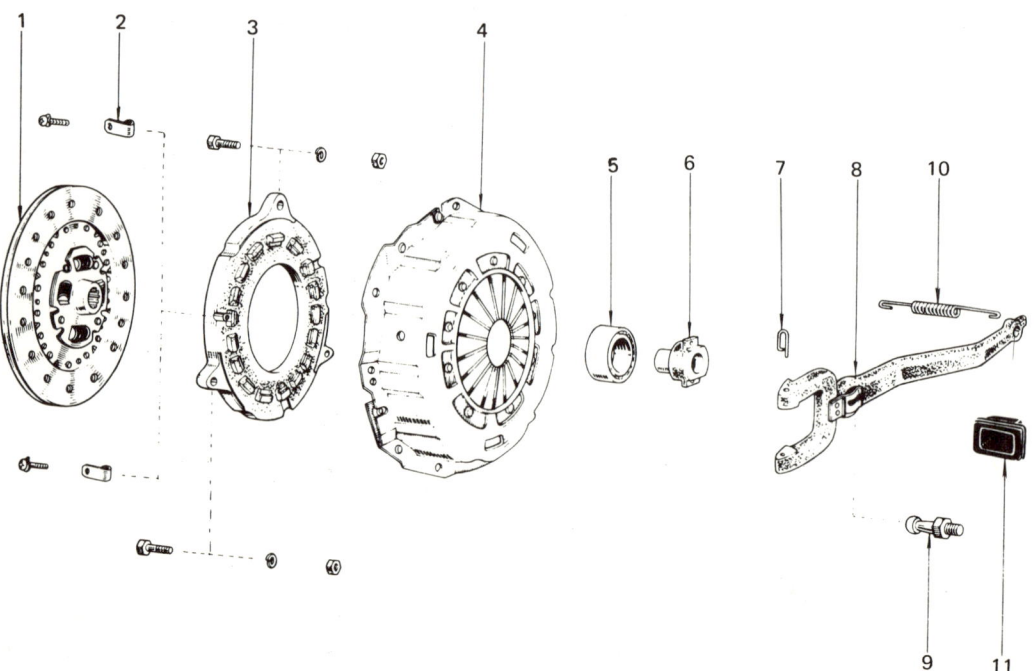

Fig. 5.16 Exploded view of alternative type diaphragm spring clutch unit (Sec. 10)

1 Driven plate	4 Cover	7 Release bearing clip	10 Return spring
2 Spring	5 Release bearing	8 Release fork	11 Flexible boot
3 Pressure plate	6 Release bearing hub	9 Ball pivot stud	

Chapter 5/Clutch

Fig. 5.17 Clutch release bearing details (Sec. 11)

1 Release bearing retaining clips 3 Release fork
2 Release bearing

12.2 Installing clutch assembly to flywheel

plate. If either are grooved they should be machined until smooth, or renewed.

4 If the pressure plate is cracked or split it is essential that an exchange unit is fitted, also if the pressure of the diaphragm (or coil springs) is suspect. It is not practical to dismantle the pressure plate assembly as it will have been accurately set up and balanced to very fine limits.

5 If a new clutch disc is being fitted it is a false economy not to renew the release bearing at the same time. This will preclude having to replace it at a later date when wear on the clutch linings is still very small.

Check the release bearing for smoothness or operation. There should be no harshness and no slackness in it. It should spin reasonably freely bearing in mind it has been pre-packed with grease.

11 Clutch release bearing - renewal

1 From the open front of the clutch bellhousing, unscrew and remove the release fork pivot bolt or alternatively if so designed, slide the release fork sideways off its pivot ball stud.
2 Detach the clips whcih secure the bearing/hub assembly to the release fork.
3 Using a distance piece of suitable diameter, press the hub from the bearing inner track and press on the new one ensuring that it seats fully on the hub and that it is fitted the right way round: contact plate facing the clutch release fingers.
4 Refitting is a reversal of removal but use new clips to retain the bearing/hub to the release fork and check the condition of the release fork arm rubber dust excluder at the clutch bellhousing aperture.
5 Finally check the condition of the input shaft spigot bearing which is located in the centre of the flywheel. If it is worn, remove it and fit a new one.

12 Clutch - installation

1 Before the driven plate and pressure plate assembly can be refitted to the flywheel, a centralising guide tool must be obtained or made up. This may be either an old input shaft from a dismantled gearbox or a stepped mandrel similar to the one shown in photo 12.4.
2 Locate the driven plate against the face of the flywheel ensuring that its flatter side is against the flywheel. (photo)

12.4 Centralising the clutch

3 Offer up the pressure plate assembly to the flywheel aligning the marks made prior to dismantling and insert the retaining bolt finger-tight only. Where a new pressure plate assembly is being fitted, locate it to the flywheel in a similar relative position to the original by reference to the index marking and dowel positions.
4 Insert the guide tool through the splined hub of the driven plate so that the end of the tool locates in the flywheel spigot bush. This action of the guide tool will centralise the driven plate by causing it to move in a sideways direction. (photo)

Insert and remove the guide tool two or three times to ensure that the driven plate is fully centralised and then tighten the pressure plate securing bolts a turn at a time and in a diametrically opposite sequence, to a torque of 11 lb/ft (1.5 kg/m) to prevent distortion of the pressure plate cover.
5 Install the gearbox (Chapter 6) or connect it to the engine and install the engine/gearbox (Chapter 1).
6 When installation is complete, check the pedal and release arm free-movement and adjust to Specification (see Section 2 of this Chapter).

For fault diagnosis see next page

13 Fault diagnosis - clutch

Symptom	Reason/s
Judder when taking up drive	Loose engine or gearbox mountings
	Badly worn friction surfaces or contaminated with oil
	Worn splines on gearbox input shaft or driven plate hub
	Worn input shaft spigot bush in flywheel
Clutch spin (failure to disengage) so that gears cannot be meshed	Incorrect release bearing to diaphragm spring due to rust. May occur after vehicle standing idle for long period
	Damaged or misaligned pressure plate assembly
	Fault in hydraulic system
Clutch slip (increase in engine speed does not result in increase in vehicle road speed - particularly on gradients)	Incorrect release bearing to diaphragm spring finger clearance
	Friction surfaces worn out or oil contaminated
Noise evident on depressing clutch pedal	Dry, worn or damaged release bearing
	Insufficient pedal free-travel
	Weak or broken pedal return spring
	Weak or broken clutch release lever return spring.
	Excessive play between driven plate hub splines and input shaft splines
Noise evident as clutch pedal released	Distorted driven plate.
	Broken or weak driven plate cushion coil springs.
	Insufficient pedal free travel
	Weak or broken clutch pedal return spring
	Weak or broken release lever return spring
	Distorted or worn input shaft
	Release bearing loose on retainer hub.

Chapter 6
Manual gearbox and automatic transmission

Contents

Part 1: Manual gearbox

Countershaft and reverse gear assemblies (three speed gearbox type N30/31) - servicing	8
Countershaft and reverse gear assemblies (four speed gearbox type W.40) - servicing	18
Countershaft and reverse gear assemblies (five speed gearbox) - servicing	25
Fault diagnosis - manual gearbox	28
Gearbox (three speed type TC1) - dismantling and examination of components	3
Gearbox (three speed type N30/31) - dismantling into major assemblies	5
Gearbox (four speed type SS1) - dismantling and inspection of components	13
Gearbox (four speed type W.40) - dismantling into major assemblies	15
Gearbox (five speed type) - dismantling into major assemblies	22
Gearbox (three speed type) - removal and installation ...	2
Gearbox (four speed type) - removal and installation ...	12
Gearbox (five speed type) - removal and installation ...	21
Gearbox (three speed type TC1) - reassembly	4
Gearbox (three speed type N30/31) - reassembly	10
Gearbox (four speed type SS1) - reassembly	14
Gearbox (four speed type W.40) - reassembly	20
Gearbox (five speed type) - reassembly	27
General description - manual gearbox	1
Input shaft (three speed gearbox type N30/31) - servicing	7
Input shaft (four speed gearbox type W.40) - servicing ...	17
Input shaft (five speed gearbox) - servicing	24
Mainshaft (three speed gearbox type N30/31) - servicing ...	6
Mainshaft (four speed gearbox type W.40) - servicing ...	16
Mainshaft (five speed gearbox) - servicing	23
Oil seals (three speed gearbox type N30/31) - renewal ...	9
Oil seals (four speed gearbox type W.40) - renewal ...	19
Oil seals (five speed gearbox) - renewal	26
Steering column gearchange - servicing and adjustment ...	11

Part 2: Automatic transmission

Automatic transmission - removal and installation	42
Brake band (A30 type auto transmission) - adjustment ...	39
Extension housing oil seal (A30/A40 type auto transmission - renewal	40
Fault diagnosis - automatic transmission	43
General description - automatic transmission	29
'Kick-down' rod (Two speed auto. transmission) - adjustment	33
Low speed brake band (Two speed auto. transmission) - adjustment	34
Maintenance - automatic transmission	30
Reverse brake band (Two speed auto. transmission) - adjustment	35
Selector linkage (A30 type auto. transmission) - adjustment	36
Selector linkage (Two speed auto. transmission) - adjustment	31
Starter inhibitor/reverse lamp switch (A30 type auto. transmission) - adjustment	37
Starter inhibitor switch (Two speed auto-transmission) - adjustment	32
Throttle link connecting rod (A30 type auto. transmission) - adjustment and testing	38

Specifications

Manual gearboxes

Gearbox types	3, 4 or 5 forward speeds (all with synchromesh) and one reverse.

Identification

Type TC1	Three forward speeds and reverse, having removable top cover plate and side mounted selector mechanism
Type N30/31	Three forward speeds and reverse, having removable bottom cover plate and side mounted selector mechanism
Type SS1	Four forward speeds and reverse, having side mounted selector mechanism
Type W.40	Four forward speeds and reverse, having remote control floor mounted gearshift
Type W50	Five forward speeds and reverse, having remote control floor mounted gearshift.

Ratios
Three speed (Type TC1):

	RT 66/66v only	other models
1st	3.647 : 1	3.337 : 1
2nd	1.807 : 1	1.653 : 1
3rd	1.000 : 1	1.000 : 1
Reverse	4.863 : 1	4.449 : 1

Three speed (Type N30/31):

	Car	Estate wagon
1st	3.337 : 1	3.647 : 1
2nd	1.653 : 1	1.807 : 1
3rd	1.000 : 1	1.000 : 1
Reverse	4.449 : 1	4.863 : 1

Four speed (Type SS1):
- 1st ... 3.673 : 1
- 2nd ... 2.114 : 1
- 3rd ... 1.403 : 1
- 4th ... 1.000 : 1
- Reverse ... 4.183 : 1

Four speed (Type W.40):
- 1st ... 3.579 : 1
- 2nd ... 2.081 : 1
- 3rd ... 1.397 : 1
- 4th ... 1.000 : 1
- Reverse ... 4.399 : 1

Five speed (Type W50):
- 1st ... 3.287 : 1
- 2nd ... 2.043 : 1
- 3rd ... 1.394 : 1
- 4th ... 1.000 : 1
- 5th ... 0.853 : 1
- Reverse ... 4.039 : 1

Capacities (approx)
- Four speed ... 2.4 US qts, 2.9 Imp pints
- Five speed ... 2.7 US qts, 3.25 Imp pints

Tolerances

Three speed gearbox (Type TC1)

Countershaft gear endfloat ... 0.0020 to 0.0060 in. (0.05 to 0.15 mm)

Thrust washer thickness availability:
- 0.0453 to 0.0472 in. (1.15 to 1.20 mm)
- 0.0472 to 0.0492 in. (1.20 to 1.25 mm)
- 0.0492 to 0.0512 in. (1.25 to 1.30 mm)
- 0.0512 to 0.0532 in. (1.30 to 1.35 mm)
- 0.0532 to 0.0551 in. (1.35 to 1.40 mm)
- 0.0551 to 0.0571 in. (1.40 to 1.45 mm)
- 0.0571 to 0.0590 in. (1.45 to 1.50 mm)
- 0.0590 to 0.0610 in. (1.50 to 1.55 mm)
- 0.0610 to 0.0630 in. (1.55 to 1.60 mm)
- 0.0630 to 0.0650 in. (1.60 to 1.65 mm)
- **0.0650 to 0.0669 in. (1.65 to 1.70 mm)**
- 0.0669 to 0.0689 in. (1.70 to 1.75 mm)
- 0.0689 to 0.0709 in. (1.75 to 1.80 mm)
- 0.0709 to 0.0728 in. (1.80 to 1.85 mm)
- 0.0728 to 0.0748 in. (1.85 to 1.90 mm)
- 0.0748 to 0.0768 in. (1.90 to 1.95 mm)

First and second gear endfloat:
- Standard ... 0.0020 to 0.0060 in. (0.05 to 0.15 mm)
- Limit ... 0.008 in. (0.2 mm)

Circlip thickness availability for input shaft (bearing outer track)
- 0.0906 to 0.0953 in. (2.30 to 2.42 mm)
- 0.0953 to 0.1012 in. (2.43 to 2.57 mm)

Circlip thickness availability for mainshaft (front):
- 0.0744 to 0.0764 in. (1.89 to 1.94 mm)
- 0.0768 to 0.0787 in. (1.95 to 2.00 mm)
- 0.0791 to 0.0811 in. (2.01 to 2.06 mm)
- 0.0815 to 0.0835 in. (2.07 to 2.12 mm)
- 0.0839 to 0.0858 in. (2.13 to 2.18 mm)
- 0.0862 to 0.0882 in. (2.19 to 2.24 mm)
- 0.0886 to 0.0906 in. (2.25 to 2.30 mm)
- 0.0909 to 0.0929 in. (2.31 to 2.36 mm)
- 0.0933 to 0.0953 in. (2.37 to 2.42 mm)

Chapter 6/Manual gearbox and automatic transmission

Circlip thickness availability for mainshaft (rear):

    0.0866 to 0.0886 in. (2.20 to 2.25 mm)
    0.0886 to 0.0906 in. (2.25 to 2.30 mm)
    0.0906 to 0.0925 in. (2.30 to 2.35 mm)
    0.0925 to 0.0945 in. (2.35 to 2.40 mm)
    0.0945 to 0.0965 in. (2.40 to 2.45 mm)
    0.0965 to 0.0984 in. (2.45 to 2.50 mm)

Circlip thickness availability for mainshaft bearing outer track:

    0.0551 to 0.0590 in. (1.40 to 1.50 mm)
    0.0630 to 0.0670 in. (1.60 to 1.70 mm)

Bush length availability for 1st gear:

    1.2618 to 1.2638 in. (32.05 to 32.10 mm)
    1.2638 to 1.2657 in. (32.10 to 32.15 mm)

Bush length availability for 2nd gear:

    1.3819 to 1.3839 in. (35.10 to 35.15 mm)
    1.3839 to 1.3858 in. (35.15 to 35.20 mm)

Three speed gearbox (Type N30/31)

Countershaft gear endfloat ... ...   0.0047 to 0.0114 in. (0.12 to 0.29 mm)

Circlip thickness availability for countershaft:

    0.0882 to 0.0902 in. (2.24 to 2.29 mm)
    0.0906 to 0.0925 in. (2.30 to 2.35 mm)
    0.0929 to 0.0949 in. (2.36 to 2.41 mm)
    0.0953 to 0.0972 in. (2.42 to 2.47 mm)
    0.0976 to 0.0996 in. (2.48 to 2.53 mm)
    0.1000 to 0.1020 in. (2.54 to 2.59 mm)

1st, 2nd and reverse gear endfloat:
    Standard ... ...   0.0039 to 0.0098 in. (0.10 to 0.25 mm)
    Limit ... ...   0.0118 in. (0.30 mm)

Circlip thickness availability for input shaft:

    0.0807 to 0.0827 in. (2.05 to 2.10 mm)
    0.0827 to 0.0846 in. (2.10 to 2.15 mm)
    0.0846 to 0.0866 in. (2.15 to 2.20 mm)
    0.0866 to 0.0886 in. (2.20 to 2.25 mm)
    0.0886 to 0.0906 in. (2.25 to 2.30 mm)
    0.0906 to 0.0925 in. (2.30 to 2.35 mm)

Circlip thickness availability for mainshaft:

    0.0531 to 0.0571 in. (1.35 to 1.45 mm)
    0.0571 to 0.0610 in. (1.45 to 1.55 mm)
    0.0610 to 0.0650 in. (1.55 to 1.65 mm)
    0.0650 to 0.0689 in. (1.65 to 1.75 mm)
    0.0689 to 0.0728 in. (1.75 to 1.85 mm)

Reverse idler gear thrust collar length availability:

    1.1197 to 1.1220 in. (28.44 to 28.50 mm)
    1.1276 to 1.1299 in. (28.64 to 28.70 mm)
    1.1354 to 1.1378 in. (28.84 to 28.90 mm)
    1.1433 to 1.1457 in. (29.04 to 29.10 mm)

Four speed gearbox (Type SS1)

Countershaft gear endfloat ... ...   0.0020 to 0.0060 in. (0.05 to 0.15 mm)
Countershaft thrust washer availability ... ...   as 3 speed type TC1) except smallest and largest sizes not supplied

1st, 2nd and 3rd gear endfloat.
    Standard ... ...   0.004 to 0.008 in. (0.10 to 0.20 mm)
    Limit ... ...   0.010 in. (0.26 mm)
Circlip thickness availability for input shaft (bearing outer track)   as three speed gearbox (Type TC1)
Circlip thickness availability for mainshaft (front):

    0.0906 to 0.0925 in. (2.30 to 2.35 mm)
    0.0925 to 0.0945 in. (2.35 to 2.40 mm)
    0.0945 to 0.0965 in. (2.40 to 2.45 mm)
    0.0965 to 0.0984 in. (2.45 to 2.50 mm)
    0.0984 to 0.1004 in. (2.50 to 2.55 mm)
    0.1004 to 0.1024 in. (2.55 to 2.60 mm)
    0.1024 to 0.1043 in. (2.60 to 2.65 mm)
    0.1043 to 0.1063 in. (2.65 to 2.70 mm)
    0.1063 to 0.1083 in. (2.70 to 2.75 mm)
    0.1083 to 0.1102 in. (2.75 to 2.80 mm)

Circlip thickness availability for mainshaft (rear) ... ...   as 3 speed gearbox (Type TC1)
Circlip thickness availability for mainshaft bearing outer track   as 3 speed gearbox (Type TC1)
Bush length availability for 1st gear:

    1.3405 to 1.3425 in. (33.95 to 34.00 mm)
    1.3425 to 1.3445 in. (34.00 to 34.05 mm)

Bush length availabilty for 2nd gear:

    1.2618 to 1.2638 in. (32.05 to 32.10 mm)
    1.2638 to 1.2657 in. (32.10 to 32.15 mm)

Bush length availability for 3rd gear:

    1.3800 to 1.3819 in. (35.05 to 35.10 mm)
    1.3819 to 1.3839 in. (35.10 to 35.15 mm)

Four speed gearbox (Type W.40)

1st, 2nd and 3rd gear endfloat:
    Standard ... 0.0059 to 0.0098 in. (0.15 to 0.25 mm)
    Limit ... 0.0118 in. (0.30 mm)
Circlip thickness availability for input shaft ... as for three speed gearbox (Type N30/31)
Circlip thickness availability for mainshaft (front):

    0.0787 to 0.0807 in. (2.00 to 2.05 mm)
    0.0807 to 0.0827 in. (2.05 to 2.10 mm)
    0.0827 to 0.0846 in. (2.10 to 2.15 mm)
    0.0846 to 0.0866 in. (2.15 to 2.20 mm)
    0.0866 to 0.0886 in. (2.20 to 2.25 mm)
    0.0886 to 0.0906 in. (2.25 to 2.30 mm)

Circlip thickness availability for mainshaft (rear):

    0.0807 to 0.0827 in. (2.05 to 2.10 mm)
    0.0827 to 0.0846 in. (2.10 to 2.15 mm)
    0.0846 to 0.0866 in. (2.15 to 2.20 mm)
    0.0866 to 0.0886 in. (2.20 to 2.25 mm)
    0.0886 to 0.0906 in. (2.25 to 2.30 mm)
    0.0906 to 0.0925 in. (2.30 to 2.35 mm)
    0.0925 to 0.0945 in. (2.35 to 2.40 mm)
    0.0945 to 0.0965 in. (2.40 to 2.45 mm)
    0.0965 to 0.0984 in. (2.45 to 2.50 mm)
    0.0984 to 0.1004 in. (2.50 to 2.55 mm)
    0.1004 to 0.1024 in. (2.55 to 2.60 mm)

Countershaft gear spacer thickness availability:

    0.0807 to 0.0846 in. (2.05 to 2.15 mm)
    0.0874 to 0.0906 in. (2.22 to 2.30 mm)
    0.0925 to 0.0965 in. (2.35 to 2.45 mm)
    0.0984 to 0.1024 in. (2.50 to 2.60 mm)

Five speed gearbox (Type W50)

1st, 2nd, 3rd and reverse idler gear endfloat ... 0.0059 to 0.0098 in. (0.15 to 0.25 mm)
5th gear endfloat ... 0.0039 to 0.0098 in. (0.10 to 0.25 mm)
    Limit ... 0.0118 in. (0.30 mm)
Circlip thickness availability for input shaft ... as for three speed gearbox (Type N30/31)
Circlip thickness availability for mainshaft (front) ... as for four speed gearbox (Type W.40)
Circlip thickness availability for mainshaft (fifth gear):

    0.0744 to 0.0764 in. (1.89 to 1.94 mm)
    0.0768 to 0.0787 in. (1.95 to 2.00 mm)
    0.0791 to 0.0811 in. (2.01 to 2.06 mm)
    0.0815 to 0.0835 in. (2.07 to 2.12 mm)
    0.0839 to 0.0858 in. (2.13 to 2.18 mm)
    0.0862 to 0.0882 in. (2.19 to 2.24 mm)
    0.0886 to 0.0906 in. (2.25 to 2.30 mm)
    0.0909 to 0.0929 in. (2.31 to 2.36 mm)
    0.0933 to 0.0953 in. (2.37 to 2.42 mm)
    0.0957 to 0.0976 in. (2.43 to 2.48 mm)
    0.0980 to 0.1000 in. (2.49 to 2.54 mm)
    0.1004 to 0.1024 in. (2.55 to 2.60 mm)
    0.1028 to 0.1047 in. (2.61 to 2.66 mm)

Circlip availability for countershaft (rear):

    0.0551 to 0.0571 in. (1.40 to 1.45 mm)
    0.0630 to 0.0650 in. (1.60 to 1.65 mm)
    0.0709 to 0.0728 in. (1.80 to 1.85 mm)
    0.0787 to 0.0807 in. (2.00 to 2.05 mm)

Countershaft gear spacer thickness availability:

    0.0807 to 0.0846 in. (2.05 to 2.15 mm)
    0.0874 to 0.0906 in. (2.22 to 2.30 mm)
    0.0925 to 0.0965 in. (2.35 to 2.45 mm)
    0.0984 to 0.1024 in. (2.50 to 2.60 mm)

Chapter 6/Manual gearbox and automatic transmission

Automatic transmission

Ratios

Toyoglide two speed:
- High ... 1.0 : 1
- Low ... 1.82 : 1
- Reverse ... 2.048 : 1

A30 type:
- 1st speed ... 2.400 : 1
- 2nd speed ... 1.479 : 1
- 3rd speed ... 1.000 : 1
- Reverse ... 1.920 : 1

A40 type:
- 1st speed ... 2.450 : 1
- 2nd speed ... 1.450 : 1
- 3rd speed ... 1.000 : 1
- Reverse ... 2.220 : 1

Capacities

- Two speed ... 5.9 Imp qts, 7.2 U.S. qts, 6.8 litres
- A30 ... 5.6 Imp qts, 6.8 U.S. qts, 6.4 litres
- A40 ... 5.1 Imp qts, 6.1 U.S. qts, 5.8 litres

Torque wrench settings

	lb ft	Kg/m
Manual gearbox		
Clutch bellhousing to engine bolts	33	4.5
Clutch bellhousing to gearbox bolts	50	6.9
Extension housing bolts	30	4.1
3 speed - type TC1		
Mainshaft front bearing retainer bolts	5	0.7
Shift lever housing to gearbox bolts	11	1.5
Gearbox cover bolts	5	0.7
3 speed - type N30/31		
Detent plug	35	4.8
Mainshaft rear nut	72	10.0
Mainshaft front nut	58	8.5
4 speed - type SS1		
Gearbox cover bolts	15	2.1
Shift lever housing bolts	22	3.0
4 and 5 speed - types W.40 and W50		
Detent plug	22	3.0
Mainshaft rear bearing retainer bolts	15	2.1
Reverse gear shift arm pivot nut	11	1.5
Restrictor pin	30	4.1

Automatic transmission

	Toyoglide Two speed	Type A30	Type A40
Side cover bolts	12 lb/ft 1.6 kg/m	—	—
Drive plate bolts to crankshaft	47 lb/ft 6.5 kg/m	45 lb/ft 6.2 kg/m	43 lb/ft 5.9 kg/m
Driveplate to torque converter bolts	9.5 lb/ft 1.3 kg/m	32 lb/ft 4.4 kg/m	15 lb/ft 2.1 kg/m
Torque converter drain plug	9.5 lb/ft 1.3 kg/m	—	—
Torque converter housing to engine bolts	25 lb/ft 3.5 kg/m	55 lb/ft 7.6 kg/m	55 lb/ft 7.6 kg/m
Oil pan bolts	—	8 lb/ft 1.1 kg/m	8 lb/ft 1.1 kg/m
Extension housing bolts	—	14.5 lb/ft 2.0 kg/m	30 lb/ft 4.1 kg/m

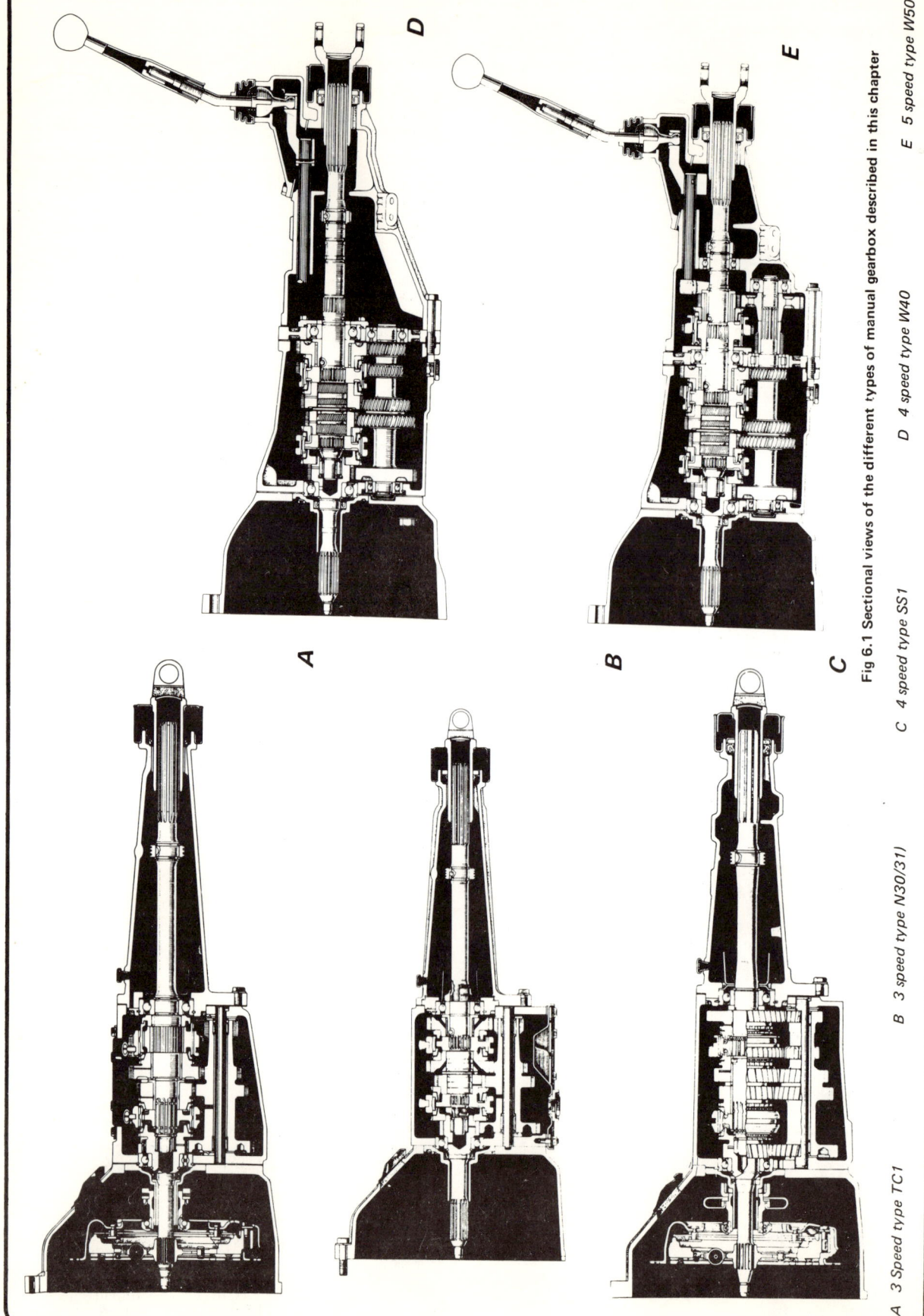

Fig 6.1 Sectional views of the different types of manual gearbox described in this chapter

A 3 speed type TC1
B 3 speed type N30/31
C 4 speed type SS1
D 4 speed type W40
E 5 speed type W50

Chapter 6/Manual gearbox and automatic transmission

Part 1: Manual gearbox

1 General description - manual gearboxes

The gearbox may be of three, four or five forward speed type according to model and date of manufacture. Synchromesh is fitted on all forward gears. Floor mounted gearchange lever or steering column type may be encountered.

The different units are described separately in this Chapter to avoid confusion.

2 Gearbox (three speed) - removal and installation

1 Disconnect the leads from the battery terminals.
2 Drain the cooling system and disconnect the radiator upper hose.
3 Disconnect the accelerator linkage at the carburettor.
4 Disconnect the starter leads and remove the starter from the clutch bellhousing.
5 Either place the vehicle over a pit or jack-up the front and rear sufficiently high that the gearbox can be withdraw from below.
6 Disconnect the speedometer cable from the gearbox.
7 Unbolt the clutch operating cylinder from the clutch bellhousing. If the fluid line is detached from its support clip, the complete flexible/rigid line together with operating cylinder can be tied up out of the way without disconnecting the pipes.
8 Unbolt the exhaust downpipe from the manifold.
9 Remove the stiffener plates from the lower half of the front of the clutch bellhousing.
10 Disconnect the gearchange control at the points shown, according to type. (Fig 6.2)
11 Drain the gearbox and then remove the propeller shaft as described in Chapter 7.
12 Support the gearbox on a jack (preferably trolley type) and remove the gearbox rear mounting.
13 Unscrew and remove the clutch bellhousing to engine securing bolts, lower the jack until the gearbox is inclined at the right attitude to be removed rearwards.
14 Withdraw the gearbox in a straight line so that its weight will at no time hang upon the input shaft while the shaft is still engaged with the clutch mechanism. During this operation, the engine will be supported on a second jack placed under the engine sump.
15 Installation is a reversal of removal but lightly grease the splines of the input shaft before offering up the unit to the flywheel mounted clutch mechanism.
16 If the clutch has been dismantled, centralise the driven plate as described in Chapter 5. Tighten the clutch bellhousing to engine bolts to the specified torque.
17 Check and adjust the clutch pedal free-movement (Chapter 5) and refill the gearbox with the correct quantity and grade of oil.

3 Gearbox (three speed type TC1) - dismantling and examination of components

1 Clean the outside of the gearbox using paraffin or a water soluble cleaner.
2 Remove the clutch release fork and bearing from within the clutch bellhousing and then unbolt the bellhousing from the gearbox.
3 Remove the gearbox cover and gasket.
4 Unbolt the front bearing retainer.
5 Extract the split pins from the shift fork securing screws and unscrew them and withdraw the springs and detent balls.

Fig 6.2 Gearchange control disconnection and 3 speed gearbox (Sec 2)

A Floor mounted control
1 Low speed connecting rod
2 Cross shaft

B Steering column control
3 Gearshift rod

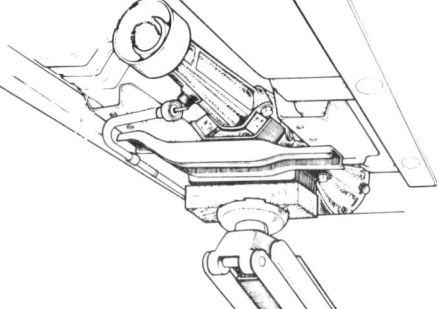

Fig 6.3 Gearbox supported on a trolley jack (Sec 2)

Fig 6.4 Removing the shift fork screws from 3 speed type TC 1 gearbox (Sec 3)

6 Set the gears in the 1st or 2nd speed position and then drive out the selector shaft towards the rear of the gearbox lifting each of the selector forks from the unit and marking them so that they can be refitted in their original locations.
7 Push the 2nd/3rd synchro unit sleeve towards the 3rd gear and then unbolt and remove the extension housing complete with mainshaft gear assembly.
8 At this stage check the countershaft gear endfloat and make a note of it for reference during reassembly.
9 Drive out the countershaft from the gearbox casing towards the rear. This will leave the countershaft gear assembly and thrust washers resting on the bottom of the gearbox casing for subsequent removal.
10 Remove the input shaft from the front of the gearbox by tapping its rear end with a soft faced mallet.
11 The countershaft gear and thrust washers may now be extracted from the gearbox interior.
12 Drive out the reverse idler gear shaft from the gearbox casing towards the rear, noting that it is secured by a Woodruff key.
13 Withdraw the reverse idler gear.
14 Remove the shift outer lever cotter bolts and withdraw the levers, also the interlock support shaft.
15 Unbolt the shift lever shaft housing bolts and lift the housing from the gearbox casing.
16 Extract the internal type circlip from the input shaft and then withdraw the needle rollers.
17 Remove the circlip from the front end of the mainshaft and then draw off the components from the section of the mainshaft

Fig 6.5 Withdrawing the extension housing with mainshaft assembly from 3 speed type TC1 gearbox (Sec 3)

Fig 6.6 Removing the countershaft from 3 speed type TC1 gearbox (Sec 3)

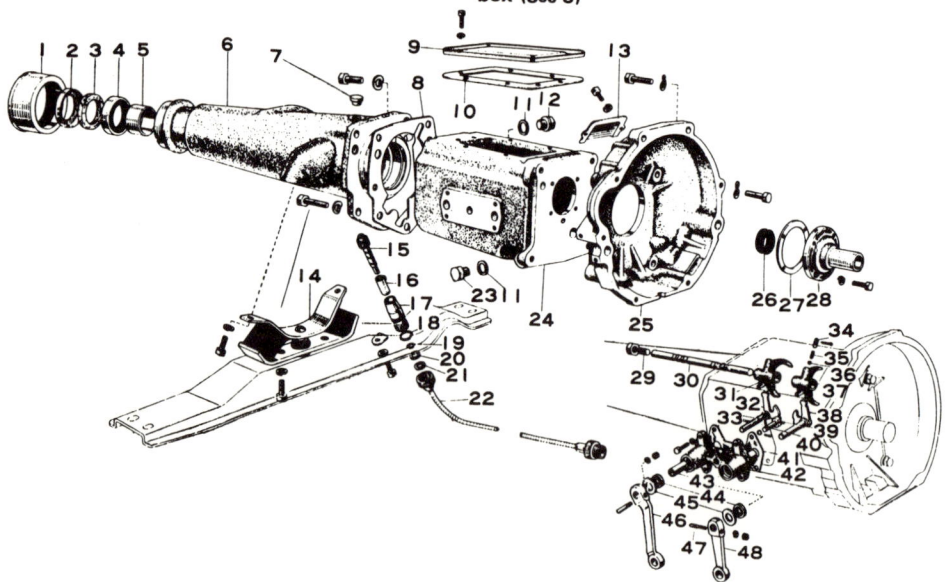

Fig 6.7 3 speed type TC1 gearbox components (Sec 3)

1 Dust deflector
2 Dust seal retainer
3 Dust seal
4 Oil seal
5 Bush
6 Extension housing
7 Breather
8 Gasket
9 Cover
10 Gasket
11 Washer
12 Filler plug
13 Inspection cover
14 Rear mounting
15 Speedometer driven gear
16 Bush
17 Sleeve
18 'O' ring
19 'O' ring
20 Collar
21 Gasket
22 Cable
23 Drain plug
24 Casing
25 Clutch bellhousing
26 Oil seal
27 Gasket
28 Front bearing retainer
29 Selector shaft adjuster screw
30 Selector shaft
31 1st/2nd reverse shift fork
32 Shift lever
33 Pin
34 Screwed plug
35 Spring
36 Detent ball
37 2nd/3rd shift fork
38 Shift lever
39 Pin
40 Interlock support shaft
41 Gasket
42 Shift lever shaft housing
43 Bush
44 Oil seal
45 Washer
44 Oil seal
45 Washer
46 External shift lever
47 Cotter bolt
48 External shift lever

Chapter 6/Manual gearbox and automatic transmission   111

which is projecting from the extension housing. These components (in order of removal) are: 2nd/3rd synchro unit, second gear, bush, first gear, bush, 1st/2nd synchro unit and reverse gear.
18 Remove the speedometer driven gear from the extension housing.
19 Extract the circlip from the bearing outer track located on the front face of the extension housing and then drive out the mainshaft towards the front of the housing, using a soft faced mallet.
20 If the input shaft bearing is to be renewed, remove it with a two legged extractor.
21 The speedometer drive gear can be withdrawn from the mainshaft after removing the oil baffle and extracting the two retaining circlips. Retain the Woodruff key. If the mainshaft rear bearing is to be removed, a press must be used.
22 Wash all components in paraffin and dry them. Check the gears for worn or chipped teeth and the shafts for scoring or

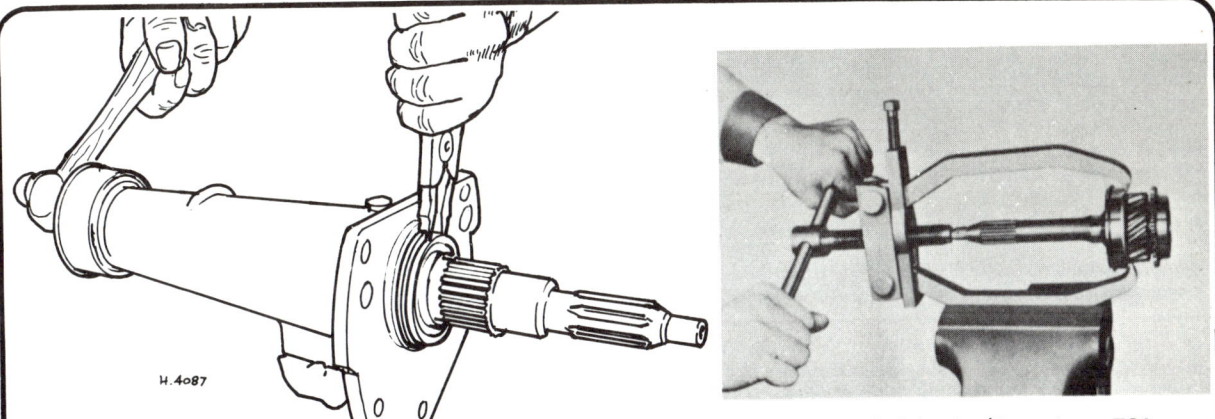

Fig 6.8 Removing mainshaft from extension housing of 3 speed type TC1 gearbox (Sec 3)

Fig 6.9 Removing input shaft bearing (3 speed type TC1 gearbox)

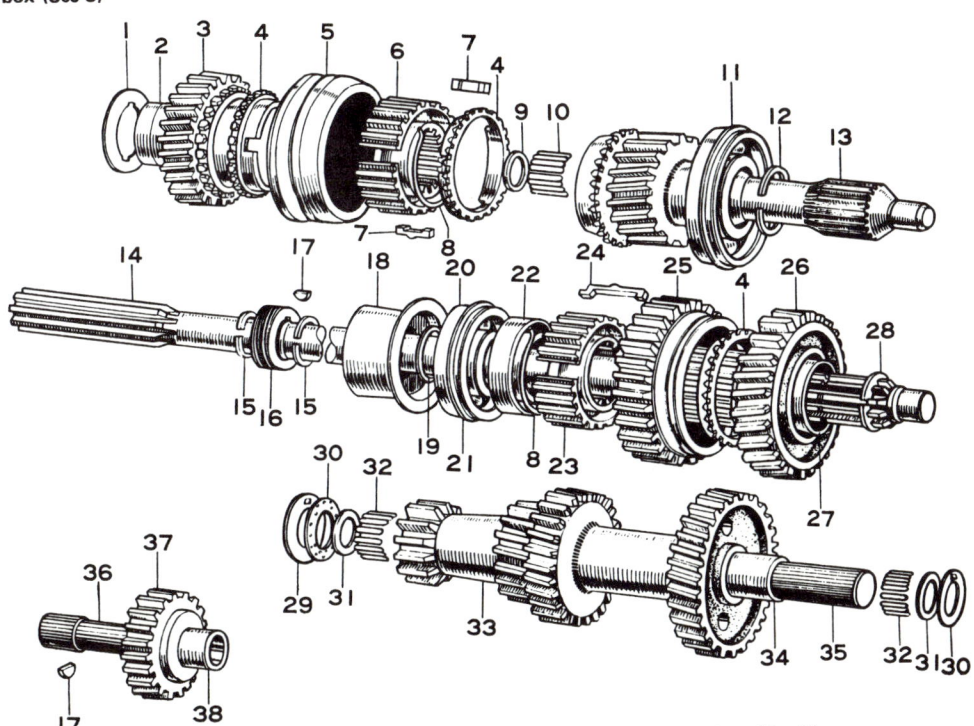

Fig 6.10 Internal components of 3 speed type TC1 gearbox (Sec 3)

1 Thrust washer
2 2nd gear bush
3 2nd gear
4 2nd/3rd synchro. rings
5 2nd/3rd synchro. sleeve
6 2nd/3rd synchro. hub
7 Blocker bar
8 Spring

9 Circlip
10 Needle rollers
11 Input shaft bearing
12 Circlip
13 Input shaft
14 Mainshaft
15 Circlip
16 Speedometer drive gear
17 Woodruff key
18 Oil deflector
19 Circlip

20 Mainshaft bearing
21 Bearing outer track circlip
22 Retainer
23 1st/2nd synchro. unit hub
24 Blocker bar
25 Reverse gear
26 1st gear
27 Bush
28 Circlip

29 Thrust washer
30 Thrust washer
31 Spacer
32 Needle rollers
33 Countergear assembly
34 Spacer tube
35 Countershaft
36 Reverse idler gear shaft
37 Reverse idler gear
38 Bush

grooves.

23 Fit the synchro rings to the gear wheel cones and check the clearance. It should be between 0.039 and 0.059 in (1.0 to 1.5 mm) with a minimum of 0.020 in (0.5 mm).

24 With the shift forks located in the synchro sleeve grooves, check the side clearance. This should be between 0.006 and 0.042 in (0.15 and 1.25 mm) otherwise renew the components. Also test the fit of the shift lever shaft in the shift fork. The clearance should be between 0.008 and 0.024 in (0.2 and 0.6 mm).

25 Renew the oil seals in the front bearing retainer, the rear extension housing and the shift lever shaft housing. A piece of tubing can be used as a drift for these operations (see Section 9).

26 Examine the gearbox casing and extension housing for cracks. These components are of light alloy and should be treated with respect.

27 Inspect the condition of the synchroniser units. If there has been a history of noisy gearchanging or the synchromesh could easily be 'beaten', renew the unit complete.

28 Correct assembly of the two synchro units must be carried out before installing them on the mainshaft. Ensure that the spring ends do not engage in the same gaps on opposite sides of the unit.

4 Gearbox (three speed type TC1) - reassembly

1 Install the shift key retainer onto the mainshaft and then press on the rear bearing so that its outer track circlip groove is nearer the front of the shaft.

2 Select and install a circlip to give minimum clearance from those listed in **Specifications Section**.

3 To the mainshaft, fit the oil baffle, circlip, Woodruff key and speedometer drive gear. Fit a circlip to the rear bearing outer track to give minimum groove clearance, from those listed in **Specifications Section**.

4 Insert the mainshaft into the extension housing.

5 Fit the speedometer driven gear to the extension housing.

6 Fit 1st/2nd synchro unit to the mainshaft, followed by the 1st gear bush and 1st gear.

7 Fit the thrust washer and 2nd gear bush, pushing the latter towards 1st gear, then measure the clearance between 1st gear and the thrust washer. This should be between 0.002 and 0.006 in (0.05 and 0.15 mm) with a maximum of 0.0083 in (0.21 mm). Where the clearance exceeds that specified, renew the 1st gear bush which is available in two lengths (see Specifications Section).

8 Fit 2nd gear, 2nd/3rd synchro and while pressing the synchro hub towards 2nd gear, measure the clearance between 2nd gear and the thrust washer. This should be as described for 1st gear in the preceding paragraph, otherwise change the 2nd gear bush for one of two alternative lengths which are available (see Specifications Section).

9 Fit a circlip to the front end of the mainshaft, selecting one to give an endfloat between 0 and 0.0024 in (0 and 0.06 mm) from those listed in Specifications Section.

10 Bolt the shift lever shaft housing to the gearbox casing, using a new gasket and applying jointing compound to the bolt threads. Tighten the bolts to the specified torque.

11 Install the interlock support shaft into the shift lever shaft housing, entering it from the interior of the gearbox. Insert the pin and a new split pin.

12 Assemble the straight pin, shift lever shafts and external levers, securing them with the cotter bolts.

13 Assemble the reverse idler gear and shaft into the gearbox casing, making sure that the boss on the gear faces the front of the gearbox and that the shaft is driven in from the rear, with the Woodruff key in position.

14 Refer to the countershaft endfloat clearance measured before dismantling. If this was outside the specified tolerance of between 0.002 and 0.006 in (0.05 and 0.15 mm) renew the thrust washer by selecting one from those listed in Specifications

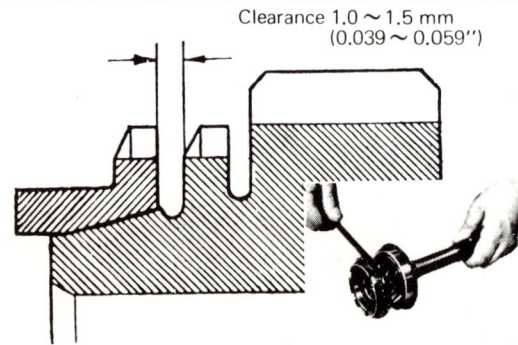

Fig 6.11 Checking synchro. ring to gear clearance (3 speed type TC1 gearbox) (Sec 3)

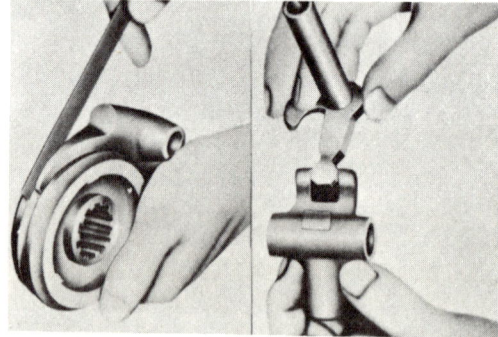

Fig 6.12 Checking fit of shift fork and shift lever (3 speed type TC1 gearbox) (Sec 3)

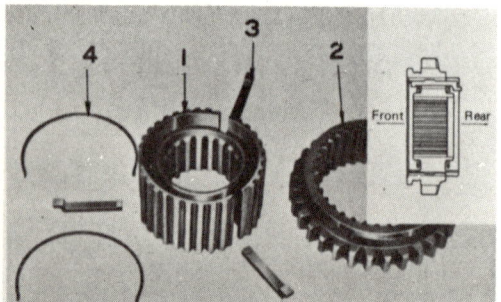

Fig 6.13 Assembly diagram 1st/2nd synchro unit (3 speed type TC1 gearbox) (Sec 3)

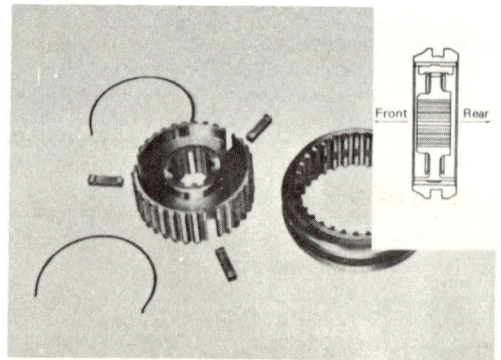

Fig 6.14 Assembly diagram 2nd/3rd synchro. unit (3 speed type TC1 gearbox) (Sec 3)

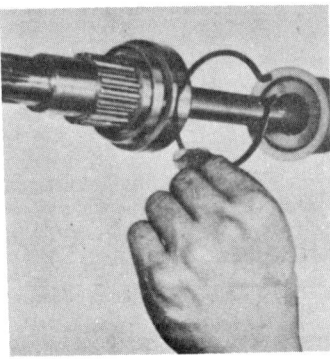

Fig 6.15 Selecting mainshaft bearing outer track circlip (3 speed type TC1 gearbox) (Sec 4)

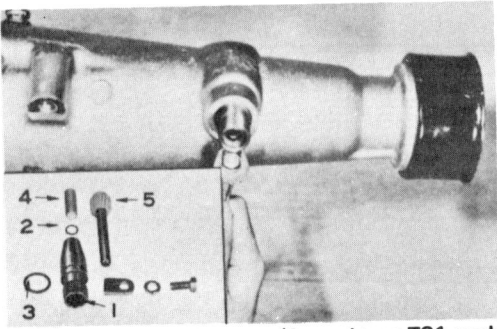

Fig 6.16 Speedometer driven gear (3 speed type TC1 gearbox) (Sec 4)
1 Sleeve
2 and 3 'O' rings
4 Bush
5 Gear

Fig 6.17 Installing 1st gear to the mainshaft of 3 speed type TC1 gearbox (Sec 4)

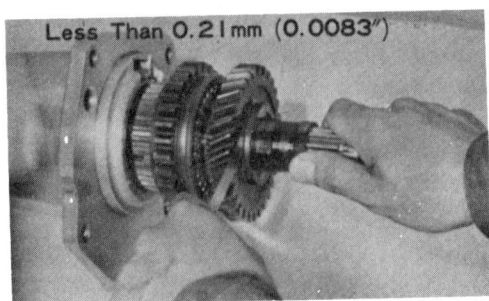

Fig 6.18 Measuring 1st gear endfloat on 3 speed type TC1 gearbox (Sec 4)

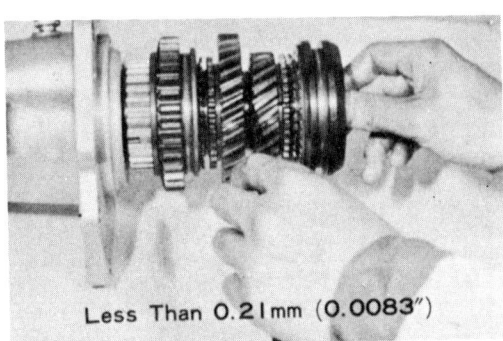

Fig 6.19 Measuring 2nd gear endfloat on 3 speed type TC1 gearbox (Sec 4)

Fig 6.20 Assembling shift lever shaft housing on 3 speed type TC1 gearbox (Sec 4)
1 Gasket
2 'O' ring
3 Housing
4 Interlock support shaft
5 Pin

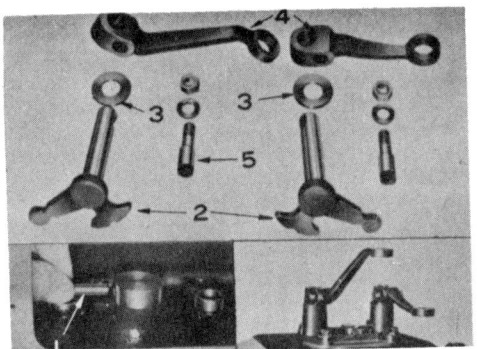

Fig 6.21 External shift lever assembly (3 speed type TC1 gearbox) (Sec 4)
1 Straight pin
2 Shift lever shafts
3 Washers
4 Shift levers
5 Cotter bolts

Fig 6.22 Assembling reverse idler gear on 3 speed type TC1 gearbox (Sec 4)

Section.

15 Insert a dummy shaft into the countershaft gear assembly and then insert the needle rollers (23 at each end) and the two spacers, using thick grease to retain them.

16 Stick the two thrust washers to the recesses inside the gearbox casing again using a dab of thick grease to retain them.

17 Insert the needle rollers into the recess in the rear face of the input shaft and secure them with the internal type circlip.

18 If the input shaft bearing has been removed, press on a new one so that its outer track circlip groove is nearer the front and then select a circlip to provide minimum clearance in the bearing groove (see circlips listed in Specifications Section).

19 Lower the countershaft gear assembly into the bottom of the gearbox, taking care not to displace the thrust washers previously located in the gearbox interior recesses.

20 Install the input shaft into the gearbox from the front.

21 Raise the countershaft gear and insert the countershaft so displacing the dummy shaft. Make sure that the needle roller bearings and the thrust washers are still in position. Fit the Woodruff key at the rear end of the countershaft to prevent it rotating. Check the countershaft gear endfloat again as described in paragraph 14, and substitute one or both thrust washers if the original measurements and washer selection have altered.

22 To the front of the gearbox, fit the bearing retainer using a new gasket and applying jointing compound to the gasket and the bolt threads. Make sure that the oil return hole and groove are correctly aligned. Tighten the bolts to the specified torque.

23 Make sure that the synchro ring is in position on the input shaft 3rd gear cone and using a new gasket, bolt the extension housing/mainshaft assembly to the gearbox. Note that the longer securing bolt is located at the bottom of the gearbox. Tighten the bolts to the specified torque and then measure the

Fig 6.23 Inserting countershaft needle rollers (3 speed type TC1 gearbox) (Sec 4)

Fig 6.24 Checking countershaft gear endfloat (3 speed type TC1 gearbox) (Sec 4)

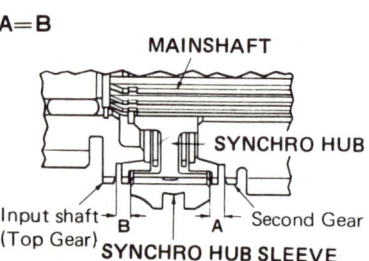

Fig 6.25 Synchro. hub to 2nd and 3rd gear clearance diagram (3 speed type TC1 gearbox) (Sec 4)

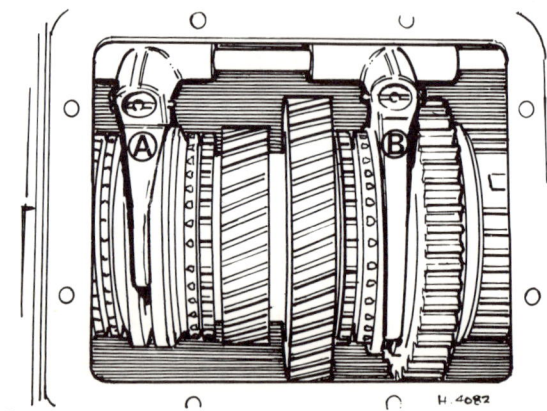

Fig 6.26 Correct location of shift forks on 3 speed type TC1 gearbox (Sec 4)

A 1st/reverse   B 2nd/3rd

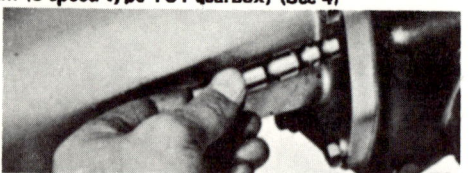

Fig 6.27 Correct installation of selector shaft to 3 speed type TC1 gearbox (Sec 4)

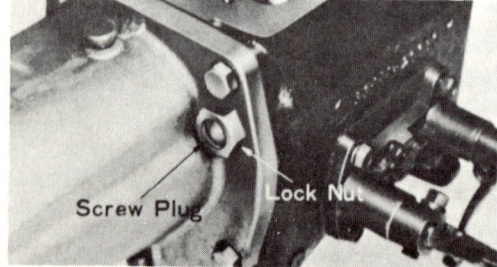

Fig 6.28 Location of selector shaft adjuster screw and locknut on 3 speed type TC1 gearbox (Sec 4)

Fig 6.29 Correct installation of gearbox top cover (3 speed type TC1) (Sec 4)

Chapter 6/Manual gearbox and automatic transmission

clearances: (A) face of synchro hub to face of 2nd gear and (B) face of synchro hub to face of 3rd gear cone teeth. The clearances should be approximately equal at 0.4 in (10.0 mm). If not, remove the extension housing and fit another one, or two, gaskets as required, applying jointing compound to the gasket faces and to the securing bolt's threads. (Fig 6.25)

24 Install the shift forks and insert the selector shaft. Note that the three unequally spaced detent grooves in the shaft must be located to the rear of the gearbox.

25 Align the detent ball groove in the shaft with the hole in the shift fork and insert the ball and spring. Screw in the plug until the split pin can be inserted easily through the plug groove. Bend over the ends of the pins. When the gears are in the neutral mode, the shift forks should be equally spaced within the synchro sleeve grooves. Where adjustment is required, turn the screw and locknut which passes through the extension housing flange or in extreme cases, change the fork to casing shims (if fitted).

26 Use a new gasket with jointing compound applied and bolt on the top cover so that the breather pipe faces the rear. Tighten the securing bolts to the specified torque.

27 Refit the clutch bellhousing, clutch release bearing and release fork mechanism.

5 Gearbox (3 speed type N30/31) - dismantling into major assemblies

1 Clean the outside of the gearbox using paraffin or a water soluble cleaner.
2 Remove the clutch release fork and bearing from within the clutch bellhousing.
3 Unbolt and remove the clutch bellhousing from the gearbox.
4 Unbolt and remove the front bearing retainer, the sump plate and its gasket.
5 Remove the speedometer driven gear assembly from the extension housing and then unbolt and remove the extension housing.
6 Before further dismantling, measure the endfloat of the countergear and the reverse idler gear and make a note of it for reference on reassembly. (Fig 6.31)
7 Drive out the countershaft using a suitable drift and lift the countergear assembly from the gearbox. (Fig 6.32)
8 Remove the reverse idler gear retaining bolt and withdraw the reverse idler shaft, gear and thrust washer. (Fig 6.33)
9 Unscrew and remove the two shift fork screwed plugs and extract the springs and balls.

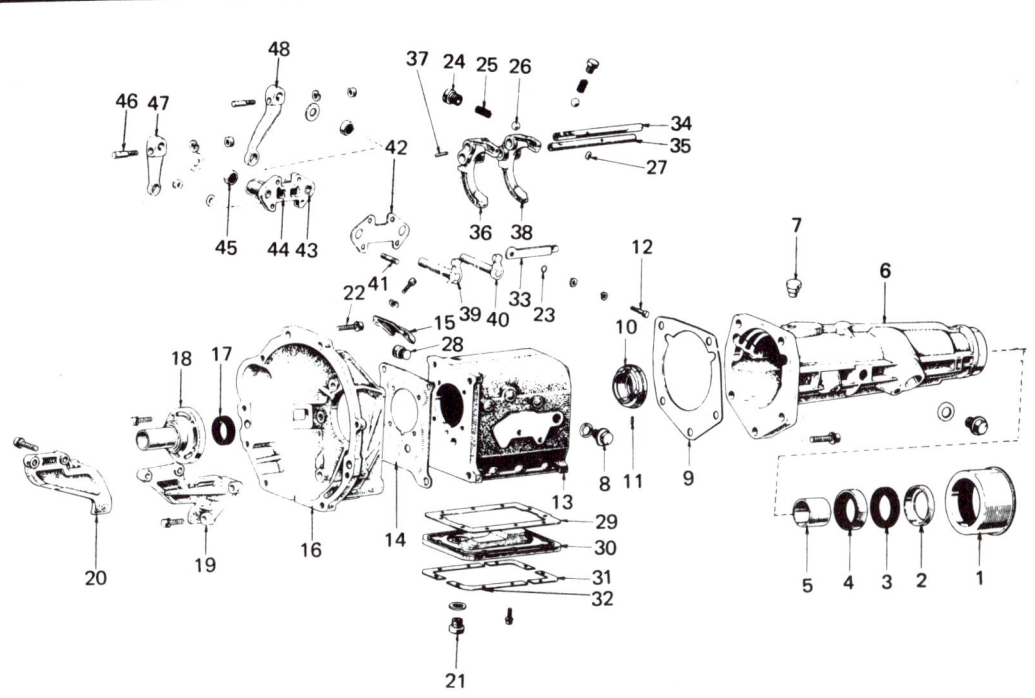

Fig 6.30 External components and selector mechanism of 3 speed gearbox (Type N30/31)

1 Dust deflector
2 Dust seal retainer
3 Dust seal
4 Oil seal
5 Bush
6 Extension housing
7 Breather plug
8 Filler plug
9 Gasket
10 Mainshaft rear bearing retainer
11 Tension pin
12 Socket screw
13 Gearbox casing
14 Gasket
15 Inspection cover
16 Clutch bellhousing
17 Front oil seal
18 Front bearing retainer
19 and 20 reinforcement brackets
21 Drain plug
22 Bolt
23 'O' ring
24 Detent ball plug
25 Spring
26 Detent ball
27 Interlock pin
28 Plug
29 Gasket
30 Sump plate
31 and 32 reinforcements
33 Oil catcher
34 2nd/3rd gear selector shaft
35 1st/2nd gear selector shaft
36 3rd/4th shift fork
37 Tension pin
38 1st/2nd shift fork
39 2nd/3rd shift lever shaft
40 1st/2nd shift lever shaft
41 Stud
42 Seal
43 Bush
44 Shift lever shaft housing
45 Seal
46 Cotter bolt
47 2nd/3rd outer shift lever
48 1st/2nd outer shift lever

Fig 6.31 Checking reverse idler gear endfloat (3 speed gearbox type N30/31) (Sec 5)

Fig 6.32 Removing the countershaft (3 speed gearbox type N30/31) (Sec 5)

10 Now remove the remaining two plugs and drive out the tension pins.
11 Withdraw the gear selector shafts one at a time and remove the interlock pin.
12 Detach the cranked and straight shift external levers.
13 Remove the nuts which secure the shaft housing (1) and then push the inner shift levers until they are horizontal and in contact with the gearbox casing. Do not attempt to remove the shaft housing or inner shift levers at this stage. (Fig 6.36
14 Push 1st/2nd synchro unit towards the reverse gear and withdraw the shift fork.
15 The second shift fork should be withdrawn with the gears in the neutral mode.
16 Remove the mainshaft assembly from the gearbox which will leave the input shaft still in position.
17 Now remove the shift lever shafts and housing (see paragraph 13).

Fig 6.33 Removing the reverse idler gear (3 speed gearbox type N30/31) (Sec 5)

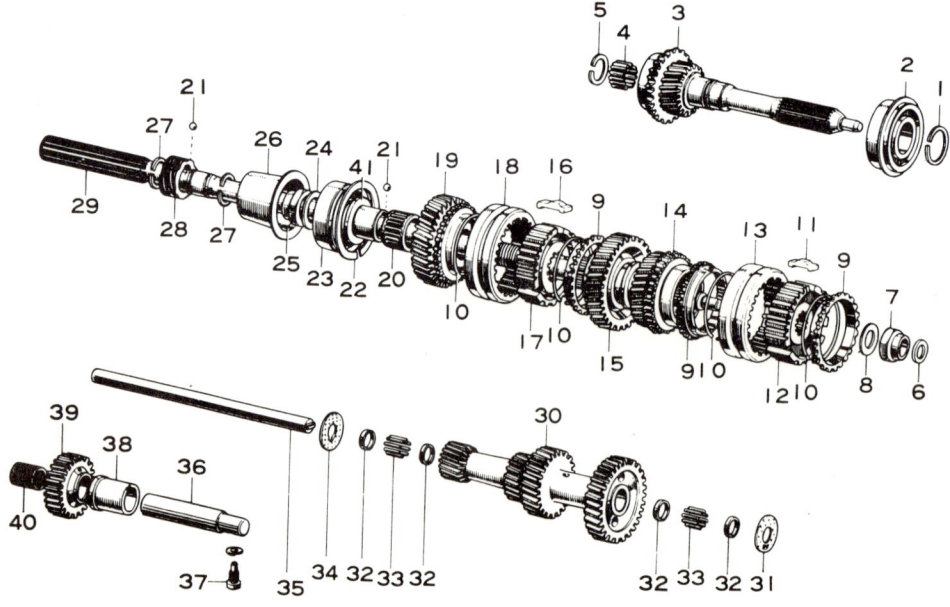

Fig 6.34 Gear assemblies (3 speed gearbox type N30/31) (Sec 5)

1 Circlip	11 Blocker bar	22 Circlip	32 Spacer
2 Bearing	12 Synchro hub	23 Bearing	33 Needle roller
3 Input shaft	13 Synchro. sleeve	24 Shim	34 Thrust washer
4 Needle roller bearing	14 Second gear	25 Nut	35 Countershaft
5 Circlip	15 First gear	26 Oil deflector	36 Reverse idler gear
6 Spacer	16 Blocker bar	27 Circlip	37 Locking ball
7 Nut	17 Synchro. hub	28 Speedo. drive gear	38 Thrust collar
8 Shim	18 Synchro. sleeve	29 Mainshaft	39 Reverse idler gear
9 2nd/3rd synchro. ring	19 Reverse gear	30 Countershaft gear	40 Needle roller
10 Synchro. spring	20 Needle roller bearing	31 Thrust washer	41 Bush
	21 Locking ball		

Chapter 6/Manual gearbox and automatic transmission

Fig 6.35 Dismantling selector shafts from 3 speed gearbox type N30/31 (Sec 5)

A 1 screw plugs
B 1 screw plug
2 Spring
2 Tension pin
3 Detent ball

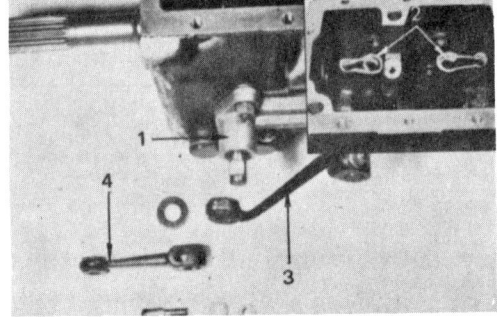

Fig 6.36 Shift inner levers (2) and external levers (3 and 4) on 3 speed gearbox type N30/31 shift lever shaft housing (Sec 5)

Fig 6.37 Location of (1) 1st/2nd synchro. unit and (2) 2nd/3rd synchro. unit on 3 speed gearbox type N30/31 (Sec 5)

Fig 6.38 Removing the mainshaft assembly from 3 speed gearbox type N30/31 (Sec 5)

Fig 6.39 Removing the input shaft bearing outer circlip (3 speed gearbox type N30/31) (Sec 5)

18 Remove the input shaft bearing outer circlip and push the input shaft into the interior of the gearbox and then withdraw it.
19 Inspect all components for wear and renew as necessary.

6 Mainshaft (three speed gearbox type N30/31) - servicing

1 Before commencing to dismantle, measure the endfloats of the 1st, 2nd, and reverse gears. Make a note of them pending reassembly.
2 Hold the mainshaft assembly very securely in the jaws of a vice (fitted with soft metal jaw protectors of adequate thickness) and remove the spacer from the front (input) end of the shaft. Relieve the staking on the nut and unscrew and remove it together with the shim.

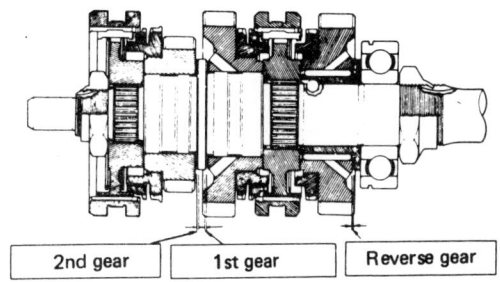

Fig 6.40 Endfloat measuring points (3 speed gearbox type N30/31) (Sec 6)

3 Withdraw the 2nd/3rd synchro unit, the ring and 2nd gear. Mark the synchro unit with a piece of masking tape to prevent confusion with 1st/2nd synchro which is identical.
4 From the rear end of the mainshaft, remove the circlips, speedometer drive gear and ball and the oil deflector.
5 Relieve the staking and unscrew and remove the nut and its shim.
6 The rear bearing will have to be removed on a press.
7 Withdraw reverse gear and the needle roller bearing, inner race and ball. Then remove the 1st/2nd synchro ring and first gear.
8 Wash all components in paraffin and dry thoroughly. Inspect the gears for chipped or worn teeth and the shaft for scoring, grooves or distortion.
9 The running clearances between the first and second gears and the mainshaft should not exceed 0.0051 in (0.13 mm).
10 Inspect the condition of the synchroniser units. If there has been a history of noisy gear-changing or the synchromesh could easily be 'beaten', renew the unit complete. In any event, fit the synchro ring onto the gear and measure the clearance. This should not be less than 0.031 in (0.8 mm).
11 Fit the shift forks to the synchro sleeves and check for side clearance. If this exceeds 0.039 in (1.0 mm) renew one or both components as necessary.
12 Correct assembly of the two synchro units must be carried out before installing them to the mainshaft. Ensure that the spring ends do not engage in the same gaps on opposite sides of the unit.
13 To the rear end of the mainshaft, fit the first gear, 1st/2nd synchro ring and sleeve. Press the synchro unit towards the first gearwheel and measure the clearance. This should be between 0.0039 and 0.0098 in (0.10 and 0.25 mm) with a maximum of 0.0118 in (0.30 mm).
14 Locate the ball and install reverse gear, the bearing and inner race. Make sure that the ball aligns with the slot in the inner race and that the synchro ring slots align with the shift keys.
15 Press a new bearing onto the rear end of the mainshaft so that its outer circlip groove is nearer the front.
16 Fit the shim and tighten the nut to the specified torque.
17 Check that the reverse gear endfloat is between 0.0039 and 0.0098 in (0.10 and 0.25 mm) with a maximum of 0.0118 in (0.30 mm). Recheck the first gear endfloat (see paragraph 13). Stake the nut to the mainshaft.
18 Locate the circlips, ball and speedometer drive gear to the rear end of the mainshaft.
19 To the front end of the mainshaft, assemble the 2nd gear, and synchro ring. Fit the 2nd/3rd synchro unit followed by the shim and nut. Make sure that the synchro ring slots are in alignment with the shift keys and tighten the nut to the specified torque.
20 Measure the second gear endfloat: this should be as for reverse gear (paragraph 17). If the clearance is correct, stake the nut to the mainshaft.
21 To the mainshaft rear bearing, fit the outer circlip and oil deflector. A circlip should be selected from those available to provide the minimum side clearance in the groove. Circlips are available in thicknesses as listed in Specifications Section.

7 Input shaft (three speed gearbox type N30/31) - servicing

1 Inspect the gearteeth for chipping and the splines and shaft surfaces for wear.
2 Locate the synchro ring to the rear end of the input shaft and check the clearance between the two components. It should be between 0.039 and 0.079 in (1.0 and 2.0 mm) with a maximum of 0.031 in (0.8 mm), otherwise renew the ring.
3 Check the internal bore of the needle bearing recess and the condition of the bearing itself.
4 If the main bearing requires renewal, it will have to be removed on a press. When pressing on the new one, make sure that the outer circlip groove is nearer the front of the shaft. Select a shaft circlip to give the minimum side clearance in the shaft groove from those listed in Specifications Section.

Fig 6.41 Removing 2nd/3rd synchro unit (1) synchro ring (2) and 2nd gear (3) from the mainshaft (3 speed gearbox type N30/31) (Sec 6)

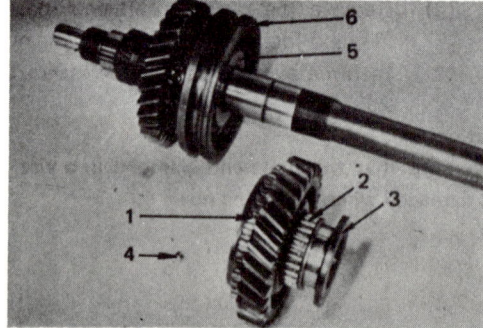

Fig 6.42 Reverse gear (1) needle roller bearing (2) inner track (3) locking ball (4) 1st/2nd synchro unit (5) with sleeve (6) on the mainshaft of a 3 speed gearbox type N30/31 (Sec 6)

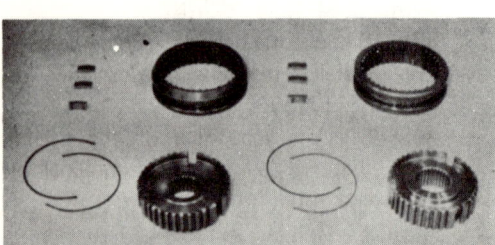

Fig 6.43 Exploded view of synchro. units (3 speed gearbox type N30/31) (Sec 6)

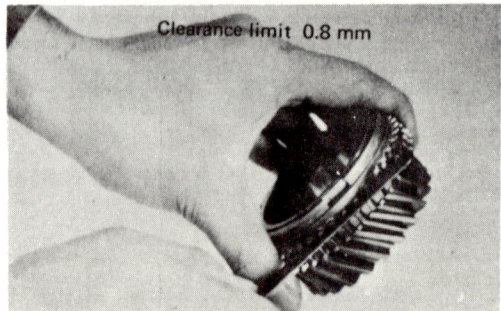

Fig 6.44 Measuring synchro. ring to gear clearance (3 speed gearbox type N30/31) (Sec 6)

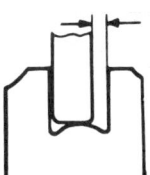

Fig 6.45 Shift fork to synchro. sleeve groove clearance measuring diagram 3 speed gearbox type N30/31 (Sec 6)

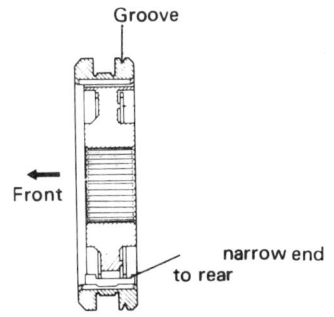

Fig 6.46 Assembly diagram for 1st/2nd synchro unit (3 speed gearbox type N30/31) (Sec 6)

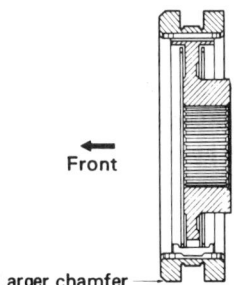

Fig 6.47 Assembly diagram for 2nd/3rd synchro. unit (3 speed gearbox type N30/31) (Sec 6)

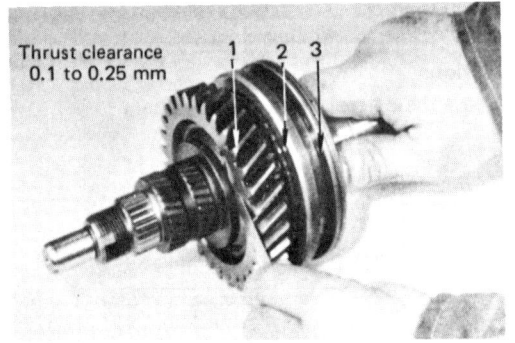

Fig 6.48 Measuring 1st gear endfloat (3 speed gearbox type N30/31) (Sec 6)

1 1st gear
2 Synchro ring
3 1st/2nd synchro unit

Fig 6.49 Installing reverse gear to mainshaft (3 speed gearbox type N30/31)(Sec 6)

1 Locking ball
2 Reverse gear
3 Needle bearing
4 Inner track

Fig 6.50 Checking reverse gear endfloat (3 speed gearbox type N30/31) (Sec 6)

Fig 6.51 Gear assembly for front end of mainshaft (3 speed gearbox type N30/31) (Sec 6)

1 2nd gear
2 Synchro. ring
3 2nd/3rd synchro. unit
4 Shims
5 Nut

Fig 6.52 Measuring 2nd gear endfloat (3 speed gearbox type N30/31) (Sec 6)

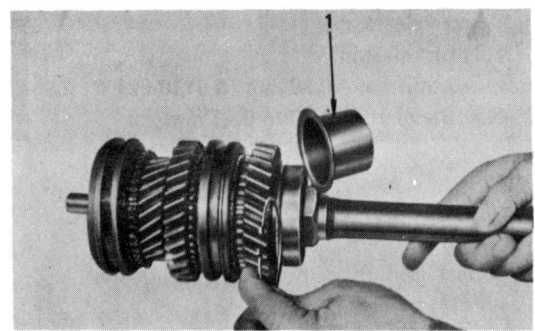

Fig 6.53 Testing a circlip in the mainshaft rear bearing groove (3 speed gearbox type N30/31) (Sec 6)

1 Oil deflector

8 Countershaft and reverse gear assemblies (three speed gearbox type N30/31) - servicing

1 The countershaft assembly cannot be dismantled and must be renewed if the gears are worn or chipped. The thrust washers and bearings can be renewed if worn.
2 The reverse idler gear, shaft and bearing should be renewed if worn or scored.

9 Oil seals (three speed gearbox type N30/31) - renewal

1 When carrying out a major overhaul of the gearbox, it is recommended that all oil seals and 'O' rings are renewed as a matter of routine.
2 Renew the 'O' rings in the shift lever housing and at the same time make sure that the housing and levers are in good condition.
3 Renew the speedometer driven gear 'O' rings and renew any worn components of the drive or driven gear.
4 Renew the oil seal in the front bearing retainer, using a tubular drift.
5 Renew the oil seal at the end of the rear extension housing in a similar manner to that described in the preceding paragraph. Should the metal bush be worn it can be renewed after heating the rear end of the extension housing in boiling water. When installing the new bush, make sure that the oil feed grooves are in alignment.

10 Gearbox (three speed type N30/31) reassembly

1 Fit the speedometer driven gear assembly to the extension housing.
2 Fit the input shaft by inserting it first into the interior of the gearbox and when positioned correctly intall the bearing outer circlip. If working single-handed the bearing retainer can be temporarily bolted up to hold the input shaft in position.
3 Locate the shift lever shaft housing onto the gearbox casing using a new gasket.
4 Insert the shift lever shafts from the gearbox interior pushing them until the levers are horizontal and touching the inside of the gearbox casing.
5 Fit the 2nd/3rd synchro ring to the rear end of the input shaft and the spacer onto the front end of the mainshaft and install the mainshaft assembly from the rear end of the gearbox.
6 Insert the two shift forks so that they engage correctly in the synchro sleeve grooves.
7 Insert the selector shafts so that they and their forks are assembled as shown complete with detent balls and springs. The installation sequence is to position 1st/2nd selector shaft in neutral and align the tension spring hole. Insert the ball, spring and plug. Drive in the tension pin (4) and screw in the plug (5). This plug should have gasket sealing compound applied to it and it should be tightened to the specified torque. (Fig 6.60)
8 Insert the interlock pin: this is most easily done by using a piece of tubing as a guide.
9 Now insert the 2nd/3rd selector shaft passing it through the shift forks and then positioning it in the neutral mode. Fit the tension pin (2) and plug (1). Inser the ball (3) spring (4) and plug (5). The plugs should be tightened to the specified torque and have gasket sealing compound applied to them. (Fig 6.62)
10 Tighten the shift lever housing nuts and then fit the external shift levers complete with washers and cotters.
11 Install the reverse idler gear by inserting the idler shaft from the rear of the gearbox casing, fitting the gear and thrust washer and screwing in the locking bolt. The endfloat of the reverse idler gear should compare with the clearance measured before dismantling (see Section 3) which should be between 0.0039 and 0.0098 in (0.10 and 0.25 mm) otherwise change the thrust collar from those available and listed in Specifications Section.
12 Assemble the countershaft gear complete with bearings and spacers. Stick the two thrust washers to the internal faces of the gearbox casing, using thick grease and ensuring that the projections on the washers locate in the casing grooves.
13 Lower the countershaft gear into the casing and insert the countershaft from the front end, taking care not to displace the thrust washers. The locking tongue on the endface of the countershaft should be positioned horizontally. Compare the endfloat of the countershaft with that measured during dismantling (see Section 3) and change the rear washer if necessary to bring the clearance in line with that which applied originally

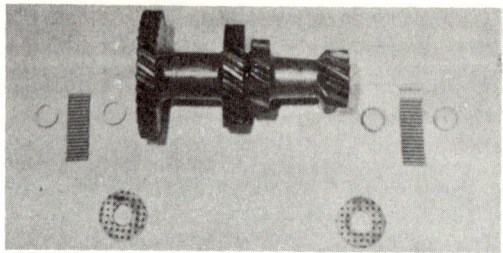

Fig 6.54 Countershaft gear assembly, thrust washers and needle roller bearings (3 speed gearbox type N30/31)(Sec 8)

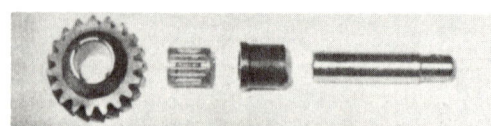

Fig 6.55 Reverse idler gear assembly (3 speed gearbox type N30/31)(Sec 8)

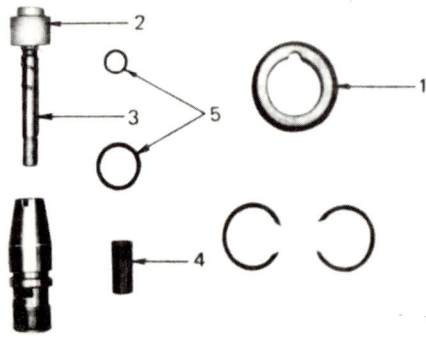

Fig 6.56 Speedometer gear components (3 speed gearbox type N30/31) (Sec 9)

1 Drive gear
2 Driven gear
3 Shaft
4 Bush
5 'O' rings

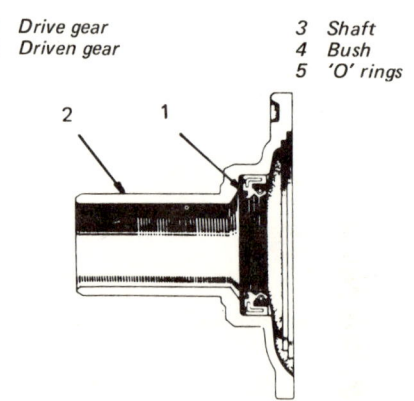

Fig 6.57 Front bearing retainer oil seal (1) and retainer (2) - 3 speed gearbox type N30/31 (Sec 9)

Chapter 6/Manual gearbox and automatic transmission

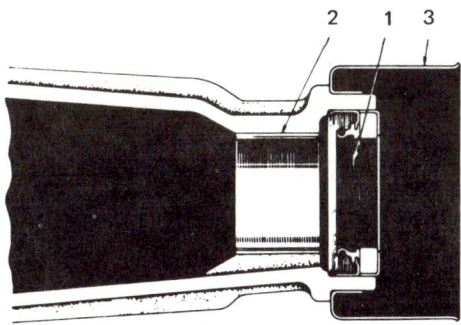

Fig 6.58 Rear extension housing oil seal (1) bush (2) and dust defelctor (3) (3 speed gearbox type N30/31) (Sec 9)

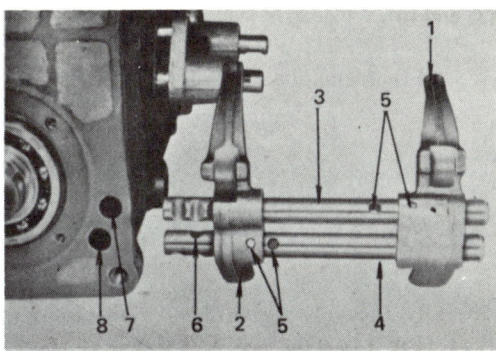

Fig 6.59 Correct assembly of shift forks and selector shafts (3 speed gearbox type N30/31) (Sec 10)

1 1st/2nd fork
2 2nd/3rd fork
3 1st/2nd selector shaft
4 2nd/3rd selector shaft
5 Tension pin holes
6 Interlock pin location
7 1st/2nd selector shaft hole
8 2nd/3rd selector shaft hole

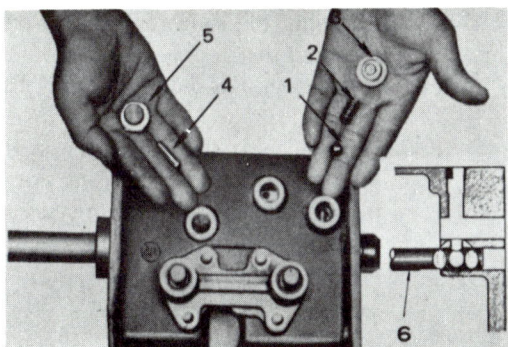

Fig 6.60 Assembling 1st/2nd selector shaft (3 speed gearbox type N30/31) (Sec 10)

1 Detent ball
2 Spring
3 Plug
4 Tension pin
5 Plug
6 Shaft

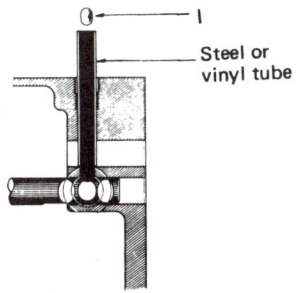

Fig 6.61 Method of inserting interlock pin (3 speed gearbox type N30/31) (Sec 10)

Fig 6.62 Assembling 2nd/3rd selector shaft (3 speed gearbox type N30/31) (Sec 10)

1 Plug
2 Tension pin
3 Detent ball
4 Spring
5 Plug
6 Shaft

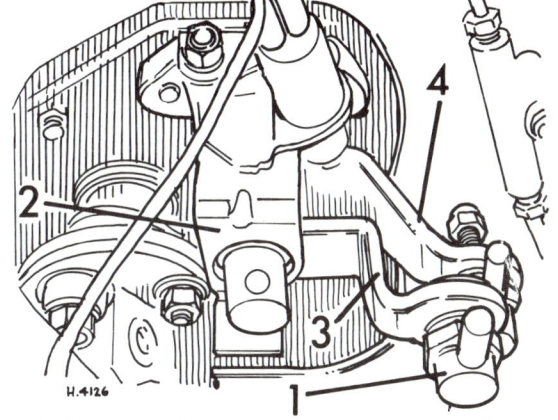

Fig 6.63 Location of lower components on steering column gearchange (Sec 11)

1 Swivel
2 Retainer
3 High speed lever
4 Low speed lever

and should be between 0.0047 and 0.0114 in (0.12 and 0.29 mm). Rear thrust washers are available in thicknesses as listed in Specifications Section.
14 Bolt on the extension housing using a new gasket and tightening the bolts to the specified torque.
15 Fit the sump plate using a new gasket.
16 Fit the front bearing retainer with a new gasket, making sure that the oil holes are in alignment.
17 Bolt on the clutch bellhousing and fit the speedometer driven gear and release bearing and fork.

11 Steering column gearchange linkage - servicing and adjustment

1 Commence dismantling by removing the two connecting rod swivels (1) and the shift lever retainer (2).
2 Remove the dust covers and the high speed lever (3) together with spacer. Disconnect the leads from the reversing lamp switch.
3 Drive out the control lever selecting key and remove the

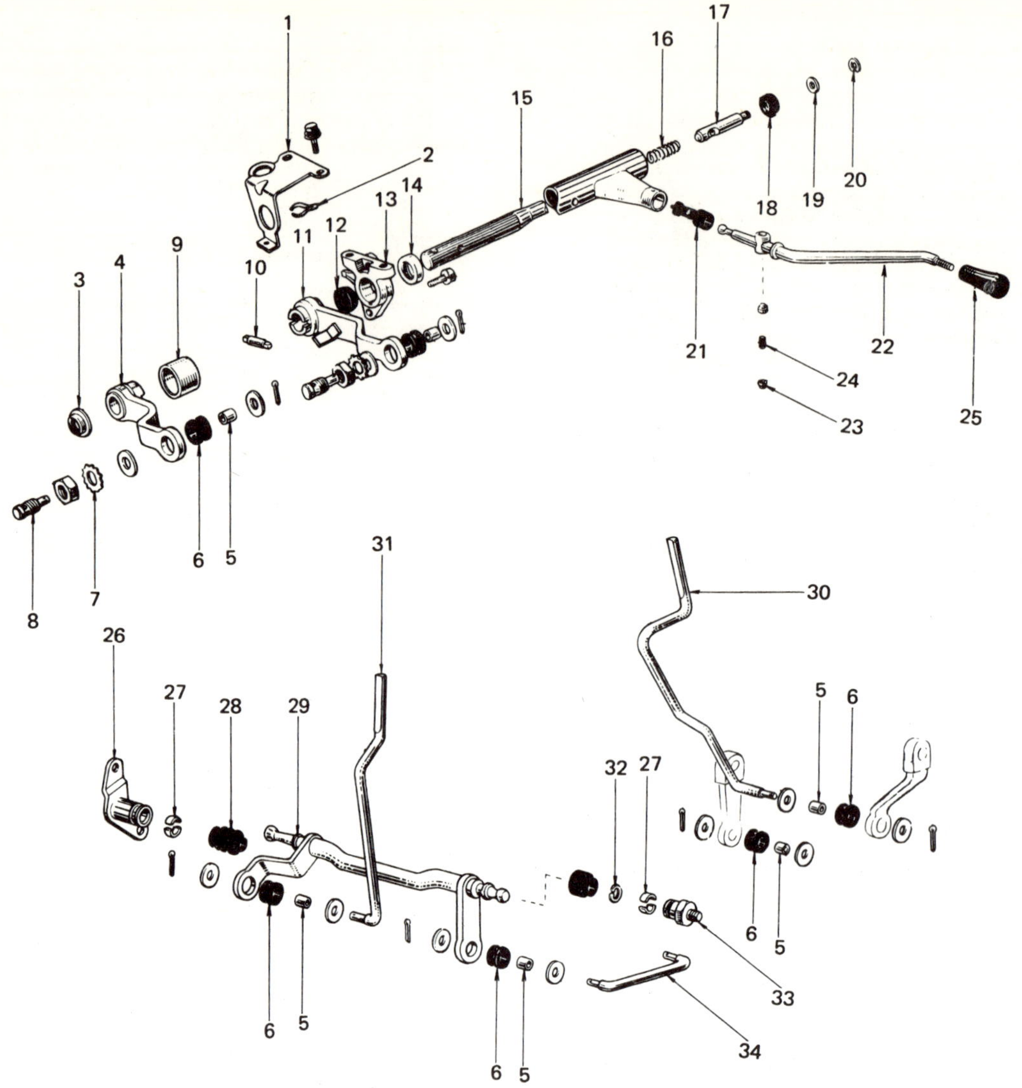

Fig 6.64 Exploded view of the steering column gearchange control (3 speed gearbox type N30/31) (Sec 11)

1 Retainer	9 Spacer	17 Upper shaft	25 Knob
2 Spring	10 Key	18 Bush	26 Cross shaft support
3 Dust excluder	11 Low speed lever	19 Washer	27 Bush
4 High speed lever	12 Bush	20 Circlip	28 Dust cover
5 Bush	13 Lower bracket	21 Cover	29 Cross shaft
6 Grommet	14 Dust seal	22 Shift lever	30 Low speed connecting rod
7 Star washer	15 Control shaft	23 Shift lever pin	31 High speed rod
8 Swivel pin	16 Spring	24 Spring	32 Circlip

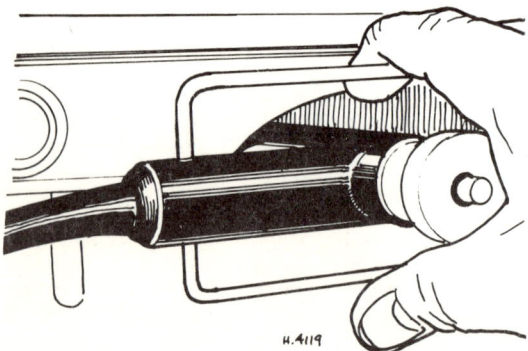

Fig 6.65 Depressing the shift lever spring loaded retaining pins (Steering column gearchange) (Sec 11)

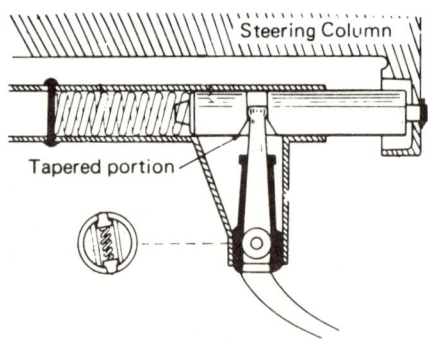

Fig 6.66 Steering column gearchange control installation diagram (Sec 11)

control low speed lever (4) and bush.
4 Remove the shrouds from the upper end of the steering column and unscrew the wiring harness clips.
5 Depress the shift lever spring pins simultaneously with a suitable tool and withdraw the lever.
6 Prise off the circlip and remove the washer, upper shaft and spring. Withdraw the control shaft into the vehicle interior.
7 Remove the low and high speed connecting rods and the cross-shaft from the gearbox end of the control system.
8 Inspect all components for wear and renew as necessary.
9 Commence reassembly by inserting the control shaft into the column followed by the compression spring and upper shaft. The upper shaft must be positioned so that the tapered end of the shift lever hole will be ready to receive the lever.
10 Fit the washer and circlip so that the upper bracket is located between them.
11 Insert the springs and pins into the recesses in the shift lever and depressing both pins at the same time, connect the shift lever to the control shaft.
12 Refit the wiring harness clip and upper steering column shrouds.
13 Install the lower bush, low speed lever and selecting key to the shaft, driving in the key until it projects equally both sides.
14 Grease all moving parts and then fit the spacer, high speed lever, dust cover and shaft lever retainer. Connect the reversing lamp switch leads.
15 Fit the cross-shaft, the low speed connecting rod, the high speed connecting rod and the shift rod.
16 With installation complete, position the hand shift lever in neutral. Loosen the low and high speed connecting rod swivel nuts. Align the control shaft adjusting hole with the one in the shift lever retainer and insert a piece of ¼ in (6.3 mm) diameter rod as a guide pin while the swivel nuts are moved on their rods to the points where no stress is applied to the rod in either direction. Tighten the swivel nuts. Check the operation of the gearchange mechanism by moving the hand shift lever to all gear positions.

12 Gearbox (four speed type) - removal and installation

1 The procedure is very similar to that described for the three speed types except that the gearbox must be lowered sufficiently to unbolt the gearchange lever mounting flange from the remote control housing on type W.40 units.

13 Gearbox (four speed type SS1) - dismantling and inspection of components

1 Unscrew the side cover bolts, half a turn at a time and in diagonal sequence and then tap off the cover with a soft faced mallet. Do not lever it off by inserting a scewdriver between the joint faces or the light alloy surfaces will be damaged.
2 From within the clutch bellhousing, remove the clutch release mechanism and bearing.
3 Unbolt the clutch bellhousing from the gearbox and remove it. Remove the speedometer drive gear from the extension housing.
4 From the front face of the gearbox, unbolt and remove the bearing retainer.
5 Unscrew and remove the bolts which secure the extension housing to the gearbox casing and then turn the extension housing in a clockwise direction (viewed from the rear) until the end of the countershaft is exposed. Measure the countershaft gear assembly endfloat and record it for reference during re-assembly
6 From the front face of the gearbox, drive the countershaft out towards the rear. Use a rod for this purpose which is slightly less in diameter than the countershaft so that it will retain the countershaft needle roller bearings and thrust washers in position as it passes through.
7 Withdraw the dummy countershaft and lower the countershaft gear to the bottom of the gearbox.
8 Withdraw the extension housing with mainshaft assembly

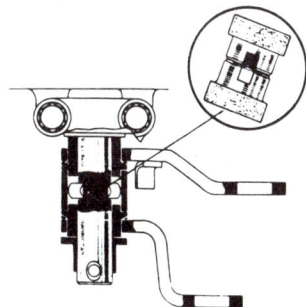

Fig 6.67 Selector key installation diagram (Steering column gearchange) (Sec 11)

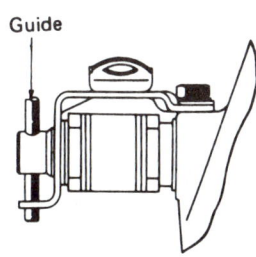

Fig 6.68 Control shaft to shift lever retainer alignment (Steering column gearchange) (Sec 11)

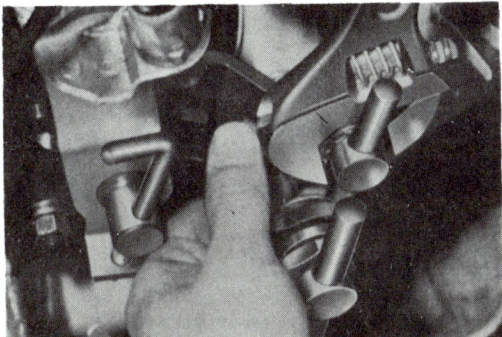

Fig 6.69 Tightening the control rod swivel nut (Steering column gearchange) (Sec 11)

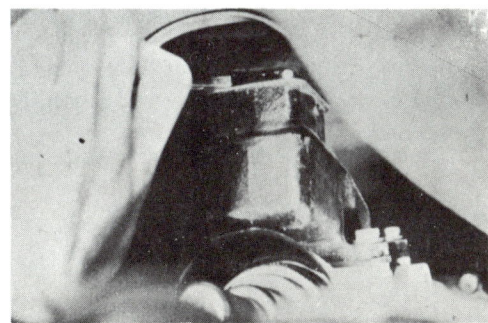

Fig 6.70 Unbolting the gearchange control lever retaining flange on 4 speed type W40 gearbox (Sec 12)

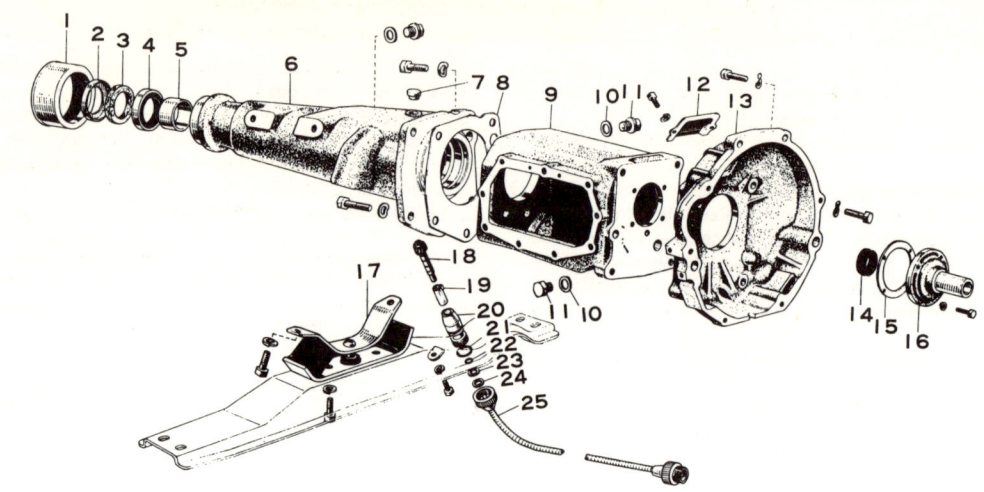

Fig 6.71 External components of 4 speed type SS1 gearbox (Sec 13)

1 Dust deflector
2 Dust seal retainer
3 Dust seal
4 Oil seal
5 Bush
6 Extension housing
7 Breather
8 Gasket
9 Casing
10 Washer
11 Drain plug
12 Inspection cover
13 Clutch bellhousing
14 Oil seal
15 Gasket
16 Front bearing retainer
17 Rear mounting
18 Speedometer drive gear
19 Bush
21 and 22 'O' rings
23 Collar
24 Gasket
25 Speedometer cable

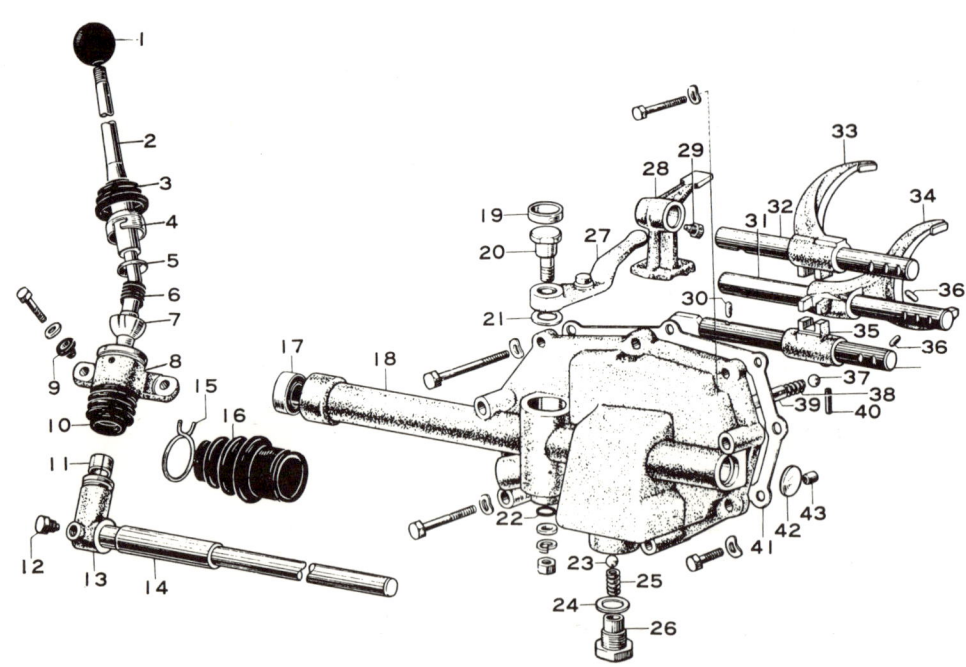

Fig 6.72 Side cover and selector mechanism 4 speed type SS1 gearbox (Sec 13)

1 Knob
2 Gearchange
3 Flexible boot
4 Cap
5 Spring seat
6 Spring
7 Ball seat
8 Retainer bracket
9 Bush
10 Flexible boot
11 Bush
12 Gearchange lever lock bolt
13 Housing
14 Remote control rod
15 Clip
17 Oil seal
18 Side cover
19 Plug
20 Shift arm pivot
21 Washer
22 'O' ring
23 Lock ball
24 Washer
25 Spring
26 Reverse restrictor plug
27 Reverse shift arm
28 Selector lever
29 Lock bolt
30 Interlock pin
31 3rd/4th selector shaft
32 1st/2nd selector shaft
33 1st/2nd shift fork
34 3rd/4th shaft fork
35 Reverse shift fork
36 Interlock pin
37 Detent ball
38 Spring
39 Plunger
40 Tension pin
41 Gasket
42 Welch plug
43 Hollow dowel

Chapter 6/Manual gearbox and automatic transmission

from the rear of the gearbox. During this operation, hold the countergear assembly to one side of the gearbox casing.

9 Remove the input shaft by tapping it gently, with a soft faced hammer, out of the front face of the gearbox in a forward direction. If necessary, remove the bearing using a two legged extractor after withdrawing the securing circlip.

10 Using a thin drift, drive the reverse idler gear shaft to the rear, far enough to enable the reverse idler gear to be removed from the shaft. Extract the shaft complete with Woodruff key.

11 Lift the countergear assembly complete with needle rollers from the bottom of the gearbox and also remove the two thrust washers.

12 From the front end of the mainshaft (still attached to the extension housing) remove the circlip and draw off the 3rd/4th synchro unit, third gear and bush, thrust washer, 2nd gear and bush, and 1st/2nd synchro unit.

13 Remove the mainshaft bearing outer track circlip and tap the mainshaft forward out of the extension housing.

14 If necessary, the speedometer drive gear with its retaining clips can now be withdrawn from the mainshaft, retaining the

Fig 6.73 Extension housing rotated to expose end of countershaft (4 speed type SS 1 gearbox) (Sec 13)

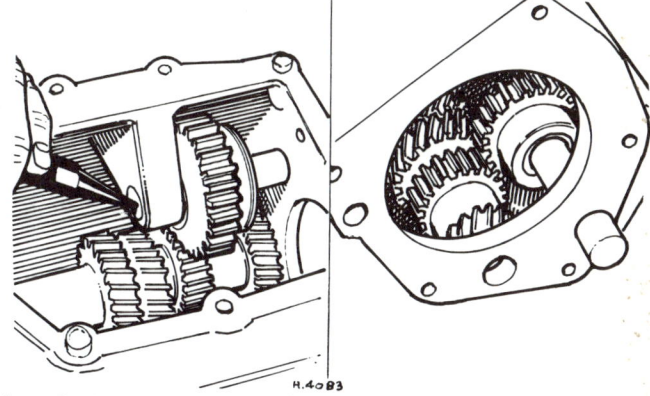

Fig 6.74 Removing reverse idler shaft and gear from 4 speed type SS 1 gearbox (Sec 13)

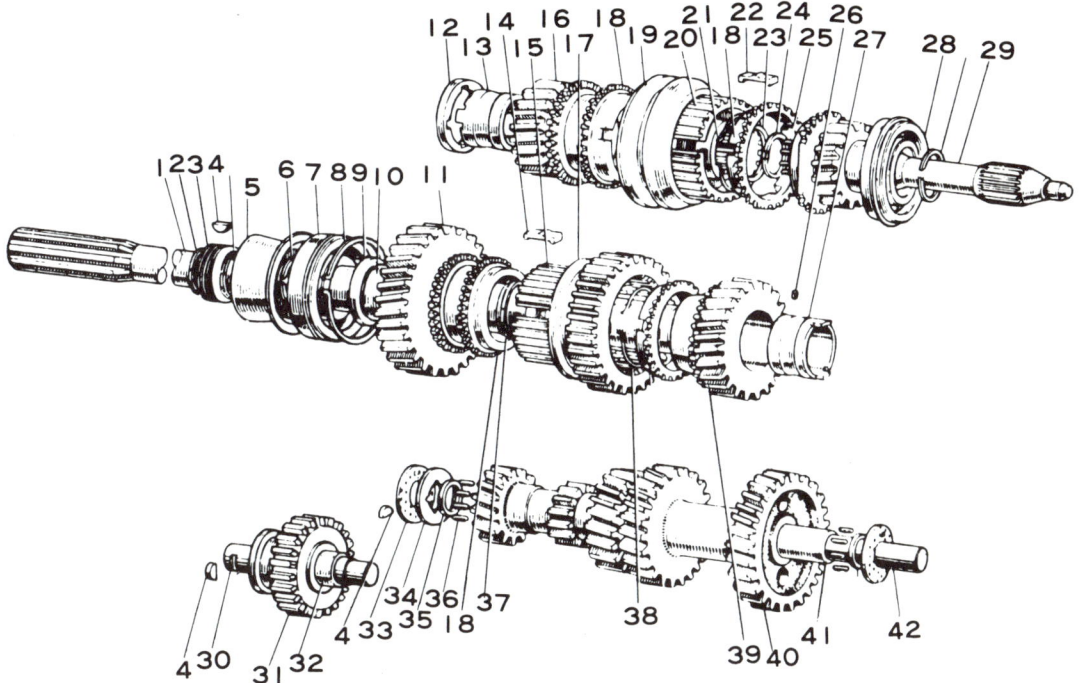

Fig 6.75 Internal components of 4 speed type SS1 gearbox (Sec 13)

1 Mainshaft
2 Circlip
3 Speedometer drive gear
4 Woodruff key
5 Oil deflector
6 Circlip
7 Mainshaft bearing
8 Bearing outer track circlip
9 Spacer
10 Bush
11 1st gear
12 Thrust washer
13 Bush
14 Blocker bar
15 1st/2nd synchro. hub
16 3rd gear
17 Reverse gear
18 Synchro. ring
19 Synchro. sleeve
20 3rd/4th synchro. hub
21 Spring
22 Blocker bar
23 Circlip
24 Circlip
25 Needle bearings
26 Pin
27 Bush
28 Input shaft bearing
29 Input shaft
30 Reverse idler gear shaft
31 Reverse idler gear
32 Bush
33 Thrust washer (bronze)
34 Thrust washer (steel)
35 Spacer
36 Needle roller bearings
37 Circlip
38 Spring
39 2nd gear
40 Counter gear assembly
41 Distance tube
42 Countershaft

Woodruff key. Remove the oil deflector and if the bearing is to be removed, a press will have to be used. Draw off the circlip, bearing, 1st gear bush and spacer from the rear end of the mainshaft.

15 If the shift fork and selector mechanism is to be dismantled, secure the side cover in a vice and move 3rd/4th gear shift fork to the 4th gear position. Drive out the tension pin (2) and then remove the selector shaft and fork taking care to retain the detent ball and spring which will be ejected. (photo) (Fig 6.76)

16 Remove the 1st/2nd selector shaft and fork in a similar manner and remove the interlock pins during the process.

17 From the lower face of the side cover, unscrew and remove

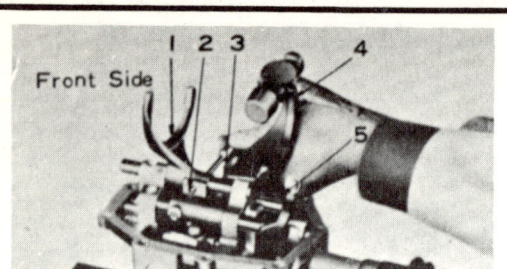

Fig 6.76 Selector shaft/shift fork assembly on 4 speed type SS1 gearbox (Sec 13)

1 3rd/4th shift fork
2 Tension pin
3 3rd/4th selector shaft
4 1st/2nd shift fork
5 Reverse selector shaft

13.15 Shift fork securing tension pin (SS1 gearbox)

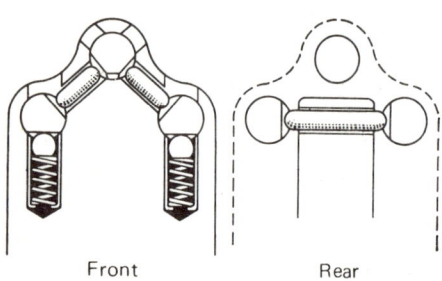

Fig 6.77 Sectional view of detent balls and interlock pins on 4 speed type SS1 gearbox (Sec 13)

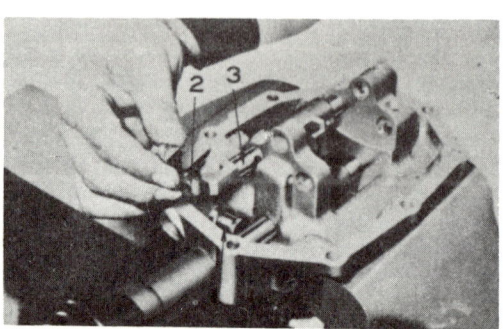

Fig 6.78 Removing reverse selector shaft and shift fork from 4 speed type SS1 gearbox (Sec 13)

1 Shift arm pivot
2 Reverse gear shift arm
3 Reverse selector shaft

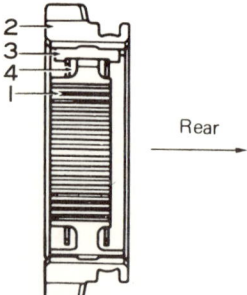

Fig 6.79 Correct assembly of 1st/2nd synchro. unit (4 speed type SS1 gearbox) (Sec 13)

1 Synchro. hub 2 synchro. sleeve
3 Blocker bar 4 Spring

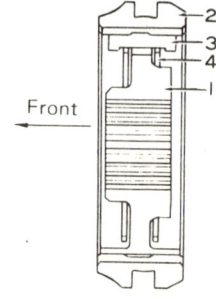

Fig 6.80 Correct assembly of 3rd/4th synchro. unit (4 speed type SS1 gearbox) (Sec 13)

1 Synchro. hub 2 Synchro. sleeve
3 Blocker bar 4 Springs

13.21 Example of wear on selector fork (SS1 gearbox)

Chapter 6/Manual gearbox and automatic transmission

the reverse restrictor plug, spring and ball.
18 Cut the locking wire and remove the shift lever lock bolt. Withdraw the remote control rod.
19 Remove the reverse shift arm and pivot bolt and then drive out the securing tension pin and withdraw the reverse selector shaft and fork. Again take care that the detent ball and spring are not lost. Remove the reversing lamp switch if necessary.
20 If the gearchange lever is to be removed from its retainer, depress the bayonet fitting type cap and turn it in an anti-clockwise direction.
21 Carry out an inspection of the dismantled components as described in Section 3, paragraphs 22 to 28 for the three speed type gearbox. (photo)

14 Gearbox (four speed type SS1) - reassembly

1 Reassemble the selector and shift mechanism to the side cover by reversing the dismantling process. Use new tension pins and 'O' ring seals and check carefully that the detent balls and interlock pins are correctly located. Do not tighten the shift arm pivot locknut until the side cover is fitted to the gearbox and the pivot adjusted (see paragraph 25).
2 Ensure that the 1st/2nd synchro retaining circlip is in position on the mainshaft and then to the rear end of the mainshaft slide on the 1st gear and the spacer, and then press on the new bearing, applying pressure only to the centre track. (photos) Make sure that the outer track circlip groove is nearer the front of the shaft.
3 Measure the clearance between the 1st gear and the spacer which should be as specified in Specifications Section. (photo)
4 Fit a bearing retaining circlip which will give the minimum groove clearance from those listed in Specifications Section. (photo)
5 To the mainshaft, fit the oil deflector, the first circlip, the speedometer drive gear with Woodruff key and the second **speedo drive gear circlip. (photos)**

14.2a 1st/2nd synchro. circlip on mainshaft (SS1 gearbox)

14.2b Installing 1st gear to rear end of mainshaft (SS1 gearbox)

14.2c Installing mainshaft rear bearing (SS1 gearbox)

14.3 Measuring 1st gear to spacer clearance (SS1 gearbox)

14.4 Mainshaft rear bearing circlip (SS1 gearbox)

14.5a Fitting oil deflector to mainshaft (SS1 gearbox)

14.5b Speedometer drive gear key (SS1 gearbox)

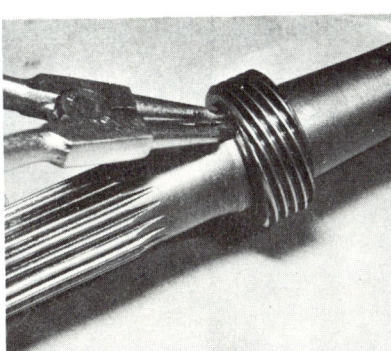
14.5c Installing speedometer drive gear second circlip (SS1 gearbox)

6 Assemble the mainshaft into the extension housing and install a bearing outer track circlip to provide minimum endfloat, from those listed in Specifications Section. (photos)

7 Fit the speedometer driven gear to the extension housing. (photos)

8 To the front of the mainshaft fit the 1st/2nd synchro unit, 2nd gear and its bush, the thrust washer and 3rd gear bush. (photos)

9 Measure the endfloat between 2nd gear and the thrust washer. Where this is not as specified (see Specifications Section) change the second gear bush for one of different length.

10 Onto the mainshaft install 3rd gear and 3rd/4th gear synchro unit, then measure the endfloat between 3rd gear and the thrust washer. If the clearance is outside that specified (see Specifications Section) change the 3rd gear bush for one of different length. (photo)

11 Fit a new circlip to the front end of the mainshaft, ensuring that the correct endfloat of between 0 and 0.0020 in (0 and 0.05 mm) is obtained by selecting one of suitable thickness from

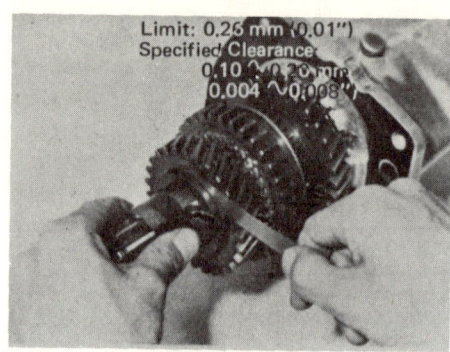

Fig 6.81 Measuring 2nd gear endfloat (4 speed type SS1 gearbox) (Sec 14)

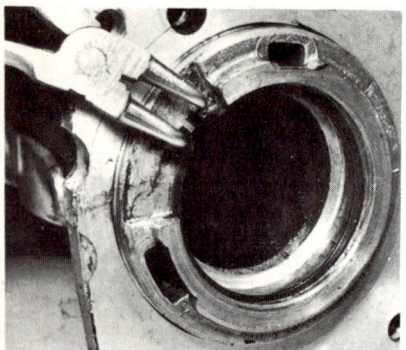

14.6a Installing mainshaft rear bearing outer circlip (SS1 gearbox)

14.6b Installing mainshaft assembly to extension housing (SS1 gearbox)

14.7a Installing speedometer driven gear (SS1 gearbox)

14.7b Speedometer driven gear lock plate and bolt (SS1 gearbox)

14.8a Installing 1st/2nd synchro. unit to mainshaft (SS1 gearbox)

14.8b Installing 2nd gear bush to mainshaft (SS1 gearbox)

14.8c Installing 2nd gear to mainshaft (SS1 gearbox)

14.8d Installing 2nd gear thrust washer to mainshaft (SS1 gearbox)

14.8e Installing 3rd gear bush to mainshaft (SS1 gearbox)

Chapter 6/Manual gearbox and automatic transmission

those listed in Specifications Section. (photo)

12 Install the reverse idler gear and shaft into the gearbox, aligning the Woodruff key correctly with the keyway. Note the direction of installation of the reverse idler gear. (photo)

13 Using a dummy shaft, stick 25 needle rollers into each end of the countergear using thick grease to hold them and their spacers. (photos)

14 Stick the countergear thrust washers into their recesses on the internal faces of the gearbox casing again using a dab of thick grease for the purpose. There is only one plain thrust washer and this fits against the inner face of the bronze washer at the smaller gear end of the countergear. (photo)

15 Lower the countergear assembly into the bottom of the gearbox taking care not to displace the thrust washers. (photo)

16 If the input shaft bearing has been removed, press on the new one and select an outer track circlip to give the minimum clearance in the groove from those listed in Specifications Section.

17 Stick the 14 needle rollers into the recess in the rear face of the input shaft using thick grease to retain them and then fit the internal type circlip. (photo)

18 Install the input shaft into the gearbox and fit the synchro ring to the input shaft cone. (photo)

19 Use a new gasket and assemble the extension housing to the gearbox, rotating the housing to expose the countershaft hole. (photo)

20 Insert the hand through the side cover aperture and raise the countergear so that the countershaft can be installed from the rear face of the gearbox, displacing the dummy shaft but not the needle rollers or thrust washers. Check that the countershaft is secured by the Woodruff key which is positioned at the extension housing end of the shaft. Check the countershaft endfloat which should lie within that specified and as measured before dismantling. Where it is outside the correct tolerance, the thrust washers will have to be changed for ones of alternative thickness as listed in Specification Section. (photo)

21 Turn the extension housing back to its correct position and tighten the securing bolts, having applied jointing compound to

14.10 Installing 3rd/4th synchro. unit to mainshaft (SS1 gearbox)

14.11 Fitting circlip to front end of mainshaft (SS1 gearbox)

14.12 Installation of reverse idler gear and shaft (SS1 gearbox)

14.13a Installing countershaft needle roller bearings (SS1 gearbox)

14.13b Installing countershaft needle roller bearing spacer (SS1 gearbox)

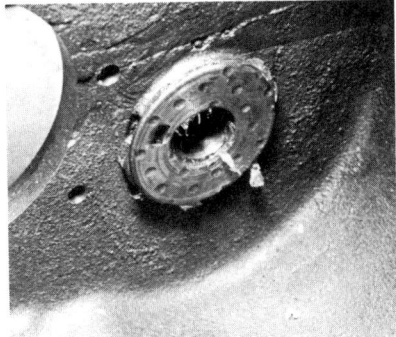
14.14 Countershaft (bronze) thrust washer correctly located (SS1 gearbox)

Fig 6.82 Measuring 3rd gear endfloat (4 speed type SS1 gearbox) (Sec 14)

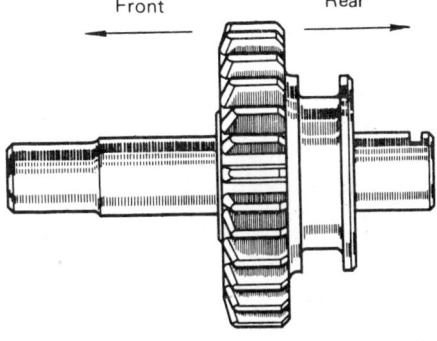
Fig 6.83 Correct orientation of reverse idler gear on 4 speed type SS1 gearbox (Sec 14)

14.15 Countergear components

14.17 Needle rollers retained in input shaft (SS1 gearbox)

14.18 Installing input shaft (SS1 gearbox)

14.19 Assembling extension housing to gearbox (SS1 gearbox)

14.20 Countershaft key (SS1 gearbox)

14.22 Installing front bearing retainer (SS1 gearbox)

14.23a Side cover/Selector assembly (SS1 gearbox)

14.23b Installing side cover (SS1 gearbox)

14.24a Installing clutch bellhousing (SS1 gearbox)

14.24b Release bearing and springs correctly installed (SS1 gearbox)

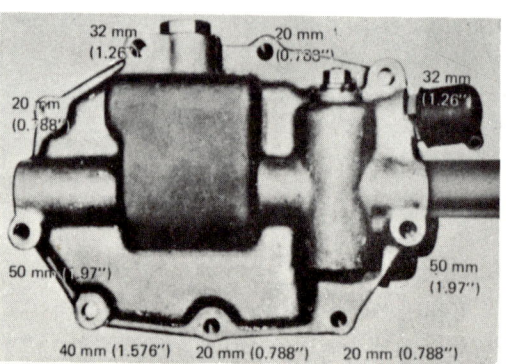

Fig 6.84 Location of differing lengths of side cover bolts (4 speed type SS1 gearbox) (Sec 14)

their threads.
22 Fit the front bearing retainer using a new gasket and making sure that the oil return groove is correctly aligned. Apply jointing compound to the bolt threads. (photo)
23 Fit the side cover using a new gasket. Make sure that the shift forks engage correctly with the synchro unit grooves. Apply jointing compound to both sides of the gasket and to the bolt threads. Note that the side cover securing bolts are of different lengths and must be refitted exactly as indicated. (photos) (Fig 6.84)
24 Refit the clutch bellhousing and release mechanism. (photos)
25 With the gearbox completely reassembled, adjust the reverse gear pivot. To do this, release the shift arm pivot locknut and using the slot in the end of the shift arm pivot, turn it in a **clockwise** direction so that reverse idler gear is moved into contact with 1st gear. Now by means of the slot, turn the shift arm pivot through 90° **anticlockwise** and secure it in this position with the locknut.

15 Gearbox (four speed type W40) - dismantling into major assemblies

1 Remove the clutch release fork and bearing from within the clutch bellhousing. Unbolt the clutch bellhousing from the gearbox.
2 Remove the speedometer driven gear from the extension housing.
3 Unscrew and remove the reverse gear restrict pin and then unbolt and remove the exhaust housing making sure that the swing arm is moved in an anticlockwise direction (when viewed from the rear) to disengage the remote control rod from the

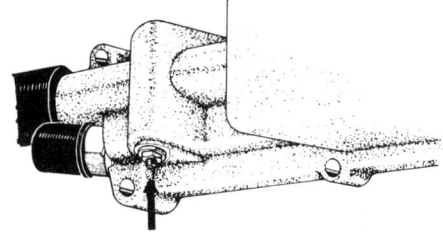

Fig 6.85 Location of reverse gear pivot adjuster screw on 4 speed type SS1 gearbox (Sec 14)

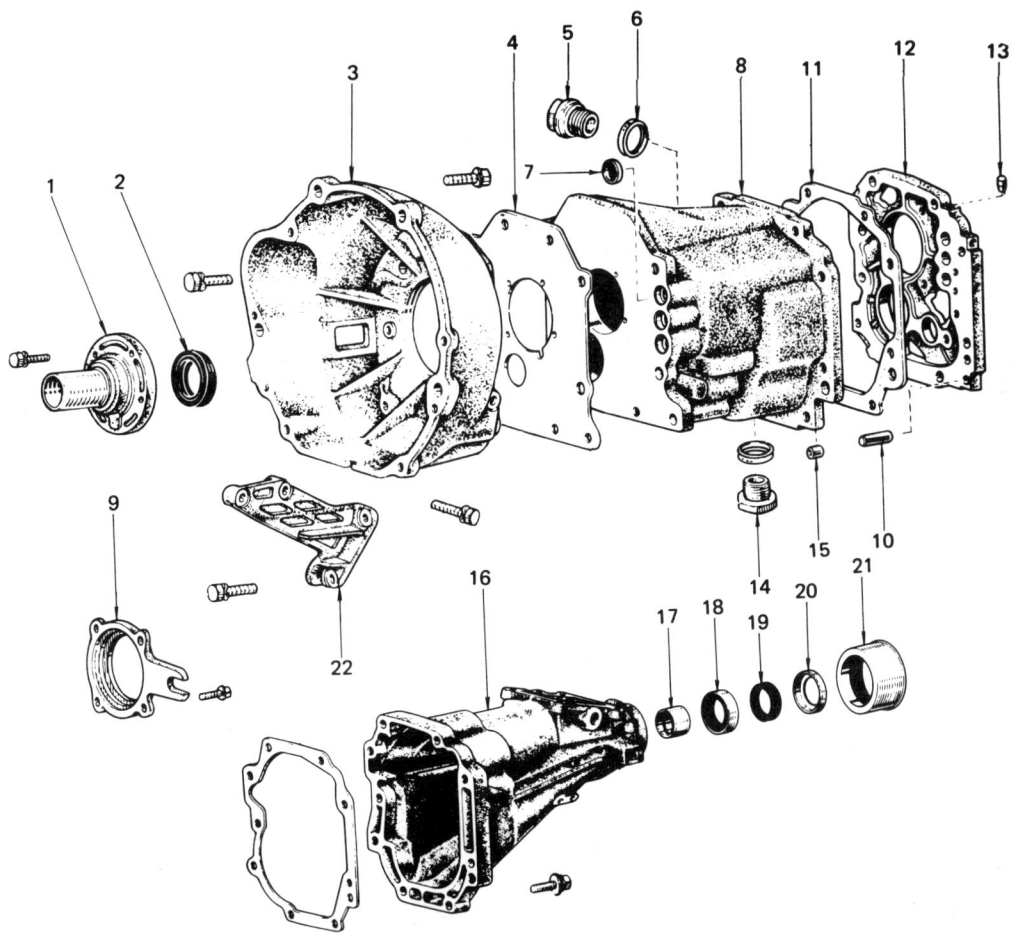

Fig 6.86 External components of the 4 speed type W40 gearbox (Sec 15)

1 Front bearing retainer
2 Oil seal
3 Clutch bellhousing
4 Gasket
5 Filler/level plug
6 Gasket
7 Plug
8 Casing
9 Mainshaft rear bearing retainer
10 Dowel pin
11 Gasket
12 Intermediate plate
13 Dowel
14 Drain plug
15 Hollow dowel
16 Extension housing
17 Bush
18 Oil seal
19 Dust seal
20 Dust seal retainer
21 Dust deflector
22 Reinforcement bracket

selector rods.
4 With the extension housing removed, drive out the tension pin and remove the remote control rod and swing arm.
5 Remove the reversing lamp switch.
6 From the front face of the gearbox, remove the front bearing retainer, the countershaft cover and spacer.
7 Remove the circlips from the outer tracks of the input shaft and countershaft front bearings.

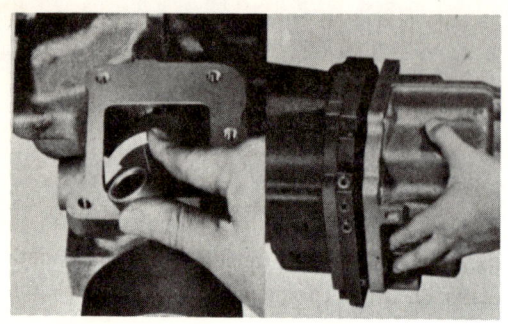

Fig 6.87 Removing extension housing (4 speed type W40 gearbox) (Sec 15)

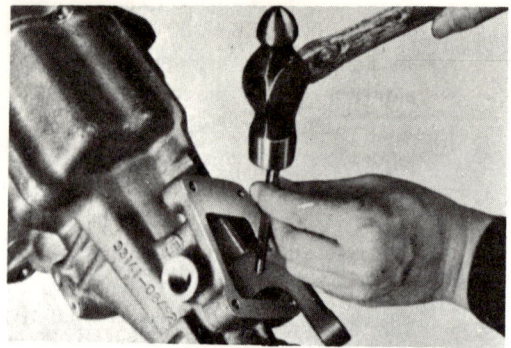

Fig 6.88 Driving out remote control shaft/swing arm tension pin (4 speed type W40 gearbox) (Sec 15)

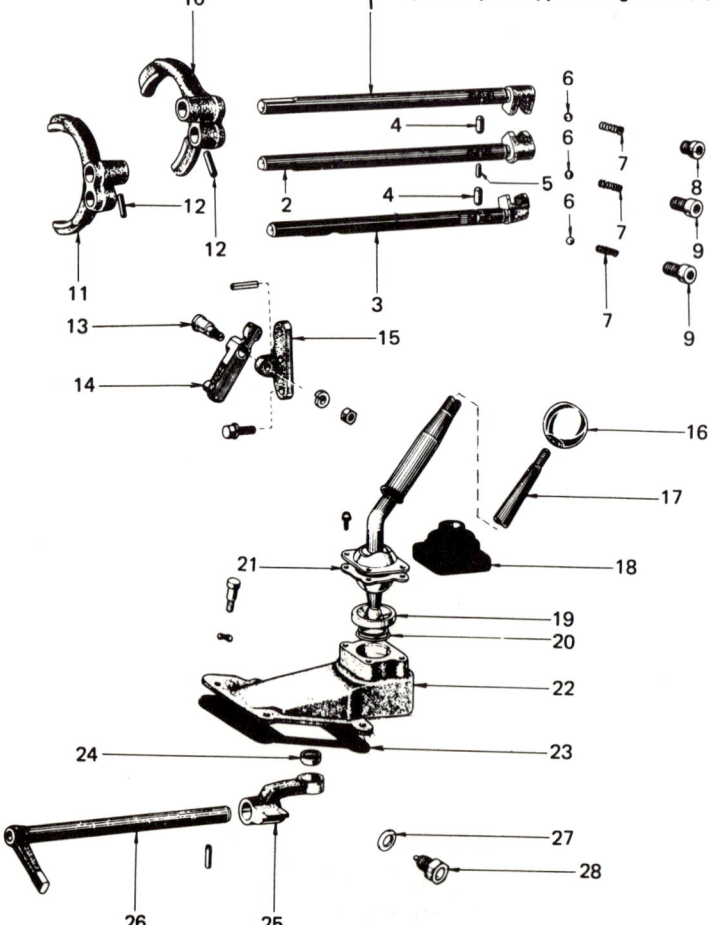

Fig 6.89 Shift and selector components (4 speed type W40 gearbox) (Sec 15)

1 1st/2nd selector shaft
2 3rd/4th selector shaft
3 Remover selector shaft
4 Interlock pin
5 Interlock pin
6 Detent balls
7 Detent springs
8 Socket screw
9 Socket screw
10 1st/2nd shift fork
11 3rd/4th shift fork
12 Tension pin
13 Reverse shift arm pivot
14 Reverse shift arm
15 Reverse shift arm bracket
16 Gearchange knob
17 Gearchange lever
18 Boot
19 Seat
20 Spring
21 Ball retaining flange
22 Remote control housing
23 Oil defelctor
24 Bush
25 Swing arm
26 Remote control rod
27 Washer
28 Reverse restrictor pin

Chapter 6/Manual gearbox and automatic transmission

8 Separate the casing from the intermediate plate and pull off the casing leaving all the gear assemblies attached to the intermediate plate.
9 Secure the intermediate plate in the jaws of a vice using jaw protectors to prevent damaging the plate.
10 Remove the speedometer drive gear and retain the locking ball.
11 Drive out the tension pin, slacken the reverse gear shift arm bracket bolt and withdraw the bracket with shift arm attached.
12 Unbolt the reverse idler gear shaft stop and withdraw the idler gear and shaft towards the front of the gearbox. (Fig 6.93)
13 Unbolt and remove the mainshaft rear bearing retainer.
14 Using an Allen key, unscrew the plugs from the edge of the intermediate plate and extract the springs and detent balls.
15 Drive out the tension pin from each of the shift forks.
16 Withdraw each of the selector shafts in the sequence - reverse, 3rd/4th, 1st/2nd. Remove each of the shift forks as the selector shafts are withdrawn and retrieve the interlock pins.
17 Remove the circlip from the mainshaft rear bearing outer track and then push the mainshaft and countershaft assemblies simultaneously (meshed together) from the rear face of the intermediate plate. (Fig 6.96)
18 Inspect all the components for wear and renew as necessary.

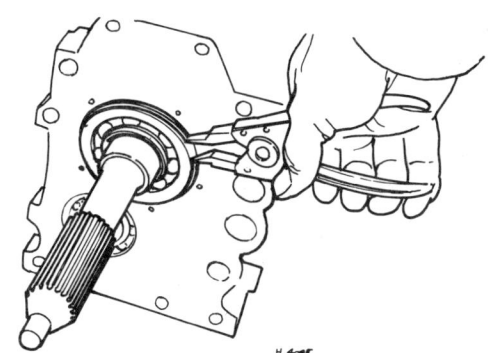

Fig 6.90 Removing front bearing outer track circlips (4 speed type W.40 gearbox) (Sec 15)

Fig 6.91 Separating gear casing and intermediate plate (4 speed type W40 gearbox) (Sec 15)

16 Mainshaft (four speed gearbox type W40) - servicing

1 Pull off the input shaft and synchroniser ring from the front

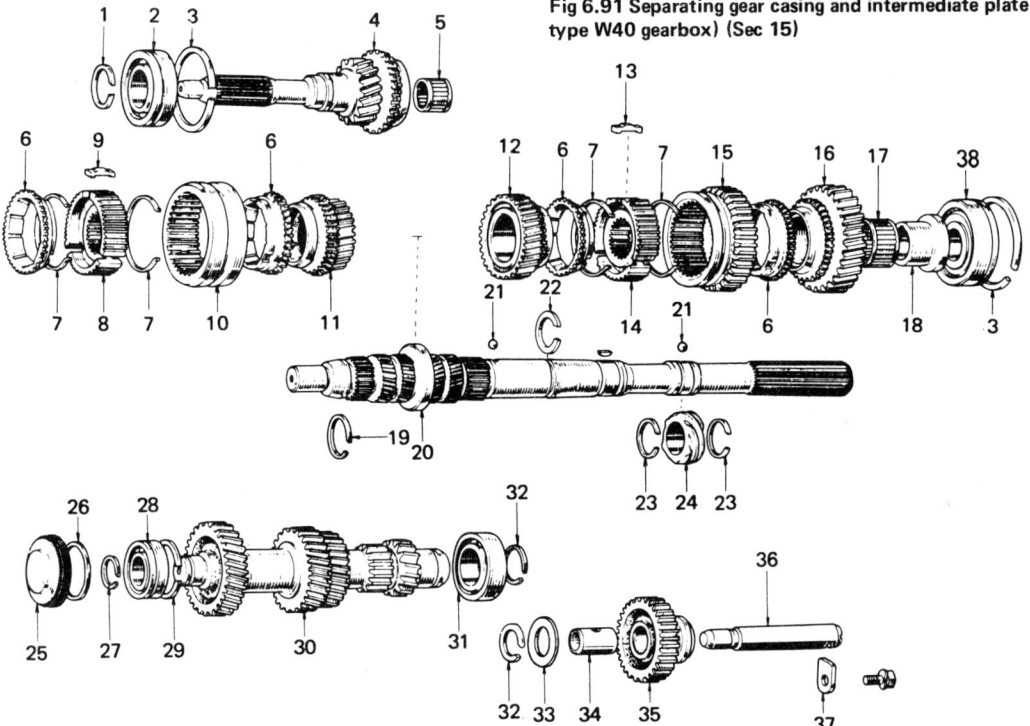

Fig 6.92 Internal components of 4 speed type W40 gearbox (Sec 15)

1 Circlip	10 3rd/4th synchro. sleeve	track	circlip
2 Input shaft bearing	11 3rd gear	19 Circlip	30 Countergear
3 Bearing outer track circlip	12 2nd gear	20 Mainshaft	31 Countershaft rear bearing
4 Input shaft	13 Blocker bar	21 Lock ball	32 Circlip
5 Needle roller bearing	14 1st/2nd synchro. hub	22 Circlip	33 Spacer
6 3rd/4th synchro. ring	15 Reverse gear	23 Circlip	34 Bush
7 Spring	16 1st gear	24 Speedometer drive gear	35 Reverse idler gear
8 3rd/4th synchro. hub	17 Needle roller bearing	25 Countershaft cover	36 Reverse idler shaft
9 Blocker bar	18 1st gear bearing inner	26 Spacer	37 Reverse idler shaft stop
		27 Circlip	38 Mainshaft rear bearing
		28 Countershaft front bearing	
		29 Bearing outer track	

of the mainshaft.
2 Extract the shaft circlip and withdraw the 3rd/4th synchro unit followed by 3rd gear.
3 If the rear bearing is to be removed, extract the shaft circlip and press it from the shaft on a press.
4 With the rear bearing removed, 1st gear, the needle roller bearing and the synchro ring can be drawn off the rear end of the mainshaft. Do not lose the locking balls from the needle bearing inner race.
5 A press must again be used to remove the reverse gear, 1st/2nd synchro unit, second gear and synchro ring.
6 Clean all components thoroughly and examine for worn or

Fig 6.93 Removing reverse idler gear from 4 speed type W40 gearbox (Sec 15)

Fig 6.94 Removing a detent socket screw (4 speed type W40 gearbox) (Sec 15)

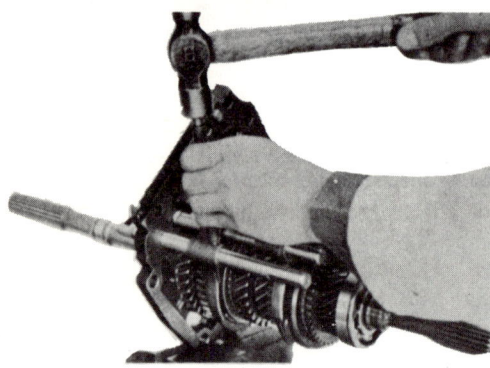

Fig 6.95 Driving out a shift fork tension pin (4 speed type W40 gearbox) (Sec 15)

Fig 6.96 Removing mainshaft and countershaft assemblies from intermediate plate of 4 speed type W40 gearbox (Sec 15)

Fig 6.97 Removing 3/4th synchro. unit and 3rd gear (4 speed type W40 gearbox) (Sec 16)

Fig 6.98 Removing mainshaft rear bearing (4 speed type W40 gearbox) (Sec 16)

Fig 6.99 Removing reverse and 2nd gear using a press (4 speed type W40 gearbox) (Sec 16)

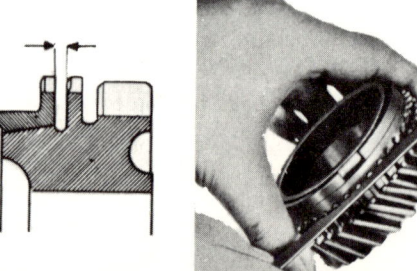

Fig 6.100 Checking synchro. ring to gear clearance (4 speed type W40 gearbox) (Sec 16)

chipped teeth and grooving or scoring of the shaft. The gears should have a running clearance between their internal bores and the shaft of between 0.0014 and 0.0039 in (0.06 and 0.10 mm) with a maximum of 0.0059 in (0.15 mm).

7 Inspect the condition of the synchroniser units. If there has been a history of noisy gearchanging or the synchromesh could easily be 'beaten', renew the unit complete. In any event, fit the synchro ring onto the gear and measure the clearance. This should not be less than 0.031 in (0.8 mm) otherwise renew the ring.

8 Fit the shift forks to the synchro sleeves and check for side clearance. If this exceeds 0.039 in (1.0 mm) renew one or both components as necessary.

9 Correct assembly of the two synchro units must be carried out before installing them to the mainshaft. Ensure that the spring ends do not engage in the same gaps on opposite sides of the unit.

10 Commence reassembly by installing 3rd gear complete with synchro ring onto the mainshaft. Apply oil liberally to all components.

11 Slide the 3rd/4th synchro unit onto the mainshaft until it rests against the shoulder on the shaft. Tap it into position if necessary using a plastic faced hammer and secure it with a circlip that will give a groove clearance of not more than 0.002 in (0.05 mm). Select a circlip from those listed in the Specifications Section.

12 Using feeler blades, measure the third gear endfloat, which should be between 0.0059 and 0.0098 in (0.15 and 0.25 mm) with a maximum of 0.0118 in (0.30 mm).

13 Install 2nd gear complete with synchro ring onto the mainshaft.

14 Using a press, install the 1st/2nd synchro unit and reverse gear assembly onto the mainshaft.

15 Measure 2nd gear endfloat which should be within the tolerances specified for 3rd gear in paragraph 12.

16 Using a dab of thick grease, stick the needle bearing inner track locking ball into its shaft recess.

17 Slide 1st gear, 3rd/4th synchro ring, needle bearing and inner track, (held as an assembly) onto the shaft. Check that the inner track slot aligns with the locking ball and that the synchro ring slots are aligned with the shift keys.

18 Press the mainshaft rear bearing onto the shaft end, making sure that the outer track circlip groove is nearer the rear end of the mainshaft.

19 Measure first gear endfloat which again should be as specified for third gear in paragraph 12.

20 Select a circlip for securing the mainshaft rear bearing to the shaft to give the minimum clearance. There are eleven alternative thicknesses available (see Specifications).

17 Input shaft (four speed gearbox type W40) - servicing

The procedure is identical to that described in Section 7.

18 Countershaft and reverse gear assemblies (four speed gearbox type W40) - servicing

1 The countershaft assembly cannot be dismantled and must be renewed if the gears are chipped or worn. The bearings can be renewed using an extractor and press.

2 The reverse idler gear, should be renewed if the teeth are

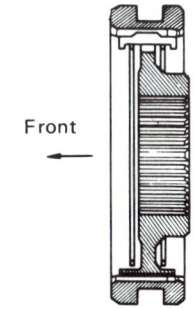

Fig 6.101 Checking clearance of shift fork in synchro sleeve groove (4 speed type W40 gearbox) (Sec 16)

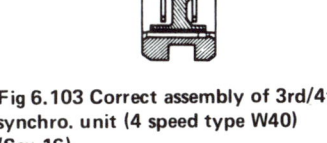

Fig 6.102 Correct assembly of 1st/2nd synchro unit (4 speed type W40 gearbox) (Sec 16)

Fig 6.103 Correct assembly of 3rd/4th synchro. unit (4 speed type W40) (Sev 16)

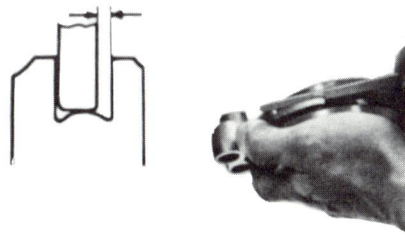

Fig 6.104 Measuring 3rd gear endfloat (4 speed type W40 gearbox) (Sec 16)

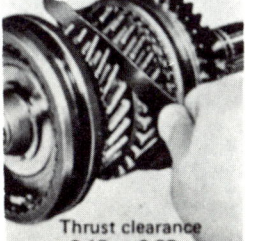

Fig 6.105 Measuring 2nd gear endfloat (4 speed type W40 gearbox) (Sec 16)

Fig 6.106 Measuring 1st gear endfloat (4 speed type W40 gearbox) (Sec 16)

worn or chipped; also the shaft if scored or grooved.

3 If the reverse gear bush is worn, it must be pressed out and the new one fitted so that the oil holes are in alignment and then the bush reamed if necessary to achieve a finished internal diameter of between 0.7890 and 0.7898 in (20.04 and 20.06 mm).

19 Oil seals (four speed gearbox type W40) - renewal

1 The recommendations and procedure are as described in Section 9, excluding paragraph 2.

20 Gearbox (four speed type W40) - reassembly

1 Check that the dowel pin projects between ¼ in and 5/16 in (6.0 to 8.0 mm) from the front face of the intermediate plate and then secure the plate in a vice fitted with jaw protectors.

2 Insert the needle roller bearing into the input shaft recess, sticking it in position with grease.

3 Liberally oil all components as they are assembled, commencing by fitting the 3rd/4th synchro ring to the rear end of the input shaft.

4 Fit the input shaft to the front end of the mainshaft.

5 Mesh the mainshaft and countershaft assemblies and insert them together into the intermediate plate.

6 Fit the circlip to the groove in the mainshaft rear bearing outer track.

7 Connect the reverse idler shaft to the reverse idler gear and fit them to the intermediate plate. Fit the spacer over the shaft and secure with a circlip.

8 Fit the stop to retain the reverse idler shaft in position.

9 Locate 1st/2nd and 3rd/4th shift forks into their respective synchro sleeve grooves. When correctly positioned, the longer bosses of these two shift forks will face each other.

10 Install 1st/2nd selector shaft and interlock pin, followed by 3rd/4th selector shaft and its interlock pin and then the third interlock pin and reverse selector shaft. Each selector shaft should be in the neutral position when inserting its interlock pin.

11 Secure the shift forks to their respective selector shafts by driving in the tension pins.

12 Into the holes in the edge of the intermediate plate, insert the detent balls and springs. Apply gasket sealing compound to the plugs and screw them in to the specified torque.

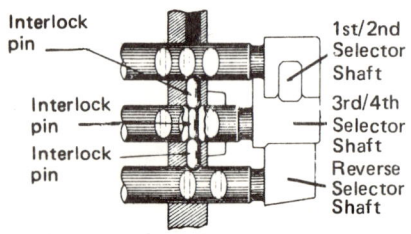

Fig 6.107 Location of selector shaft interlock pins (4 speed type W40 gearbox) (Sec 20)

Fig 6.108 Mainshaft rear bearing retainer installed on intermediate plate of 4 speed type W40 gearbox (Sec 20)

Fig 6.109 Installing shift arm and tension pin (4 speed type W40 gearbox) (Sec 20)

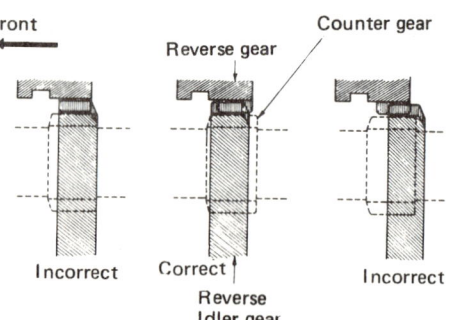

Fig 6.110 Adjustment diagram for reverse idler gear (4 speed type W40 gearbox) (Sec 20)

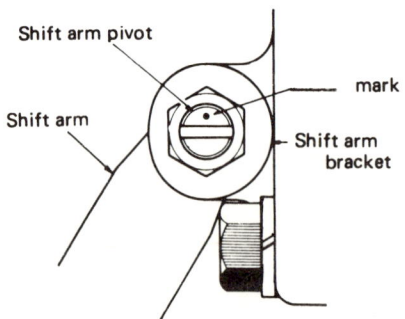

Fig 6.111 Correct reverse idler gear adjustment (4 speed type W40 gearbox) (Sec 20)

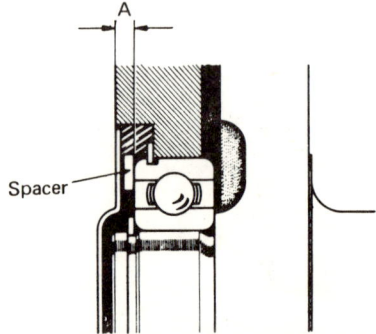

Fig 6.112 Countershaft front bearing spacer adjustment diagram (4 speed type W40 gearbox) (Sec 20)

13 Bolt the mainshaft rear bearing retainer to the intermediate plate, tightening the bolts to the specified torque.
14 Assemble the reverse shift arm to its bracket, tightening the bolt only finger tight. Locate them on the intermediate plate and drive in the tension pin so that it projects as shown in Fig 6.109.
15 Select reverse gear by moving the shift fork and check the mesh between the reverse gear and reverse idler gear. When correctly meshed, the front faces of the reverse idler gear and reverse gear on the mainshaft should be in alignment. In this situation, the slot in the shift arm pivot bolt will be at right angles to the intermediate plate. Adjust as necessary to achieve this setting and then tighten the pivot nut to the specified torque.
16 Position a new gasket to the front face of the intermediate plate and locate the gearbox casing on the plate.
17 Fit the circlips to the input shaft and countershaft front bearings.
18 Assemble the remote control rod and swing arm into the extension housing by driving in the connecting tension pin.
19 Locate a new gasket on the rear face of the intermediate plate and offer up the extension housing until it is within an inch (25.4 mm) of its installed position. Move the swing arm clockwise to engage the remote control rod with the shift forks and push the extension housing fully home.
20 Bolt the extension housing to the gearbox casing, sandwiching the intermediate plate and two gaskets in between them. Tighten the bolts to the specified torque.
21 Push the countershaft fully to the rear and measure the distance between the front face of the countershaft front bearing and the front face of the gearbox, using a dial gauge or feeler blades. Select a spacer to correspond with the dimension established from thicknesses available as listed in Specifications Section.
22 Fit the selected spacer to the front of the countershaft bearing, followed by the cover.
23 Use a new gasket and bolt on the input shaft bearing retainer, making sure that the oil return holes are in alignment.
24 Use a new gasket and bolt the clutch bellhousing to the front face of the gearbox. Tighten the bolts to the specified torque.
25 Screw in the reverse restrict pin, with its sealing washer, to the specified torque.
26 Fit the speedometer driven gear into the extension housing, also the reversing lamp switch.
27 The gearchange lever can be inserted and the retaining flanges bolted up as the gearbox is being installed in the vehicle. Note that the gearchange lever ball spring is installed with its larger diameter end downward.

21 Gearbox (five speed type) - removal and installation

This is identical to the procedure for the four speed type gearbox (see Section 12).

22 Gearbox (five speed type) - dismantling into major assemblies

1 Unbolt the clutch bellhousing from the gearbox casing.
2 Remove the speedometer driven gear and two restrictor pin assemblies from the extension housing.
3 Carry out the operations described in paragraphs 3 to 9 of Section 15.
4 Using a socket wrench, unscrew and remove the plugs from the edge of the intermediate plate and extract the springs and detent balls.
5 Drive out the tension pins from the shift forks and withdraw the selector shafts taking care not to lose the two interlock pins.
6 Remove the speedometer drive gear and its spacer from the mainshaft after the shaft circlips have been removed. Take care not to lose the locking ball.
7 Using a two legged puller, draw off the bearing from the rear end of the mainshaft.
8 Remove the circlip from the mainshaft.
9 From the rear end of the countershaft, remove the circlip and draw off the bearing.
10 Withdraw the countershaft fifth gear and reverse gear.
11 From the mainshaft, remove the circlip and withdraw fifth gear, the synchro ring, needle roller bearing and fifth gear inner bearing track, taking care not to lose the track locking ball.

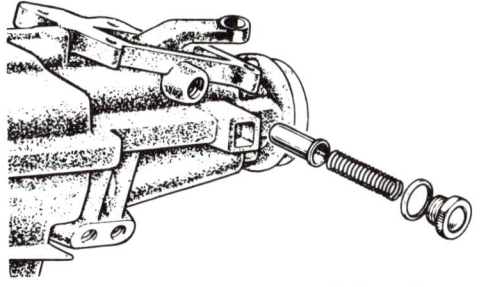

Fig 6.113 Removing a restrictor pin assembly from the extension housing (5 speed gearbox) (Sec 22)

Fig 6.114 Removing a detent socket screw (5 speed gearbox) (Sec 22)

Fig 6.115 Removing a shift fork tension pin (5 speed gearbox) (Sec 22)

Fig 6.116 Removing 5th gear from the mainshaft (5 speed gearbox) (Sec 22)

12 Remove the reverse gear and fifth gear synchro unit.
13 Slacken the bolt which secures the reverse idler shaft stop to the intermediate plate, withdraw the shaft to the rear and remove the reverse idler gear and spacer.
14 Unbolt the mainshaft rear bearing retainer and remove the circlip from the bearing.
15 From the rear end of the countershaft, push the bearing outer track to the rear and withdraw the bearing components. The countershaft assembly may now be removed from the intermediate plate.
16 Remove the input shaft and synchro ring from the mainshaft and then withdraw the mainshaft assembly from the intermediate plate.

23 Mainshaft (five speed gearbox) - servicing

1 Extract the circlip and remove the 3rd/4th synchro unit, the synchro ring and third gear from the front end of the mainshaft.
2 From the rear end of the mainshaft draw off the bearing. A press will be required for this operation. (Fig 6.122)
3 Remove first gear, the needle roller bearing, bearing inner track and synchro ring. Take care not to lose the inner track locking ball. (Fig 6.123)
4 Press off the second gear complete with synchro ring, reverse speed gearbox and they must be assembled as shown. (Figs 6.126 6.127 and 6.128).
5 Clean all components thoroughly and examine for worn or

Fig 6.117 Removing countershaft bearing outer track (5 speed gearbox) (Sec 22)

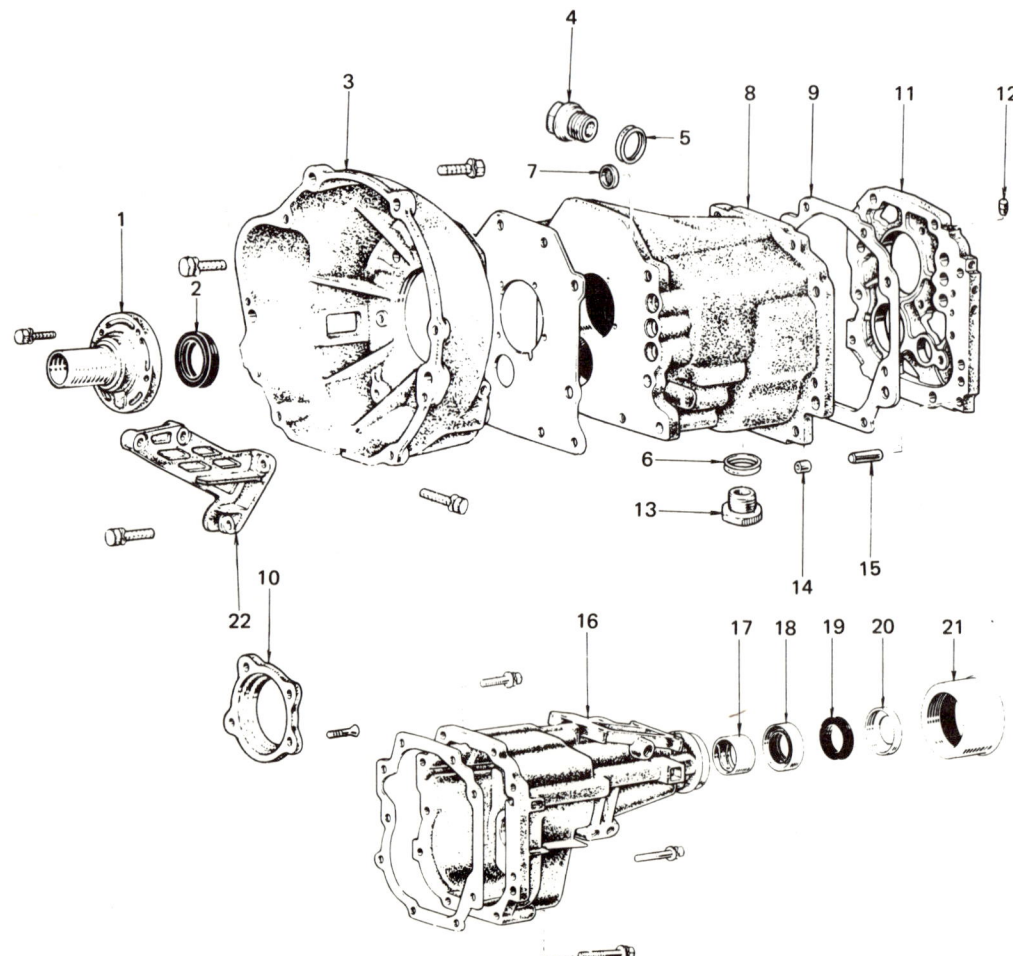

Fig 6.118 External components of the 5 speed type W50 gearbox (Sec 22)

1 Front bearing retainer
2 Oil seal
3 Clutch bellhousing
4 Filler/lever plug
5 Washer
6 Washer
7 Plug
8 Casing
9 Gasket
10 Mainshaft rear bearing retainer
11 Intermediate plate
12 Dowel
13 Drain plug
14 Hollow dowel
15 Dowel
16 Extension housing
17 Bush
18 Oil seal
19 Dust seal
20 Dust seal retainer
21 Dust deflector
22 Reinforcement bracket

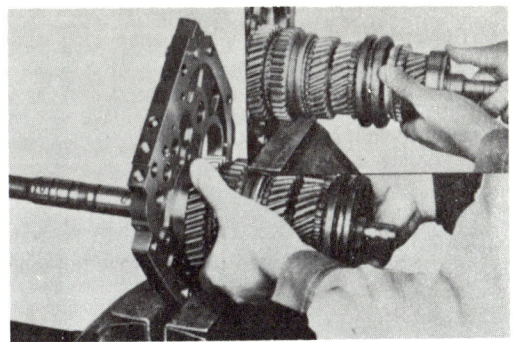

Fig 6.119 Removing input shaft and the mainshaft assembly (5 speed gearbox) (Sec 22)

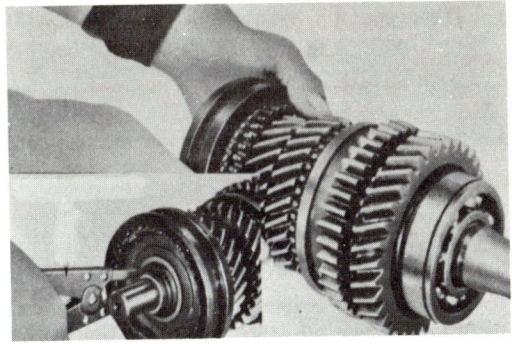

Fig 6.120 Removing 3rd gear from the front of the mainshaft (5 speed gearbox) (Sec 22)

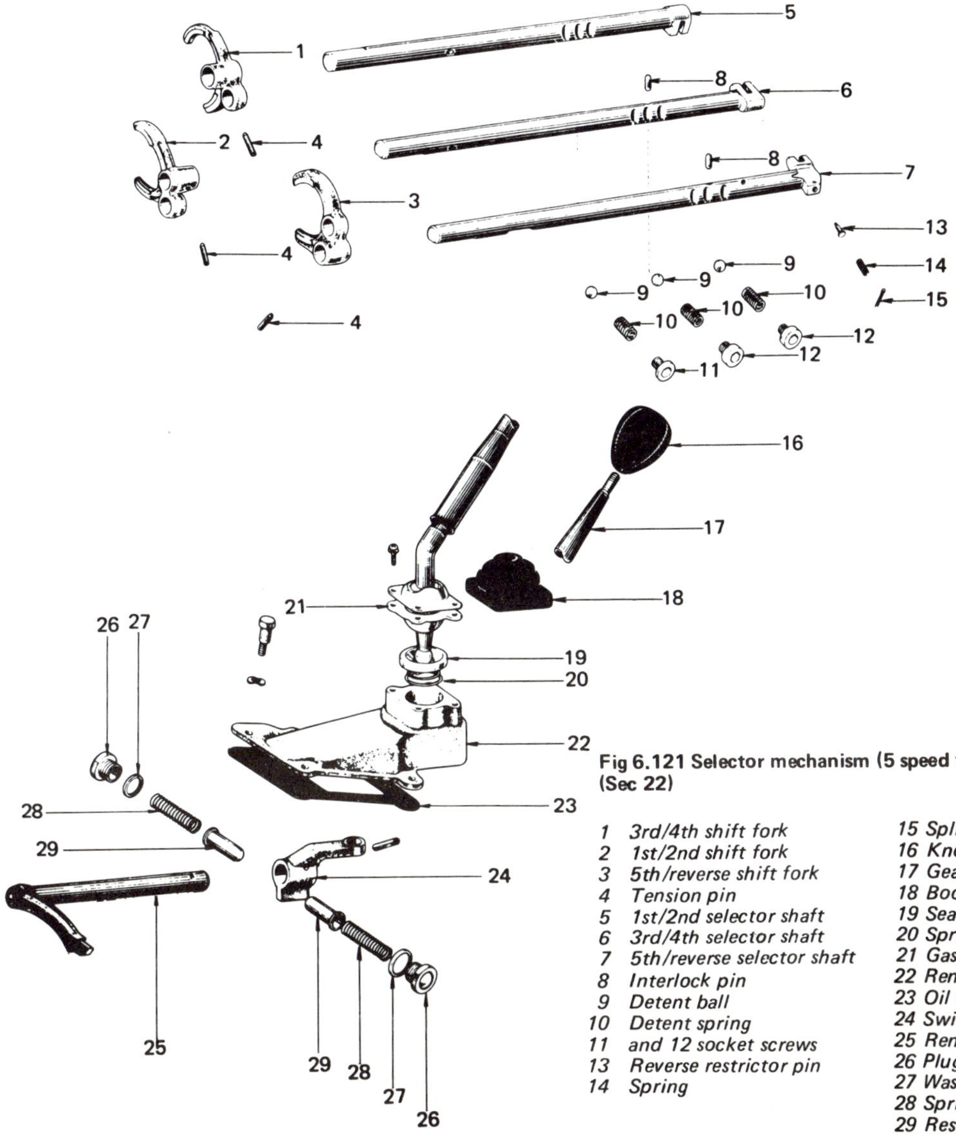

Fig 6.121 Selector mechanism (5 speed type W50 gearbox) (Sec 22)

1 3rd/4th shift fork
2 1st/2nd shift fork
3 5th/reverse shift fork
4 Tension pin
5 1st/2nd selector shaft
6 3rd/4th selector shaft
7 5th/reverse selector shaft
8 Interlock pin
9 Detent ball
10 Detent spring
11 and 12 socket screws
13 Reverse restrictor pin
14 Spring
15 Split pin
16 Knob
17 Gearchange lever
18 Boot
19 Seat
20 Spring
21 Gasket
22 Remote control housing
23 Oil deflector
24 Swing arm
25 Remote control shaft
26 Plug
27 Washer
28 Spring
29 Restrictor pin

Fig 6.122 Pressing off the mainshaft rear bearing (5 speed gearbox) (Sec 23)

Fig 6.123 Removing 1st gear from mainshaft (5 speed gearbox) (Sec 23)

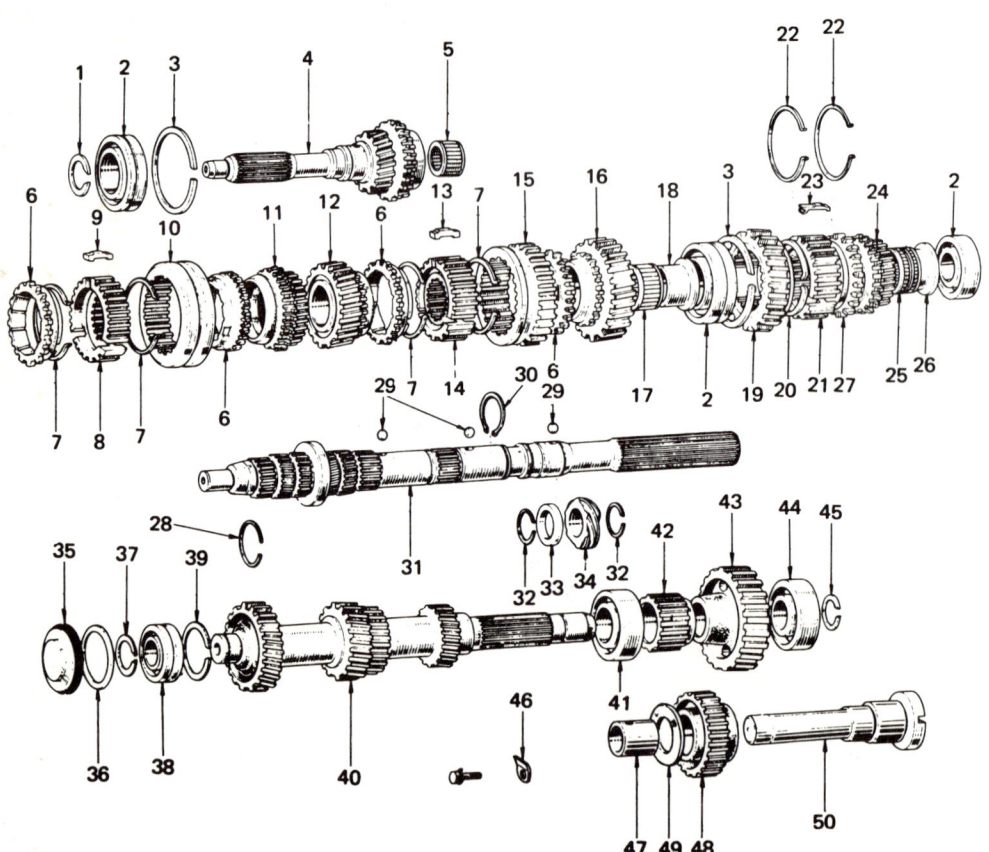

Fig 6.124 Internal components of the 5 speed type W50 gearbox (Sec 22)

1　Circlip
2　Input shaft bearing
3　Bearing outer track circlip
4　Input shaft
5　Needle roller bearing
6　Synchro. ring
7　Spring
8　3rd/4th synchro. hub
9　Blocker bar
10　3rd/4th synchro. sleeve
11　3rd gear
12　2nd gear
13　Blocker bar
14　1st/2nd synchro. hub
15　Reverse gear
16　1st gear
17　Needle bearing
18　Needle bearing inner track
19　Reverse gear
20　Circlip
21　5th gear synchro. hub
22　Spring
23　Blocker bar
24　5th gear
25　Needle roller bearing
26　Needle bearing inner track
27　Synchro. ring
28　Circlip
29　Lock balls
30　Mainshaft rear bearing circlips
31　Mainshaft
32　Circlip
33　Spacer
34　Speedometer drive gear
35　Countershaft cover
36　Spacer
37　Circlip
38　Countershaft front bearing
39　Bearing outer track circlip
40　Countergear
41　Bearing
42　Reverse gear
43　Fifth gear
44　Bearing
45　Circlip
46　Stop
47　Bush
48　Reverse idler gear
49　Spacer
50　Reverse idler gear shaft

chipped teeth and grooving or scoring of the shaft. The gears should have a running clearance between their internal bores and the shaft of between 0.0008 and 0.0020 in (0.02 and 0.05 mm) for 1st and 5th gears and 0.0014 and 0.0039 in (0.06 and 0.10 mm) for 2nd and 3rd gears.

6 Check the synchro units as described in Section 16, paragraphs 7, 8 and 9 but there are of course three units in the five speed gearbox and they must be assembled as shown.

7 Commence reassembly of the mainshaft by installing the 3rd/4th synchro ring to third gear and then fitting them to the shaft.

8 Fit the 3rd/4th synchro unit, positioning it tight against the mainshaft shoulder. Secure it with a circlip to give a groove clearance of between 0 and 0.002 in (0 and 0.05 mm) from those available which are as listed in Specifications Section.

9 Carry out the operations described in Section 16, paragraphs 12 to 19 inclusive.

24 Input shaft (five speed gearbox) - servicing

The procedure is identical to that described in Section 7, for the 3 speed type gearbox.

25 Countershaft and reverse gear assemblies (five speed gearbox) - servicing

1 The procedure is similar to that described in Section 18 for four speed type gearboxes but when fitting the countershaft cylindrical roller bearing inner track, position it so that its flanged side is towards the front.

2 The bush of the reverse idler gear must be reamed to a finished diameter of between 0.9858 and 1.0260 in (25.04 and 26.06 mm).

26 Oil seals (five speed gearbox) - renewal

1 The procedure is identical to the operations described in Section 9, excluding paragraph 2.

27 Gearbox (five speed type) - reassembly

1 Check that the intermediate plate dowel pins project by between ¼ and 5/16 in (6.0 and 8.0 mm) from the front face of the intermediate plate and then secure the plate in a vice fitted with jaw protectors.

2 Install the needle roller bearing assembly to the input shaft and then fit the 3rd/4th synchro ring to the cone on the end of the input shaft.

3 Fit the mainshaft assembly to the intermediate plate and then fit the input shaft to the mainshaft.

4 Install the countershaft assembly onto the intermediate plate and then fit the roller bearing onto the shaft from the rear side of the plate and then fit the spacer.

5 Fit the circlip to the outer track of the mainshaft rear bearing.

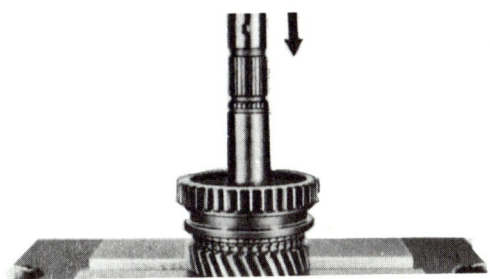

Fig 6.125 Pressing off reverse and 2nd gears (5 speed gearbox) (Sec 23)

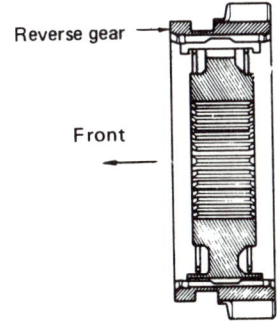

Fig 6.126 Correct assembly of 1st/2nd. synchro unit (5 speed gearbox) (Sec 23)

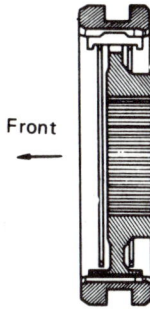

Fig 6.127 Correct assembly of 3rd/4th synchro. unit (5 speed gearbox) (Sec 23)

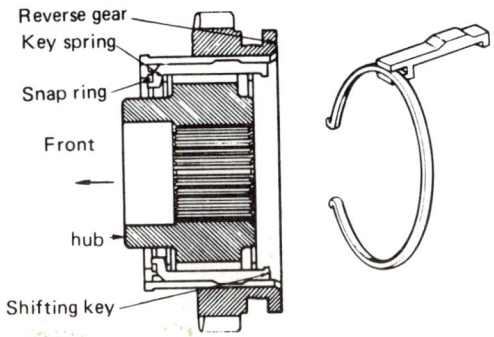

Fig 6.128 Correct assembly of 5th gear synchro. unit (Sec 23)

Fig 6.129 Installing input shaft to the mainshaft (5 speed gearbox) (Sec 27)

Chapter 6/Manual gearbox and automatic transmission

6 Install the mainshaft rear bearing retainer onto the intermediate plate.

7 Assemble the reverse idler gear and spacer onto the reverse idler shaft and then insert the assembly into the intermediate plate from the rear side. The oil holes in the reverse idler gear must face to the rear.

8 Lock the reverse idler shaft with the stop plate and bolt then check the reverse idler gear endfloat. This should be between 0.0059 and 0.0098 in (0.15 and 0.25 mm) with a maximum of 0.0118 in (0.30 mm).

9 Locate the 5th gear synchro unit (assembled with the reverse gear) onto the mainshaft until it is tight against the inner track of the bearing in the intermediate plate.

10 Fit the locking ball into the mainshaft recess. Use a dab of thick grease to retain it.

11 To the mainshaft, fit the fifth gear, synchro ring, needle roller bearing and inner track, (all assembled together) until the assembly rests against the face of the synchro unit.

12 Secure the assembly to the mainshaft by selecting a circlip from the thirteen available thicknesses to give the minimum clearance.

13 Check fifth gear endfloat; this should be between 0.0039 and 0.0098 in (0.10 and 0.25 mm) with a maximum clearance of 0.0118 in (0.30 mm).

14 Fit the countershaft reverse gear, fifth gear and drive on the bearing using a piece of tubing as a drift.

15 Fit a circlip to the countershaft and another to the mainshaft. Select the circlips from the four available thicknesses as listed in Specifications Section.

16 Drive the rear bearing onto the mainshaft again using a piece

Fig 6.130 Fitting mainshaft rear bearing retainer (5 speed gearbox) (Sec 27)

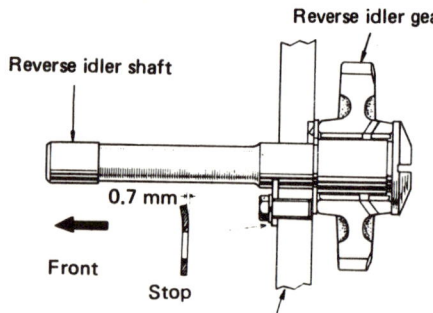
Fig 6.131 Reverse idler gear assembly diagram (5 speed gearbox) (Sec 27)

Fig 6.132 Measuring reverse idler gear endfloat (5 speed gearbox) (Sec 27)

Fig 6.133 Fitting 5th gear to the mainshaft (Sec 27)

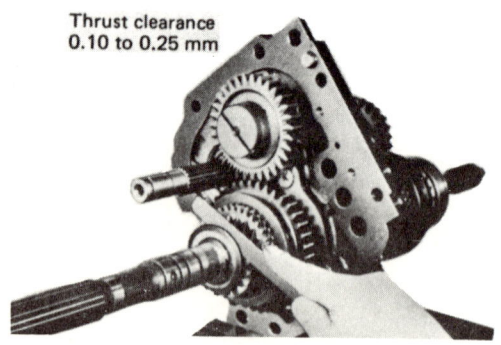
Fig 6.134 Measuring 5th gear endfloat (Sec 27)

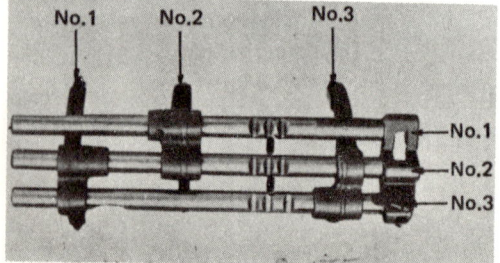
Fig 6.135 Correct assembly of selector shafts and shift forks (5 speed gearbox) (Sec 27)

1 1st/2nd   2 3rd/4th   3 5th/reverse

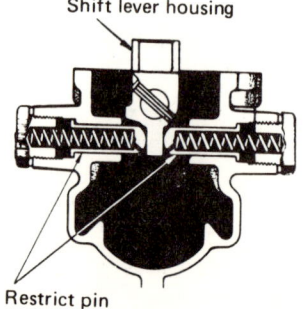
Fig 6.136 Installation of restrictor pin assemblies in extension housing of 5 speed gearbox (Sec 27)

of tubing as a drift and making sure that it rests against the inner track of the bearing.
17 To the mainshaft, fit the spacer, locking ball and speedometer drive gear and secure them with a circlip.
18 Locate the shift forks in their respective synchro hub grooves, ensuring that the bosses of the forks face the correct way as shown in Fig 6.135.
19 Insert the 1st/2nd selector shaft and the 5th/reverse selector shaft. The gears should be in neutral when assembling each shaft and the interlock pins correctly inserted.
20 Insert the 3rd/4th selector shaft.
21 Insert the detent balls and springs into their holes in the edge of the intermediate plate. Tighten the socket screws to the specified torque and in order to prevent oil leaks, ensure that their threads are coated with jointing compound.
22 Secure the shift forks to the selector shafts by driving in the tension pins.
23 Carry out the operations described in paragraphs 16 to 24 inclusive of Section 20.
24 Insert the restrictor pins and springs, one on each side of the extension housing and tighten the plugs to the specified torque.
25 Refit the speedometer driven gear to the extension housing and the reversing lamp switch to the gearbox casing.
26 The gearshift lever will normally be bolted to the extension housing as the gearbox is offered up during installation.

28 Fault diagnosis - manual gearbox

Symptom	Cause
Ineffective synchromesh on one or more gears	Worn baulk rings. Worn blocker bars
Jumps out of one or more gears.	Weak detent springs Worn shift forks Worn engagement dogs Worn synchro hubs
Whining, roughness, vibration allied to other faults.	Bearing failure and/or overall wear
Noisy and difficult gear engagement.	Clutch not operating correctly
Sloppy and impositive gear selection	Overall wear throughout the selector mechanism

Part 2: Automatic transmission

29 General description - automatic transmission

All models may be equipped with Toyoglide automatic transmission.

Some vehicles have a two speed version, others have the more usual three speed unit (A30) while those manufactured from 1973 onwards have the A40 design. The main difference between the A30 and A40 models is that the latter is of bandless construction and requires no external adjustment to the unit itself. No rear oil pump is incorporated in the A40 design and in the event of breakdown, the vehicle must not be towed in excess of 30 mph (48 km/h) or further than 50 miles (80 km) unless the propeller shaft is disconnected. Failure to observe this requirement may cause damage to the transmission due to lack of lubrication. Due to the complexities of dismantling and reassembly of automatic transmission units, the operations described in this Chapter are limited to maintenance, adjustment and removal and installation of the unit.

30 Maintenance

1 The importance of maintaining the correct fluid level cannot be over-emphasised.

Two speed unit

2 Run the vehicle until normal transmission fluid operating temperature is reached (5 miles - 8km of running) and then apply the handbrake fully and move the selector lever through all positions, waiting a few seconds in each. Return the lever to 'N' and with the engine still running, withdraw the dipstick, wipe it, reinsert it and withdraw it again. The fluid level should be near the 'Full' mark. Top-up with recommended fluid as necessary.

Three speed units

3 If the transmission fluid is cold, withdraw the dipstick, wipe

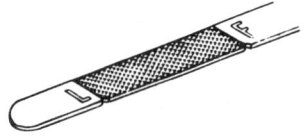

Fig 6.137 Automatic transmission dipstick (2 speed unit) (Sec 30)

Fig 6.138 Automatic transmission dipstick (3 speed unit) (Sec 30)

it, re-insert it and withdraw it again. The fluid level should be within the cold range. If the vehicle has travelled at least 5 miles (8 km) the fluid level should be within the hot range of the dipstick when the same checking procedure is followed. Top-up with fluid of the specified grade.
4 Keep the external surfaces of the transmission unit clean and free from mud and grease to prevent overheating. If an oil cooler is fitted make sure that the connecting pipes are secure and in good condition.

31 Selector linkage (two speed automatic transmission) - adjustment

1 Place the speed selector lever in the 'N' position.
2 Loosen the control rod swivel nut and then move the intermediate shaft lever on the side of the transmission casing to the 'N' position. Retighten the swivel nut. (Fig 6.141)
3 The eccentric type stop pin will now have to be slackened and turned to provide the same clearance between it and the stop plate cut-outs when the speed selector is in the 'L' or 'N' positions. (Fig 6.142)

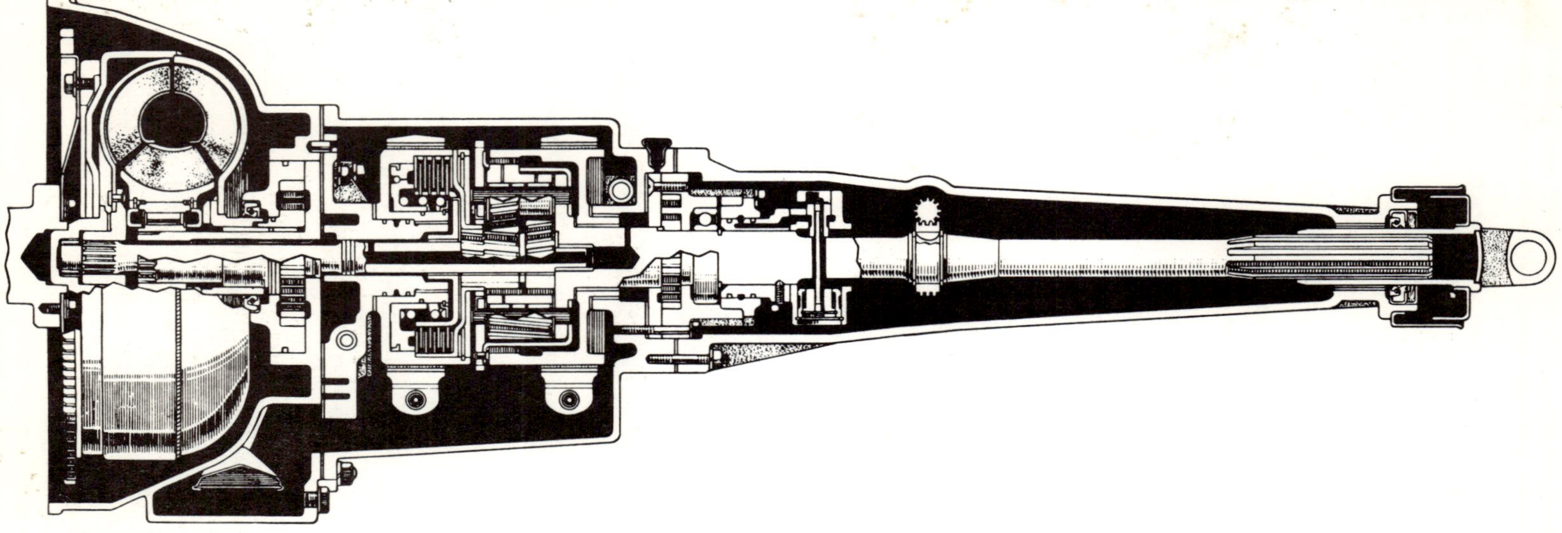

Fig 6.139 Sectional view of Toyoglide 2 speed automatic transmission

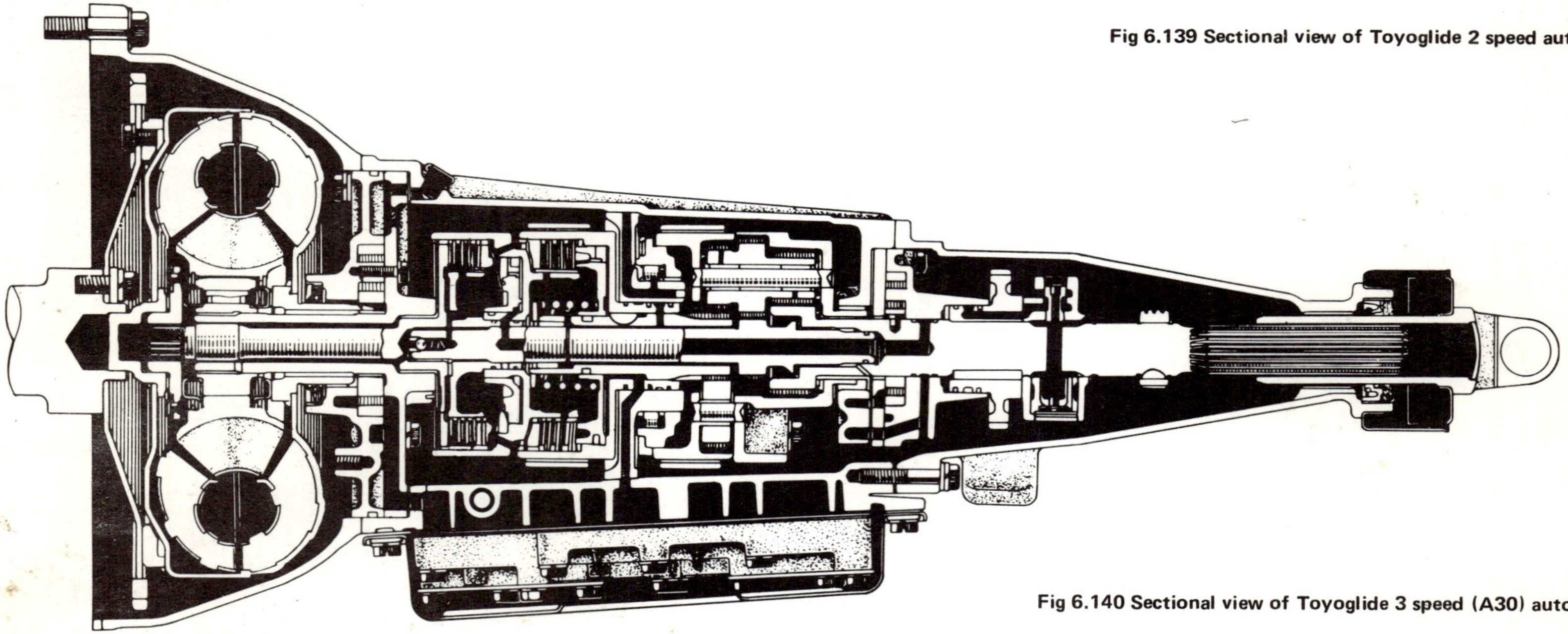

Fig 6.140 Sectional view of Toyoglide 3 speed (A30) automatic transmission

32 Starter inhibitor switch (two speed automatic transmission) - adjustment

1 The starter motor should only operate when the key is turned and the selector lever is in the 'N' or 'P' position. Where it operates with the selector in other positions, use a test bulb to check the on and off actuation between the 'D' and 'N' position. If necessary alter the screw (1) after slackening the locknut (2) to provide the correct actuation. (Fig 6.143)

2 Now set the selector lever to the 'D' position and adjust the contact position of the control shaft lever (1) and the switch lever (2) by moving the lever support plate within the limits of its elongated bolt holes. (Fig 6.144)

3 When the adjustment has been completed, check the operation of the switch in all positions of the speed selector lever.

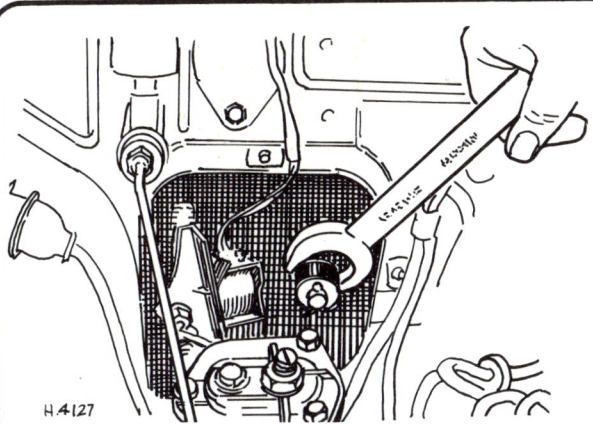

Fig 6.141 Loosening swivel nut on auto. transmission speed selector control rod (two speed unit) (Sec 31)

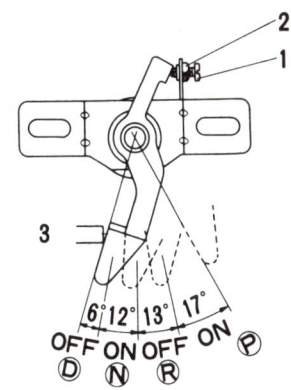

Fig 6.143 Starter inhibitor switch adjustment diagram (two speed automatic transmission) (Sec 32)

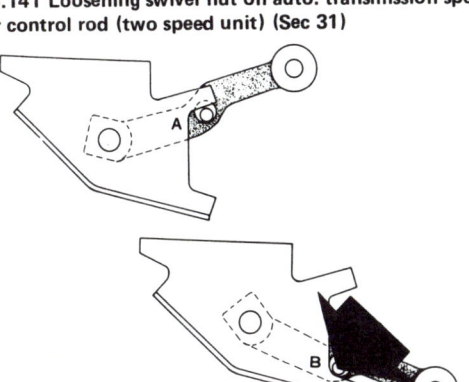

Fig 6.142 Stop in adjustment diagram (2 speed auto. transmission) (Sec 31)

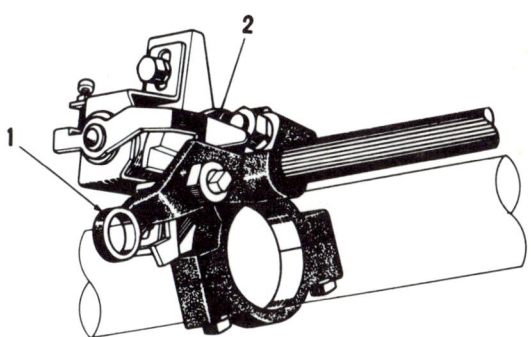

Fig 6.144 Starter inhibitor switch control shaft lever (1) and switch lever (two speed auto. transmission) (Sec 32)

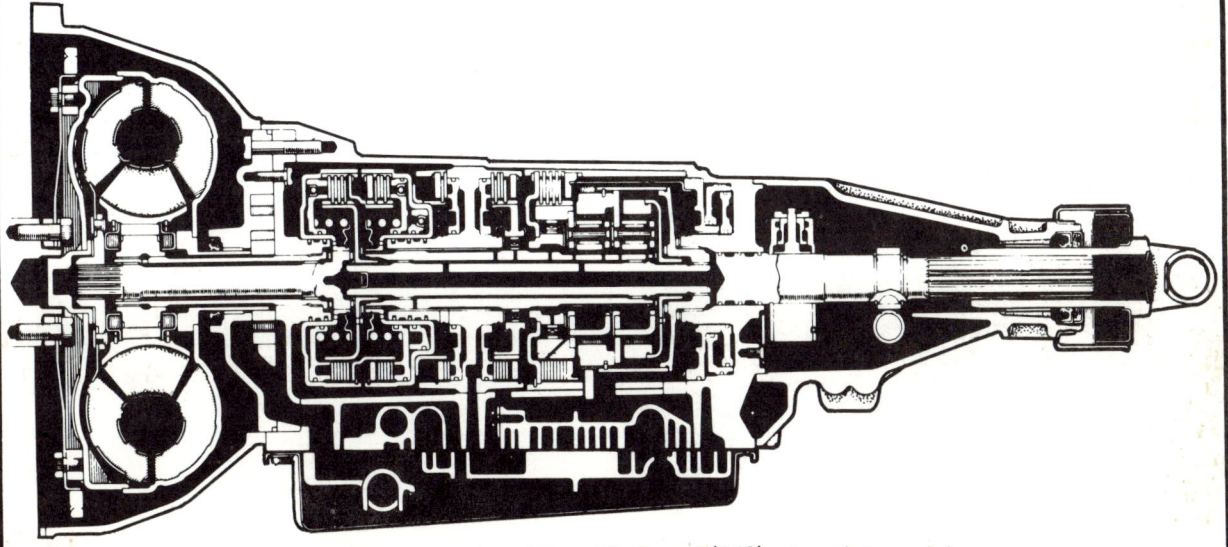

Fig 6.145 Sectional view of Toyoglide 3 speed (A40) automatic transmission

33 'Kick-down' rod (two speed auto transmission) - adjustment

1. Remove the air cleaner from the carburettor.
2. Disconnect the 'kick-down' rod from the throttle bellcrank.
3. Slacken the turnbuckle locknuts.
4. Open the carburettor throttle butterfly valve plate to its fullest extent and then with the marks on the outer lever (5) and the transmission casing in alignment, adjust the length of the 'kick-down' rod until it will connect to the bellcrank without altering the position of the throttle valve plate or the outer lever.

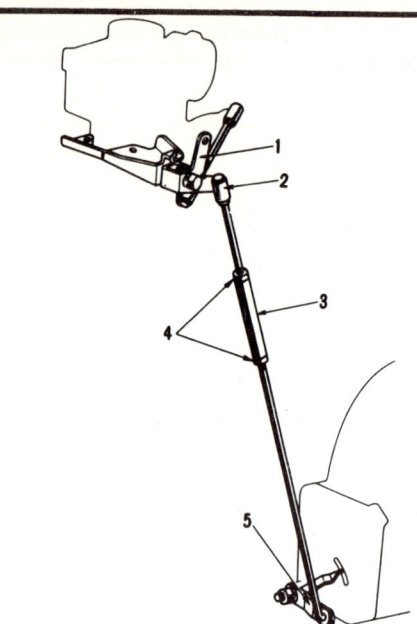

Fig 6.146 'Kick-down' rod (two speed auto. transmission) (Sec 33)

1. Throttle bell crank
2. Ball joint
3. Turn buckle
4. Locknuts
5. Outer lever

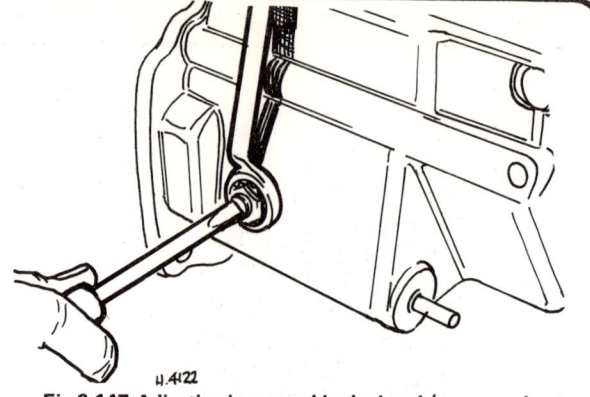

Fig 6.147 Adjusting low speed brake band (two speed auto. transmission) (Sec 34)

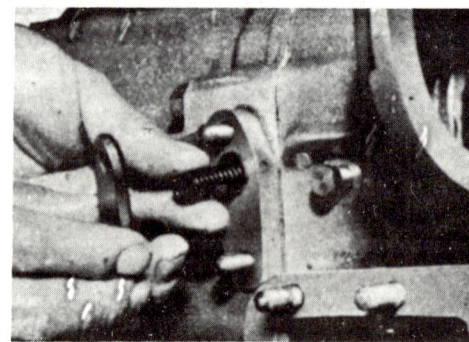

Fig 6.148 Removing pressure regulator valve assembly (two speed auto. transmission) (Sec 35)

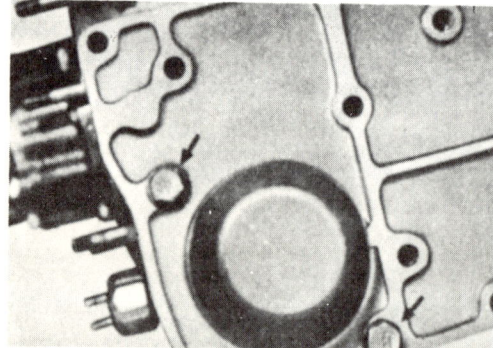

Fig 6.149 Side cover (two speed auto. transmission) (Sec 35)

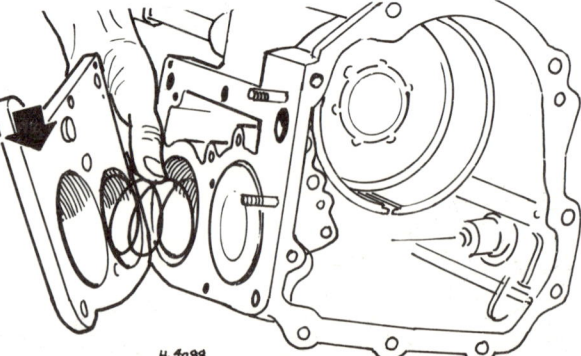

Fig 6.150 Removing side cover and servo piston spring (two speed auto. transmission) (Sec 35)

Fig 6.151 Adjusting reverse brake band (two speed auto. transmission) (Sec 35)

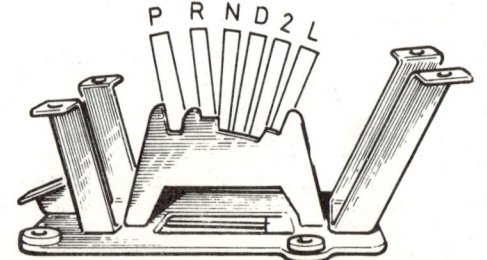

Fig 6.152 Speed selector lever gate (3 speed A30 auto. transmission) (Sec 36)

5 The 'kick-down' facility operates when the accelerator pedal is fully depressed at speeds below 37 mph (60 km/h). Generally, if the transmission does not downshift when the pedal is depressed, the 'kick-down' rod requires lengthening or if downshift to the lower speed occurs with only partial pedal depression, the rod requires shortening.

34 Low speed brake band (two speed auto transmission) - adjustment

1 This is not an adjustment which will normally be required but the settings should be checked where any faults occur in the forward or reverse speed operation.
2 Jack-up the front of the vehicle and support adequately on stands.
3 Remove the cap from the low speed brake band anchor bolt. Loosen the locknut and the anchor bolt.
4 Fully tighten the anchor bolt and then unscrew it three complete turns. Tighten the locknut and refit the cap.
5 Remove the stands and jack.

35 Reverse brake band (two speed auto transmission) - adjustment

1 Jack-up the front of the vehicle and support on stands.
2 Disconnect the speed selector control rod from the intermediate shaft on the side of the transmission casing.
3 Thoroughly clean the side cover and then drain the transmission fluid.
4 Disconnect the oil cooler tube and clamp.
5 Remove the pressure regulator valve assembly.
6 Unscrew and remove all the side cover bolts except the two arrowed. Unscrew the remaining two bolts a half-a-turn at a time, in alternate sequence, to relieve the pressure of the servo piston spring. When the bolts are removed completely, pull the cover straight off to avoid damaging the pressure regulating valve connecting tube located at the top right-hand corner of the cover. (Fig 6.149)
7 Remove the servo piston spring.
8 Loosen the now exposed anchor bolt locknut and fully tighten the anchor bolt using a 10 in (250.0 mm) long screwdriver. Now unscrew the bolt exactly 4¾ turns and tighten the locknut.
9 Refit the dismantled components and refill the unit with fluid.

36 Selector linkage (A30 type auto transmission) - adjustment

1 The adjustments described in this and the following Sections are not to be considered as routine and should only be carried out when wear in the components or incorrect operation of the automatic transmission requires them.
2 The floor mounted speed selector lever operates in a six position gate, through a right-hand control rod and a cross shaft to the hydraulic valve lever. On the lect-hand side of the transmission unit a secondary control rod actuates the transmission parking lock.
3 It is essential that the hand control moves smoothly and positively through all positions and when a speed is selected, the valve lever should be in the centre of its detent, not being under any overriding force from the control rod.
4 To synchronise the hand control and the valve lever positions, remove the swivel bolt which connects the hand lever to the control rod. Set the valve lever to the 'N' on the transmission speed range indicator and then set the hand lever to the 'N' position. Reconnect the swivel bolt and tighten fully.
5 Now loosen the adjusting nuts on the forward end of the parking lock rod, place the selector hand lever in 'P' and pull the parking lock shaft to the lock position. Tighten the adjusting nuts without disturbing the setting of the rod.

6 When adjustment of the parking lock rod is completed, check that with the selector lever in 'R', the parking pawl is completely disengaged. To do this push the vehicle backwards and forwards. With the steering column type selector linkage, the adjustment procedure is similar except that the swivel nut on the control rod is slackened and the effective length of the control rod altered.

37 Starter inhibitor/reverse lamp switch (A30 type auto transmission) - adjustment

1 On vehicles having a floor mounted speed selector lever remove the selector lever knob and remove the centre console.
2 The switch is now accessible. Place the selector lever in 'N' and then adjust the position of the switch (by moving it within the limit of its elongated bolt holes) until the marks on the switch and the selector lever pivot are in alignment. (Figs 6.155 and 6.156)

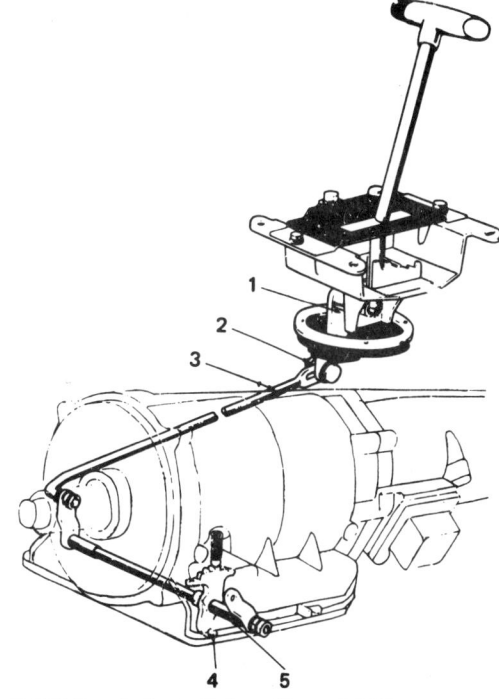

Fig 6.153 Speed selector linkage (3 speed A30 auto. transmission) (Sec 36)
1 Selector lever
2 Swivel bolt
3 Control rod
4 Valve lever
5 Cross shaft

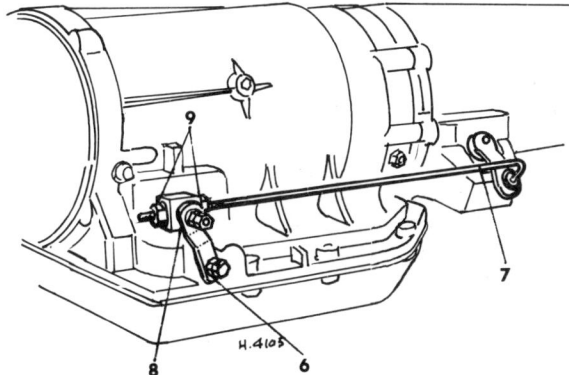

Fig 6.154 Parking lock control linkage (3 speed A30 auto. Transmission) (Sec 36)
6 Shaft lever
7 Lock rod
8 Swivel
9 Nuts

3 On vehicles having a steering column type selector control, adjustment of the switch is similar to that described in Section 32, but using the relative diaphragm. (Fig 6.157)

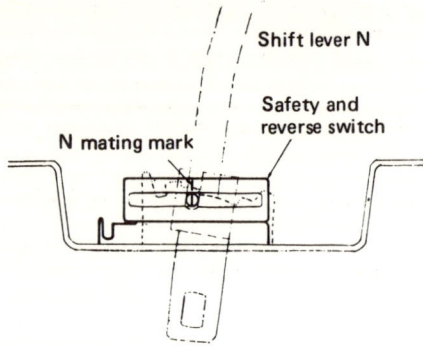

Fig 6.155 Starter inhibitor/reverse lamp switch (3 speed A30 auto. transmission) (Sec 37)

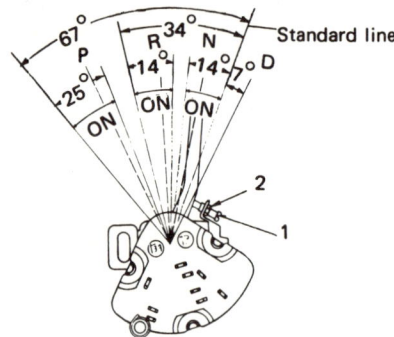

Fig 6.156 Starter inhibitor/reverse lamp switch adjustment diagrams (3 speed A30 auto. transmission) (Sec 37)

Fig 6.157 Starter inhibitor/reverse lamp switch on 3 speed A30 auto. transmission with steering column control (Sec 370

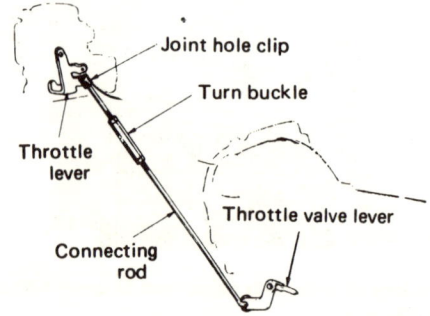

38 Throttle link connecting rod (A30 type auto transmission) - adjustment and testing

1 The correct adjustment of this component is essential to ensure correct operation of the 'kick-down' facility when fast acceleration is required by immediate change to a lower speed.
2 Operate the throttle lever on the carburettor by hand so that the carburettor throttle butterfly valve is fully open. Have an assistant check that the throttle valve lever indicator is in alignment with the mark on the side of the transmission casing. Where this is not the case, loosen the turnbuckle locknut on the connecting rod, rotate the turnbuckle and when adjustment is correct, tighten the locknut.
3 Before road testing for correct operation of the 'kick-down', check the fluid level and run the vehicle to normal operating temperature over a distance of at least 6 miles (9km) to ensure that the transmission fluid is fully warmed.
4 Accelerate gently but progressively and listen for the points of change (up) to the next speed. These should occur from 1 to 2 at between 6 and 10 mph (10 and 16 km/h) and from 2 to 3 between 11 and 18 mph (17 and 28 km/h). Repeat the test on the same stretch of road but accelerating at full throttle. The speed change points should occur 1 to 2 at between 33 and 41 mph (53 and 66 km/h) and 2 to 3 at between 54 and 63 speed according to the degree of acceleration (throttle opening) then it can be assumed that the transmission and control gear are operating correctly.
5 Now check the 'kick-down' change points. With the throttle valve about half open at a road speed of 43 mph. (68 km/h) in 3rd speed depress the accelerator pedal sharply and check that the transmission downshifts to 2nd speed.
6 Under similar conditions at a road speed of between 50 and 55 mph (80 and 88 km/h) move the selector lever to the '2' position. The transmission should immediately downshift to 2nd speed. As the road speed decreases to between 18 and 33 mph (29 and 52 km/h) the transmission will downshift to 1st speed.
7 If the preceding tests do not prove positive and the throttle link connecting rod has been correctly adjusted, a fault must lie in the governor, valve, throttle valve or the shift valves; consult your Toyota dealer.

39 Brake band (A30 type auto transmission) - adjustment

1 Adjustment of these components should only be carried out as the result of relevant fault symptoms accurring as described in Section 43.
2 The rear band adjuster is located on the right-hand inclined surface of the transmission casing. Loosen the locknut and tighten the anchor bolt to a torque of 3.6 lb/ft (0.5 kg/m) then unscrew it exactly one turn and tighten the locknut.
3 The front band adjuster is only accessible after draining the transmission unit and removing the oil pan. The clearance between the faces of the adjuster bolt and piston should be 0.0118 in (3.0 mm). Screw the bolt in or out as necessary.

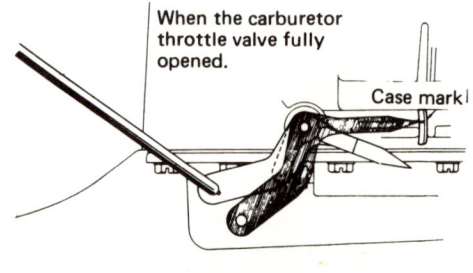

Fig 6.158 'Kick-down' rod adjustment on 3 speed A30 auto. transmission (Sec 38)

40 Extension housing oil seal (A30/A40 type auto transmission) - renewal

1 Renewal of the oil seal may be carried out with the transmission unit in position in the vehicle.
2 Remove the propeller shaft as described in Chapter 7.
3 Knock off the dust deflector towards the rear and prise out the dust seal. Using a suitable extractor and levering against the end face of the mainshaft, extract the oil seal.
4 Drive in the new oil seal with a tubular drift, fit a new dust seal and refit the dust deflector.
5 Refit the propeller shaft after first greasing the front sliding sleeve both internally and externally. Make sure that the propeller shaft and pinion driving flanges have their mating marks aligned.

41 Adjustments (A40 type auto transmission)

1 There are only two adjustments which require attention in this type of transmission.
2 Check and adjust the throttle cable. To do this, remove the air cleaner and fully depress the accelerator pedal (use a block or piece of wood) checking that the carburettor throttle valve is fully open.
3 Measure the distance between the end of the accelerator outer cable and the stop collar which should be 2.05 in (52.0 mm). If necessary, adjust the outer cable by slackening the two locknuts on the support bracket.
4 To adjust the speed selector linkage, slacken the swivel nut on the control rod. (Fig 6.163)
5 Push the selector lever on the side of the transmission fully

Fig 6.159 Rear brake band adjustment on 3 speed A30 auto. transmission (Sec 39)

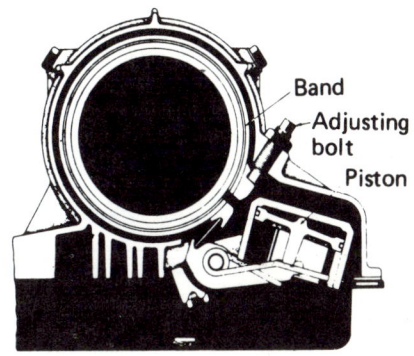

Fig 6.160 Front brake band adjustment on 3 speed A30 auto. transmission (Sec 39)

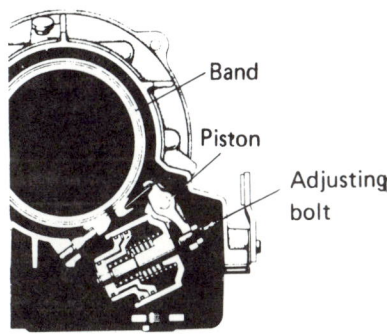

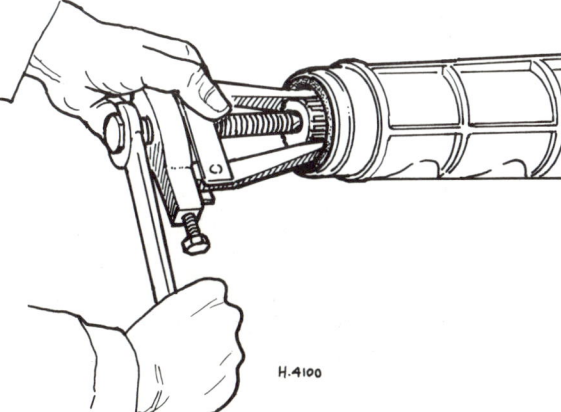

Fig 6.161 Removing extension housing oil seal (3 speed A30 auto. transmission) (Sec 40)

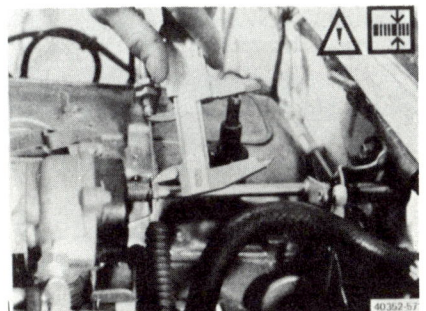

Fig 6.162 Checking throttle cable adjustment (3 speed A40 auto. transmission) (Sec 41)

forward and then pull it back three notches to the 'N' position.
6   Have an assistant hold the speed selector lever in 'N' and then retighten the swivel nut. Check the operation of the transmission in all positions of the speed range.

42 Automatic transmission - removal and installation

1   The procedure for removing and installing the three types of

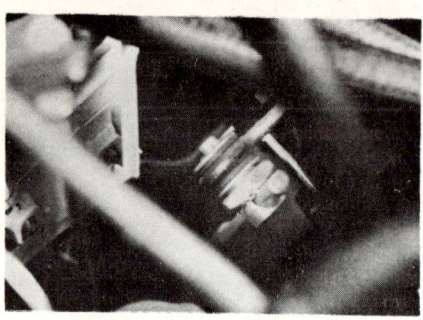
Fig 6.163 Location of swivel nut on speed selector control rod of A40 auto. transmission) (Sec 41)

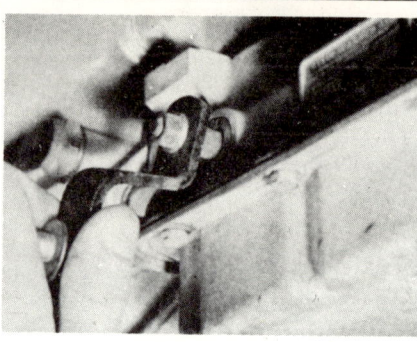
Fig 6.164 Location of speed selector lever on A40 auto. transmission (Sec 41)

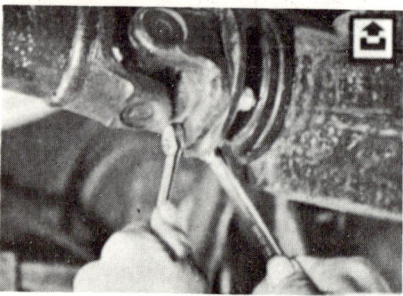
Fig 6.165 Disconnecting propeller shaft (Sec 42)

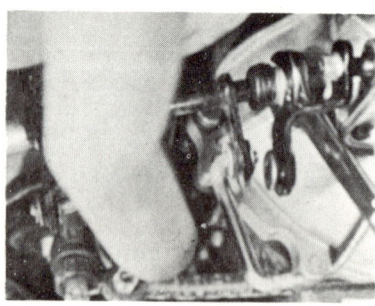
Fig 6.166 Disconnecting speed selector linkage (A40 auto. transmission) (Sec 42)

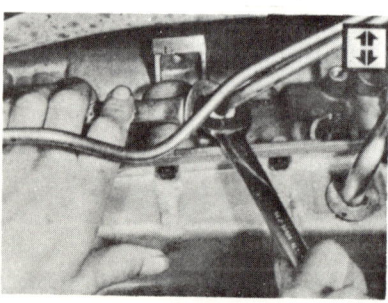
Fig 6.167 Disconnecting fluid cooler pipes (A40 auto. transmission) (Sec 42)

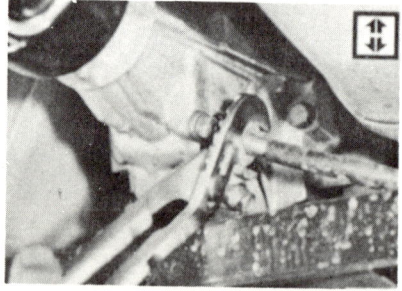
Fig 6.168 Disconnecting the speedometer cable from A40 auto. transmission (Sec 42)

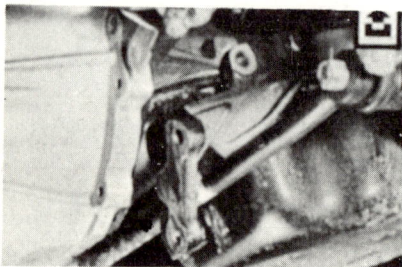
Fig 6.169 Unbolting the stiffener brackets (A40 auto. transmission) (Sec 42)

Fig 6.170 Removing the rear mounting crossmember (A40 auto. transmission) (Sec 42)

Chapter 6/Manual gearbox and automatic transmission

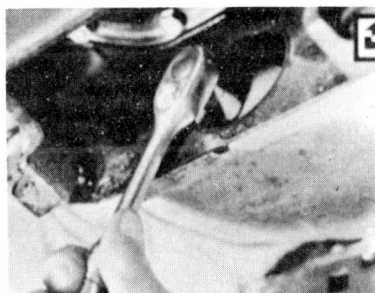

Fig 6.171 Removing a driveplate to torque converter securing bolt (A40 auto. transmission) (Sec 42)

Fig 6.172 Lowering the transmission from the engine (A40 type) (Sec 42)

Fig 6.173 withdrawing the torque converter (A40 auto. transmission) (Sec 42)

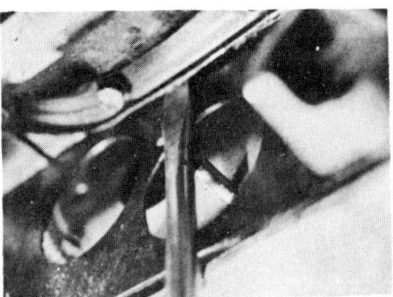

Fig 6.174 Removing 2 speed type auto. transmission, leaving torque converter in position (Sec 42)

automatic transmission is similar. Certain components are not fitted to A40 type units and disconnection instructions will not therefore apply. Special procedure is given in paragraph 21, for removal of the two speed type transmission torque converter.

2 Disconnect the lead from the battery negative terminal.
3 Drain the cooling system and disconnect the radiator top hose.
4 Remove the air cleaner and disconnect the throttle control at the carburettor.
5 Unless the vehicle is over a pit or raised on a hoist, jack-up the front and rear so that there is an adequate working clearance between the underside of the body floor and the ground to permit the torque converter housing to be withdrawn.
6 Drain the fluid from the transmission unit.
7 Remove the starter motor.
8 Disconnect the propeller shaft from the rear axle (see Chapter 7) and withdraw it from the transmission rear extension housing.
9 Disconnect the speed selector linkage at the transmission unit, also the 'kick-down' rod (A30 type transmission and two speed type).
10 Disconnect the exhaust downpipe from the manifold and remove the support bracket from the transmission unit.
11 Disconnect the fluid cooler pipes from the transmission and plug them. Remove the pipe supports from the transmission.
12 Disconnect the speedometer drive cable.
13 Unbolt the two reinforcement brackets from the torque converter housing. Pull the fluid filler tube from the transmission and retain the 'O' ring seals.
14 Remove the splash shield from below the radiator.
15 Remove the support plate for the handbrake equaliser.
16 Remove the shield from the lower half of the front of the torque converter housing (or two rubber plugs on A40 type).
17 Support the automatic transmission with a jack and then remove the rear crossmember and mounting. Through the open lower half of the torque converter housing, remove the six bolts which secure the drive plate and converter together. These can only be removed in turn by rotating the drive plate. To do this, apply a ring spanner to the crankshaft pulley securing bolt. Now screw in two guide pins (easily made from two old bolts) into diametrically opposite bolt holes in the front of the drive plate and then rotate the engine until they are horizontal. These pins will act as pivot points during removal of the transmission unit.
18 Place a jack under the engine sump (use a block of wood to protect it) and remove the bolts which secure the torque converter housing to the engine.
19 Lower both jacks progressively until the transmission unit will clear the lower edge of the engine rear bulkhead. Insert two levers between the engine rear plate and the temporary pivot pins and prise the transmission unit from the engine. Catch the fluid which will run from the torque converter during this operation. **On no account should levers be placed between the drive plate and the torque converter as damage or distortion will result.**
20 The torque converter can now be pulled forward to remove it from the housing. The drive plate can be unbolted from the crankshaft flange if the plate has to be renewed because of worn starter ring gear.
21 On two speed type automatic transmission units, the transmission is removed leaving the torque converter still attached to the drive plate. Remove first the four bolts which secure the driveplate to the pump impeller. Now turn the driveplate through 180° and remove the remaining four bolts. Withdraw the torque converter. The driveplate can be removed from the crankshaft rear flange if necessary after unscrewing the six securing bolts.
22 Installation is a reversal of removal but tighten all bolts to the specified torque and carry out the adjustments described earlier in this Chapter according to type, after first having refilled the unit with the correct grade and quantity of fluid.

43 Fault diagnosis - automatic transmission

Symptom	Cause
Vehicle fails to move in any selector position	Low hydraulic pressure. Transmission locked by parking pawl.
Vehicle fails to move in 'D', '2' or 'L'	Front clutch inoperative.
No drive in 2nd speed with selector in 'D' or '2' with vehicle moving	Front band inoperative or requires adjustment
No drive in 3rd speed with selector in 'D' and vehicle moving	Rear clutch inoperative. Low hydraulic pressure.
Vehicle fails to move in 'R'	Rear clutch inoperative. Low oil pressure. Rear brake band requires adjustment or rear servo piston not actuating.
No 1st/2nd speed upshift	Low governor pressure. Front servo piston inoperative or front brake band requires adjustment.
No 2nd/3rd speed upshift	Low governor pressure. Rear clutch inoperative. Low oil pressure to rear clutch and front servo.
No 3rd/2nd downshift	Low throttle valve pressure. High governor pressure. Front servo piston inoperative or front brake band requires adjustment.
No 2nd/1st downshift	High governor pressure. One-way clutch inoperative.
Incorrect speed shift points	Faulty shift valves. Throttle link connecting rod incorrectly adjusted. Line pressure abnormal.
Incorrect kick down point	Throttle pressure check ball faulty. Incorrectly adjusted 'kick-down' rod.
Jerky upshift and downshift throughout range	High hydraulic line pressure. Faulty internal control valve.
Jerky upshift or downshift to 2nd speed with selector in 'D' or '2'	High hydraulic line pressure. Front brake band worn.
Jerky 2nd/3rd upshift	High hydraulic line pressure.
Jerky 2nd/1st downshift	Faulty one way clutch.
Evidence of high fuel consumption	Incorrect grade of fluid. Faulty one-way clutch. Friction or slipping between idle or operating clutches and bands.

Chapter 7 Propeller shaft and universal joints

Contents

Centre bearing - removal and refitting ... 4
Fault diagnosis - propeller shaft and universal joints ... 6
General description ... 1
Maintenance ... 2
Propeller shaft - removal and refitting ... 3
Universal joints - inspection, dismantling and reassembly ... 5

Specifications

Type ... Tubular with two or three universal joints according to model. Centre bearing with 3 joint type. Front sliding sleeve

Universal joints
Type ... Greased sealed, needle roller bearing
Bearing cup circlip thickness availability:

0.0935 to 0.0955 in. (2.375 to 2.425 mm)
0.0955 to 0.0974 in. (2.425 to 2.475 mm)
0.0974 to 0.0994 in. (2.475 to 2.525 mm)
0.0994 to 0.1014 in. (2.525 to 2.575 mm)

Torque wrench settings	lb ft	Kg/m
Propeller shaft drive flange bolts	20	2.8
Centre bearing attachment bolts	20	2.8
Centre flange nut (to splined end of shaft) - tighten in two stages:	
1st	145	20.0
2nd	170	24.0

1 General description

1 Vehicles built up until 1972 may be equipped with a two or three joint propeller shaft according to model.
2 The three joint type incorporates a rubber mounted centre bearing which is attached to the bodyframe.
3 Later vehicles are equipped with a two universal joint type shaft.
4 The universal joints and the sliding sleeve which fits over the rear end of the gearbox mainshaft absorb the varying angles and length of the propeller shaft which is caused by the up and down motion of the rear axle due to the deflection of the rear road springs.
5 The universal joints each comprise a four way trunnion, or 'spider', each leg of which runs in a needle roller bearing race, prepacked with grease and fitted into the bearing journal yokes of the sliding sleeve and propeller shaft and flange. The universal

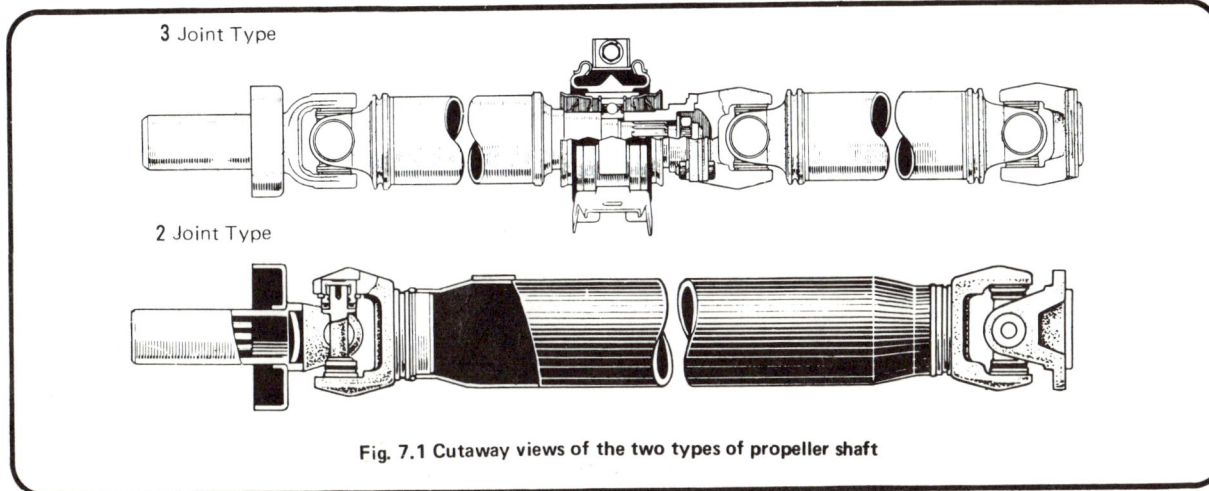

Fig. 7.1 Cutaway views of the two types of propeller shaft

Fig. 7.2 Exploded view of the two joint type of propeller shaft

1 Shaft complete
2 Dust cover
3 Yoke
4 Spider
5 Needle bearing cover
6 Oil seal
7 'O' ring
8 Circlip
9 Bearing cup
10 Balance weight
11 Propeller shaft
12 Yoke

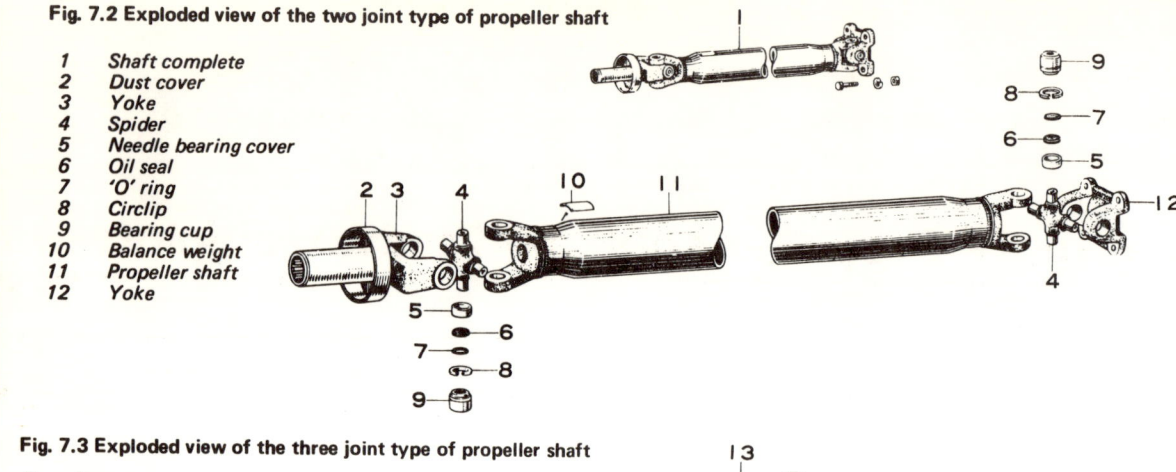

Fig. 7.3 Exploded view of the three joint type of propeller shaft

2 Dust cover
3 Yoke
4 Spider
5 Needle bearing cover
6 Oil seal
7 'O' ring
8 Circlip
9 Bearing cup
11 Propeller shaft
12 Yoke
13 Shaft complete
14 Intermediate shaft
15 Centre bearing
16 Flange
17 Washer
18 Nut

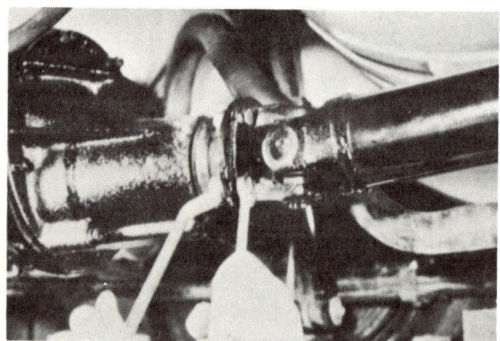

Fig. 7.4 Disconnecting the propeller shaft rear flanges (Sec. 3)

Fig. 7.5 Propeller shaft centre bearing and adjacent components (Sec. 4)

1 Intermediate shaft
2 Securing bolts
3 Rear shaft section
4 Centre bearing
5 Flange yoke
6 Nut

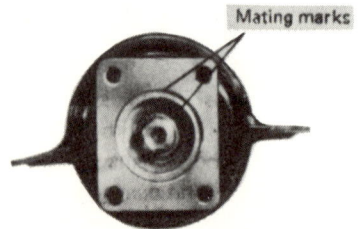

Fig. 7.6 Mating marks made before separation of the intermediate shaft and centre flange (Sec. 4)

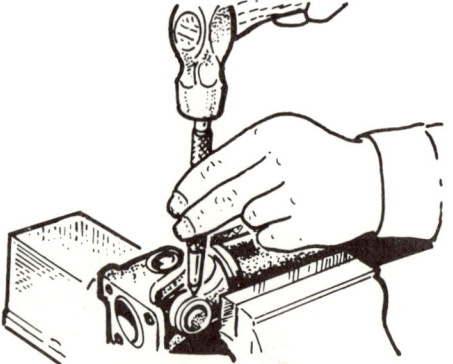

Fig. 7.7 Marking propeller shaft yokes to ensure exact replacement (Sec. 5)

Chapter 7/Propellor shaft and universal joints

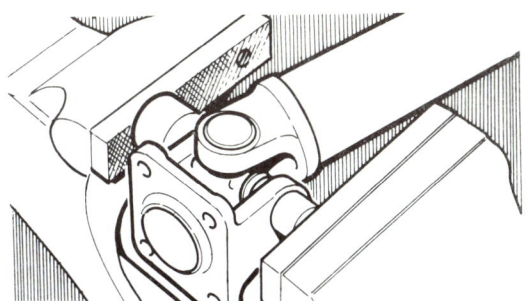

Fig. 7.8 Pressing in a universal joint bearing cup (Sec. 5)

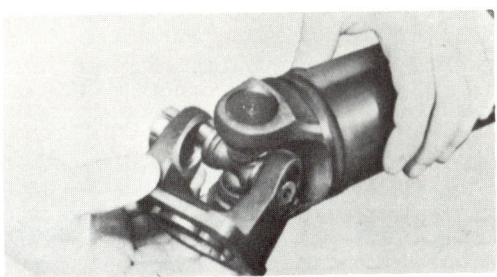

Fig. 7.9 Assembling a universal joint (Sec. 5)

joints are replaceable and the components are supplied in kit form.

2 Maintenance

No lubrication of the universal joints is required as they are prepacked with grease on assembly. The sliding sleeve of the forward end of the propeller shaft is lubricated from the gearbox. It is recommended that periodic inspection is carried out, however, whenever the car may be undergoing service, to check for any slackness in the universal bearings or at the flange bolts at the rear.

3 Propeller shaft - removal and refitting

1 Unless the vehicle is over a pit or supported on a hoist, jack up the rear to provide adequate working clearance.
2 Mark the edges of the propeller shaft rear driving flange and the rear axle pinion flange.
3 On three joint type propeller shafts, remove the attachment bolts from the centre bearing, retaining the washers and noting their location.
4 Unscrew and remove the four bolts from the rear driving flange. Separate the rear flanges by pulling the propeller shaft forward slightly and then withdraw the propeller shaft from the extension housing of the gearbox or automatic transmission. As the sliding joint is withdrawn from a manual type gearbox, be ready to catch a small quantity of oil.
5 Refitting is a reversal of removal but remember to align the rear flange mating marks and replace the centre bearing washers in their original locations.

4 Centre bearing - removal and refitting

1 Remove the bolts (2) and separate the shaft centre flanges.
2 Mark the position of the flange to the splined end of the shaft and remove the nut (6) and withdraw the washer, flange and centre bearing (Fig. 7.5).
3 The centre bearing cannot be dismantled but must be renewed complete if it is worn.

4 Refitting is a reversal of removal making sure that all nuts are tightened to the specified torque.

5 Universal joints - inspection, dismantling and reassembly

1 Preliminary inspection of the universal joints can be carried out with the propeller shaft on the car.
2 Grasp each side of the universal joint, and with a twisting action, determine whether there is any play or slackness in the joint. Also try an up and down rocking motion for the same purpose. If there is any sign whatsoever of play, the joints need replacement.
3 Remove the propeller shaft as described in Section 3.
4 Dot punch adjacent edges of the yokes so that they will be refitted in their original positions. Remove the circlips.
5 The bearing cups may be removed by one of two methods. Either hit the yoke (supported in the hand) adjacent to the bearing cup hole with a wooden or plastic mallet until the cup begins to emerge or press the cup out in a vice using an old bearing cup on one side and tubular spacer on the other to receive the ejected cup. With both methods, screw the cups out of their seats once they have emerged far enough to be able to grip them with a self locking wrench.
6 Inspect the holes in the yokes for elongation. Evidence of this is only likely in the event of previous neglect or abuse in which case the yokes must be renewed.
7 Obtain the appropriate repair kit for each joint. This will comprise spider, bearing cups, needle bearings and seals.
8 Locate the spider within the yoke and check that the 'O' ring seals are in position and that the dot punch marks mate.
9 Fill the bearing cup 1/3rd full with grease and check that the needle bearings are correctly held in position (with grease) around the inside of the cup.
10 Using a vice and an old bearing cup, press the new bearing cup into the yoke at the same time holding the spider in alignment so that the cup will slide onto the trunnion.
11 Repeat the operations for the remaining three bearings of each universal joint.
12 Insert new circlips **which must be of the same thickness for each opposite pair of bearing cups** and must be selected from the sizes listed in Specifications to ensure an axial end float of not more than 0.002 in. (0.05 mm).

6 Fault diagnosis - propeller shaft and universal joints

Symptom	Cause
Vibration	Worn universal joints
	Worn or loose centre bearing
	Propeller shaft bent
	Extension housing bush worn
	Loose drive flange bolts
	Propeller shaft out of balance
Knocking during starting, deceleration, gear-changing, or at the moment of deceleration	Worn universal joints
	Worn splines on shafts
	Loose drive flange bolts

Chapter 8 Rear axle

Contents

Differential carrier - removal and refitting 5
Fault diagnosis - rear axle 7
General description 1
Halfshafts, bearings and oil seals - removal and refitting ... 2
Pinion oil seal - renewal 4
Rear axle - removal and refitting 6
Roadwheel studs - renewal 3

Specifications

Rear axle type ... ... Hypoid semi-floating

Final drive ratios

	Saloon and hard top	Estate wagon
18R series engine (4 speed manual)	3.909 : 1	3.900 : 1
18R series engine (5 speed manual)	4.111 : 1	4.111 : 1
18R series engine (auto. transmission)	4.100 : 1	3.900 : 1
All other models:		
Manual gearbox	3.700 : 1	3.700 : 1
Automatic transmission	3.910 : 1	3.900 : 1

Torque wrench settings

	lb ft	Kg/m
Differential carrier to axle casing nuts	25	3.1
Brake backplate to axle casing bolts	35	4.8
Axle casing breather	20	2.8
Leaf spring 'U' bolts	35	4.8
Coil spring type suspension		
Upper control arm to axle housing	135	22.7
Lower control arm to axle housing	135	22.7
Lateral control arm to axle housing	75	10.4

1 General description

The rear axle is of hypoid semi-floating type. The differential unit may incorporate two or four pinions according to date of manufacture and vehicle model. The final drive ratio differs between the various models and reference should be made to Specifications Section for precise details.

The crownwheel and pinion and differential are mounted as an assembly in the differential carrier and this is bolted to the front of the banjo type axle casing. The advantage of this type of differential carrier is that the differential carrier may be removed complete with crownwheel and pinion and differential after disconnection of the propeller shaft and partial withdrawal of the halfshafts (axle-shafts).

Operations on the rear axle should be limited to those described in this Chapter. Dismantling and reassembly of the differential and crownwheel and pinion is not considered to be within the scope of the home mechanic due to the need for special tools and gauges. When a fault develops through wear or damage, exchange the differential carrier complete for a factory reconditioned unit.

2 Halfshafts, bearings and oil seals - removal and refitting

1 The halfshafts may be withdrawn without disturbing the differential gear. They are removed in order to renew the bearings or oil seals or if the differential is to be removed. Read the whole of this Section before starting work.

2 Jack up the car at the rear and support it firmly on proper stands. Remove the rear wheels, free the handbrake and remove the brake drums. (Details in Chapter 9).

3 Remove the nuts and bolts securing the bearing retainer plate and brake backplate to the axle casing flange. The halfshaft hub, bearing and backplate are now held in position as an assembly by the fit of the outer race of the bearing into the axle casing. Ideally the use of a proper impact hammer removal tool is needed to draw the assembly out. This consists of a flange which bolts to the wheel studs and to which is fitted a long shaft extension with a sliding weight on it. The sliding weight is hit against a flange at the extremity of the shaft and this draws the axle out. Whatever you do, this principle - of attaching a suitable bracket and striking point to the wheel studs - must be followed. No part of the axle assembly itself must be struck. A sustained pull is also quite ineffective and will probably only result in heaving the car off the stands. So get something suitable organised in advance or you will be wasting your time. One possibility is to use an old wheel rim bolted to the studs and then strike it from the inside with something suitably heavy. The success or otherwise of this method depends on access and the ability to get a good swing at it. Whatever method is used the car should be firmly supported (Figs. 8.3 and 8.4).

4 If both axle shafts are being removed and dismantled for axle bearing renewal, mark all the components 'left' or 'right' as they are not interchangeable from side to side.

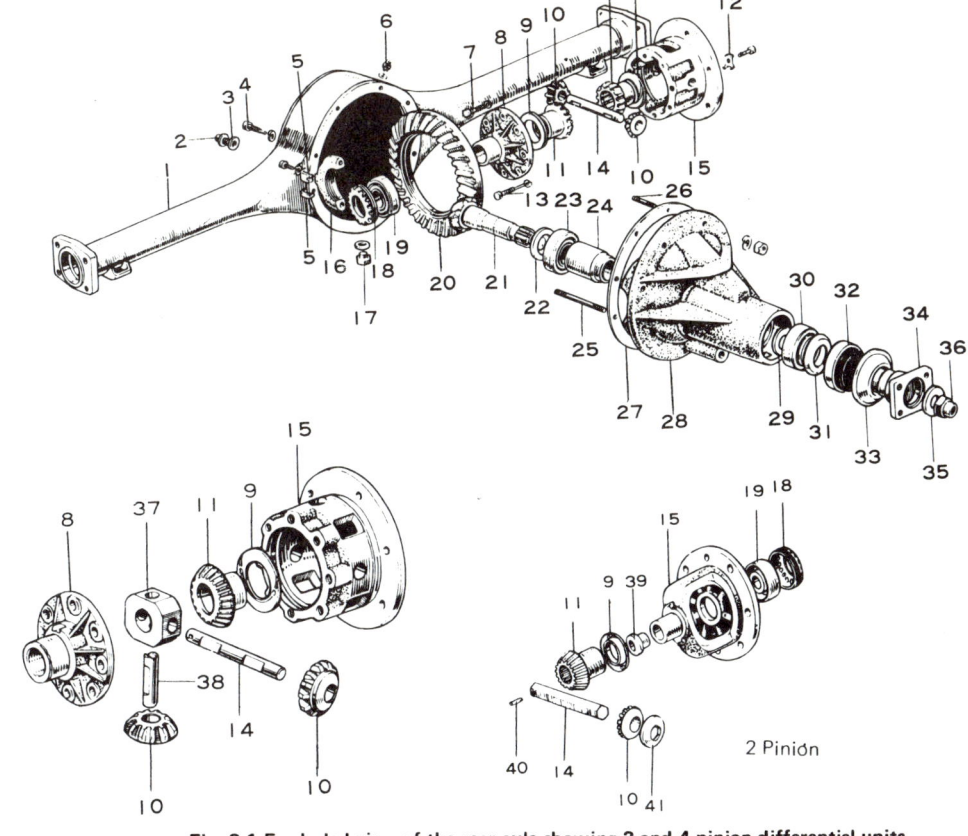

Fig. 8.1 Exploded view of the rear axle showing 2 and 4 pinion differential units

1 Axle casing	12 Lockplate	22 Washer	32 Pinion oil seal
2 Screw	13 Shaft pin	23 Taper roller	33 Dust deflector
3 Washer	14 Cross pin	24 Compressible spacer	34 Universal joint flange
4 Bolt	15 Differential case	25 Stud	35 Washer
5 Side bearing lock	16 Bearing cap	26 Stud	36 Nut
6 Breather plug	17 Drain plug	27 Gasket	37 Cross pin holder
7 Bolt	18 Bearing adjusting nut	28 Differential carrier	38 Pin
8 Differential case cover	19 Taper roller	29 Shim	39 Oil retainer
9 Washer	20 Crown wheel	30 Taper toller bearing	40 Lock pin
10 Pinion	21 Pinion	31 Oil deflector	41 Pinion thrust washer
11 Side gear			

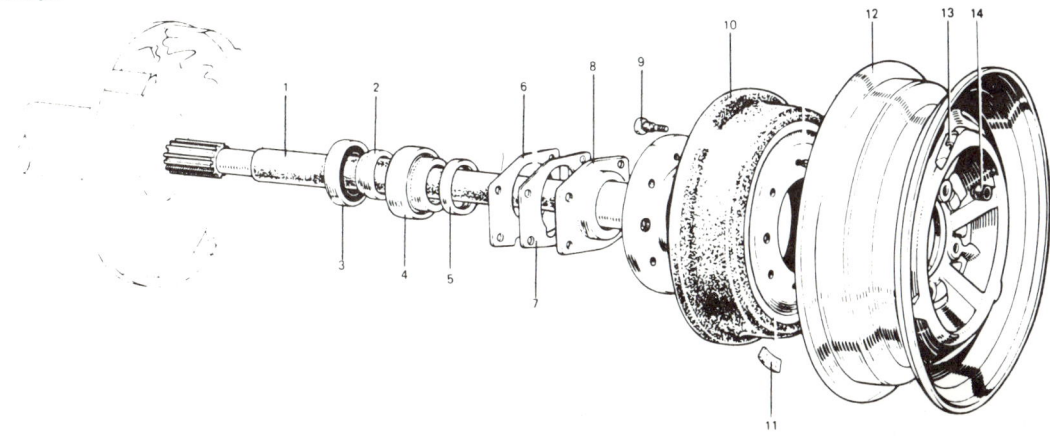

Fig. 8.2 Exploded view of a rear axle-shaft

1 Axle-shaft	5 Spacer	9 Roadwheel stud	12 Roadwheel
2 Bearing retaining collar	6 Gasket	10 Brake drum	13 Wheel balance weight
3 Oil seal	7 Gasket	11 Drum balance weight	14 Wheel nut
4 Bearing	8 Bearing retainer plate		

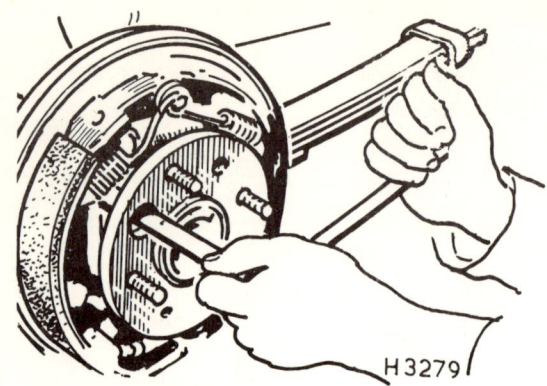

Fig. 8.3 Removing a backing/bearing retainer plate nut (Sec. 2)

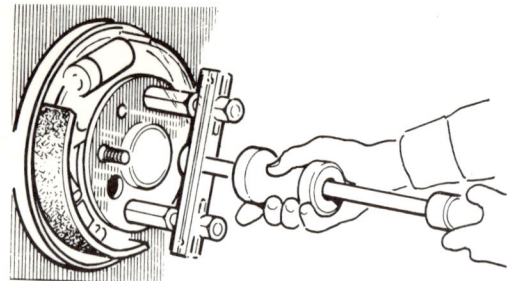

Fig 8.4 Using a slide hammer to withdraw an axle-shaft (Sec 2)

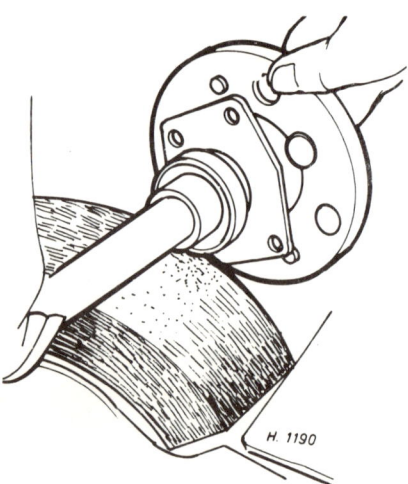

Fig. 8.5 Grinding off an axle bearing collar (Sec. 2)

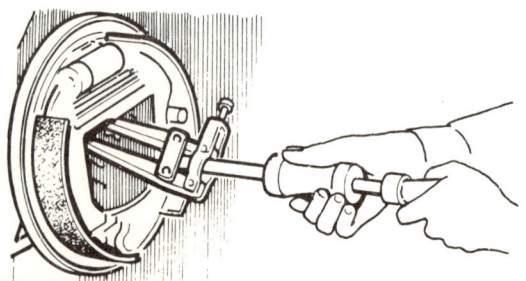

Fig. 8.6 Removing an oil seal from the rear axle casing (Sec. 2)

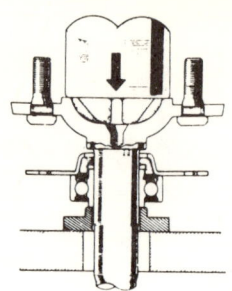

Fig. 8.7 Pressing a bearing onto an axle-shaft (Sec. 2)

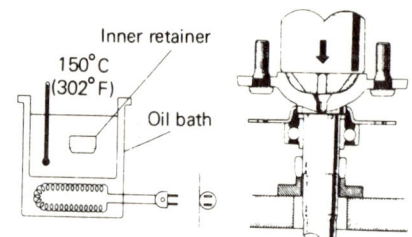

Fig. 8.8 Fitting an axle bearing retaining collar (Sec. 2)

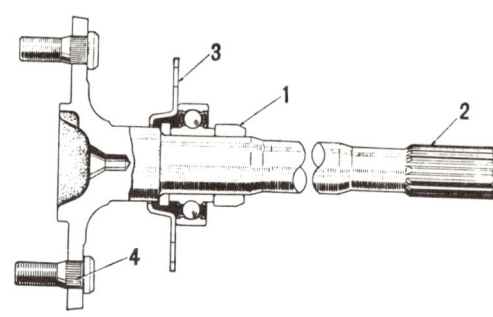

Fig. 8.9 Sectional view of rear axle hub components (Sec. 2)

1 Bearing retaining collar
2 Half shaft
3 Bearing retainer plate
4 Roadwheel stud

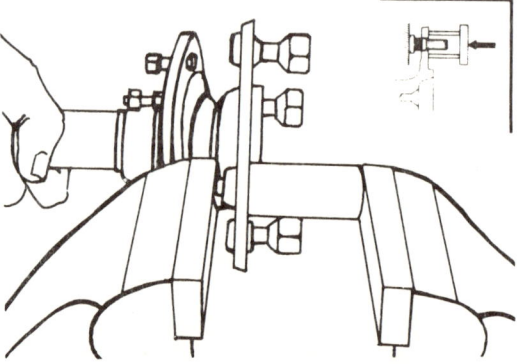

Fig. 8.10 Pressing a wheel stud into the rear axle-shaft flange (Sec. 3)

5 Grind or hacksaw a groove across the bearing inner retaining collar and then cut it from the axle shaft using a sharp chisel. Do not damage the shaft in any way.
6 Press the bearing from the shaft using a suitable press.
7 It is false economy not to renew the oil seals once the halfshafts have been withdrawn. Remove the seals with a suitable two legged extractor and drive in the new ones with a tubular drift.
8 Having examined the halfshaft for cracks, spline wear and distortion, fit the oil retaining plate, the spacer and then press on the bearing. Pressure must be exerted on the hub end of the halfshaft while the centre track of the bearing is supported on a suitable distance piece.
9 Take a new bearing retaining collar and heat it in an oil bath to 320°F (160°C). It will then have to be quickly dropped onto the axle shaft and using a method similar to that used for fitting the bearing, press it onto the shaft until it contacts the inner track of the bearing.
10 The brake backing plate has not been removed during this operation, but should there be signs of oil seepage from the gasket located between the backplate and the axle casing end flange, the old gasket must be removed and a new one fitted. To establish the thickness of the gasket required, measure the thickness of the backing plate and from the following table, select the appropriate gasket (available from your Toyota dealer).

Brake backing plate thickness	Axle casing end flange gasket thickness
0.105 to 0.109 in (2.66 to 2.78 mm)	0.012 in (0.3 mm)
0.100 to 0.105 in (2.54 to 2.66 mm)	0.020 in (0.5 mm)
0.095 to 0.100 in (2.42 to 2.54 mm)	0.024 in (0.6 mm)

11 Smear gasket cement to both sides of a new bearing retainer plate gasket and locate it on the outside face of the brake backplate.
12 When replacing the halfshaft the splines at the inner end should first pick up the splines in the differential side gears. Then enter the bearing into the axle casing recess until the outer edge of the race is nearly flush with the casing. Then bolt up the backplate evenly, which will draw the bearing completely into position. It is recommended that new self-locking nuts are used to secure the backplate and tightened to the specified torque.
13 Refit the brake drum, the roadwheel and lower the jacks. When assembly is completed, check the oil level in the rear axle.

3 Roadwheel studs - renewal

1 Renewal of a sheared stud or one with a damaged thread is simply carried out by first removing the halfshaft as described in the preceding Section.
2 Adequately support the rear face of the hub plate and knock the old stud from its splined hole.
3 Press the new stud into position using a vice and a piece of tubing as a distance piece.

4 Pinion oil seal - renewal

1 The pinion oil seal may be renewed with the differential carrier still in position on the rear axle casing and the casing still attached to the rear suspension.
2 Jack up the rear of the vehicle and mark the edges of the propeller shaft rear flange and the pinion driving flange. Then disconnect the flanges and tie the propeller shaft up out of the way.
3 Ensure that the handbrake is fully off and then attach a spring balance to a length of cord wound round the pinion driving flange. Give an even pull and read off the bearing preload on the spring balance. Note the figure for later comparison which should be between 2 and 5 lbs (0.9 to 2.3 kg). New bearings should have a pre-load of between 7 and 10 lbs (3.2 to 4.5 kg).

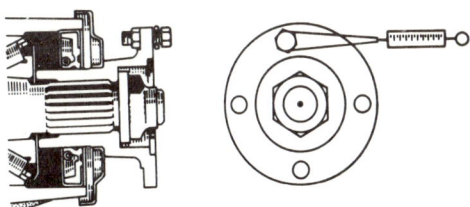

Fig. 8.11 Method of measuring rear axle pinion bearing preload using a spring balance (Sec. 4)

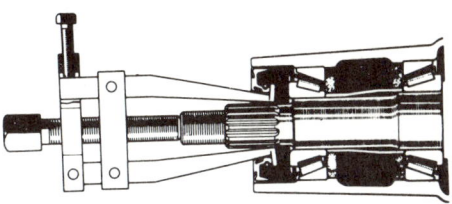

Fig. 8.12 Extracting a rear axle pinion oil seal (Sec. 4)

4 Mark the pinion coupling in relation to the pinion splines and knock back the staking on the pinion nut with a drift or narrow chisel.
5 Hold the pinion coupling quite still by bolting a length of flat steel to two of the coupling flange holes and then unscrew the pinion nut. A ring spanner of good length will be required for this.
6 Remove the lever from the coupling flange and withdraw the coupling. If it is tight, use a two or three legged puller but on no account attempt to knock it from the splined pinion. Withdraw the dust deflector.
7 Remove the defective oil seal using a two legged extractor.
8 Refit the new oil seal first having greased the mating surfaces of the seal and the axle housing. The lips of the oil seal must face inwards. Using a piece of brass or copper tubing of suitable diameter, carefully drive the new oil seal into the axle housing recess until the face of the seal is flush with the housing. Make sure that the end of the pinion is not knocked during this operation.
9 Refit the coupling to its original position on the pinion splines after first having located the dust cover.
10 Fit a new pinion nut and holding the coupling still with the lever, tighten the nut until the pinion end float only just disappears. Do not overtighten.
11 Rotate the pinion to settle the bearings and then check the preload using the cord and spring balance method previously described and by slight adjustment of the nut and rotation of the pinion, obtain a spring balance preload figure to match that which applied before dismantling. Do not overtighten the nut as it cannot be backed off without having to renew the internal compressible spacer.
12 Stake the nut, refit the propeller shaft, making sure to align the mating marks.
13 Lower the vehicle and check the oil level in the axle.

5 Differential carrier - removal and refitting

1 Jack-up the car and support it on stands as for halfshaft removal. Drain the oil from the back axle by removing the drain plug. The halfshaft should then be removed sufficiently far for the inner ends to disengage from the differential side pinions. The propeller shaft should then be dismantled from the rear axle pinion flange. It is not necessary to draw it out from the gearbox provided it can be conveniently rested out of the way on one

side.

2 Undo the ten nuts and washers holding the differential carrier to the casing. The whole unit can be drawn forward off the studs and taken out.

3 When replacing the assembly ensure that the mating faces are perfectly clean and free from burrs. A new gasket coated with sealing compound should also be used. Otherwise refitting is a reversal of the removal operation. Tighten the nuts to the specified torque.

4 Refill the unit with the correct grade and quantity of oil (approximately 2½ pints/1.4 litres).

6 Rear axle - removal and refitting

1 Jack-up the rear of the vehicle, place axle stands under the rear body frame side members and securely chock the front wheels. Place the jack under the differential and take its weight.

2 Remove the road wheels and disconnect the propeller shaft at the rear axle pinion coupling flange. Remember to mark the edges of the flange before disconnecting them so that they will be refitted in their original positions. Move the rear end of the propeller shaft to one side and support it to avoid strain on the centre universal joint or bearing.

3 Remove the brake drums and disconnect the handbrake cables from the actuating levers and then detach them from the brake backplate. Refit the drums to protect the brake shoe assemblies.

4 Disconnect the brake hydraulic line at the union on top of the axle casing. Plug both ends of the line to prevent loss of fluid or ingress of dirt.

Saloon and hardtop built after October 1973

5 Refer to Chapter 11, and disconnect the rear shock absorber lower mountings from the axle casing.

6 Lower the jack previously placed under the differential until the rear coil springs can be lifted from their seats.

7 Disconnect the upper and lower suspension links from the axle casing and then detach the lower end of the lateral control rod from its axle housing bracket.

8 Draw the rear axle assembly out sideways from under the vehicle.

Saloon and hardtop built before October 1973 and all estate wagons

9 Disconnect the rear shock absorber lower mountings from the road leaf spring support plates.

10 Unscrew and remove the four road spring 'U' bolts.

11 Remove each of the lower rear spring shackle bolts and lower the rear ends of the road springs to the ground.

12 Lower the jack previously placed under the differential until the rear axle assembly can be drawn out sideways from under the vehicle.

13 Refitting is a reversal of removal but refer to Chapter 11, for details of loading/tightening conditions for the suspension components and to Chapter 9, for a description of bleeding the hydraulic system.

7 Fault diagnosis - rear axle

Symptom	Cause
Noisy differential	
(a) During normal running	Lack of oil, damaged or worn gears, incorrect adjustment.
(b) During deceleration	Incorrect adjustment or damage to drive pinion bearings.
(c) During turning of vehicle	Worn or damaged axle-shaft bearing, worn differential gears.
Noisy rear hub	Worn axle-shaft bearings, buckled roadwheel, defective tyre, bent axle-shaft.
Oil leakage at hub and pinion oil seals	May be caused by blocked breather plug on axle casing or overfilled unit

Chapter 9 Braking system

Contents

Brake disc - examination, removal and refitting 12	General description 1
Brake drum - inspection and renovation 15	Handbrake - adjustment 21
Brake pedal - removal, refitting and adjustment 23	Handbrake and cables - dismantling and reassembly ... 22
Disc pads (dual cylinder, Girling type) - inspection and renewal ... 4	Hydraulic system - bleeding 18
Disc pads (single cylinder caliper) - inspection and renewal ... 3	Master cylinder (dual circuit, tandem type) - removal, servicing and installation 17
Drum brakes - adjustment 2	Master cylinder (single circuit type) - removal, servicing and installation 16
Fault diagnosis - braking system 28	
Flexible hoses - inspection and renewal 19	Pressure regulating valve 27
Front disc caliper (dual cylinder, Girling type) removal and refitting ... 10	Rear drum brake shoes (duo servo type) - inspection and renewal ... 7
Front disc caliper (dual cylinder, Girling type) - servicing ... 11	Rear drum brake shoes (leading trailing type) - inspection and renewal ... 6
Front disc caliper (single cylinder type) - removal and refitting ... 8	Rear drum wheel cylinders - removal, servicing and refitting 14
Front disc caliper (single cylinder type) - servicing ... 9	Rigid brake lines - inspection and renewal 20
Front drum brake shoes - inspection and renewal ... 5	Vacuum servo (brake booster) unit - description 24
Front drum wheel cylinders - removal, servicing and refitting ... 13	Vacuum servo unit - dismantling and reassembly ... 26
	Vacuum servo unit - removal and installation 25

Specifications

System type ... ... Four wheel drum or four wheel disc and drum according to model. Vacuum servo assistance on certain models also dual hydraulic circuit with pressure regulating valve. Handbrake mechanically operated on rear wheels only.

Front drums
Inner diameter ... ... 9.0 in. (228.6 mm)
Maximum wear or regrinding diameter ... ... 9.079 in. (230.6 mm)
Friction lining thickness ... ... 0.252 in. (6.4 mm)
Wheel cylinder diameter ... ... 0.872 to 0.873 in. (22.147 to 22.180 mm)

Rear drums
Inner diameter ... ... 9.0 in. (228.6 mm)
Maximum wear or regrinding diameter ... ... 9.079 in. (230.6 mm)
Friction lining thickness ... ... 0.228 in. (5.8 mm)
Wheel cylinder diameter ... ... 0.747 to 0.748 in. (18.977 to 19.010 mm)

Front disc brakes (single cylinder caliper)
Cylinder inner diameter ... ... 1.893 in. (48.07 mm)
Disc diameter ... ... 9.498 in. (241.0 mm)
Disc thickness:
   New ... ... 0.3940 in. (10.0 mm)
   Minimum ... ... 0.355 in. (9.0 mm)
Disc runout (maximum) ... ... 0.006 in. (0.15 mm)
Pad thickness:
   Overall ... ... 0.3934 in. (10.0 mm)
   Minimum (friction material) ... ... 0.08 in. (2.0 mm)

Dual cylinder caliper
Cylinder inner diameter ... ... 2.126 in. (54.0 mm)
Disc thickness:
   New ... ... 0.3934 in. (10.0 mm)
   Minimum ... ... 0.3740 in. (9.5 mm)
Disc runout (maximum) ... ... 0.0060 in. (0.15 mm)

Pad thickness:
 Overall ... 0.3937 in. (10.0 mm)
 Minimum (friction material) ... 0.08 in. (2.0 mm)

Master cylinder
 Piston diameter:
  Single type (4 wheel drum brakes) ... 0.747 to 0.748 in. (18.977 to 19.010 mm)
  All other types ... 0.872 to 0.873 in. (22.146 to 22.180 mm)

Vacuum servo unit (booster)
 Diaphragm diameter ... 6.102 in. (155.0 mm)
 Stroke ... 1.575 in. (40.0 mm)
 Pushrod (to master cylinder piston) clearance ... 0.012 in. (0.3 mm)

Brake pedal settings
 Floor to pedal upper surface ... 6.3 to 6.6 in. (161 to 168 mm)
 Free movement:
  Standard ... 0.08 to 0.28 in. (2.0 to 7.0 mm)
  With vacuum servo ... 0.12 to 0.24 in. (3.0 to 6.0 mm)
 Minimum distance from floor to pedal upper surface when pedal fully depressed ... 2.4 in. (60.0 mm)

Torque wrench settings	lb ft	Kg/m
Drum brakes		
Wheel cylinder to backplate	8	1.1
Backplate to stub axle carrier	50	6.9
Disc brakes		
Shield to stub axle carrier	50	6.9
Hub to disc bolts	38	5.3
Caliper to stub axle carrier (single cylinder)	50	6.9
Caliper to stub axle carrier (dual cylinder)	80	11.0
Master cylinder (single type)		
Non-return valve plugs	80	11.0
Reservoir securing bolt	20	2.8
Master cylinder (tandem type)		
Non-return valve plugs	65	9.0
Reservoir securing bolts	20	2.8
Stop bolt	9	1.2
Fluid pressure switches	32	4.5
Banjo type union bolts	36	5.0
General		
Bleed nipples	9	1.2
Brake pedal cross shaft bolt	45	6.2
Master cylinder to servo unit	12	1.7

1 General description

The braking system is of four wheel hydraulic type with optional servo assistance. The front brakes may be of drum or disc type, according to model, operating territory or date of manufacture. The rear brakes are of drum type on all models. The types of brakes fitted vary and are of differing makes. The handbrake operates on the rear wheels only, through mechanical linkage and the lever itself may be of floor mounted or pull out facia mounted design.

The hydraulic circuit may be of single or dual design dependent upon the regulations in force where the vehicle is intended to operate.

A pressure regulating valve is incorporated in the hydraulic system to prevent the rear wheels locking under heavy braking applications.

2 Drum brakes - adjustment

1 The rear drum brakes on all models are self-adjusting. The action of applying the handbrake actuates the adjustment mechanism.

2 Front brakes of two leading shoe type are not self-adjusting and the following operations must be carried out at regular intervals:

3 Jack-up the front of the vehicle and remove the two plugs from the adjusting holes.

4 Insert a small screwdriver until it engages with the teeth of the adjuster wheel. Turn the adjuster wheel until the brake shoe locks the drum. Now turn the adjuster wheel in the reverse direction until the roadwheel can be rotated without any binding or dragging of the shoe lining.

5 Repeat the adjustment procedure on the second shoe and then on the opposing brake drum.

6 Front drum brakes of duo servo type are self-adjusting.

3 Disc pad (single cylinder caliper) - inspection and renewal

1 Jack-up the front of the vehicle and remove the roadwheels.

2 Extract the spring clips and withdraw the cylinder guides.

3 Pull the cylinder assembly from the caliper unit and tie it up

Chapter 9/Braking system

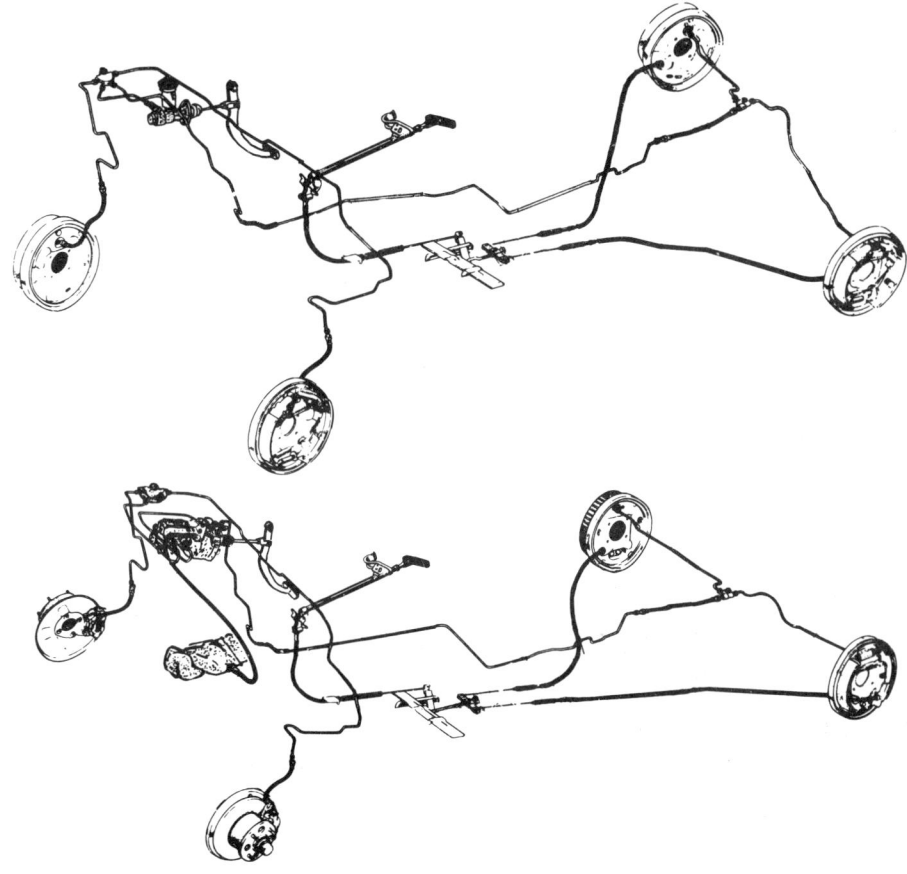

Fig. 9.1 Four wheel drum and disc/drum (with servo assistance) layouts

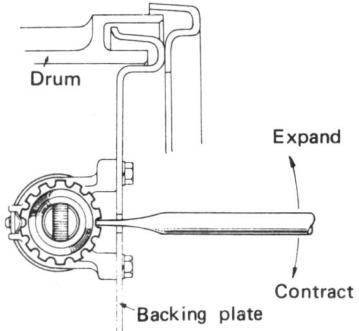

Fig. 9.2 Method of adjusting front wheel drum brakes (Sec. 2)

Fig. 9.3 Removing spring clips and cylinder guides from single cylinder type caliper (Sec. 3)

Fig. 9.4 Removing cylinder from caliper unit (Sec. 3)

with a piece of wire so that the flexible hydraulic hose will not be strained.

4 Inspect the thickness of the friction material of the pads. If they are worn to 0.08 in (2.0 mm) or less they must be renewed as a complete front axle set of four.

5 Pull the pads from the caliper housing (on one side of the vehicle only) (Fig. 9.5).

6 Using a flat bar or piece of wood, depress the piston into the cylinder, keeping it quite square. This operation is to provide enough room to insert the new, thicker pads and will cause the fluid level to rise in the reservoir unless the caliper bleed plug is opened during the time that the piston is being depressed.

7 Insert the new pads, fit the cylinder assembly, the cylinder

guides and the spring clips.
8 Depress the foot brake two or three times in order to bring the pads into contact with the disc.
9 Repeat the foregoing operations on the opposite front brake.
10 Refit the roadwheels, lower the jack and then check the level of the fluid in the hydraulic reservoir.

4 Disc pad (dual cylinder, Girling type) - inspection and renewal

1 Jack-up the front end of the vehicle and remove the roadwheels. Inspect the pad friction material thickness; if it is less than 0.08 in (2.0 mm) the pads must be renewed as an axle set of four.

Fig. 9.5 Withdrawing the disc pads from a single cylinder type caliper (Sec. 3)

2 Remove the spring clips and withdraw the pad retaining pins. (photo)
3 Extract the anti-squeal shims and then withdraw the disc pads, gripping their projections with a pair of pliers. (photo) If a disc pad wear indicator is fitted, disconnect the leads which run to the sensor from the pads as they are withdrawn.
4 Wipe out any dust from the interior of the caliper unit and using a flat bar depress each of the pistons into its cylinder squarely. This action will cause the level of the fluid in the hydraulic reservoir to rise unless the bleed nipple on the caliper unit is released.
5 Insert the new pads with their anti-squeal shims correctly located at the rear of the pad backing plates and with the arrows pointing upwards.
6 Fit the anti-rattle springs, retaining pins and spring clips.
7 Apply the footbrake two or three times to bring the pads against the disc and then repeat all the foregoing operations on the opposite front brake.

5 Front drum brake shoes - inspection and renewal

1 Jack-up the front of the vehicle and remove the roadwheels.
2 From one hub tap off the grease cap and withdraw the split pin from the castellated nut.
3 Unscrew the nut, extract the thrust washer and then withdraw the combined hub drum assembly from the stub axle. Take care that the outer hub bearing does not drop out or it may be damaged. Prevent any dirt or grit from entering the bearings.
4 Inspect the condition of the friction linings. If they are in good condition, brush any dust from them and from the drum interior and reassemble the hub/drum.

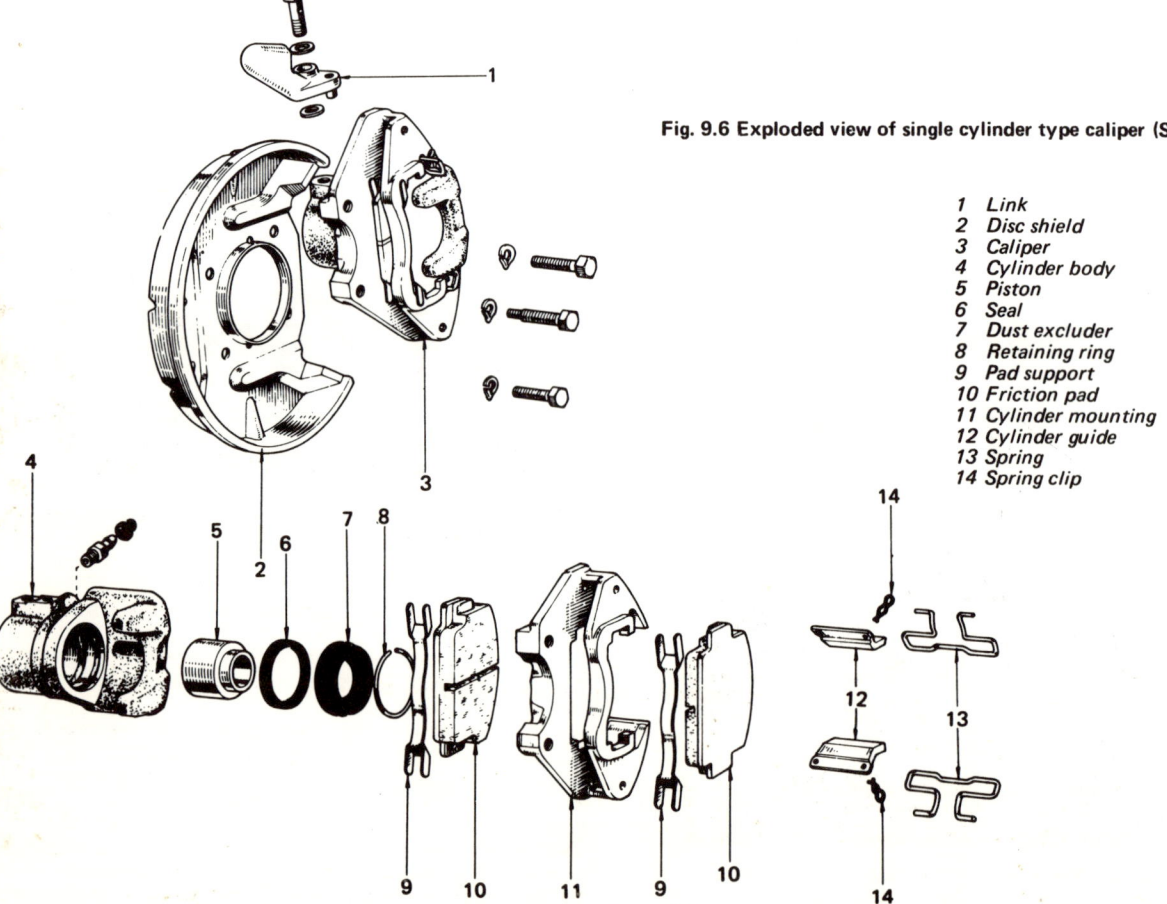

Fig. 9.6 Exploded view of single cylinder type caliper (Sec. 3)

1 Link
2 Disc shield
3 Caliper
4 Cylinder body
5 Piston
6 Seal
7 Dust excluder
8 Retaining ring
9 Pad support
10 Friction pad
11 Cylinder mounting
12 Cylinder guide
13 Spring
14 Spring clip

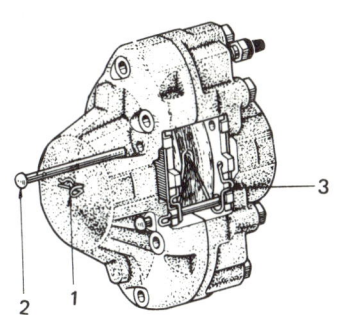

Fig. 9.7 Removing disc pads from a dual cylinder caliper (Sec. 4)

1 Spring clip
2 Retaining pin
3 Anti-rattle spring

4.2 Disc pad anti-rattle springs and retaining pins

4.3 Disc pad anti-squeal shim

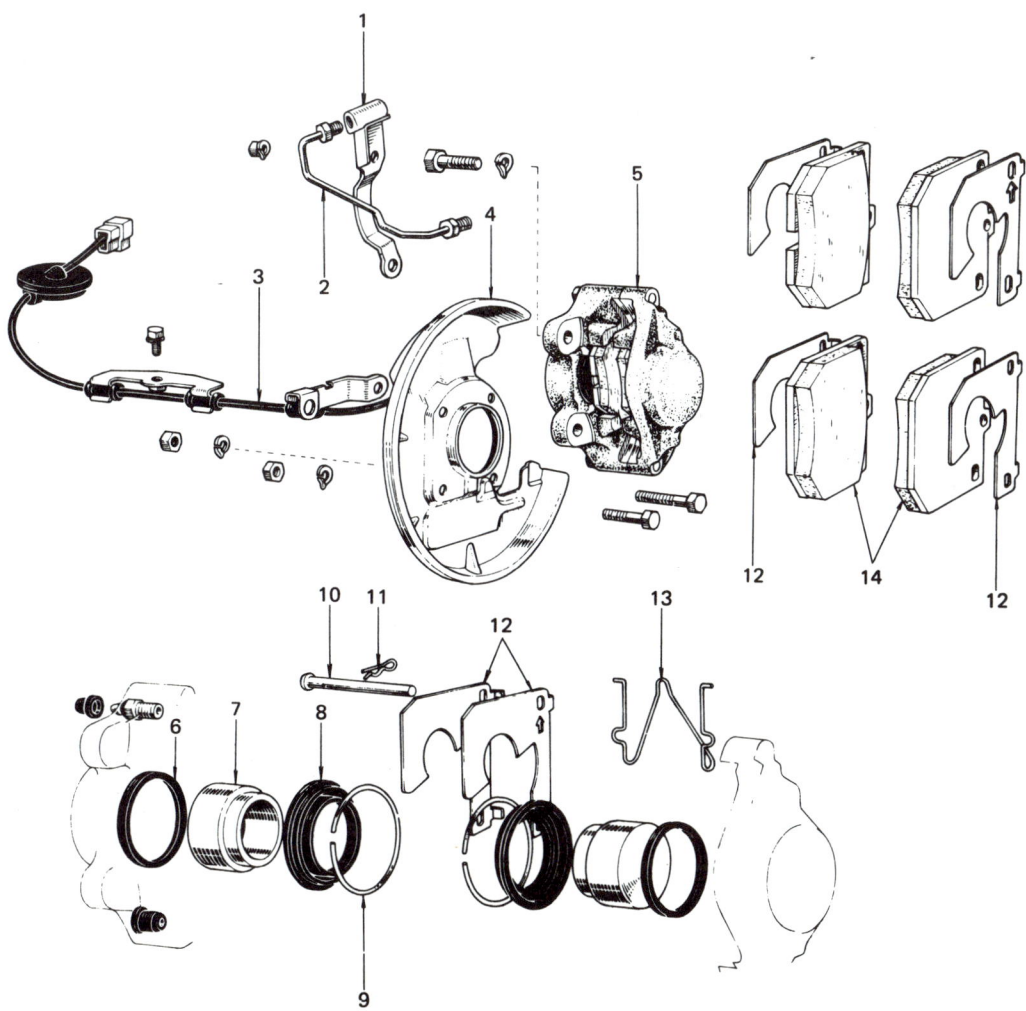

Fig. 9.8 Exploded view of dual cylinder type caliper (Sec. 4)

1 Connector
2 Bridge pipe
3 Lead for pad wear indicator
4 Disc shield
5 Caliper
6 Seal
7 Piston
8 Dust excluder
9 Retaining ring
10 Pad retaining pin
11 Spring clip
12 Anti-squeal shim
13 Anti-rattle spring
14 Pads

Fig. 9.9 Installing pads and anti-squeal shims (dual cylinder caliper) (Sec. 4)

Fig. 9.11 Removing the torsion spring (1) and automatic adjuster lever (2) from a duo servo type front brake (Sec. 5)

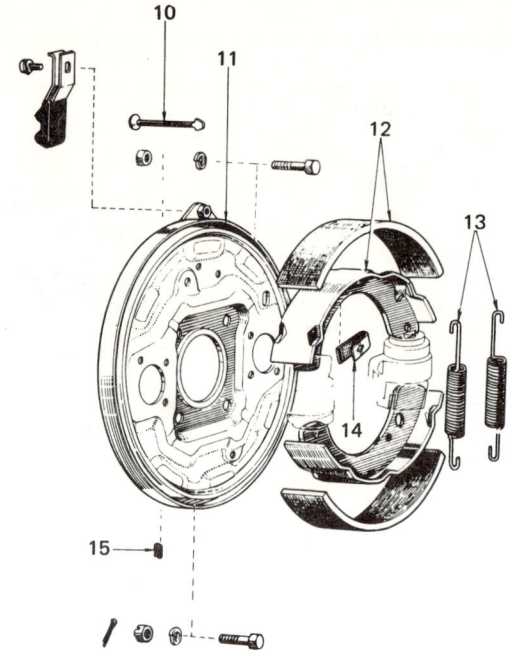

Fig. 9.10 Exploded view of two leading shoe type front brake (Sec. 5)

10 Shoe steady post   13 Shoe return spring
11 Back plate   14 Shoe steady spring
12 Brake shoe and lining 15 Adjustment hole plug

Fig. 9.12 Exploded view of a duo servo type front brake (Sec. 5)

1 Seal
2 Wheel cylinder
3 Automatic adjuster cable
4 Shoe return spring
5 Cable guide
6 Shoe return spring
7 Shoe steady spring retainers
8 Shoe steady spring
9 Shoe steady post
10 Back plate
11 Shoe and lining
12 Shoe return spring
13 Adjuster
14 Shoe and lining
15 Spring
16 Torsion spring
17 Automatic adjuster lever

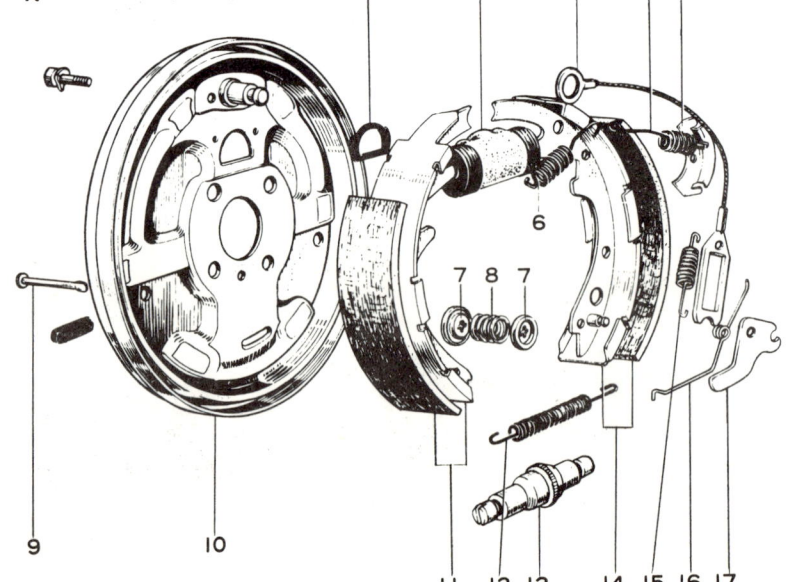

5 If the linings are worn down to (or nearly down to) the rivets or the linings are grease strained, then they must be renewed. If grease contamination is evident, then the oil seal in its retainer must be renewed as described in Chapter 11.

6 It is not recommended that new linings are fitted to the original shoes but rather the old shoes are exchanged for factory relined ones. This will prove much more satisfactory as the linings will be securely rivetted and ground to contour to minimise the bedding-in process.

7 *On two leading shoe type brakes,* remove the shoe steady springs from their posts and slacken the shoe adjusters right off. Prise one shoe from its location, pull it slightly forward and allow it to move towards the hub centre so that the second shoe can be removed and lift away both shoes with return springs still

attached.

8 *On duo servo (automatically adjusted) type brakes,* unhook the torsion spring (1) and remove the adjuster lever (2). Disconnect the upper shoe return springs and then remove the automatic adjuster cable and guide (Fig. 9.11).

Disconnect the lower shoe return spring (1) the adjusting screw (2) and the shoe steady springs and dished retainers (3) and withdraw the brake shoes (Fig. 9.13).

9 With both types of brake assembly, note carefully the way round each shoe is fitted with reference to leading and trailing ends, also mark the holes in which the shoe return springs engage.

10 Installation of the shoes is a reversal of removal but apply a smear of brake grease to the shoe sliding surfaces as indicated.

11 *On two leading shoe type brakes,* refit and adjust the hub/drum assembly, as described in paragraph 13, of this Section and then adjust the brake, as instructed in Section 2, of this Chapter.

12 *On duo servo type brakes,* locate the shoes on the backplate and fit the steady springs, posts and dished retainers. Connect the upper return springs, adjuster cable and guide, applying a smear of brake grease to the channel of the latter. Fit the adjuster screw and lower shoe return spring.

Hook the adjuster lever (2) onto the spring (1) and connect the lever to the pin (3) and then attach the torsion spring (4) to the end of the lever. Turn the adjuster screw until the brake drum can be installed over them with the minimum clearance (Fig. 9.17).

13 On both types of brakes, tighten the hub nut to a torque of 20 lb/ft (2.8 kg/m) whilst rotating the hub/drum backwards and forwards. Release the nut and then just tighten it with the fingers using a socket

14 Insert a new split pin, bend over the ends and then tap on the grease cap. When the front hub is correctly adjusted, the bearing

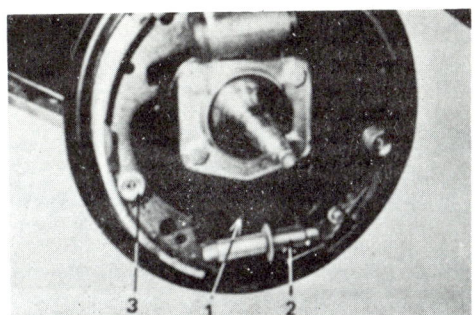

Fig. 9.13 Removing shoe return spring (1) adjuster (2) and shoe steady spring (3) from duo servo type front brake (Sec. 5)

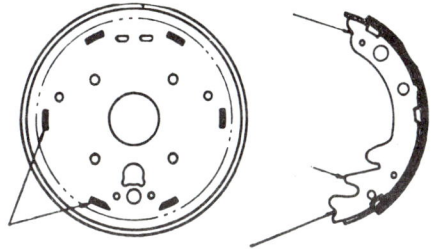

Fig. 9.14 Grease application points (duo servo type front brake) (Sec. 5)

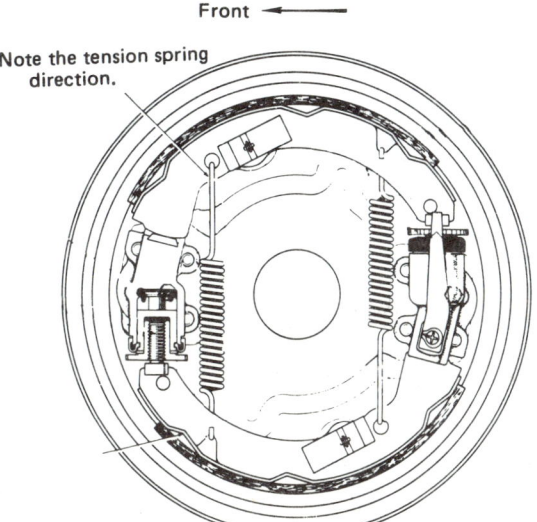

Fig. 9.15 Correctly installed brake shoes (left-hand side front two leading shoe type) (Sec. 5)

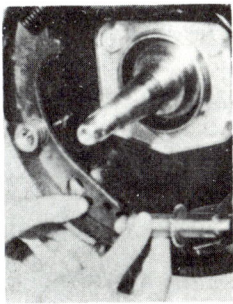

Fig. 9.16 Installing the adjuster (duo servo type front brake) (Sec. 5)

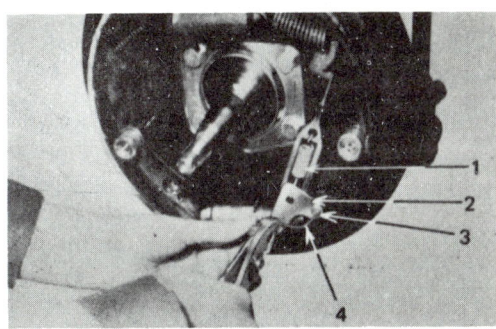

Fig. 9.17 Connecting the automatic adjuster mechanism (duo servo type front brake) (Sec. 5)

1 Spring
2 Lever
3 Pin
4 Torsion spring

Fig. 9.18 Adjusting a front wheel bearing (Sec. 5)

preload can be checked by attaching a spring balance to a roadwheel stud and pulling it in the forward direction of travel. The force required to start the hub/drum turning should be between 0.66 and 1.54 lbs (0.3 and 0.7 kg). Note the grease packing areas.

15 Repeat all the foregoing operations on the opposing front wheel as the brake shoes must always be renewed as a complete axle set.

16 Refit the roadwheels and lower the jacks.

6 Rear drum brake shoes (leading-trailing type) - inspection and renewal

1 Jack-up the rear of the vehicle, remove the roadwheel and the brake drum (two screws). (photo)

2 Inspect the condition of the friction linings. If they are in good condition, brush any dust from them and from the drum interior and refit the drum and roadwheel.

3 If the linings are worn down to (or nearly down to) the rivets or the linings are oil stained, then they must be renewed. If oil contamination is evident, then the rear axle oil seal must be renewed as described in Chapter 8.

4 It is not recommended that new linings are fitted to the original shoes but rather the old shoes are exchanged for factory relined ones. This will prove much more satisfactory as the linings will be securely rivetted, and ground to contour, to minimise the bedding-in process.

5 Remove the lower and upper shoe return springs using a hooked tool or a pair of narrow nosed pliers. (photos)

6 Press the automatic adjuster ratchet (1) down and push the lever (2) towards the centre of the hub (Fig. 9.22).

7 Remove the shoe steady spring and withdraw the leading shoe. Remove the trailing shoe in a similar manner but disconnect the handbrake cable as the shoe is withdrawn. Remove the handbrake strut. (photo)

8 Remove the automatic adjuster lever and ratchet from the old leading shoe and fit them to the new one.

9 Remove the handbrake lever from the old trailing shoe and fit them to the new one.

10 Install the handbrake strut and spring to the trailing shoe.

11 Installation of the new brake shoes is a reversal of removal but apply a smear of brake grease to the shoe sliding surfaces of the backplate and to the wheel cylinder slots.

12 Refit the brake drum and then apply the handbrake several times in succession to adjust the shoes and provide the minimum clearance between the linings and the drum.

13 Repeat the operations on the opposing wheel, then refit the roadwheels and lower the jack.

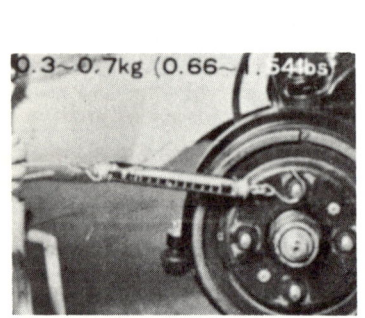

Fig. 9.19 Checking the front hub bearing preload (Sec. 5)

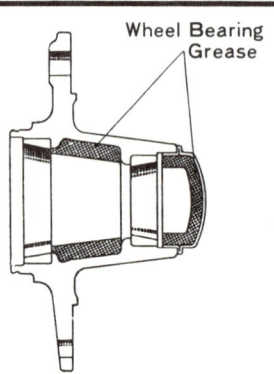

Fig. 9.20 Grease packing locations in front hub (Sec. 5)

6.1 Rear brake drum showing retaining screw holes

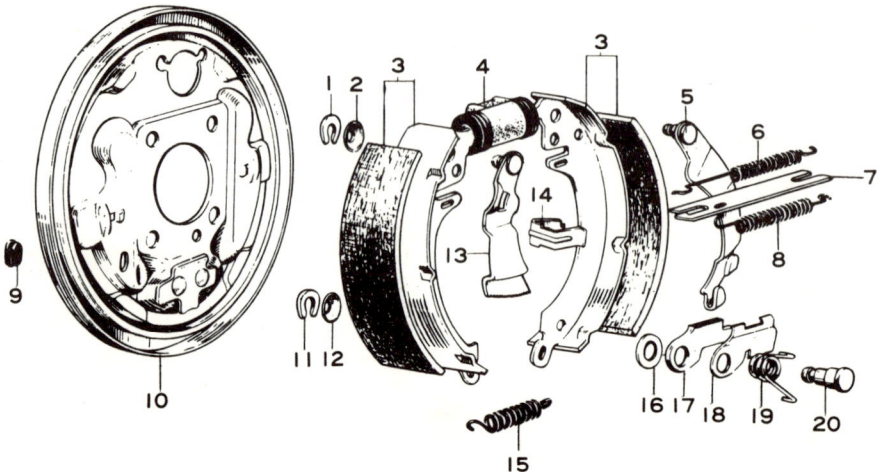

Fig. 9.21 Exploded view of rear brake (leading/trailing type) (Sec. 6)

1 'C' washer	6 Shoe return spring	11 'C' washer	16 Washer
2 Wave washer	7 Handbrake strut	12 Wave washer	17 Automatic adjuster latch
3 Brake shoe and lining	8 Shoe return spring	13 Automatic adjuster lever	18 Stop
4 Wheel cylinder	9 Adjuster hole plug	14 Shoe steady spring	19 Torsion spring
5 Handbrake lever	10 Backing plate	15 Shoe return spring	20 Pivot

6.5a Rear brake upper shoe return spring

6.5b Rear brake lower shoe return spring correctly located

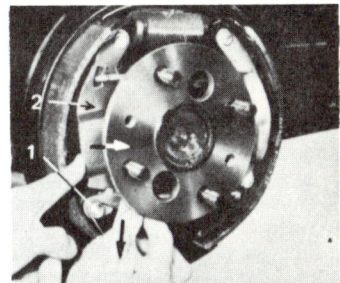
Fig. 9.22 Adjuster ratchet (1) and lever (2) on leading/trailing type rear drum brake) (Sec. 6)

Fig. 9.23 Removing the leading shoe (leading/trailing type rear drum brake) (Sec. 6)

6.7 Withdrawing rear drum brake trailing shoe. Note handbrake cable, strut and adjuster lever

Fig. 9.24 Disconnecting handbrake cable from the trailing shoe (leading/trailing type rear drum brake) (Sec. 6)

Fig. 9.25 Location of adjuster ratchet and stop on leading shoe of leading/trailing type rear drum brake (Sec. 6)

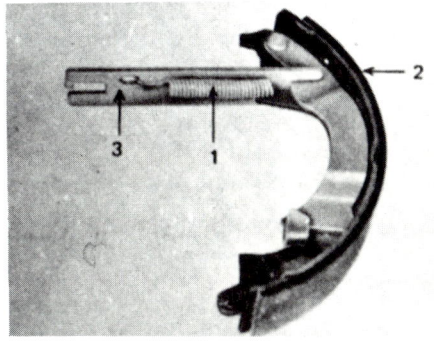
Fig. 9.26 Handbrake lever spring (1) and strut (3) fitted to trailing shoe of trailing shoe of leading/trailing type rear drum brake (Sec. 6)

7 Rear drum brake shoes (duo servo type) - inspection and renewal

1 Carry out the operations 1 to 4 of the preceding Section.
2 Remove the torsion spring (1) and adjuster lever (2) (Fig. 9.28).
3 Remove the shoe upper return springs and automatic adjuster cable and guide.
4 Remove the handbrake strut.
5 Remove the shoe lower return spring (1) the automatic adjuster screw (2) and shoe steady spring assembly (3) (Fig. 9.30).
6 Withdraw the brake shoes, disconnecting the handbrake cable from the shoe lever as the shoe is removed.
7 Remove the handbrake lever and the automatic adjuster lever from their respective shoes and refit them to the new shoes.
8 Apply a smear of brake grease to the shoe sliding surfaces of the brake backplate and to the wheel cylinder slots as indicated. (Fig. 9.32).
9 Installation of the new shoes is a reversal of removal.
10 Refit the brake drum and then apply the handbrake several times in succession to adjust the shoes and to provide the minimum clearance between the linings and the drum.
11 Repeat the operations on the opposing wheel then refit the roadwheels and lower the jack.

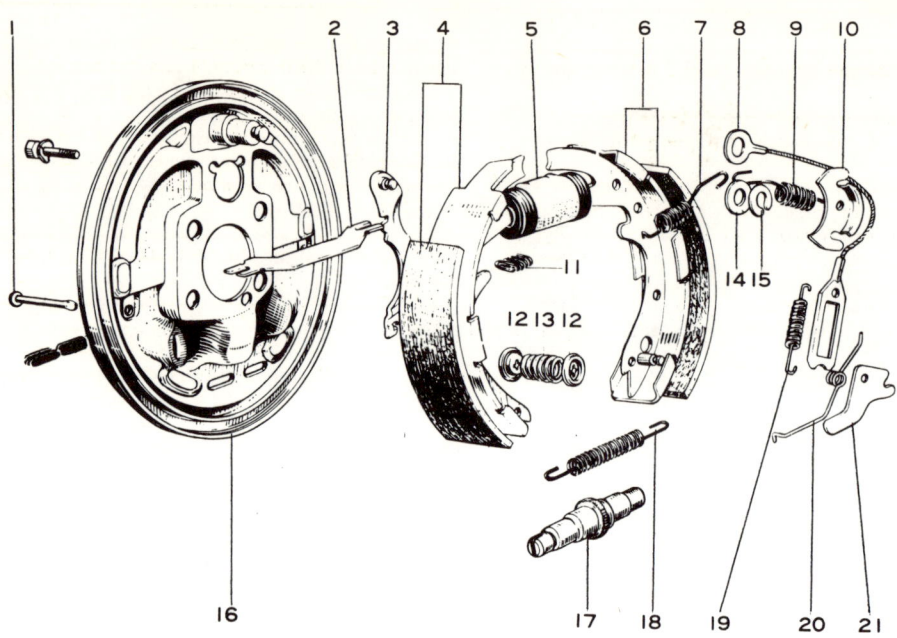

Fig. 9.27 Exploded view of duo servo type rear drum brake (Sec. 7)

1 Steady post
2 Handbrake strut
3 Handbrake lever
4 Brake shoe and lining
5 Wheel cylinder
6 Brake shoe and lining
7 Shoe return spring
8 Automatic adjuster cable
9 Shoe return spring
10 Cable guide
11 Spring
12 Shoe steady spring retainer
13 Shoe steady spring
14 Wave washer
15 'C' type washer
16 Back plate
17 Adjuster screw
18 Shoe return spring
19 Tension spring
20 Torsion spring
21 Automatic adjuster lever

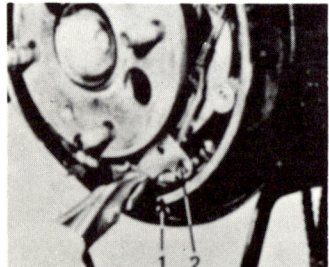

Fig. 9.28 Removing torsion spring (1) and adjuster lever (2) from duo servo type rear drum brake (Sec. 7)

Fig. 9.29 Removing the handbrake strut (duo servo type rear drum brake) (Sec. 7)

Fig. 9.30 Location of shoe lower return spring (1) automatic adjuster screw (2) and shoe steady spring (3) on duo servo type rear drum brake (Sec. 7)

Fig. 9.31 Disconnecting handbrake cable from shoe of duo servo type rear drum brake (Sec. 7)

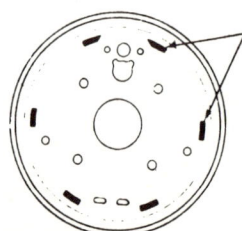

Fig. 9.32 Grease application points (duo servo type rear drum brake) (Sec. 7)

8 Front disc caliper (single cylinder type) - removal and refitting

1 Jack-up the front of the vehicle and support it securely. Remove the roadwheel.
2 Disconnect the flexible hydraulic hose from the caliper and plug the hose to prevent loss of fluid. An alternative method of preventing loss of fluid is to remove the brake fluid reservoir cap and place a sheet of polythene film over the neck of the reservoir and then screw on the cap. This causes a partial vacuum and prevents the fluid leaking from the master cylinder.
3 Remove the cylinder assembly and disc pads, as described in Section 3.
4 Remove the two bolts which secure the caliper unit to the stub axle carrier and remove the unit complete with cylinder support springs and pad support plates.
5 Refitting is a reversal of removal but tighten the caliper bolts to the specified torque and bleed the hydraulic system (Section 18).

9 Front disc caliper (single cylinder type) - servicing

1 Carefully prise out the dust excluder retaining ring and remove the dust excluder.
2 Apply aid from a tyre pump at the hydraulic hose connection on the caliper body and eject the piston.
3 Inspect the mating surfaces of the piston and cylinder. If any scoring is evident or 'bright' wear areas, renew the caliper cylinder assembly complete.
4 If these components are in good condition, extract the seal from the cylinder recess and discard it.
5 Wash all components in clean hydraulic fluid or methylated spirit and obtain a repair kit which will contain all the necessary seals and other renewable items.
6 Locate the new seal in its cylinder recess, manipulating it into position using the fingers only to avoid damage.
7 Dip the piston in clean hydraulic fluid and enter it squarely into the cylinder.
8 Fit the new rubber dust excluder and retaining ring.
9 Examine all other components of the caliper unit and renew any that are worn or damaged.

10 Front disc caliper (dual cylinder Girling type) - removal and refitting

1 Remove the pads and wear indicator leads (if fitted), as described in Section 4.
2 Disconnect the hydraulic pipe from the caliper unit, either plugging the line or sealing the reservoir, as described in Section 8.
3 Unscrew and remove the two caliper mounting bolts and remove the caliper from the stub axle carrier, retaining any mounting shims which may be fitted.
4 Refitting is a reversal of removal but tighten the caliper securing bolts to the specified torque and bleed the hydraulic system, as described in Section 18.

11 Front disc caliper (dual cylinder Girling type) - servicing

1 Servicing of this type of caliper is very similar to that described for the single cylinder type in Section 9 except that there are of course two cylinders.
2 Place a thin piece of wood between the opposing pistons before ejecting them to prevent damaging their end faces.
3 **On no account loosen or remove the bolts which secure the two halves of the caliper unit together.**
4 Reassembly is similar to that described for the single cylinder type in Section 9.

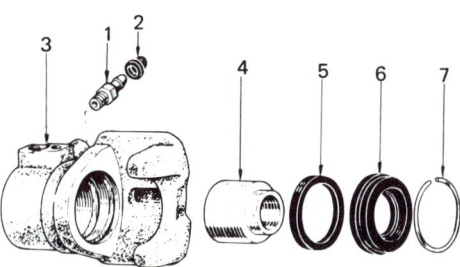

Fig. 9.33 Exploded view of single cylinder type caliper (Sec. 8)

1 Bleed nipple
2 Dust cap
3 Cylinder body
4 Piston
5 Seal
6 Dust excluder
7 Dust excluder retaining ring

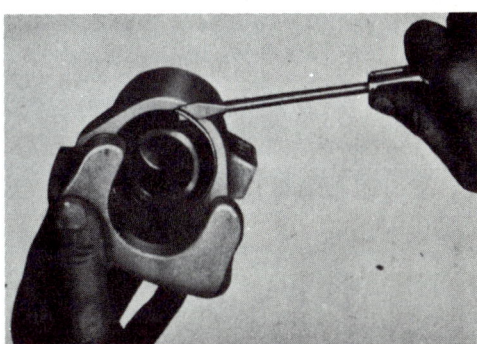

Fig. 9.34 Prising out the dust excluder retaining ring from single cylinder type caliper (Sec. 9)

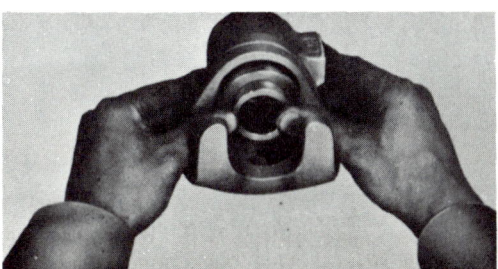

Fig. 9.35 Inserting the piston into single cylinder type caliper unit (Sec. 9)

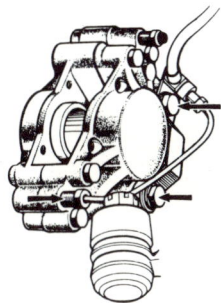

Fig. 9.36 Mounting bolts (dual cylinder type caliper) (Sec. 10)

12 Brake disc - examination, removal and refitting

1 Jack-up the front of the vehicle, remove the roadwheel and caliper.
2 Inspect the disc surfaces for deep scoring or grooves. Light scoring is normal.
3 Using a dial gauge or similar instrument, check for run out (buckle). This should not exceed 0.0059 in (0.15 mm) otherwise the disc should be renewed.
4 The disc thickness should not be reduced below 0.453 in (11.5 mm) either by normal wear or if it is decided to surface grind it to remove scoring.
5 To remove the disc/hub assembly, tap off the grease cap (10) remove the split pin and nut retainer (9). Unscrew the nut (8) and extract the thrust washer (7). Withdraw the disc/hub assembly taking care not to let the outer bearing drop out. (Fig 9.38).
6 Unscrew the bolts which secure the disc to the hub and separate the two components.
7 Refitting is a reversal of dismantling but tighten the disc to hub bolts to a torque of 33 lb/ft (4.5 kg/m) and adjust the front bearing preload in a similar manner to that described for drum/hub assemblies in Section 5.

13 Front drum wheel cylinders - removal, servicing and refitting

1 Remove the brake shoes, as described in Section 5, according to type.
2 Although it is possible to dismantle the wheel cylinder while it is still attached to the backplate, it is recommended that it is removed. To do this, disconnect the fluid line from the cylinder and either plug the line or seal the reservoir filler neck with a sheet of polythene to prevent loss of fluid.
3 Remove the wheel cylinder from the brake backplate.
4 Remove the adjuster wheel and screw, and the dust excluder, and then eject the piston by tapping the cylinder on a piece of wood or by applying air from a tyre pump to the fluid inlet.
5 Examine the mating surfaces of the piston and cylinder. If they are scored or any 'bright' wear areas are evident, renew the cylinder complete.
6 Where the components are in good order, discard the seals and wash all items in clean hydraulic fluid or methylated spirit.
7 Obtain a repair kit and manipulate the new seal into position using only the fingers.
8 Dip the piston assembly into clean hydraulic fluid and insert it into the cylinder. Fit the dust excluder, adjuster wheel and screw.
9 Bolt the wheel cylinders to the backplate tightening the bolts

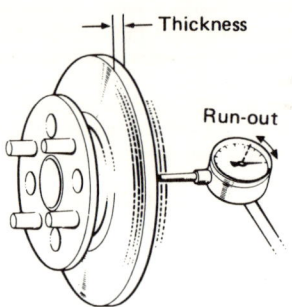

Fig. 9.37 Checking disc run out (Sec. 12)

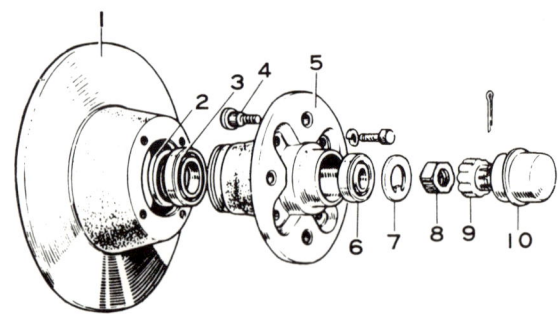

Fig. 9.38 Exploded view of a disc/hub assembly (Sec. 12)

1 Disc
2 Oil seal
3 Tapered roller bearing
4 Wheel stud
5 Hub
6 Tapered roller bearing
7 Thrust washer
8 Nut
9 Nut retainer
10 Grease cap

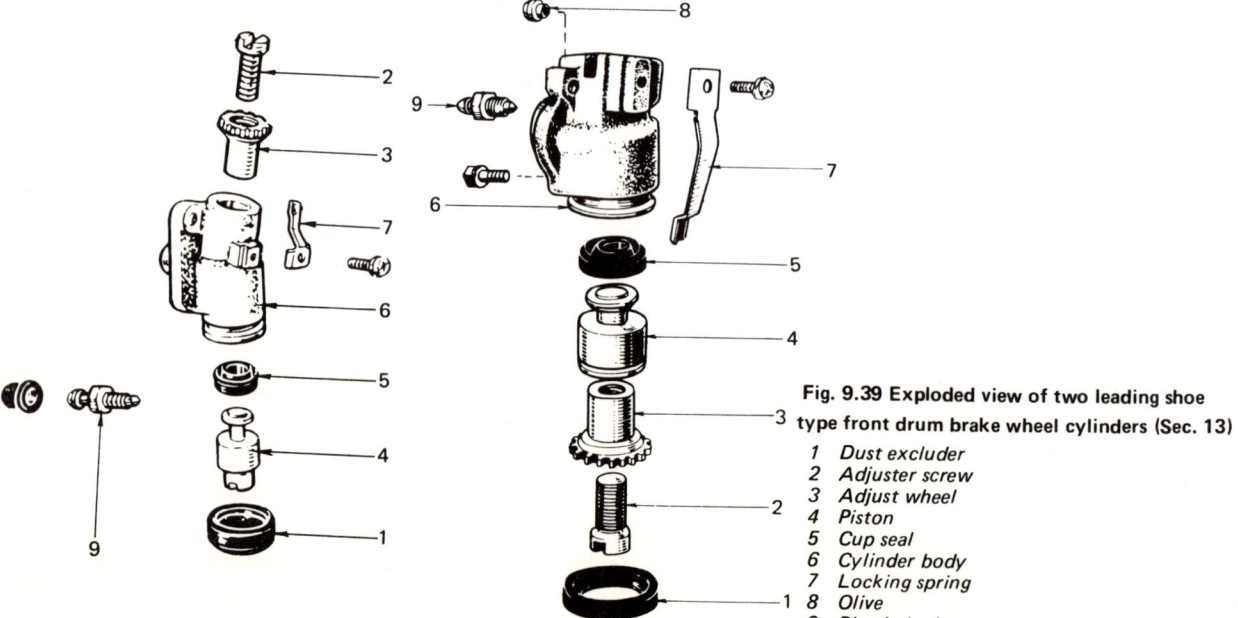

Fig. 9.39 Exploded view of two leading shoe type front drum brake wheel cylinders (Sec. 13)

1 Dust excluder
2 Adjuster screw
3 Adjust wheel
4 Piston
5 Cup seal
6 Cylinder body
7 Locking spring
8 Olive
9 Bleed nipple

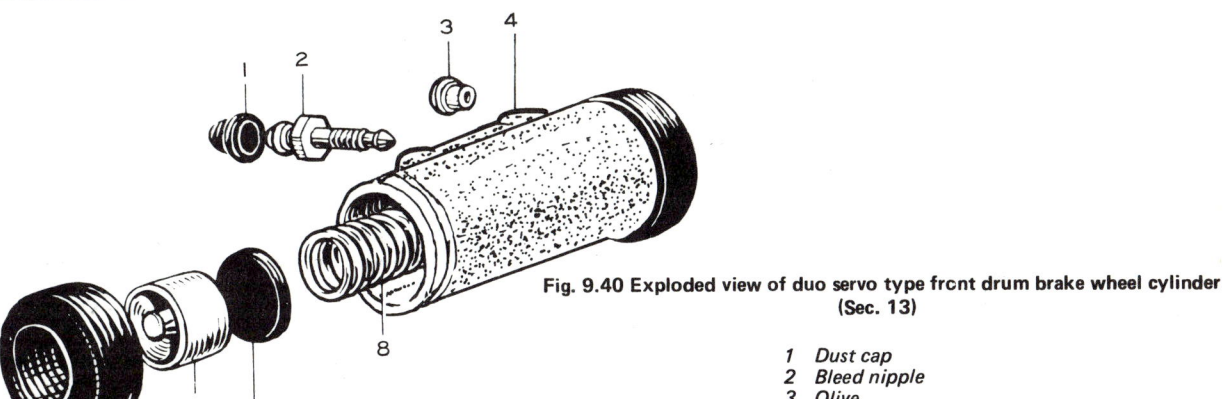

Fig. 9.40 Exploded view of duo servo type front drum brake wheel cylinder (Sec. 13)

1 Dust cap
2 Bleed nipple
3 Olive
4 Body
5 Dust excluder
6 Piston
7 Cup seal
8 Spring

to the specified torque setting.
10 Reconnect the fluid line and bleed the brakes as described in Section 18.

14 Rear drum wheel cylinders - removal, servicing and refitting

1 The procedure is similar to that described for front wheel cylinders in the preceding Section.

15 Brake drums - inspection and renovation

1 Whenever the front or rear brake drums are removed, they should be examined for cracks and for internal scoring or grooves.
2 After a considerable mileage, the drums may also become out of round.
3 To remove scoring or to correct out of round, the drums must either be ground or renewed. If the drums are ground then their internal diameter must not exceed 9.079 in (230.6 mm) after grinding.

16 Master cylinder (single circuit type) - removal, servicing and installation

1 Several types of master cylinder may be encountered according to application. Although they differ in component detail, the servicing procedure is similar for all types.
2 *On vehicles without a servo unit,* disconnect the master cylinder pushrod from the brake pedal. Disconnect the fluid pipe from the union on the master cylinder body. Unbolt the master cylinder from the engine compartment rear bulkhead and remove it.
3 *On vehicles with a vacuum servo unit,* disconnect the fluid pipe from the master cylinder body. Remove the support bracket and then remove the nuts from the studs on the front face of the vacuum servo unit and withdraw the master cylinder.
4 *On non servo type master cylinders,* extract the circlip from the end of the cylinder and eject the piston assembly and spring. Remove the reservoir by unscrewing the internal bolt.
5 *On vacuum servo type master cylinders,* remove the reservoir. Extract the circlip from the end of the cylinder body and eject the piston assembly. Remove the fluid outlet plug and union and extract the non-return valve and spring. Using a thin screwdriver, depress the small spring (1) and remove the piston return spring retainer from the piston. Remove the inlet valve from the inlet valve connecting rod. Wash all components in clean hydraulic

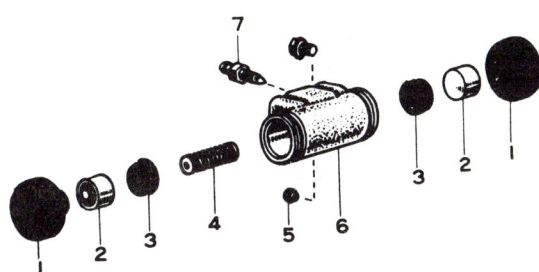

Fig. 9.41 Exploded view of leading/trailing type rear drum brake wheel cylinder (Sec. 4)

1 Dust excluder
2 Piston
3 Cup seal
4 Spring
5 Olive
6 Body
7 Bleed nipple

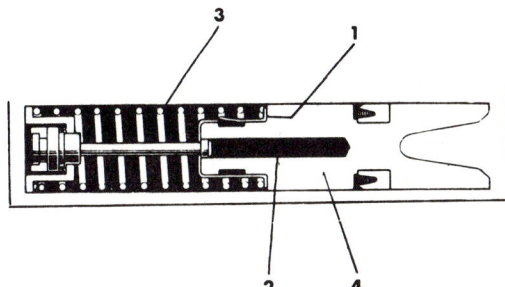

Fig. 9.42 Dismantling piston return spring retainer (single cylinder servo type master cylinder) (Sec.16)

1 Small spring
2 Spring retainer
3 Return spring
4 Piston

fluid or methylated spirit (Fig. 9.42).
6 On all types of cylinder, inspect the sliding surfaces of the piston and cylinder for scoring or 'bright' wear areas. If these are evident, renew the master cylinder complete.
7 Where the components are in good order, discard all rubber seals and obtain a repair kit.
8 Install the new seals using the fingers only to manipulate them into position.
9 Dip the internal components in clean hydraulic fluid before reassembling them.
10 Installation of the master cylinder is a reversal of removal but check and adjust the brake pedal height (see Section 23) and bleed the hydraulic system (Section 18).

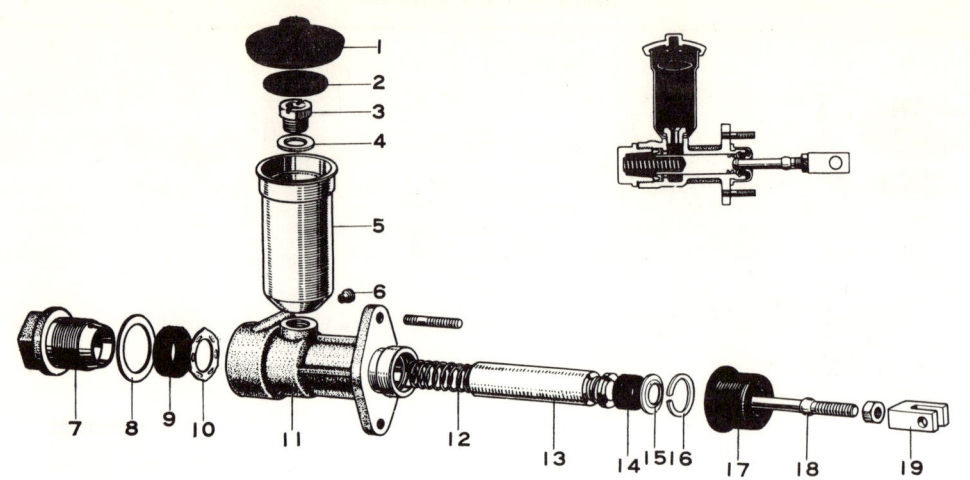

Fig. 9.43 Exploded view of single cylinder type master cylinder used in conjunction with four wheel drum brakes (Sec. 16)

1 Cap	6 Olive	11 Body	16 Circlip
2 Float	7 Cap bolt	12 Spring	17 Rubber boot
3 Securing bolt	8 Sealing washer	13 Piston	18 Push rod
4 Washer	9 Cup seal	14 Cup seal	19 Clevis fork
5 Reservoir	10 Spacer	15 Stop plate	

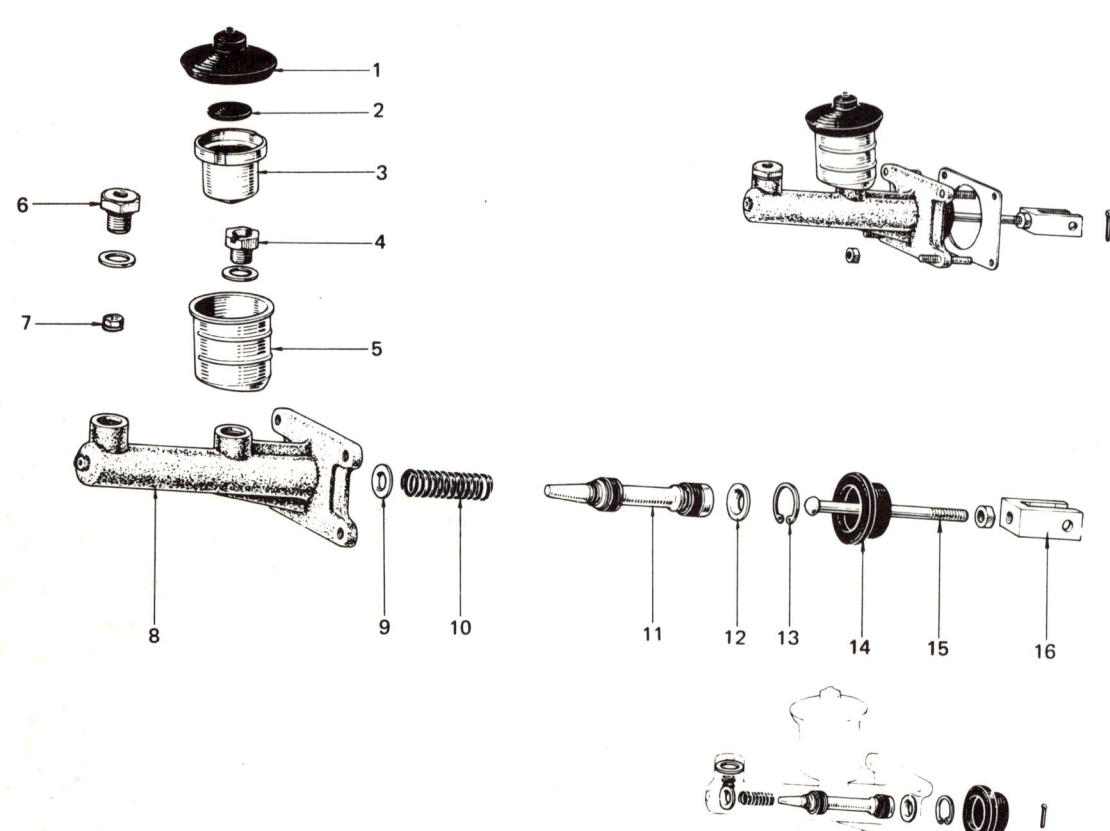

Fig. 9.44 Exploded view of alternative type of single cylinder master cylinder used in conjunction with four wheel drum brakes (Sec. 16)

1 Cap	5 Reservoir	9 Washer	13 Circlip
2 Float	6 Fluid outlet plug	10 Spring	14 Rubber boot
3 Filter	7 Non return valve	11 Piston	15 Push rod
4 Securing bolt	8 Body	12 Washer	16 Clevis fork

Chapter 9/Braking system

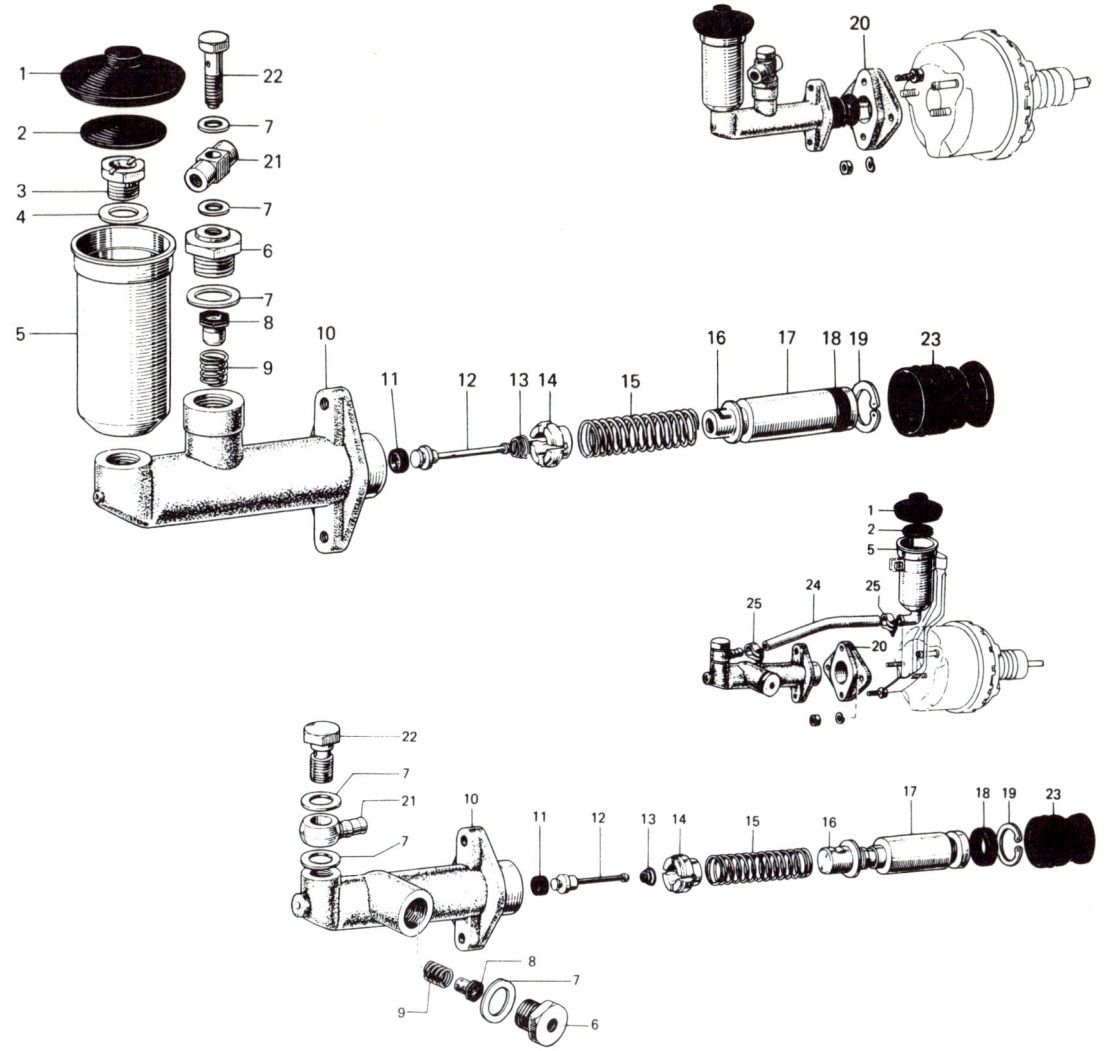

Fig. 9.45 Exploded view of single cylinder type master cylinder used in conjunction with disc/drum braking system having vacuum servo assistance (Sec 16)

1 Cap
2 Float
3 Securing bolt
4 Washer
5 Reservoir
6 Fluid outlet plug
7 Washer
8 Non return valve
9 Spring
10 Body
11 Seal
12 Inlet valve rod
13 Spring
14 Inlet valve casing
15 Spring
16 Spring retainer
17 Piston
18 Cup seal
19 Circlip
20 Spacer/bracket
21 Union
22 Hollow bolt
23 Rubber boot
24 Connecting pipe
25 Hose clip

17 Master cylinder (dual circuit, tandem type) - removal, servicing and installation

1 Two types of tandem master cylinder may be encountered (fitted in conjunction with a vacuum sero unit). One type has fluid level indicators incorporated in the reservoirs while the later type has two fluid pressure switches screwed into the base of the master cylinder body.
2 The later type unit is described in this Section but reference to the earlier type unit will make it clear where the component assembly details differ.
3 Disconnect the reservoir to master cylinder hoses, the fluid pressure switch leads and the fluid outlet pipes from the master cylinder.
4 On vehicles equipped with emission control systems, disconnect the hoses from the vacuum switching valve to provide better access to the master cylinder.
5 Remove the bracket and unbolt and remove the master cylinder from the front face of the vacuum servo unit.
6 Unscrew and remove the two fluid pressure switches from the master cylinder body, also the two fluid union bolts.
7 Remove the stop bolt from the side of the master cylinder body.
8 Remove the circlip from the end of the master cylinder body and eject the internal piston assemblies.
9 Unscrew and remove the fluid outlet plugs and non-return valve assemblies.
10 At this stage, check the condition of the sliding surfaces of the piston and cylinder. If they are scored or any 'bright' wear

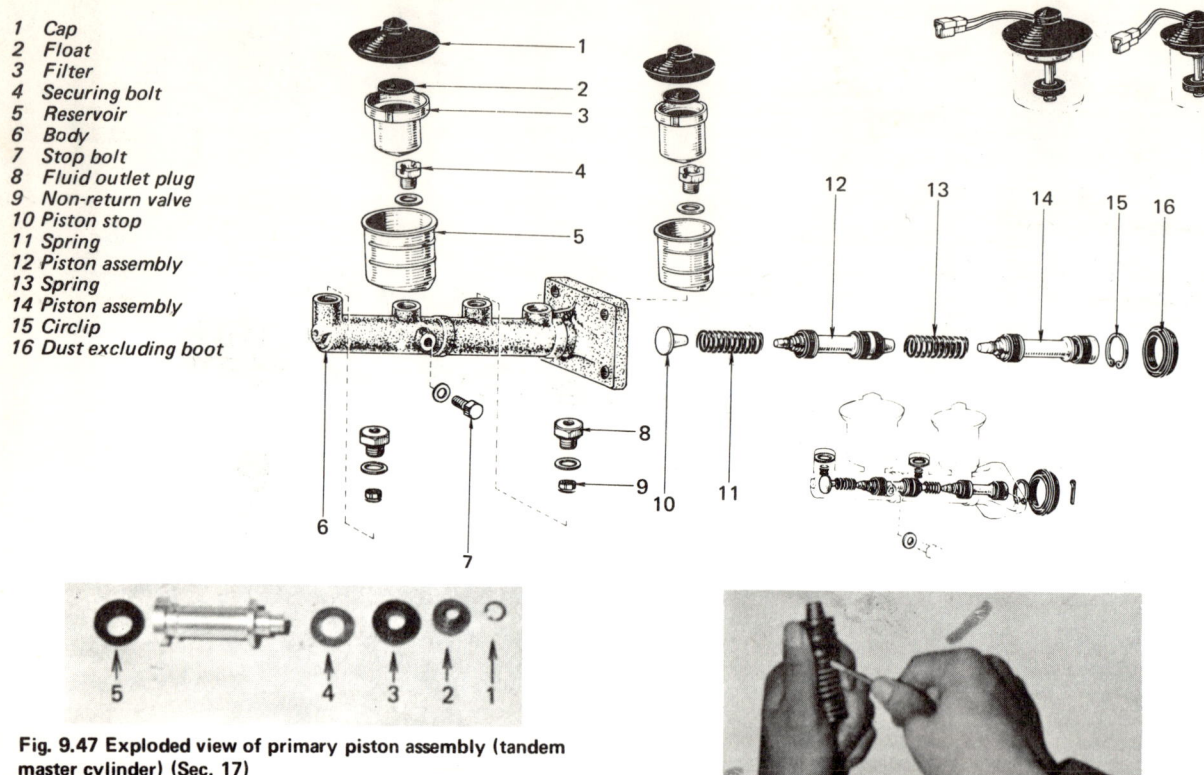

Fig. 9.46 Exploded view of tandem type master cylinder (Sec. 17)

1 Cap
2 Float
3 Filter
4 Securing bolt
5 Reservoir
6 Body
7 Stop bolt
8 Fluid outlet plug
9 Non-return valve
10 Piston stop
11 Spring
12 Piston assembly
13 Spring
14 Piston assembly
15 Circlip
16 Dust excluding boot

Fig. 9.47 Exploded view of primary piston assembly (tandem master cylinder) (Sec. 17)

1 Circlip
2 Spring retainer
3 Cup seal
4 Spacer
5 Cup seal

areas are evident, renew the master cylinder complete.
11 Where the components are in good condition, continue to dismantle by removing the circlip from the end of the first piston followed by the piston return spring retainer, cup seal, spacer and seal.
12 Using a thin screwdriver, depress the tab of the piston return spring retainer.
13 Remove the inlet valve connecting rod and inlet valve, followed by the spring, valve case, spring and spring retainer all from the second piston.
14 Remove the inlet valve seat from the cylinder.
15 Wash all components in clean hydraulic fluid or methylated spirit and discard all rubber seals. Obtain a repair kit. which will contain all necessary seals and renewable items.
16 Reassembly is a reversal of dismantling but dip all components in clean hydraulic fluid before assembling and tighten parts to the torque settings specified in Specifications Section at the beginning of this Chapter. Rubber seals should be manipulated into position using the fingers only to prevent damaging them.
17 Installation is a reversal of removal but check and adjust the brake pedal height and bleed the hydraulic system as described in Sections 23 and 18 respectively.

18 Hydraulic system - bleeding

1 Removal of all the air from the hydraulic system is essential to the correct working of the braking system, and before undertaking this examine the fluid reservoir cap to ensure that both vent holes, one on top and the second underneath but not in line, are clear; check the level of fluid and top up if required.
2 Check all brake line unions and connections for possible

Fig. 9.48 Depressing return spring retainer tab (tandem master cylinder) (Sec. 17)

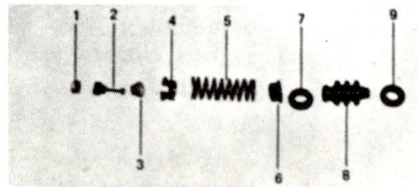

Fig. 9.49 Exploded view of second piston assembly (Sec. 17)

1 Inlet valve
2 Connecting rod
3 Spring
4 Inlet valve casing
5 Spring
6 Spring retainer
7 Cup seal
8 Piston
9 Cup seal

seepage, and at the same time check the condition of the rubber hoses, which may be perished.
3 If the condition of the wheel cylinders is in doubt, check for possible signs of fluid leakage.
4 If there is any possibility of incorrect fluid having been put into the system, drain all the fluid out and flush through with methylated spirit. Renew all piston seals and cups since these will be affected and could possibly fail under pressure.
5 Gather together a clean glass jar, a length of tubing which fits tightly over the bleed nipples, and a tin of the correct brake fluid.
6 To bleed the system clean the areas around the bleed valves, and start on the rear brakes by removing the rubber cup over the bleed valve, and fitting a rubber tube in position.
7 Place the end of the tube in a clean glass jar containing sufficient fluid to keep the end of the tube underneath during the operation.

Chapter 9/Braking system

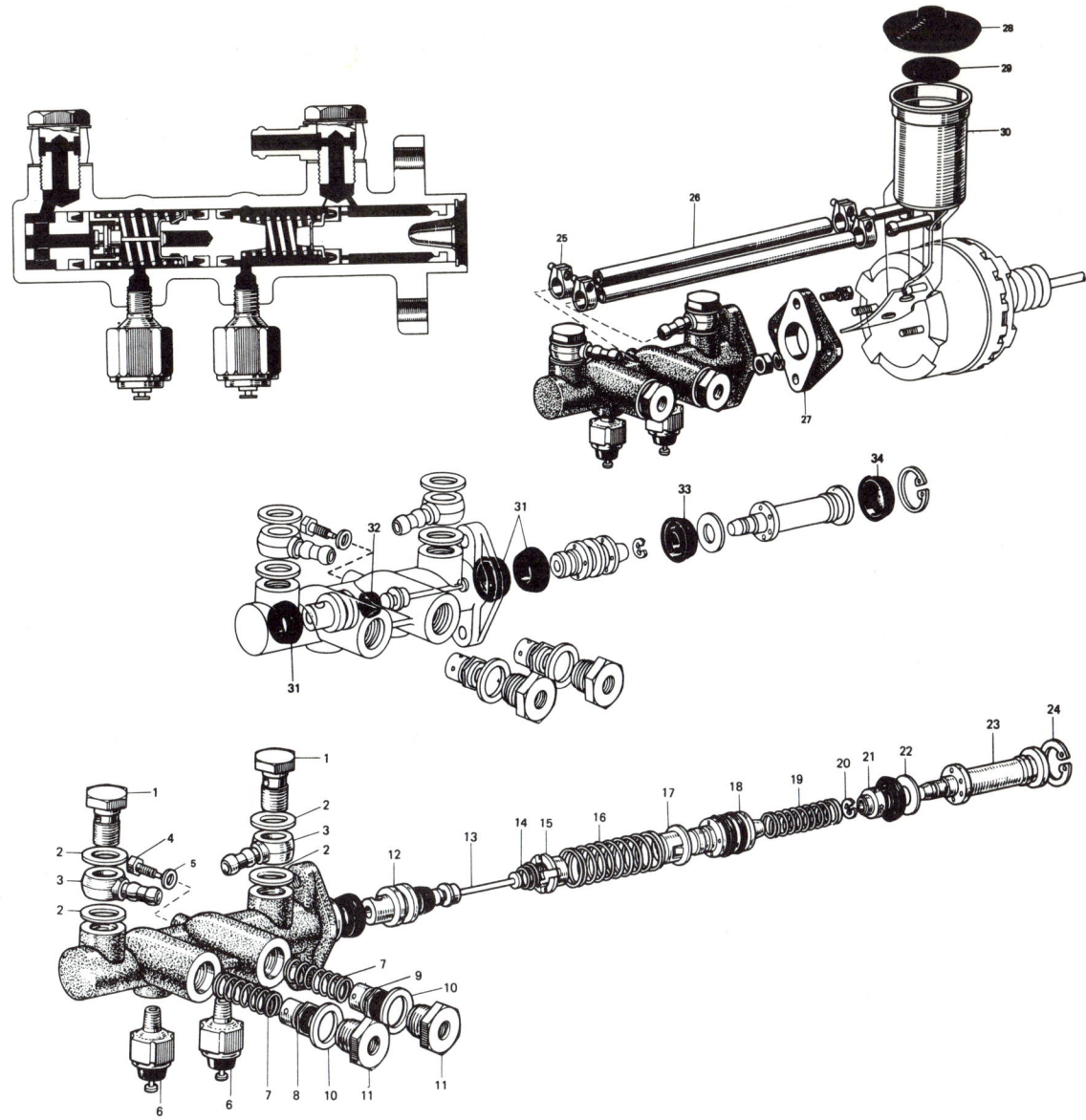

Fig. 9.50 Exploded view of alternative type of tandem master cylinder (Sec. 17)

1 Union bolt	10 Sealing washers	19 Spring	27 Spacer/support bracket
2 Washer	11 Fluid outlet plug	20 Circlip	28 Cap
3 Banjo union	12 Inlet valve	21 Return spring retainer	29 Float
4 Stop bolt	13 Connecting rod	22 Spacer	30 Reservoir
5 Washer	14 Spring	23 Primary piston assembly	31 Cup seals
6 Fluid pressure switch	15 Inlet valve casing	24 Circlip	32 Inlet valve
7 Spring	16 Spring	25 Hose clip	33 Cup seal
8 Non-return valve	17 Piston return spring retainer	26 Hose	34 Cup seal
9 Non-return valve	18 Secondary piston assembly		

8 Open the bleed valve with a spanner and quickly press down the brake pedal. After slowly releasing the pedal, pause for a moment to allow the fluid to recoup in the master cylinder and then depress again. This will force air from the system. Continue until no more air bubbles can be seen coming from the tube. At intervals make certain that the reservoir is kept topped-up, otherwise air will enter at this point again.

9 Once the rear brakes have been bled, bleed the front brake furthest from the master cylinder followed by the remaining front brake.

10 Tighten the bleed screws when the pedal is in the fully depressed position. Use only clean fluid for topping up purposes and discard fluid from the bleed jar. Fluid used for topping up should have been kept in an air tight container and remained unshaken for the previous 24 hours.

19 Flexible hoses - inspection and renewal

1 Inspect the condition of the flexible hoses leading from under the front wings to the brackets on the front suspension units, and also the single hose on the rear axle casing. If they are swollen, damaged or chafed, they must be renewed.
2 Undo the lock nuts at both ends of the flexible hoses and then holding the hexagon nut on the flexible hose steady undo the other union nut and remove the flexible hose and washer.
3 Replacement is a reversal of the removal procedure, but carefully check all the securing brackets are in a sound condition and that the locknuts are tight. Bleed the hydraulic system (Section 18).

20 Rigid brake lines - inspection and renewal

1 At regular intervals wipe the steel pipes clean and examine them for signs of rust or denting caused by flying stones.
2 Examine the securing clips. Bend the tongues of the clips if necessary to ensure that they hold the brake pipes securely without letting them rattle or vibrate.
3 Check that the pipes are not touching any adjacent components or rubbing against any part of the vehicle. Where this is observed, bend the pipe gently away to clear.
4 Any section of pipe which is rusty or chafed should be renewed. Brake pipes are available to the correct length and fitted with end unions from most Toyota dealers and can be made to pattern by many accessory suppliers. When installing the new pipes use the old pipes as a guide to bending and do not make any bends sharper than is necessary.
5 The system will of course have to be bled when the circuit has been reconnected.

21 Handbrake - adjustment

1 The handbrake is normally adjusted automatically by the action of the automatic adjuster mechanism located within the rear brake drums. However, in the event of cable stretch, additional adjustment may be required as described in the following paragraphs:
2 Underneath the vehicle, release the locknut from the turnbuckle or the equaliser according to type.
3 Turn the turnbuckle or equaliser adjuster nut until with floor mounted type handbrake levers, the handbrake is fully on after the lever is pulled through three to six notches of the ratchet. On facia mounted pull out type handbrake controls, the handbrake should be fully applied after being pulled through eight to fifteen notches.
4 When adjustment is completed, jack-up the rear wheels and check that the roadwheels will turn freely when the handbrake control is fully released.
5 Tighten the turnbuckle or equaliser locknuts.

22 Handbrake and cables - dismantling and reassembly

(a) Facia mounted type control

1 Remove the handbrake 'ON' switch and bracket from the forward end of the hand control lever.
2 Pull the handbrake lever out two or three notches, lift the pawl at the side of the outer casing and push the handbrake fully down so that the front section of the handbrake cable can be detached from the hand control lever.
3 Now detach the tension spring at the intermediate lever and remove the other end of the first section of the cable from the lever.
4 Renewal of any internal component of the handbrake control lever is carried out after first dismantling the assembly by drifting out the pin which secures the control handle and the outer casing together.
5 Renewal of either rear handbrake cable is carried out by detaching the cable ends from the equaliser and the lever within each rear brake drum and removing the outer cable securing clips.
6 When the new cables have been refitted, refer to Section 21 and carry out the adjustment procedure.

(b) Floor mounted type control

7 Access to this type of handbrake lever can be obtained after removal of the centre arm rest and flexible dust cover from the handbrake quadrant type ratchet. Remove the primary pullrod clevis pin from the handbrake lever and then remove and refit the rear cables as described in part (a) of this Section.

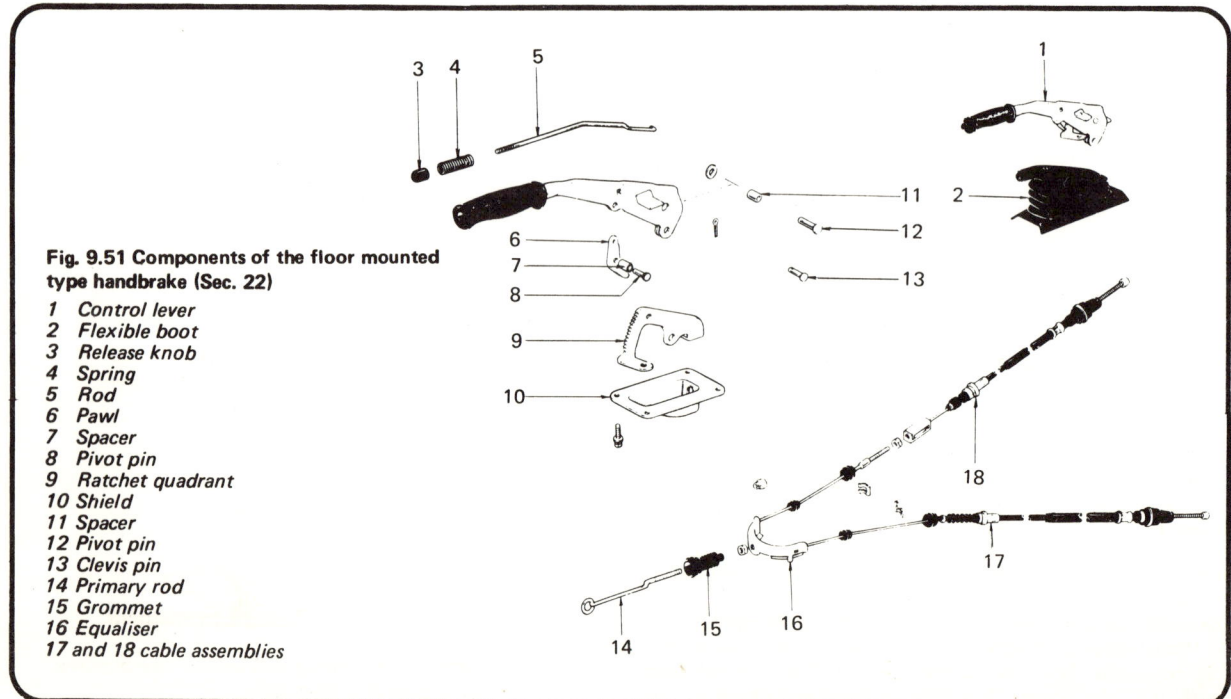

Fig. 9.51 Components of the floor mounted type handbrake (Sec. 22)

1 Control lever
2 Flexible boot
3 Release knob
4 Spring
5 Rod
6 Pawl
7 Spacer
8 Pivot pin
9 Ratchet quadrant
10 Shield
11 Spacer
12 Pivot pin
13 Clevis pin
14 Primary rod
15 Grommet
16 Equaliser
17 and 18 cable assemblies

Chapter 9/Braking system

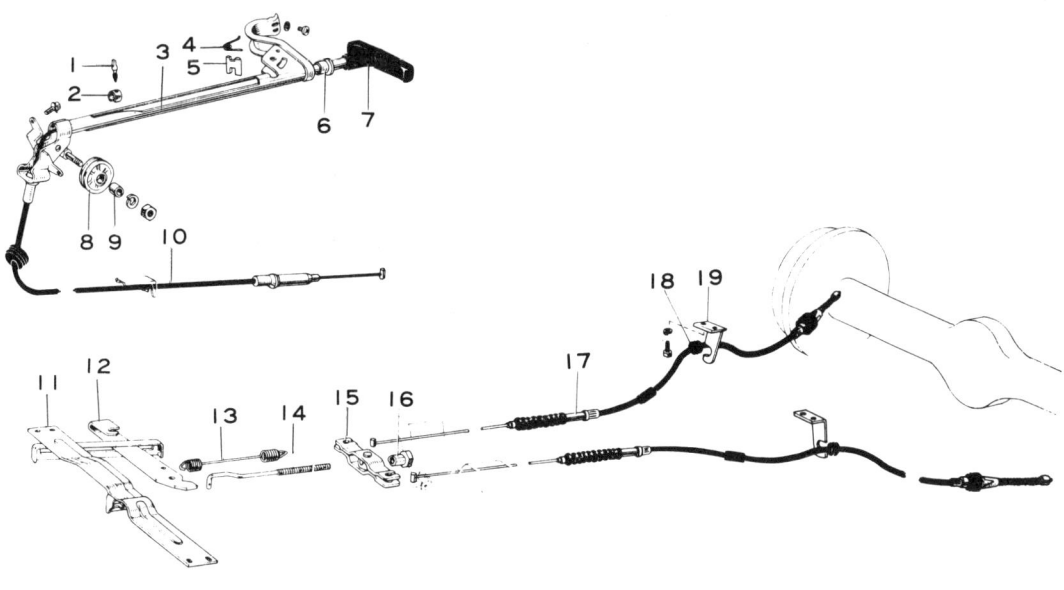

Fig. 9.52 Components of the facia mounted type handbrake (Sec 22)

1 Plunger pin
2 Anti-rattle collar
3 Lever guide tube
4 Spring
5 Pawl
6 Bush
7 Hand control lever
8 Pulley
9 Collar
10 Primary cable
11 Support bracket
12 Intermediate lever
13 Spring
14 Connecting rod
15 Equaliser
16 Adjusting nut
17 Cable assembly
18 Grommet
19 Cable support

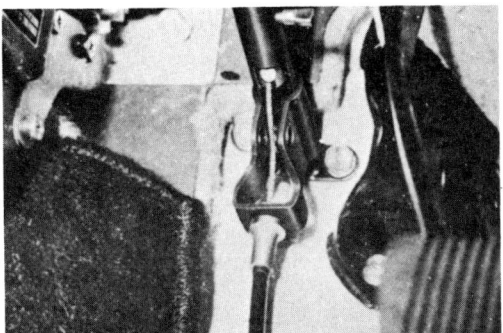

Fig. 9.53 Connection of cable to handbrake control lever (pull out type) (Sec. 22)

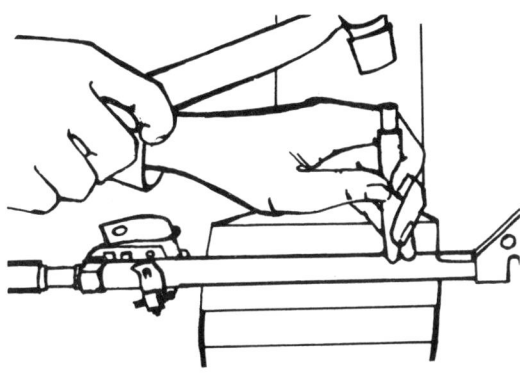

Fig. 9.54 Driving out the retaining pin to dismantle the pull out type of handbrake control (Sec. 22)

23 Brake pedal - removal, refitting and adjustment

1 The footbrake pedal is removed in conjunction with the clutch pedal as they both operate on a common cross-shaft. Refer to Chapter 5, Section 2, for full details of removal and refitting of both pedals.
2 Whenever the brake pedal has been removed or the brake master cylinder has been removed, the height of the brake pedal above the floor must be checked and adjustment carried out if necessary.
3 Release the locknut on the stoplamp switch and unscrew the stoplamp switch so that it no longer contacts the brake pedal arm. On vehicles with vacuum servo unit, depress the brake pedal several times to destroy the vacuum.
4 Release the locknut on the master cylinder or servo unit pushrod and turn the rod until the distance between the surface of the floor panel (carpet peeled back) and the upper surface of the pedal pad is between 6.3 and 6.6 in (161 to 168 mm).
5 When the pedal height is correctly set, a certain amount of free-movement should be apparent when the pedal is depressed gently with the fingers. On vehicles without vacuum servo, this

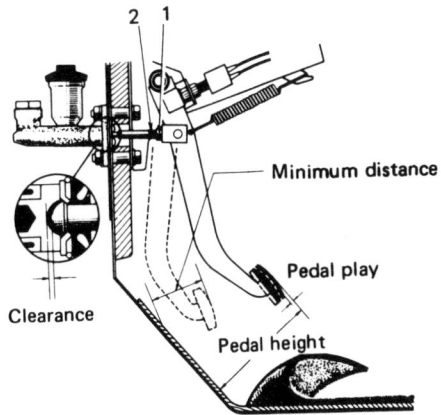

Fig. 9.55 Brake pedal setting diagram (non-servo master cylinders) (Sec. 23)

free-movement should be between 0.08 and 0.28 in (2.0 to 7.0 mm) and on vehicles with vacuum servo between 0.12 and 0.24 in (3.0 and 6.0 mm). If necessary re-adjust the pushrod to obtain this clearance.

6 When the brake pedal is fully depressed, the distance between the upper surface of the pedal and the floor should not be less than 2.4 in (60.0 mm). If it is, then the brakes require adjustment (adjustable drum type), the automatic adjusting mechanism is seized or faulty or the disc pads or shoe linings are worn out.

7 When adjustment is completed, tighten the pushrod locknut and then screw in the stoplamp switch until its plunger is in a partially depressed state and then check (with the ignition switched on) that when the pedal is depressed through 1/8 in (3.2 mm) the stop lamps illuminate. When the correct setting of the switch has been established, tighten the switch locknut.

24 Vacuum servo (brake booster) unit - description

The vacuum servo unit is designed to supplement the effort applied by the driver's foot to the brake pedal.

The unit is an independent mechanism so that in the event of its failure the normal braking effort of the master cylinder is retained. A vacuum is created in the servo unit by its connection to the engine inlet manifold and with this condition applying on one side of the diaphragm, atmospheric pressure applied on the other side of the diaphragm is harnessed to assist the foot

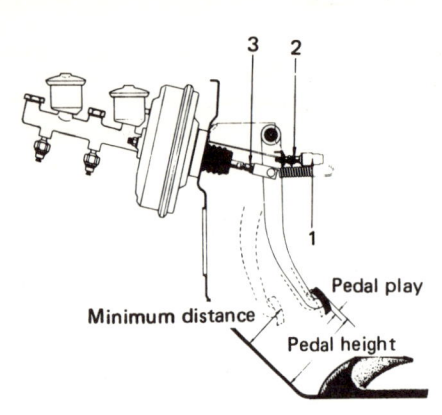

Fig. 9.56 Brake pedal setting diagram (master cylinders with servo) (Sec. 23)

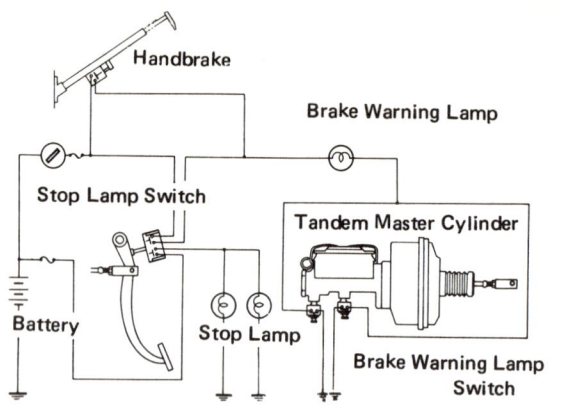

Fig. 9.57 Brake stop lamp switch and pressure failure switch circuit (Sec. 23)

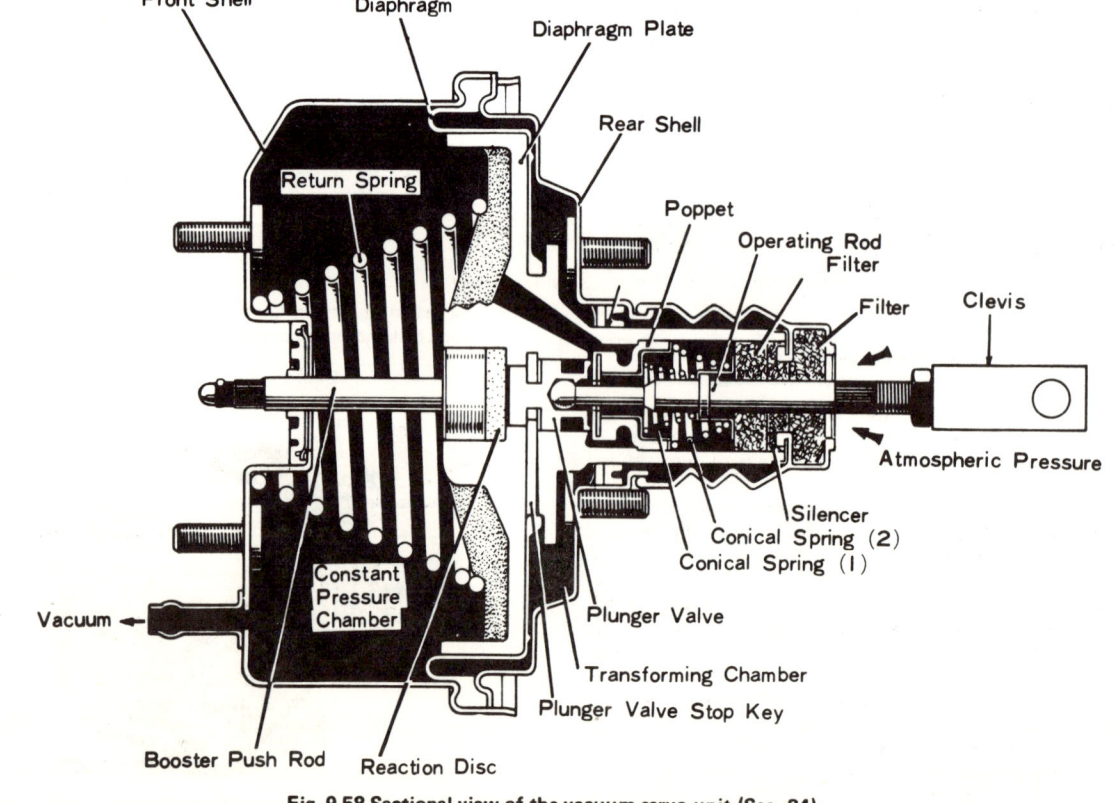

Fig. 9.58 Sectional view of the vacuum servo unit (Sec. 24)

pressure on the master cylinder. With the brake pedal released, the diaphragm is fully recuperated and held against the rear shell by the return spring. The operating rod assembly is also fully recuperated and a condition of vacuum exists each side of the diaphragm.

When the brake pedal is applied, the valve rod assembly moves forward until the control valve closes the vacuum port. Atmospheric pressure then enters the chamber to the rear of the diaphragm and forces the diaphragm plate forward to actuate the master cylinder pistons through the medium of the vacuum servo unit pushrod.

When pressure on the brake pedal is released, the vacuum port is opened and the atmospheric pressure in the rear chamber is extracted through the non-return valve. The atmospheric pressure inlet port remains closed as the operating rod assembly returns to its original position by action of the coil return spring.

The diaphragm then remains in its position with vacuum conditions on both sides until the next depression of the brake pedal when the cycle is repeated.

25 Vacuum servo unit - removal and installation

1 Destroy the vacuum effect in the servo unit by repeated applications of the foot pedal.
2 Disconnect the vacuum hose from the servo unit.
3 Disconnect the hydraulic circiult fluid pipes from the master cylinder unions and plug the pipes to prevent ingress of dirt.
4 Disconnect the leads from the master cylinder pressure switches.
5 From inside the vehicle disconnect the operating rod from the brake pedal arm and then unscrew and remove the four servo unit securing nuts from their studs.
6 Remove the vacuum servo unit complete with master cylinder and regulator valve from its location on the engine rear bulkhead.
7 Remove the regulator valve securing bolt and the four nuts which hold the master cylinder to the front face of the vacuum servo unit and withdraw the master cylinder from the servo unit.
8 Refitting is a reversal of removal but check the pedal height and bleed the hydraulic system (Sections 23 and 18).

26 Vacuum servo unit - dismantling and reassembly

1 If as a result of checking the fault diagnosis Section the vacuum servo unit is found to be faulty, then it is recommended that a factory exchange unit is obtained rather than undertaking the servicing of the unit yourself. However, where the necessary tools and skill are available dismantling procedure should be carried out as described in this Section. The operations apply to a unit of JKK manufacture but where the other makes of unit are encountered, the information is generally applicable although the construction may differ in detail.
2 Scratch mating marks on the front and rear shells.
3 Holding the mounting studs of the front shell in a plate drilled to receive them, rotate the rear shell anti-clockwise to release it using a tool similar to the one shown. Remove the diaphragm return spring (Fig. 9.60).
4 Withdraw the diaphragm plate from the rear shell and remove the retainer, bearing and seal. The diaphragm plate is made of brittle plastic and should be handled carefully.
5 Remove the diaphragm from the diaphragm plate.
6 Remove the filter/silencer retainer, then the key by pointing

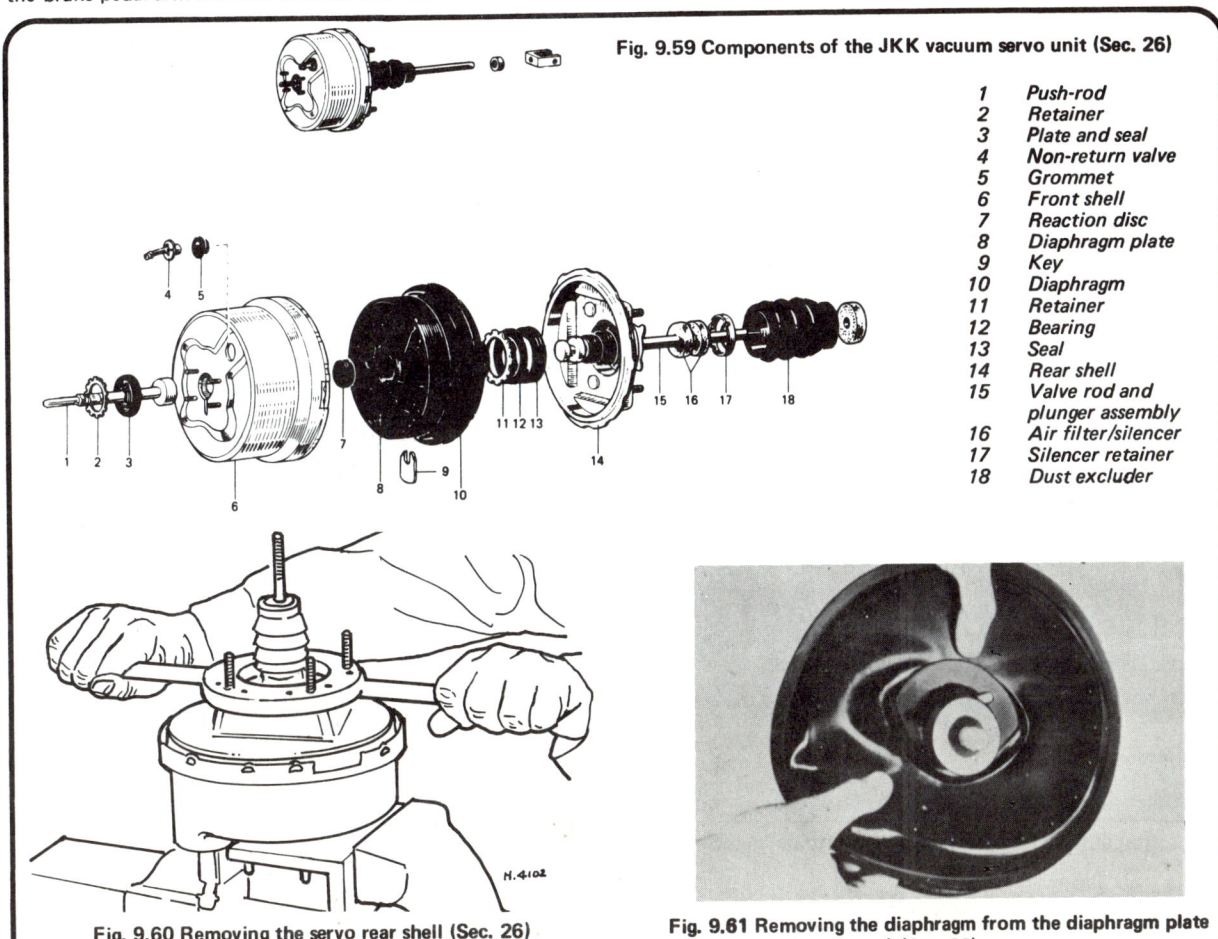

Fig. 9.59 Components of the JKK vacuum servo unit (Sec. 26)

1   Push-rod
2   Retainer
3   Plate and seal
4   Non-return valve
5   Grommet
6   Front shell
7   Reaction disc
8   Diaphragm plate
9   Key
10 Diaphragm
11 Retainer
12 Bearing
13 Seal
14 Rear shell
15 Valve rod and plunger assembly
16 Air filter/silencer
17 Silencer retainer
18 Dust excluder

Fig. 9.60 Removing the servo rear shell (Sec. 26)

Fig. 9.61 Removing the diaphragm from the diaphragm plate (servo unit) (Sec. 26)

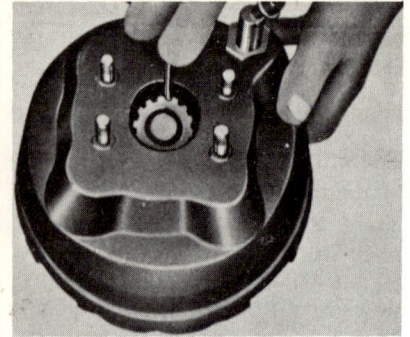

Fig. 9.62 Removing the retainer from servo front shell (Sec. 26)

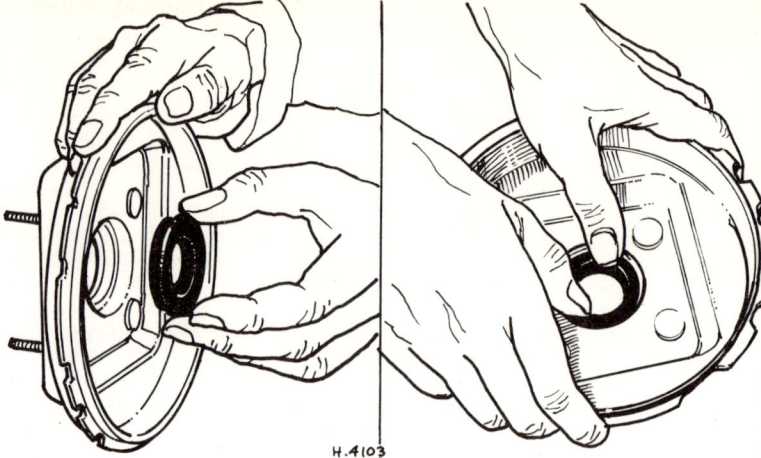

Fig. 9.63 Assembling the seal (1) and bearing (2) together with the retainer to the servo rear shell (Sec. 26)

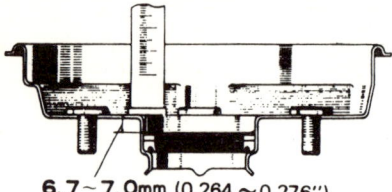

6.7 ~ 7.0mm (0.264 ~ 0.276")

Fig. 9.64 Rear servo shell assembly diagram (Sec. 26)

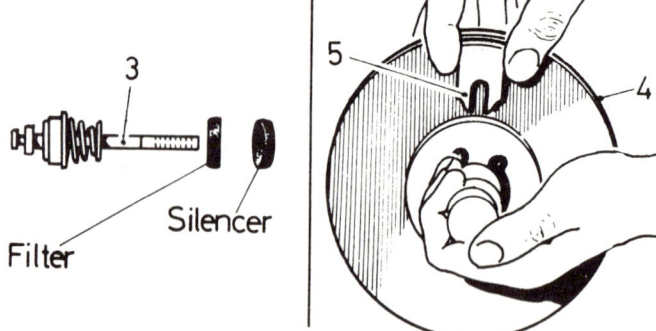

Fig. 9.65 Servo unit plunger assembly (Sec. 26)
3 Plunger assembly　　　5 Key
4 Diaphragm plate

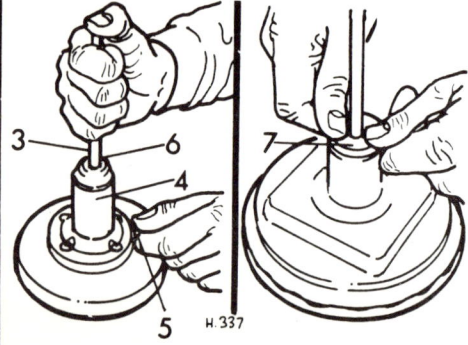

Fig. 9.66 Fitting air filter/silencer retainer to diaphragm plate (Sec. 26)

3 Plunger　　　　　　6 Filter/silencer
4 Diaphragm plate　　7 Retainer
5 Key

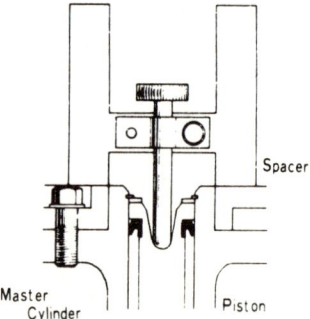

Fig. 9.67 Fitting the plate and seal assembly (11) to the front shell (10) of a vacuum servo unit (Sec. 26)

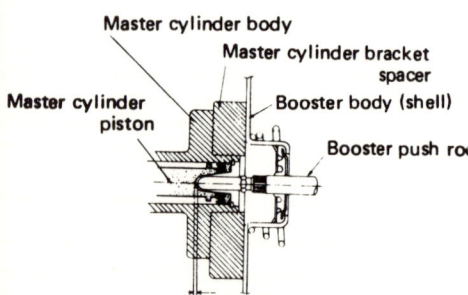

Fig. 9.68 Servo unit push rod to master cylinder piston clearance diagram (Sec. 26)

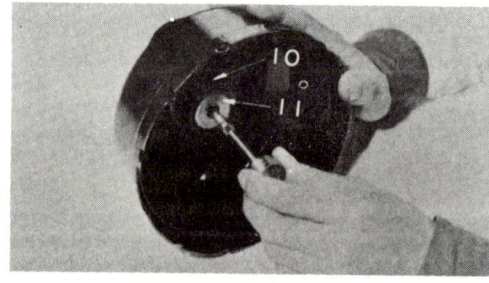

Fig. 9.69 Suitable tool for measuring depth of master cylinder recess during push rod clearance adjustment (Sec. 26)

Chapter 9/Braking system

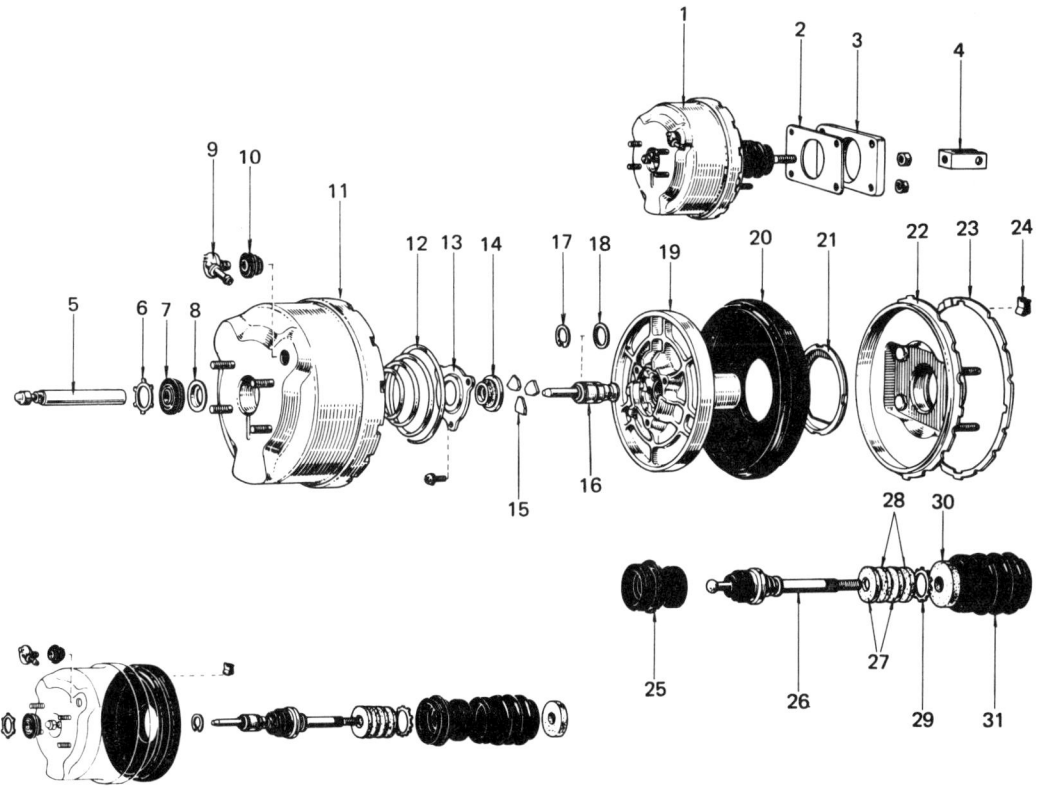

Fig. 9.70 Exploded view of the alternative type ASCO brake vacuum servo unit (Sec. 26)

1 Vacuum servo unit
2 Gasket
3 Spacer/support bracket
4 Clevis fork
5 Push rod
6 Spacer
7 Seal
8 Retainer
9 Vacuum non-return valve
10 Grommet
11 Front shell
12 Spring
13 Retainer
14 Reaction disc
15 Reaction
16 Air valve
17 Circlip
18 Washer
19 Piston
20 Diaphragm
21 Diaphragm retainer
22 Rear shell
23 Connecting ring
24 Lock
25 Bearing
26 Valve operating rod
27 and 28 filter/separator
29 Retainer
30 Silencer
31 Flexible boot

the keyhole downwards and pressing the valve operating rod. Withdraw the valve plunger assembly.
7 Remove the retainer, plate and seal and push the rod from the front shell.
8 Clean all components in methylated spirit and check for cracks, corrosion and distortion, and the diaphragm and seals for deterioration (these are best renewed in any event).
9 Smear silicone oil of recommended grade to the seal (1) and bearing (2) and fit them into the rear shell then secure them with a retainer (Fig. 9.63).
10 Apply silicone oil to the plunger disc outer edge and assemble
11 Fit a new air filter/silencer and press the retainer into the diaphragm plate.
12 Fit the diaphragm to the diaphragm plate and the reaction disc, first having smeared it with silicone oil.
13 Smear the outer edge of the diaphragm with silicone oil and then fit the diaphragm plate assembly and the valve body to the rear shell.
14 Fit the plate and seal assembly (11) to the front shell (10) using a smear of silicone oil and then install the pushrod (Fig. 9.67).
15 Secure the front shell in the holding tool and insert the diaphragm return spring. Align the shell mating marks and engage the front and rear shells with a clockwise twisting motion. If they are difficult to engage, apply a smear of silicone oil to the diaphragm edges.
16 Using the tool which was required for dismantling the front and rear shells, tighten the rear shell until it comes up against the stop on the front shell.
17 Whenever the vacuum servo unit has been dismantled and reassembled check that there will be a clearance of 0.012 in (0.3 mm) between the end of the servo unit pushrod and the end of the master cylinder piston. Check by using the official tool or making up a depth gauge so that the projection of the servo unit pushrod can be compared with the depth of the recess to the end of the master cylinder piston. Carry out any adjustment by loosening the locknut and rotating the front section of the vacuum servo unit pushrod.

27 Pressure regulating valve

1 As previously described, this valve is incorporated in the hydraulic circuit close to the master cylinder. It varies the hydraulic pressure between the front and rear circuits in order to prevent the rear wheels locking during heavy brake applications.
2 The valve cannot be adjusted or repaired and in the event of the valve leaking or a tendency for the rear wheels to lock, renew

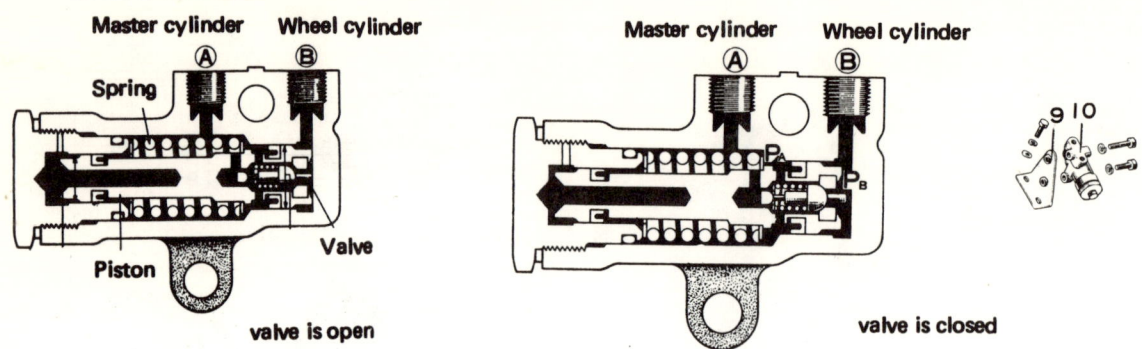

Fig. 9.71 Sectional views of the pressure regulating valve (Sec. 27) (inset) valve bracket (9) and valve (10)

the valve complete.

3 Disconnect the fluid pipes from the valve body by unscrewing the unions and then remove the valve securing bolts and lift the valve away.

4 Installation of the new valve is a reversal of removal but bleed the hydraulic system as described in Section 18.

Chapter 9/Braking system

28 Fault diagnosis - braking system

Symptom	Cause
Brake grab	Brake shoe linings or pads not bedded-in Contaminated with oil or grease Scored drums or discs Servo unit faulty
Brake drag	Master cylinder faulty Brake foot pedal return impeded Blocked filler cap vent Master cylinder reservoir or compartments overfilled Seized wheel caliper or cylinder Incorrect adjustment of handbrake Weak or broken shoe return springs Crushed or blocked pipelines
Brake pedal feels hard	Friction surfaces contaminated with oil or grease Glazed friction material surfaces Rusty disc surfaces Seized caliper or wheel cylinder Faulty servo unit
Excessive pedal travel	Low fluid level in reservoir Automatic rear shoe adjusters faulty Excessive disc runout Worn front wheel bearings System requires bleeding Worn pads or linings
Pedal creep during sustained application	Fluid leak Faulty master cylinder Faulty servo
Pedal "spongy" or "springy"	System requires bleeding Perished flexible hose Loose master cylinder Cracked brake drum Linings not bedded-in Faulty master cylinder
Fall in master cylinder fluid level	Normal disc pad wear Leak Internal fluid leak from servo

Servo unit fault diagnosis

Symptom	Cause
Hard pedal, lack of assistance when engine running	Lack of vacuum due to: Loose connections Restricted hose Blocked air filter/silencer Major fault in unit
Slow action of servo	Faulty vacuum hose Blocked air filter/silencer
Lack of assistance during heavy braking	Air leaks in: Non-return valve grommet Non-return valve Dust cover Hoses and connections
Loss of fluid	Major failure in unit
Brake pedal pushes back against foot pressure	Hydraulic inlet and outlet pipes incorrectly connected at regulator valve Major fault in unit

Chapter 10 Electrical system

Contents

Alternator - dismantling, servicing and reassembly ...	9
Alternator - general description, maintenance and precautions ...	6
Alternator regulator - testing and adjustment ...	10
Alternator - removal and refitting ...	8
Alternator - testing in vehicle ...	7
Ammeter - testing ...	24
Battery - charging ...	5
Battery - maintenance ...	3
Battery - removal and installation ...	2
Bulbs - renewal ...	34
Electrical relays - description and testing ...	18
Electrolyte - replenishment ...	4
Electro sensor panel - description ...	20
Fault diagnosis - electrical system ...	44
Fuel level transmitter and gauge - testing ...	21
Fuses and fusible link ...	17
General description ...	1
Hazard warning and direction indicator lamps ...	19
Headlights - adjustment ...	33
Headlight sealed beam unit - renewal ...	32
Horns - adjustment ...	39
Instruments (early type) - removal and installation ...	25
Instruments (later type) - removal and installation ...	26
Instruments (printed circuit connection) - removal and installation ...	27
Light switch (early models) - removal and installation ...	28
Oil pressure switch, warning lamp or gauge - testing ...	23
Radio and tape players - removal and installation ...	40
Rear window demister (early models) - removal ...	41
Seat belt electrical interlock system ...	43
Starter motor - dismantling ...	14
Starter motor - general description ...	11
Starter motor - reassembly ...	16
Starter motor - removal and installation ...	13
Starter motor - servicing and testing ...	15
Starter motor - testing in vehicle ...	12
Steering column switches (1969 - 1970) - removal and installation ...	29
Steering column switches (1971 - 1973) - removal and installation ...	30
Steering column switches (1973 onwards) - removal and installation ...	31
Water temperature transmitter and gauge - testing ...	22
Window regulator motor - servicing ...	42
Windscreen washer - servicing ...	38
Windscreen wiper motor and linkage (early models) - removal and installation ...	35
Windscreen wiper motor and linkage (later models) - removal and installation ...	36
Wiper motor - dismantling and reassembly ...	37

Specifications

System type ... 12 volt negative earth

Battery ... 60 amp/hr

Alternator
- Output ... 12 volts, 40 amps
- Earth ... Negative
- Rotational direction (viewed from pulley) ... Clockwise
- Rectification ... Full wave by six integral silicone diodes
- Minimum brush length (wear limit) ... 0.34 in. (8.5 mm)

Alternator voltage control unit
- Regulating voltage ... 13.8 to 14.8 volts
- Relay operating voltage ... 4.5 to 5.8 volts

Starter motor
- Motor type ... d.c. series wound, pre-engaged with solenoid
- Rating ... 12 volts: 1.0 k.w. (1.4 k.w. on reduction gear type motor)
- Rotational direction (viewed from pinion) ... Clockwise
- Speed of rotation ... More than 6000 rev/min.
- Commutator diameter:
    - 8R series engine ... 1.53 in. (38.8 mm)
    - 18R series engine ... 1.22 in. (31.0 mm)
- Minimum brush length (wear limit) ... 0.47 in. (12.0 mm)
- Pinion to stop collar clearance (solenoid actuated) ... 0.04 to 0.16 in. (1.0 to 4.0 mm)

Windscreen wiper motor
　No load operating current ... Less than 5 amps
　High speed ... 57 to 71 rev/min with load of 10 cm/kg
　Low speed ... 39 to 47 rev/min with load of 10 cm/kg

Windscreen washer
　Motor type ... Ferrite magnetic
　Pump type ... Gear
　Operating current ... Less than 3 amps
　Maximum continuous operating period ... 20 seconds
　Reservoir capacity ... 1.1 litres

Fuses (1969 to 1973)

Number from top of fuse block	Amperage	Circuit protected
1	10	Headlight main beam RH
2	10	Headlight main beam LH
3	10	Headlight dipped beam RH
4	10	Headlight dipped beam LH
5	10	Parking, tail and rear licence lamps
6	20	Horn and stop lamp
7	20	Cigar lighter, clock, interior lamp
8	20	Heater, reversing lamps and instruments
9	15	Wiper and washer motors
10	15	Direction indicator lamps

Fuses (1973 on)

Number from top of fuse block	Amperage	Circuit protected
1	5	Radio and tape player
2	10	Cigar lighter and door warning lamp
3	15	Side and marker lamps, instrument panel lamps, tail and rear licence plate lamps
4	15	Horn, hazard warning lamps, stop lamp, seat belt warning system
5	10	Interior and courtesy lamps
6	15	Spare
7	20	Wiper and washer motors
8	5	Ignition coil resistor
9	15	Direction indicator lamps, alternator, regulator and main relay
10	20	Heater blower, instruments, reversing lamps and brake warning lamp
11	15	Rear window demister

Bulbs

	Wattage		
	1969 to 1972	1973	1974
Headlight inner sealed beam	37.5	37.5	37.5
Headlight outer sealed beam	37.5/50	37.5/50	37.5/50
Front direction indicators	25	23/8	27
Front parking lights	8	23/8	8
Side marker lights	8	8	8
Reversing lamps	25	23	27
Stop and tail lamps	23/8	23/8	27/8
Rear direction indicator	25	23	27
Rear licence plate lamp	10	7.5	7.5
Interior lamp	10	10	10
Front interior lamp (hardtop)	5	10	5
Tailgate lamp (estate wagon)	5	10	10
Courtesy lamps (hardtop)	5	5	5
Engine compartment lamp	—	10	7.5
Glove compartment lamp	5	3	3.4

1 General description

The electrical system is of 12 volt negative earth type. The major components comprise a battery, an alternator and a pre-engaged type starter motor.

The battery supplies a steady current to the ignition system and to the vehicle's electrical equipment. All electrical circuits incorporate fuses and a fusible link is inserted in the battery lead to the fuse block.

2 Battery - removal and installation

1 The battery is located at the front on the right-hand side of the engine compartment.
2 Disconnect the lead from the negative terminal by unscrewing the clamp bolt.

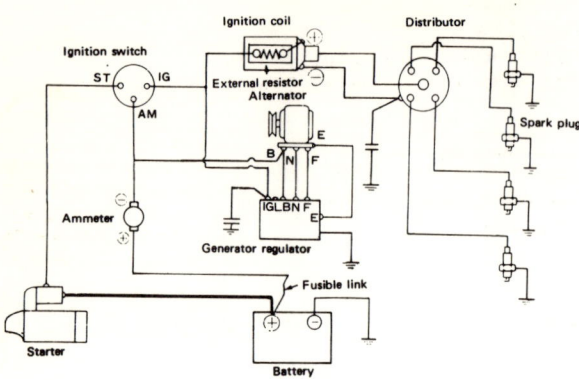

Fig 10.1 Diagram of electrical circuit

3 Disconnect the lead from the positive terminal and remove the battery securing bolts and frame.
4 Lift the battery carefully from its tray and avoid spilling electrolyte on the paintwork.
5 Installation is a reversal of removal, but when connecting the terminals, clean off any corrosion or white deposits which may be present and when the clamp bolts are tight, smear the terminal and clamp with petroleum jelly to prevent corrosion recurring.

3 Battery - maintenance

1 Carry out the regular weekly maintenance described in the Routine Maintenance Section at the front of this manual.
2 Clean the top of the battery, removing all dirt and moisture.
3 As well as keeping the terminals clean and covered with petroleum jelly, the top of the battery, and especially the top of the cells, should be kept clean and dry. This helps prevent corrosion and ensures that the battery does not become partially discharged by leakage through dampness and dirt.
4 Once every three months, remove the battery and inspect the battery securing bolts, the battery clamp plate, tray and battery leads for corrosion (white fluffy deposits on the metal which are brittle to touch). If any corrosion is found, clean off the deposits with ammonia and paint over the clean metal with an anti-rust/anti-acid paint.
5 At the same time inspect the battery case for cracks. If a crack is found, clean and plug it with one of the proprietary compounds marketed for this purpose. If leakage through the crack has been excessive then it will be necessary to refill the appropriate cell with fresh electrolyte as detailed later. Cracks are frequently caused to the top of the battery cases by pouring in distilled water in the middle of winter *after* instead of *before* a run. This gives the water no chance to mix with the electrolyte and so the former freezes and splits the battery case.
6 If topping-up the battery becomes excessive and the case has been inspected for cracks that could cause leakage, but none are found, the battery is being over-charged and the voltage regulator will have to be checked and reset.
7 With the battery on the bench at the three monthly interval check, measure its specific gravity with a hydrometer to determine the state of charge and condition of the electrolyte. There should be very little variation between the different cells and if a variation in excess of 0.025 is present it will be due to either:
  a) *Loss of electrolyte from the battery at some time caused by spillage or a leak, resulting in a drop in the specific gravity of the electrolyte when the deficiency was replaced with distilled water instead of fresh electrolyte.*
  b) *An internal short circuit caused by buckling of the plates of a similar malady pointing to the likelihood of total battery failure in the near future.*
8 The specific gravity of the electrolyte for varying conditions of charge at a mean temperature of 68°F (20°C) are listed below.

  1.260   fully charged
  1.210   ¾ charged
  1.160   ½ charged
  1.110   ¼ charged
  1.060   fully discharged

4 Electrolyte - replenishment

1 If the battery is in a fully charged state and one of the cells maintains a specific gravity reading which is 0.025 or more lower than the others, and a check of each cell has been made with a voltage meter to check for short circuits (a four to seven second test should give a steady reading of between 1.2 to 1.8 volts), then it is likely that electrolyte has been lost from the cell with the low reading at some time.
2 Top-up the cell with a solution of 1 part sulphuric acid to 2.5 parts of water. If the cell is already fully topped-up draw some electrolyte out of it with a pipette.
3 When mixing the sulphuric acid and water **never add water to sulphuric acid** - always pour the acid slowly onto the water in a glass container. **If water is added to sulphuric acid it will explode.**
4 Continue to top up the cell with the freshly made electrolyte and then recharge the battery and check the hydrometer readings.

5 Battery - charging

1 In winter time when heavy demand is placed upon the battery, such as when starting from cold, and much electrical equipment is continually in use, it is a good idea to occasionally have the battery fully charged from an external source at the rate of 3.5 or 4 amps.
2 Continue to charge the battery at this rate until no further rise in specific gravity is noted over a four hour period.
3 Alternatively, a trickle charger charging at the rate of 1.5 amps can be safely used overnight.
4 Specially rapid 'boost' charges which are claimed to restore the power of the battery in 1 to 2 hours are most dangerous as they can cause serious damage to the battery plates.
5 Before charging the battery from an external source always disconnect the battery positive (+) lead to prevent damage to the alternator.

6 Alternator - general description, maintenance and precautions

1 The alternator generates three-phase alternating current which is rectified into direct current by three positive and three negative silicone diode rectifiers installed within the end frame of the alternator. The in-built characteristics of the unit obviate the need for a cut-out or current stabiliser.
2 A voltage regulator unit is incorporated in the charging circuit to control the exciting current and the current applied to the voltage coil.
3 Check the drivebelt tension every 5000 miles (8000 km) and adjust, as described in Chapter 2, by loosening the mounting bolts. Pull the alternator body away from the engine block; do not use a lever as it will distort the alternator casing.
4 No lubrication is required as the bearings are grease sealed for life.
5 Take extreme care when making circuit connections to a vehicle fitted with an alternator and observe the following. When making connections to the alternator from a battery always match correct polarity. Before using electric-arc welding equipment to repair any part of the vehicle, disconnect the connector from the alternator and disconnect the positive battery terminal. Never start the car with a battery charger connected. Always disconnect the battery (+) lead before using a mains charger. If

Chapter 10/Electrical system   189

boosting from another battery, always connect in parallel using heavy cable.

7 Alternator - testing in vehicle

1 In the event of failure of the normal performance of the alternator, carry out the following test procedure paying particular attention to the possibility of damaging the charging and electrical system unless the notes (a) to (c) are observed.

a) The alternator output 'B' terminal is connected to the battery at all times. When the ignition switch is operated, the 'F' terminal is also at battery voltage.
b) Never connect the battery leads incorrectly or the rectifiers and flasher unit will be damaged.
c) Never run the engine at high revs. with the alternator 'B' terminal disconnected otherwise the voltage at the 'N' terminal will rise abnormally and damage to the voltage relay will result.

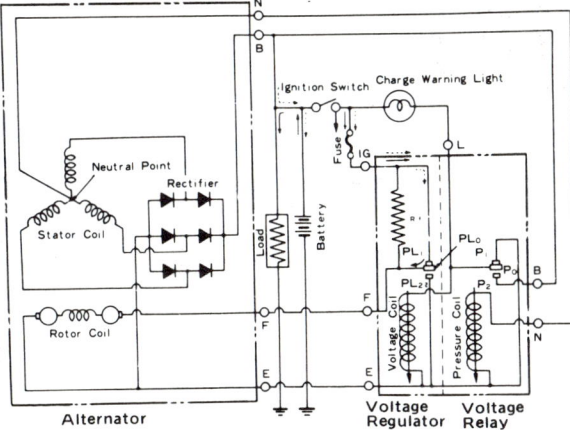

Fig 10.2 Diagram of charging circuit

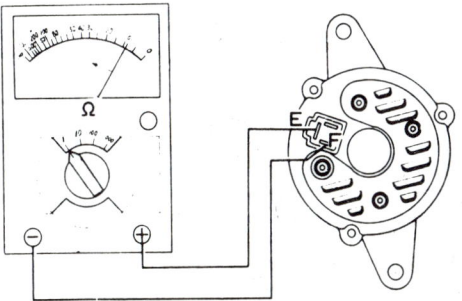

Fig 10.3 Measuring voltage between alternator connector plug terminal E and F (Sec 7)

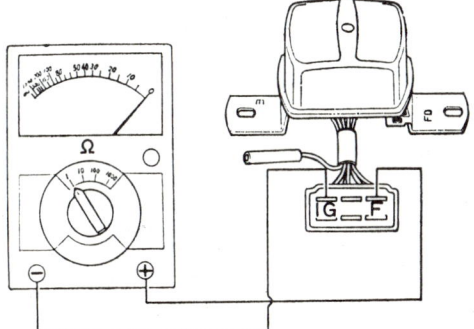

Fig 10.4 Checking for open circuit between 1G and F terminal of voltage regulator connector plug (Sec 7)

2 Check the security of the alternator mountings, the terminal leads and the drivebelt tension (Chapter 2).
3 Check the flasher fuse (15 amp) and the heater fuse (20 amp) and renew them if they are blown.
4 Switch on the vehicle radio and tune into a local transmitter. Start the engine and increase its speed from idling to 2000 rev/min. If a distinct humming sound is heard from the radio speaker then this indicates that the alternator rectifier is shorted or open.
5 Connect a voltmeter and ammeter to the alternator 'B' terminal. Start the engine and gradually increase its speed to 2300 rev/min. The voltmeter should read between 13.8 and 14.8 volts and the ammeter under 10 amps. If the amperage is greater than the specified figure, the battery is either discharged or there is an internal short circuit. If the voltmeter needle fluctuates the regulator contacts may be dirty or arced or the alternator 'F' terminal may be loose.
6 If the voltage reading is too high then (i) the regulator contact gaps may be too wide (ii) there is an open circuit at the regulator and voltage relay coil, (iii) 'N' and 'B' regulator terminals are open (iv) the regulator has a defective earth connection.
7 Switch off the engine and disconnect the wiring harness connecting plug. Turn on the ignition switch and measure the voltage between the 'F' and 'E' sockets of the connecting plug. This should be 12 volts. If the reading is low or zero, check for (i) faulty fuse connection (ii) open circuit 'F' or 'IG' terminals (iii) the regulator contact points fused together.
8 Repeat the tests described in the preceding paragraphs 5 and 6 but run the engine at only 1100 rev/min with all lights and accessories switched on; the ammeter reading should be in excess of 30 amps. If the reading is less than 30 amps it is indicative of open rectifiers, stator coil circuit or short circuited rectifiers.

8 Alternator - removal and refitting

1 Disconnect the cable from the battery negative terminal.
2 Loosen the alternator mounting bracket bolts and the adjustment strap bolts and then push the alternator in towards the engine block so that the driving belt can be removed from the pulley.
3 Disconnect the electrical leads from the alternator terminals, remove the mounting bolts and lift the unit from its location.
4 Refitting is a reversal of removal but adjust the driving belt tension, as described in Chapter 2.

9 Alternator - dismantling, servicing and reassembly

1 Remove the three tie bolts which secure the two end frames together.
2 Insert screwdrivers in the notches in the drive end frame and separate it from the stator.
3 Hold the front end of the rotor shaft still with an Allen key and remove the securing nut, pulley, fan and spacer.
4 Press the rotor shaft from the drive end frame.
5 Remove the bearing retainer, bearing, cover and felt ring from the drive end frame.
6 Remove the rectifier holder and brush holder securing screws and detach the stator from the rectifier end frame.
7 Remove the brush lead and stator coil 'N' terminals from the brush holder by prising with a small screwdriver.
8 Test the rotor coil for an open circuit by connecting a circuit tester between the two slip rings located at the rear of the rotor. The indicated resistance should be from 4.1 to 4.3 ohms but if there is no conductance then the coil is open and the rotor must be renewed as an assembly.
9 Now connect the tester between each slip ring in turn and the rotor shaft. If the tester needle moves then the rotor must be renewed as it is earthed.

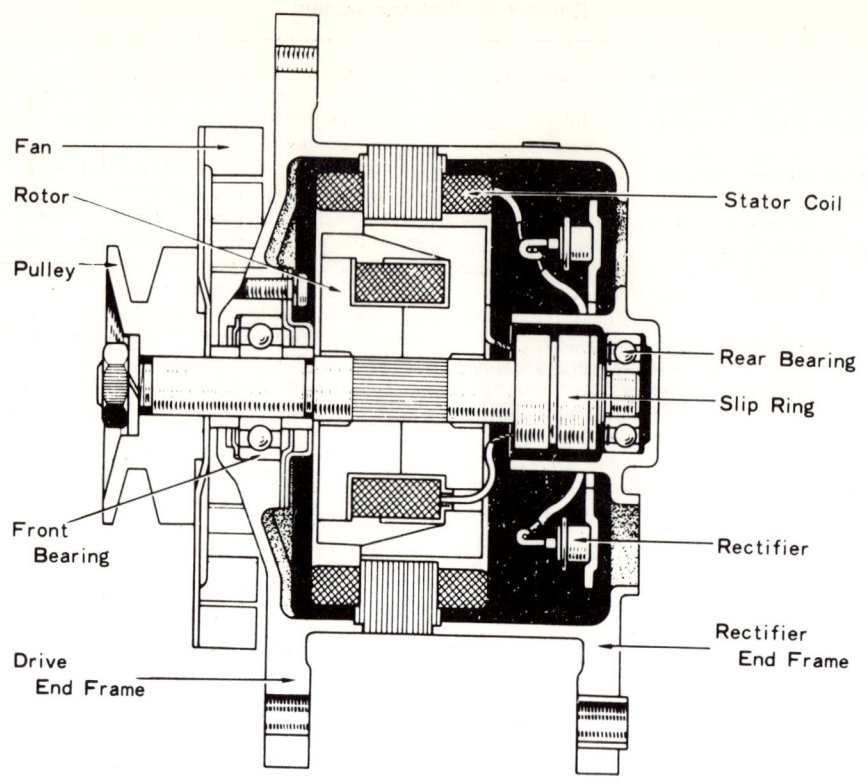

Fig 10.5 Sectional view of the alternator

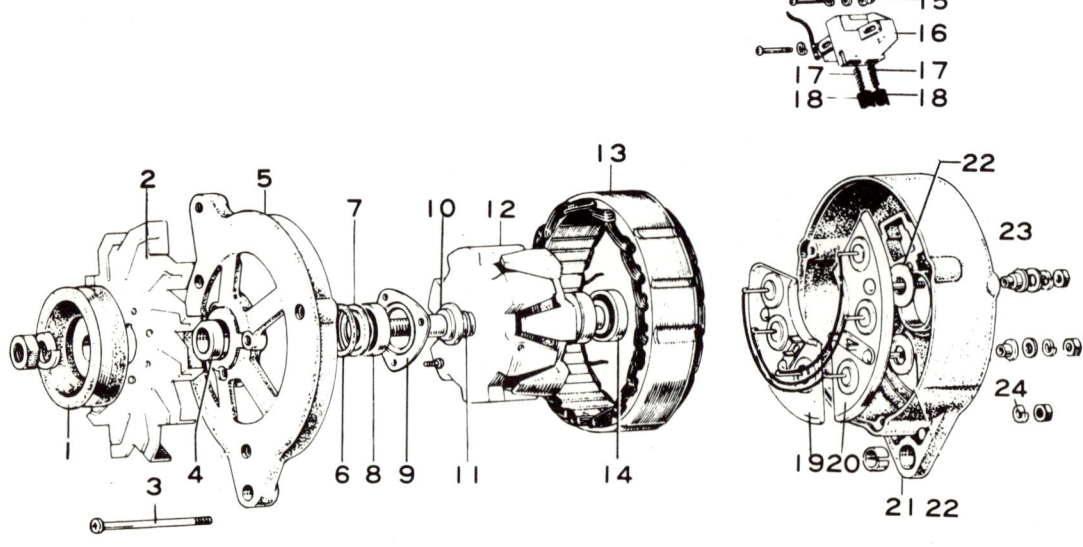

Fig 10.6 Exploded view of the alternator

1 Driving pulley
2 Fan
3 Tie bolt
4 Spacer
5 Drive end frame
6 Felt ring
7 Cover
8 Front bearing
9 Bearing retainer
10 Spacer
11 Circlip
12 Rotor
13 Stator
14 Rear bearing
15 Terminal insulator
16 Brush holder
17 Brush spring
18 Brush
19 Rectifier negative holder
20 Rectifier positive holder
21 Rectifier end frame
22 Insulating washer
23 'B' terminal insulator
24 Insulator

Chapter 10/Electrical system

10 Inspect the rotor bearing for wear and renew if necessary by removing it from the shaft with a two legged puller.

11 Clean the slip rings and rotor surfaces with a solvent moistened cloth.

12 Test the insulation of the stator coil by connecting the tester between the stator coil and the stator core. If the tester needle moves then the coil is earthed through a breakdown in the insulation and must be renewed.

13 To test the stator coil for open circuit, the coil leads must be disconnected from the rectifier leads. Apply the soldering iron to the joint for the minimum time to prevent any heat travelling to the rectifier which is easily damaged.

14 Check the four stator coil leads for conductance. If the tester needle does not flicker then the coil has an open circuit and it must be renewed.

15 The testing of the rectifiers should be limited to measuring the resistance between their leads and holders in a similar manner to that described in paragraph 13. These tests will indicate short or open circuited diodes but not rectifying or reverse flow characteristics which can only be checked with specialised equipment.

16 If more than one of the preceding tests proves negative then it will be economically sound to exchange the alternator complete for a factory reconditioned unit rather than renew more than one individual component.

17 Finally, examine the brushes for wear. If they are less than 0.34 in. (8.5 mm) in length renew them. Remove the old brushes and insert the new ones in their holders, checking to see that they slide freely. Ensure that the brush does not project more than 0.5 in. (12.5 mm) from its holder and then solder the brush lead, cutting off any surplus wire.

18 Commence reassembly of the alternator by fitting the stator coil 'N' terminal to the brush holder, then a terminal insulator followed by the brush negative lead.

19 Fit the two insulating washers between the rectifier positive holder and the end frame and install the 'B' terminal and the retaining bolt insulators and secure the holder with its four retaining nuts. Secure the negative rectifier holder with its four nuts.

20 Fit the brush holder with its insulating plate and tighten the securing screws passing them through the terminal insulators. Locate the stator coil in the rectifier end frame.

21 To the drive end frame fit the felt ring, cover (convex face to pulley) bearing (packed with multi-purpose grease) and bearing retainer (3 screws).

22 Fit the spacer ring to the rotor shaft and then press the drive end frame onto the shaft. Fit the collar, fan and pulley and tighten the securing nut to a torque of 35 lb/ft (4.838 kg/m).

23 Connect the drive end frame assembly to the rectifier end frame assembly and secure with the three tie bolts. Use a piece of wire to support the brushes in the raised position during this operation.

10 Alternator regulator - testing and adjustment

1 Testing of the relay operating voltage and the regulator output voltage and amperage levels should be left to an auto-electrician as special equipment is needed. However, circuit testing and mechanical adjustments may be carried out in the following manner:

2 Disconnect the regulator connector plug. Remove the cover from the regulator unit and inspect the condition of the points. If they are pitted, clean with very fine emery cloth otherwise clean them with methylated spirit.

3 Connect a circuit tester between the 'IG' and 'F' terminals of the connector plug when no resistance should be indicated. If a resistance is shown, then the regulator points PL1 and PL0 are making poor contact. Now press down the regulator armature and check the resistance which should be about 10 ohms. If it is much higher, the control resistance is defective and must be renewed.

4 Connect the circuit tester between the connector plug 'L' and

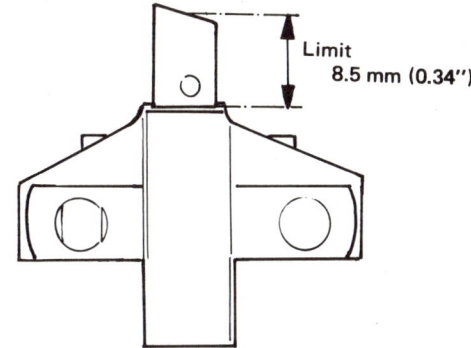

Fig 10.7 Alternator brush wear diagram (Sec 9)

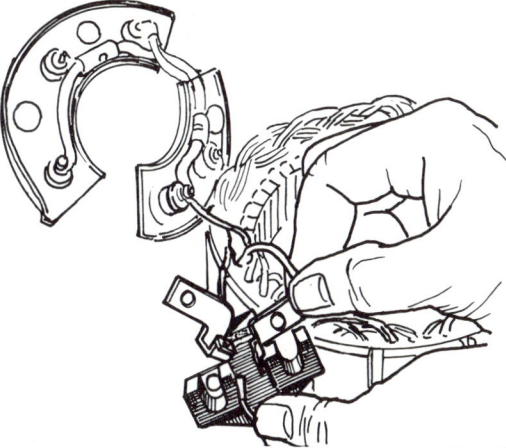

Fig 10.8 Assembling the alternator brush holder (Sec 9)

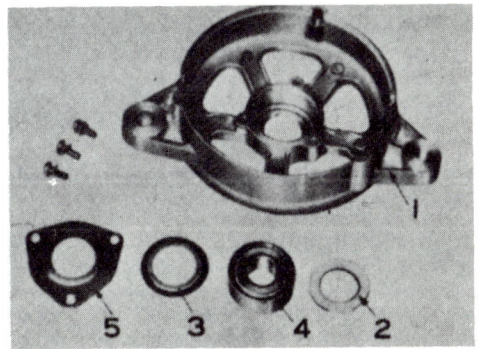

Fig 10.9 Components of the alternator drive end frame (Sec 9)

1 Frame
2 Felt ring
3 Felt ring cover
4 Bearing
5 Bearing retainer

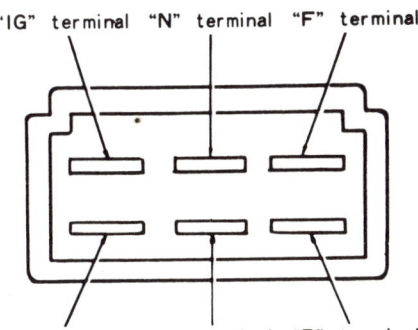

Fig 10.10 Identification of alternator connecting plug terminals (Sec 10)

'E' terminals when no resistance should be indicated. If a resistance is shown then the contact points P1 and P0 are making poor contact. Press down the relay armature and check the resistance which should be about 100 ohms. If it is higher, the voltage coil has an open circuit or if lower, the points P1, P0 are fused together or the coil is shorted.

5 Connect the circuit tester between the 'N' and 'E' terminals when a resistance of 23 ohms should be indicated. If the resistance is much higher, the pressure coil has an open circuit, if lower then it is short circuited.

6 Connect the circuit tester between the 'B' and 'L' terminals and depress the voltage relay armature. There should be no indicated resistance but if there is, this will show that the contact of the points P0 and P2 is poor.

7 Connect the circuit tester between the 'B' and 'E' terminals when the indicated resistance should be infinity. Where this is not so, the points P0 and P2 are fused together. Depress the relay armature and check the resistance which should be about 100 ohms. If the resistance is higher then the voltage coil has an open circuit and if lower it has a short circuit.

8 Connect the circuit tester between the 'F' and 'E' terminals when the indicated resistance should be infinity. Where this is not the case the points PL0 and PL2 are fused together. Depress the regulator armature and check the resistance which should be zero. If there is a resistance indicated on the tester then the points PL0 and PL2 are making poor contact.

9 **With the connector plug still disconnected** carry out the following mechanical checks.

10 Refer to Fig. 10.11 and depress the voltage relay armature. Using a feeler gauge check the deflection gap between the contact spring and its supporting arm. This should be between 0.008 and 0.024 in. (0.20 and 0.60 mm) if not, bend the contact point holder (P2). Release the armature and check the point gap which should be between 0.016 and 0.047 in. (0.4 to 1.2 mm) if not, bend the contact point holder (P1).

11 Check the armature gap on the voltage regulator which should be in excess of 0.012 in. (0.30 mm) otherwise bend the contact point holder PL2 to adjust (Fig. 10.32). Check the voltage regulator point gap which should be between 0.012 and 0.018 in. (0.30 and 0.45 mm) otherwise bend the contact point holder PL2 to adjust. Depress the voltage regulator armature and check the deflection gap between the contact spring and its supporting arm. This should be between 0.008 and 0.024 in. (0.2 and 0.6 mm). If not renew the regulator as an assembly. Finally depress the voltage regulator armature and check the angle gap at its narrowest point. This gap should not exceed 0.008 in. (0.2 mm) otherwise renew the unit as an assembly.

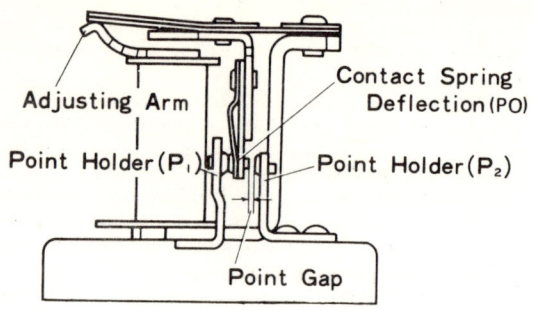

Fig 10.11 Voltage relay (Sec 10)

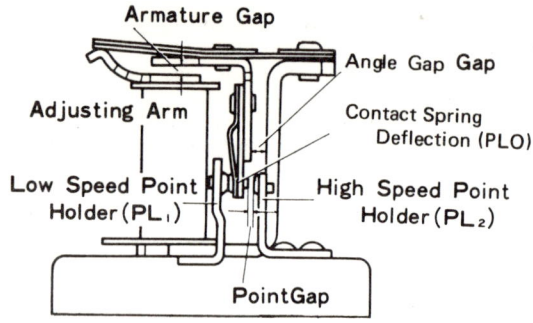

Fig 10.12 Voltage regulator (Sec 10)

11 Starter motor - general description

The starter motor is of heavy duty type, designed to cope with engine and gearbox drag in sub-zero temperatures. The starter operates on the principle of pre-engagement which through the medium of a solenoid switch meshes the starter drive gear with the ring gear on the flywheel (or torque convertor - automatic transmission) fractionally in advance of the closure of the main starter motor contacts. This slight delay in energising the starter motor does much to extend the life of the starter drive and ring gear components. As soon as the engine fires and its speed of rotation exceeds that of the armature shaft of the starter motor, a built-in clutch mechanism prevents excessive rotation of the shaft and the release of the starter switch key causes the solenoid and drive engagement fork to return to their de-energised positions. The armature shaft is fitted with rear and central rotational speed retarding mechanisms to stop its rotational movement rapidly after the starter has been de-energised.

On some later model vehicles built for operation in North America, a modified type of starter motor is used. In this unit, an idler gear is incorporated to provide a lower reduction gear characteristic.

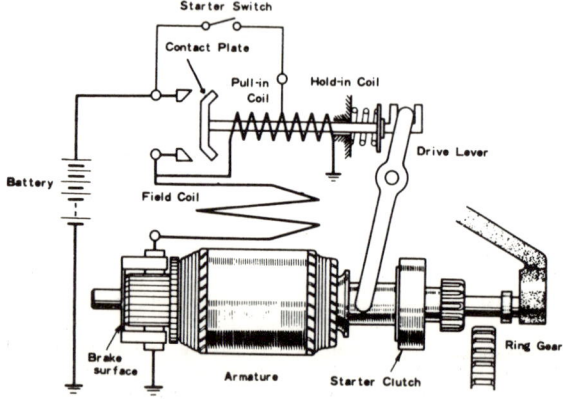

Fig 10.13 Diagrammatic view of starter circuit (Sec 11)

12 Starter motor - testing in vehicle

1 If the starter motor fails to operate, check the state of charge of the battery by checking the specific gravity with a hydrometer or switching on the headlamps. If they glow brightly for several seconds and then gradually dim, then the battery is in an uncharged state.

2 If the tests prove the battery to be fully charged, check the security of the battery leads at the battery terminals, scraping away any deposits which are preventing a good contact between the cable clamps and the terminal posts.

3 Check the battery negative lead at its body frame terminal, scraping the mating faces clean if necessary.

4 Check the security of the cables at the starter motor and solenoid switch terminals.

5 Check the wiring with a voltmeter for breaks or short circuits.

6 Check the wiring connections at the ignition/starter switch terminals.

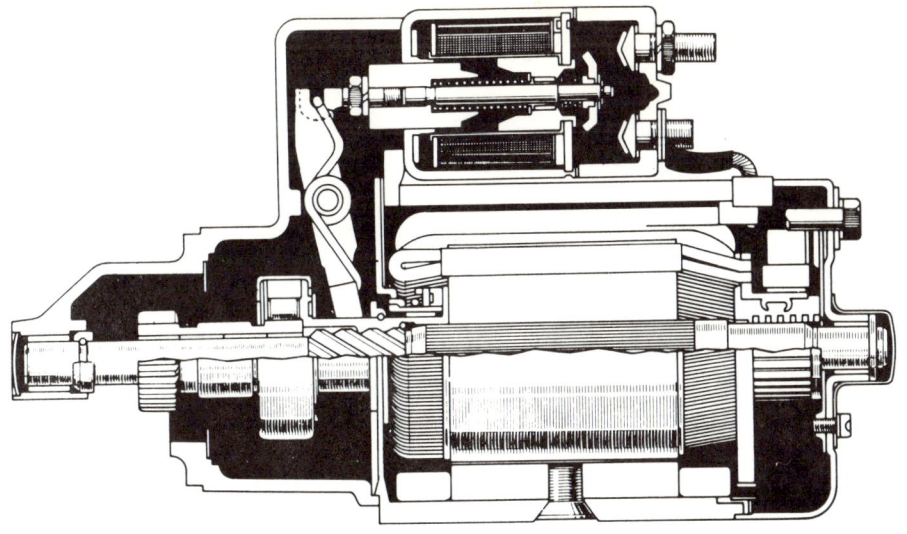

Fig 10.14 Sectional view of standard model starter motor (Sec 11)

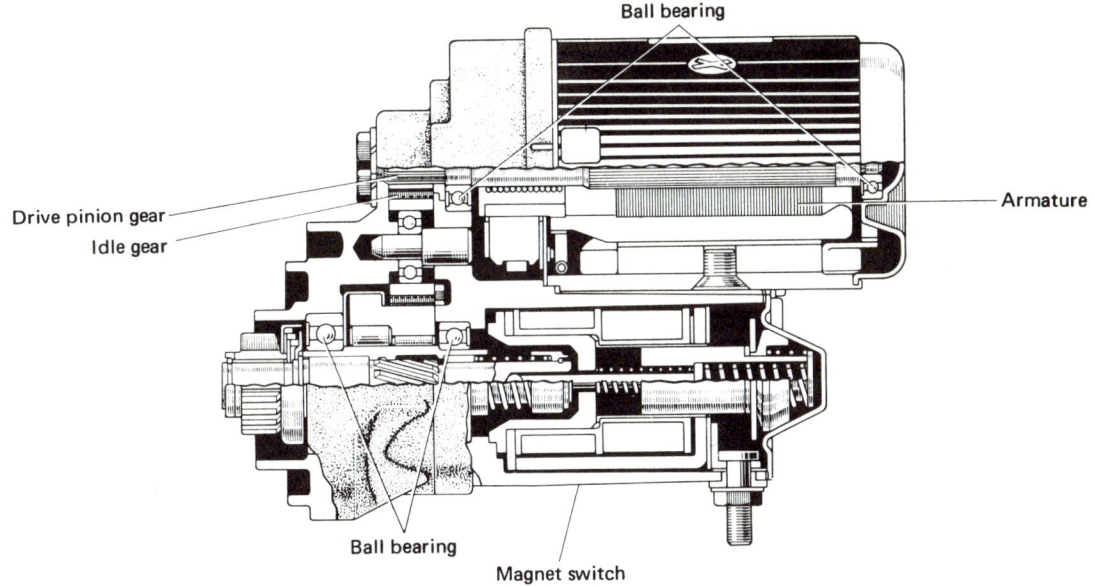

Fig 10.15 Sectional view of reduction gear type starter motor (Sec 11)

Fig 10.16 Exploded view of standard model starter motor (Sec 14)

1 Solenoid
2 Engagement lever fork
3 Armature
4 Clutch assembly
5 Pinion stop collar
6 Circlip
7 Drive end frame
8 Bush
9 Plug
10 End frame cover
11 Commutator end frame
12 Insulator
13 Rubber packing
14 Backing plate
15 Lockplate
16 Washer
17 Brake spring
18 Seal
19 Brush
20 Brush spring
21 Brush holder
22 Field coil
23 Pole shoe
24 Yoke

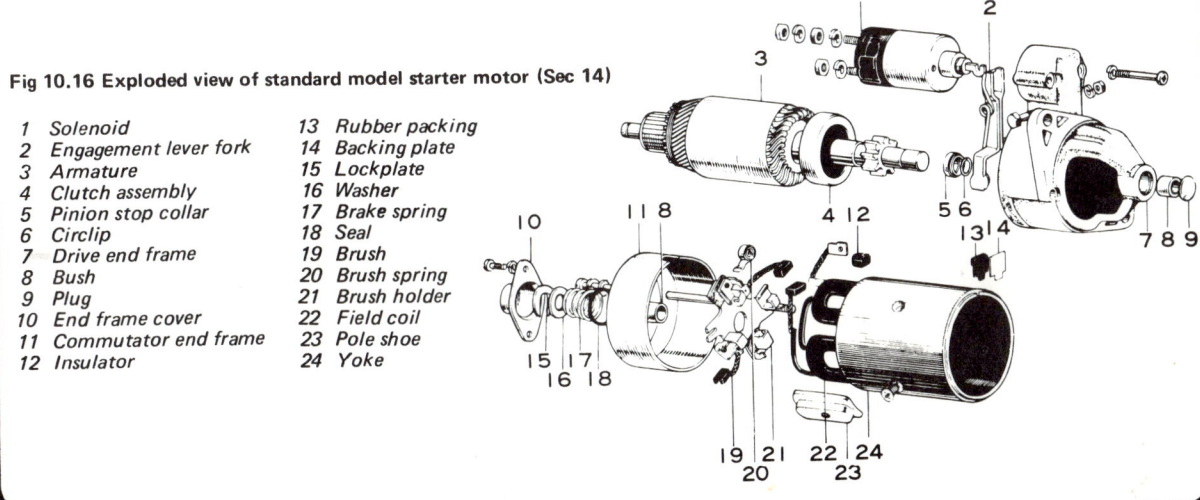

Chapter 10/Electrical system

7 If everything is in order, remove the starter motor as described in the next Section and dismantle, test and service as described in Section 14.

13 Starter motor - removal and installation

1 Disconnect the lead from the battery negative terminal.
2 Disconnect the cables from the starter solenoid terminals.
3 Unscrew and remove the starter motor securing bolts and withdraw the unit from the clutch bellhousing (or torque converter housing - automatic transmission).
4 Installation is a reversal of removal.

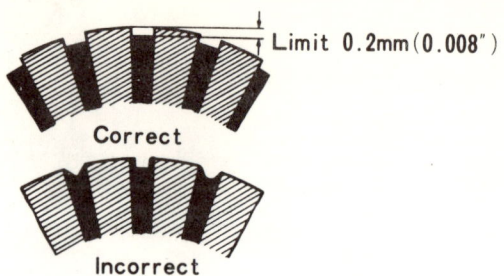

Fig 10.17 Mica segment undercutting diagram (starter motor commutator) (Sec 15)

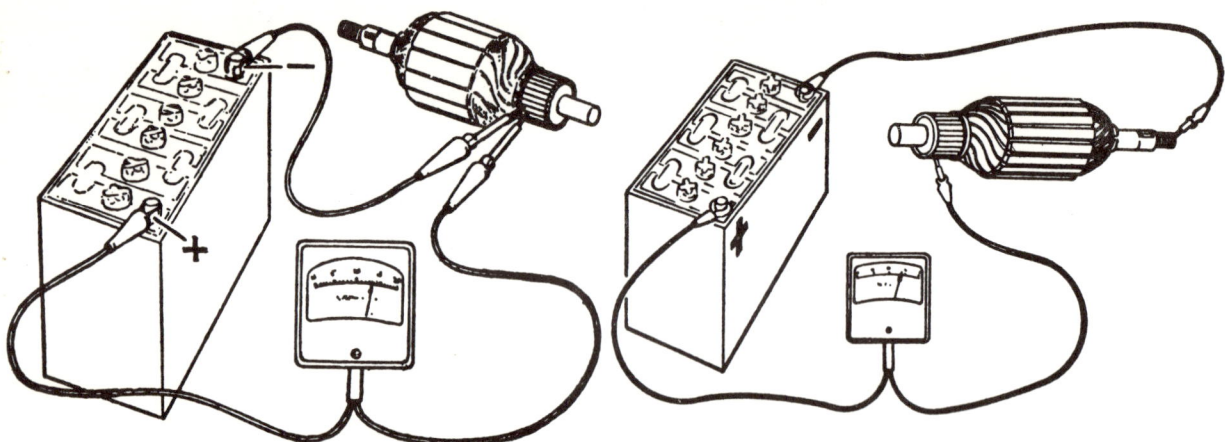

Fig 10.18 Testing the starter motor armature for open circuit (left) and for insulation breakdown of windings (right) (Sec 15)

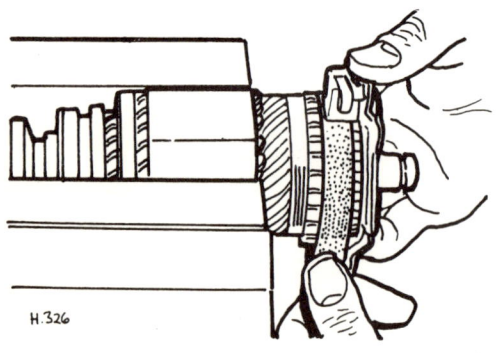

Fig 10.19 Dressing starter motor brushes to the correct contour (Sec 15)

Fig 10.20 Locating the drive engagement lever to the starter motor shaft (Sec 16)

1 Clutch
2 Engagement lever
3 Washer

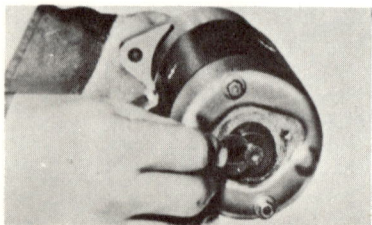

Fig 10.21 Fitting the lockplate to the starter motor shaft (Sec 16)

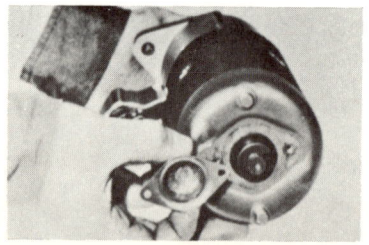

Fig 10.22 Fitting the starter motor end cover (Sec 16)

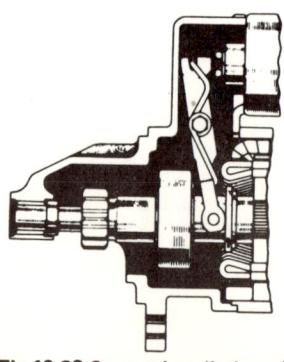

Fig 10.23 Correct installation of starter motor solenoid hook (Sec 16)

14 Starter motor - dismantling

1 Disconnect the field coil lead from the starter solenoid main terminal.
2 Remove the two securing screws from the solenoid and withdraw the solenoid far enough to enable it to be unhooked from the drive engagement lever fork.
3 Remove the end frame cover, the lockplate, washer, spring and seal.
4 Unscrew and remove the two tie bolts and withdraw the commutator end frame.
5 Pull out the brushes from their holders and remove the brush holder assembly.
6 Pull the yoke from the drive end frame.
7 Remove the engagement lever pivot bolt from the drive end frame and detach the rubber buffer and its backing plate. Remove the armature, complete with drive engagement lever from the drive end frame.
8 With a piece of tubing, drive the pinion stop collar up the armature shaft far enough to enable the circlip to be removed and then pull the stop collar from the shaft together with the pinion and clutch assembly.

15 Starter motor - servicing and testing

1 Check for wear in the armature shaft bearings. The specified clearance between shaft and bearing is between 0.037 and 0.053 in. (0.095 and 0.135 mm) with a maximum of 0.008 in. (0.2 mm). Normally the bearings will require renewal by pressing out the old ones from the end frames and pressing in the new but before doing this check the diameter of the armature shaft which should be 0.492 in. (12.50 mm). If this is worn then a new armature will be required and it will be more economical to exchange the starter complete for a reconditioned unit.
2 Armature shaft bearings are available in standard and undersizes as follows:
Standard: 0.4935 to 0.4945 in. (12.535 to 12.560 mm) diameter
Undersize (0.30 mm single line identification): 0.4817 to 0.4827 in. (12.235 to 12.260 mm)
Undersize (0.50 mm double line identification): 0.4738 to 0.4748 in. (12.035 to 12.060 mm)
3 Check the armature shaft for bend or ovality and renew if evident.
4 Check the commutator segments and undercut the mica insulators if necessary, using a hacksaw blade ground to correct thickness. If the commutator is burned or discoloured, clean it with a piece of fine glass paper (not emery or carborundum) and finally wipe it with a solvent moistened cloth.
5 To test the armature is not difficult but a voltmeter or bulb and 12 volt battery are required. The two tests determine whether there may be a break in any circuit winding or if any wiring insulation is broken down. Fig. 10.18 shows how the battery, voltmeter and probe connectors are used to test whether (a) any wire in the windings is broken or (b) whether there is an insulation breakdown. In the first test the probes are placed on adjacent segments of a clean commutator. All voltmeter readings should be similar. If a bulb is used instead it will glow very dimly or not at all if there is a fault. For the second test any reading or bulb lighting indicates a fault. Test each segment in turn with one probe and keep the other on the shaft. Should either test indicate a faulty armature the wisest action in the long run is to obtain a replacement starter. The field coils may be tested if an ohmmeter or ammeter can be obtained. With an ohmmeter the resistance (measured between the terminal and the yoke) should be 6 ohms. With an ammeter, connect it in series with a 12 volt battery again from the field terminal to the yoke. A reading of 2 amps, is normal. Zero amps or infinity ohms indicate an open circuit. More than 2 amps or less than 6 ohms indicates a breakdown of the insulation.

If a fault in the field coils is diagnosed then a reconditioned starter should be obtained as the coils can only be removed and refitted with special equipment.
6 Check the insulation of the brush holders and the length of the brushes. If these have worn to below 0.47 in. (12 mm), renew them. Before fitting them to their holders, dress them to the correct contour by wrapping a piece of emery cloth round the commutator and rotating the commutator back and forth.
7 Check the starter clutch assembly for wear or sticky action, or chipped pinion teeth and renew the assembly if necessary.

16 Starter motor - reassembly

1 Fit the clutch assembly to the armature shaft followed by a new pinion stop collar and circlip. Pull the stop collar forward and stake the collar rim over the circlip. Grease all sliding surfaces.
2 Locate the drive engagement lever to the armature shaft as shown in Fig. 10.20 with the spring towards the armature and the steel washer up against the clutch.
3 Apply grease to all sliding surfaces and locate the armature assembly in the drive end frame. Insert the drive engagement lever pivot pin, well greased.
4 Fit the rubber buffer together with its backing plate and then align and offer into position the yoke to the drive end frame.
5 Fit the brush holder to the armature and then insert the brushes.
6 Grease the commutator end frame bearing and then fit the end frame into position. Insert and tighten the two tie bolts.
7 Fit the seal, washer lockplate and end cover (half packed with multi-purpose grease). Check the armature shaft endfloat, if this exceeds 0.03 in. (0.8 mm) remove the end cover and add an additional thrust washer.
8 Install the solenoid switch making sure that its hook engages under the spring of the engagement lever fork.
9 Set up a test circuit similar to the one shown in Fig. 10.24 and check that the motor rotates smoothly at a current loading of 45 amps. With the solenoid switch energised, insert a feeler gauge between the end face of the clutch pinion and the pinion stop collar. There should be a clearance of between 0.04 and 0.16 in. (1 and 4 mm). If the clearance is incorrect, remove the solenoid switch and adjust the length of the adjustable hooked stud by loosening its locknut.

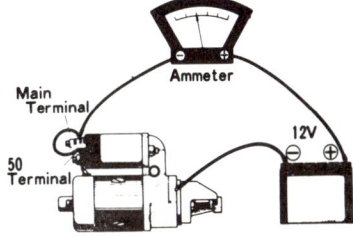

Fig 10.24 Testing the starter motor after reassembly (Sec 16)

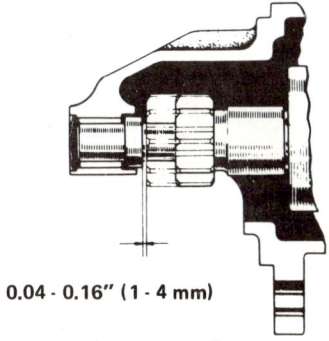

0.04 - 0.16" (1 - 4 mm)

Fig 10.25 Starter motor pinion to stop clearance (Sec 16)

17 Fuses and fusible link

1 The fuse block is located under the facia panel. The fuse ratings and circuits protected vary according to model and date of manufacture but the fuse block is clearly marked and the cover incorporates two spare fuses.
2 In the event of a fuse blowing, always find the reason and rectify the trouble before fitting the new one. Always replace a fuse with one of the same amperage rating as the original.
3 A double protection is provided for the electrical harness by a fusible link installed in the lead running from the battery positive terminal. The fusible link must never be by-passed and should it melt, the cause of the circuit overload must be established before renewing the link with one of similar type and rating. On some vehicles an ammeter fuse is incorporated.

Note: The electrical equipment described in the remainder of this Chapter may only be fitted in part to vehicles according to date of manufacture and operating territory. Only the very latest vehicles marketed in North America are equipped with the more sophisticated warning devices. Readers should check the specifications of their particular vehicle to ascertain which Sections of this Chapter are relevant.

18 Electrical relays - description and testing

1 A number of relays are fitted to the vehicle and their locations are illustrated. Each relay is of sealed type and cannot be repaired but must be renewed if, after carrying out the tests described in this Section, it is proved to be faulty (Fig. 10.30).

Tail light control relay
2 With the connector securely plugged into the relay, short circuit the 'Ts' terminal to earth. The relay should be heard to operate and the tail light illuminate if the unit is in good order.

Headlight relay
3 With the connector securely plugged into the relay, short circuit the 'Hs' terminal to earth. The relay should be heard to operate and the headlights should illuminate. If the relay is inoperative, check that battery voltage is applied across the terminals 'TB' and 'HB'.

Main relay
4 Turn the ignition switch on and listen for the points closing within the relay.
5 Connect terminal (3) to earth and then apply battery voltage (12v) to the terminal. There should be continuity between terminals (1) and (2) (Fig. 10.32).

19 Hazard warning and direction indicator lamps

1 If the flashers fail to work properly first check that all the bulbs are serviceable and of the correct wattage. Then check that the nuts which hold the lamp bodies to the car are tight and free from corrosion. These are the means by which the circuit is completed and any resistance here could affect the proper working of the coils in the flasher unit.
2 Check the security of all leads after reference to the appropriate wiring diagram.

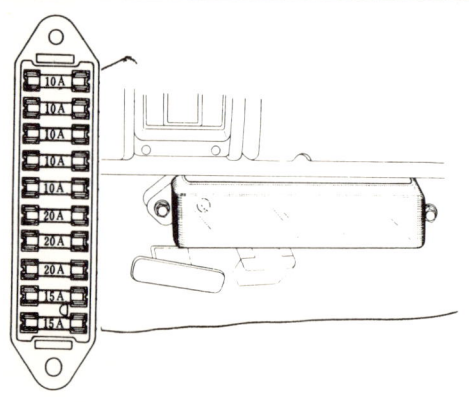

Fig 10.26 Early type fuse box and location. For circuit details see Specifications section (Sec 17)

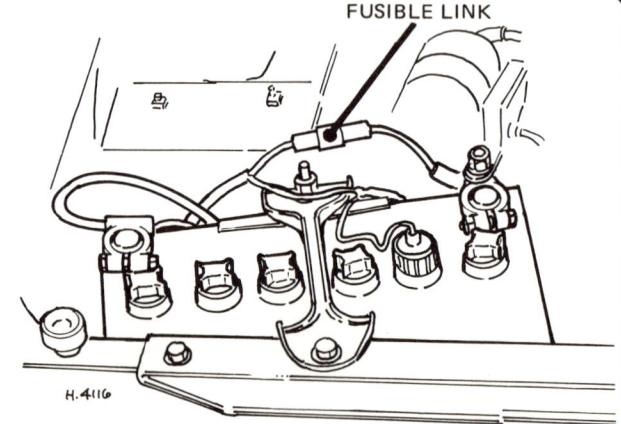

Fig 10.28 Location of fusible link (Sec 17)

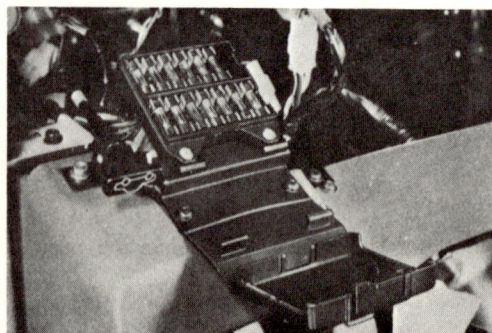

Fig 10.27 Later type fuse box and location. For circuit details, see Specifications section (Sec 17)

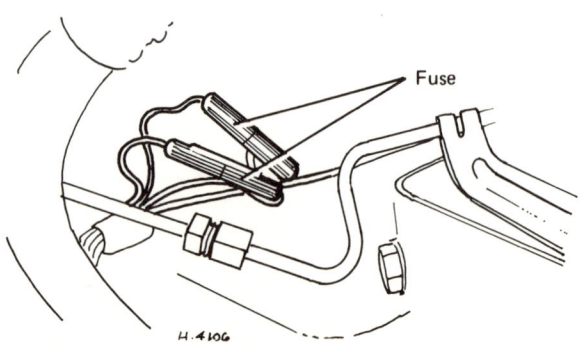

Fig 10.29 The ammeter protective fuse used on some models (Sec 17)

Chapter 10/Electrical system   197

3 If everything is in order then the hazard warning or flasher indicator units themselves must be faulty and as they cannot be repaired, they must be renewed. The units are located beneath the facia panel.

20 Electro sensor panel - description

1 This is a system of transmitter switches, a computer and a warning light panel which indicate to the driver immediately there is a failure in any component or drop in fluid level, pressure or vacuum conditions which are likely to affect the safety of the vehicle.

2 The warning lamp panel is mounted in the roof interior lining and indicates the following conditions:

(i) Failure of rear licence plate, stop and tail lamps, also headlights.
(ii) Low levels in the radiator, engine, battery, windscreen, washer, brake fluid reservoir.
(iii) Low vacuum pressure in the brake servo unit.
(iv) Front disc pads worn below specified limit.

3 Whenever one of the indicator bulbs lights up, investigate the reason and rectify it at once.
4 Any failure of a section of the system should be checked out by first testing the bulb and the connecting wiring. The transmitter switches are not repairable and where tests of the circuit have proved satisfactory then the transmitter switch must be renewed.
5 When replacing the battery combined plug/sensor ensure that it is only refitted into one of the centre four cell filler holes.

21 Fuel level transmitter and gauge - testing

1 In the event of malfunction of the fuel gauge, first check that there is in fact fuel in the tank and then that the connecting leads are secure and unbroken.
2 Using a circuit tester, measure the resistance between the transmitter unit terminal and earth. The resistance should correspond approximately with the amount of fuel known to be in the tank. If the tank is empty, the resistance should be 120 ohms, if half-full 45 ohms and when full 17 ohms.
3 If the transmitter unit is satisfactory, test the fuel gauge.
4a *On early vehicles,* connect a circuit tester between terminals C and E on the back of the gauge and the resistance should be approximately 25 ohms. Now apply battery voltage between the two terminals (using a 3w bulb in the circuit otherwise the gauge filament will melt) and if the needle of the gauge deflects smoothly then the gauge is serviceable.
4b *On later vehicles* having printed circuit type instrumentation measure the resistance between the terminals shown in Fig. 10.35; this should be approximately 25 ohms. Carry out the

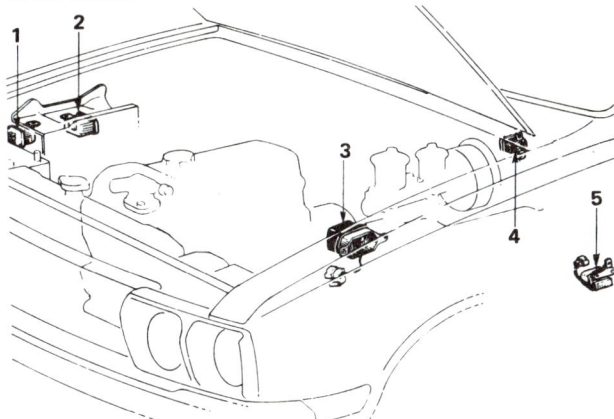

Fig 10.30 Location of relays (Sec 18)

1 Tail light
2 Horn
3 Voltage regulator
4 direction indicator
5 Main relay

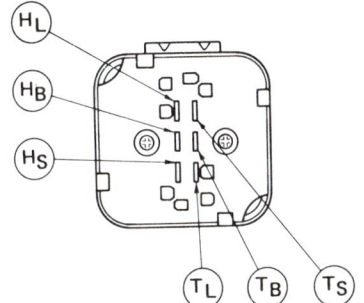

Fig 10.31 Connections of tail light control relay (Sec 18)

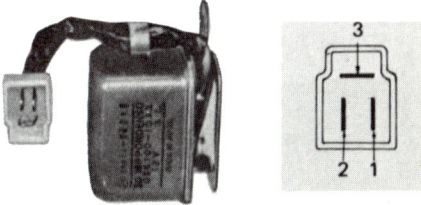

Fig 10.32 The main relay and connector (Sec 18)

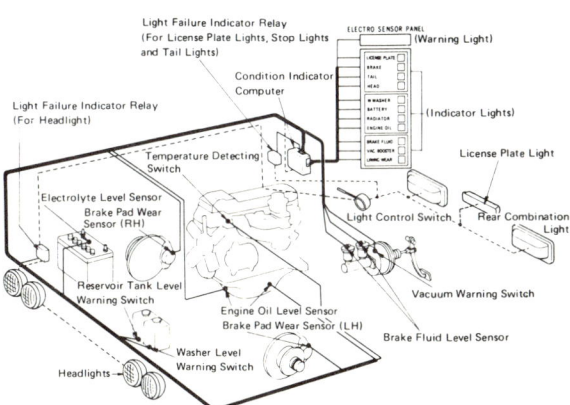

Fig 10.33 Layout of electro sensor circuit (Sec 20)

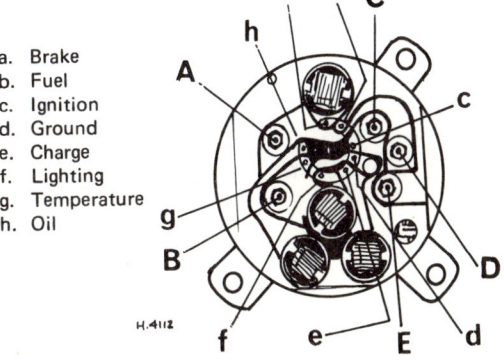

a. Brake
b. Fuel
c. Ignition
d. Ground
e. Charge
f. Lighting
g. Temperature
h. Oil

Fig 10.34 Early type instrument terminals (Secs 21 and 22)

check using the test bulb as described for early model gauges in the preceding paragraph.

22 Water temperature transmitter and gauge - testing

1 In the event of malfunction of the water temperature gauge, first check the security of the connecting leads and that the cooling system is not short of coolant.

2 Using a circuit tester, connected between the transmitter switch terminal and earth, measure the resistance which should be between 400 and 700 ohms.

3 If the transmitter is satisfactory, check the temperature gauge. On early model vehicles, connect the circuit tester between terminals A and B (Fig. 10.34) when the indicated resistance should be 25 ohms (using a 3w bulb in the circuit otherwise the gauge filament will melt) and if the needle of the gauge deflects smoothly then the gauge is serviceable.

4 *On later vehicles* having printed circuit instrumentation, measure the resistance between the terminals as shown in Fig. 10 37 this should be 25 ohms. Carry out the check using the test bulb as described for early model gauges in the preceding paragraph.

23 Oil pressure switch, warning lamp or gauge - testing

1 The oil pressure indicator may be in the form of a gauge or warning lamp according to model.

2 In the event of the warning lamp remaining on, check for low oil level, assuming the engine to be in good condition. If the oil pressure warning lamp does not come on when the ignition switch is turned on, check for a blown bulb or disconnected lead.

3 Where a gauge is fitted and registers no pressure, check for low engine oil level or a broken or disconnected lead from the switch to the gauge.

4 To test the pressure switch, connect a circuit tester between the switch terminal and earth. With the engine stationary (ignition on or off) there should be no reading on the circuit tester. Start the engine and a resistance will be indicated which should increase progressively as the engine is revved.

5 *On early type* oil gauges, measure the resistance across the terminals exactly as described for the early model water temperature gauge. On later type gauges fitted in conjunction with printed circuit type instrumentation, measure the resistance between the two terminals shown, this should be 42 ohms. Carry out the check using a test bulb and battery voltage, as described in the two previous Sections (Fig. 10.40).

24 Ammeter - testing

1 In the event of malfunction of the ammeter, first check that the alternator drivebelt is not broken or slipping, then that the charging system is operating correctly.

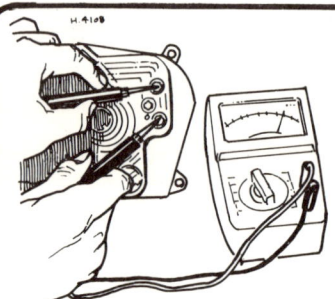

Fig 10.35 Checking fuel gauge (printed circuit type connection) (Sec 22)

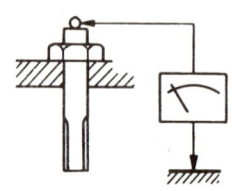

Fig 10.36 Checking water temperature transmitter (Sec 22)

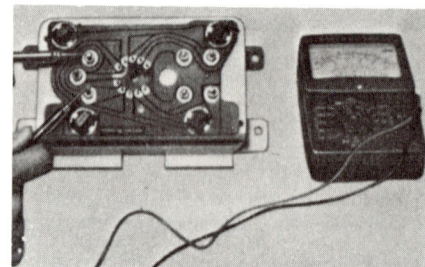

Fig 10.37 Checking water temperature gauge (printed circuit type connection) (Sec 22)

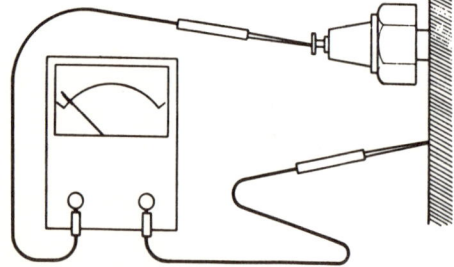

Fig 10.38 Testing the oil pressure switch (warning lamp type) (Sec 23)

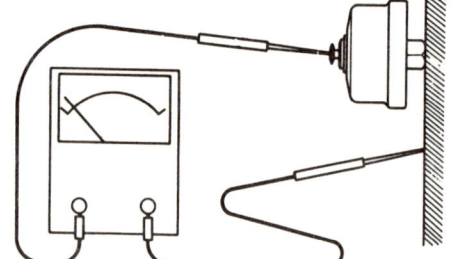

Fig 10.39 Testing the oil pressure switch (gauge type) (Sec 23)

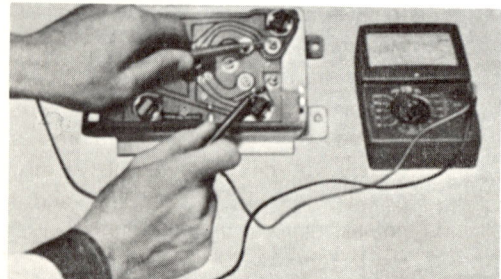

Fig 10.40 Testing the oil pressure gauge (printed circuit type connection) (Sec 23)

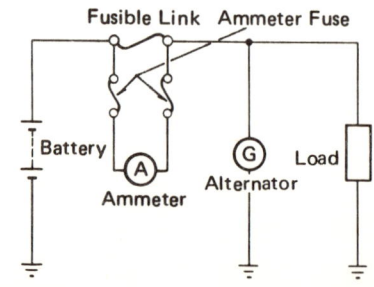

Fig 10.41 Shunt type ammeter circuit layout (Sec 24)

Chapter 10/Electrical system

2 Check the amount by connecting battery voltage (with a 12v, 8w bulb incorporated) between the terminals. If the amount indicates 30 amps. then the ammeter is serviceable.

25 Instruments (early type) - removal and installation

1 On early models, the instruments may be of rectangular or circular type.
2 Disconnect the lead from the battery negative terminal.
3 Remove the parcels shelf and the fuse block bracket.

Rectangular instrumentation
4 Prise off the safety pad from the facia below the instrument panel. Disconnect the speedometer cable and wiring connectors. If a radio is not fitted it will be easier to remove the glove compartment and to reach behind the instruments and withdraw them after the three upper and two lower securing screws have been removed.

Circular instrumentation
5 Remove the side ventilator and the lighting switch.

6 Disconnect the speedometer cable and the electrical leads and remove the instruments from the rear of the panel, individually or as a unit by unscrewing the two upper and two lower screws.
7 Installation of both types of instrumentation is a reversal of removal.

26 Instruments (later type) - removal and installation

1 Disconnect the lead from the battery negative terminal.
2 Remove the ashtray.
3 Remove the glove compartment door, lock, light switch and the glove compartment itself.
4 Remove the radio knobs and locknuts.
5 Remove the radio securing bolts, disconnect the electrical and aerial leads from the back of the unit and withdraw it from the facia panel.
6 Remove the fuse bracket securing bolt and withdraw the lower safety pad. Remove the heater control lamp and the nut from the steering column clamp.
7 Disconnect the three heater control wires from the heater and disconnect the speedometer cable.

Fig 10.42 Rectangular styled instrumentation (Sec 25)

1 Water temperature gauge
2 Fuel gauge
3 Direction indicator
4 Speedometer
5 Handbrake 'ON' lamp
6 Main beam warning lamp
7 Odometer
8 Trip meter
9 Ignition warning lamp
10 Oil pressure warning lamp

Fig 10.43 Circular styled instrumentation (Sec 25)

1 Handbrake warning lamp
2 Main beam warning lamp
3 Direction indicator lamp
4 Oil pressure gauge
5 Speedometer
6 Tachometer
7 Water temperature gauge
8 Ignition warning lamp
9 Fuel gauge
10 Trip meter
11 Odometer

Fig 10.44 Location of securing screws (rectangular instrumentation) (Sec 25)

Fig 10.45 Circular type instrument panel retaining screws (Sec 25)

8 Unscrew and remove the six securing screws from the upper edge of the instrument panel and eight from the lower edge. Withdraw the instrument panel far enough to be able to disconnect the wiring harness connector plugs. Lift away the instrument panel.

9 Installation is a reversal of removal.

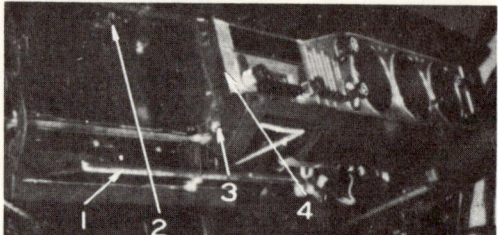

Fig 10.46 Location of glove compartment door (1) lock (2) lift switch (3) and glove compartment (4) on later type vehicles (Sec 26)

Fig 10.47 Location of radio tuning knob (1) on/off switch (2) and securing bolts (3) on later type vehicles (Sec 26)

Fig 10.49 Upper (1) and lower (2) instrument panel securing screws on later type vehicles (Sec 26)

Fig 10.51 Location of heater control lamp assembly retaining screws (Sec 27)

27 Instruments (printed circuit connection) - removal and installation

1 Disconnect the lead from the battery negative terminal.
2 Remove the instrument embellishment by unscrewing each of the screws from under the instrument hoods.
3 Remove the knob from the side ventilator.
4 The fuel gauge, speedometer, tachometer and clock can now be removed individually after disconnecting the securing nuts and screws and withdrawing from the printed circuit board. The speedometer drive cable will also have to be disconnected.
5 To remove the combined oil pressure gauge and ammeter, also the water temperature gauge, remove the heater control indicator lamp lens, the instrument embellishment and then the heater control indicator lamp assembly, in that order. The instruments may now be removed individually after disconnecting their electrical leads.
6 The instruments may be removed as two clusters if preferred by unscrewing their mounting plate screws.

28 Light switch (early models) - removal and installation

1 This switch is mounted on the facia panel and controls the operation of the side and headlights.
2 The switch can be removed by first disconnecting the lead from the battery negative terminal, then disconnecting the leads from the switch and then unscrewing the ring nut which secures the switch to the facia.

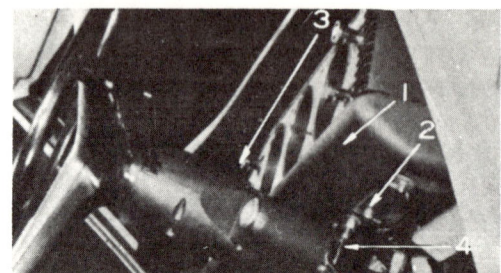

Fig 10.48 Location of lower safety pad 1) fuse bracket securing bolt (2) heater control warning lamp (3) and steering column clamp nut (4) on later model vehicles (Sec 26)

Fig 10.50 Gauge securing screws (printed circuit connections) (Sec 27)

Fig 10.52 Instrument cluster securing screws (Sec 27)

SEDAN - SALOON

HARDTOP - COUPE

Fig 10.53 Instrument panel printed circuit (Sec 27)

RHD Terminal connections

1. Right-hand direction indicator lamp
2. Main beam warning lamp
3. Left-hand direction indicator lamp
4. Switch
5. Instrument lamp (+)
6. Combination instrument (−)
7. Fuel gauge
8. Spare (saloon) handbrake indicator lamp (hardtop)
9. Combination instrument (+)
10. Ignition warning lamp
11. Oil pressure warning lamp
12. Door open indicator lamp (−)
13. Combination instrument (−)
14. Seat belt indicator lamp
15. Fuel contents warning lamp
16. Handbrake indicator lamp (saloon) spare (hardtop)
17. Clock (+) door open indicator lamp (+)
18. Water temperature gauge

LHD Terminal connections

1. Water temperature gauge
2. Right-hand indicator lamp
3. Left-hand indicator lamp
4. Main beam indicator lamp
5. Switch
6. Clock (+) door open indicator lamp
7. Handbrake indicator lamp
8. Spare
9. Combination instrument (−)
10. Instrument lamp (+)
11. Ignition warning lamp
12. Switch
13. Seat belt indicator lamp
14. Seat belt indicator lamp
15. Oil pressure warning lamp
16. Fuel gauge (saloon) spare (hardtop)
17. Combination instrument (+)
18. Door open indicator lamp

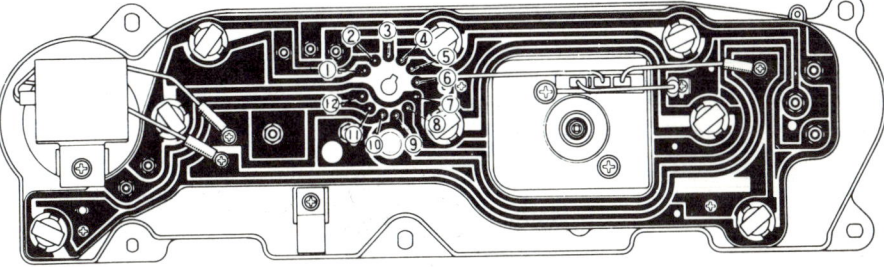

Fig 10.54 Instrument panel printed circuit (vehicles with tachometer)

RHD Terminal connections

1. Right-hand direction indicator lamp
2. Tachometer
3. Combination instrument (−)
4. Main beam indicator lamp
5. Left-hand direction indicator lamp
6. Switch
7. Instrument lamp (+)
8. Fuel gauge
9. Fuel warning lamp
10. Combination instrument (+)
11. Handbrake 'ON' warning lamp
12. Clock (+)

LHD Terminal connections

1. Right-hand direction indicator lamp
2. Tachometer
3. Left-hand direction indicator lamp
4. Main beam indicator lamp
5. Combination instrument (−)
6. Instrument lamp
7. Clock (+)
8. Switch
9. Handbrake 'ON' warning lamp
10. Combination instrument (+)
11. Spare
12. Fuel gauge

Fig 10.55 Combination instrument (oil pressure, water temperature gauges and ammeter) - printed circuit (Sec 27)

RHD MODELS

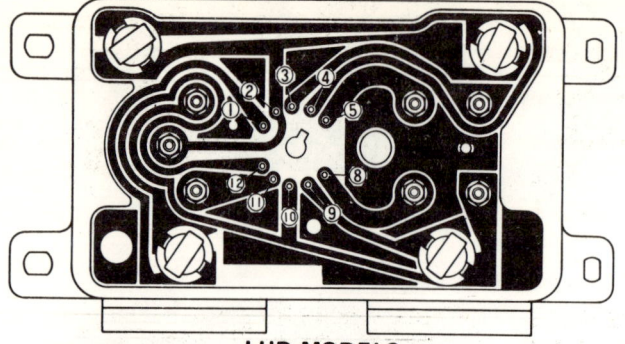

RHD Terminal connections

1. Door open indicator lamp (−)
2. Combination instrument (−)
3. Oil pressure gauge
4. Instrument lamp (+)
5. Ammeter (+)
6. Spare
7. Spare
8. Ammeter (−)
9. Seat belt indicator lamp
10. Combination instrument (+)
11. Water temperature gauge
12. Door open indicator lamp (+)

LHD MODELS

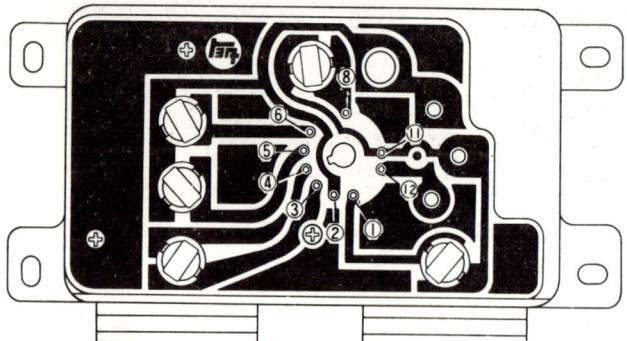

LHD Terminal connections

1. Seat belt indicator lamp
2. Combination instrument (+)
3. Door open indicator lamp
4. Door open indicator lamp
5. Oil pressure warning lamp
6. Ignition warning lamp
7. Spare
8. Instrument lamp
9. Spare
10. Spare
11. Combination instrument (−)
12. Water temperature gauge

Fig 10.56 Direction indicator switch retaining screws (1969-1970 models) (Sec 29)

Fig 10.57 Ignition/starter switch securing screw (A) on 1969-1970 models (Sec 29)

SS: To stoplight
F: Flasher terminal
RR: To rear right bulb
FR: To front right bulb
RL: To rear left bulb
FL: To front left bulb

A: Light switch
B: Power source
C: Lower beam
D: Upper beam
E: Horn

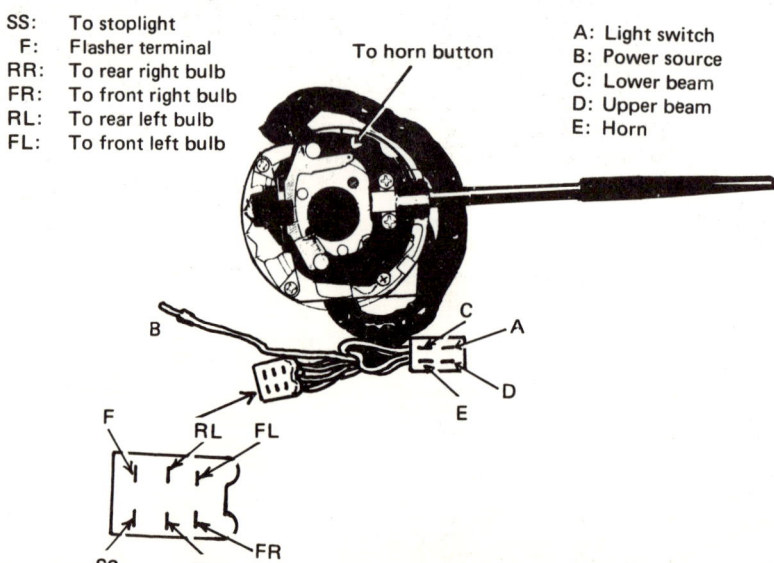

Fig 10.58 Combination switch (1971 to 1973 models) (Sec 30)

Chapter 10/Electrical system

29 Steering column switches (1969-1970) - removal and installation

1 On early models, three switches are incorporated in the steering column upper housing. These are the combined direction indicator/headlight dipper switch, the windscreen wiper/washer switch and the ignition/starter switch.
2 *To remove the direction indicator/dipper switch,* remove the parcels tray and the steering column lower clamp; disconnect the switch wiring at the connector.
3 Remove the steering wheel (see Chapter 11), unscrew the three switch retaining screws and withdraw the switch.
4 *The wiper/washer switch* is now exposed and can be removed after unscrewing the self-tapping screw and disconnecting the leads.
5 With the direction indicator/dipper switch and wiper/washer switch removed, the ignition/starter switch can be withdrawn after releasing the single securing screw and pulling the switch in the direction arrowed (Fig. 10.57).

30 Steering column switches (1971 - 1973) - removal and installation

1 *The combined direction indicator/horn/headlamp dipper switch* is accessible after removal of the steering wheel (Chapter 11) and the steering column shrouds. Reach under the instrument panel and disconnect the electrical harness plugs and then unscrew the switch noting carefully its position in relation to the direction indicator self-cancelling cam.
2 To remove *the ignition/starter switch,* remove the steering column shrouds and turn the ignition key to the 'ACC' position.
3 Using th thin probe, depress the lockpin and withdraw the switch.
4 To remove *the steering lock,* the securing bolts must be centre punched and a hole drilled in each so that they can be removed with a bolt extractor.
5 Installation of both switches is a reversal of removal but the following points must be watched. When fitting the steering lock, check that its tongue engages correctly with the steering shaft (operate the lock with a screwdriver to check its alignment) before tightening the bolts until their heads shear. When inserting the ignition/starter switch set the switch and the steering lock to the 'ACC' position and push in the switch until its lockpin engages in its hole.

31 Steering column switches (1973 onwards) - removal and installation

1 The procedures for removing this combination switch and steering lock are similar to those described in the preceding Section except that the switch differs in detail from the earlier type.

32 Headlamp sealed beam unit - renewal

1 Remove the radiator grille.
2 Unscrew the three screws which secure the tabs of the headlamp retaining ring just far enough to permit the lamp unit to be turned in a clockwise direction and withdrawn complete with retaining ring. (photo)
3 Remove the ring and pull off the connector from the back of the lamp unit. (photo)
4 Refitting is a reversal of removal but when installation is

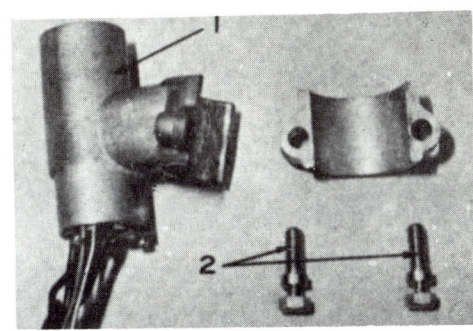

Fig 10.59 Components of the steering column lock (Sec 30)

1 Body
2 Shear bolts (new)

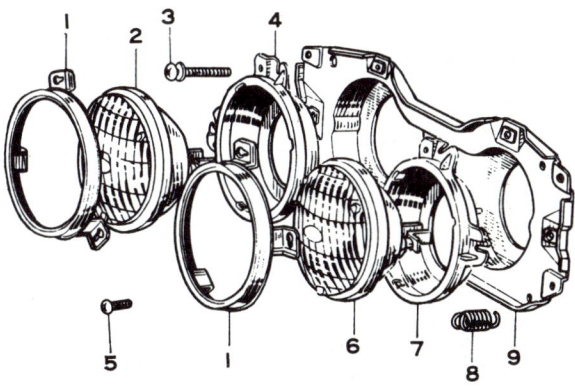

Fig 10.60 Exploded view of inner and outer headlights (Sec 32)

1 Retaining ring
2 Sealed beam unit
3 Adjusting screw
4 Mounting
5
6 Sealed beam
7 Mounting
8 Spring
9 Housing

32.2 Removing sealed beam headlamp unit and retaining ring

32.3 Disconnecting sealed beam headlamp unit

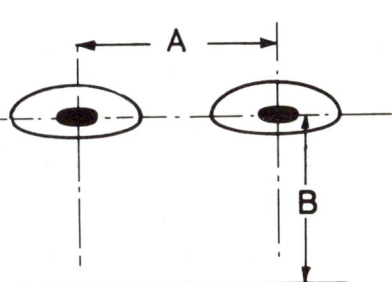

Fig 10.61 Outer headlamp setting diagram (Sec 33)

complete, adjust the beam, as described in the following Section.
5 **Never interchange the inner and outer sealed beam units.**

33 Headlights - adjustment

1 It is recommended that the headlights are adjusted by a service station having modern beam setting equipment but where these facilities are not available, follow the procedure described in this Section.
2 Position the vehicle with tyres correctly inflated, on a level surface square to, and at a distance of 25 ft (7.6 m) from, a wall or screen. Obviously the adjustment will be carried out during the hours of darkness.
3 Measure the height of the outer headlight centres and then transpose this measurement (dimension 'B') to the wall as a horizontal line (Fig. 10.61).
4 Mark the position of the vehicle centre line on the wall and then measure off dimension 'A' which represents the distance between the centres of the outer headlights.
5 Switch the headlights to main beam and adjust the outer headlight screws until the required light pattern is obtained.
6 Now mark the positions of the inner headlight centres on the wall. Switch to low beam (dipped filament) and mask the outer headlights. Adjust the inner headlight screws until the required light pattern is obtained. (photo)

34 Bulbs - renewal

1 Access to all vehicle lighting units is obtained by removing the lenses (retaining screws) or removing the lamp bulb socket retainers from inside the luggage boot. (photos)
2 Instrument panel indicator and warning lamp bulbs can be

Fig 10.62 Headlamp securing screws (A) and adjusting screws (B) (Sec 33)

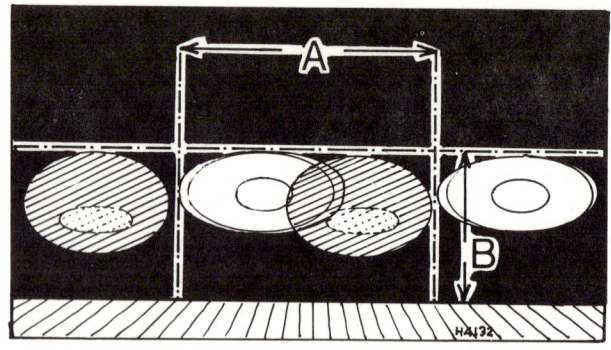

Fig 10.63 Inner headlamp setting diagram solid indicates LHD shaded RHD (Sec 33)

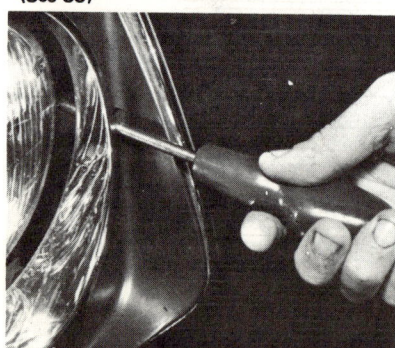

33.6 Adjusting a headlamp

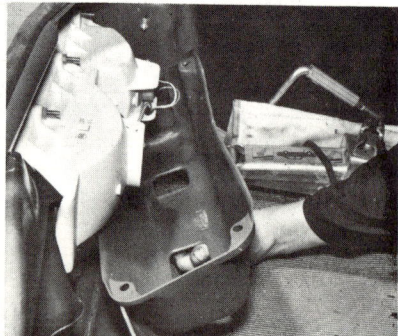

34.1A Removing cover from rear lamp cluster

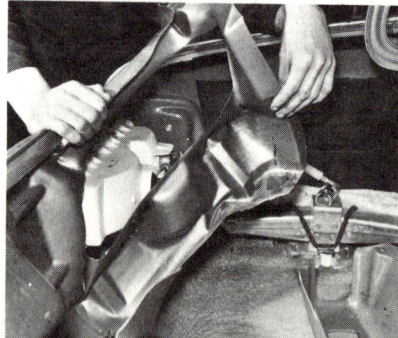

34.1B Removing trim from rear lamp cluster

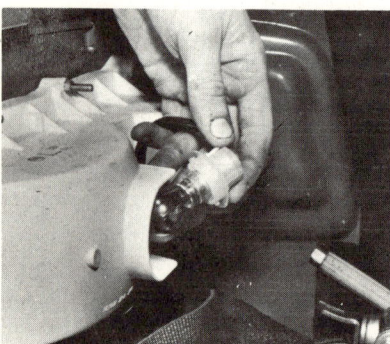

34.1C Removing bulb and holder from rear lamp cluster

34.1D Lens removed from bumper mounted type side/flasher lamp

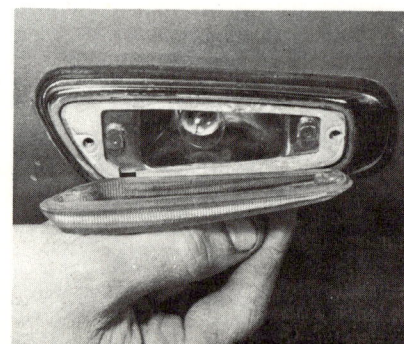

34.1E Removing lens from side marker lamp

Chapter 10/Electrical system 205

renewed from the rear of the panel but the fuse block bracket will have to be removed to gain access to certain of them.
3 Always replace a defective bulb with one of the same type and rating as the original (see Specifications).

35 Windscreen wiper motor and linkage (early models) - removal and installation

1 Raise the bonnet and then remove the air intake grille which is located just in front of the windscreen. The grille is retained by plastic clips and the centre pin must be removed before the outer clip can be prised out.
2 The wiper motor is accessible after the aperture cover is removed. Remove the mounting bolts from the wiper motor, disconnect the crank arm and the electrical connections.
3 The linkage and wiper arm pivots can be removed after detaching the wiper arms and blades and unscrewing the pivot mounting bolts.

36 Windscreen wiper motor and linkage (later models) - removal and installation

1 Remove the inspection hole cover plate from the top of the rear engine compartment bulkhead just above the wiper motor.
2 The motor connecting crank will be in its parked position but rotate it through 180° by switching on the wiper switch and turning the ignition key on and off quickly until the desired position is attained.
3 Separate the wiper crank from the link with a screwdriver.
4 Withdraw the electrical connecting plug from the wiper motor, remove the mounting bolts and withdraw the unit from the bulkhead.
5 Refitting is a reversal of removal.

37 Wiper motor - dismantling and reassembly

The windscreen wiper motors vary slightly in design according to which vehicle model they are fitted and to the date of manufacture but the following procedure applies generally to all types:
1 Remove the gear housing cover plate but do not detach the soldered wires unless the brush holder or gear housing is being renewed.
2 Detach the crank from the wiper motor by removing the retaining nut and pulling the crank arm from the splined tapered shaft of the drive gear. Retain the thrust and wave washers. Detach the rubber seat.
3 Remove the gear housing from the stator by withdrawing the two securing screws. Retain the ball from the end of the armature shaft. Remove the thrust adjuster screw from the gear housing.
4 Pull the armature from the stator using enough force to overcome the magnetic attraction. Retain the ball from the other end of the armature shaft.
5 Clean the grease from all components and inspect for wear or damage. Check the drive shaft endfloat and if it exceeds 0.008 in. (0.2 mm) renew the thrust washer.
6 Check the brushes for wear and if they are less than 0.31 in. (8.0 mm) in length, renew them.
7 Commence reassembly by fitting the brushes and springs to the brush holders so that the leads pass over the lips of the cut-away portions.
8 Assemble the armature to the gear housing, first packing the shaft bush with grease.
9 Pack the stator rear bearing with grease and insert the thrust ball. Carefully wipe out the interior of the stator to remove any ferrous filings which may be adhering to it due to magnetic attraction.
10 Align the stator and gear housing and secure them together with the two bolts and nuts inserted through the slots in the

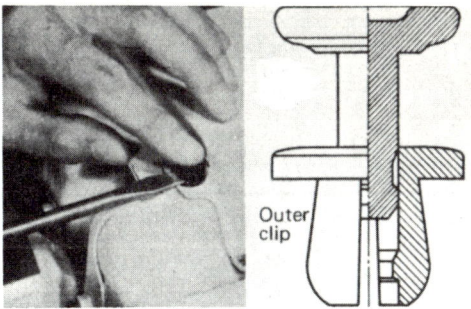

Fig 10.64 Removing an air intake grille clip (early models) (Sec 35)

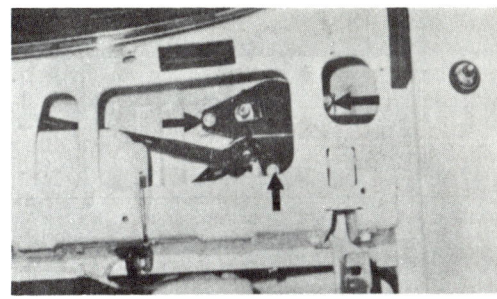

Fig 10.65 Wiper motor and linkage (early models) (Sec 35)

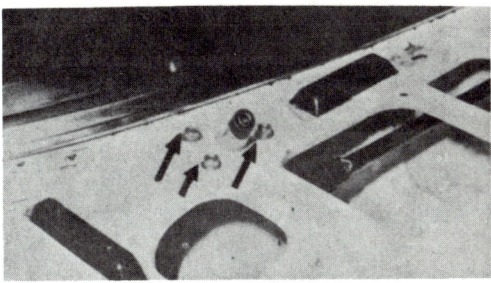

Fig 10.66 Wiper arm pivot mounting bolts (early models) (Sec 35)

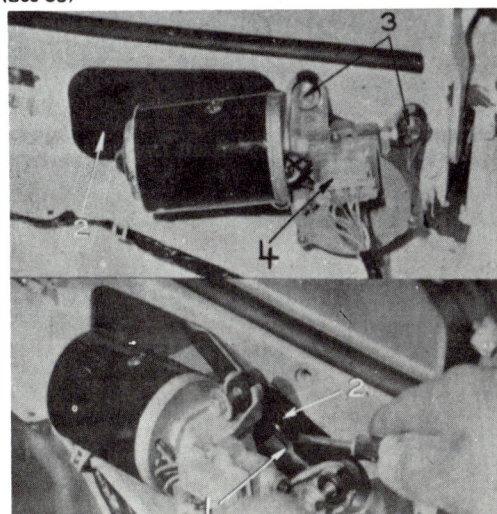

Fig 10.67 Wiper motor and linkage (later models) (Sec 36)

1 Link   3 Mounting bolts
2 Crank to motor 4 Connector plug

stator casing. A piece of adhesive tape attached to the nuts will help to hold them in position while engaging the bolts in them. Seal the stator to gear housing joint and the nut slots with gasket cement.

11 Grease the drive shaft/gear assembly liberally, also the thrust and wave washers and insert the components into the gear housing.

12 Drop the remaining ball into the thrust adjuster screw hole, insert the adjuster screw and tighten it until all armature end-float disappears. Secure the screw with the locknut only finger tight at this stage.

13 Check the height of the automatic switch lever from the inside surface of the gear housing cover plate. This should be 0.39 in. (10 mm), adjust if necessary.

14 Connect the wiring plug to the gear housing cover plate connector and turn the wiper motor switch on. Connect an

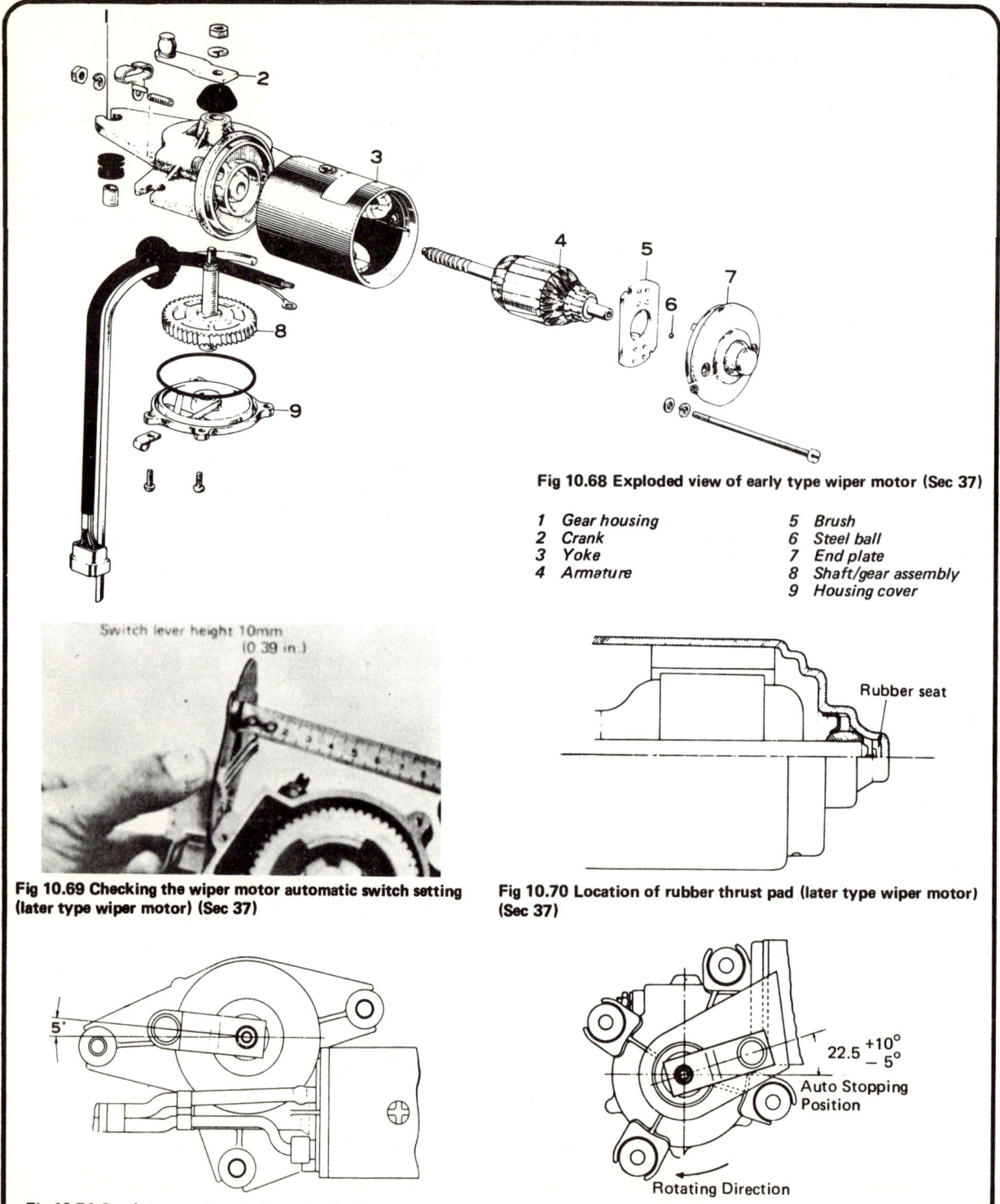

Fig 10.68 Exploded view of early type wiper motor (Sec 37)

1 Gear housing
2 Crank
3 Yoke
4 Armature
5 Brush
6 Steel ball
7 End plate
8 Shaft/gear assembly
9 Housing cover

Fig 10.69 Checking the wiper motor automatic switch setting (later type wiper motor) (Sec 37)

Fig 10.70 Location of rubber thrust pad (later type wiper motor) (Sec 37)

Fig 10.71 Crank to armature shaft setting (early type wiper motor) (Sec 37)

Fig 10.72 Crank to armature shaft setting (later type wiper motor) (Sec 37)

Chapter 10/Electrical system

ammeter between the battery and fusible link and then rotate the adjuster screw until the wiper motor is running under no load conditions and then screw it in to the point where the ammeter needle just starts to rise and secure the adjuster screw with its locknut. Endfloat adjustment can only be satisfactorily carried out in this manner because of the compressibility of the armature rear bearing rubber thrust pad.

15 Switch the motor off by using the wiper switch so that the motor will come to rest in its normal parked position. Fit the crank to the drive shaft so that it takes up the position shown according to model (Figs. 10.71 and 10.72).

38 Windscreen washer - servicing

1 The windscreen washer is of electrically operated type having the pump mounted within the washer fluid reservoir.
2 Keep the reservoir clean and the electrical connections secure, also the washer connecting pipes.
3 Never operate the washer without fluid in the reservoir nor depress the switch for periods in excess of 20 seconds.

39 Horns - adjustment

1 According to vehicle type, the horns may be of vibrator or wind-tone (trumpet) type.
2 To adjust the horn for tone, connect an ammeter in a battery/switch circuit. Loosen the locknut which secures the smaller screw on the back of the horn, switch on the current and turn the adjuster screw in or out until the sound is acceptable with the ammeter reading as specified according to type of horn:

Vibrator type 1.5 to 3.0 amps
Trumpet type 2.5 to 3.5 amps

3 Adjustment of the air gap should only be required if the horn has been dismantled. To do this, release the large locknut and with the horn secured in a vice, apply battery voltage to its terminals. Apply the current intermittently and turn the large adjuster bolt in a clockwise direction until any clicking noise produced by the contacts ceases. From this point unscrew the adjuster bolt in accordance with the following specifications and then tighten the locknut:

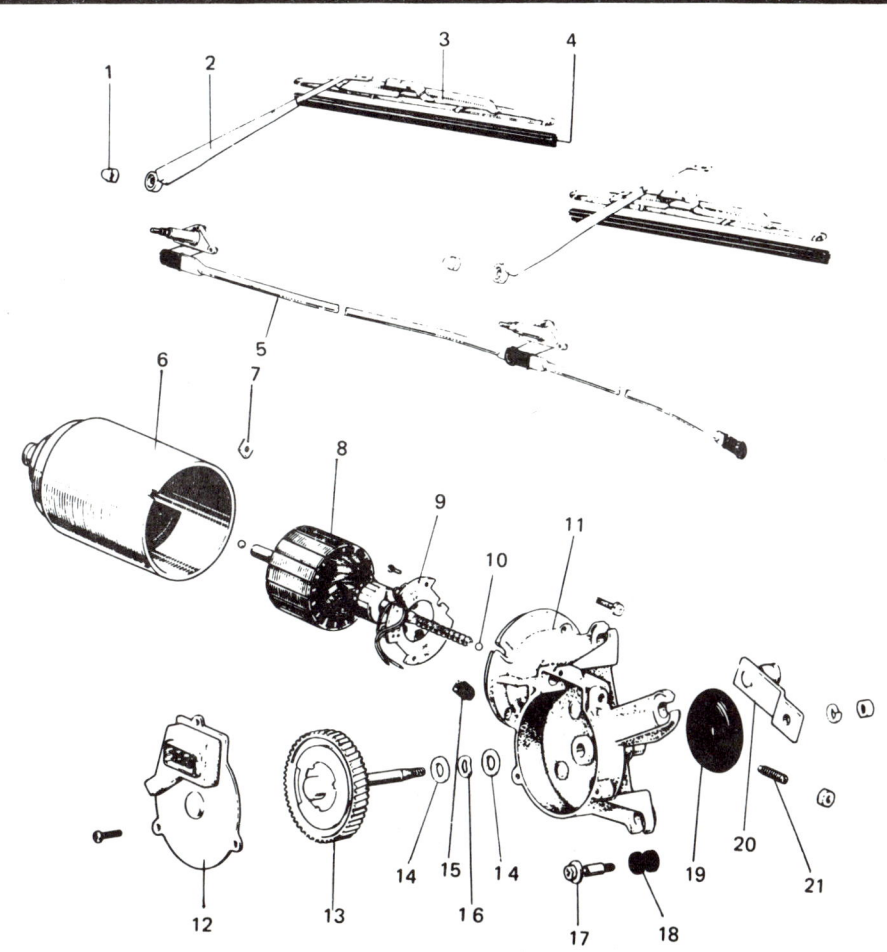

Fig 10.73 Exploded view of later type windscreen wiper assembly (Sec 37)

1 Wiper arm spindle cap nut	6 Stator	12 Gear housing cover plate	17 Bolt
2 Wiper arm	7 Retaining nut		18 Bush
3 Wiper blade	8 Armature	13 Gear/shaft assembly	19 Rubber seat
4 Rubber insert	9 Brush holder	14 Thrust washer	20 Crank
5 Link assembly	10 Thrust ball	15 Grommet	21 Armature thrust adjuster screw
	11 Wiper motor housing	16 Wave washer	

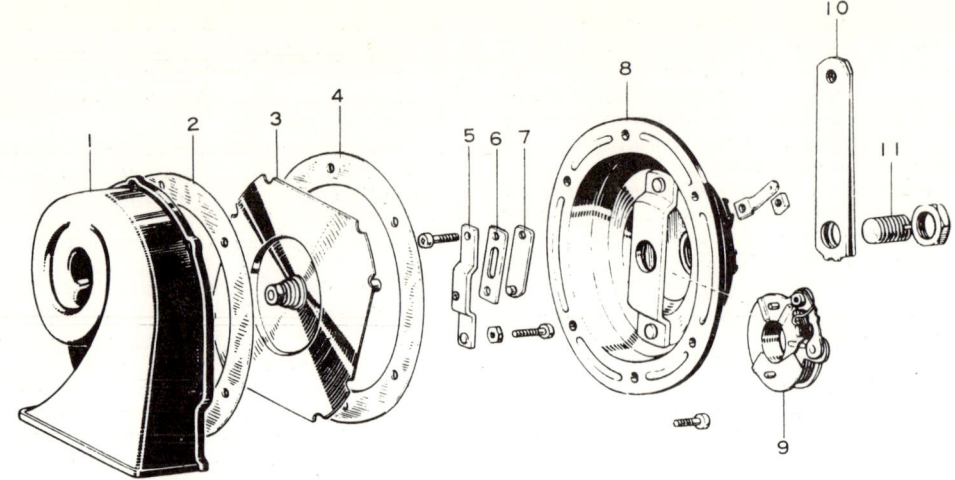

Fig 10.74 Exploded view of trumpet type horn (Sec 39)

1 Trumpet	4 Gasket	7 Point	10 Stay
2 Gasket	5 Bracket	8 Body	11 Adjuster (air gap)
3 Diaphragm	6 Insulator	9 Coil	

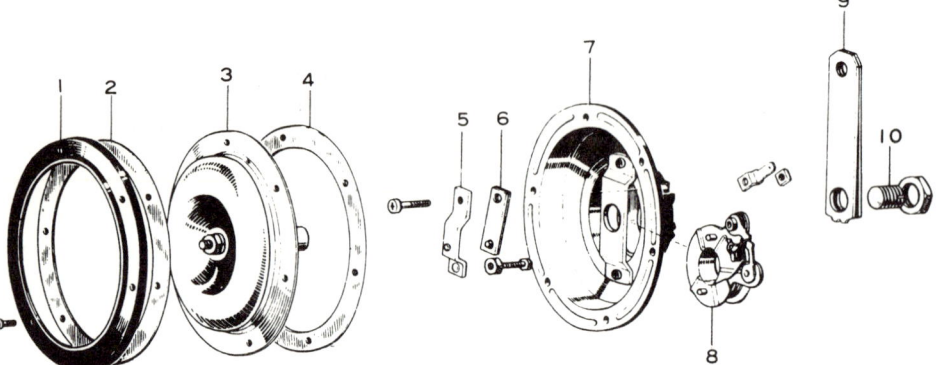

Fig 10.75 Exploded view of vibrator type horn (Sec 39)

1 Cover	4 Gasket	7 Body	9 Stay
2 Gasket	5 Bracket	8 Coil	10 Adjuster (air gap)
3 Diaphragm	6 Insulator		

Fig 10.76 Exploded view of window regulator motor assembly (Sec 42)

1 Rubber cover
2 Motor end frame
3 Brush holder
4 Steel ball
5 Armature
6 Coil
7 Yoke
8 Housing
9 Steel ball
10 Shaft/gear assembly
11 Washer
12 Washer
13 Gasket
14 Cover

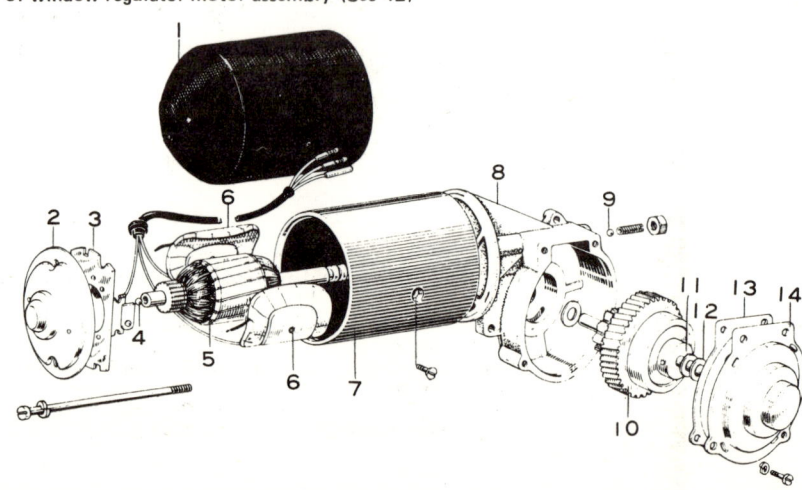

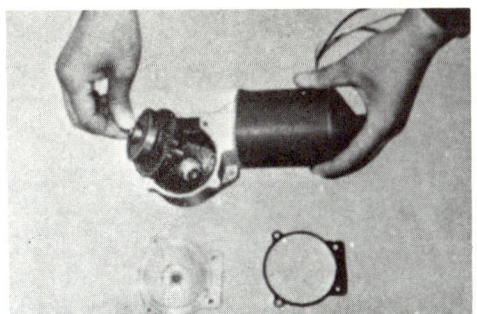

Fig 10.77 Removing the gear assembly from window regulator unit

Number of turns unscrewed of adjuster bolt from air gap closed position

Trumpet horn:
High note 1 1/3
Low note 1 ¾
Vibrator type horn:
High note 7/8
Low note 1

4 Carry out the foregoing air gap closure operation quickly to prevent overheating of the horn coil. Later type trumpet horns have non-adjustable air gaps.

40 Radio and tape players - removal and installation

1 Disconnect the lead from the battery negative terminal.
2 *On early models,* the radio is mounted above the heater/ventilator control unit. Remove the upper and lower cover panels from the facia. The knobs from the control levers of the heater unit will have to be removed before these panels can be detached.
3 Unscrew the three screws which secure the frame of the radio and clock and pull the clock and radio forward until the leads can be disconnected from both conponents and then remove the complete radio/clock unit.
4 The speaker can be removed after the glove compartment has been withdrawn. The aerial is located on the left front wing, access to the aerial mounting being obtainable after the splash shield has been removed from under the wing.
5 *On later model vehicles,* if the radio is mounted in the facia then access to it is obtainable after removal of the instrument panel embellishment. Where it is mounted in the centre console, the radio (and tape player) can be withdrawn after unscrewing the mounting screws and disconnecting the leads.
6 The radio speaker is located at the rear of the instrument panel and the tape player is housed below the parcels tray under the rear window. Remove the rear seat to gain access to the speaker.

41 Rear window demister (early models) - removal

1 Early models were equipped with a blower unit to demist the rear window. This was fitted prior to the installation of heated rear windows as standard equipment.
2 To remove the assembly, lift out the rear seat cushion and back. Remove the rear parcels tray and disconnect the electrical leads from the demister blower.
3 Remove the blower and demister tubes and nozzles from the luggage boot.

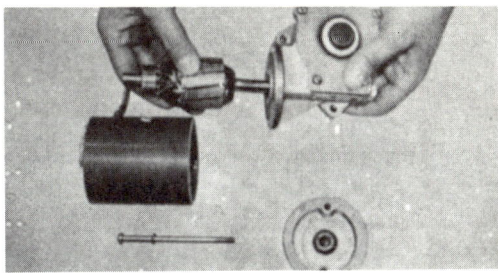

Fig 10.78 Removing the armature from window regulator motor

42 Window regulator motor - servicing

1 Removal and refitting of the power operated window regulator mechanism and motor is covered in Chapter 12.
2 To dismantle the electric motor and gearbox, remove the gear housing cover and extract the gear assembly taking care to retain the shims which are fitted, one to each side of the gearshaft.
3 Remove the rubber cover and end frame, taking care not to lose the ball located at the end of the armature shaft.
4 Withdraw the stator from the gear housing ensuring that the brushes are not damaged in the process.
5 Pull the armature from the gear housing, taking care not to lose the ball at its end.
6 Clean all components and inspect for wear or damage. If the brushes are worn below a length of 0.32 in. (8.0 mm) renew them.
7 Check the armature and field coils for open circuit in a similar manner to that described for the starter motor in Section 15 of this Chapter and service the commutator by identical means.
8 Reassembly is a reversal of dismantling but pack the gear housing with high melting point grease and apply jointing compound between the mating faces of the gear housing and stator, to the wiring grommet sealing edges and to the threads of the gear housing cover securing screws.

43 Seat belt electrical interlock systems

1 Vehicles produced after 1973 for operation in North America are fitted with an elaborate electrical warning and safety interlock system. Bascially if either of the two front seat belts are not fastened, the following actions occur:
(i) *a warning buzzer and lamp actuate if the ignition key is turned to the 'start' position.*
(ii) *the starter will not operate when the key is turned (it will operate if the driver's belt is connected and there is no weight on the front passenger seat, also the inertia belt not in use is fully retracted).*

2 The engine can of course be started for repairs etc. by reaching into the vehicle interior to turn the starter switch. Although the seat belts are not fastened, neither is there any weight on the seats to actuate the interlock switches and so the engine can be started.
3 The system also incorporates a deceleration sensor which locks the inertia type seat belt reels in advance of impact, should a collision occur.
4 Individual components of the system are sealed units and can only be renewed as such. Maintenance should be limited to occasionally checking the security of the connecting wiring, in conjunction with the wiring diagrams provided later in this manual.
5 On vehicles operating in Canada, the system is similar except that there is no starter interlock circuit.

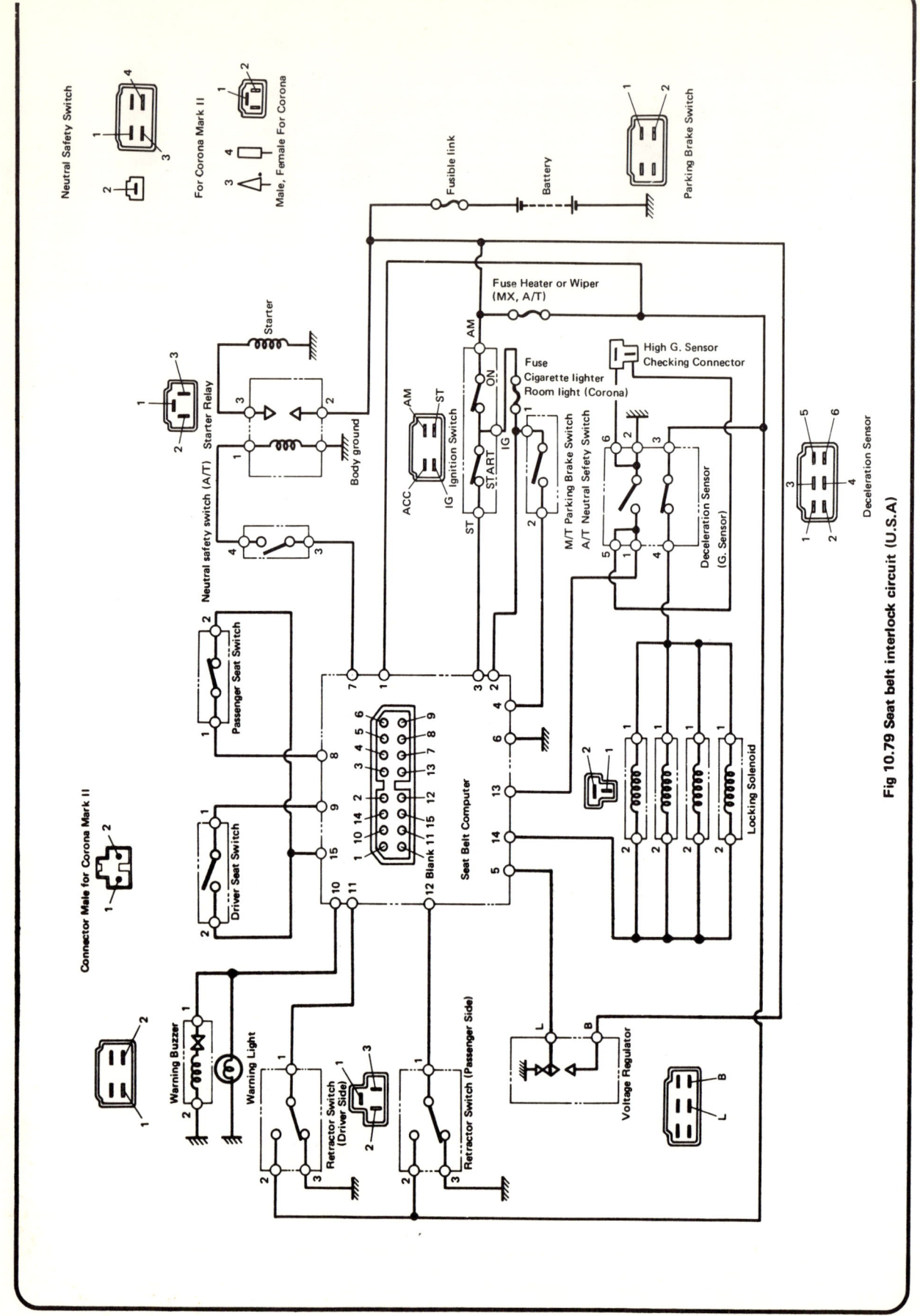

Fig 10.79 Seat belt interlock circuit (U.S.A)

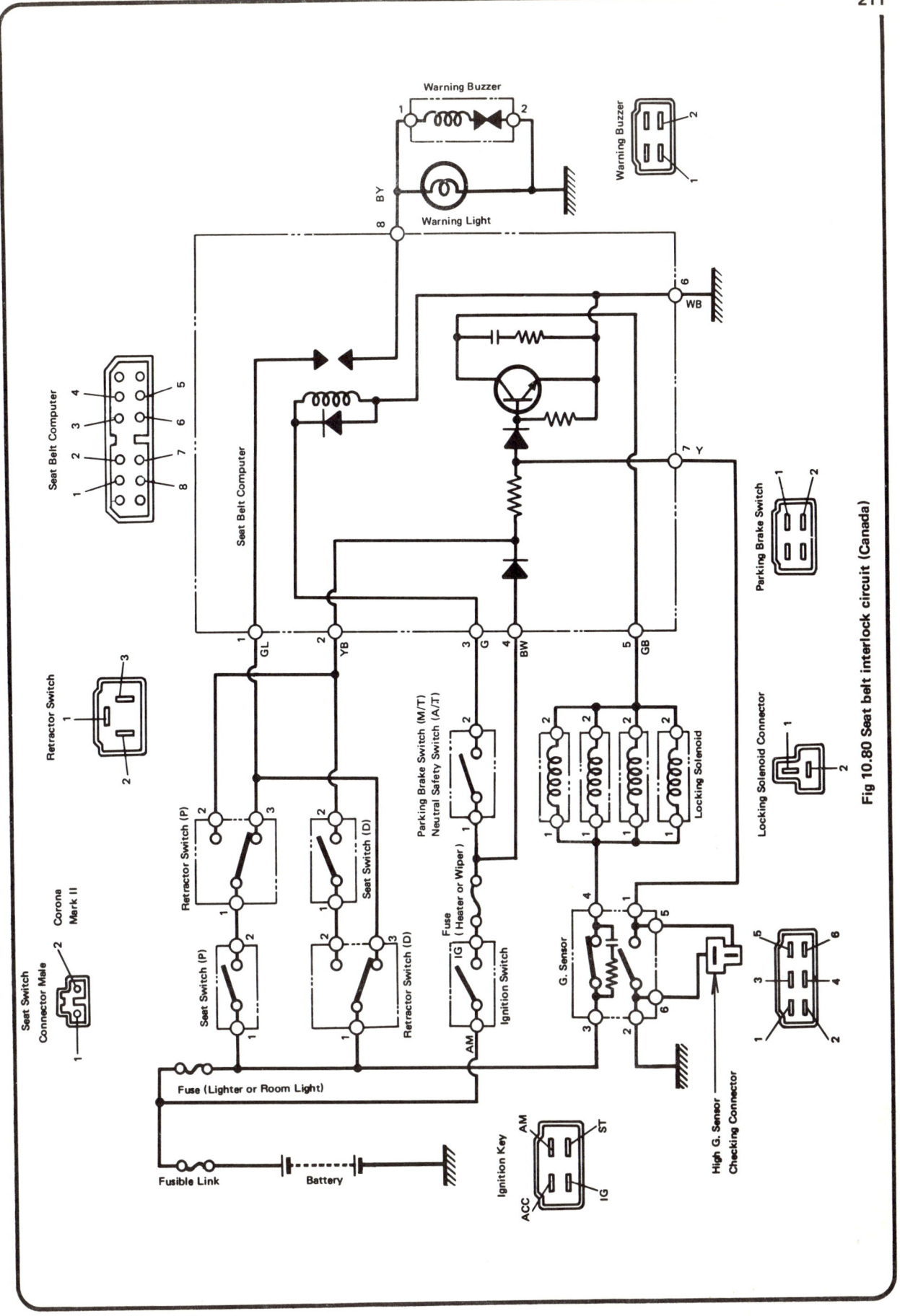

Fig 10.80 Seat belt interlock circuit (Canada)

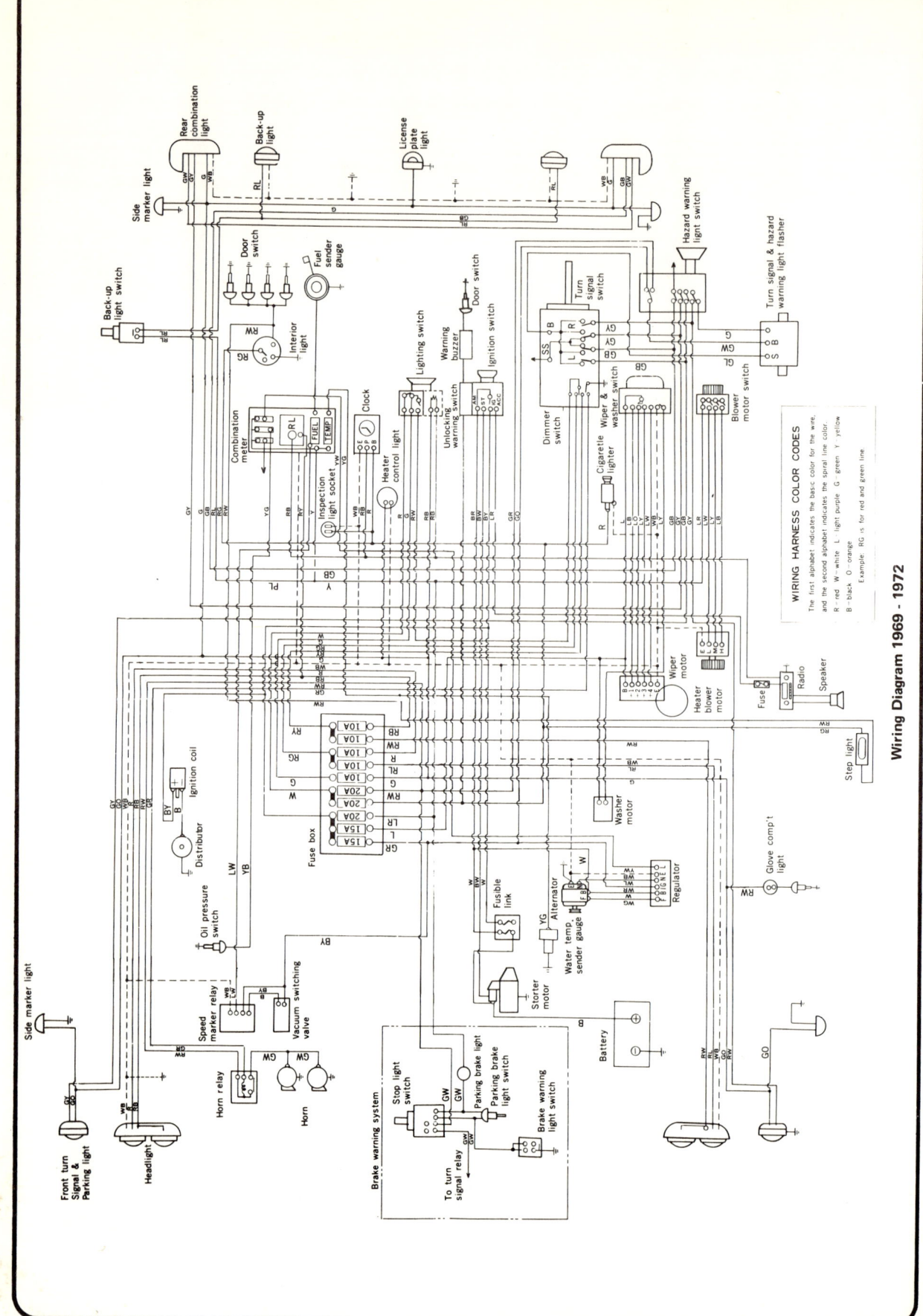

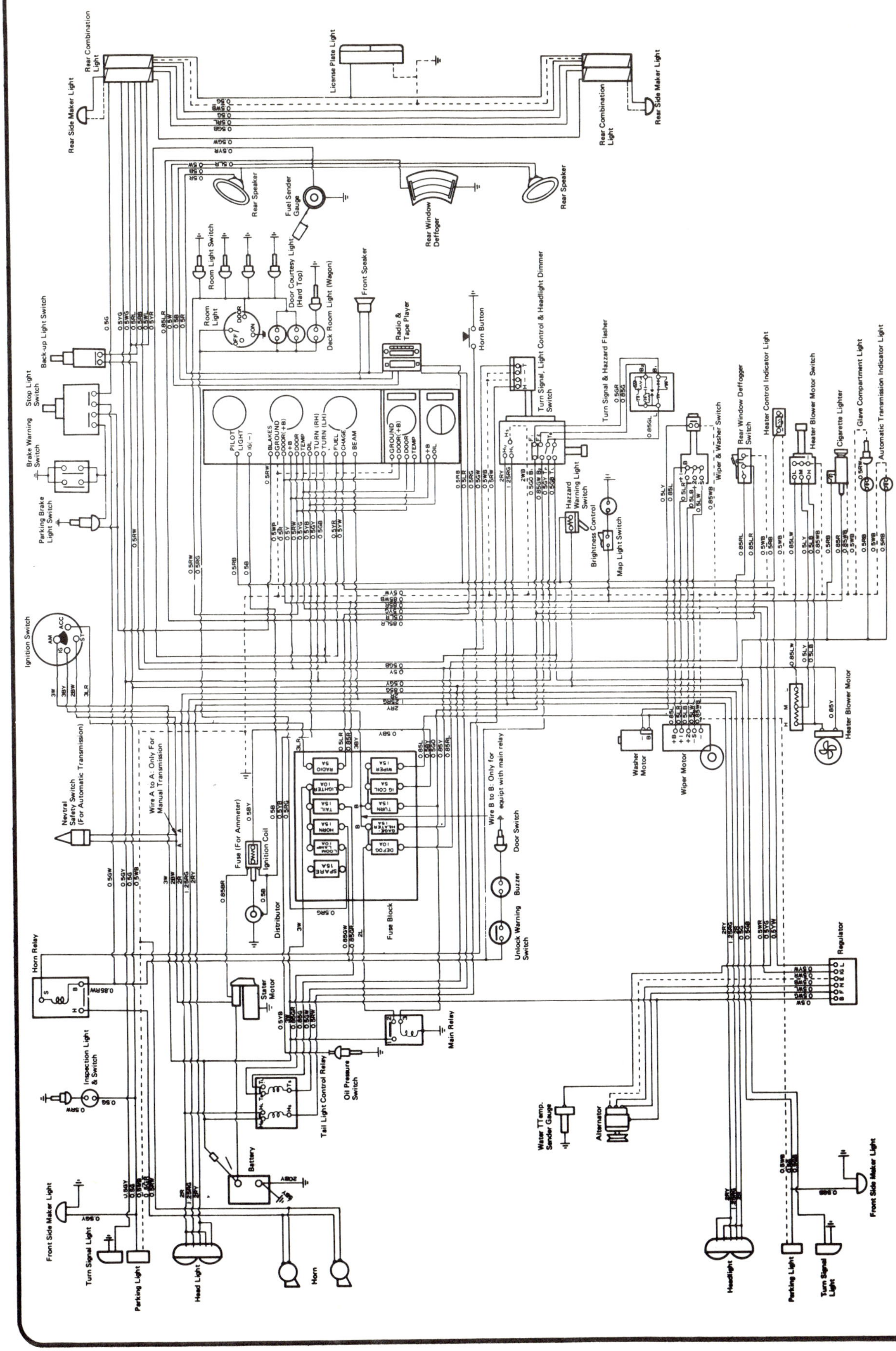

Wiring Diagram 1973 - 1974

44 Fault diagnosis - electrical system

Symptom	Cause
Starter motor fails to turn engine No electricity at starter motor	Battery discharged Battery defective internally Battery terminal leads loose or earth lead not securely attached to body Loose or broken connections in starter motor circuit Starter motor switch or solenoid faulty
Electricity at starter motor: faulty motor	Starter brushes badly worn, sticking or brush wires loose Commutator dirty, worn or burnt Starter motor armature faulty Field coils earthed
Starter motor turns engine very slowly Electrical defects	Battery in discharged condition Starter brushes badly worn, sticking or brush wires loose Loose wires in starter motor circuit
Starter motor operates without turning engine Mechanical damage	Pinion or flywheel gear teeth broken or worn
Starter motor noisy or excessively rough engagement Lack of attention or mechanical damage	Pinion or flywheel gear teeth broken or worn Starter motor retaining bolts loose
Battery will not hold charge for more than a few days Wear or damage	Battery defective internally Electrolyte level too low or electrolyte too weak due to leakage Plate separators no longer fully effective Battery plates severely sulphated
Insufficient current flow to keep battery charged	Battery plates severely sulphated Drive belt slipping Battery terminal connections loose or corroded Alternator not charging Short in lighting circuit causing continual battery drain Regulator unit not working correctly
Ignition light fails to go out, battery runs flat in a few days Alternator not charging (see Section 9 for full test procedure)	Drive belt loose and slipping or broken Brushes worn, sticking, broken or dirty Brush springs weak or broken
Regulator fails to work correctly (see Section 10 for full test procedure)	Regulator incorrectly set Open circuit in wiring of regulator unit

Failure of individual electrical equipment to function correctly is dealt with alphabetically, item-by-item, under the headings listed below:

Horn Horn operates all the time	Horn push either earthed or stuck down Horn cable to horn push earthed
Horn fails to operate	Blown fuse Cable or cable connection loose, broken or disconnected Horn has an internal fault
Horn emits intermittent or unsatisfactory noise	Cable connections loose Horn incorrectly adjusted
Lights Lights do not come on	If engine not running, battery discharged Light bulb filament burnt out or bulbs broken Wire connections loose, disconnected or broken Light switch shorting or otherwise faulty

Chapter 10/Electrical system

Lights come on but fade out	If engine not running battery discharged Light bulb filament burnt out or bulbs or sealed beam units broken Wire connections loose, disconnected or broken Light switch shorting or otherwise faulty
Lights give very poor illumination	Lamp glasses dirty Lamps badly out of adjustment Incorrect bulb with too low wattage fitted Existing bulbs old and badly discoloured
Lights work erratically - flashing on and off, especially over bumps	Battery terminals or earth connection loose Lights not earthing properly Contacts in light switch faulty

Wipers

Wiper motor fails to work	Blown fuse Wire connections loose, disconnected, or broken Brushes badly worn Armature worn or faulty Field coils faulty
Wiper motor works very slowly and takes excessive current	Commutator dirty, greasy or burnt Armature bearings dirty or unaligned Armature badly worn or faulty Armature thrust adjuster screw overtightened
Wiper motor works slowly and takes little current	Brushes badly worn Commutator dirty, greasy or burnt Armature badly worn or faulty

Chapter 11 Suspension and steering

Contents

Fault diagnosis - suspension and steering ... 28	Steering box - removal and installation ... 24
Front crossmember (up to 1973) - removal and installation 12	Steering column (up to 1970) - removal, servicing and installation ... 21
Front hubs - servicing and adjustment ... 5	Steering column (1971 to 1973) - removal, servicing and installation ... 22
Front wheel alignment ... 26	Steering column (1973 onwards) - removal, servicing and installation ... 23
General description ... 1	
Maintenance and inspection ... 2	
Rear coil springs (saloon and hardtop 1973 onwards) - removal and refitting ... 16	Steering linkage - removal and installation ... 19
Rear lateral control rod (saloon and hardtop 1973 onwards) - removal and refitting ... 17	Steering wheel - removal and refitting ... 20
	Stub axle carrier - removal and refitting ... 6
Rear leaf spring (early type) - removal, servicing and refitting ... 14	Suspension lower arm and coil spring (up to 1973) - removal and refitting ... 8
Rear leaf spring (later type) - removal, servicing and refitting ... 15	Suspension lower arm and coil spring (1973 onwards) - removal and refitting ... 10
Rear leaf spring - silencer pad renewal ... 13	Suspension upper arm (up to 1973) - removal and refitting ... 7
Rear upper and lower suspension control links (saloon and hardtop 1973 onwards) - removal and refitting ... 18	Suspension upper arm (1973 onwards) - removal and refitting 9
Shock absorbers - removal, testing and refitting ... 3	Upper and lower suspension arm balljoints - testing and renewal ... 4
Stabiliser bars - removal and installation ... 11	Wheels and tyres ... 27
Steering box - dismantling and reassembly ... 25	

Specifications

Front suspension
Type ... Independent, double wishbone with coil springs, telescopic shock absorbers and stabiliser bar

Rear suspension
Type:
Saloon and hardtop up to 1973 and all estate wagons ... Semi-elliptic leaf springs, with telescopic shock absorbers and stabiliser bar
Saloon and hardtop after 1973 ... Coil springs with links, telescopic shock absorbers and lateral control rod

Steering
Type ... Recirculating ball
Ratio:
  Up to 1973 ... 19.5 to 21.5 : 1
  After 1973 (RHD) ... 19.5 to 21.5 : 1
  After 1973 (LHD) ... 20.0 to 23.5 : 1
Steering wheel diameter ... 15.56 in. (395.0 mm)

Steering angles:	Up to 1970	1970 to 1973	1973 onwards
Castor	10' to 1° (+45' − 15')	20' (± 30')	−40' to 1° 50'
Camber	1° 15' (± 30')	1° 20' (± 30')	−25' to 1° 20'
Toe-in	0.236 to 0.315 in. (6.0 to 8.0 mm)	0.196 to 0.204 in. (4.0 to 6.0 mm)	−0.04 to 0.12 in. (1.0 to 3.0 mm)
Steering axis inclination	6° 45'	6° 55'	7°
Turning circle	31 ft 9 in. (9.6 m)	31 ft 8 in. (9.5 m) estate wagon 32 ft 8 in. (9.8 m)	31 ft 10 in. (9.7 m) estate wagon 32 ft 10 in. (9.9 m)
Wheelbase:			
Saloon	98.8 in. (250.9 cm)	95.7 in. (243.1 cm)	98.4 in. (250.1 cm)
Estate wagon	98.8 in. (250.9 cm)	96.9 in. (246.1 cm)	98.4 in. (250.1 cm)

Chapter 11/Suspension and steering

Tyre size:			
Saloon	6.00 x 13	6.45 x 13 (165 - 13)	6.45 x 14 - 185/70 165 x 14 - B78 - 14
Estate wagon	6.00 x 13	6.45 x 13 (165 - 13)	165 SR14 - B78 - 14
Pressures: Saloon			
Front	22 lb/in^2 (1.6 kg/cm^2)	26 lb/in^2 (1.83 kg/cm^2)	26 lb/in^2 (1.83 kg/cm^2)
Rear	22 lb/in^2 (1.6 kg/cm^2)	26 lb/in^2 (1.83 kg/cm^2)	26 lb/in^2 (1.83 kg/cm^2)
Pressures: Estate			
Front	22 lb/in^2 (1.6 kg/cm^2)	26 lb/in^2 (1.83 kg/cm^2)	26 lb/in^2 (1.83 kg/cm^2)
Rear	26 lb/in^2 (1.83 kg/cm^2)	30 lb/in^2 (2.11 kg/cm^2)	26 lb/in^2 (1.83 kg/cm^2)

Torque wrench settings

	lb/ft	kg/m
Front suspension:		
Hub nut (initial tightening)	20	2.8
Suspension upper arm pivot bushes (up to 1973)	85	11.8
Suspension upper arm pivot shaft bolts (up to 1973)	40	5.5
Suspension lower arm pivot shaft bushes (up to 1973)	85	11.8
Suspension lower arm pivot shaft bushes (up to 1973)	35	4.8
Suspension upper arm pivot bolts (after 1973)	100	13.9
Suspension lower arm pivot bolts (after 1973)	40	5.5
Front crossmember bolts	65	9.0
Upper balljoint to stub axle carrier	35	4.8
Lower balljoint to stub axle carrier	50	6.9
Steering arm to stub axle carrier	50	6.9
Shock absorber upper mounting	22	3.0
Shock absorber lower mounting	15	2.1
Strut to frame (up to 1973)	60	8.3
Strut to suspension lower arm (up to 1973)	50	6.9
Rear suspension:		
Link pivot bolts (saloon/hardtop after 1973)	130	18.0
Lateral control rod bolts (saloon/hardtop after 1973)	60	8.3
Shock absorber upper mounting	22	3.0
Shock absorber lower mounting	15	2.1
'U' bolt nuts:		
Saloon	38	5.3
Estate wagon	60	8.3
Rear shackle pin (leaf spring)	50	6.9
Front eye bolt:		
Saloon (leaf spring)	70	9.7
Estate wagon	30	4.1
Steering:		
Steering wheel nut	22	3.0
Steering column bracket bolts (up to 1973)	22	3.0
Steering column bracket bolts (after 1973)	14	1.9
Wormshaft locking ring	70	9.7
Cover plate bolts (steering box)	15	2.1
Rocker shaft adjuster locknut	22	3.0
Flexible coupling pinch bolt	20	2.8
Steering box to bodyframe bolts	35	4.8
Drop arm nut	100	13.8
Idler arm nut	65	9.0
Idler arm support bracket to bodyframe	35	4.8
Steering linkage balljoints	35	4.8

1 General description

All models in the range have independent front suspension which is of upper and lower wishbone type and incorporates coil springs, double acting telescopic type hydraulic shock absorbers and a stabiliser bar.

The rear suspension on estate wagons is of leaf spring type with hydraulic shock absorbers. This type of rear suspension is also used on saloon and hardtop models up until October 1973. After this date, saloon and hardtop models are equipped with rear suspension of coil spring and link type. All models have a rear stabiliser bar.

The steering gear is of recirculating ball design and later models have a steering column which is of collapsible type.

2 Maintenance and inspection

1 Refer to the Routine Maintenance Section at the front of this manual.
2 Regularly inspect the condition of the balljoint rubber covers for splits or deterioration and renew if necessary. Also check the condition of the rear suspension trailing link bushes for wear and renew the rubber bushes if there is any movement.
3 Check the security of all suspension nuts and bolts, checking particularly those on the balljoints and on the rear road spring 'U' bolts. Tighten them if necessary to the torques specified.
4 Every 24,000 miles (38,000 km) clean and repack the front wheel hub bearings and adjust them as described in this Chapter. At similar mileage intervals, check the front wheel alignment (Section 26).

3 Shock absorbers - removal, testing and refitting

1 The shock absorbers on the sedan and coupe are attached at their lower ends by rubber bushes inside eyes with a pivot bolt. The upper mountings comprise the threaded shock absorber rod, various cushions and washers, a securing nut and locknut.
2 The shock absorbers on the wagon are secured at upper and lower ends by eye type mountings.
3 Removal of both types of shock absorber is simply a matter of removing the attachment nuts or bolts and withdrawing the unit. Do not remove a shock absorber with the vehicle jacked-up and the road wheel hanging free. If working clearance is required always jack-up the car under the coil spring pans or leaf spring 'U' bolt plates in order to keep the springs under compression.
4 To test a shock absorber, grip the lower mounting in a vice with the unit in a vertical position. Extend and contract the shock absorber to the full extent of its travel about ten times. **There should be a definite resistance in both directions**, otherwise renew the unit. Any sign of oil leakage around the operating rod seal will also indicate the need for renewal as the units are not repairable.
5 Refitting is a reversal of removal but tighten the retaining nuts and bolts to the correct torque.

4 Upper and lower suspension arm balljoints - testing and renewal

1 To test for wear in these components, jack-up the front suspension on one side by placing a jack under the coil spring pan.
2 Grip the roadwheel and move it vertically up and down and then in and out in a horizontal direction.
3 Assuming the wheel bearings are correctly adjusted, see Section 5, then there should only be movement in any direction, not exceeding the limits specified.
4 Where excessive wear is found, the balljoints must be renewed.

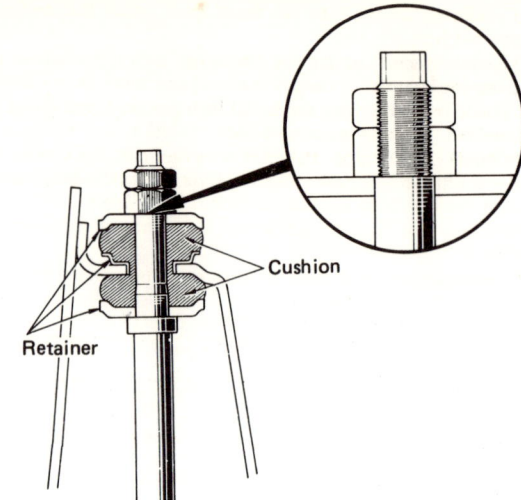

Fig. 11.1 Shock absorber upper mounting (Sec. 3)

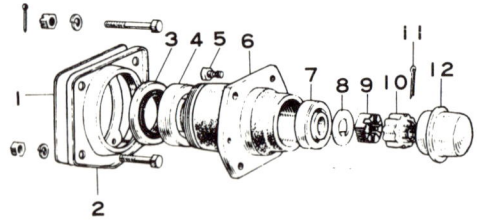

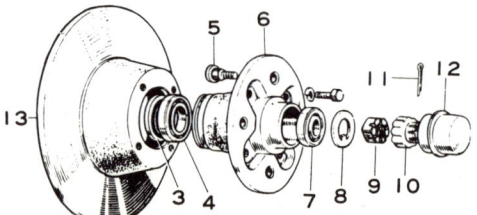

Fig. 11.3 Exploded views of alternative types of front hub assembles (Sec. 5)

1 Gasket
2 Retainer
3 Oil seal
4 Inner bearing
5 Bolt
6 Hub
7 Outer bearing
8 Thrust washer
9 Nut
10 Nut retainer
11 Split pin
12 Grease cap
13 Disc

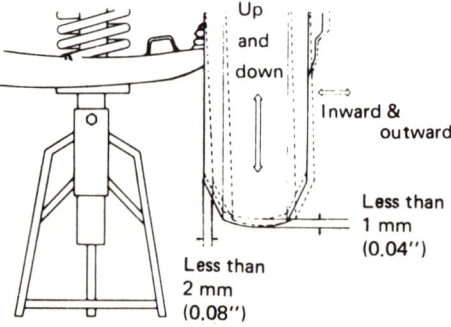

Fig. 11.2 Wear checking diagram for front suspension swivel ball joints (Sec. 4)

Fig. 11.4 Front hub grease packing areas (Sec. 5)

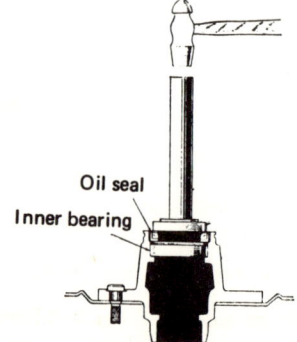

Fig. 11.5 Installing a front hub oil seal (Sec. 5)

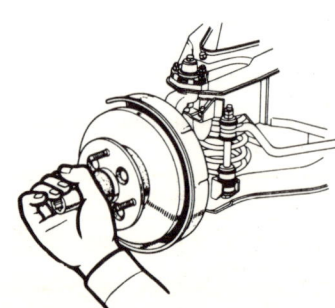

Fig. 11.6 Final adjustment of front hub nut (Sec. 5)

Chapter 11/Suspension and steering

5 The use of a balljoint separator will now be essential as there is no room to attempt to jar them apart using the wedge or hammer method.

6 Unscrew and almost remove the lower balljoint stud nut and using the separator tool detach the balljoint taper stud from the stud axle carrier. Remove the balljoint from the lower wishbone by removing the three securing bolts.

7 Removal of the upper balljoint is carried out in a similar way but do not strain the brake flexible hose once it is detached by allowing the weight of the hub to hang upon it.

8 Refitting the upper and lower balljoints is a reveral of removal.

9 Tighten the balljoint taper stud nuts to the specified tightening torque.

5 Front hubs - servicing and adjustment

1 Jack-up the front of the vehicle and remove the roadwheel.
2 *On vehicles with front drum brakes,* tap off the grease cap, extract the split pin and unscrew and remove the nut, retainer and thrust washer.
3 Pull the hub/drum assembly forward an inch or two and then push it back. This will expose the hub outer bearing which can then be extracted. Now pull the hub/drum assembly straight off the stub axle.
4 *On vehicles with front disc brakes,* removal of the hub/disc assembly is similar to the procedure just described for hub/drum assembles except that the caliper unit must first be unbolted and tied up out of the way. There is no need to disconnect the hydraulic pipe on single cylinder caliper units but on dual cylinder calipers (Girling type) the rigid brake line will have to be disconnected from the caliper.
5 Wash out all old grease from the bearings and hub interior, taking care not to damage the oil seal. Check the bearings and tracks for wear, damage or scoring.
6 If they are in good condition, repack the inside of the hub with grease.
7 If there is evidence of grease seepage onto the discs, drift out the old seal and tap in a new one using a tubular drift.
8 If either the inner or outer bearings require renewal, drift out the tracks with a brass drift and press in the new ones. Where both front hubs are being serviced at the same time, do not mix the bearing components as the race and the track are matched in production.
9 The disc or drum should not be removed from the hub assembly unless they are to be renewed or re-faced as described in Chapter 9.
10 Reassembly is a reversal of dismantling but the bearings must be adjusted in the following way.
11 Tighten the hub nut to 20 lb/ft (2.8 kg/m) rotating the hub at the same time. Unscrew the nut and then tighten it using only the socket gripped in the hand.
12 Check the bearing preload by attaching a spring balance to one of the road wheel studs. The pull required to rotate the hub should be between 0.66 and 1.54 lb (0.3 to 0.7 kg).
13 When adjustment is correct, fit the adjuster cap and insert a new split pin.
14 Fill the grease cap 1/3rd full with grease and knock it into position.
15 On vehicles with dual cylinder type calipers, bleed the brake hydraulic system.
16 Refit the roadwheel and lower the jack.

6 Stub axle carrier - removal and refitting

1 Jack-up the front of the vehicle supporting it securely under the main crossmember.
2 Place a second jack under the lower wishbone of the suspension and raise the jack until the rubber bump stop separates from the crossmember.
3 Remove the hub/drum or hub/disc assembly as described in

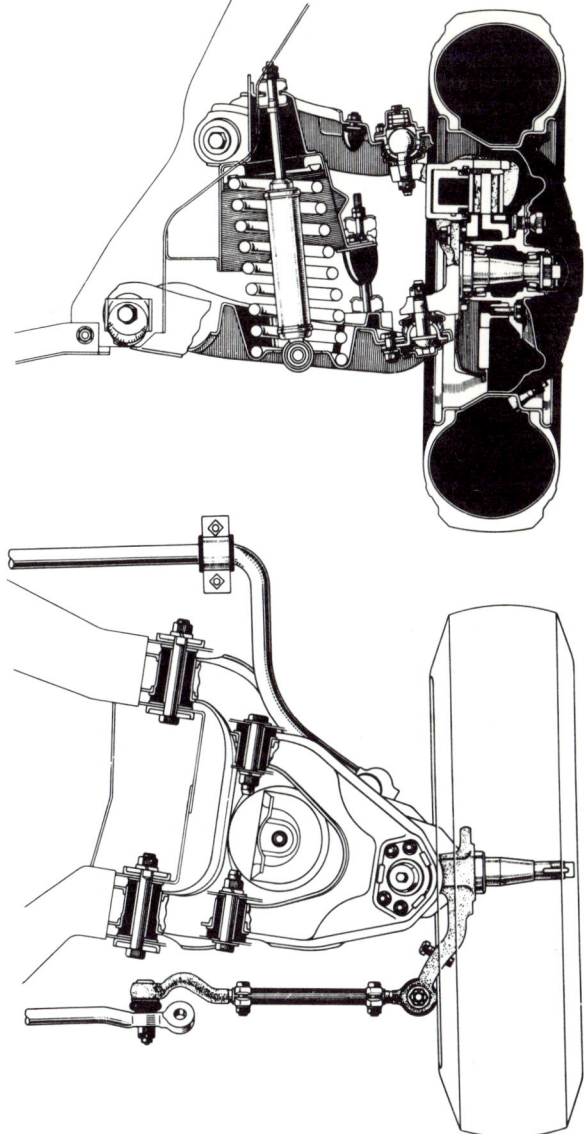

Fig. 11.7 Sectional views of one side of the front suspension (Sec. 6)

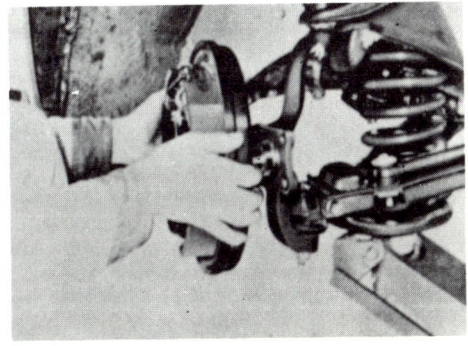

Fig. 11.8 Removing a front drum brake back plate assembly (Sec. 6)

the preceding Section.

4 Unbolt the shield (disc brakes) or the backplate (drum brakes). In the case of the latter, tie it up out of the way to avoid straining the hydraulic flexible hose.

5 Using a balljoint separator, disconnect the trackrod-end from the steering arm of the stub axle carrier.

6 Separate the suspension wishbone upper and lower balljoints and withdraw the stub axle carrier.

7 Refitting is a reversal of removal.

7 Suspension upper arm (up to 1973) - removal and refitting

1 Jack-up the front of the vehicle by placing a jack under the suspension lower arm.

2 Disconnect the upper balljoint from the stub axle carrier.

3 Working within the engine compartment, unscrew the bolts which secure the suspension upper arm pivot.

4 Withdraw the suspension upper arm but note and record the number and position of the shims which are used to set the camber angle and are located behind the pivot bolt holes.

5 If the bushes are worn, unscrew them and screw in new ones tightening them to 85 lb/ft (11.8 kg/m) but making sure that the pivot shaft is centralised in the upper arm by screwing in the bushes an equal amount.

6 Refitting is a reversal of removal but make sure that the shims are installed in their original locations and tighten the pivot bolts to a torque of 40 lb/ft (5.5 kg/m).

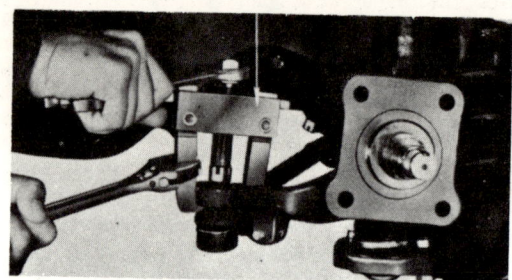

Fig. 11.9 Separating a track rod end ball joint (Sec. 6)

Fig. 11.10 Exploded view of one side of the front suspension and detachable cross member (up to 1973)

1 Pivot bush
2 Seal
3 Pivot shaft
4 Shim (camber angle)
5 Bolt
6 Suspension upper arm
7 Upper ball joint
8 Rubber boot
9 Retainer
10 Rubber bump stop
11 Stub axle carrier
12 Pivot shaft
13 Seal
14 Suspension lower arm
15 Lower ball joint
16 Rubber boot
17 Retainer
18 Retainer
19 Rubber cushion
20 Retainer
21 Rubber bump stop
22 Insulator
23 Spacer
24 Coil spring
25 Retainer
26 Distance piece
27 Rubber cushion
28 Clamp
29 Bracket
30 Rubber bush
31 Stabiliser bar
32 Bolt
33 Bush
34 Rubber cushion
35 Engine mounting bracket
36 Crossmember

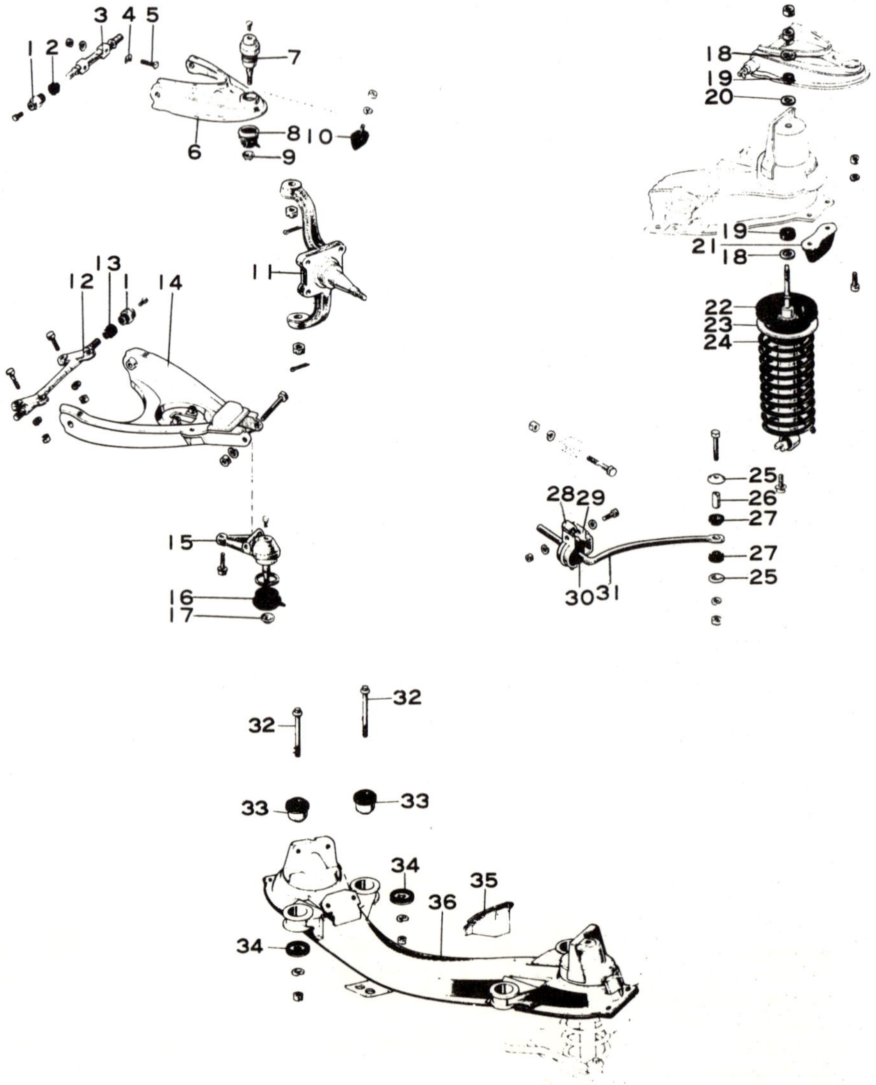

Chapter 11/Suspension and steering

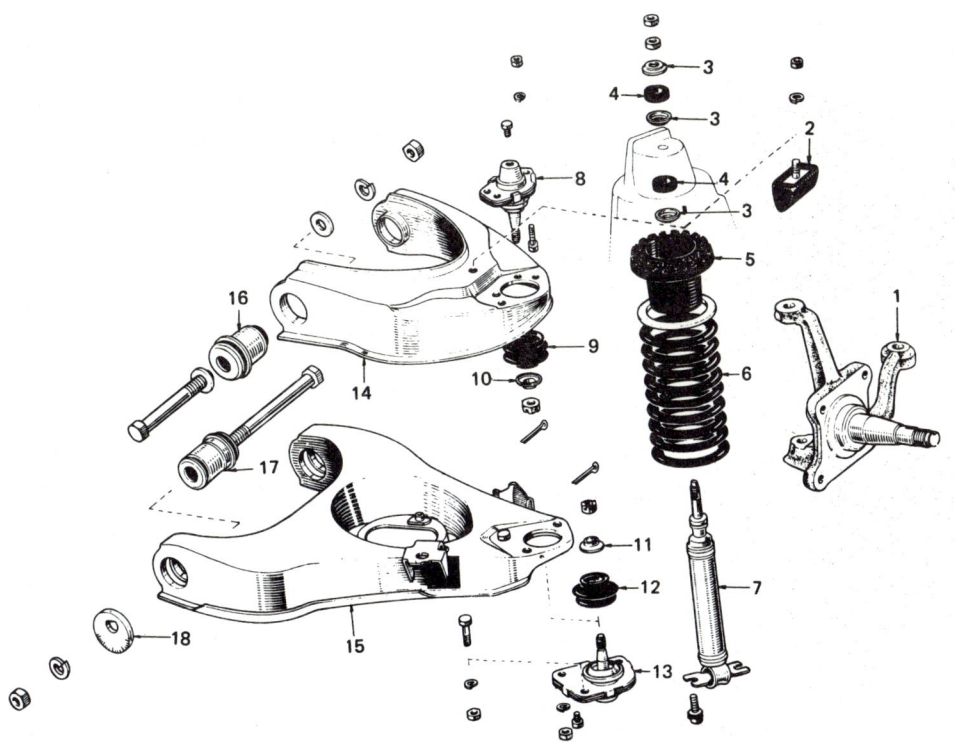

Fig. 11.11 Exploded view of one side of the front suspension (1973 onwards)

1 Stub axle carrier
2 Bump stop
3 Retainer
4 Rubber bush
5 Insulator
6 Coil spring
7 Shock absorber
8 Upper ball joint
9 Rubber boot
10 Retainer
11 Collar
12 Rubber boot
13 Lower ball joint
14 Suspension
15 Suspension lower arm
16 Pivot bush
17 Pivot bush
18 Eccentric cam plate

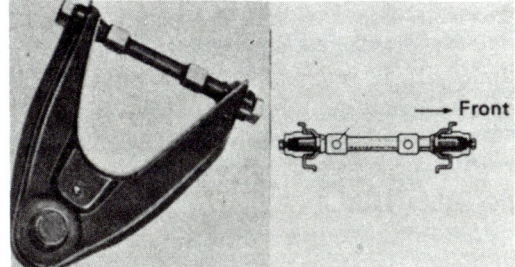

Fig. 11.12 Pivot shaft assembly diagram (up to 1973) (Sec. 7)

Fig. 11.13 Coil spring compressor installed in place of front shock absorber (Sec. 8)

8 Suspension lower arm and coil spring (up to 1973) - removal and refitting

1 Jack-up the front of the vehicle and support it securely under the front crossmember. Remove the roadwheel.
2 Remove the shock absorber and substitute a spring compressor. This can easily be made from a length of studding, two cross plates and nuts.
3 Compress the road spring until the bottom coil is no longer in contact with the spring pan of the lower arm. Disconnect the stabiliser bar from the lower arm. On very early models, remove the struts, having first measured their installed length.
4 Disconnect the lower balljoint and lower the suspension arm.
5 Remove the coil spring after releasing the compressor.
6 Unbolt the lower suspension arm pivot from the crossmember and remove the crossmember.
7 If the pivot bushes are worn, unscrew them and renew them.
8 Screw in the new bushes to a torque of 85 lb/ft (11.8 kg/m) making sure that the pivot shaft is centralised by screwing in the bushes equally from both ends.
9 Commence reassembly by bolting the pivot shaft to the crossmember. (Torque 35 lb/ft - 4.8 kg/m).
10 Install the coil spring so that it fits correctly in the upper insulator and then compress it using the spring compressor.
11 Jack-up the lower arm and connect the balljoint to the stub axle carrier.
12 Connect the stabiliser to the lower arm and do not overtighten the nut or locknut. On early models refit the strut, setting it to the specified installed length.
13 Remove the coil spring compressor making sure that the

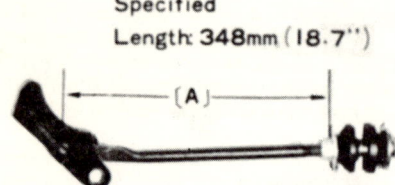

Fig. 11.14 Strut installation setting diagram (early front suspension)

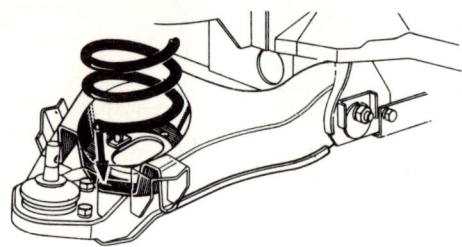

Fig. 11.15 Correct location of coil spring in lower spring pan (front suspension after 1973) (Sec. 10)

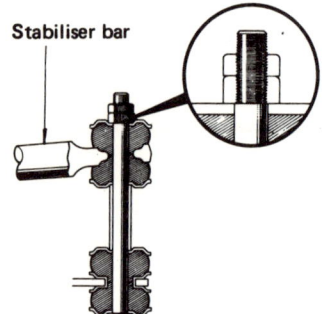

Fig. 11.16 Stabiliser bar end fitting nut tightening diagram (Sec. 11)

bottom coil locates correctly in the lower arm pan.
14 Fit the shock absorber and roadwheel and lower the vehicle to the ground.

9 Suspension upper arm (1973 onwards) - removal and refitting

1 Working from within the engine compartment unscrew and remove the suspension upper arm securing nuts **but do not attempt to knock out the pivot bolts** at this stage.
2 Jack-up the front of the vehicle and then place an axle stand under the suspension lower arm so that the coil spring is under compression. Remove the roadwheel.
3 If a brake pad wear warning sensor is fitted, detach the cable clamp from the suspension upper arm.
4 Disconnect the upper balljoint and support the brake hydraulic hose to prevent it from being strained.
5 Extract the suspension upper arm bolts and lever the arm from its location.
6 If the suspension arm bushes have deteriorated, they must be renewed by a service station which has the necessary press and guide tools.
7 The suspension upper arms are handed left and right and are not interchangeable.
8 Refitting is a reversal of removal but the arm will have to be tapped into position between the bodyframe mountings.
9 Insert the pivot bolts but only tighten the nuts finger-tight at this stage.
10 Reconnect the upper balljoint to the stub axle carrier.
11 Refit the roadwheel, lower the vehicle to the ground and then rock it on its suspension several times before tightening the pivot bolts to a torque of 100 lb/ft (13.9 kg/m).
12 Check the front wheel alignment as described in Section 26 of this Chapter.

10 Suspension lower arm and coil spring (1973 onwards) - removal and refitting

1 Jack-up the front of the vehicle, supporting it securely under the front crossmember.
2 Remove the roadwheel.
3 Remove the shock absorber by disconnecting the upper and lower mountings.
4 Disconnect the stabiliser bar from the suspension lower arm.
5 A coil spring compressor will now be required. One may be made up if necessary from a length of studding, cross plates and nuts. Compress the coil spring so that its bottom coil is no longer in contact with the suspension lower arm spring pan (see Fig. 11.13).
6 Support the suspension lower arm on a jack and then disconnect the lower balljoint from the stub axle carrier.
7 Unscrew the nuts from the pivot bolts, remove the cam plates, noting carefully the setting of each cam plate index.
8 Tap out the pivot bolts and withdraw the suspension lower arm.
9 Carefully release the coil spring compressor and remove the coil spring.
10 If the suspension arm bushes have deteriorated, they must be renewed by a service station having the necessary press and guide tools.
11 Commence reassembly by offering up the suspension lower arm to the bodyframe and inserting the pivot bolts.
12 Fit the cam plates and screw on the nuts only finger tight.
13 Install the coil spring so that it fits correctly in the upper insulator and then compress it using the spring compressor.
14 Jack-up the lower arm and using a piece of wood, prise the coil spring (lower coil) into its pan so that the end of its coil is correctly located.
15 Connect the lower balljoint to the stub axle carrier.
16 Connect the stabiliser bar to the lower arm. Do not over-tighten the securing nut or locknut.
17 Remove the coil spring compressor and refit the shock absorber.
18 Refit the roadwheel and lower the vehicle to the ground.
19 Rock the vehicle on its suspension several times and then turn the cam plates to their original settings and tighten the pivot bolts to the specified torque setting.

11 Stabiliser bars - removal and installation

1 The procedure for front and rear bars is similar. Disconnect the end attachments and then the brackets and rubber insulator which secure the stabiliser bar to the bodyframe.
2 Installation is a reversal of removal but do not over compress the end fitting nuts or locknuts.

12 Front crossmember (up to 1973) - removal and installation

1 On these models, the crossmember is of bolt on type. Raise the front of the vehicle and support the bodyframe on stands. Remove the two front roadwheels.
2 Unscrew and remove the bolts which secure both engine front mountings to the crossmember.
3 Disconnect the hydraulic pipe which runs from the brake circuit 3-way union to the wheel cylinders.
4 Remove the drop arm from the steering shaft and unbolt the steering idler assembly.

Chapter 11/Suspension and steering

5 Using a hoist and slings or chains, raise the engine slightly.
6 Locate a jack (preferably trolley type) under the centre of the front crossmember and then unbolt the crossmember (four bolts), lower the jack slightly and remove the complete front suspension assembly.
7 Installation is a reversal of removal. Tighten the crossmember bolts to the specified torque and bleed the brake hydraulic system.

13 Rear leaf spring - silencer pad renewal

1 Jack-up the rear of the vehicle and support the bodyframe on stands or blocks.
2 Place a second jack under the differential housing and raise it until any downward pressure caused by the weight of the rear axle is removed from the road springs.
3 Prise up the two ends of the rivetted clip and then separate the leaves by driving in a cold chisel.
4 Extract the silencer pad and fit the new one, noting that the side with the projection faces downwards.
5 Remove the chisel, bend down the ends of the clip and remove the jacks.

14 Rear leaf spring (early type) removal, servicing and refitting

1 Jack-up the rear of the vehicle by placing the jack under the differential housing. Support the body frame with stands and then remove the roadwheels.
2 Remove the road spring 'U' bolt retaining nuts and detach the retaining plate and rubber insulating pad. Detach the handbrake cable clamp from its support plate.
3 Jack-up the differential until the leaf springs are relieved of the weight of the rear axle and then remove the 'U' bolts.
4 Remove the shackle bolt from the spring rear eye and the bracket bolt from the front eye and remove the road spring.
5 Scrub the spring clean in a paraffin bath using a wire brush. Examine each leaf edge throughout its length for cracks. If a crack or broken leaf is found, do not attempt to dismantle it by removing the centre bolt or rivetted clips but either exchange it for a new unit or have it professionally repaired by the insertion of a new leaf.
6 The spring eye bushes are of the split rubber type and should be renewed if perished or worn, no press is required but a little hydraulic brake fluid will assist in fitting them into the spring eyes.
7 Refitting should commence by connecting the front eye bolt followed by the rear shackle bolt; tighten the nuts only finger tight. Note that the shorter length of the spring (eye to centre bolt) is located to the front of the rear axle.
8 Fit the insulating pads and retainers to the spring and then lower the jack under the rear axle ensuring that the spring centre bolt engages in its locating hole in the rear axle mounting plate.
9 Fit the 'U' bolts and their nuts finger tight.
10 Reconnect the handbrake cable clamps and then fit the roadwheels and remove the support stands and lower the vehicle to the ground.
11 Bounce the vehicle up and down several times to settle the suspension and then tighten the nuts to the specified torque settings.
12 During the period when the rear road springs are removed from the rear axle, the axle must not be moved rearwards otherwise the sliding sleeve of the propeller shaft may become disconnected and the rear flexible brake hose may be strained and damaged.

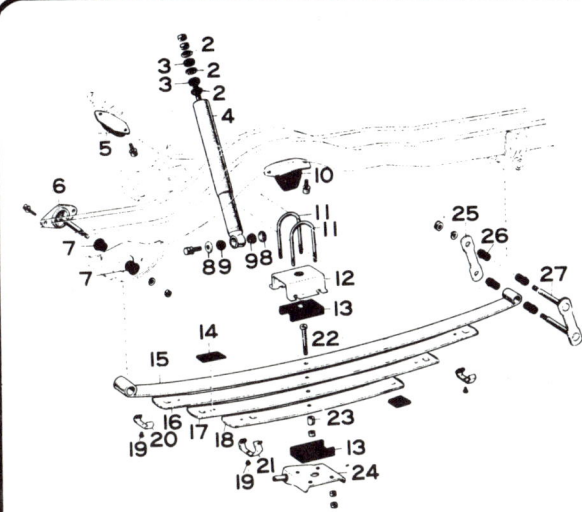

Fig. 11.17 Rear leaf spring components (saloon and hardtop) (Sec. 13)

2	Retainer
3	Rubber cushion
4	Shock absorber
5	Bump stop
6	Bracket bolt
7	Bush
8	Washer
9	Rubber bush
10	Bump stop
11	U bolt
12	Retainer
13	Rubber pad
14	Silencer pad
15, 16, 17, 18	Spring leaves
19	Rivet
20	Clip
21	Clip
22	Centre bolt
23	Spacer
24	Shackle plate
26	Bush
27	Shackle pin assembly

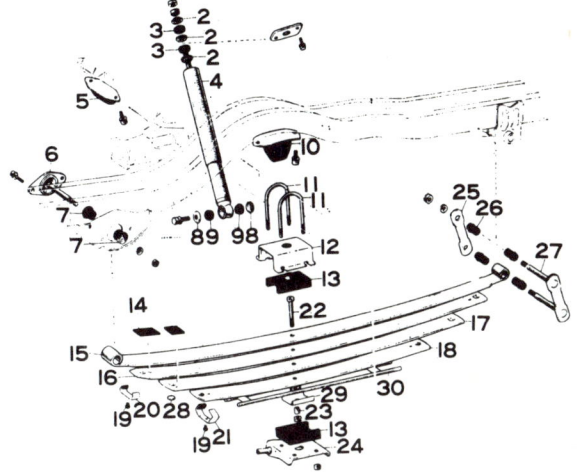

Fig. 11.18 Rear leaf spring components (estate wagon) (Sec. 13)

2	Retainer
3	Rubber cushion
4	Shock absorber
5	Bump stop
6	Bracket bolt
7	Bush
8	Washer
9	Rubber bush
10	Bump stop
11	U bolt
12	Retainer
13	Rubber pad
14	Silencer pad
15, 16, 17, 18	Spring leaves
19	Rivet
20	Clip
21	Clip
22	Centre bolt
23	Spacer
24	Shackle plate
26	Bush
27	Shackle pin assembly
28	Silencer pad
29	Spacer
30	Helper

15 Rear leaf spring (later type) - removal, servicing and refitting

1 A rear stabiliser bar is fitted to later models and this has made necessary a change in design of some rear spring components.
2 The operations described in the preceding Section will however apply after removal of the stabiliser bar.

16 Rear coil springs (saloon and hardtop 1973 onwards) - removal and refitting

1 Jack-up the rear of the vehicle by placing the jack under the rear axle differential housing.
2 Support the bodyframe and remove the road wheels.
3 Disconnect the shock absorber lower mountings.
4 Lower the jack located under the differential until the coil springs can be removed complete with rubber insulators from their pans in the lower control links.
5 Refitting a coil spring is a reversal of removal.

17 Rear lateral control rod (saloon and hardtop 1973 onwards) - removal and refitting

1 Jack-up the rear of the vehicle under the differential housing.

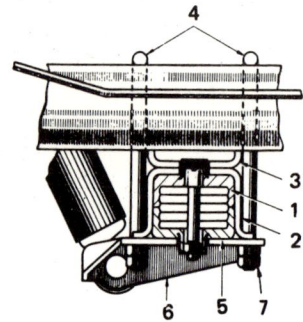

Fig. 11.19 Sectional view of rear spring anchorage (Sec. 14)

1 Rubber pad
2 Retainer
3 Rear axle housing
4 'U' bolts
5 Rubber pad
6 Seat
7 Nuts

Support the bodyframe and then disconnect the left-hand shock absorber lower mounting.
2 Disconnect the mounting bolts from both ends of the lateral control rod and remove the rod.
3 If the bushes are worn they should be renewed at a service station having suitable pressing equipment.
4 Refitting is a reversal of removal but finally tighten the mounting bolts to the specified torques with the weight of the vehicle on the suspension after it has been lowered to the ground.

18 Rear upper and lower suspension control links (saloon and hardtop 1973 onwards) - removal and refitting

1 Raise the rear of the vehicle by placing a jack under the rear axle differential housing. Support the bodyframe on stands, leave the jack in position.
2 Detach the pivot bolts from both ends of the upper control link and remove the link.
3 To remove the lower control link, lower the jack under the differential until the coil spring is under only very little compression. Before removing a left-hand link, detach the handbrake cable clamp.
4 Remove the pivot bolt from each end of the lower control link and remove the link.
5 Should the rubber bonded bushes in either the upper or lower control links require renewal this should be left to a service station having the necessary pressing equipment.
6 Refitting is a reversal of removal and all pivot bolts should be finally tightened with the weight of the vehicle on the suspension (after it has been lowered to the ground).

19 Steering linkage - removal and installation

1 The steering linkage on all models is similar although the design of some components differs in detail. Late models (after 1973) have steering arms which are integral with the stub axle carrier whereas earlier models have detachable ones.
2 Before dismantling the steering linkage it is essential to obtain a balljoint separator. This may be of screw type or consist of a pair of wedges. It is possible to jar the balljoint taper pin free from its eye by striking opposite sides of the eye simultaneously with two club hammers but the available space to do this is very restricted and the use of a proper extractor is recommended.
3 Unscrew and remove the nut which secures the drop arm to the shaft of the steering gear.
4 Using a suitable extractor, draw the drop arm from the

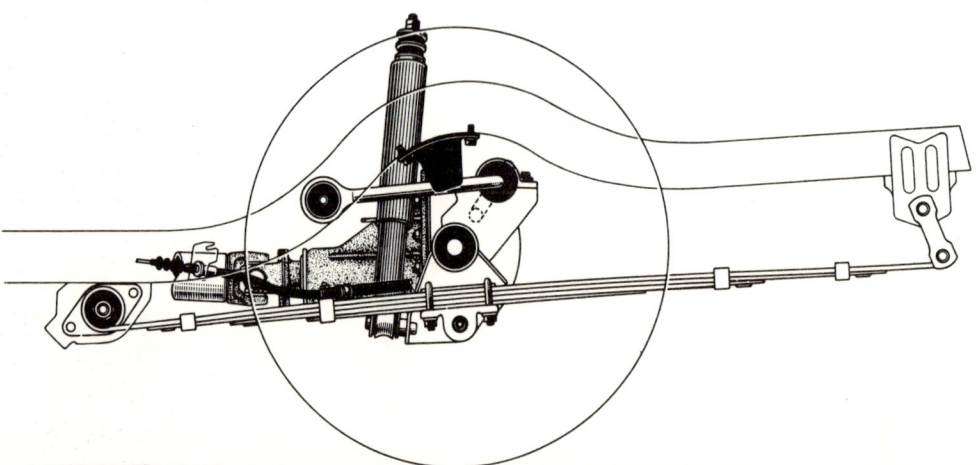

Fig. 11.20 Rear leaf spring assembly with stabiliser bar (Sec. 15)

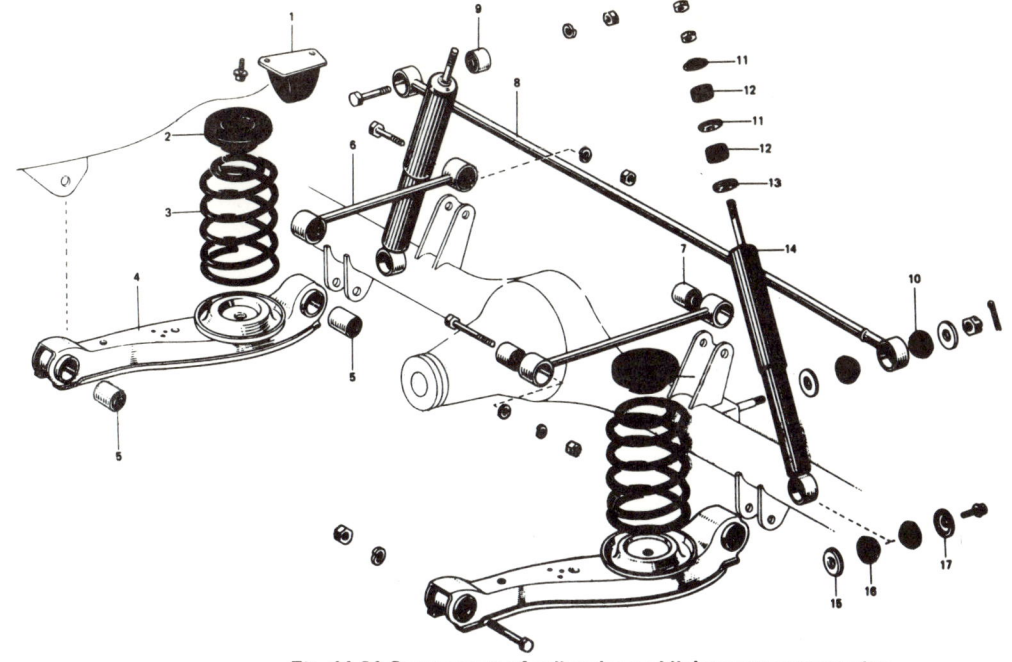

Fig. 11.21 Components of coil spring and link type rear suspension (saloon and hardtop 1973 onwards) (Sec. 16)

1 Rebound stop
2 Coil spring rubber insulator
3 Road spring
4 Lower link
5 Bush
6 Upper link
7 Bush
8 Lateral control rod
9 Bush
10 Rubber split cone type bush
11 Washer
12 Rubber cushion
13 Washer
14 Rear shock absorber
15 Washer
16 Bush
17 Washer

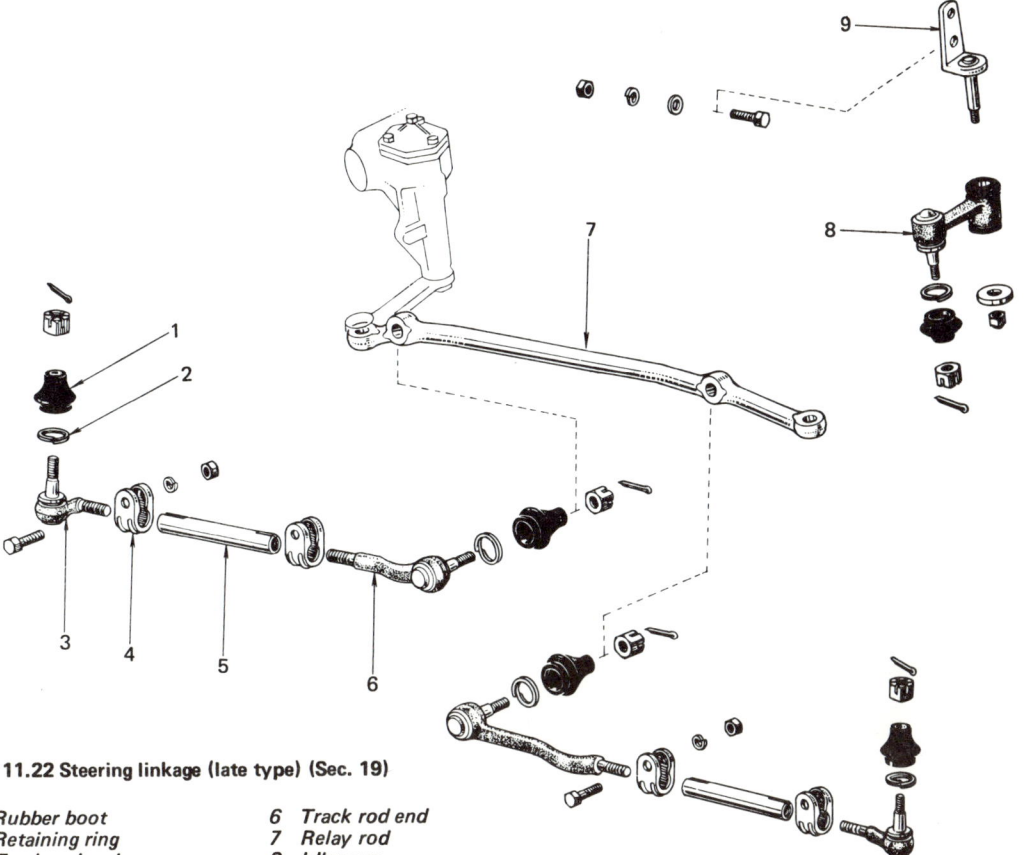

Fig. 11.22 Steering linkage (late type) (Sec. 19)

1 Rubber boot
2 Retaining ring
3 Track rod end
4 Clamp
5 Track rod
6 Track rod end
7 Relay rod
8 Idler arm
9 Idler support

splined shaft.
5 Unbolt the idler arm bracket.
6 Using a balljoint separator, disconnect the track rod ends from the steering arms of the stub axle carriers.
7 Withdraw the complete steering linkage.
8 The individual components of the linkage may be separated using the balljoint separator and loosening the trackrod clamps.
9 Check each balljoint for slackness or excessive stiffness, also for split or deteriorated rubber dust excluders and renew as necessary. Check the idler arm bushes.
10 When fitting a balljoint dust cover, pack the interior with multi-purpose grease.
11 Reassembly is a reversal of dismantling but observe the following points:
12 Fit the idler arm to the support so that it conforms to the specified setting angle according to date of vehicle manufacture. Tighten the self-locking nut to the specified torque without altering the setting.
13 Screw the trackrod-ends into their tubes by an equal amount.
14 Refit the drop arm so that the mating marks are in alignment.
15 When refitting of the linkage is complete, check and adjust the front wheel alignment as described in Section 26.

20 Steering wheel - removal and refitting

1 Access to the steering wheel securing nut is obtained by various means according to the particular type of horn button and steering wheel design. Disconnect the battery negative lead.
2 On some early models, depress the central horn button and turn it anticlockwise.
3 With other types, disconnect the wiring harness at the connector plug under the instrument panel and then using a screwdriver prise off the pad in an upward direction.
4 On later models, the horn pad is secured with screws which are accessible from the rear of the steering wheel spokes.

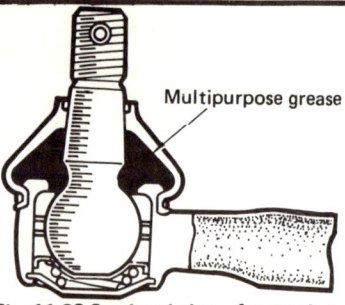

Fig. 11.23 Sectional view of a steering linkage balljoint (Sec. 19)

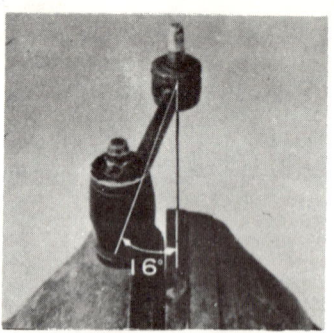

Fig. 11.24 Idler arm to support bracket setting diagram (up to 1972) (Sec. 19)

Fig. 11.25 Idler arm to support bracket setting diagram (1972 to 1973) (Sec. 19)

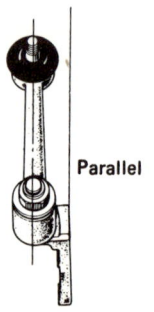

Fig. 11.26 Idler arm to support bracket setting diagram (1973 onwards) (Sec. 19)

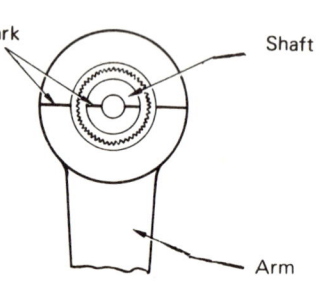

Fig. 11.27 Drop arm to steering box rocker shaft alignment (Sec. 19)

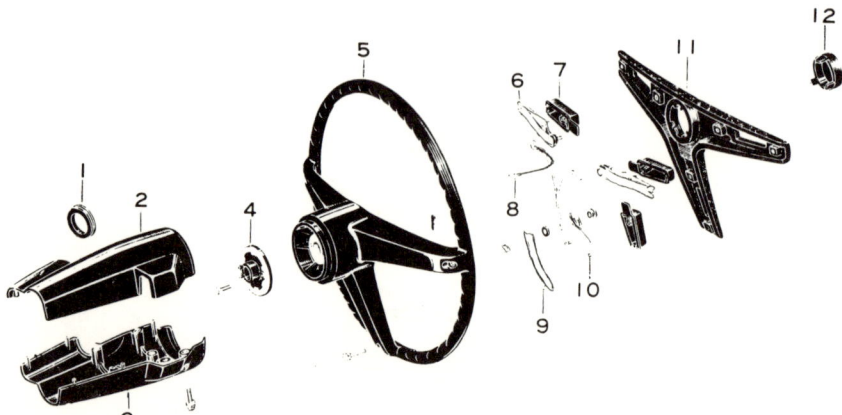

Fig. 11.28 Steering wheel assembly (1973) (Sec. 20)

1 Ring	4 Retainer	7 Horn button	10 Horn button contact plate spring
2 Upper shroud	5 Steering wheel	8 Cable	11 Crash pad
3 Lower shroud	6 Horn contact plate	9 Horn button contact plate	12 Badge

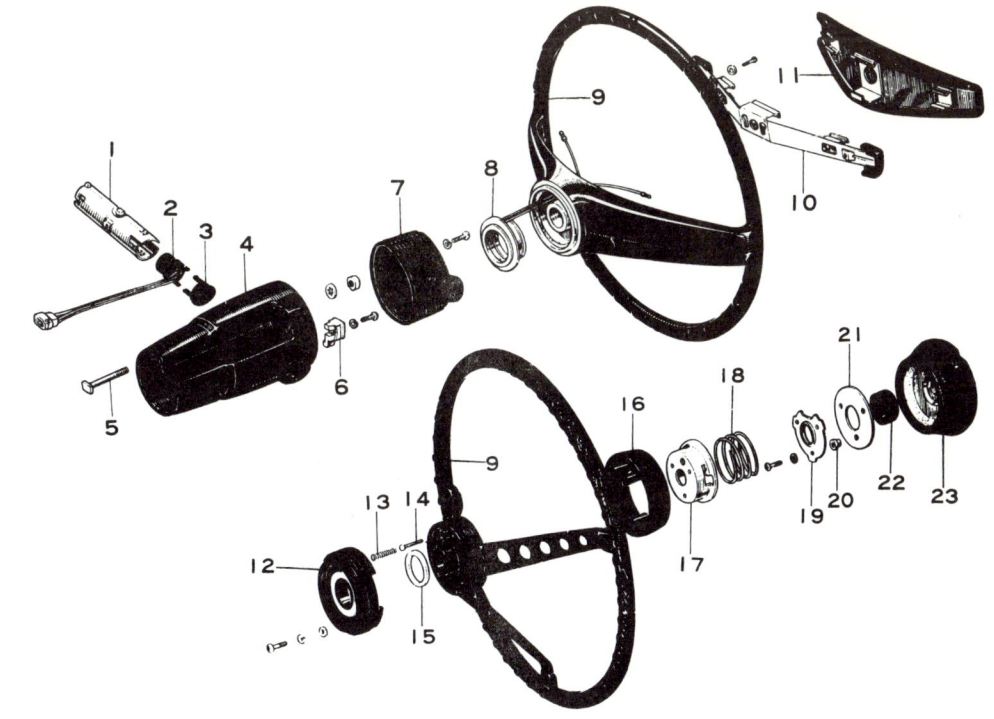

Fig. 11.29 Types of steering wheel assemblies (up to 1973) (Sec. 20)

1 Steering column lock
2 Ignition switch
3 Cover
4 Shroud
5 Bolt
6 Bracket
7 Windscreen wiper switch housing
8 Horn button contact ring
9 Steering wheel
10 Horn contact plate
11 Crash pad
12 Lower cover
13 Spring
14 Pin
15 Gasket
16 Upper cover
17 Seat
18 Spring
19 Stop plate
20 Washer
21 Contact plate
22 Cushion
23 Horn button

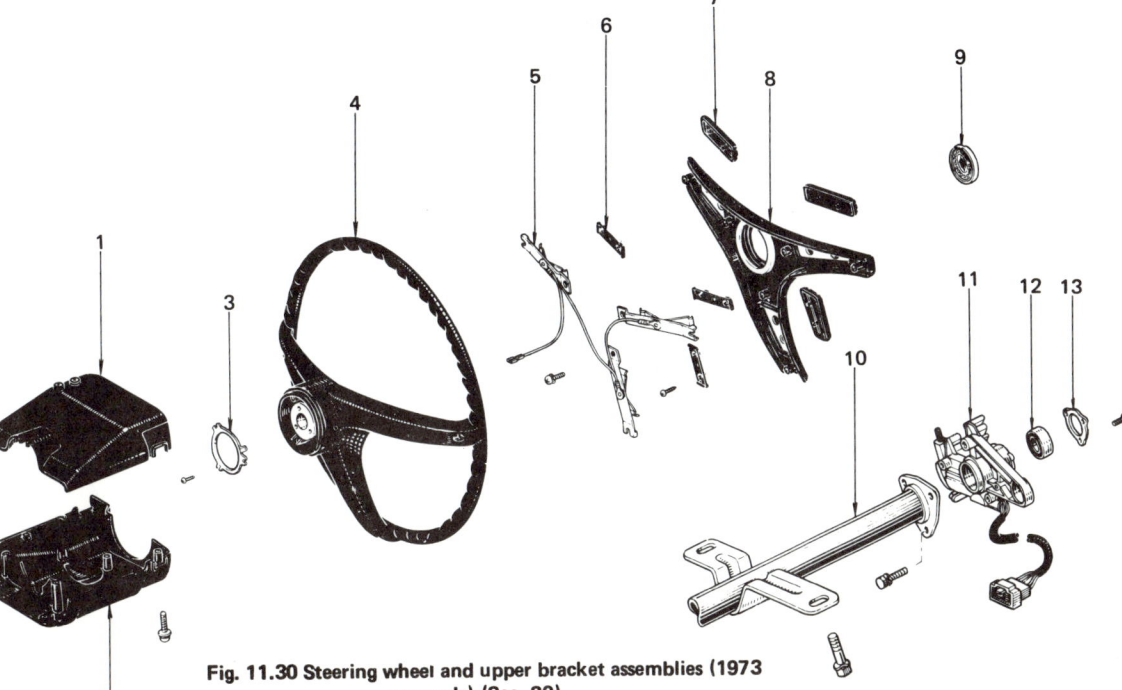

Fig. 11.30 Steering wheel and upper bracket assemblies (1973 onwards) (Sec. 20)

1 Upper shroud
2 Lower shroud
3 Horn contact ring
4 Steering wheel
5 Horn switch plate
6 and 7 Horn button assembly
8 Crash pad
9 Badge
10 Steering column
11 Upper bracket
12 Upper bearing
13 Bearing retainer

5 Once the pad or horn button has been removed, unscrew the securing nut and then make alignment marks on the end of the shaft and the steering wheel so that the wheel can be refitted in exactly the same position.

6 Remove the steering wheel by tapping it gently at the rear with the palms of the hands. If it does not come off, on no account attempt to jar it off or to hammer the end of the shaft as damage to the column will result, particularly if it is of collapsible type. If the wheel is stuck, use an extractor with centre screw, taking care to protect the surfaces of the steering wheel and hub.

7 Installation of the steering wheel is a reversal of removal but make sure that the mating marks made before removal, are in alignment. On late type vehicles make sure that the hole in the steering wheel and the direction indicator switch cancelling cam are in alignment.

8 Tighten the steering wheel securing nut to a torque of 22 lb/ft (3.0 kg/m).

21 Steering column (up to 1970) - removal, servicing and installation

1 Remove the steering wheel as described in the preceding Section, also the direction indicator and windscreen wiper switches as described in Chapter 10.

2 Remove the steering shaft bearing circlips and then loosen the housing retaining nut and withdraw the steering column upper housing together with the bearing.

3 At the lower end of the steering column, remove the pinch bolt from the shaft to worm coupling clamp.

4 Remove the retainer (steering column gearshift lever) and disconnect the high and low speed levers.

5 Disconnect the handbrake cable from the intermediate lever and from the clamp.

6 Remove the parcels tray.

7 Remove the steering column clamp.

8 Remove the clutch and brake pedal return springs, the stop lamp switch and after disconnecting the pushrods from the

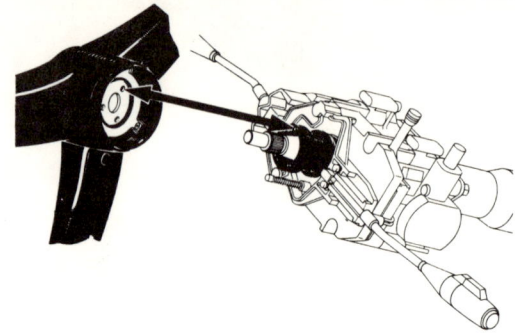

Fig. 11.31 Steering wheel and indicator switch cam alignment (late models) (Sec. 20)

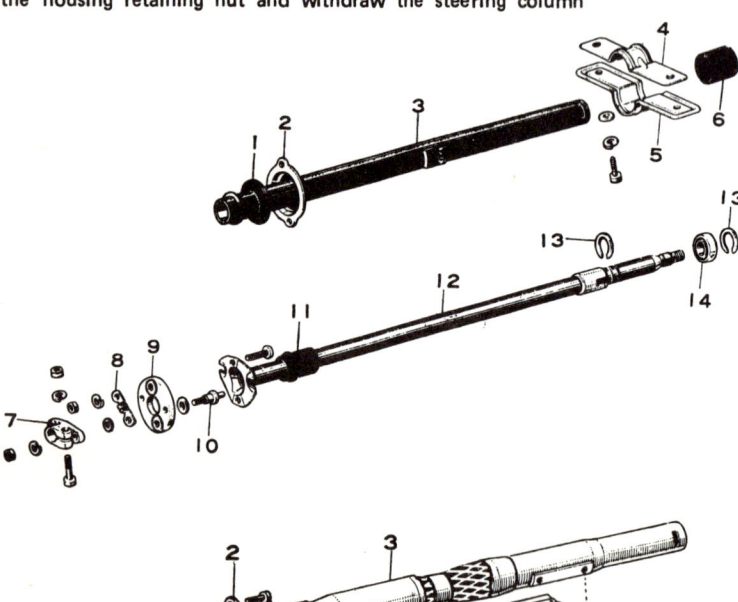

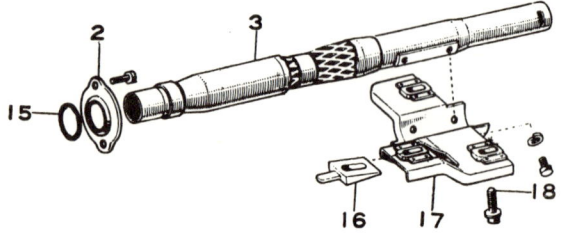

Fig. 11.32 Components of the rigid and collapsible type steering columns (up to 1971) (Sec. 21)

1 Grommet
2 Cover plate
3 Steering column
4 and 5 Clamps
6 Grommet
7 Coupling
8 Earth connection
9 Flexible coupling
10 Stop bolt
11 Dust seal
12 Inner shaft
13 Circlip
14 Upper bearing
15 'O' ring
16 Wedge
17 'Break away' bracket
18 Bolt
19 Plug

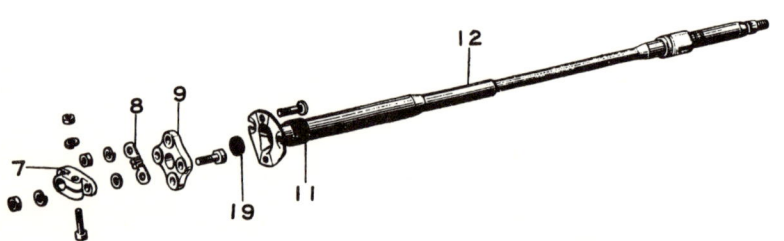

pedals, remove the clutch and brake master cylinders.
9 Remove the brake and clutch pedal support bracket and withdraw the steering column assembly into the interior of the vehicle.
10 Dismantle by pulling the shaft from the column tube.
11 Remove the flexible coupling from the mainshaft and then detach the yoke by tapping it from the rear.
12 Renew any worn components and reassemble by reversing the dismantling procedure. Remember to fit the coupling earth connection and to apply grease to the lower dust seal and to the upper bearing.
13 Installation of the steering column is a reversal of removal but with collapsible type columns, the bolt (1) must be tightened first and bolt (2) inserted so it passes through the hole in the wedge which must be located between the instrument panel and the break-away bracket. Tighten the bolts to the specified torque of 22 lb/ft (3.0 kg/m) (Fig. 11.33).

22 Steering column (1971 to 1973) - removal, servicing and installation

1 Remove the steering wheel (Section 20) the steering column shrouds and the direction indicator switch as described in Chapter 10.
2 At the lower end of the steering column remove the pinch bolt from the shaft coupling, remove the reversing lamp switch and disconnect the gearchange control shafts from the levers.
3 Unscrew the column clamp bolts and the column aperture cover bolts and withdraw the steering column into the vehicle interior.

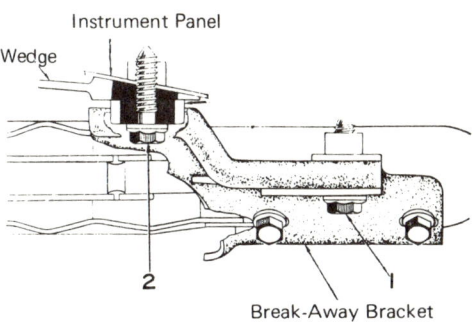

Fig. 11.33 Installation of upper bracket on collapsible column (up to 1970) (Sec. 21) 1 bolt to be tightened first 2 bolt to be tightened after insertion of wedge

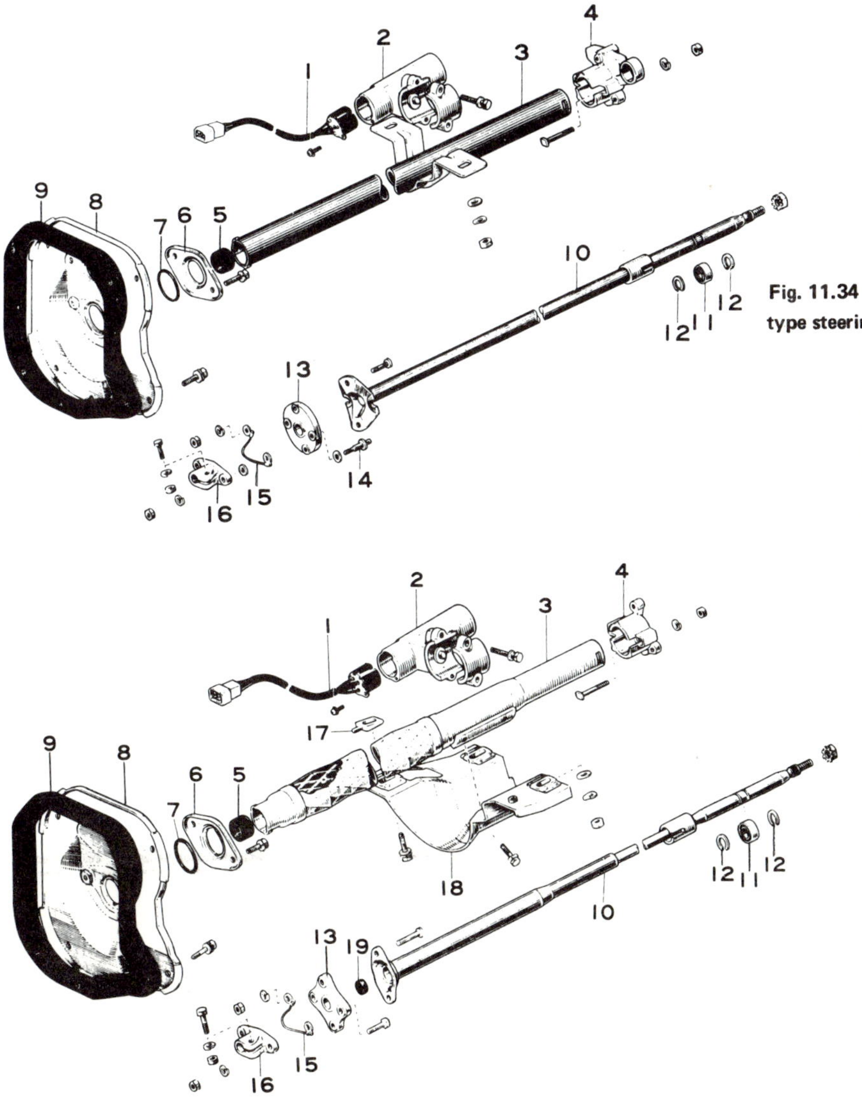

Fig. 11.34 Components of the rigid and collapsible type steering columns (1971 to 1973) (Sec. 22)

1 Ignition switch
2 Steering lock
3 Steering column
4 Steering column bracket
5 Dust seal
6 Cover plate
7 'O' ring
8 Cover plate
9 Seal
10 Shaft
11 Upper bearing
12 Circlip
13 Flexible coupling
14 Stop bolt
15 Earth connection
16 Coupling yoke
17 Wedge
18 'Break-away' bracket
19 Plug

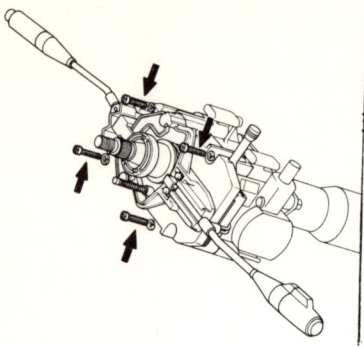

Fig. 11.35 Combination switch retaining screws (steering column 1973 onwards) (Sec. 23)

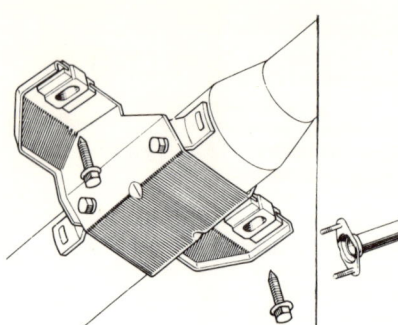

Fig. 11.36 Steering column upper clamp (1973 onwards) (Sec. 23)

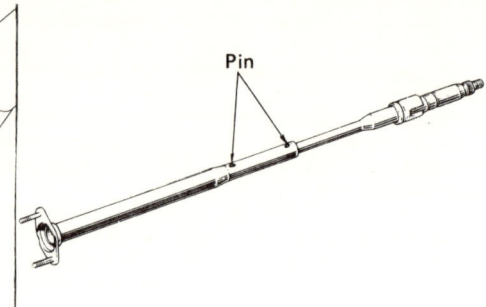

Fig. 11.37 Collapsible type steering shaft (1973 onwards) (Sec. 23)

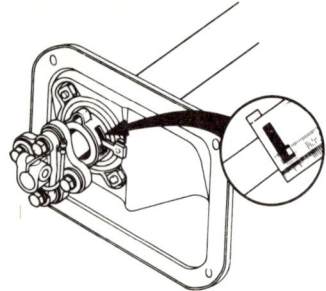

Fig. 11.38 Correct location of aperture cover pin in steering column cut-out (1973 onwards) (Sec. 23)

4   Remove the column bracket, the circlip and upper bearing.
5   Remove the column from the aperture cover and remove the flexible coupling from the inner shaft.
6   Inspection, reassembly and installation is similar to that described in paragraphs 12 and 13 of the preceding Section.

23 Steering column (1973 onwards) - removal, servicing and installation

1   Remove the steering wheel (Section 20) and the combination switch as described in Chapter 10.
2   Turn the ignition key to the 'ACC' position, depress the spring plunger of the lock and remove the cylinder.
3   Remove the shaft bearing retainer and bracket bolts.

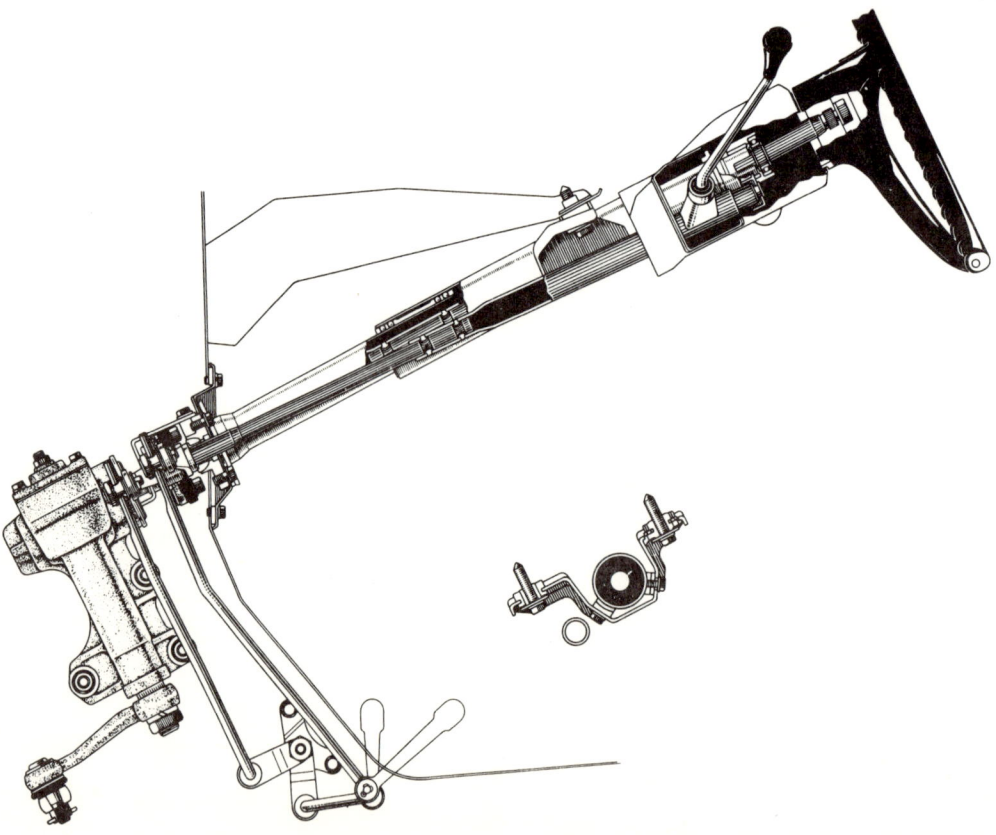

Fig. 11.39 Sectional view of steering column (1973 onwards) (Sec. 23)

Chapter 11/Suspension and steering

4 Extract the circlip and withdraw the upper bracket.
5 At the lower end of the steering column, remove the pinch bolt from the coupling.
6 Remove the bolts from the steering column aperture cover and from the steering column clamp.
7 Withdraw the shaft from the steering column and remove the dust seal.
8 Remove the flexible coupling from the inner shaft.
9 Unbolt the aperture cover plate from the column tube.
10 Inspect all components for wear and renew as appropriate. Check for the loosening of the plastic pins which secure the collapsible sections of the steering shaft.
11 Assembly is a reversal of dismantling but apply grease to the upper bearing and to both sides of the dust seal.
12 Install the column assembly and connect the coupling and tighten the pinch bolt.
13 Locate the column bracket but insert the bolts only finger-tight.
14 Tighten the column aperture cover bolts.
15 Push the steering column fully downward and then tighten the column bracket bolts to 14 lb/ft (1.9 kg/m).
It is imperative that the pin in the aperture cover locates in the cut-out in the outer column.

24 Steering box - removal and installation

1 Remove the drop arm from the shaft.
2 Remove the pinch bolt from the steering shaft coupling. On LHD late model vehicles, the flexible coupling bolts and the air cleaner must also be removed.
3 Unbolt the steering box and remove it from the vehicle.
4 Installation is a reversal of removal but align the mating marks on the drop arm and shaft endface.
5 Check the oil level and top-up with the specified grade.

25 Steering box - dismantling and reassembly

1 Loosen the rocker shaft adjuster screw locknut.
2 Remove the cover plate bolts and remove the rocker shaft/cover plate assembly.
3 Remove the worm bearing adjuster nut locking ring and then unscrew and remove the adjuster nut from the steering box housing. A special type of spanner will be required for this, having two pins to engage in the holes in the nut.
4 Withdraw the worm/nut assembly complete with bearings from the steering box. Do not try to remove the nut.
5 Examine the worm and nut and bearings for wear, scoring or damage but do not run the nut up and down the worm from end to end during the checking.
6 Renew the oil seals and the 'O' ring.
7 If any of the worm or rocker shaft bearings are worn or damaged then the housing should be taken to a Toyota Dealer to have them renewed.
8 If the worm or nut show signs of wear or damage then they must be renewed as an assembly.
9 Commence reassembly by greasing the lips of the oil seals and dipping each component in clean gear oil.
10 Fit the worm/nut assembly into the steering box followed by the adjuster nut and locking ring.
11 Wind a thin cord round the splined pinion of the worm gear and attach a spring balance to it. Adjust the adjuster nut until

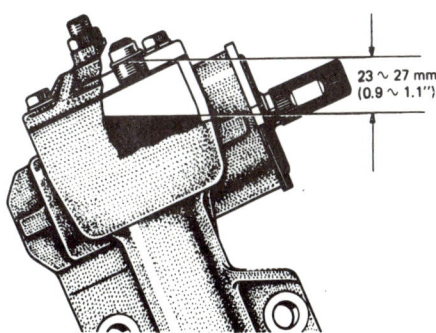

Fig. 11.40 Correct steering box oil level (Sec. 24)

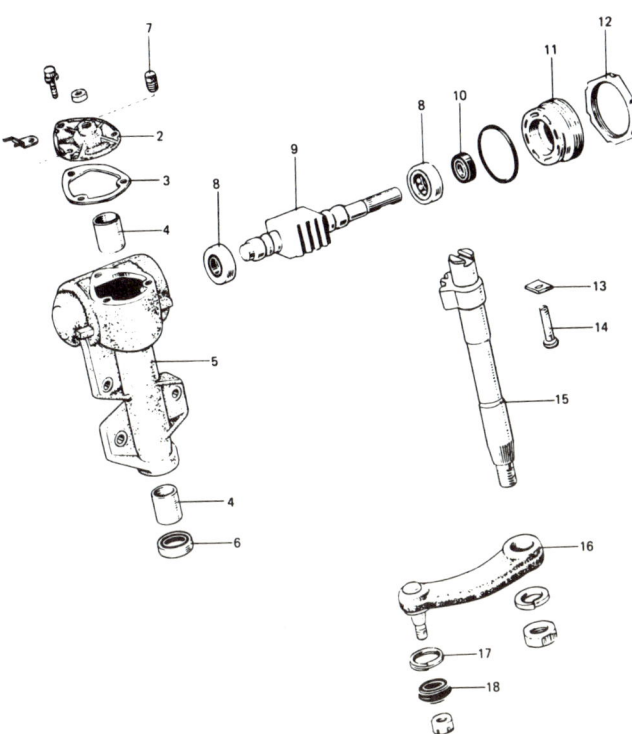

Fig. 11.41 Exploded view of the steering box (Sec. 25)

2 Cover
3 Gasket
4 Bush
5 Housing
6 Oil seal
7 Breather/filler plug
8 Bearing
9 Worm/nut assembly
10 Oil seal
11 Worm bearing adjuster nut
12 Locking ring
13 Thrust washer
14 Rocker shaft adjuster screw
15 Rocker shaft
16 Drop arm
17 Retaining ring
18 Dust excluder

the spring balance registers between 9 and 13 lbs (4.1 and 6.0 kg) when given an even pull, this is the required worm bearing pre-load. Without moving the adjuster nut, tighten the locking ring to 70 lb/ft (9.7 kg/m).

12 Using a feeler gauge, measure the clearance between the convex face of the adjuster screw and its rocker shaft contact face. The clearance should not exceed 0.004 in. (0.09 mm) otherwise change the thrust-washer.

The following thrust-washer thicknesses are available: 0.079 in. (2.00 mm), 0.080 in. (2.04 mm), 0.082 in. (2.08 mm), 0.083 in. (2.12 mm), 0.085 in. (2.16 mm), 0.087 in. (2.20 mm).

13 Refit the rocker shaft, ensuring that the nut is positioned in the centre of the steering worm.

14 Loosen the cover plate adjuster screw right off and then fit the cover plate complete with new gasket (smeared both sides with jointing compound). Tighten the cover plate bolts to 15 lb/ft (2.1 kg/m) torque.

15 Screw in the rocker shaft adjuster screw and check the preload by winding a cord round the splines of the worm shaft and attaching it to a spring balance in a manner similar to that described in paragraph 11, but on this occasion, the reading on the spring balance should be between 18 and 24 lbs (8.2 and 10.9 kg). Fit the locknut to the adjuster screw and tighten it to 22 lb/ft (3.0 kg/m). Rocker shaft adjustment can be carried out if slackness develops when the steering box is in the vehicle by removing the steering wheel and winding the cord round the shaft splines, taking the preload reading as just described.

26 Front wheel alignment

1 Accurate front wheel alignment is essential for good steering and even tyre wear. Before considering the steering angles, check that the tyres are correctly inflated, that the front wheels are not buckled, the hub bearings are not worn or incorrectly adjusted and that the steering linkage is in good order, without slackness or wear at the joints.

2 Wheel alignment consists of four factors:

Camber, which is the angle at which the front wheels are set from the vertical when viewed from the front of the car. Positive

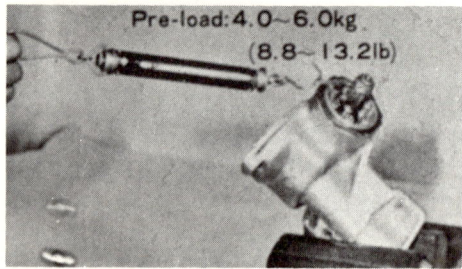

Fig. 11.42 Checking worn bearing pre-load (Sec. 25)

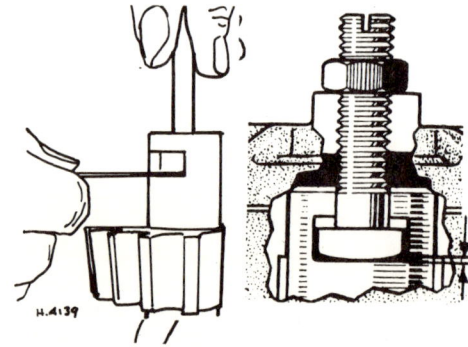

Fig. 11.43 Checking adjuster screw to rocker shaft cut-out clearance (Sec. 25)

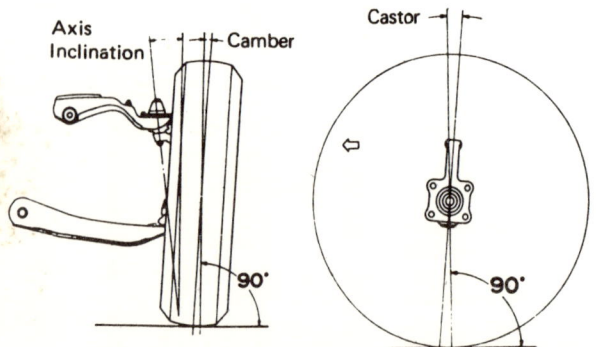

Fig. 11.44 Diagram of steering angles (Sec. 26)

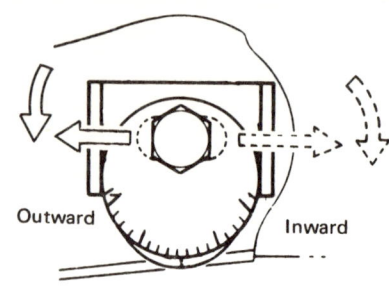

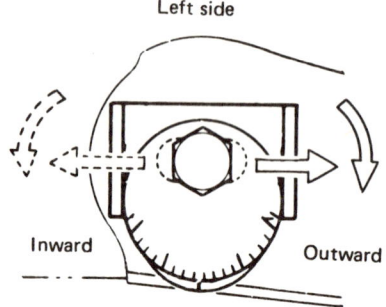

Fig. 11.45 Effect of suspension lower arm cam adjustment (after 1973) (Sec. 26)

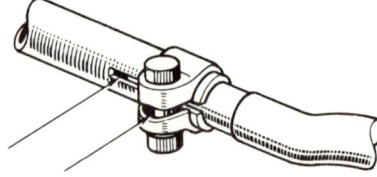

Fig. 11.46 Correct installation of track rod clamps (Sec. 26)

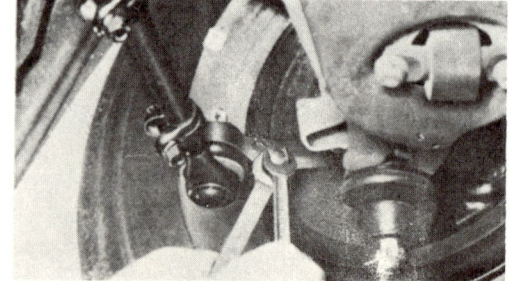

Fig. 11.47 Adjusting a steering lock adjustment stop bolt (Sec. 26)

Chapter 11/Suspension and steering

camber is the amount (in degrees) that the wheels are tilted outwards at the top from the vertical.

Castor, is the angle between the steering axis and a vertical line when viewed from each side of the car. Positive castor is when the steering axis is inclined rearward.

Steering axis inclination, is the angle, when viewed from the front of the car, between the vertical and an imaginary line drawn between the upper and lower suspension swivel balljoints.

Toe-in, is the amount by which the distance between the front inside edges of the road wheels (measured at hub height) is less than the diametrically opposite distance measured between the rear inside edges of the front road wheels.

3 Due to the need for prevision gauges to measure the small angles set in the steering and suspension layout it is preferable that adjustment of camber and castor is left to a service station having the necessary equipment.

4 *On early models*, the camber angle is varied by the inclusion of shims between the suspension upper arm pivot shaft and the bodyframe. Variation in the thickness and quantity of shims between one end of the pivot shaft and the other will also affect the castor angle.

5 On later models (after 1973) the camber and castor angles are varied by turning the eccentric cam adjusters on the suspension lower arm pivot bolts. These angles are normally set for 'life' during production and if the suspension is to be dismantled, always record the cam setting in relation to its reference mark before starting work.

6 Front wheel tracking (toe-in) may be checked and adjusted by carrying out the following operations.

7 Place the car on level ground with the wheels in the straight ahead position.

8 Obtain or make a toe-in gauge. One may be easily made from tubing, cranked to clear the sump and bellhousing, having an adjustable nut and setscrew at one end.

9 With the gauge, measure the distance between the two wheel inner rims (at hub height) at the rear of the wheel.

10 Rotate the wheel through 180° (half a turn) and measure the distance between the wheel inner rims (again at hub height) at the front of the wheel. This measurement should be less by an amount which corresponds with the specified toe-in for the particular vehicle model, (see Specifications Section).

Where the toe-in is found to be incorrect, slacken all four track rod clamp bolts and rotate each track rod equally. It is a good plan to first measure each track rod between the balljoint centres in case they have been adjusted unevenly by a previous owner. When adjustment is correct, tighten the clamp bolts, ensuring that the clamp openings are in alignment with the slots in the track rod tubes and that the track rod ends are positioned in the centres of their arcs of travel.

11 Steering lock stop bolts are fitted to the rear of the stub axle carriers and are adjustable to limit the full lock travel in both directions.

27 Wheels and tyres

1 Regularly check the tyre pressures including the spare.

2 Every 6000 miles (10000 km) remove the roadwheels, extract any flints which are embedded in the tread and move the position of the wheel to even out the wear of the tyre. This rotation should only be carried out if the wheels have been balanced off the vehicle. If the wheels have been balanced on the vehicle then moving the roadwheels cannot be carried out unless the wheels are re-balanced afterwards.

3 Regularly inspect the depth of tyre tread. When it has worn down to 1 mm, renew the tyre.

4 When new tyres are fitted, always renew the valve at the same time.

5 Never mix radial and crossply tyres on the same axle.

6 Never attempt to mend a puncture by the insertion of a plug from the outside. The cover must be removed and a 'mushroom' type plug inserted from the inside. The wheel must be re-balanced after insertion of the plug.

28 Fault diagnosis - suspension and steering

Before diagnosing faults from the following chart, check that any irregularities are not caused by:
1 *Binding brakes*
2 *Incorrect 'mix' of radial and crossply tyres*
3 *Incorrect tyre pressures*
4 *Misalignment of the bodyframe*

Symptom	Cause
Steering wheel can be moved considerably before any sign of movement of the wheels is apparent	Wear in the steering linkage, gear and column coupling
Vehicle difficult to steer in a consistent straight line - wandering	As above Wheel alignment incorrect (indicated by excessive or uneven tyre wear) Front wheel hub bearings loose or worn Worn suspension unit swivel joints
Steering stiff and heavy	Incorrect wheel alignment (indicated by excessive or uneven tyre wear) Excessive wear or seizure in one or more of the joints in the steering linkage or suspension unit balljoints Excessive wear in the steering gear unit
Wheel wobble and vibration	Road wheels out of balance Road wheels buckled Wheel alignment incorrect Wear in the steering linkage, suspension unit bearings or track control arm bushes Broken front spring
Excessive pitching and rolling on corners and during braking	Defective shock absorbers and/or broken spring

Chapter 12 Body and fittings

Contents

Air conditioning system - general description and maintenance 27	Impact absorbing type bumpers - removal and refitting ... 21
Bonnet - removal, refitting and adjustment 18	Maintenance - hinges and locks 6
Doors - removal, refitting and adjustment 17	Maintenance - bodywork and underframe 2
Doors - tracing rattles and their rectification 7	Maintenance - upholstery and carpets 3
Estate wagon tailgate - removal, refitting and adjustment ... 20	Major body damage - repair 5
Fault diagnosis - air conditioning system 28	Minor body damage - repair 4
Front door glass and regulator - removal and refitting ... 12	Opening quarterlight ventilators - removal and refitting ... 13
Front door lock - removal, refitting and adjustment ... 10	Power operated window regulators (hardtop) - removal and
Front wing - removal and installation 8	refitting 16
General description 1	Quarterlight glass (hardtop) - removal and installation ... 15
Heater (1969 - 72) - dismantling, servicing and reassembly 25	Rear boot lid - removal, refitting and adjustment ... 19
Heater (1973 onwards) - dismantling, servicing and	Rear door glass and regulator - removal and refitting ... 14
reassembly 26	Rear door lock (saloon and estate wagon) - removal,
Heater - general description 22	refitting and adjustment 11
Heater (1969 - 72) - removal and refitting 23	Windscreen glass - removal and installation 9
Heater (1973 onwards) - removal and refitting 24	

Specifications

Dimensions and weights

1969 to 1971	Saloon	Hardtop	Estate Wagon
Overall length	171.3 in. (4.351 m)	171.3 in. (4.351 m)	171.5 in. (4.356 m)
Width	63.2 in. (1.605 m)	63.2 in. (1.605 m)	63.2 in. (1.605 m)
Height	55.3 in. (1.404 m)	54.9 in. (1.394 m)	56.1 in. (1.425 m)
Weight	2305 lbs (1046 kg)	2305 lbs (1046 kg)	2430 lbs (1102 kg)
Ground clearance	7.1 in. (180.3 mm)	7.1 in. (180.3 mm)	6.7 in. (170.2 mm)
Wheelbase	98.8 in. (2.509 m)	98.8 in. (2.509 m)	98.8 in. (2.509 m)
Track (front)	52.2 in. (1.326 m)	52.2 in. (1.326 m)	52.2 in. (1.326 m)
Track (rear)	52.0 in. (1.321 m)	52.0 in. (1.321 m)	52.0 in. (1.321 m)

1972 to 1973	Saloon	Hardtop	Estate Wagon
Overall length	170.7 in. (4.336 m)	170.7 in. (4.336 m)	171.3 in. (4.283 m)
Width	61.8 in. (1.570 m)	61.8 in. (1.570 m)	61.8 in. (1.570 m)
Height	54.7 in. (1.389 m)	54.1 in. (1.374 m)	55.9 in. (1.420 m)
Weight	2470 lbs (1120 kg)	2470 lbs (1120 kg)	2580 lbs (1170 kg)
Ground clearance	6.9 in. (175.3 mm)	6.9 in. (175.3 mm)	6.9 in. (175.3 mm)
Wheelbase	95.7 in. (2.450 m)	95.7 in. (2.450 m)	96.9 in. (2.461 m)
Track (front)	51.2 in. (1.301 m)	51.2 in. (1.301 m)	51.2 in. (1.301 m)
Track (rear)	50.4 in. (1.280 m)	50.4 in. (1.280 m)	50.4 in. (1.280 m)

1973 onwards	Saloon	Hardtop	Estate Wagon
Overall length	171.9 in. (4.366 m)	171.9 in. (4.366 m)	175.0 in. (4.445 m)
Special for California	172.6 in. (4.384 m)	172.6 in. (4.384 m)	175.8 in. (4.465 m)
Width	63.8 in. (1.620 m)	63.8 in. (1.620 m)	63.8 in. (1.620 m)
Height	55.0 in. (1.397 m)	54.0 in. (1.372 m)	56.3 in. (1.430 m)
Weight	2505 lbs (1136 kg)	2505 lbs (1136 kg)	2620 lbs (1188 kg)
Ground clearance	6.9 in. (175.3 mm)	6.9 in. (175. 3mm)	6.5 in. (165.1 mm)
Wheelbase	98.4 in. (2.499 m)	98.4 in. (2.499 m)	98.4 in. (2.499 m)
Track (front)	53.0 in. (1.346 m)	53.0 in. (1.346 m)	53.0 in. (1.346 m)
Track (rear)	52.0 in. (1.321 m)	52.0 in. (1.321 m)	52.0 in. (1.321 m)

Chapter 12/Body and fittings

1 General description

The body and underframe is of steel, welded, unitary construction. The body styles covered by this manual are described in the Introduction. Saloon, hardtop (coupe) and estate wagon versions are produced in each of the three bodystyles. A heating and ventilation system is installed as standard but a full air conditioning system can be specified as an option.

On later models destined for operation in North America, the front and rear bumpers are of impact absorbing type and in order to accommodate their increased section and depth, some redesign of adjacent bodywork has been carried out.

On all models the front wings are detachable. The information given in this Chapter applies to all the models built between 1969 and 1974 but in order to avoid an excessive number of illustrations, individual operations are not necessarily supported by all the differing types of body style illustrations although of course the text will apply to all types.

2 Maintenance - bodywork and underframe

The general condition of a car's bodywork is the one thing that significantly affects its value. Maintenance is easy but needs to be regular and particular. Neglect, particularly after minor damage, can lead quickly to further deterioration and costly repair bills. It is important also to keep watch on those parts of the car not immediately visible, for instance the underside, inside all the wheel arches and the lower part of the engine compartment.

2 The basic maintenance routine for the bodywork is washing - preferably with a lot of water, from a hose. This will remove all the loose solids which may have stuck to the car. It is important to flush these off in such a way as to prevent grit from scratching the finish. The wheel arches and underbody need washing in the same way to remove any accumulated mud which will retain moisture and tend to encourage rust. Parodoxically enough, the best time to clean the underbody and wheel arches is in wet weather when the mud is thoroughly wet and soft. In very wet weather the underbody is usually cleaned of large accumulations automatically and this is a good time for inspection.

3 Periodically it is a good idea to have the whole of the underside of the car steam cleaned, engine compartment included, so that a thorough inspection can be carried out to see what minor repairs and renovations are necessary. Steam cleaning is available at many garages and is necessary for removal of accumulation of oily grime which sometimes is allowed to cake thick in certain areas near the engine, gearbox and back axle. If steam facilities are not available, there are one or two excellent grease solvents available which can be brush applied. The dirt can then be simply hosed off.

4 After washing paintwork, wipe off with a chamois leather to give an unspotted clear finish. A coat of clear protective wax polish will give added protection against chemical pollutants in the air. If the paintwork sheen has dulled or oxidised, use a cleaner/polish combination to restore the brilliance of the shine. This requires a little more effort, but is usually caused because regular washing has been neglected. Always check that door and ventilator opening drain holes and pipes are completely clear so that water can drain out. Bright work should be treated the same way as paintwork. Windscreens and windows can be kept clear of the smeary film which often appears if a little ammonia is added to the water. If they are scratched, a good rub with a proprietary metal polish will often clear them. Never use any form of wax or other body or chromium polish on glass.

3 Maintenance - upholstery and carpets

1 Mats and carpets should be brushed or vacuum cleaned regularly to keep them free of grit. If they are badly stained remove them from the car for scrubbing or sponging and make quite sure they are dry before replacement. Seats and interior trim panels can be kept clean by a wipe over with a damp cloth. If they do become stained (which can be more apparent on light coloured upholstery) use a little liquid detergent and a soft nail brush to scour the grime out of the grain of the material. Do not forget to keep the head lining clean in the same way as the upholstery. When using liquid cleaners inside the car do not over-wet the surface being cleaned. Excessive damp could get into the seams and padded interior causing stains, offensive odours or even rot. If the inside of the car gets wet accidently it is worthwhile taking some trouble to dry it out properly, particularly where carpets are involved. **Do not** leave oil or electric heaters inside the car for this purpose.

4 Minor body damage - repair

See also photo sequences on pages 236 and 237.

Repair of minor scratches in the car's bodywork

If the scratch is very superficial, and does not penetrate to the metal of the bodywork repair is very simple. Lightly rub the area of the scratch with a paintwork renovator (eg 'Top-Cut'), or a very fine cutting paste, to remove loose paint from the scratch and to clear the surrounding bodywork of wax polish. Rinse the area with clean water.

Apply touch-up paint to the scratch using a thin paint brush; continue to apply thin layers of paint until the surface of the paint in the scratch is level with surrounding paintwork. Allow the new paint at least two weeks to harden; then, blend it into the surrounding paintwork by rubbing the paintwork in the scratch area with a paintwork renovator (eg. 'Top-Cut'), or a very fine cutting paste. Finally apply wax polish.

An alternative to painting over the scratch is to use Holts 'Scratch-Patch'. Use the same preparation for the affected area; then simply, pick a patch of suitable size to cover the scratch completely. Hold the patch against the scratch and burnish its backing paper; the patch will adhere to the paintwork, freeing itself from the backing paper at the same time. Polish the affected area to blend the patch into the surrounding paintwork.

Where a scratch has penetrated, right through to the metal of the bodywork, causing the metal to rust, a different repair technique is required. Remove any loose rust from the bottom of the scratch with a penknife, then apply rust inhibiting paint (eg. 'Kurust') to prevent the formation of rust in the future. Using a rubber or nylon applicator fill the scratch with body-stopper paste. If required, this paste can be mixed with cellulose thinners to provide a very thin paste which is ideal for filling narrow scratches. Before the stopper-paste in the scratch hardens, wrap a piece of smooth cotton rag around the tip of the finger; dip the finger in cellulose thinners and then quickly sweep it across the surface of the stopper-paste in the scratch; this will ensure that the surface of the stopper-paste is slightly hollowed. The scratch can now be painted over as described earlier in this Section.

Repair of dents in the car's bodywork

When deep denting of the car's bodywork has taken place, the first task is to pull the dent out, until the affected bodywork almost attains its original shape. There is little point in trying to restore the original shape completely, as the metal in the damaged area will have stretched on impact and cannot be reshaped fully to its original contour. It is better to bring the level of the dent up to a point which is about 1/8 inch (3 mm) below the level of the surrounding bodywork. In cases where the dent is very shallow anyway, it is not worth trying to pull it out at all.

If the underside of the dent is accessible, it can be hammered out gently from behind, using a mallet with a wooden or plastic head. Whilst doing this, hold a suitable block of wood firmly against the outside of the dent. This block will absorb the impact from the hammer blows and thus prevent a large area of bodywork from being 'belled-out'.

Chapter 12/Bodywork and fittings

Preparation for filling

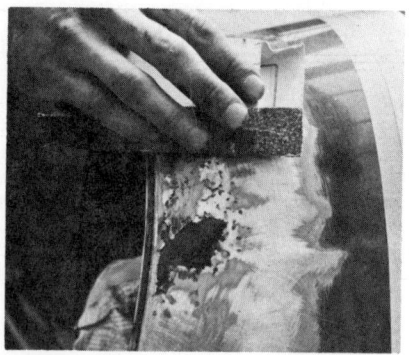
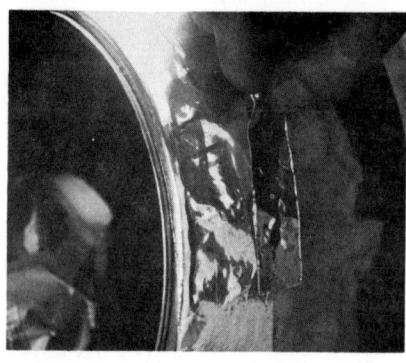
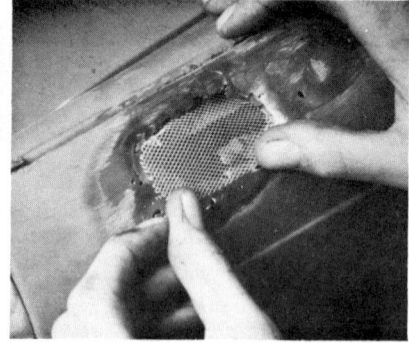
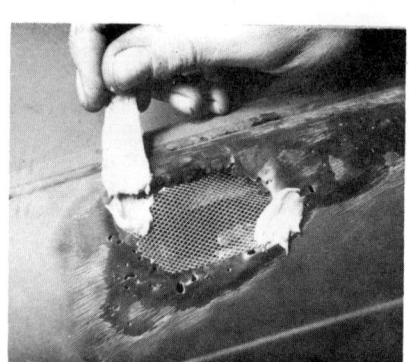

Filling and shaping

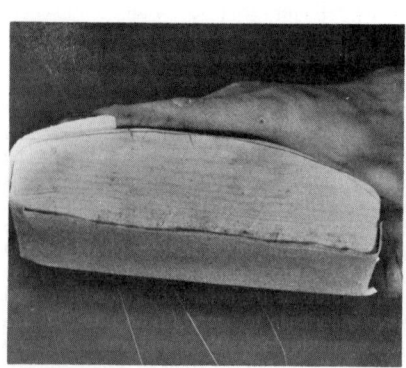
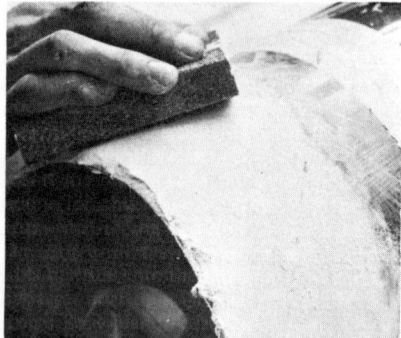

Chapter 12/Body and fittings

Masking and spraying

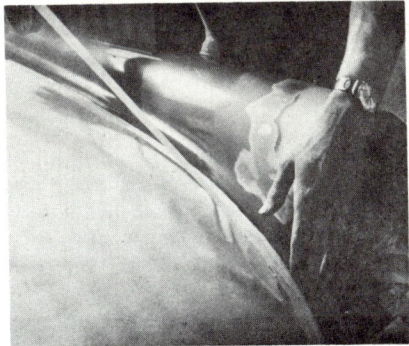
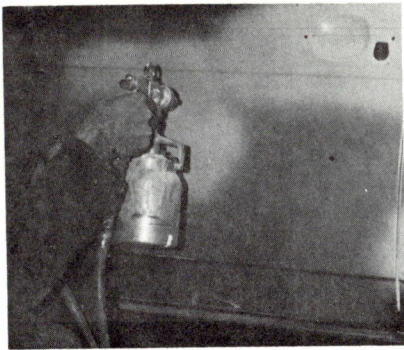
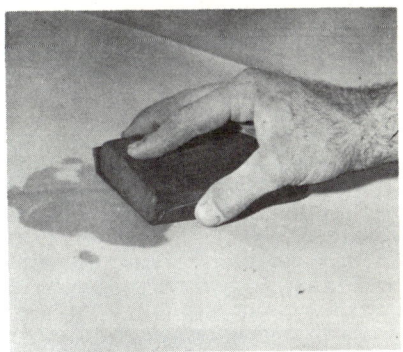

Should the dent be in a section of the bodywork which has a double skin or some other factor making it inaccessible from behind, a different technique is called for. Drill several small holes through the metal inside the dent area - particularly in the deeper sections. Then screw long self-tapping screws into the holes just sufficiently for them to gain a good purchase in the metal. Now the dent can be pulled out by pulling on the protruding heads of the screws with a pair of pliers.

The next stage of the repair is the removal of the paint from the damaged area, and from an inch or so of the surrounding 'sound' bodywork. This is accomplished most easily by using a wire brush or abrasive pad on a power drill, although it can be done just as effectively by hand using sheets of abrasive paper. To complete the preparations for filling, score the surface of the bare metal with a screwdriver or the tang of a file, or alternatively, drill small holes in the affected area. This will provide a really good 'key' for the filler paste.

To complete the repair see the Section on filling and re-spraying.

Repair of rust holes or gashes in the car's bodywork

Remove all paint from the affected area and from an inch or so of the surrounding 'sound' bodywork, using an abrasive pad or a wire brush on a power drill. If these are not available a few sheets of abrasive paper will do the job just as effectively. With the paint removed you will be able to gauge the severity of the corrosion and therefore decide whether to replace the whole panel (if this is possible) or to repair the affected area. Replacement body panels are not as expensive as most people think and it is often quicker and more satisfactory to fit a new panel than to attempt to repair large areas of corrosion.

Remove all fittings from the affected area, except those which will act as a guide to the original shape of the damaged bodywork (eg. headlamp shells etc.,). Then, using tin snips or a hacksaw blade, remove all loose metal and any other metal badly affected by corrosion. Hammer the edges of the hole inwards in order to create a slight depression for the filler paste.

Wire brush the affected area to remove the powdery rust from the surface of the remaining metal. Paint the affected area with rust inhibiting paint (eg. 'Kurust'); if the back of the rusted area is accessible treat this also.

Before filling can take place it will be necessary to block the hole in some way. This can be achieved by the use of one of the following materials: Zinc gauze, Aluminium tape or Polyurethane foam.

Zinc gauze is probably the best material to use for a large hole. Cut a piece to the approximate size and shape of the hole to be filled, then position it in the hole so that its edges are below the level of the surrounding bodywork. It can be retained in position by several blobs of filler paste around its periphery.

Aluminium tape should be used for small or very narrow holes. Pull a piece off the roll and trim it to the approximate size and shape required, then pull off the backing paper (if used) and stick the tape over the hole; it can be overlapped if the thickness of one piece is insufficient. Burnish down the edges of the tape with the handle of a screwdriver or similar, to ensure that the tape is securely attached to the metal underneath.

Polyurethane foam is best used where the holes are situated in a section of bodywork of complex shape, backed by a small box section (eg. where the sill panel meets the rear wheel arch - most cars). The usual mixing procedure for this foam is as follows: Put equal amounts of fluid from each of the two cans provided in the kit, into one container. Stir until the mixture begins to thicken, then quickly pour this mixture into the hole, and hold a piece of cardboard over the larger apertures. Almost immediately the polyurethane will begin to expand, gushing frantically out of any small holes left unblocked. When the foam hardens it can be cut back to just below the level of the surrounding bodywork with a hacksaw blade.

Bodywork repairs - filling and re-spraying

Before using this Section, see the Sections on dent, deep scratch, rust hole, and gash repairs.

Many types of bodyfiller are available, but generally speaking those proprietary kits which contain a tin of filler paste and a tube of resin hardener (eg. "Holts Cataloy") are best for this type of repair. A wide, flexible plastic or nylon applicator will be found invaluable for imparting a smooth and well contoured finish to the surface of the filler.

Mix up a little filler on a clean piece of card or board - use the hardener sparingly (follow the maker's instructions on the packet), otherwise the filler will set very rapidly.

Using the applicator, apply the filler paste to the prepared area; draw the applicator across the surface of the filler to achieve the correct contour and to level the filler surface. As soon as a contour that approximates the correct one is achieved stop working the paste. If you carry on too long the paste will become sticky and begin to 'pick-up' on the applicator. Continue to add thin layers of filler paste at twenty-minute intervals until the level of the filler is just 'proud' of the surrounding bodywork.

Once the filler has hardened, excess can be removed using a Surform plane or Dreadnought file. From then on, progressively finer grades of abrasive paper should be used, starting with a 40 grade production paper and finishing with 400 grade 'wet-and-dry' paper. Always wrap the abrasive paper around a flat rubber, cork, or wooden block - otherwise the surface of the filler will not be completely flat. During the smoothing of the filler surface the 'wet-and-dry' paper should be periodically rinsed in water; this will ensure that a very smooth finish is imparted to the filler at the final stage.

At this stage the 'dent' should be surrounded by a ring of bare metal, which in turn should be encircled by a finely 'feathered' edge of the good paintwork. Rinse the repair area with clean water, until all of the dust produced by the rubbing-down operation is gone.

Spray the whole repair area with a light coat of grey primer - this will show up any imperfections in the surface of the filler. Repair these imperfections with fresh filler paste or bodystopper, and once more smooth the surface with abrasive paper. If bodystopper is used, it can be mixed with cellulose thinners to form a really thin paste which is ideal for filling small holes. Repeat this spray and repair procedure until you are satisfied that the surface of the filler, and the feathered edge of the paintwork are perfect. Clean the repair area with clean water and allow to dry fully.

The repair area is now ready for spraying. Paint spraying must be carried out in a warm, dry, windless and dust free atmosphere. This condition can be created artifically if you have access to a large indoor working area, but if you are forced to work in the open, you will have to pick your day very carefully. If you are working indoors, dousing the floor in the work area with water will 'lay' the dust which would otherwise be in the atmosphere. If the repair area is confined to one body panel, mask off the surrounding panels; this will help to minimise the effect of a slight mis-match in paint colours. Bodywork fittings (eg chrome strips, door handles etc) will also need to be masked off. Use genuine masking tape and several thicknesses of newspaper for the masking operation.

Before commencing to spray, agitate the aerosol can thoroughly, then spray a test area (an old tin, or similar) until the technique is mastered. Cover the repair area with a thick coat of primer; the thickness should be built up using several thin layers of paint rather than one thick one. Using 400 grade 'wet-and-dry' paper, rub down the surface of the primer until it is really smooth. While doing this, the work area should be thoroughly doused with water, and the wet-and-dry paper periodically rinsed in water. Allow to dry before spraying on more paint.

Spray on the top coat, again building up the thickness by using several thin layers of paint. Start spraying in the centre of the repair area and then, using a circular motion, work outwards until the whole repair area and about 2 inches of the surrounding original paintwork is covered. Remove all masking material 10 to 15 minutes after spraying on the final coat of paint.

Allow the new paint at least 2 weeks to harden fully; then, using a paintwork renovator (eg "Top-Cut") or a very fine cutting paste, blend the edges of the new paint into the existing paintwork. Finally, apply wax polish.

5 Major body damage - repair

Where serious damage has occurred or large areas need renewal due to neglect, it means certainly that completely new sections or panels will need welding in and this is best left to professionals. If the damage is due to impact it will also be necessary to completely check the alignment of the bodyshell structure. Due to the principle of construction the strength and shape of the whole can be affected by damage to a part. In such instances the services of a Toyota Dealer with specialist checking jigs are essential. If a body is left misaligned it is first of all dangerous as the car will not handle properly and secondly uneven stresses will be imposed on the steering, engine and transmission causing abnormal wear or complete failure. Tyre wear may also be excessive.

6 Maintenance - hinges and locks

1 Oil the hinges of the bonnet, boot and doors with a drop or two of light oil periodically. A good time is after the car has been washed.
2 Oil the bonnet release catch pivot pin and the safety catch pivot pin periodically.
3 Do not over lubricate door latches and strikers. Normally a little oil on the rotary cam spindle alone is sufficient.

7 Doors - tracing rattles and their rectification

1 Check first that the door is not loose at the hinges and that the latch is holding the door firmly in position. Check also that the door lines up with the aperture in the body.
2 If the hinges are loose or the door is out of alignment it will be necessary to reset the hinge positions, as described in Section 17.
3 If the latch is holding the door properly it should hold the door tightly when fully latched and the door should line up with the body. If it is out of alignment it needs adjustment as described in Section 10. If loose, some part of the lock mechanism must be worn out and requiring renewal.
4 Other rattles from the door would be caused by wear or looseness in the window winder, the glass channels and sill strips or the door buttons and interior latch release mechanism.

8 Front wing - removal and installation

1 Unbolt and remove the front bumper assembly.
2 Remove the radiator grille.
3 Unscrew the air intake grille which is located just forward of the windscreen (refer to Section 35 Chapter 10).
4 Unscrew and remove all the securing bolts from the wing flanges.
5 Unscrew the bolt (A) which is accessible from inside the vehicle after removing the cover from the aperture in the trim panel below the facia (shaver nose models 1969 to 1972 only) (Fig. 12.3).
6 On left-hand front wings, remove the radio aerial after detaching the splash shield.
7 Cut round the mastic seal and lift the wing from the vehicle.
8 Clean the mating flanges of the new wing and bodyframe and apply a bead of mastic and refit the wing by reversing the removal operations.

Chapter 12/Body and fittings

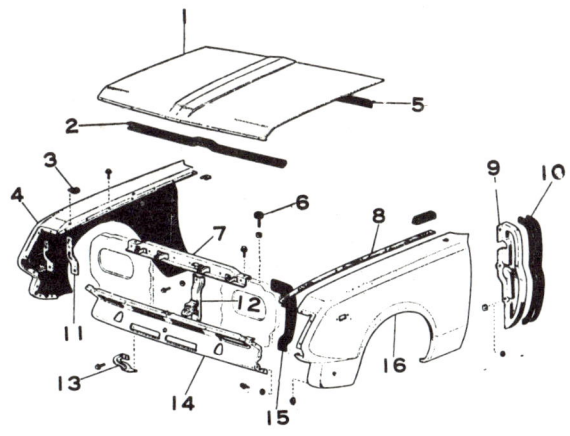

Fig 12.1 'Shavernose' body style front and components (Sec 8)

1 Bonnet
2 Seal
3 Bump stop
4 Front wing
5 Seal
6 Bonnet bump stop
7 Baffle
8 Packing strip
9 Splash shield
10 Seal
11 Packing strip
12 Lockplate
13 Stay
14 Shroud
15 Panel
16 Front wing
17 Safety catch
18 Bonnet stay
19 Bonnet lock cable
20 Battery hold down frame
21 Battery hold down bolt
22 Battery carrier
23 Battery carrier support plate
24 Bonnet hinge
25 Air intake rainwater outlet
26 Hose clip
27 Hose
28 Bonnet lock
29 Spring

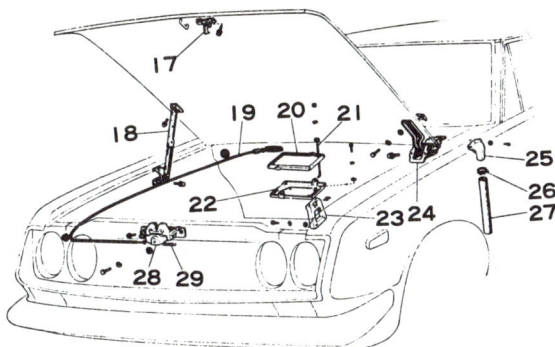

Fig 12.2 Front end components (1970 to 1973 models) (Sec 8)

1 Badge
2 Grille
3 Direction indicator lamps
4 Bumper

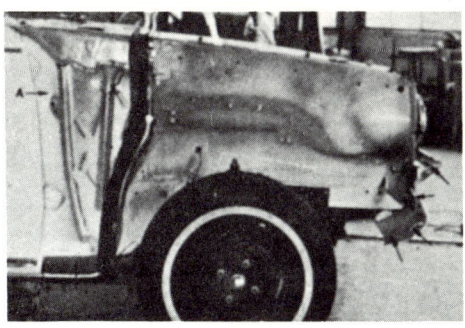

Fig 12.3 Location of front wing mounting bolts (shaver nose models) (Sec 8)

A is bolt accessible from interior of vehicle

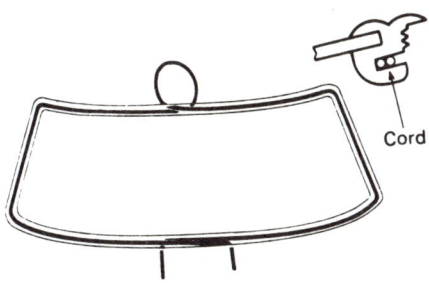

Fig 12.4 Cord fitting diagram for windscreen installation (Sec 9)

9 When the wing has been installed, apply under-sealing compound to the lower surface and respray the top surface to match the colour of the bodywork.

9 Windscreen glass - removal and installation

1 Remove the wiper arms.
2 Using a small screwdriver, prise out the bright moulding from the rubber windscreen surround.
3 Remove the interior mirror and then prise the rubber surround lip (at the inside top centre) from the body frame edge. Work in both directions and exert even pressure along the top part of the screen until it moves outwards.
4 Thoroughly clean the windscreen recess of the bodyframe and examine the rubber surround. If it is cut or has perished or hardened or old pieces of sealant cannot easily be removed, then renew it.
5 Commence installation of the windscreen by locating the rubber surround to the glass. Fit a thin cord to the body seating groove of the rubber surround so that the two ends overlap at the bottom centre.
6 Locate the windscreen accurately at the body aperature with the two ends of the pull cord hanging inside the vehicle.
7 Have an assistant press on the glass from the outside and pull the two ends of the fitting cord evenly so that the combination of pressure and cord withdrawal will engage the rubber surround lip with the body flange.
8 With the windscreen installed, inject black sealant into the space between the rubber and the glass and between the rubber and the body.
9 Install the side and top bright moulding strips by applying pressure so that its turned over edge engages with the rubber surround or clips, according to type.
10 Clean off any excess sealant with a rag soaked in paraffin or white spirit.

Chapter 12/Body and fittings

10 Front door lock - removal, refitting and adjustment

1 Unscrew and remove the door lock plunger from the interior door ledge. (photo)
2 Remove the arm rest (two screws). (photo)
3 Remove the interior door handle bezel by unscrewing its retaining screw and withdrawing it to the right. (photo)
4 Remove the window winder handle by using a hooked tool to detach its securing clip. (photo)
5 Detach the interior trim panel by inserting the fingers between the panel and the door and jerking the clips from their holes. When the panel is free, disconnect the courtesy light connector. (photo)
6 Remove the waterproof sheet from the door aperture.
7 Within the door cavity, detach the operating rod from the lock cylinder, remove the cylinder retaining clip in an upward direction and withdraw the cylinder.
8 Temporarily refit the window winder handle and close the window fully.
9 Detach the operating rods from the interior and exterior door handles.
10 Remove the bolts from the bottom glass channel.
11 Remove the bolts which secure the door lock assembly and withdraw it through the door rear aperature.
12 Refitting is a reversal of removal.
13 Adjustment can be made by altering the position of the door striker plate. Before loosening the striker plate securing screws, mark the original position of the plate and move it only a fraction at a time.
14 Adjust the exterior handle to give a slight free-movement.

11 Rear door lock (saloon and estate wagon) - removal, refitting and adjustment

1 The operations are similar to those described for the front door lock in the preceding Section.
2 The exterior handle is secured by two bolts accessible from within the door cavity. When correctly fitted, the handle should have a small free movement and adjustment is provided for.

12 Front door glass and regulator - removal and refitting

1 Remove the door interior trim as previously described.
2 Lower the window glass fully and remove the two bolts which connect the channel to the regulator arm.
3 Prise out the moulding and weatherstrip.
4 Tilt the glass and withdraw it upwards from the door cavity.
5 On early models (shaver nose) having an opening quarterlight ventilator, remove the ventilator as described in Section 13 together with the division bar, the latter being detachable after unscrewing the adjusting bolt at its lower end.
6 Remove the window regulator mounting bolts and withdraw the regulator mechanism from the door aperature.
7 If the winder mechanism is faulty, renew it as an assembly, greasing it liberally before refitting.
8 Refitting of the glass and door trim is a reversal of removal.
9 Any adjustment required to ensure that the glass moves up and down squarely and smoothly may be carried out by loosening the securing screws and moving the positions of the channels and slides.

13 Opening quarterlight ventilators - removal and refitting

1 Extract the spring clip which secures the control handle to the shaft of the ventilator operating mechanism. (photos).
2 Remove the door interior trim as previously described.
3 Unscrew the operating mechanism and then disconnect the ventilator lower pivot.
4 Unscrew and remove the division bar securing screws, wind the main window right down and then withdraw the ventilator

10.1 Interior door lock plunger

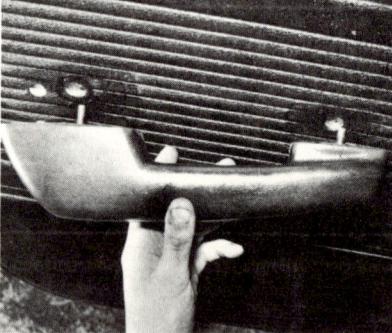
10.2 Removing arm rest

10.3 Removing interior door lock handle escutcheon

10.4 Window regulator handle

10.5 Removing door interior trim

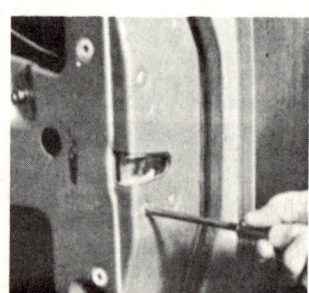
Fig 12.5 Door lock securing screws (Sec 10)

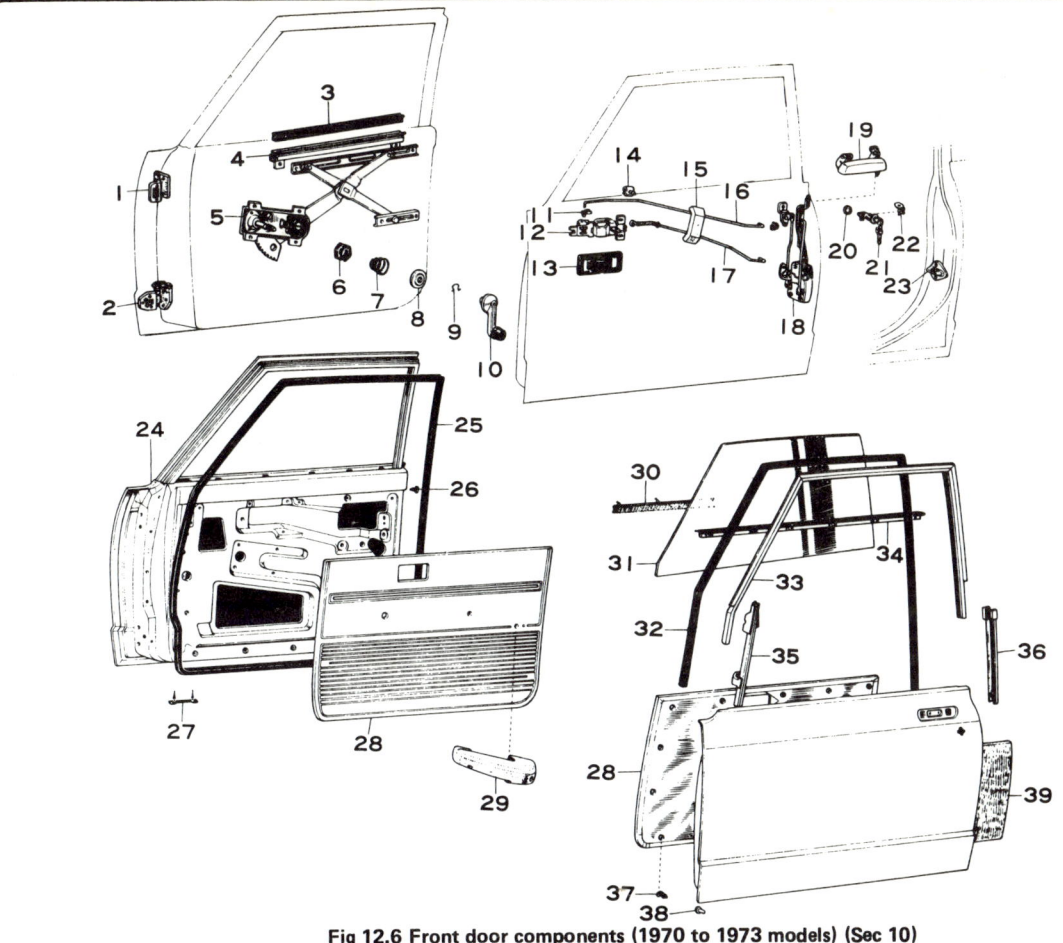

Fig 12.6 Front door components (1970 to 1973 models) (Sec 10)

1 and 2 hinges	12 Interior door handle	key	30 Glass inner weatherstrip
3 Weatherstrip	13 Handle trim plate	22 Cylinder retainer	31 Door glass
4 Glass channel	14 Clamp	23 Striker plate	32 Glass run
5 Window regulator	15 Anti-rattle clip	24 Door	33 Frame
6 Seal	16 Rod	25 Rubber weatherstrip	34 Moulding/Weatherstrip
7 Spring	17 Rod	26 Weatherstrip clip	35 Support frame
8 Escutcheon	18 Lock assembly	27 Door drain hole dust seal	36 Support frame
9 Handle retaining clip	19 Exterior handle	28 Interior trim panel	37 Trim panel clip
10 Window regulator handle	20 Pad	29 Arm rest	38 Trim panel clip cap
11 Clip	21 Lock cylinder and		39 Anti-drumming pad

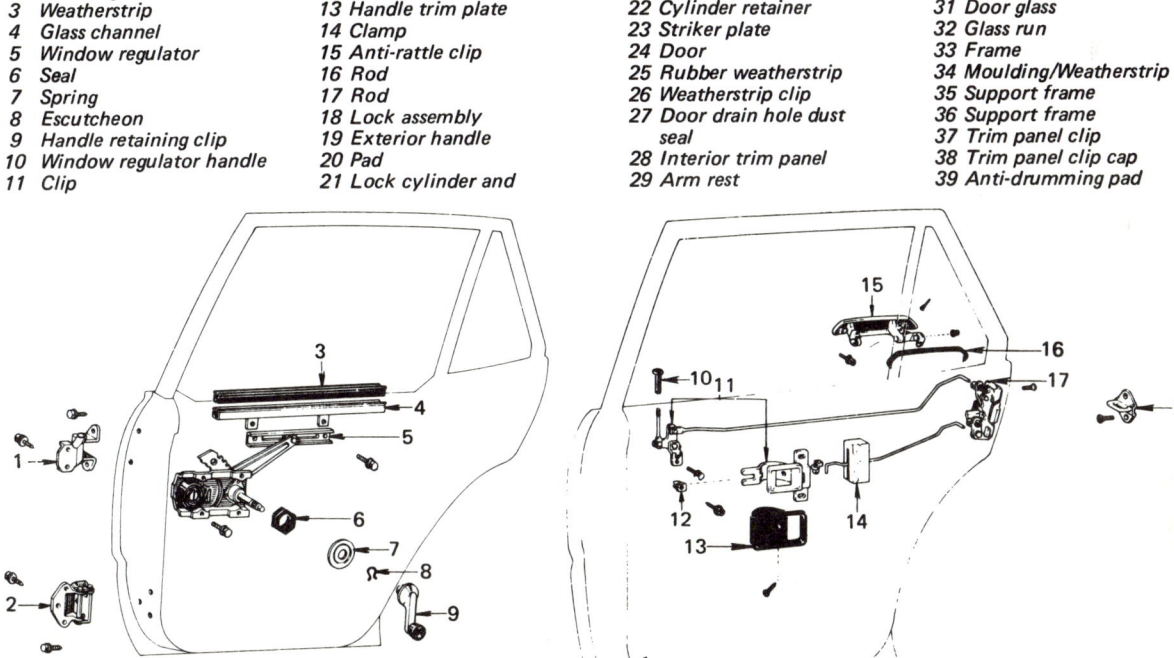

Fig 12.7 Rear door components (1973 onwards) (Sec 11)

1 and 2 hinges	7 Escutcheon	11 Interior handle	15 Exterior handle
3 and 4 Glass channel	8 Handle securing clip	12 Clip	16 Pad
5 Window regulator	9 Regulator handle	13 Handle bezel	17 Lock assembly
6 Seal	10 Lock plunger	14 Anti-rattle clip	18 Lock striker plate

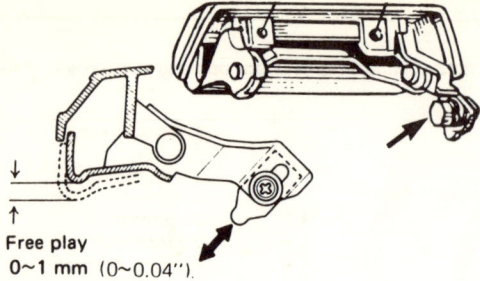

Fig 12.8 Rear door exterior handle adjustment diagram (Sec 11)

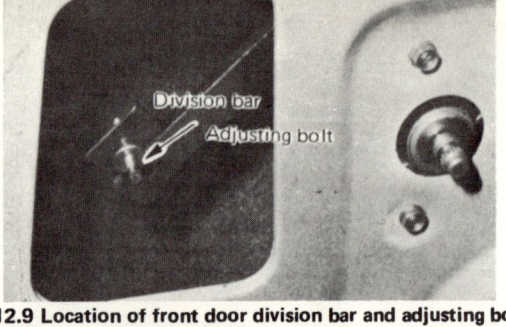

Fig 12.9 Location of front door division bar and adjusting bolt (Sec 12)

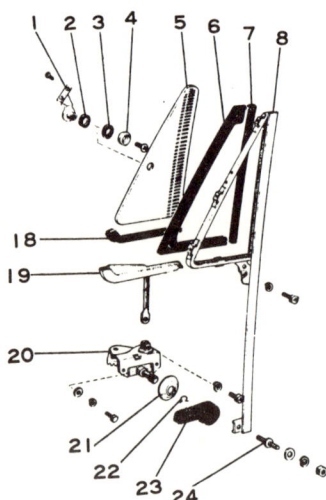

13.1A Quarterlight ventilator control

13.1B Method of securing quarterlight ventilator control

Fig 12.10 Components of a front door opening quarter light ventilator (Sec 13)

1. Upper pivot
2. Seal
3. Seal
4. Plate
5. Glass
6. and 7 Weatherstrips
8. Division bar
18. Rubber insert
19. Frame
20. Opening control
21. Escutcheon
22. Handle securing clip
23. Control handle
24. Adjusting bolt

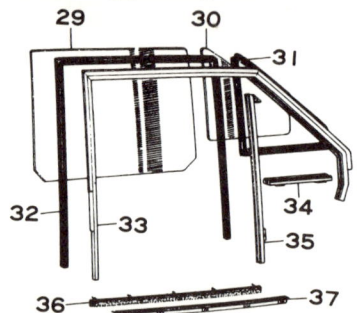

Fig 12.11 Rear door glass components (Sec 14)

29. Door glass
30. Quarter light glass
31. Weatherstrip
32. Glass channel
33. Door frame
34. Lower frame
35. Division bar
36. Inner weatherstrip
37. Moulding

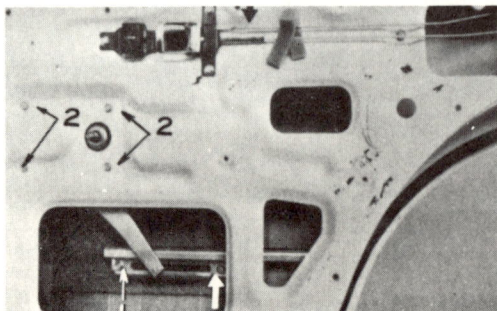

Fig 12.12 Location of rear door glass channel bolt (1) and regulator mechanism bolts (2) (Sec 14)

Chapter 12/Body and fittings

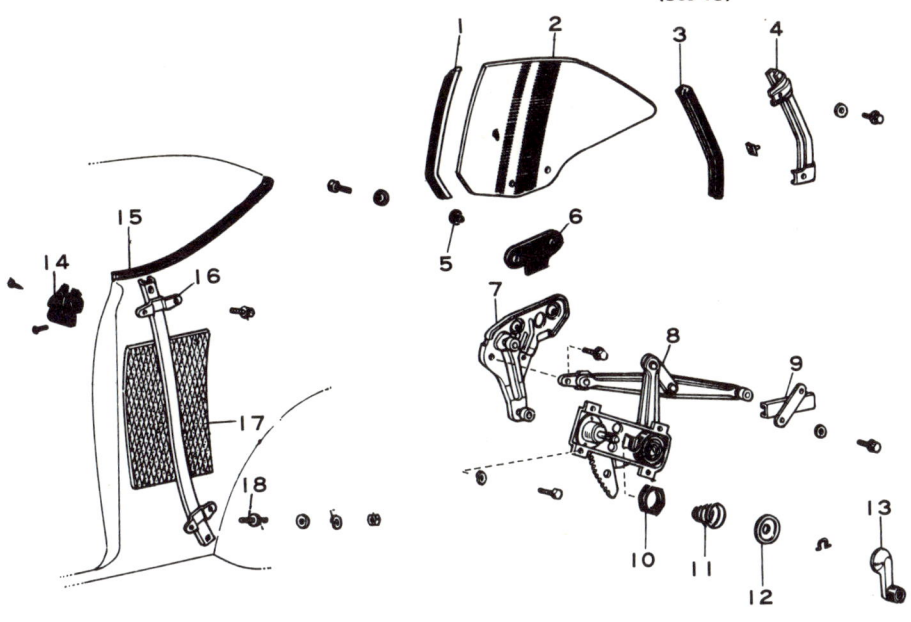

Fig 12.13 Components of a rear opening quarterlight (hardtop) (Sec 15)

1 Weatherstrip
2 Glass
3 Rubber insert
4 Channel
5 Spacer
6 Insulator
7 Glass connecting plate
8 Regulator
9 Lifting arm bracket
10 Seal
11 Spring
12 Escutcheon
13 Regulator handle
14 Seal
15 Weatherstrip
16 Glass guide
17 Anti-drumming pad
18 Adjuster bolt

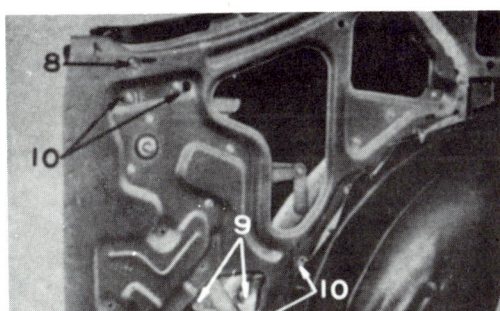

Fig 12.14 Hardtop quarterlight upper stops (8) regulator bolts (9) and glass guide bolts (10) (Sec 15)

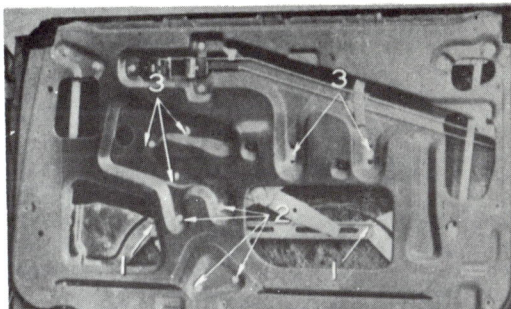

Fig 12.15 Location of glass bottom channel bolts (1) window regulator motor bolts (2) and regulator mechanism bolts (3) on hardtop door. (Sec 16)

assembly from the door.
5 Refitting is a reversal of removal.

14 Rear door glass and regulator - removal and refitting

1 Remove the door interior trim as previously described.
2 Lower the window glass fully.
3 Remove the bar which divides the fixed quarterlight glass from the main window.
4 Pull the quarterlight glass complete with rubber frame from the door.
5 Remove the quarterlight lower frame.
6 Using a hooked tool, remove the clips which secure the glass weatherstrip and moulding.
7 Remove the bolts which secure the window regulator in position and disconnect the regulator arm from the glass bottom channel.
8 The glass can now be withdrawn upwards from the door cavity and the regulator mechanism lifted out through the door aperture.
9 Refitting is a reversal of removal.

15 Quarterlight glass (hardtop) - removal and installation

1 Remove the rear seat.

2 From the interior rear side trim panel, remove the regulator handle, seat back retaining bracket and the trim panel screws. Remove the trim panel.
3 Unscrew and remove the upper stops (8) bolts (9) and (10).
4 Lower the glass guide completely and then lift out the glass followed by the glass guide and glass run channel (Fig. 12.14).
5 Extract the window regulator from the body cavity.
6 Installation is a reversal of removal but grease the regulator mechanism and then adjust the operation of the window by altering the position of the upper stops, the lower guide and the glass run channel as necessary.

16 Power operated window regulators (hardtop) - removal and refitting

1 Power operated window regulators may be encountered fitted to the door windows or rear quarterlights of the hardtop models.
2 *To remove the mechanism from a door,* detach the interior trim and remove the bolts which secure the regulator arms to the glass bottom channel.
3 Raise the glass and insert a screwdriver to prevent it from dropping.
4 Unscrew the bolts which secure the motor and regulator assembly, disconnect the electrical leads and withdraw the mechanism from the door cavity.

5 *To remove the mechanism from the rear quarterlight*, carry out the operations described in paragraphs 1 and 2 of Section 15, then remove the bolts from the regulator and motor and withdraw the assembly from the body cavity.
6 Servicing of the electric motor and gear is described in Chapter 10, Section 42. Where the regulator is worn or faulty, renew it complete.
7 Refitting is a reversal of removal.

17 Doors - removal, refitting and adjustment

1 Open the door fully and support it under its lower edge with a jack or blocks.
2 Mark round the hinge plates to provide a guide when re-fitting.
3 Remove the door interior panel (Section 10) and disconnect the courtesy light wiring.
4 Unscrew and remove the bolts which secure the hinges to the door frame edge and remove the door. If the hinges are to be removed from the body pillars, again mark their positions before removal.
5 Refit the door by reversing the removal process but do not tighten the hinge bolts fully until the fit of the door in the body aperture has been checked. The front and rear gaps of the door should be equal and parallel and the top gap parallel. At the same time, the top and bottom edges of the door should be in alignment with the front or rear door on the same side of the body (saloon or estate wagon). It is a good idea to remove the lock striker plate from the door pillar during the adjustment procedure. Finally tighten the hinge bolts and refit and adjust the striker plate (Section 10).
6 Refit the door panel after connecting the courtesy light wiring.
    On some models, access to the hinge bolts on the pillar can only be obtained after removal of the parcels shelf under the instrument panel and the ventilator side duct and louvre.

18 Bonnet - removal, refitting and adjustment

1 Disconnect the engine compartment light wiring.
2 Unscrew and remove the bolts which secure the bonnet lid to the hinges and with the help of an assistant, lift the lid away.
3 Refitting is a reversal of removal but adjust the mounting bolts to provide an equal gap on both sides of the lid.
4 The lid should close by gentle pressure and remain closed without any tendency to rattle when the vehicle is on the road.
5 Adjust the closure action by loosening the locknut on the rubber buffer setscrew and turning it and then adjust the lock position by slackening the lock securing screws.

19 Rear boot lid - removal, refitting and adjustment

1 The boot lid is counter-balanced by the inclusion of two torsion rods. These must be removed before the hinge bolts are unscrewd. This can be done by using a large adjustable wrench to disengage the cranked ends of the rods.
2 Mark the location of the hinges before removing them.
3 Refitting is a reversal of removal and the lock and striker plate may be adjusted to give positive closure by loosening their securing bolts.
4 The torsion bar action may be altered by varying the position of the free end of the bar using the two slots provided. When the torsion bar is engaged in the upper slot, the counter-balance action is increased.

20 Estate wagon tailgate - removal, refitting and adjustment

1 Remove the torsion bar/hinge cover by carefully prising out the securing clips.
2 Remove the rear interior light.
3 Support the tailgate in its fully open position, using a length of wood.
4 Although the position of the tailgate within the bodyframe can be varied by slackening the hinge bolts **they must never be completely removed without the torsion bars first having been disconnected.**
5 Use a long screwdriver or steel rod inserted through the 'U' of the torsion bars to depress them and to disengage them from their anchorages.
6 Mark the position of the hinge plates, remove the securing bolts, disconnect the wiring harness and with the help of an

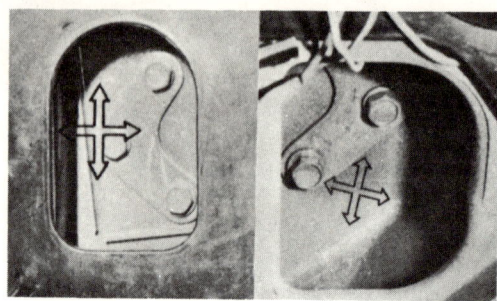

Fig 12.16 Location of front door hinge bolts (early models) (Sec 17)

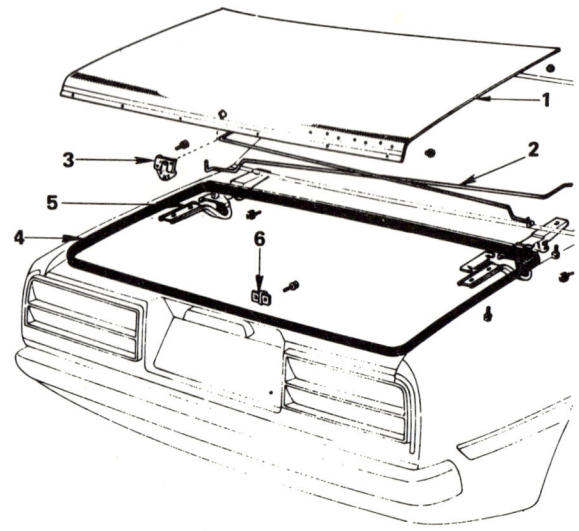

Fig 12.17 Luggage boot lid components (1973 onwards) (Sec 19)

1 Boot lid
2 Counter balance torsion bar
3 Lock
4 Weatherstrip
5 Hinge
6 Striker plate

Fig 12.18 Rear luggage boot torsion bar adjustment slots (Sec 19)

Chapter 12/Body and fittings

assistant, lift the tailgate away.

7 Installation is a reversal of removal; adjust the position of the tailgate and lock mechanism by loosening the securing bolts of the hinges and lock and striker plates. When the fit is correct, insert the torsion rods, reconnect the wiring harness and refit the trim panel.

21 Impact absorbing type bumpers - removal and refitting

1 Disconnect the direction indicator wiring harness at the connector.
2 Unbolt the two shock abosrber support/retainers from the

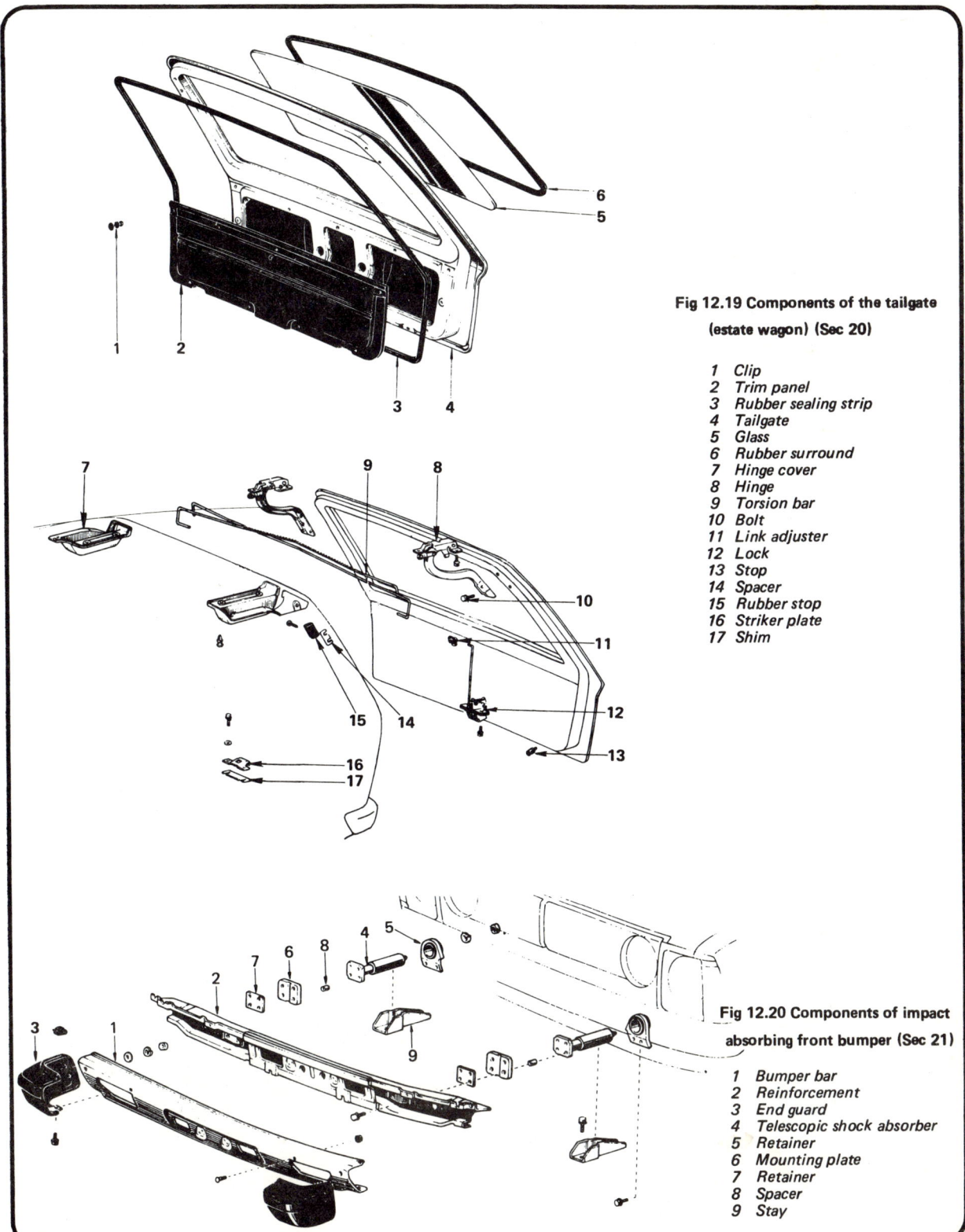

Fig 12.19 Components of the tailgate (estate wagon) (Sec 20)

1 Clip
2 Trim panel
3 Rubber sealing strip
4 Tailgate
5 Glass
6 Rubber surround
7 Hinge cover
8 Hinge
9 Torsion bar
10 Bolt
11 Link adjuster
12 Lock
13 Stop
14 Spacer
15 Rubber stop
16 Striker plate
17 Shim

Fig 12.20 Components of impact absorbing front bumper (Sec 21)

1 Bumper bar
2 Reinforcement
3 End guard
4 Telescopic shock absorber
5 Retainer
6 Mounting plate
7 Retainer
8 Spacer
9 Stay

bodywork and remove the complete bumper assembly from the bodywork.
3 The bumper assembly can be dismantled into separate components for renewal of any damaged items.
4 Measure the length of the shock absorbers and if they do not conform to specification or offer little resistance when compressed, then they should be renewed.

22 Heater - general description

1 The heater system delivers fresh air to the windscreen for demisting purposes and the car interior. The flow to each may be varied in respect of volume and temperature by the facia mounted controls. A flow-through fresh air ventilation system is fitted which delivers unheated air through the two facia mounted controllable ducts and exhausts the stale air through the flap valves at the rear of the rear side windows.
2 The heater assembly comprises a matrix heated by water from the engine cooling system and a booster fan controlled by a three position switch located on the facia panel. During normal forward motion of the car, air is forced through the air intake just forward of the windscreen and passes through the heater matrix absorbing heat and carrying it to the car interior. When the car is stationary or travelling at low speed then the booster fan may be actuated and with the heater control in the 'RECIRC' position, the entry of outside air will be cut off to prevent the admission of fumes or dust.
3 The components used in early and later model assemblies are similar except that later models incorporate heater ducts for the rear seat passengers.

23 Heater (1969 - 72) - removal and refitting

1 Disconnect the lead from the battery negative terminal.
2 Place the heater controls to the hot positions and drain the cooling system.
3 Remove the parcels tray from under the instrument panel.
4 Disconnect the deminster hoses from the heater.
5 Disconnect the water inlet and outlet water hoses from the heater.
6 Disconnect the electrical leads from the heater motor and the control cables from the heater valves.
7 Remove the ashtray and the cigar lighter.
8 Unscrew and remove the bolt which secures the radio tuning panel and the heater bracket.
9 Unscrew the two bolts which secure the heater on the left and right-hand sides and withdraw the heater downwards. Prepare to catch coolant which may spill from the open ends of the heater pipes.
10 Refitting is a reversal of removal.

24 Heater (1973 onwards) - removal and refitting

1 The heater may be removed from the vehicle either as a complete unit or by removing the blower motor independently.
2 *To remove the blower motor on its own,* remove the parcels tray and the trim panel. Disconnect the electrical leads and release the three motor mounting bolts and withdraw the motor/fan assembly.
3 *To remove the complete heater unit,* disconnect the lead from the battery negative terminal, drain the coolant and disconnect the heater hoses. Remove the centre console (see Chapter 10, Section 40). Remove the parcels tray, the heater air duct, the glove compartment, the rear compartment duct, the ventilator duct and the combined instruments from the instrument panel. Remove the radio, the heater control assembly (by disconnecting the control cables from the heater) and the demister nozzle.
4 Tilt the heater unit forward and remove it downwards and to the left. Prepare to catch any coolant which may spill from the open water pipe nozzles.
5 Refitting is a reversal of removal.

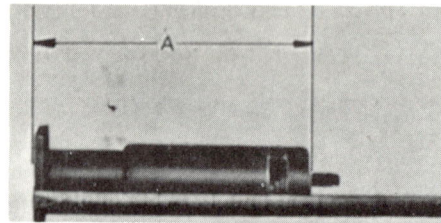

Fig 12.21 Correct free length of bumper shock absorber when in good condition A 7.95 in (202 mm) (Sec 21)

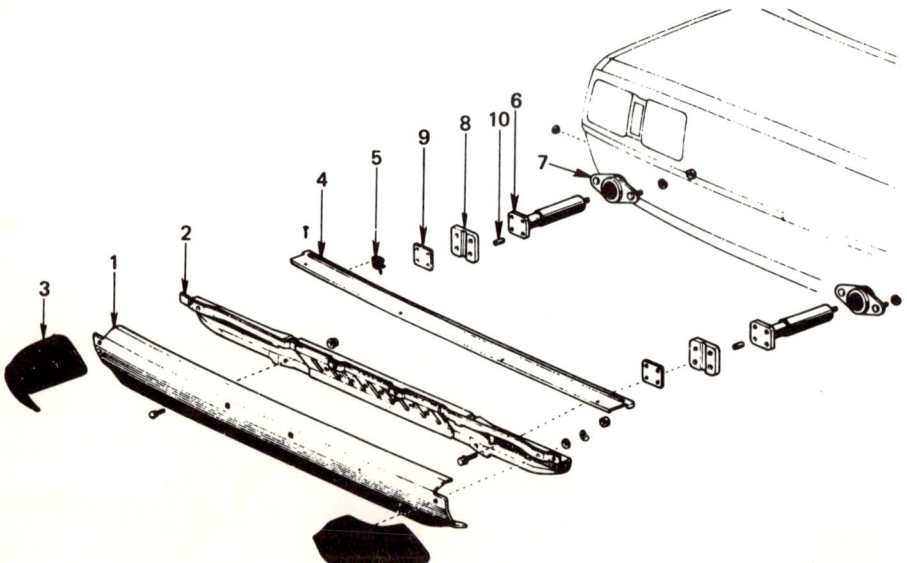

Fig 12.22 Components of impact absorbing rear bumper

1 Bumper bar
2 Reinforcement
3 End guard
4 Apron
5 Cushion
6 Telescopic shock absorber
7 Retainer
8 Retainer
9 Mounting plate
10 Spacer

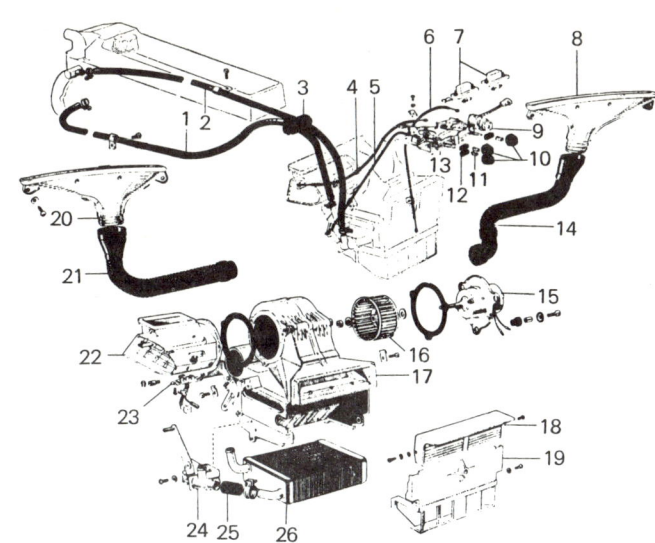

Fig 12.23 Exploded view of the heater unit (1969-72) (Sec 23)

1 and 2 water hoses
3 Bulkhead grommet
4 Air inlet flap control cable
5 Heat control cable
6 Demister control
7 Indicator lamp
8 Demister nozzle
9 Blower fan switch
10 Control lever knob
11 Control lever retainer
12 Control lever guide
13 Control assembly
14 Demister hose
15 Blower motor
16 Blower fan
17 Heater casing
18 Louvre
19 Cover
20 Demister nozzle
21 Demister nozzle
22 Air inlet flap
23 Resistor
24 Water valve
25 Hose
26 Matrix

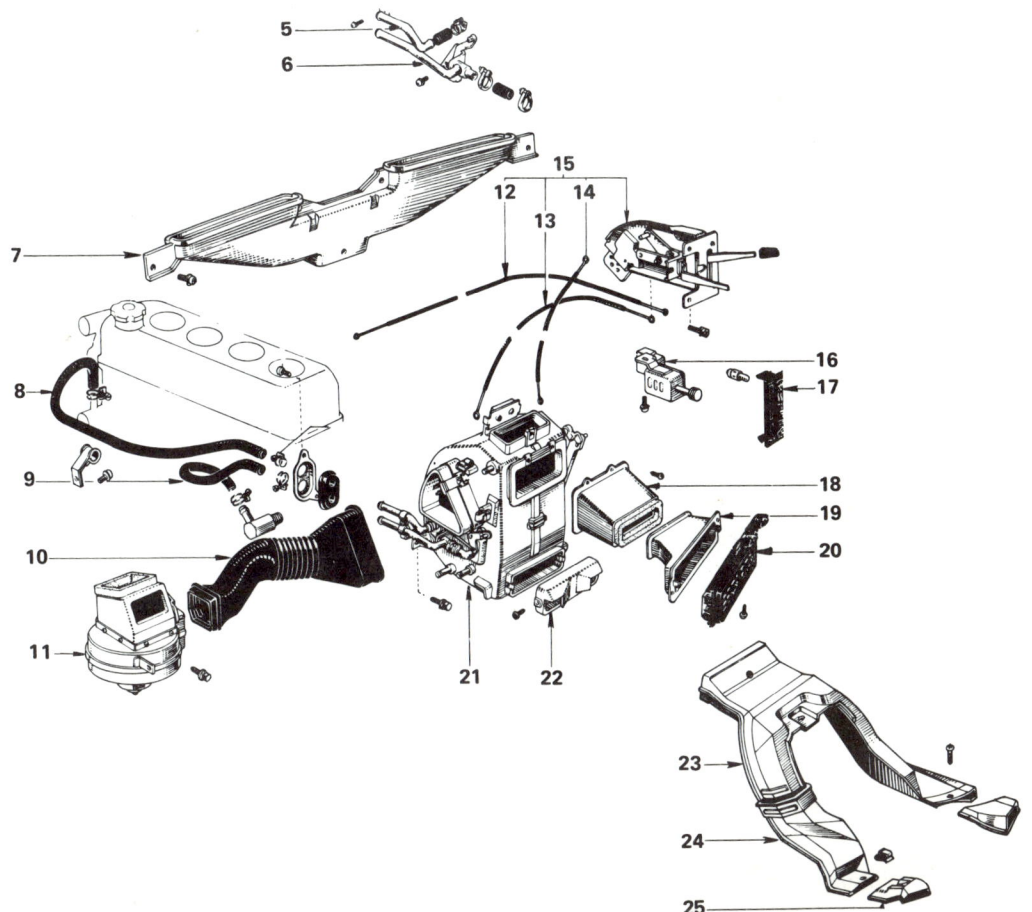

Fig 12.24 Exploded view of the heater unit (1973 onwards) (Sec 24)

5 Water hose
6 Water valve
7 Demister hose
8 Water return
9 Water flow hose
10 Air duct
11 Blower
12 Air inlet flap control cable
13 Heat control cable
14 Demister control cable
15 Control assembly
16 Blower switch
17 Indicator lamp
18 Duct
19 Duct
20 Louvre
21 Housing
22, 23, 24 and 25 components of rear duct

25 Heater (1969 - 72) - dismantling, servicing, reassembly

1 Remove the air deflector (1) from the main housing.
2 Remove the blower assembly (2) (Fig. 12.25).
3 Disconnect the electrical lead (3), remove the flap (4) cover (5) and the grille (6) (Fig. 12.26).
4 Carefully pull the matrix from the heater housing.
5 Malfunction of the heater may be due to one or more various factors. These include a blockage in the heater hoses or matrix, incorrectly adjusted or connected controls, faulty booster motor, air in the heater system or a faulty thermostat in the engine cooling system.
6 In the event of the heater matrix being blocked, then it should be inverted and reverse flushed with a cold water hose. Where this procedure does not clear it then an exchange unit should be obtained. Do not use chemical cleaners in the heater matrix or the fine cooling tubes will either clog or become perforated.
7 Reassembly is a reversal of dismantling.

26 Heater (1973 onwards) - dismantling, servicing and reassembly

1 With the blower unit removed independently from the heater unit, remove the three screws which secure the motor to the blower housing and withdraw the motor.
2 The matrix may be extracted from the heater unit (already removed from vehicle) by first removing the water valve (1) and the outlet hose (2) (Fig. 12.29).
3 Detach the securing clip, band and bolt and gently pull the matrix from the heater housing.
4 For servicing details, refer to paragraphs 5 and 6 of the preceding Section.
5 Reassembly is a reversal of dismantling.

27 Air conditioning system - general description and maintenance

1 The optionally specified system comprises a heater and cooling unit, a belt driven compressor comprises, a condenser and a receiver together with the necessary temperature controls
2 The oil filled compressor is driven from the crankshaft pulley and incorporates a magnetic type clutch.
3 Servicing of the system is outside the scope of the home mechanic as special equipment is needed to purge or recharge the system with refrigerant gas and dismantling of any part of the system must not be undertaken, in the interest of safety, without first having discharged the system pressure.
4 To maintain optimum performance of the system, the owner should limit his operations to the following:
(i) Checking the tension of the compressor driving belt. The total deflection of this belt should be between 5/8 and ¾ in. (15.8 and 19.1 mm) at the centre of its longest run. Adjust by moving the idler pulley.
(ii) Checking the security of all hoses and unions.
(iii) Always keeping the ignition timing correctly set.
(iv) Checking the security of the electrical connections.
(v) Regularly cleaning the air intake filter.
5 Use a soft brush to remove accumulations of dust and flies from the condenser fins.
6 During the winter months, operate the air conditioning system for a few minutes each week to lubricate the interior of the compressor pumps as lack of use may cause deterioration in the moving parts.

Fig 12.25 Location of air intake (1) and blower fan (2) on early type heater (Sec 25)

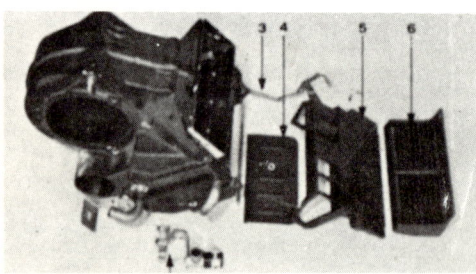

Fig 12.26 Location of wiring harness (3) air inlet flap (4) cover (5) and louvre (6) on early type heater (Sec 25)

Fig 12.27 Removing the matrix from early type heater (Sec 25)

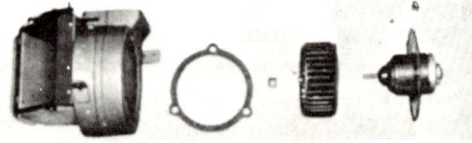

Fig 12.28 Components of the blower fan on later type heater (Sec 26)

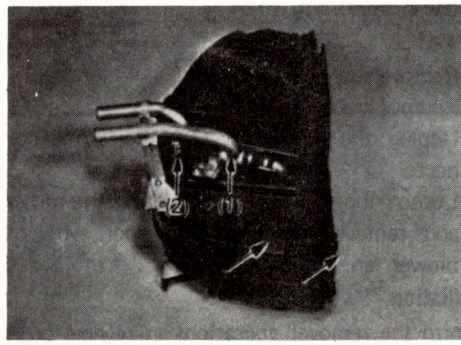

Fig 12.29 Disconnection points (1 and 2) prior to withdrawing matrix from later type heater housing in direction of arrows (Sec 26)

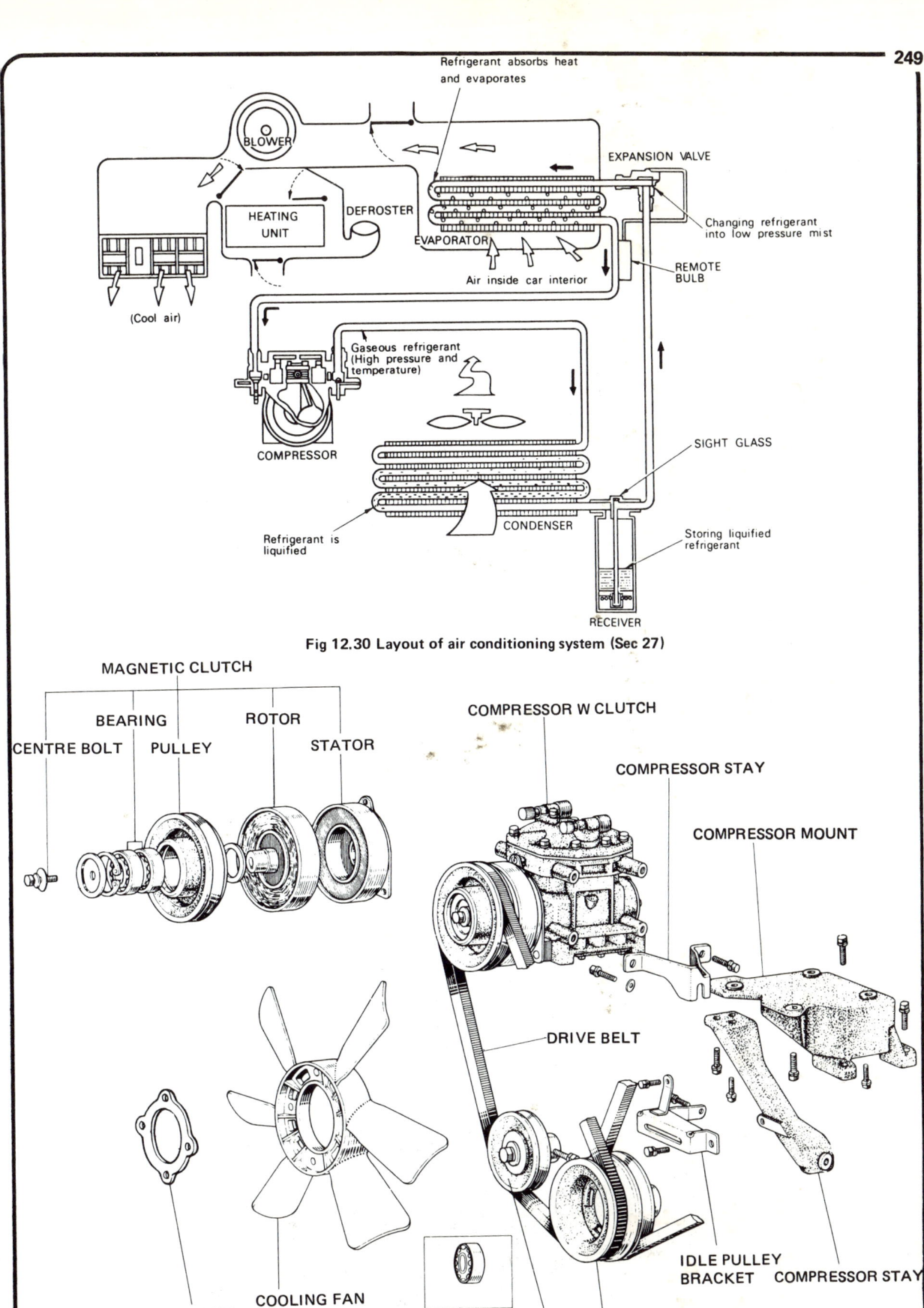

Fig 12.30 Layout of air conditioning system (Sec 27)

Fig 12.31 Details of the air conditioning system compressor pump (Sec 27)

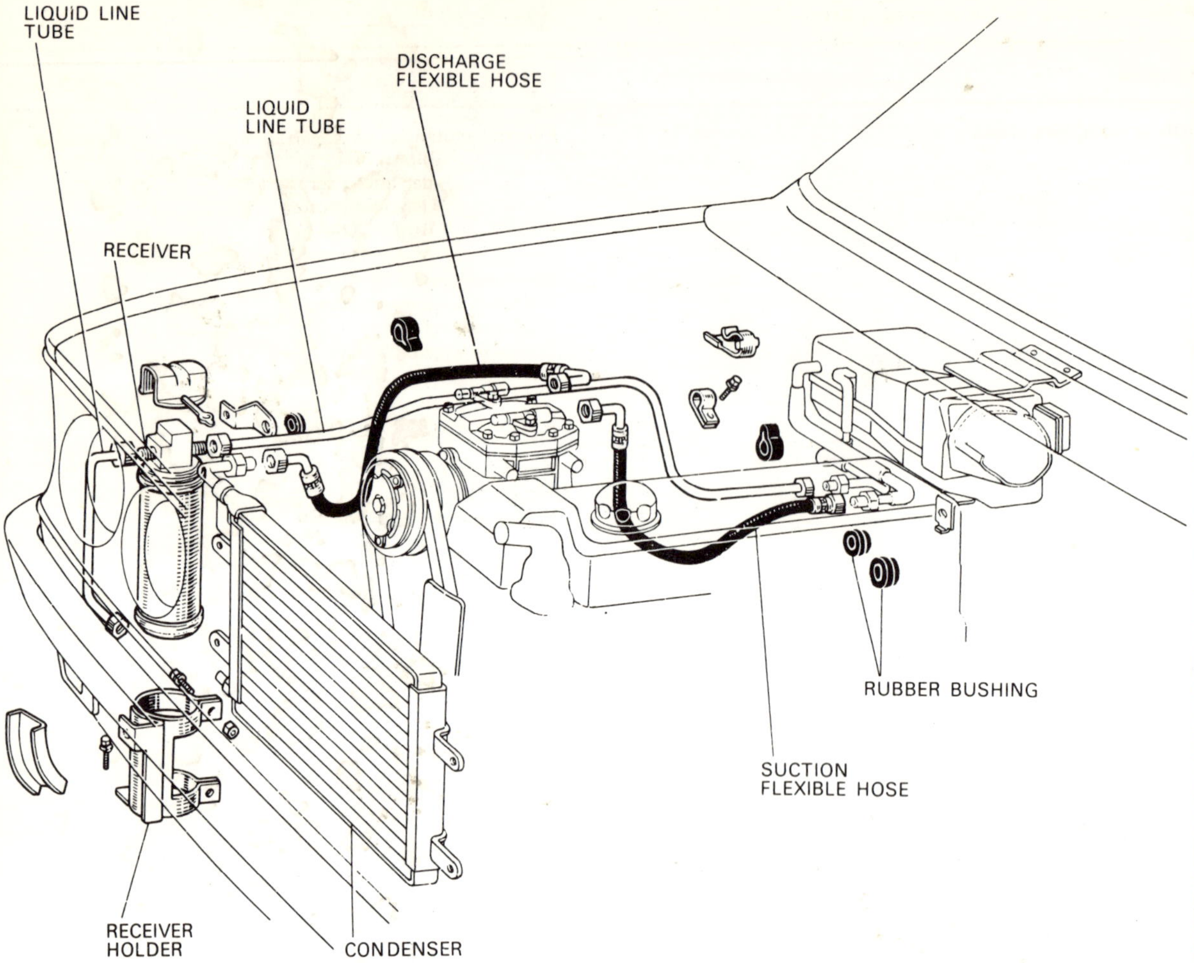

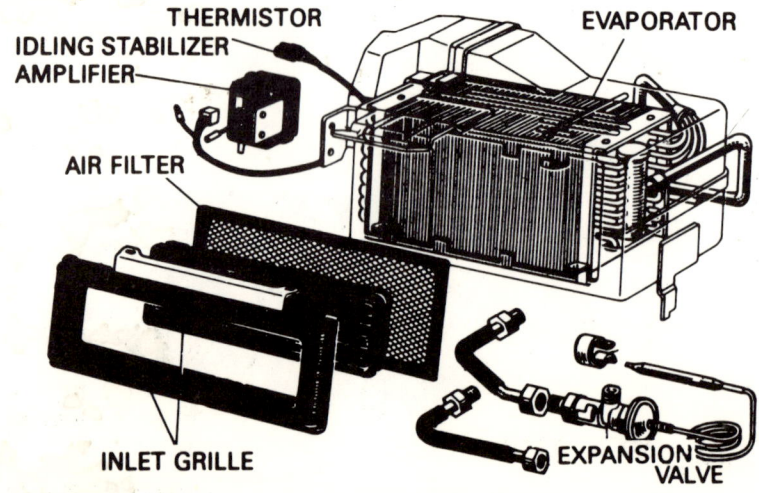

Fig 12.32 Location of major components of air conditioning system (Sec 27)

Fig 12.33 Location of air filter and other components on air conditioning system (Sec 27)

Chapter 12/Body and fittings

28 Fault diagnosis - air conditioning system

Symptom	Cause
Little or no cooling effect	Magnetic clutch not engaging due to: 　　blown fuse 　　defective microswitch 　　defective resistor 　　defective thermistor 　　broken electrical lead Loose compressor drive belt Defective compressor pump Insufficient refrigerant Defective expansion valve Choked receiver Clogged air filter Control dampers inoperative
Restricted air ejection	Blower fuse blown Blower motor defective Blower switch or resistor defective Clogged air filter
Noisy operation	Dry or worn blower motor bearing Worn compressor Compressor mountings loose Low oil level in compressor Magnetic clutch bearings worn Slack drive belt Worn idler pulley bearing
Overheating of engine (see also Fault diagnosis, Chapter 2)	Condenser fins clogged

Metric conversion tables

Inches	Decimals	Millimetres	Millimetres to Inches		Inches to Millimetres	
			mm	Inches	Inches	mm
1/64	0.015625	0.3969	0.01	0.00039	0.001	0.0254
1/32	0.03125	0.7937	0.02	0.00079	0.002	0.0508
3/64	0.046875	1.1906	0.03	0.00118	0.003	0.0762
1/16	0.0625	1.5875	0.04	0.00157	0.004	0.1016
5/64	0.078125	1.9844	0.05	0.00197	0.005	0.1270
3/32	0.09375	2.3812	0.06	0.00236	0.006	0.1524
7/64	0.109375	2.7781	0.07	0.00276	0.007	0.1778
1/8	0.125	3.1750	0.08	0.00315	0.008	0.2032
9/64	0.140625	3.5719	0.09	0.00354	0.009	0.2286
5/32	0.15625	3.9687	0.1	0.00394	0.01	0.254
11/64	0.171875	4.3656	0.2	0.00787	0.02	0.508
3/16	0.1875	4.7625	0.3	0.01181	0.03	0.762
13/64	0.203125	5.1594	0.4	0.01575	0.04	1.016
7/32	0.21875	5.5562	0.5	0.01969	0.05	1.270
15/64	0.234375	5.9531	0.6	0.02362	0.06	1.524
1/4	0.25	6.3500	0.7	0.02756	0.07	1.778
17/64	0.265625	6.7469	0.8	0.03150	0.08	2.032
9/32	0.28125	7.1437	0.9	0.03543	0.09	2.286
19/64	0.296875	7.5406	1	0.03937	0.1	2.54
5, 16	0.3125	7.9375	2	0.07874	0.2	5.08
21/64	0.328125	8.3344	3	0.11811	0.3	7.62
11/32	0.34375	8.7312	4	0.15748	0.4	10.16
23/64	0.359375	9.1281	5	0.19685	0.5	12.70
3/8	0.375	9.5250	6	0.23622	0.6	15.24
25/64	0.390625	9.9219	7	0.27559	0.7	17.78
13/32	0.40625	10.3187	8	0.31496	0.8	20.32
27/64	0.421875	10.7156	9	0.35433	0.9	22.86
7/16	0.4375	11.1125	10	0.39370	1	25.4
29/64	0.453125	11.5094	11	0.43307	2	50.8
15/32	0.46875	11.9062	12	0.47244	3	76.2
31/64	0.484375	12.3031	13	0.51181	4	101.6
1/2	0.5	12.7000	14	0.55118	5	127.0
33/64	0.515625	13.0969	15	0.59055	6	152.4
17/32	0.53125	13.4937	16	0.62992	7	177.8
35/64	0.546875	13.8906	17	0.66929	8	203.2
9/16	0.5625	14.2875	18	0.70866	9	228.6
37/64	0.578125	14.6844	19	0.74803	10	254.0
19/32	0.59375	15.0812	20	0.78740	11	279.4
39/64	0.609375	15.4781	21	0.82677	12	304.8
5/8	0.625	15.8750	22	0.86614	13	330.2
41/64	0.640625	16.2719	23	0.90551	14	355.6
21/32	0.65625	16.6687	24	0.94488	15	381.0
43/64	0.671875	17.0656	25	0.98425	16	406.4
11/16	0.6875	17.4625	26	1.02362	17	431.8
45/64	0.703125	17.8594	27	1.06299	18	457.2
23/32	0.71875	18.2562	28	1.10236	19	482.6
47/64	0.734375	18.6531	29	1.14173	20	508.0
3/4	0.75	19.0500	30	1.18110	21	533.4
49/64	0.765625	19.4469	31	1.22047	22	558.8
25/32	0.78125	19.8437	32	1.25984	23	584.2
51/64	0.796875	20.2406	33	1.29921	24	609.6
13/16	0.8125	20.6375	34	1.33858	25	635.0
53/64	0.828125	21.0344	35	1.37795	26	660.4
27/32	0.84375	21.4312	36	1.41732	27	685.8
55/64	0.859375	21.8281	37	1.4567	28	711.2
7/8	0.875	22.2250	38	1.4961	29	736.6
57/64	0.890625	22.6219	39	1.5354	30	762.0
29/32	0.90625	23.0187	40	1.5748	31	787.4
59/64	0.921875	23.4156	41	1.6142	32	812.8
15/16	0.9375	23.8125	42	1.6535	33	838.2
61/64	0.953125	24.2094	43	1.6929	34	863.6
31/32	0.96875	24.6062	44	1.7323	35	889.0
63/64	0.984375	25.0031	45	1.7717	36	914.4

Index

A

Accelerator pedal and linkage - 80
Air cleaner
    automatic temperature controlled - 53
    cleanable type - 52
    paper element type - 53
Air conditioning system - 248 - 251
Alternator
    description - 188
    dismantling and reassembly - 189
    maintenance - 188
    precautions - 188
    regulator testing - 191
    removal and refitting - 189
    servicing - 189
    testing in vehicle - 189
Antifreeze - 48
Automatic transmission
    description - 143
    driveplate refitting - 39
    driveplate servicing - 35
    fault diagnosis - 152
    maintenance - 143
    removal and installation - 150
    specifications - 107
    torque wrench settings - 107
Automatic transmission (A30 type)
    brake band adjustment - 148
    selector linkage adjustment - 147
    starter inhibitor/reverse lamp switch adjustment - 147
    throttle link connecting rod adjustment - 148
Automatic transmission (A30/A40 type)
    extension housing oil seal renewal - 149
Automatic transmission (A40 type)
    adjustments - 149
Automatic transmission (two speed)
    'kick-down' rod adjustment - 147
    low speed brake band adjustment - 147
    reverse brake band adjustment - 147
    selector linkage adjustment - 143
    starter inhibitor switch adjustment - 145

B

Battery
    charging - 188
    electrolyte replenishment - 188
    maintenance - 188
    removal and installation - 187
Big-end bearings
    renovation - 31
Body
    description - 235
    front wing - 238
    maintenance - 235, 238
    rear boot lid - 244
    repair - major damage - 238
    repair - minor damage - 235
    specifications - 234
    tailgate (estate wagon) - 244
Bonnet - 244
Braking system
    bleeding hydraulic system - 176
    description - 162
    disc - removal and refitting - 172
    disc pad (dual cylinder caliper) - 164
    disc pad (single cylinder caliper) - 162
    drum brakes adjustment - 162
    drums - renovation - 173
    fault diagnosis - 185
    flexible hoses - 178
    front disc caliper (dual cylinder type) - 171
    front disc caliper (single cylinder type) - 171
    front drum brake shoes - 164
    front drum wheel cylinders - 172
    handbrake - 178
    master cylinder (dual circuit, tandem type) - 175
    master cylinder (single circuit type) - 173
    pedal - 179
    pressure regulating valve - 183
    rear drum brake shoes (duo servo type) - 169
    rear drum brake shoes (leading - trailing type) - 168
    rear drum wheel cylinders - 173
    rigid brake lines - 178
    specifications - 161
    torque wrench settings - 162
    vacuum servo unit - description - 180
    vacuum servo unit - dismantling and reassembly - 181
    vacuum servo unit - removal and installation - 181
Bumpers
    impact absorbing type - 245

C

Camshaft
    removal - 23
    renovation - 33
Capacities - 12
Carburettor (dual barrel)
    accelerator pump adjustment - 57
    automatic choke adjustment - 57
    removal and installation - 57
    slow running adjustment - 57
Carburettor (dual barrel - 8R engine series type)
    adjustments and setting - 64
    dismantling and reassembly - 57
    final adjustment after installation - 65
    adjustments and setting - 68
    dismantling and reassembly - 65
    final adjustment after installation - 68
Carburettors
    description - 56
Carburettors (SU twin - 8R-B engine)
    removal and installation - 70
Carburettors (SU twin - 8R-B engine up to 1970)
    adjustments - 68
    dismantling and reassembly - 71

Index

Carburettors (SU twin - 8R-B engine 1970 on)
    adjustments - 70
    dismantling and reassembly - 74
Carpets
    maintenance - 235
Clutch
    adjustment - 96
    bleeding hydraulic system - 98
    description - 95
    fault diagnosis - 102
    installation - 101
    master cylinder dismantling and reassembly - 96
    master cylinder removal and refitting - 96
    operating cylinder dismantling and reassembly - 98
    operating cylinder removal and refitting - 98
    pedal - 99
    release bearing renewal - 101
    removal - 99
    renovation - 99
    specifications - 95
    torque wrench settings - 95
Coil polarity and testing - 93
Condenser - 86
Connecting rods
    reassembly - 37
    renovation - 31
Contact breaker points
    adjustment - 85
    removal and refitting - 86
Cooling system
    description - 47
    draining - 47
    fault diagnosis - 50
    filling - 47
    flushing - 47
Crankcase ventilation system - 30
Crankshaft
    reassembly - 37
    removal - 27
    renovation - 30
Cylinder blade
    renovation - 35
Cylinder bores
    renovation - 31
Cylinder head
    installation - 40
    removal - 24
    servicing - 33

D

Distributor
    dismantling (early type) - 89
    dismantling and reassembly (late type) - 90
    dwell angle - 88
    reassembly (early type) - 90
    removal and installation - 86
    servicing - 90
Doors
    front glass and regulator - 240
    front lock - 240
    opening quarterlight ventilators - 240
    power operated window regulators (hardtop) - 243
    quarterlight glass (hardtop) - 243
    rear glass and regulator - 243
    rear lock (saloon and estate wagon) - 240
    removal, refitting and adjustment - 244
    rattles - 238
Drivebelt
    adjustment - 49

E

Electrical system
    ammeter - 198
    bulbs - renewal - 204
    description - 187
    electro sensor panel - 197
    fault diagnosis - 214
    fuel level transmitter and gauge - 197
    fuses and fusible link - 196
    hazard warning and direction indicator lamps - 196
    headlamp sealed beam unit - 203
    headlights - adjustment - 204
    instruments (early type) - 199
    instruments (later type) - 199
    instruments (printed circuit connection) - 200
    light switch (early models) - 200
    oil pressure indicator - 198
    rear window demister (early models) - 209
    relays - 196
    seat belt electrical interlock systems - 209/211
    specifications - 186
    steering column switches (1969 - 1970) - 203
    steering column switches (1971 - 1973) - 203
    steering column switches (1973 on) - 203
    water temperature transmitter and gauge - 198
    window regulator motor - 209
Emission control system
    fault diagnosis - 83
Emission control system (8R-C 1971 engine)
    air injection system - 78
    air pump servicing - 79
Emission control system (8R-C and 18R-C engines)
    circuits testing - 77
    components maintenance and testing - 75
    description and application - 74
Engine
    ancillary components refitting - 43
    ancillary components removal - 22
    description - 19
    dismantling - 22
    fault diagnosis - 45
    oil seals renewal - 35
    operations with engine in position - 19
    operations with engine removed - 19
    reassembly - 37
    removal method - 19
    renovation - 30
    separation from automatic transmission - 21
    separation from gearbox - 21
    start-up after overhaul - 44
    specifications - 15
    torque wrench settings - 17
Engine/automatic transmission
    reconnecting - 44
Engine/manual gearbox
    reconnecting - 44
Engine/transmission
    installation - 44
    removal - 19
Exhaust system and manifolds - 81

F

Flywheel
    refitting - 39
    servicing - 35
Fuel evaporative emission control system - 56
Fuel filter
    servicing - 53
Fuel pump
    description - 53
    removal and refitting - 54
    servicing - 54
    testing - 54
Fuel system
    description - 52
    fault diagnosis - 83

Index

specifications - 51
torque wrench settings - 52
Fuel tank
   removal and refitting - 55
   servicing - 56

G

Gearbox (manual)
   description - 109
   fault diagnosis - 143
   specifications - 103
   steering column gearchange linkage - 121
   torque wrench settings - 107
Gearbox (manual - 3-speed)
   removal and installation - 109
Gearbox (manual - 3-speed type N30/31)
   countershaft and reverse gear servicing - 120
   dismantling - 115
   input shaft servicing - 120
   mainshaft servicing - 117
   oil seals renewal - 120
   reassembly - 120
Gearbox (manual - 3-speed type TC1)
   dismantling - 109
   reassembly - 112
Gearbox (manual - 4-speed type)
   removal and installation - 123
Gearbox (manual - 4-speed type SS1)
   dismantling - 123
   reassembly - 127
Gearbox (manual - 4-speed type W40)
   countershaft and reverse gear servicing - 135
   dismantling - 131
   input shaft servicing - 135
   mainshaft servicing - 133
   oil seals renewal - 136
   reassembly - 136
Gearbox (manual - 5-speed type)
   countershaft and reverse gear servicing - 141
   dismantling - 137
   input shaft servicing - 141
   mainshaft servicing - 138
   oil seals renewal - 141

H

Heater
   description - 246
   removal and refitting (1969 - 72) - 246
   removal and refitting (1973 on) - 246
   servicing (1969 - 72) - 248
   servicing (1973 on) - 248
Horns
   adjustment - 207
Hubs (front)
   servicing and adjustment - 219

I

Ignition system
   description - 85
   fault diagnosis - 93
   specifications - 84
   timing - 86

J

Jacking points - 12

L

Lubricants recommended - 14
Lubrication chart - 14
Lubrication system - 27

M

Main bearings
   reassembly - 37
   removal - 27
   renovation - 30
Maintenance
   routine - 10

O

Oil filter - 27
Oil pump
   reassembly - 39
   servicing - 27
Oil pump driveshaft
   servicing - 35

P

Piston/connecting rod assemblies
   removal - 26
Piston rings
   reassembly and refitting - 37
   removal - 27
   renovation - 31
Pistons
   reassembly and refitting - 37
   renovation - 31
Propeller shaft
   centre bearing - 155
   description - 153
   maintenance - 155
   removal and refitting - 155
   specifications - 153
   torque wrench settings - 153

R

Radiator - 48
Radio - 209
Rear axle
   bearings - 156
   description - 156
   differential carrier - 159
   fault diagnosis - 160
   halfshafts - 156
   oil seals - 156
   pinion oil seal - 159
   removal and refitting - 160
   specifications - 156
   torque wrench settings - 156
Rocker shaft
   removal - 23
   servicing - 35

S

Spare parts
   buying - 5
Spark plugs - 93
Starter motor
   description - 192
   dismantling - 195
   reassembly - 195
   removal and installation - 194
   servicing and testing - 195
   testing in vehicle - 192
Steering
   box - 231
   column (up to 1970) - 224
   column (1971 to 1973) - 229
   column (1973 onwards) - 230
   description - 217
   fault diagnosis - 233
   front wheel alignment - 232
   linkage - 224
   specifications - 216
   torque wrench settings - 217
   wheel - 226

Index

Sump
    refitting - 40
    removal - 24
Suspension
    description - 217
    fault diagnosis - 233
    front crossmember (up to 1973) - 222
    lower arm and coil spring (up to 1973) - 221
    lower arm and coil spring (1973 on) - 222
    maintenance - 217
    rear coil springs (saloon and hardtop 1973 on) - 224
    rear lateral control rod (saloon and hardtop 1973 on) - 224
    rear leaf spring - silencer pad renewal - 223
    rear leaf spring (early type) - servicing - 223
    rear leaf spring (later type) - servicing - 224
    rear upper and lower control links (saloon and hardtop 1973 on) - 224
    shock absorbers - 218
    specifications - 216
    stabiliser bars - 222
    stub axle carrier - 219
    torque wrench settings - 217
    upper and lower suspension arm balljoints - 218
    upper arm (up to 1973) - 220
    upper arm (1973) - 222

T

Tape players - 209
Thermostat - 48
Timing components
    renovation - 33
Timing gear
    reassembly - 39
    removal - 24
Towing points - 13
Tyre pressures - 217
Tyres - 233

U

Universal joints
    description - 153
    dismantling and reassembly - 155
    fault diagnosis - 155
    maintenance - 155
    specifications - 153
    torque wrench settings - 153
Upholstery
    maintenance - 235

V

Valves
    clearances adjustment - 40
    installation - 40
    servicing - 33
Vehicle identification numbers - 5

W

Water pump
    fluid coupling - 49
    removal and refitting - 49
Wheel studs
    renewal - 159
    Wheels - 233
Windscreen glass - 239
Windscreen washer - 207
Windscreen wiper
    motor - dismantling and reassembly - 205
    motor and linkage (early models) - 205
    motor and linkage (later models) - 205
Wiring diagrams - 212, 213

**Printed by
J. H. HAYNES & Co. Ltd
Sparkford Yeovil Somerset
ENGLAND**